KU-002-261

A guide to the
Architecture of London

A guide to the

Architecture of London

Edward Jones &
Christopher Woodward

Weidenfeld & Nicolson

First published in Great Britain in 1983
by George Weidenfeld & Nicolson Ltd;
Second edition 1992; Third edition 2000

This edition first published in 2009
by Weidenfeld & Nicolson
10 9 8 7 6 5 4 3 2 1

A CIP catalogue record for this book is available from the British Library.

ISBN: 978 0 297 85516 3

Design by tamasincole.co.uk
Edited by Debbie Woska and David Atkinson
Index by Elizabeth Wiggans
Colour reproduction by DL Interactive UK
Printed in Spain by Cayfosa

Weidenfeld & Nicolson
The Orion Publishing Group Ltd
Orion House
5 Upper St Martin's Lane
London WC2H 9EA

An Hachette UK Company

The Orion Publishing Group's policy is to use papers that are natural, renewable and recyclable products and made from wood grown in sustainable forests. The logging and manufacturing processes are expected to conform to the environmental regulations of the country of origin.

Contents

Authors' introduction

The reasons for writing this book are both practical and theoretical. Despite an abundance of books about London, there has not hitherto been a convenient guide documenting the city's buildings chronologically. This was our first aim. Our second was to review London's architecture comparatively and comprehensively.

In selecting buildings for inclusion in this guide, we have broadly categorized London's architecture as follows: works of excellence judged by international standards, by architects such as Hawksmoor, Nash, Soane, Butterfield and Lutyens; lesser and early works by these masters; districts, streets and squares which constitute the matrix for these outstanding buildings; engineering works which because of their scale have transformed the city more drastically than single buildings could; architecture which is the biggest, longest or most conspicuous of its kind; and buildings which show the development of a particular type – the artist's studio, the shopping arcade and the department store, for example.

London has grown steadily since its Roman foundation. As observed by the Danish architect and historian Steen Eiler Rasmussen (1898–1990), London expanded unhindered into open countryside. Unlike many of the cities of mainland Europe, it has not been invaded from the land for the last millennium. It has always resisted systematic reconstruction in any one period (unlike, say, Haussman's Paris or Cerda's Barcelona). The drawings below demonstrate this. Drawn to the same scale, 4km by 1km (3 miles by 0.6 mile), they show: an area of London from Marble Arch to Kilburn; Paris from the Arc de Triomphe to the Louvre; Barcelona, with Cerda's square grid grafted onto the city's historic core; and a section of Manhattan from 21st Street to 75th Street. London is notable for its looseness of structure and mainly residential fabric. The streets and squares of its housing form a background to its monumental and institutional buildings.

While visiting and revisiting the buildings catalogued here, we have been continually surprised and delighted by the amazing richness of London's domestic and monumental architectural past, and sanguine about the crass mindlessness of much recent residential and commercial work. We hope that this guide will help the reader to enjoy and understand the first, and to avoid the second.

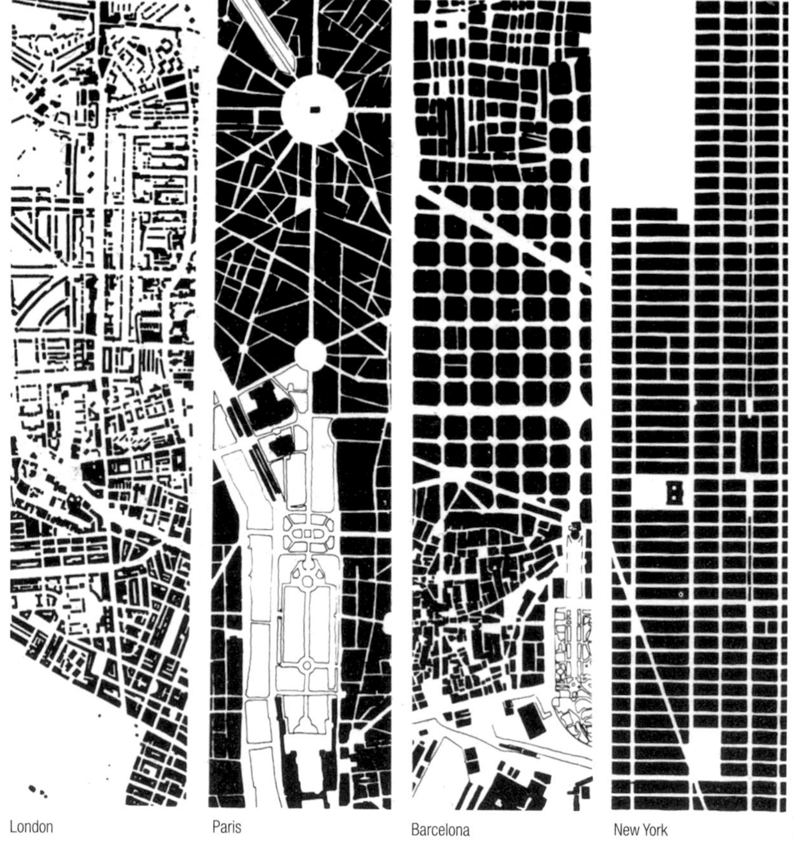

London | Paris | Barcelona | New York

How to use this guide

This guide contains over 1000 *entries*: buildings, streets or areas. These are arranged by *section*. London's administrative districts, the boroughs, are very large, each with a population of about 250,000, and do not form useful or visible subdivisions. The 30 km (18.5 mile) square approximating to the area of the former County of London has therefore been arbitrarily divided into nine smaller squares.

The middle one nets central London, defined as the area between Shepherd's Bush to the west, the Tower of London to the east, Hampstead Heath to the north and Battersea Park to the south. This central area has been further divided into sixteen squares. The inner squares have been lettered **A** to **P**, and the outer ones **Q** to **X**.

These letters correspond to the book's *sections* – each section has its own colour to provide some help in navigation. Coverage of outer London is not comprehensive: only exceptional buildings and those of interest nearby are included.

<table>
<tr><td>Q</td><td colspan="4">R</td><td>S</td></tr>
<tr><td rowspan="4">T</td><td>A</td><td>B</td><td>C</td><td>D</td><td rowspan="4">U</td></tr>
<tr><td>E</td><td>F</td><td>G</td><td>H</td></tr>
<tr><td>I</td><td>J</td><td>K</td><td>L</td></tr>
<tr><td>M</td><td>N</td><td>O</td><td>P</td></tr>
<tr><td>V</td><td colspan="4">W</td><td>X</td></tr>
</table>

A more detailed map is shown overleaf

Each section is introduced by a large-scale map, with the *entries* shown by numbered red dots, followed by a description of the area and its historical development. The pages following contain the entries, arranged chronologically.

To locate an entry, look up its name in the general index: you will find it, together with its *reference*, a letter and a number. The letter tells you its section, the number shows you where it is in that section, and is marked on the section map. To help you find a number on the map, each *entry* in the text is followed by a map reference, and, in sections A to P, a lower case letter which corresponds to the subdivisions of the section map.

building — date — section & entry number

St Katherine's Hospital 1826 **F24** h
Outer Circle, Regent's Park, NW1
Ambrose Poynter

architect — address — grid reference

A note on transport

- ⊖ Transport for London stations, including the Underground, London Overground and Docklands Light Railway
- ⇌ National rail stations

Visiting buildings

The inclusion of a building in this guide does not mean that its interior can be visited. Please respect the privacy of those living or working in the buildings mentioned. Many buildings that are otherwise closed open their doors during the London Open House weekend, usually held in September.

Inner and outer London sections

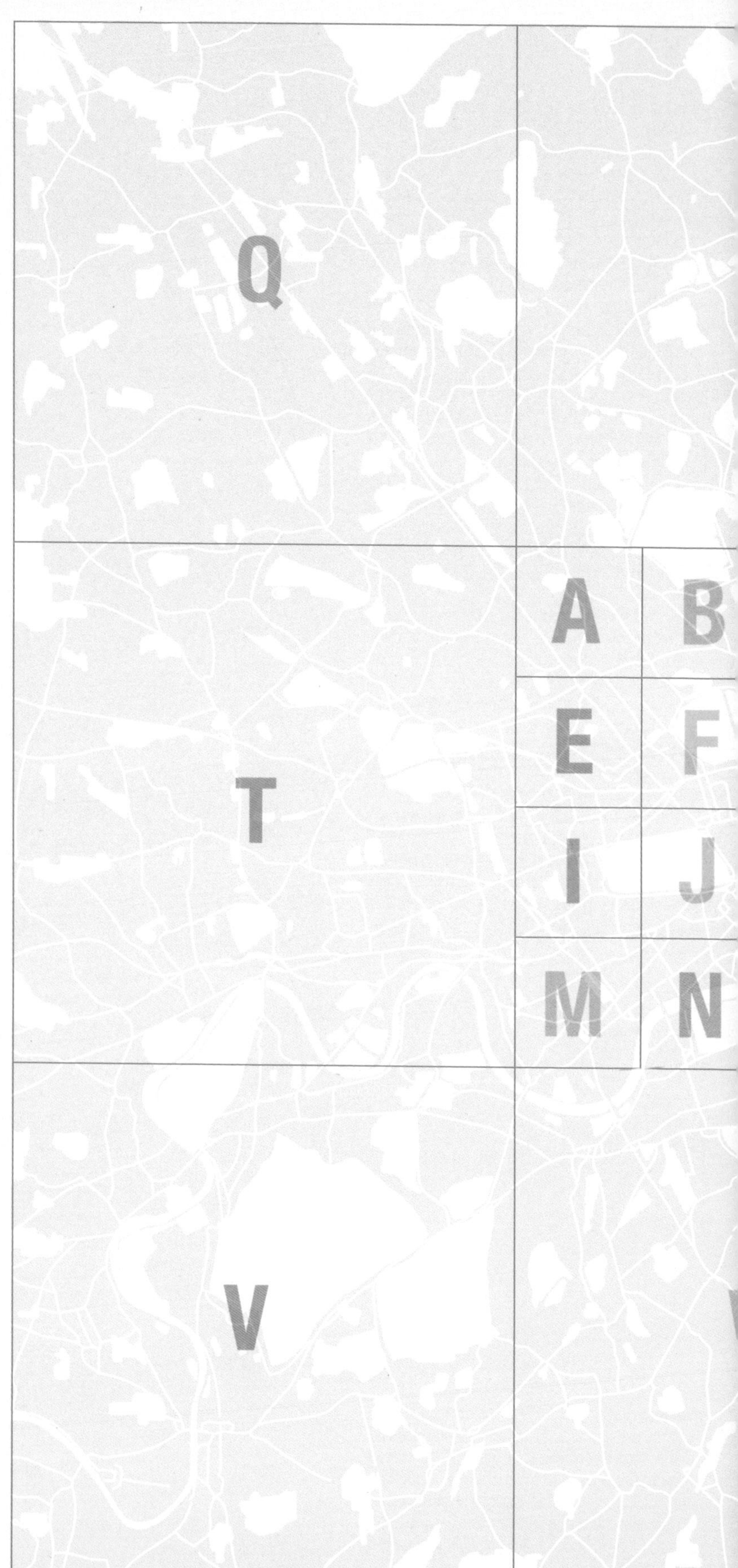

		S
C	D	U
G	H	
K	L	
O	P	
		X

Roman and Anglo-Saxon London

Julius Caesar visited England in 54BC, but nearly a century passed before the Romans invaded in AD43, during the reign of Claudius. As a settlement London barely existed before the Roman invasion, and afterwards St Albans, Colchester, Lincoln, York and Gloucester were almost certainly more important administrative centres. But it was essential to the Romans to build roads to deploy their military strength in the new colony, and London's convenient position – at a point where the Thames could be bridged and at a navigable distance from the open sea – placed it at the centre of a monumental road system. Oxford, Watling and Ermine Streets all date from this time and established London's essential armature.

By AD62, when the Britons of the eastern counties revolted under Boudicca, London had attained enough importance to warrant destruction, but the Roman town recovered and prospered as a centre of trade and administration. The Thames was bridged, as were the Walbrook and Fleet rivers, and a small fort was built near Cripplegate. By 140 the town was encircled by a defensive wall, which is now the main visible evidence of the Roman occupation of London. Archaeology has supplied the plan of the town, and the **Museum of London** H42 displays objects of everyday life.

The two centuries after Boudicca's rising were relatively peaceful, but by the end of the third century the town was menaced by Franks, Picts, Scots and Saxons. As the Roman Empire dwindled in the fourth century London declined. When the Romans withdrew in 410 the Saxons invaded, and there is no further record of the town until 605, when Augustine was ordained London's first bishop.

The Anglo-Saxons were master-craftsmen (see the treasures from the Sutton Hoo ship burial in the British Museum), but archaeological remains do not indicate that they were great builders. By 804, however, Bede could describe London as a flourishing trading town, and in 886 the walls were restored as a defence against repeated Danish invasions. But the next significant building was not until 1066, when Edward the Confessor's abbey at Westminster was completed, establishing London as the country's royal capital.

Replica of a statue of Trajan, Roman Wall, Tower Hill

0 200 400 600 800 1000 1200

OFFA 774–796
HOUSE OF WESSEX 829–1016
HOUSE OF DENMARK 1013–1042

150 population 45–60,000
population 5–10,000

c100BC Vitruvius *De Architectura Libri Decem*
316 Constantine emperor of western Empire
330 Roman Empire divided between Rome and Byzantium
742 **CHARLEMAGNE** – 814

54BC Julius Caesar visits Britain
43 Roman invasion of Britain
60 Boudicca's revolt: Londinium becomes capital of province of Roman Britain
75–85 Agricola, Governor of Britain, builds forts from the Clyde to the Forth
122 Hadrian visits Londinium
122–6 Hadrian's Wall
125 Londinium destroyed by fire
c410 Roman administration leaves Britain
587 Pope Gregory the Great sends Augustine to Britain
597 Canterbury established as Prime See
c600 Saxon London established to west of present City, its port at Aldwych
604 First **St Paul's** L28 founded by Ethelbert
605 Bishopric of London established
842, 851 & 871 Danish raiders sack London

c50 **first London Bridge**
c100 **Forum and Basilica** built
190–220 **Roman Wall** L1, L2 **built**
240 **Temple of Mithras**
606 **St Mary Overie established on site of present Southwark Cathedral** L5
660–70 **All Hallows-by-the-Tower** L3 **founded**

0 200 400 600 800 1000 1200

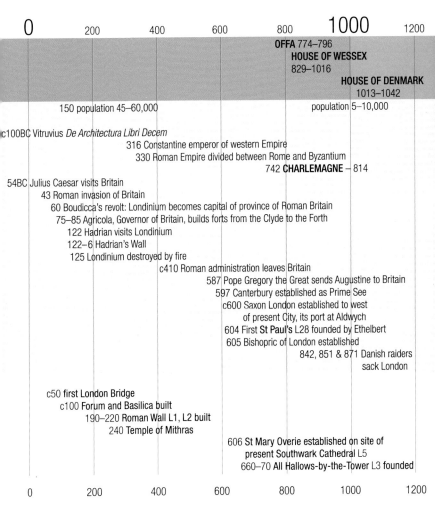

Medieval and Tudor London

The poles of late Saxon London were Westminster Abbey on marshy ground in the west, and a wooden St Paul's on Ludgate Hill in the east. In 1066 the Norman French invaded England, and their first building in London was the Tower. Started about 1078, and set on the bank of the Thames where the Roman wall met the river, it was built to awe the Saxon population, and to defend London from the east. The Normans brought a new architectural style – their heavy round-arched derivation of Romanesque – examples of which can be seen in **St John's Chapel** in the Tower L4, **St Bartholomew the Great** H1, and the much restored old **St Pancras Church** G1. In 1097 William Rufus, William the Conqueror's successor, built the first **Westminster Hall** K5, continuing the functional separation of Westminster from the City of London (see the introduction to section K) started by Edward the Confessor. Westminster gradually became the focus of Court life, and the religious and administrative centre of the kingdom. The self-governing City, with its own cathedral, continued as a centre of trade and craft industry, as it had been under the Saxons. Retail trades and handicrafts were carried on in the small timber and plaster houses, and in the streets and markets (much as they are today in the small towns of North Africa). Transport was by boat, mule and foot.

In 1245 Henry III launched an ambitious building programme, of which the Gothic **Westminster Abbey** K2 and parts of the Tower remain. Earlier in the same century, royal charters had given the City of London considerable political and trading autonomy, similar to that of the contemporary free towns of France, Germany and Italy, vestiges of which remain today in the City's separate police force and the arcane rituals of its local government. The medieval guilds, the Livery Companies, exist still, with their Halls and their charitable and social activities. At the end of the fourteenth century, the establishment of the four Inns of Court, outside the City to its west, started the growing connection between Westminster and the City along the banks of the Thames.

Sixteenth-century England under the Tudors underwent sudden changes. Increased trade – the result of exploration and discovery abroad – and the burning of forests for fuel at home brought a surge of prosperity. The population of London grew fivefold, from about 50,000 in 1530 to 200,000 in 1600, although the proportion of that population living within the walls declined from two-thirds to less than half, reflecting the justified lack of fear of invasion from the land that accounted for the structure and general character of London's development.

The centre of trade remained on the banks of the Thames: the port, in the Pool of London below the bridge, was the largest in the country. Suburbs spread north from the City up Bishopsgate to Shoreditch, east towards Whitechapel and Wapping, west along the Strand, and south of the river on Bankside. Views of London, usually taken from the tower of St Mary Overie, Southwark, show it like a seaside town spreading from Westminster to the Tower along the Thames – its means of communication, drainage and water supply.

From 1509, the royal dockyards were established at Deptford and Woolwich to build men-of-war and to relieve the congestion of the medieval harbours and shipyards. Henry VIII made huge changes in the physical pattern of London: confiscated Church lands were made available for the building of royal and aristocratic palaces or the development of houses. Palaces were built or enlarged at Whitehall, Richmond, Windsor and **Greenwich** U2, and Wolsey's Hampton Court was confiscated. The royal hunting grounds of **Hyde**

Westminster Abbey K2

Old London Bridge (demolished): engraving of 1749

Park J2, **Green Park** J1 and **St James's Park** K9 were established, giving London its open, leafy centre. Between Whitehall and the City, a mile of palaces was built along the banks of the Thames: Northumberland House, the Palace of Savoy, Somerset House (from 1547), Arundel House, Essex House, Temple and Bridewell, and while none of the originals remains, their names are still in use. North of the Strand were more grand aristocratic houses, including that of the Bedford Estate on the Covent Garden. Lambeth existed at the beginning of the century, but by the end Southwark housed all the pastimes outlawed from the City: cock fighting, bear baiting, and the theatres – the Rose of 1587, the Swan, and the **Globe** L141 in 1599.

The reign of Elizabeth was marked by little royal building, although the country and London rested on the continued prosperity produced by war and exploration. The culture of the Renaissance appeared first not in architecture but in the literature of Marlowe and Shakespeare. At the end of the century, Inigo Jones was twenty-seven.

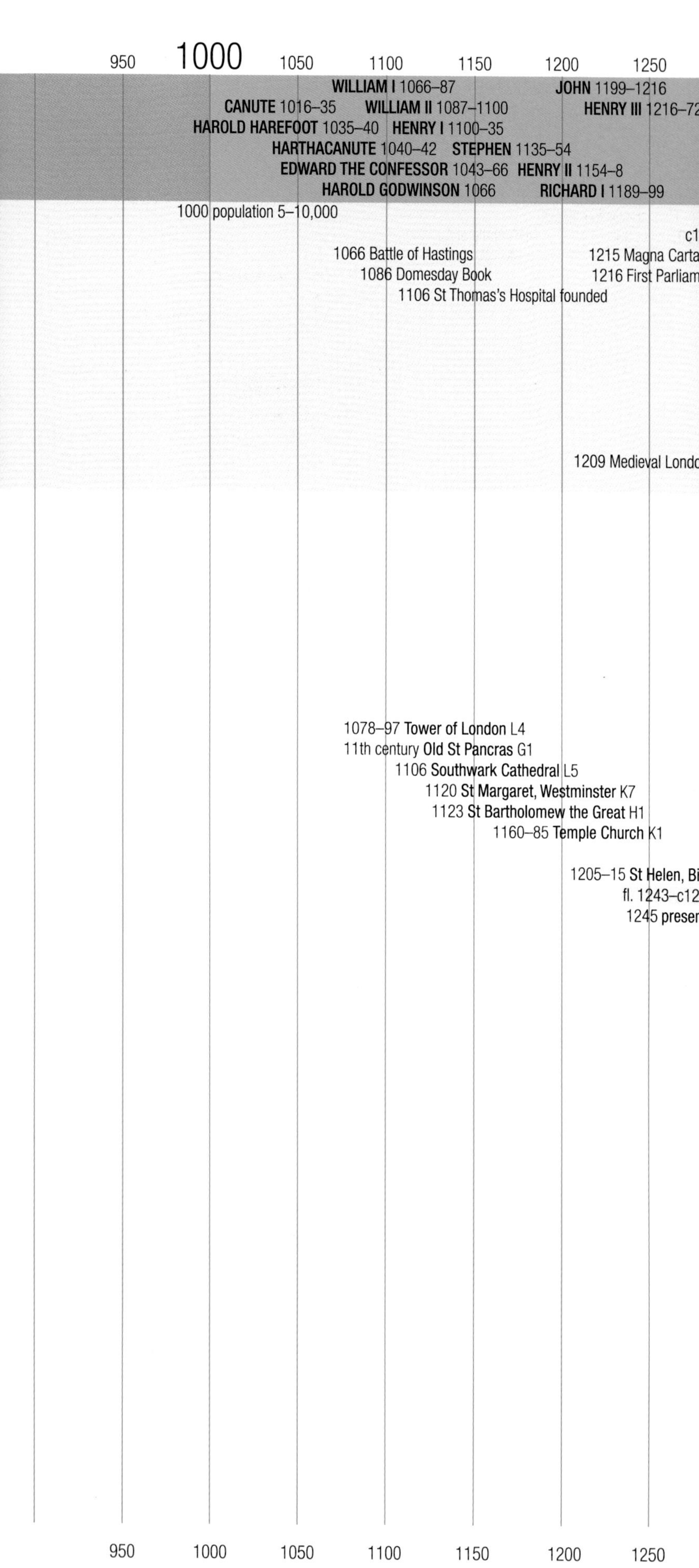

950
1000
1050
1100
1150
1200
1250
WILLIAM I 1066–87
JOHN 1199–1216
CANUTE 1016–35
WILLIAM II 1087–1100
HENRY III 1216–72
HAROLD HAREFOOT 1035–40
HENRY I 1100–35
HARTHACANUTE 1040–42
STEPHEN 1135–54
EDWARD THE CONFESSOR 1043–66
HENRY II 1154–8
HAROLD GODWINSON 1066
RICHARD I 1189–99
1000 population 5–10,000
c12
1066 Battle of Hastings
1215 Magna Carta
1086 Domesday Book
1216 First Parliame
1106 St Thomas's Hospital founded
1209 Medieval Londor
1078–97 Tower of London L4
11th century Old St Pancras G1
1106 Southwark Cathedral L5
1120 St Margaret, Westminster K7
1123 St Bartholomew the Great H1
1160–85 Temple Church K1
1205–15 St Helen, Bis
fl. 1243–c125
1245 present
950
1000
1050
1100
1150
1200
1250

1350 1400 1450 1500 1550 **1600** 1610

HENRY IV 1399–1413 **HENRY VII** 1485–1509 **JAMES I** 1603–25
HENRY V 1413–22 **HENRY VIII** 1509–47
I 1272–1307 **HENRY VI** 1422–61 **EDWARD VI** 1547–53
WARD II 1307–27 **EDWARD IV** 1461–83 **MARY I** 1553–8
EDWARD III 1327–77 **EDWARD V** 1483 **ELIZABETH** 1558–1603
RICHARD II 1377–99 **RICHARD III** 1483–5

1350 population 40,000
1600 population 200,000
SCOTUS –1308
1415 Battle of Agincourt
1588 Spanish Armada defeated
c1425 **WILLIAM CAXTON** –1491
1475 **THOMAS CARDINAL WOLSEY** –1530
1478 **THOMAS MORE** –1535
c1537 **NICHOLAS HILLIARD** –1619
c1540 **FRANCIS DRAKE** –1598
c1552 **WALTER RALEIGH** –1618
1564 **WILLIAM SHAKESPEARE** –1616
1573 **JOHN DONNE** –1631
1573 **BEN JONSON** –1637
1492 Columbus crosses Atlantic
onstructed
1498 Vasco da Gama discovers Cape route to India

1404 **L B ALBERTI** –1472
L B Alberti *De Re Aedificatoria*
1475 **MICHELANGELO** –1564
1508 **ANDREA PALLADIO** –1580
1348–9 Black death: 50,000 die
1550 Villa Capra
1570 Palladio *Quattro Libri dell'Architettura*

1370 Legal Society of Lincoln's Inn founded
1397–1419 Dick Whittington Mayor of London

L7
OF REYNS
ster Abbey begun K2
495 Lambeth Palace K3

) St Etheldreda G2
) Eltham Palace X1
c1350 Temple Church K1

c1320 **HENRY YEVELE** 1400
1390 completion of nave, Westminster Abbey K2
1394–1402 Westminster Hall K5

c1400 Lincoln's Inn K6
1410–20 Bishop's Palace Fulham W1
1411–40 Guildhall L8
15th century St Olave, Hart Street L6
mid-15th century Holy Sepulchre without Newgate L10
1492–1518 Old Hall and Gatehouse, Lincoln's Inn K6
1503–12 Henry VIII's Chapel, Westminster Abbey K8
1514 Hampton Court Palace V1
1520–32 St Andrew Undershaft L11
16th century St Nicholas, Chiswick T1
1530 St James's Palace K10

1570 **JOHN THORPE** 1610

1573 **INIGO JONES** 1652
1586 Houses, Staple Inn G3
1590 Holland House I1

1350 1400 1450 1500 1550 1600 1610

Seventeenth-century London

By all accounts and by later standards early Stuart London was not a beautiful city. It was a city of merchants, suspicious of the Crown, living mostly in ramshackle timber houses built on the medieval street pattern. With a few exceptions there was no great architecture, although master-craftsmen displayed their skill in such fine buildings as **Cromwell House** R4 and the **College of Arms** L22. Ten times larger than provincial cities like Bristol or Norwich, London was nevertheless small enough to walk across in a morning and more than adequately covered by sections K and L of this guide. The marshy land south of the river remained undeveloped except for Southwark, and London Bridge was the only permanent river crossing (and was to remain so until Westminster Bridge was built in 1738). Principal east-west transport was along the Thames, which contemporary prints show as a working river, busy with boats landing at wharfs and jetties on the north bank.

Terrible overcrowding and inadequate sanitary arrangements made the plague a constant threat. Open drains ran down the middle of most streets to issue where possible into the Thames, London's principal water supply. Royalty escaped the city's stench by retreating from the palace at Whitehall (destroyed by fire in 1698) to the many royal houses outside London – **St James's Palace** K10 and **Hampton Court** V1 to the west, and **Greenwich** U2, Richmond and Nonesuch to the south. Wealthy merchants withdrew to the country villages of Hampstead and Highgate. Meanwhile the theatre (the second Globe theatre was established on Bankside in 1616), bear baiting, cock fighting and public executions provided diversions for the average citizen.

The century's architecture was dominated by the work of two men, Inigo Jones and Christopher Wren. Previously, important buildings had been produced by craftsmen in the service of State and Church, but now the 'architect' emerged – a man of flair or genius, who might be an expert in almost anything but who was not a master-craftsman (although Jones had been apprenticed to a joiner). The diverse careers of both Jones and Wren anticipated the broad scope of learning and cultural interests of the Age of Enlightenment. Wren was a brilliant student of mathematics and law, who went on to become Professor of Astronomy at Oxford before designing his first building; Jones travelled extensively in Italy, designed masques and costumes for the theatre, and in 1601 annotated Palladio's *Quattro Libri dell'Architettura*.

Reconstructed statue of Inigo Jones at Chiswick House T6

Jones was the father of English Palladianism, and his few remaining buildings are mostly to be found in London. His **Covent Garden Piazza** K14 (1630) was the first example of a European square in England, but it was never repeated in this form. It marked the birth of the London square, which increased in popularity as a residential type for the rest of the century. With the beginning of the Civil War in 1642 Jones's work was finished: the Commonwealth did not encourage architecture, apart from the extensive defensive earthworks surrounding London in 1643 – the last time the city was to be defended from the land.

The restoration of the monarchy in 1660 was followed by the Great Plague in 1665 and the Great Fire the following year. Most of the old city was destroyed, and the rebuilding presented an extraordinary opportunity for architecture and town planning. 13,200 houses, 87 churches and 44 halls of livery companies had been lost; the reoccupation of the burnt-out city was slow, the rich (apart from the aldermen) never returned, and as a result the city's westward expansion beyond the city walls was accelerated.

Many plans were made for rebuilding, mostly inspired by the avenues and *rond points* of continental examples. Wren's was the most ambitious, but none of them was realized, owing to the intricate patchwork of land ownership in the City, and the urgent need for new premises in which business could continue.

For the last forty years of the century the output of Wren's office was prodigious. His rebuilding of the City churches and **St Paul's Cathedral** L28 was followed by other important buildings, and he became the dominant figure in a growing circle of classical architects. By the beginning of the following century other major talents were emerging. Wren's brilliant clerk Nicholas Hawksmoor, John Vanbrugh, Thomas Archer, James Gibbs and William Kent were the chief architects of English classicism, a movement dependent on the initiative and works of Wren and Jones.

Events in this century dictated London's present form. After the Commonwealth the city was no longer threatened by invasion from the land and could therefore spread at will, and rebuilding after the Great Fire gave unprecedented opportunities for land speculation by private entrepreneurs. Speculative builders leased land from the ecclesiastical and aristocratic Great Estates to build squares, the century's most significant urban innovation. Their semi-public gardens surrounded by simple brick houses combined elements of town and country in a revolutionary way, forming a strong contrast to the old city's dense and treeless network of alleys. The effects of such building were startling: by the end of the century London had been transformed from a timber-built medieval port into a classical and predominantly brick city.

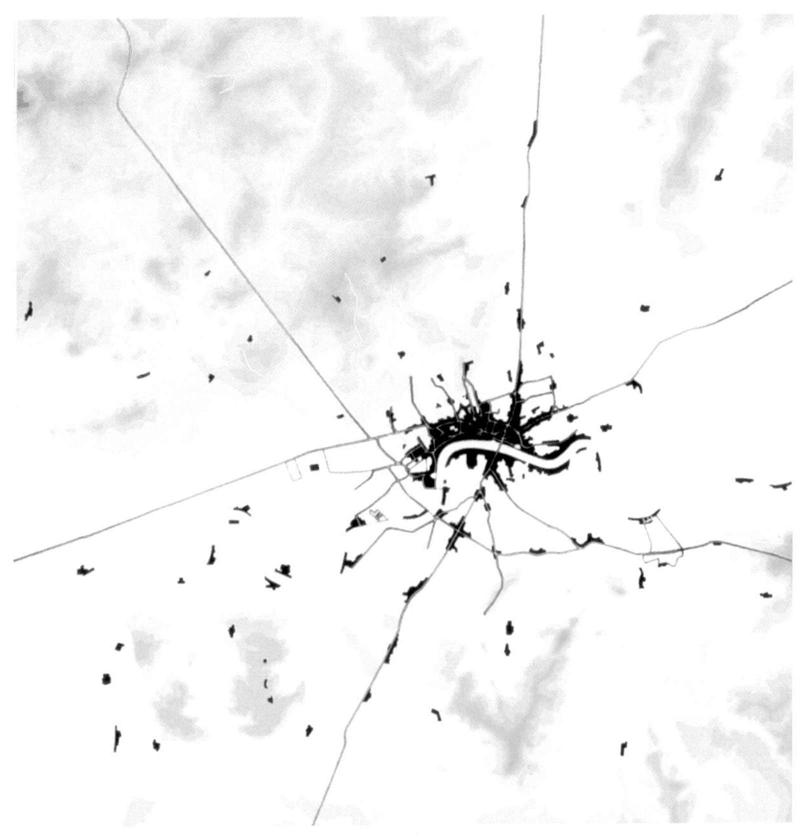

1590 **1600** 1610 1620 1630 1640

JAMES I
1603–25

CHARLES I
1625–49

1600 population c250,00
1603 Plague: 30,000 die
1605 The Great Frost: Thames frozen
1621 John Donne appointed Dean of St Paul's
1631 **JOHN DRYDEN** –170
1635 Hyde Park open
1642 **ISA**
1650 population 350

1607 Charlton House U1
1619–23 Chapel, Lincoln's Inn K6
1637 Cromwell Ho
1640 Lincol

1570 **JOHN THORPE** 1610

1573 **INIGO JONES**
1601 Annotates Palladio's *Quattro Libri dell'Architettura*
1616–35 **Queen's House**, **Greenwich** U2
1619 **Banqueting House**, **Whitehall** K12
1623–7 **Queen's Chapel** K13
1631 **St Paul's** K14 and **Piazza, Covent Ga**
1640 **Lindsey House** K16

1611 **JOHN WEBB**

1632 **CHRISTOPHER WRE**

1635 **ROBERT HOOK**

1590 1600 1610 1620 1630 1640

1660 1670 1680 1690 **1700** 1710

onwealth -60 | **CHARLES II** 1660–85 | **JAMES II** 1685–88 | **WIILIAM & MARY** 1689–1702 | **ANNE** 1702–14

1700 population c674,000

1665 Great Plague

1680 Versailles begun

1694 Bank of England founded

ON –1727

1666 Great Fire: 13,200 houses burnt

) Hampton Court, Richmond and Greenwich Palaces

ublic

1662 Royal Society founded

1698 Whitehall Palace destroyed: Court moved to St James's Palace

NLING GIBBONS –1720

1660–9 Samuel Pepys's private diary

lds K6

) Field Court, Gray's Inn G6

1660 **Bloomsbury Square**

1670 **Leicester Square** K19

1673 **Golden Square** K20

1678–88 **Gray's Inn Square** G6

1680 **Bedford Row** G4

1681 **Soho Square** K24

1684 **St James's Square** K18

1690 **Seven Dials** K25

1690 **New Square** K26

1672

1665–8 **Greenwich Palace** U2

1723

1661–1702 **Kensington Palace** I2

1670–2 **St Michael Cornhill** L9

1670–3 **St Vedast alias Foster** L14

1670–6 **St Mary-at-Hill** L15

1670–83 **St Mary-le-Bow** L17

1670–1703 **St Bride, Fleet Street** L18

1670–87 **St Lawrence Jewry** L19

1671–1705 **St Magnus** L25

1672–1717 **St Stephen Walbrook** L26

1674–87 **St James Garlickhithe** L27

1675–1711 **St Paul's Cathedral** L28

1676–84 **St James, Piccadilly** K21

1677–80 **St Anne and St Agnes** L30

1677–83 **St Benet, Paul's Wharf** L31

1677–87 **Christ Church** L32

1677–87 **St Martin, Ludgate Hill** L33

1677 –87 **St Peter upon Cornhill** L34

1681–86 **St Mary Abchurch** L37

1682 **St Mary Aldermary** L38

1683–7 **St Clement Eastcheap** L39

1684–9 **St Margaret Pattens** L40

1685–95 **St Andrew-by-the-Wardrobe** L41

1686–94 **St Michael Paternoster Royal** L43

1686–90 **St Margaret Lothbury** L42

1689–94 **Hampton Court Palace East Wing** V1

1695 **Morden College** X2

1696–1702 **Royal Naval Hospital, Greenwich** U3

1703

1670 *Map of London*

1671 **Monument** L23

1661 **NICHOLAS HAWKSMOOR** 1736

King's Gallery and Orangery, 1695–c1705 Kensington Palace I2

1664 **JOHN VANBRUGH** 1726

1668 **THOMAS ARCHER** 1743

1682 **JAMES GIBBS** 1754

1685 **WILLIAM KENT** 1748

1694 **RICHARD BURLINGTON** 1753

1660 1670 1680 1690 1700 1710

Eighteenth-century London

Four Georges of the Hanoverian dynasty occupied the throne of England from 1714 to 1830, giving their name to the 'Georgian' period and its architecture. The century was one of relative security and of economic and colonial expansion. The years between the Treaty of Utrecht in 1713 and the Battle of Waterloo in 1815 saw the emergence of England as a world trading power, with London at its centre. With the new mercantile wealth, a new social order emerged. The rural rich set up London houses, and artisans and shopkeepers proliferated to serve both the gentry and a growing middle class. In 1700 London's population was 555,500; by 1750 it had grown to only 700,000, but by 1801, the year of the first official census, it had increased dramatically to 959,000.

To celebrate the Tory Parliamentary victory over the Whigs in 1710, an Act of Parliament directed the building of 'fifty new churches in or near the Cities of London and Westminster or the suburbs thereof ... churches of stone and other proper materials with Towers and Steeples to each of them'. Of the fifty only twelve were built (between 1712 and 1735), most of them by architects of the generation after Wren – Hawksmoor, Archer and Gibbs. The call for towers and steeples required them to continue Wren's attempts to reconcile the classical temple form with the Christian steeple.

The architecture of the first half of the century is distinguished by the flowering of Palladianism as the official taste of the ruling class, and by the continued shaping and extension of the city by speculators. The modern architectural profession has its roots in this century, when such gentleman-artist-architects as Lord Burlington and William Chambers flourished. The architectural milieu centred round Lord Burlington and his associates, Colen Campbell (**Burlington House** K36 and **Chiswick House** T6) and William Kent (**Horse Guards** K50). Kent exemplified the universal designer – painter, architect, landscape gardener and furniture designer. Books published in the service of the new gentlemanly profession were to be the single most important agent in establishing the dictatorship of Palladian taste. In 1715 the first volume of Colen Campbell's *Vitruvius Britannicus* appeared, recording the best classical buildings erected in England, and in the same year Leoni made the first English translation of Palladio's *Quattro Libri*.

The force of Palladianism had waned by the middle of the century when, coinciding with England's increasing mercantile power, more exotic architectural influences developed. Architects like Chambers (the **Pagoda**, Kew T8), the Adam brothers (**Syon House** T9 and **Osterley Park** T10), and Horace Walpole and his Committee of Taste (**Strawberry Hill** V7) could digest oriental, classical and Gothic styles with equal facility. The beginnings of modern eclecticism – neo Gothic, neo-classicism, and the Picturesque – were well established before the end of the century.

Somerset House K62, detail of courtyard door

Great James Street G7, detail of doorcases

St George-in-the-East U9, detail of door to staircase

Following the great Building Act of 1774 the expansion of the city began in earnest in Bloomsbury (**Bedford Square** G12, 1775) and Marylebone (**Manchester Square** J16, 1776). Pattern books derived from *Vitruvius Britannicus* also appeared, giving instructions as to style, type and construction of buildings, and making the classical idiom accessible to the speculative builder, who might be a carpenter, actor, financier or lord. Besides the building on the Great Estates in central London, scattered developments also took place in what John Summerson called 'Greater Georgian London' – the villages of Hampstead, Highgate, Dulwich and Greenwich; along the roads from the centre to Islington, Highbury and Kennington; and in the parcels of land between the main radial roads: Somers Town, Camden Town and Canonbury. The ubiquitous Georgian terraced house, usually of four storeys including a basement, was arranged in streets, squares and crescents, and the grander terraces had an attic floor set back behind the parapet to accommodate extra servants. These narrow-fronted deep houses, unlike the houses built by master-craftsmen of the previous century, were early examples of industrial production, using standard sash windows, brick party walls, and iron railings. Beyond the composition of the street, architectural elaboration was restricted to the front door, the principal staircase, and the important rooms. In the following century John Nash used industrial methods and speculation to create picturesque urban scenery.

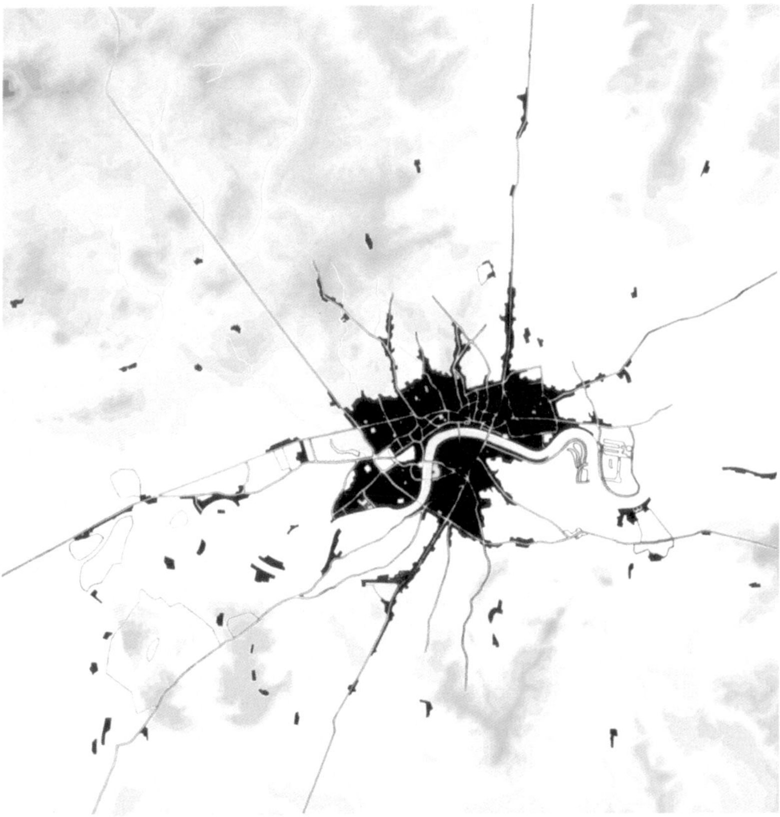

1690 **1700** 1710 1720 1730 1740

WILLIAM & MARY 1689–1702 | **ANNE** 1702–14 | **GEORGE I** 1714–27 | **GEORGE II** 1727–60

1700 population 550,000
1707 Union with Scotland
1713 Treaty of Utrecht
1716 **THOMAS GRAY** –1771
1727 **THOMAS GAINSBOROUGH** –
1728 **JAMES COOK** –1779
1736 **JAMES WATT**
1736 **JOHN CONSTA**

1711 Church Building Act
1704 Queen Anne's Gate K31
1717 Cavendish Square J3
1720 Grosvenor Square J7 1739 Berkeley
1715–25 Colen Campbell *Vitruvius Britannicus*
1715 Leoni's translation of Palladio's *Quattro Libri*

1632 **CHRISTOPHER WREN** 1723 1726 Leoni's translation of *The Archite*
1675–1710 St Paul's Cathedral L28 1727 William Kent *Designs of Inigo*
1696–1702 Royal Naval Hospital, Greenwich U3 1744
1709–11 Marlborough House K33

1661 **NICHOLAS HAWKSMOOR** 1736
1712–14 St Alfege, Greenwich U6
1714–29 St George-in-the-East U9
1714–30 St Anne, Limehouse U10
1714–29 Christ Church, Spitalfields H6
1716–24 St Mary Woolnoth L52
1716–31 St George, Bloomsbury G8
1735–45 West Tower

1664 **JOHN VANBRUGH** 1726
1717–20 Royal Arsenal, Woolwich U16
1717–26 Vanbrugh Castle U12

1668 **THOMAS ARCHER** 1743
1710–12 Roehampton House V3
1712–28 St Paul, Deptford U7
1714–28 St John, Smith Square K35

1682 **JAMES GIBBS**
1714–17 St Mary-le-Strand K34
1721–6 St Martin-in-the-Fields K40
1730–59 St Bartholomew's Hospital H12

1685 **WILLIAM KENT** 17
1733–6 Treasury Building K46
1744–5 44 Berkeley Sq
1745–55 The Horse G

1694 **RICHARD BURLINGTON**
1715–17 Burlington House with Colen Campbell K36
1722–30 College, Westminster School K41
1725–9 Chiswick House T6

1697 **HENRY FLITCROFT**
1731–3 St Giles in the Fields

1700 **GEORGE DANCE THE ELDER**
1736–40 St Leonar
1739–53 Ma
1741–4 St

1717 **HORACE WALPOLE**
17

1723 **WILLIAM CHAMBERS**

1728 **ROBERT ADAM**

1741 **GEO**

17

1690 1700 1710 1720 1730 1740

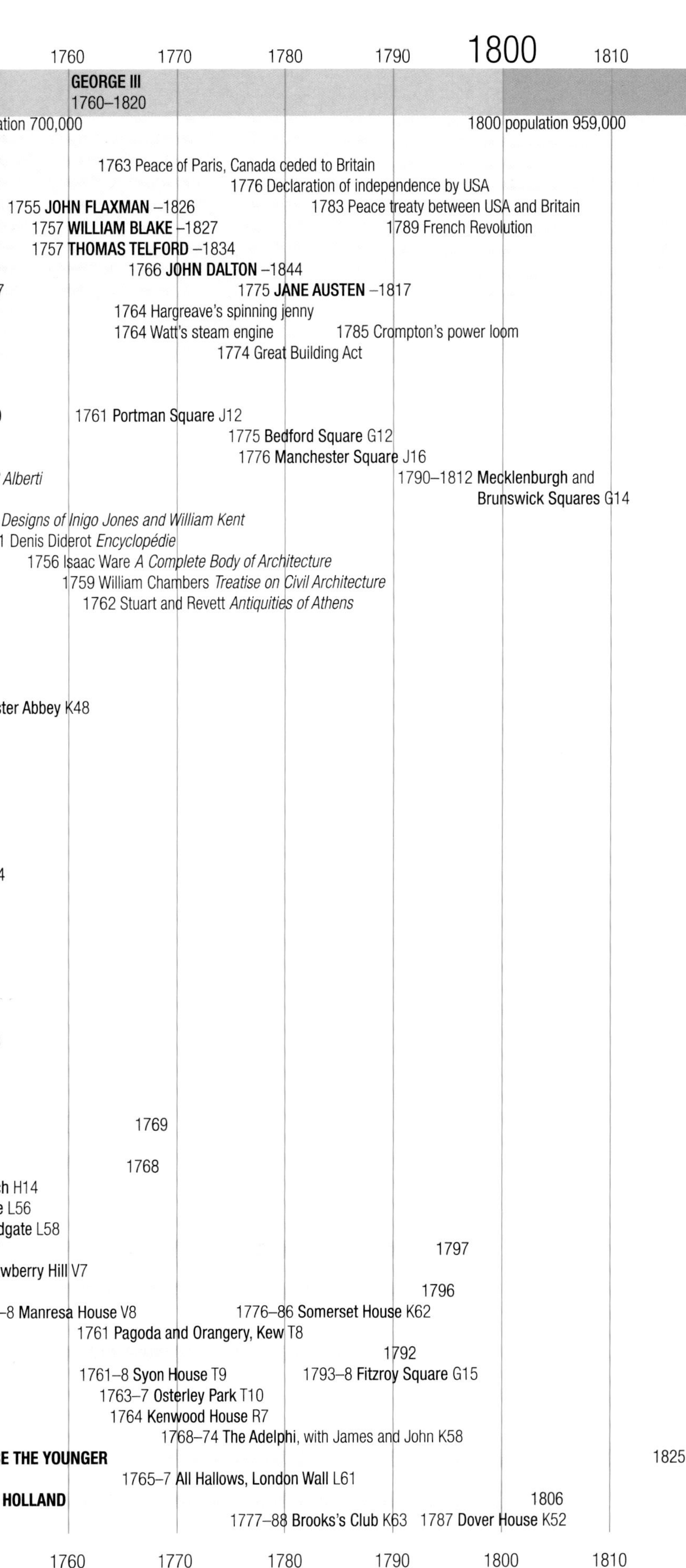

1760
1770
1780
1790
1800
1810
GEORGE III
1760–1820
ation 700,000
1800 population 959,000
1763 Peace of Paris, Canada ceded to Britain
1776 Declaration of independence by USA
1783 Peace treaty between USA and Britain
1789 French Revolution
1755 JOHN FLAXMAN –1826
1757 WILLIAM BLAKE –1827
1757 THOMAS TELFORD –1834
1766 JOHN DALTON –1844
1775 JANE AUSTEN –1817
1764 Hargreave's spinning jenny
1764 Watt's steam engine
1785 Crompton's power loom
1774 Great Building Act
1761 Portman Square J12
1775 Bedford Square G12
1776 Manchester Square J16
Alberti
1790–1812 Mecklenburgh and Brunswick Squares G14
Designs of Inigo Jones and William Kent
1 Denis Diderot Encyclopédie
1756 Isaac Ware A Complete Body of Architecture
1759 William Chambers Treatise on Civil Architecture
1762 Stuart and Revett Antiquities of Athens
ster Abbey K48
1769
1768
ch H14
e L56
dgate L58
1797
awberry Hill V7
1796
–8 Manresa House V8
1776–86 Somerset House K62
1761 Pagoda and Orangery, Kew T8
1792
1761–8 Syon House T9
1793–8 Fitzroy Square G15
1763–7 Osterley Park T10
1764 Kenwood House R7
1768–74 The Adelphi, with James and John K58
CE THE YOUNGER
1825
1765–7 All Hallows, London Wall L61
HOLLAND
1806
1777–88 Brooks's Club K63
1787 Dover House K52
1760
1770
1780
1790
1800
1810

Nineteenth-century London

The century which was to see London transformed from a large but otherwise typical European port and trade centre into the capital of a huge empire began with England at war with France. While the battle of Waterloo in 1815 brought an end to France's bid for European domination, the transformation of central London from a Georgian town into something grander had already started. In 1812 Regent Street was built with the encouragement of the Prince Regent and the initiative of the speculator-architect John Nash. His stuccoed streets and later terraces and villas brought a new, if theatrical, dignity to the city of uniform yellow-brick houses. The suburb of Regent's Park was finished in 1828 and opened to the public a decade later.

The 1820s and '30s in Europe saw the invention of new institutions of democracy, which required new building types. London now acquired the **British Museum** G25, the **Zoo** F28, arcades, hospitals (**St George's** J29 and **Charing Cross** K87) and cemeteries. After these came the buildings for trade and transport: canals, the railway stations (Euston from 1836), markets, hotels, banks, offices, restaurants, and the hygienic parks. With the increased trade brought about by the Industrial Revolution and the growth of the Empire, the population continued to grow. Many were housed in the further speculative development of the Great Estates – Cubitt's Belgravia and extensions to Bloomsbury – or new ventures like the less dense **Ladbroke estate** I7. Many more swelled the slums of the East End and notorious pockets of the West End. A series of cholera outbreaks in the 1840s and '50s showed that *laissez–faire* development would not provide adequate sanitation and in 1859 the Metropolitan Board of Works was established. Under its Chief Engineer, Joseph Bazalgette, a huge new system of sewers was built, with the main outfall at Beckton, well to the east of the city. As a further precaution, the Victoria, Albert and Chelsea Embankments to the Thames were built to speed the river and rid it of putrid mud. In 1851, Prince Albert's Great Exhibition of Arts and Industry, housed in the Crystal Palace in Hyde Park, brought a flood of visitors to London, and promoted the West End as a centre of shopping and entertainment. The subsequent development of Kensington as a cultural showpiece and centre of imperial learning added impetus to the extension of London westward from Belgravia.

The Victorians attacked the slums in two ways. Philanthropic societies built model housing for artisans. The two chief societies were rivals: one had Henry Roberts as architect producing decent humane city-buildings like those at **Streatham Street** G34; the other, presided over by Baroness Burdett-Coutts, had H A Darbishire introducing models for the destruction of the city's coherence and its re-formation into free-standing 'blocks' – the precursors of today's tower blocks. The other attack was simply to remove slums by driving new roads through them, and the last quarter of

Holly Village R11, Highgate

Reform Club K91, Pall Mall, detail of front door

Swan House N21, Embankment, detail of front door

the century saw the building of Shaftesbury Avenue, Charing Cross Road, and New Oxford Street in the West End; Queen Victoria Street (the continuation eastward of Bazalgette's Embankment) and King Street in the City; and the joining of Westminster with Hyde Park Corner by Victoria Street and later Grosvenor Gardens.

From the middle of the century, huge suburbs were built for the housing of artisans and clerks, who were enabled to commute to work in the city by an extensive but unplanned public transport system. New suburban railway lines were built, omnibuses ran on new highways and across and under the Thames by new bridges and tunnels. In 1863 the world's first underground railway opened: the Metropolitan Line from Paddington to Farringdon.

In 1870 the London School Board was set up to serve the new populations, and the type it established for the urban school is still recognizable. In 1889 the London County Council was established, taking over from the Metropolitan Board of Works, and was given increased powers to clear slums, and to provide rented working-class housing and parks. By the end of the century, London was physically much the city we inherit today. Its population had grown from just under a million in 1800 to the 6.5 million of Greater London: the largest city ever known.

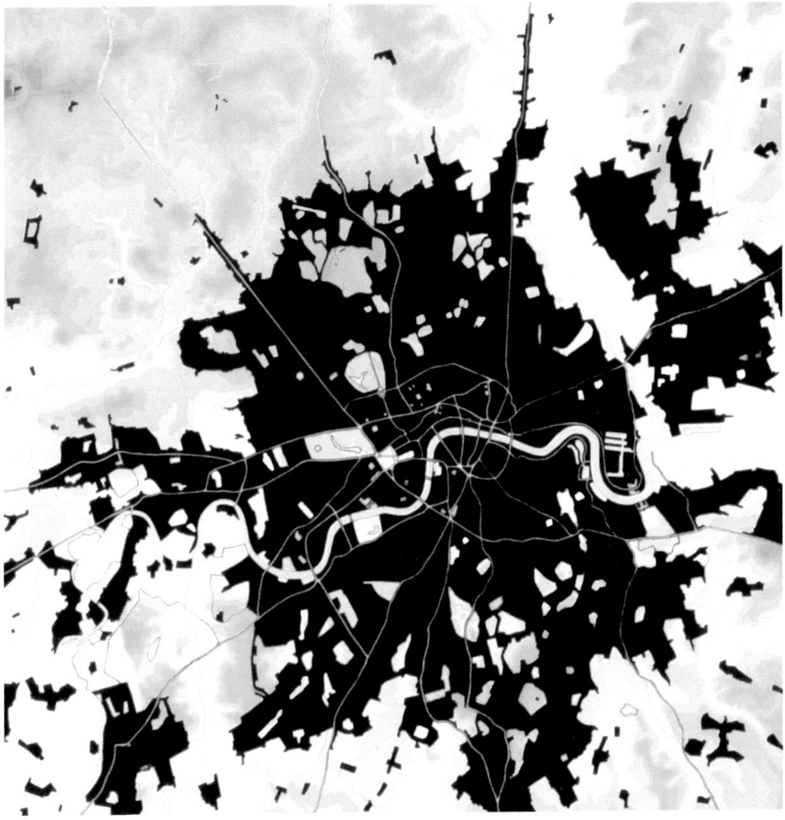

1790 **1800** 1810 1820 1830 1840

GEORGE III 1760–1820 | **GEORGE IV** 1820–30 | **WILLIAM IV** 1830–7 | **VICTORIA** 1837–1901

1800 population 959,300

1775 **J M W TURNER** –1851
1815 Battle of Waterloo
1780 **ELIZABETH FRY** –1845
1813 **DAVID LIVINGSTONE** –1873
1832 Reform Act
1781 **GEORGE STEPHENSON** –1848
1832–3 Factory Acts
1818 **KARL MARX** –1883
1801 **JOSEPH PAXTON** –1865
1819 **JOHN RUSKIN** –1900
1843 E
1806 **I K BRUNEL** –1859
1834 **WILLIAM MORR**
1809 **CHARLES DARWIN** –1882
1812 **CHARLES DICKENS** –1870

1752 **JOHN NASH** 1835
1836 A W Pugin *Co*
1812–28 Regent's Park F5
1840 Letarc
1816–18 Royal Opera Arcade K69
1842 Jose
1822–4 All Souls, Langham Place F16
1827–32 Carlton House Terrace K7
1828– Waterloo Place K79
1831 Theatre Royal, Haymar

1753 **JOHN SOANE** 1837
1800–3 Pitshanger Manor T11
1811–14 Dulwich Picture Gallery W3
1812–13 12–14 Lincoln's Inn Fields K67
1814 Stables, Royal Hospital N9
1816 Mausoleum G19
1823–5 St Peter Walworth P1
1824–8 Holy Trinity, Marylebone Road F
1825–8 St John, Bethnal Green U19

1778 **WILLIAM WILKINS** 1839
1827–9 University College
1827–9 St George's Hospital J29
1832–8 National Gallery K8

1781 **ROBERT SMIRKE**
1807–9 Royal Mint L69
1821–4 St Mary, Wyndham Place F19
1823–47 British Museum G25

1788 **THOMAS CUBITT**
1820–60 Barnsbury C1, Bloomsbury G35 and

1795 **CHARLES BARRY**
1826–8 Holy Trinity, Cloudesley Squar
1829–32 Travellers' Club K82
1835–60 Houses of P
1837–41 Reform

1800 **DECIMUS BURTON**
1825–8 Screen and Arch, Hyde Park C
1828–30 The Athenaeum K80
1844–

1811 **GEORGE GILBERT SCOTT**

1814 **WILLIAM BUTTERFIELD**

1824 **GEORGE EDMUND STREET**

1830 **ALFRED WATERHOUSE**

1831 **RICHARD NORMAN SH**

1831 **PHILIP WEBB**

1790 1800 1810 1820 1830 1840

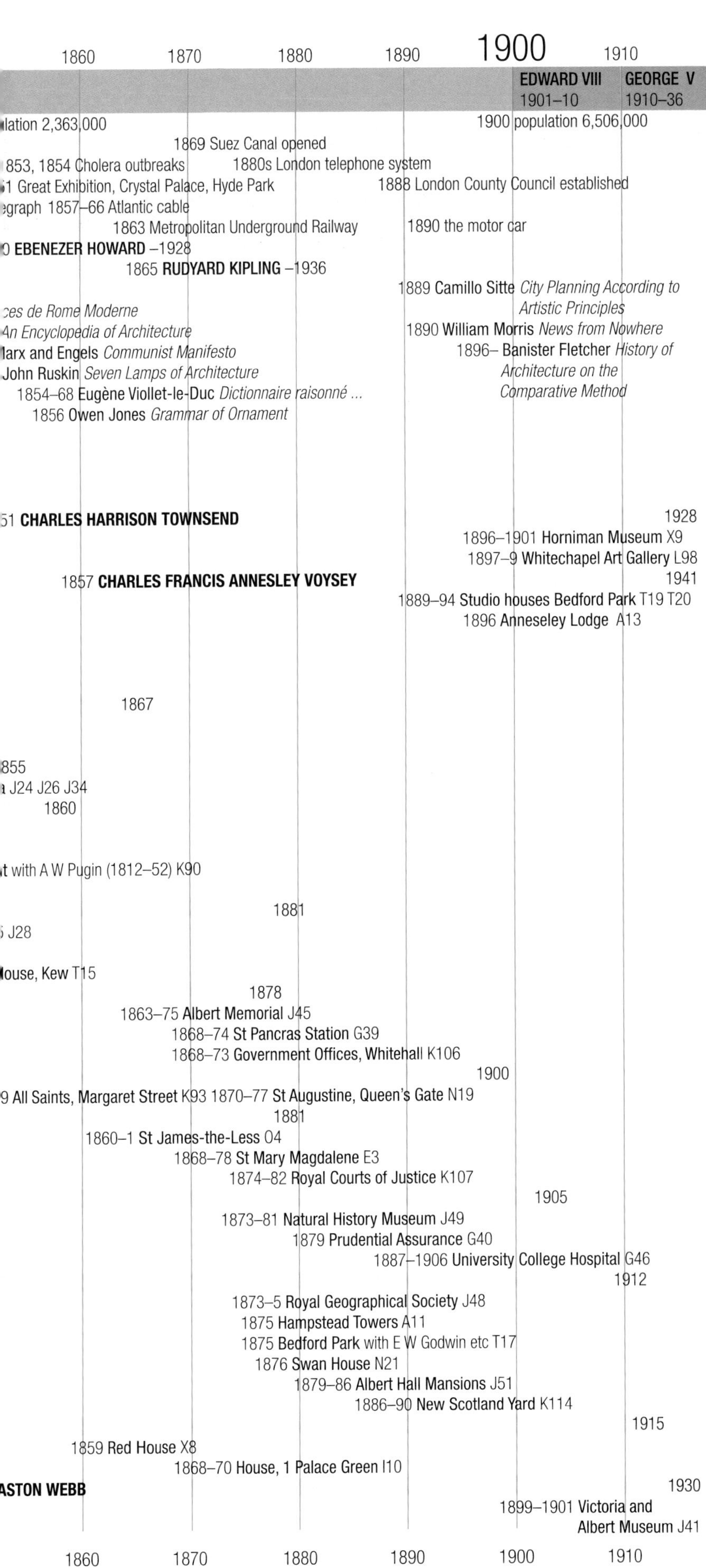

1860
1870
1880
1890
1900
1910
EDWARD VIII 1901–10
GEORGE V 1910–36
lation 2,363,000
1900 population 6,506,000
1869 Suez Canal opened
853, 1854 Cholera outbreaks
1880s London telephone system
1 Great Exhibition, Crystal Palace, Hyde Park
1888 London County Council established
graph 1857–66 Atlantic cable
1863 Metropolitan Underground Railway
1890 the motor car
0 EBENEZER HOWARD –1928
1865 RUDYARD KIPLING –1936
1889 Camillo Sitte City Planning According to Artistic Principles
ces de Rome Moderne
An Encyclopedia of Architecture
1890 William Morris News from Nowhere
larx and Engels Communist Manifesto
1896– Banister Fletcher History of Architecture on the Comparative Method
John Ruskin Seven Lamps of Architecture
1854–68 Eugène Viollet-le-Duc Dictionnaire raisonné ...
1856 Owen Jones Grammar of Ornament
51 CHARLES HARRISON TOWNSEND
1928
1896–1901 Horniman Museum X9
1897–9 Whitechapel Art Gallery L98
1857 CHARLES FRANCIS ANNESLEY VOYSEY
1941
1889–94 Studio houses Bedford Park T19 T20
1896 Anneseley Lodge A13
1867
855
J24 J26 J34
1860
t with A W Pugin (1812–52) K90
1881
J28
ouse, Kew T15
1878
1863–75 Albert Memorial J45
1868–74 St Pancras Station G39
1868–73 Government Offices, Whitehall K106
1900
9 All Saints, Margaret Street K93 1870–77 St Augustine, Queen's Gate N19
1881
1860–1 St James-the-Less O4
1868–78 St Mary Magdalene E3
1874–82 Royal Courts of Justice K107
1905
1873–81 Natural History Museum J49
1879 Prudential Assurance G40
1887–1906 University College Hospital G46
1912
1873–5 Royal Geographical Society J48
1875 Hampstead Towers A11
1875 Bedford Park with E W Godwin etc T17
1876 Swan House N21
1879–86 Albert Hall Mansions J51
1886–90 New Scotland Yard K114
1915
1859 Red House X8
1868–70 House, 1 Palace Green I10
ASTON WEBB
1930
1899–1901 Victoria and Albert Museum J41
1860
1870
1880
1890
1900
1910

Twentieth-century London

In the year 1900 London was firmly established as the capital of the world's largest empire. During the Edwardian period (1901–10) improvements to London befitting its imperial status were belatedly carried out – **Kingsway** K132, the **Mall** K17, **Admiralty Arch** K129 and a new front to **Buckingham Palace** K76 (completed, astonishingly, in three months). The architects of this confident decade were men like Aston Webb, Lutyens, Norman Shaw and Mewès and Davis. By then the English Arts and Crafts movement, originating in William Morris's reaction to the excesses of nineteenth-century industrialization, was widely admired abroad. Hermann Muthesius was commissioned by the *Deutsche Werkbund* to record English domestic architecture. His *Das Englische Haus* (The English House) was published in Germany in 1904. Without it, this significant indigenous English achievement, together with its lifestyle, would have been mostly lost or undervalued. The Free Style of Shaw, Webb and C R Ashbee's domestic work had reached its prime by the end of the nineteenth century; in the early years of the twentieth century it was applied to public buildings – notably fire stations, colleges, hospitals and libraries.

London was also the world's largest city, with a population of 6.5 million compared with 4 million in New York and 2.7 million in Paris. This massive population and the persistent slum conditions gave a fresh impetus to public housing schemes. The initiative for such work came from the philanthropic and public authority movements of the nineteenth century.

As a result of continued reformist and political pressure the London County Council was formed in 1889. The Housing for the Working Classes branch was established within the Architects Department of the LCC in 1893, following the Act of Parliament of the same name three years earlier.

At the turn of the century the LCC built the **Boundary Street Estate** H36 and the Millbank Estate to rehouse slum dwellers. They justify the claim that the LCC's output up to the First World War was one of the greatest achievements of the Arts and Crafts movement in English architecture. The socialist philosophy of William Morris and the architectural ideas of Lethaby and Philip Webb had finally been put into practice as urban design.

The suburb, that peculiarly Anglo-Saxon development for which the London prototype had been Norman Shaw's **Bedford Park** T17 of 1877, re-emerged. Ebenezer Howard's book *Tomorrow: A Peaceful Path to Real Reform*, published in 1898, pointed to the garden city as the prescription for the social and economic ills of city life. Raymond Unwin's **Hampstead Garden Suburb** R19 of 1906–9 was the closest Howard's prophecy came to being realized, and it has remained a model for similar developments to the

Broadgate H44

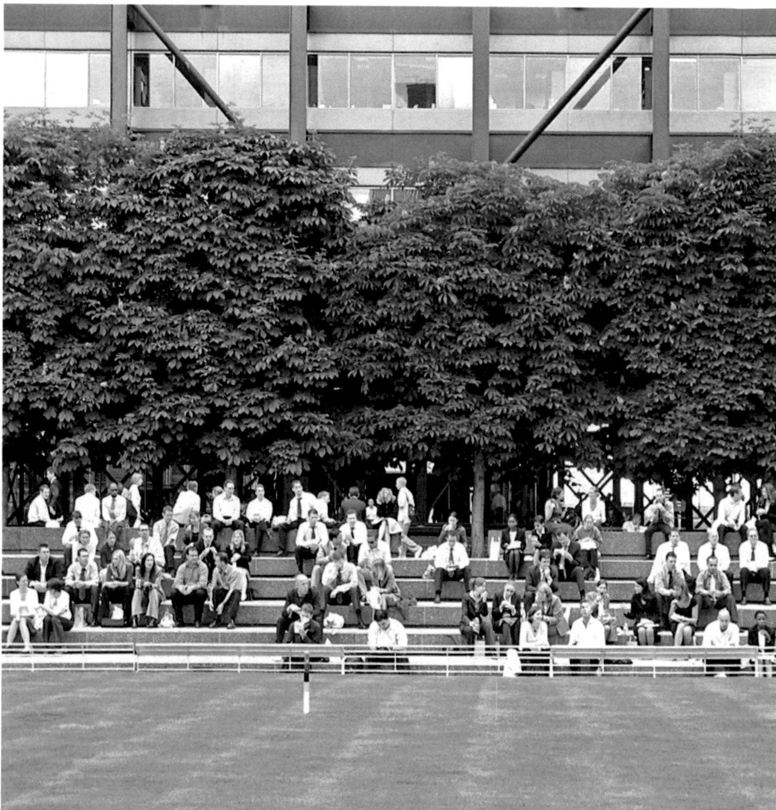

present day. Unwin's own *Town Planning in Practice* of 1909 was also an important text. It was partly influenced by German developments, a point which underlines the widespread cultural interdependence and interest that existed between the two countries before the First World War.

By 1918, however, the British Empire was in decline, and architecture suffered along with everything else. Despite the continued high stature of architects like Lutyens, Townsend and Voysey, the ideals of the Arts and Crafts movement could not withstand the traumatic effects of the first mechanized war. Architectural initiative had passed to other European centres (notably Moscow, Paris and Berlin), but London, isolated during the war, was now suspicious of foreign influence.

During the 1920s and '30s building in London concentrated on continued suburban expansion. In these two decades England and Wales built 4 million houses, a third of the total national housing stock. Many of these 'homes for heroes', in the form of semi-detached single family dwellings, were made possible by major extensions to the London Underground ('Metroland'). The underground network in central London had been considered complete in 1914, but under the directorship of Frank Pick it was radically extended. Pick understood the value of the Underground in giving unity to a diverse and extended city. As Haussmann's boulevards were to Paris in the nineteenth century, so Pick's underground network was to London. The consistent quality of Charles Holden's many stations for this £40 million expansion and of Edward Johnston's sans-serif typeface for the Underground (commissioned by Pick in 1913 and designed by 1916) gave the network a unified image.

As a result of two scandals in which formerly open squares which had been thought to be protected from development had been built over (at Endsleigh Gardens for **Friends' House** G58 and at **Mornington Crescent** G31 for the Carreras factory), the London Squares Preservation Act of 1931 preserved them as open spaces in perpetuity.

Modern architecture was gingerly introduced into the capital, principally as a middle-class experiment. The style derived from 1920s Paris, 'moderne', had to coexist uneasily with neo-Georgian. From the end of the 1920s to the outbreak of the Second World War a number of distinguished émigré architects arrived in London – Gropius, Chermayeff, Breuer, Mendelsohn, Lubetkin and Moholy-Nagy among others. They brought with them an infectious enthusiasm for the 'new architecture'. Lubetkin and his firm Tecton were responsible for buildings at **London Zoo** F43, F46 and for the **Highpoint** flats R27, which were the best of their period. The Anglo-Saxon contribution came from Connell Ward and Lucas, Emberton, Wells Coates. McGrath, Maxwell Fry and Owen Williams produced buildings of comparable quality but without quite the same intensity.

However, the prolific output of the firm of John Burnet, Tait and Lorne contributed an important middle-of-the-road modernity – seen in the

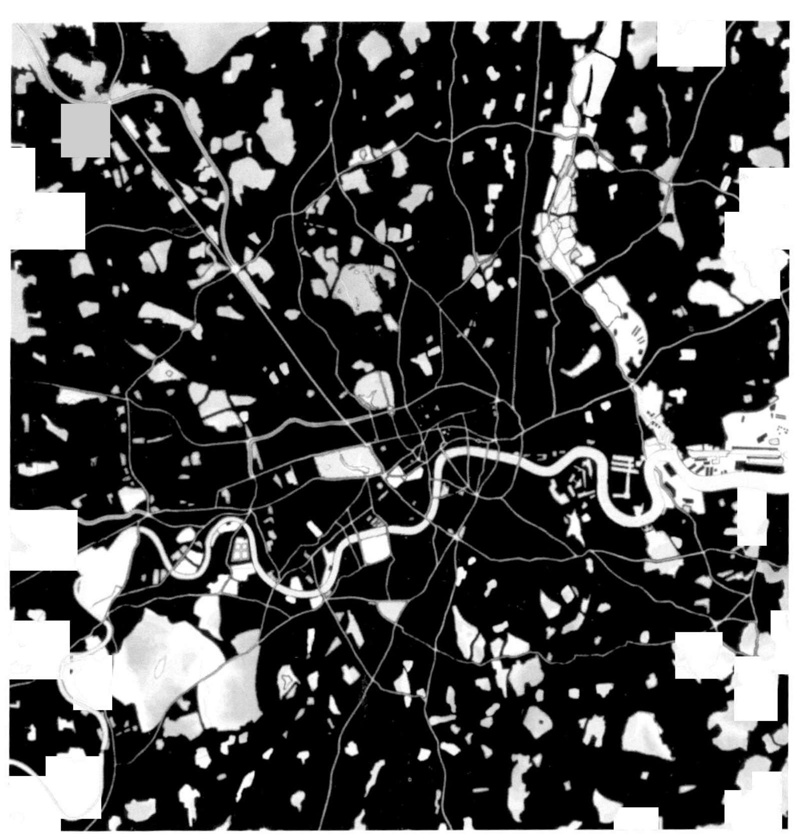

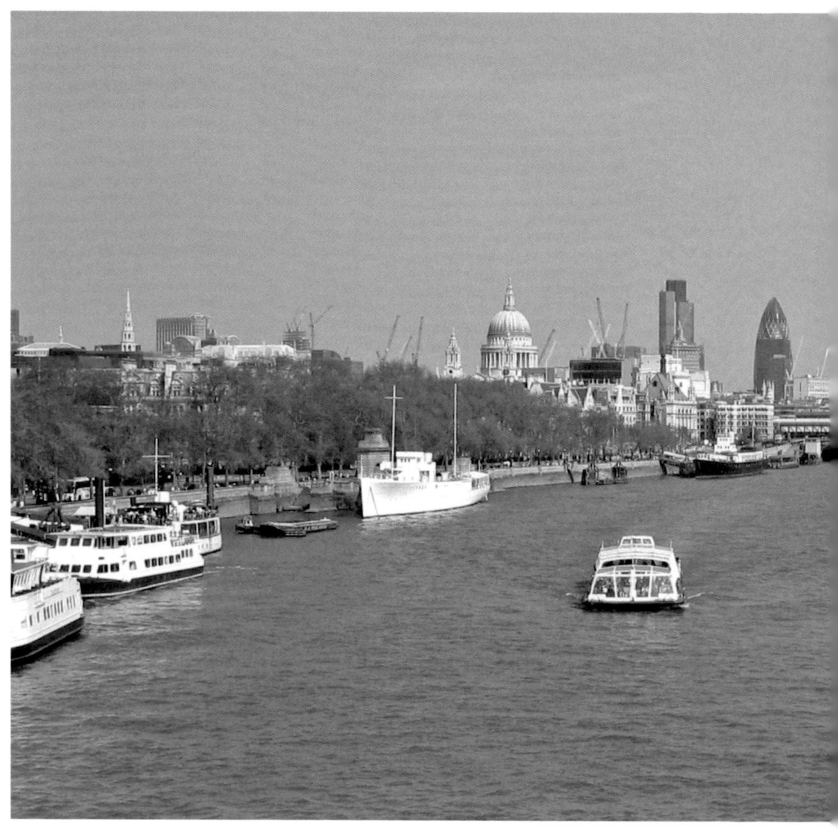

mixture of frame construction with stripped classicism in **Kodak House** K135, and the influence of Dudok's brickwork in the **Royal Masonic Hospital** T23. At the same time the work of Charles Holden and Giles Gilbert Scott offered alternative paths to modernity. The monumental brickwork of Scott's **Battersea Power Station** N30, and the elegant simplicity of **Waterloo Bridge** K160 are better appreciated today than they were by contemporary historians.

In 1940 the Blitz seriously damaged the City of London and virtually destroyed the Docks and the East End – curiously the West End of London remained relatively intact. The most conspicuous architectural casualties of the bombing were the City churches (twenty were destroyed), the Halls of City Livery Companies (nineteen were badly damaged), and to the west Gray's Inn and the Temple. The evacuation of large sections of the population followed. In 1943 Abercrombie and Forshaw's *County of London Plan* was proposed for the reconstruction – regrettably its general intentions were neither valued nor implemented.

In the early 1950s the post-war reconstruction of London began, with the Festival of Britain buildings on the South Bank (1951) as its uneasy celebration (although the **Royal Festival Hall** K163, the only remaining built evidence of the Festival, is still among the best modern public buildings in London).

In domestic building the LCC were still taking the lead, devising housing programmes in the East End, south London and in Roehampton. However, the good intentions of the Welfare State, coupled with watered-down allegiances to Le Corbusier's principles and the democratic building style of Sweden, were not enough to produce good architecture. The lack of suitable architectural models, combined with mad planning policies, resulted in a further deterioration in the quality of building in London. At the same time the population continued to decline as large numbers of people moved out to satellite New Towns like Harlow and Stevenage, established under the New Towns Act (1946). In the following decades the forms of speculative office and hotel developments have proved to be indistinguishable from the residential towers of the Welfare State. When viewed from Primrose Hill in the north or the plateau of Blackheath in the south, the skyline of London became a spectacle of stubby, evenly distributed towers. However, during the 1960s critical reaction to mixed development (towers and row houses) began to emerge in the form of 'low-rise high-density' housing, supported by the research of Leslie Martin at Cambridge University, and produced most notably by the London Borough of Camden. The resulting solutions in the main were as alien to London as the tower blocks they wished to condemn.

The 1960s saw an appetite for motorway building, which came to a head with the proposed motorway box (equivalent to the Boulevard Périphérique in Paris). For this, large and sound

View from Waterloo Bridge 2007

sections of, for example, St John's Wood and neighbouring areas were to be destroyed, but luckily vocal public opinion was beginning to act as censor to comprehensive redevelopment. Articulate local action groups prevented the construction of the motorway box and also saved the area of Covent Garden. In commercial building, the Smithsons' innovative **Economist** group (1965 K176), partly inspired by the organization of the Rockefeller Center in New York, was a welcome change from the general uncritical importation of the same city's Lever House model (see for example **Thorn House** K168, **New Zealand House** K171 and **Marathon House** F51).

In the first edition of this book we noted that there had been little building in London in the 1970s and that the city was 'poised for fresh initiatives which should respect its architectural traditions'. These initiatives were taken in the huge area of Docklands, one of the few places where any significant public investment was made, and in the City, where towards the end of the 1980s a boom in office-building reached a climax. In neither case were traditions respected and very few new buildings of distinction were produced.

There was very little public investment throughout the 1980s, with the exception of the construction of the M25, the orbital motorway which now nets London in a circle 50km (30 miles) across, providing new opportunities for development and speculation unhindered by the existing city. The failure to invest in London's public realm produced a squalor that compared very unfavourably with the continuing improvement of other European capitals.

The private commercial market collapsed at the end of the 1980s, and the start of the 1990s saw very little public or private development being undertaken. While in the 1970s architectural debate in Britain had been relatively pluralistic, the publication of HRH the Prince of Wales's *Vision of Britain* in 1990 helped polarize it between a synthetic architectural 'tradition', which was essentially reactionary, and modernism. This caricature increased the opposition between the ingratiating 'neo-vernacular' style considered appropriate for most housing and some offices, and the mainly empty-headed modernism of the suburban 'business park'.

By the end of the century, the establishment of the National Lottery in 1993 and the preparations for the celebration of the Millennium encouraged the re-equipping of the majority of the capital's principal cultural institutions – art galleries, museums and performance spaces.

Fears that the Prince of Wales's earlier 'vision' might be realized were groundless: in any case those champions of London's architecture in the late twentieth century who had been the objects of his dislike – Stirling, St John Wilson, Lasdun and the Smithsons – were dead.

1890 1900 1910 1920 1930 1940

EDWARD VII 1901–10 | GEORGE V 1910–36 | GEORGE VI 1936–52

1900 population 6,506,000

1914–18 First World War

1917 Russian Revolution

1939–45 Sec

1939 Evacuati

1940 The Bli

1904 **Herman Muthesius** *Das Englische Haus*

1933 London Passenger T

1908 **Adolph Loos** 'Ornament und Verbrechen'

19

1831 **RICHARD NORMAN SHAW**

1912

1923 **Le Corbusier** *Vers une architecture*

1905–8 Piccadilly Hotel K125

1932 **Hitchcock** & **Johnso**

1849 **ASTON WEBB**

1930

1934 **F R S Yorke** *The M*

1901–13 Queen Victoria Memorial K121, Admiralty Arch K129

1936 **Nikolaus Pe**

1912–13 Buckingham Palace front K76

1937 **Le Corbusi**

1857 **JOHN BURNET TAIT (JOHN BURNET TAIT & LORNE)**

1938

1940 **Siegfri**

1904–11 Edward VII Galleries G51

1930–34 Royal Masonic Hosp

1868 **EDWIN LUTYENS**

1944 194

1909–20 Central Square Hampstead Garden Suburb R22

1

1919–21 The Cenotaph K140

1924–7 Lutyens House H37, 1924–39 M

1928 Offices and showroom, Pall

1935 Reuters & Press

1875 **CHARLES HOLDEN**

1927–9 Broadway House K146

1930s Underground Station

1932 Senate House G65

1878 **ARTHUR DAVIES (MEWES & DAVIES)**

1906 Ritz Hotel K127

1928 Hasilwood House L113

1908–11 Royal Automobile Club K131

1922–31 National Westminster Bank L108

1880 **GILES GILBERT SCOTT**

1929–55 Battersea Power Static

1939–45 Wate

1889 **JOSEPH EMBERTON**

1930 Olympia Exhibition Hall

1935 Simpson's, Picc

1890 **OWEN WILLIAMS**

1932 Daily Express Buildin

1934 Wembley Arena T

1895 **WELLS COATES**

1933 Isokon Flats B17

1938 Flats, Pala

1895 **LCC ARCHITECTS DEPARTMENT**

1897 Boundary Street Estate H36

1901 **BERTHOLD LUBETKIN & TECTON**

1932–5 Gorilla House F43

1933–8 Highpoint 1 & 2

1938 Finsbury

1914 **DENYS LASDUN**

ALISON (1928–93) & **PETER** (1925–20

1926 **JAMES STIRLING** **(STIRLING A**

1933 **RICHARD ROGERS**

1935 **NORMAN FOST**

1890 1900 1910 1920 1930 1940

1960 1970 1980 1990 **2000** 2010

ELIZABETH II
1952–
ılation 8,197,000 — 2000 population 7,322,000
d War — 1973 Britain joins European Economic Community
ulation from London begins
51 Festival of Britain — 1969 Neil Armstrong walks on the moon
Board — 1965 Local Government reorganized: Greater London Council (GLC) established
owns Act — GLC abolished 1985 — 2000 Greater London Authority established
1965 **Le Corbusier** dies
ernational Style: Architecture since 1922
use
ioneers of the Modern Movement from Wm Morris to Walter Gropius
d les cathédrales étaient blanches
on *Space Time and Achitecture*

k Abercrombie *Greater London Plan,* **John Summerson** *Georgian London*
n Rowe 'Mathematics of the Ideal Villa'
Le Corbusier *Le Modulor*
Bank L111
49, 1928–30 Housing, Page Street O10
tion L119
1960
1958 **F R S Yorke and F Gibberd** *The Modern Flat*
11 — 1960 **Reyner Banham** *Theory and Design in the First Machine Age*
1961 **Jane Jacobs** *The Death and Life of Great American Cities*
1966 **Aldo Rossi** *L'architettura della città (The Architecture of the City)*
1966 **Robert Venturi** *Complexity and Contradiction in Architecture*
1972 **Robert Venturi** and **Denise Scott Brown** *Learning from Las Vegas*
1977 **Richard Sennett** *The Fall of Public Man*
1960 — 1978 **Colin Rowe** and **Fred Koetter** *Collage City*
1981 **Aldo Rossi** *Autobiografia scientifica*
1994 **Rem Koolhaas** *Delirious New York*
dge K160
1956 — 1995 **Rem Koolhaas** and **Bruce Mau** *S,M,L,XL*

57
1969

4–6 Pioneer Health Centre X10
1958

I24
1966
951 Royal Festival Hall K163
1952–9 Alton East V10 & Alton West V12 Estates, Roehampton
1964 Queen Elizabeth Hall & Hayward Gallery K177
1990

uin Pool F46

Centre G66

2001
1952–60 Cluster Blocks U29 U30
1958–60 Flats Green Park K170
1967–77 National Theatre K178
ITHSON — 1993, 2003
1964 Economist Building K176
1968–72 Housing, Robin Hood Gardens U34
WAN) 1992
1958 Flats, Langham House V13
1979 Tate Gallery Clore Gallery O16
1994–98 No 1 Poultry L140

ARD ROGERS PARTNERSHIP, ROGERS STIRK HARBOUR)
1978–86 Lloyd's L129
1984–7 Offices and flats, Thames Wharf T35
1993 Lloyd's Register L139
1994 Channel 4 K185
1998–2000 **O2** U50

STER & PARTNERS)
1987–90 ITN Offices G77
1990 Offices & flats, Hester Road N36
1997–2004 Offices, 30 St Mary Axe L142
2002 City Hall L146

1960 1970 1980 1990 2000 2010

Twenty-first-century London

In 2000 Londoners directly elected their first Mayor, Ken Livingstone, and an Assembly, the first city-wide government since the abolition of the GLC in 1985, but one with far fewer powers, limited to transport, the police and emergency services. What was left of 'planning' after its determined weakening in the 1980s remained with the London boroughs and with central government. While the Mayor had no direct control over planning and architecture, he chose to be advised by Richard Rogers and did initiate a programme for the improvement of public spaces, the most successful realized in the reordering and part-pedestrianizing of **Trafalgar Square** K70 to the highest standards of European design.

Wishing to appear business-friendly and to emulate the forms of those other 'world cities' and capitals of finance, Frankfurt, Tokyo and New York, the Mayor was, however, able to champion the erection of tall buildings, especially if these were of eccentric or self-promoting 'iconic' design, and this encouragement, combined with central government's quite gratuitous policy of 'densification' produced an unprecedented wave of development. The effects were concentrated largely in the City, in a desperate rivalry with Canary Wharf, and, paradoxically, in the poorer boroughs, Tower Hamlets, Hackney and Southwark. While other richer boroughs such as Westminster managed to resist the wilder excesses of development, not since the post-war reconstruction of the 1950s had the London skyline seen so many cranes. The twin policies of densification and the preference for the reuse of 'brownfield' land as sites for new housing resulted in a scattering of cheap-looking blocks of no architectural significance squeezed onto sites previously considered unsuitable: for example, very close to roads or railway lines – see photograph page 64.

Two practices emerged, those led by Norman Foster and Richard Rogers (both founder members of the small practice Team Four established in 1963), to become synonymous with British architecture both in London and abroad. Foster, like Wren, refined particular types, the commercial office and the new 'academy' schools, for example; Rogers, like Nash, was responsible for the greater awareness of the importance of the public realm, parodied as the space for the 'café society'. Foster provided conspicuous London landmarks while Rogers's active political role as advisor to the Mayor remained influential in the inconclusive debates about cities in general and London in particular. While the centre stage was appropriated by the production of the large corporate practices, there was evidence of other kinds of practice. These included cells of resistance to the crude commercial brief: Fretton, Chipperfield, Howarth Tompkins, Caruso St John and so on. Others, Hadid, Alsop, Libeskind, and Future Systems, ambitiously adopted the full mantle and glamour of the star system.

With the Mayor's active support, in 2005 London won its bid to host the Olympic Games in 2012, with a former industrial site north of Stratford as its nucleus. This and the development of the King's Cross railway lands, started in 2008, comprised the two largest building sites in the capital. In 2008 Mayor Livingstone's eight-year tenure was ended by the election of the Conservative Boris Johnson, whose early administration had, at the time of writing, shown little sense of strategy, less enthusiasm for over-sized developments than his predecessor and more for planting street trees.

Dystopias 1: Underground advertisement, London as Theme Park

1990 2000 2010 2020 2030 2040

ELIZABETH II
1952–

2000 population 7,322,000
2001 World Trade Center, New York, destroyed
2008 'Credit Crunch'
2000 London's first directly elected Mayor, **Ken Livingstone**, and Assembly
2005 London wins bid to host 2012 Olympic Games
2008 **Boris Johnson** elected Mayor
2008 High speed rail link St Pancras to mainland Europe

1933 **RICHARD ROGERS (ROGERS STIRK HARBOUR)**
1989–2008 Terminal 5, Heathrow T41
1993–2000 Lloyd's L129
1998–2000 02 (Millennium Dome) U50
2003– Chiswick Business Park T39

1935 **NORMAN FOSTER (FOSTER & PARTNERS)**
1997–2004 Offices, 30 St Mary Axe L142
2002 Millennium Foot Bridge L143
2002 City Hall L146
2003 Albion Riverside N41
2007 Wembley Stadium T42

Pavilions, Serpentine Gallery J79
2000 **ZAHA HADID** (1950–)
2001 **DANIEL LIEBSKIND** (1946–)
2002 **TOYO ITO** (1941–)
2003 **OSCAR NIEMEYER** (1907–)
2005 **ALVARO SIZA** (1933) & **EDUARDO SOUTO DE MOURA** (1952–)
2006 **OMA REM KOOLHAAS** (1944–)
2007 **OLAFUR ELIASSON** (1967–) & **KJETIL THORSEN**
2008 **FRANK GEHRY** (1929–)

1990 2000 2010 2020 2030 2040

Dystopias 2: Underground advertisement, London as Surveillance City

Inner London

Sections A–P

continued section R

continued section T

continued section E

continued section R
continued section B
continued section E
Hampstead
Vale of Health
South Hampstead
18
19
20
8
5
1
2
3
10
4
6
7
17
15
11
16
12
14
9
c
d
g
h
k
l
o
p

Hampstead (west) ■ Cricklewood ■ West Hampstead

In the seventeenth century, Hampstead village, on the ridge of a steep hill overlooking London, was much favoured as a place of retreat from the city. At the beginning of the eighteenth century the villages of Hampstead and Kentish Town, the hamlets of the Vale of Health and North End, and the manors of Belsize and Chalk Farm were all surrounded by heathland and fields and were still quite separate from London. After the discovery of the Hampstead Wells the village rapidly became a fashionable eighteenth-century spa. Most of Hampstead's fine Georgian buildings have survived, owing both to a protective cordon of open land which hindered speculation, and to the steepness of Hampstead Hill, which prevented the incursions of trams and buses in the early twentieth century.

Inseparable from Hampstead are the heath and its hamlets, the Vale of Health and North End. In 1866 further building on the heath was restricted when 97 hectares (240 acres) was bought by the government; Parliament Hill was added in 1890, Golders Hill Park in 1897, the Heath Extension north of Spaniards Road in 1905, and the Kenwood grounds in 1924, making a total of over 283 hectares (700 acres).

The land slopes down from the heights of Hampstead in the east to Edgware Road, the Romans' Watling Street. To the north of the railway lines (the North London Line and the main lines to the north from St Pancras and Marylebone) are the red-brick houses of West Hampstead; to the south are fancier red-brick 'mansion' flats such as Greencroft Gardens. Finchley Road, once a local high street, became a semi-urban motorway feeding the M1, Britain's first motorway, characterized by its quasi-Egyptian styled bridges of the late 1950s by Owen Williams.

To the west of Edgware Road (which becomes a High Street at Kilburn and Cricklewood) are the late Victorian and early Edwardian suburbs of Kilburn and Brondesbury. Between these and the Green Belt lies a ring of between-the-wars suburban semi-detached houses – 'Homes for Heroes', or 'Metroland' – in which most Londoners now live, and in which most of the remainder would like to live. A sample is seen in the north-west beyond Hendon Way, a quintessentially 1930s suburban motor road lined with flowering cherry trees.

Georgian Hampstead, Church Row A6

Fenton House 1693 **A1** d 
Hampstead Grove NW3
⊖ Hampstead

The formal approach to Fenton House, one of the finest detached houses in Hampstead, is from the green triangle of Holly Bush Hill to the south. The wrought iron gates give a view of the southern front set deep in its site, but the entrance is from the side, in Hampstead Grove, where an opening in the high boundary wall reveals the house. It is square in plan with projecting wings, linked by a colonnade of later date; the eaves, cornice and hipped roof are found in several houses in Hampstead. The house is now owned by the National Trust and open to the public, and hosts musical and theatrical evenings.

Georgian Hampstead 1 **A2** d
18th Century
(west of Heath Street NW3)
⊖ Hampstead

Apart from single buildings like **Fenton House** A1 and complete streets like **Church Row** A6, Hampstead to the west of **Heath Street** (note numbers 75–89 and 113–25) is a complex series of alleys and steps best appreciated on foot: the visitor will discover many small terraces and spaces not included in this guide. Starting from Hampstead Underground station, north up Holly Bush Hill are **Volta House**, **Bolton House**, **Windmill Hill House** and **Enfield House**: an informal mid-eighteenth-century terrace of nine bays. Set back from Holly Bush Hill behind long front gardens, they are a reminder that Hampstead was an eighteenth-century village. The front of the terrace is of brown brick, with red-brick dressings and straight door hoods on carved brackets. To the east is **Romney House** (1797), large and weatherboarded, and approached from the street through a walled courtyard. Built originally for the painter George Romney, it is one of London's earliest studio houses. The large north-facing windows at the back look over Heath Street.

Further to the north (past Fenton House) is **Old Grove House** in Hampstead Grove. The front of this complex early eighteenth-century house has an enlarged order of three bays, an attic floor of brown brick with red dressings, and a large doorway with a Tuscan pediment. In 1730 a wing of stables and cottages was added, surrounding a small yard.

Finally **The Mount** (c1710) is a gentle ramp leading from Hampstead Square back to Heath Street, from which it is divided by railings and a strip of green. It contains **Cloth Hill**, an early-eighteenth-century mansion with two projecting wings, and higher up and at right angles **Caroline House** and **Holly Cottage**, both two-bay mid-Georgian houses.

Georgian Hampstead 2 **A3** h
18th century
(west of Holly Bush Hill NW3 and north of Church Row)
⊖ Hampstead

1–4 **Lower Terrace** (late eighteenth century), 1–6 **Mount Vernon** (early eighteenth century), **Holly Walk**, **Holly Place**, **Hollyberry Lane** (all mid-eighteenth century), **Benham's Place** (1813) and **Prospect Place** (1820), together form a dense and miniature composition of interconnected alleys and single-sided streets, the whole conveying the essence of eighteenth-century Hampstead. The painter John Constable lived at 2 Lower Terrace from 1835–8.

Georgian Hampstead 3 **A4** h
18th century
(cast of Heath Street NW3)
⊖ Hampstead

An area which developed as a result of the discovery of the wells, and in the eighteenth century turned the village into a fashionable spa. Many of the place names (Well Road, Flask Walk, etc) derive from this time.

Flask Walk, a pedestrian street of eighteenth-century cottages, leads off Hampstead High Street to the south of the Underground station. At its end is the Flask Inn, the original meeting place of the Kit-Kat Club (founded in 1705 by Whig politicians and writers), portraits of whose members are to be found in the National Portrait Gallery. Flask Walk continues into **Well Walk** (c1780) where, on the south side, is a fine terrace of eighteenth-century houses, with unusual protruding porches. Note also the Victorian fountain on the north side, commemorating the spring or wells. Also on the north side is **Burgh House** (1703), a large five-bay mansion approached from New End Square. Formerly the residence of the physician attached to the Hampstead Wells, this house is now open to the public.

More Georgian houses are to be found in a group to the north, off East Heath Road, overlooking the heath, **Cannon Hall**, although much altered, is an early eighteenth-century house, with an impressive approach through a courtyard from Cannon Place. George du Maurier lived there. **Squires Mount**, a row of mid-eighteenth-century cottages forming a small court off East Heath Road, should also be noted. Also in East Heath Road is **Foley House** (1698), a fine house set back behind its walled entrance court.

Flask Walk

Elm Row early 18th century **A5** d
off Heath Street NW3
⊖ Hampstead

A fine early-eighteenth-century terrace, comparable to **Church Row** A6 in scale, although here the front gardens, enclosed with high walls, partly obscure the terrace from the street, and number 3 has an unfortunate roof extension. The windows of the houses are either straight-headed or segmentally arched. Elm Lodge (1700), on the corner, has a miniature Palladian entrance stair, and Vine House (1700–10) is an impressive five-bay, two-storey house, its doorway on carved brackets.

Church Row 1720 **A6** h
NW3
⊖ Hampstead
This is the best and most regular Georgian street in Hampstead; the houses on the south side all dating from about 1720. Of four storeys, they have low segmental brick arches to the windows, which seem to form a larger proportion of the façade than the brickwork. The north side of the street defines the southern boundary of Hampstead cemetery and is more irregular, both in form and period. Unusually for London, the central reservation of the street is planted with a line of plane trees, and the terraces give a fine perspective view of the parish church of St John. In Hampstead's loose village structure Church Row's design is the closest thing to an urban set piece.

St John 1744–7 **A7** h
Church Row NW3
Sanderson(?) after Flitcroft's design(?)
⊖ Hampstead
More remarkable for its position, closing the vista of Church Row, than for its architecture (veiled by trees), the church is unexpectedly large with a tall east spire set behind battlements. The interior was much altered by S P Cockerell in 1872, the altar and reredos are by T G Jackson, about 1878, and the ceiling was decorated in Renaissance style by Alfred Bell. Tall unfluted Ionic columns support arches which cut into the tunnel vault. The pulpit is original and particularly fine: an octagon on a square platform standing on four fluted Ionic columns. John Constable, George du Maurier and Norman Shaw are among those buried in the graveyard.

Admiral's House **A8** d
mid-18th century
Admiral's Walk, west of Hampstead Grove NW3
⊖ Hampstead
A conspicuously large, white stuccoed house with later additions. Its nautical associations are expressed by the galleries, railings, flagpole on the roof, and the large first-floor conservatory. The house was painted by Constable, and George Gilbert Scott lived here for eight years. Grove Lodge, a cottage attached to the house and also painted white, further extends the composition, and was the home of John Galsworthy from 1918–33.

Vale of Health NW3 1780 **A9** d
⊖ Hampstead
A village or hamlet within Hampstead Heath, the Vale of Health is more remarkable for its cohesion – a tight pattern of small streets and passageways – and the conspicuous absence of the twentieth century, than for any particular piece of architecture (although Vale Lodge, Manor Lodge and Woodbine Cottage are noteworthy). As a quiet backwater, it has attracted residents such as Leigh Hunt and D H Lawrence.

St Mary 1816 **A10** h
Holly Walk NW3
⊖ Hampstead
One of the first Roman Catholic churches to be built in London after the Reformation (and probably the smallest), this beautiful and diminutive church is recessed in the centre of a row of three-storey cottages. The stuccoed front and Tuscan doorway were added in 1830. Note the statue of the Virgin Mary in a niche above the door, and the segmental pediment over the bell.

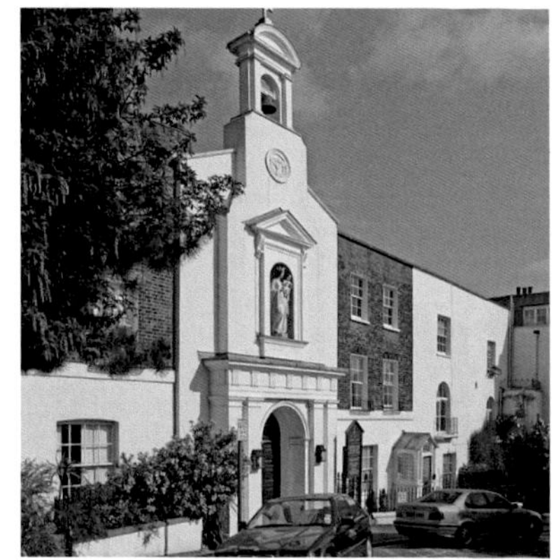

Hampstead Towers 1875 **A11** h
6 Ellerdale Road NW3
R Norman Shaw
⊖ Hampstead
Hampstead Towers was built by Shaw for himself, and although he used the same Queen Anne style as in **Swan House** N21, the composition here is freer. The principal staircase divides the plan and the street façade in two: on the left the two main storeys have a brick bay with tall windows while the three-storey bay to the right has horizontal glazing between bands of stucco. The remaining windows appear randomly placed, their position determined by the rooms inside. Hampstead Towers' pointed gables, tall chimneys, porthole windows and beautifully modulated brickwork are all characteristic of Shaw. Underneath the mezzanine studio where Shaw designed his subsequent buildings is the dining room which, with its low inglenook fireplace, is particularly fine. Unfortunately the house is difficult to visit as it is now occupied by an Italian convent, the Institute of St Marcellina.

Studio house 1885 **A12** h
39 Frognal NW3
R Norman Shaw
⊖ Hampstead
The tile-hung exterior of this house, in the style of a Surrey Weald cottage, is appropriate to Kate Greenaway, the nineteenth-century children's book illustrator for whom it was built. The house faces north-east, but the studio within the attic has been rotated to face north.

Opposite is University College School (1907) by Arnold Mitchell, an impressive group of Edwardian baroque buildings.

Annesley Lodge 1896 **A13** b
Platts Lane NW3
C F A Voysey
⊖ Hampstead, West Hampstead
Voysey built this house for his father, and Pevsner calls it his best house in London. It is certainly a compendium of the elements of his style, with its long unbroken red-tiled roof, buttresses at the corners of the while pebble dashed walls, and heart motifs on the front door. The plan is cranked, a response to its suburban corner site, the two wings enclosing the front garden, with the front door at their intersection. See also Voysey's **Bedford Park** houses T19, T20; at **Barons Court** T20 and **Dixcote** W8.

Camden Arts Centre **A14** l
1897, 2004
Finchley Road NW3
Arnold S Taylor; Tony Fretton Architects/MUF
⊖ Finchley Road and Frognal
This conversion gave new life to a revered local institution. From the outside there is an abrupt contrast between the red-brick exuberance of the original building, once Hampstead's Central Library forming part of Edwardian Arkwright Road, and the cool matter-of-factness of the new addition with its aluminium box frames forming a glazed billboard to the semi-urban motorway of the Finchley Road. The glazed screen also acts as an acoustic barrier as well as a window to the back garden laid out by MUF, which is now integrated into the public life of the gallery. Internally there is an absence of detail, as might be now expected in the contemporary gallery.

Sun House 1935 **A15** h
9 Frognal Way NW3
E Maxwell Fry
⊖ Hampstead
The first example of an expensive modern house in London – all earlier ones had been in the country. The site slopes up from the road, and the main rooms of the house are at the front, facing the view and raised above the garage and retaining wall. The roof is 'accessible for the serving of tea'. The house is built of concrete, and the outside is smoothed and painted except for the steel balconies supported on slender columns. The railings were originally painted pale green, and the retaining wall grey. See also **66 Old Church Street** N34.

Frogneeded Close NW3 1937 **A16** h

E L Freud

⊖ Hampstead

Approached from Frognal, this fine enclave of six brick houses in semi-detached blocks with front doors at each end suggests an enclosed courtyard, or M H Baillie Scott's close planning for **Hampstead Garden Suburb** R19. The raised brick band around the upper-storey windows and the nautical handling of the front doors are the first clues to the period. The large windows set into dark brick walls are more like those of 1920s Germany than the architecture of Hampstead Garden Suburb.

Note Samuel and Harding's **New House** of 1937, at 13 Arkwright Road, an early domestic application of glass blocks for the then Headmaster of University College School opposite.

House 1938 **A17** h

66 Frognal NW3

Connell, Ward and Lucas

⊖ Hampstead

Le Corbusier's Five Points of Architecture are expressed in this house. The free ground floor plan, the long windows, the structure independent of the façade and the roof garden are all present to some extent as part of the necessary pedigree. From the outside it is convincing; however, the internal planning is merely sensible and bourgeois. The house, previously somewhat altered, was adapted and restored by Avanti Architects in 2003.

House 1967 **A18** c
9 West Heath Road NW3
James Gowan
⊖ Hampstead
This strange and obsessive building was one of Gowan's first after the dissolution of his partnership with James Stirling. It uses piers of purple-grey brick rising through three storeys and separated by continuous strips of glazing, to define a series of spaces, each with a very specific function. The imagery would suit local authority housing rather than a residence for a successful furniture manufacturer.

Housing, Branch Hill 1970–7 **A19** d
Branch Hill NW3
London Borough of Camden Architects Department; Gordon Benson and Alan Forsyth
⊖ Hampstead
A steeply sloping garden, large and overgrown, in an affluent section of Hampstead was the improbable site for this luxurious local authority housing scheme of forty-two dwellings. The scheme adopts a well-tried section for building on sloping ground derived from traditional Mediterranean hill towns, and from Le Corbusier's Roq et Rob proposals (1948).

House 1998 **A20** d
Upper Terrace NW3
Rick Mather Architects
⊖ Hampstead
For a moment you have the feeling that this house had been overlooked by historians and the authors of this book and that either Connell Ward and Lucas or Wells Coates had built on Upper Terrace in the 1930s. Set back behind its protective boundary wall this white stuccoed cube with its corner window is a worthy successor to the tradition of modern houses in Hampstead. The interior with its complex sectional devices and its relationship to the view are many of the attributes of this house denied to the public.

B
continued section R
continued section A
continued section F
Vale of Health
East Heath
Hampstead Ponds
Hampstead Ponds
South Hampstead
Hospital
Drill Hall
Synagogue
Sports Ground
1
2
3
4
7
8
10
11
13
15
17
19
20
22
23
24
25
27
29
30

continued section R

continued section C

continued section F

Hampstead (east) ■ Hampstead Heath ■ Parliament Hill Fields ■ Belsize Park ■ Maitland Park ■ Gospel Oak ■ Chalk Farm ■ Dartmouth Park ■ Swiss Cottage

By the early nineteenth century Hampstead was expanding beyond its village limits, and London was spreading northwards, beginning with the laying out of Regent's Park (see section F). With the development of the Eton College Estate in the 1830s, followed by the Belsize Estate in the 1840s, Hampstead's engulfment in the general expansion of London had begun, to be completed in the 1870s and '80s by the red-brick mansions of Fitzjohn's Avenue extending to Finchley Road, and to Belsize Park via Haverstock Hill. Hampstead has attracted artists and writers as residents and still has great charm; its steep, labyrinthine alleys and well-preserved Georgian streets are best discovered on foot.

Kentish Town was still a village on the road to Highgate as late as 1780 but by the beginning of the nineteenth century a series of brick terraces (notably **Grove Terrace** B5) was being extended along Highgate Road. In the second half of the nineteenth century Gospel Oak (the venue of traditional country fairs as late as the 1850s), Maitland Park and Dartmouth Park to the south of Highgate were developed. By the beginning of the twentieth century, the whole area of this section had been built up in a series of loosely connected estates, some of which fell victim in the 1950s and '60s to well-intentioned redevelopment by local authorities. The most conspicuous and tragic examples of this misplaced zeal were the comprehensive redevelopment of Gospel Oak and the massive intrusion of the rebuilt Royal Free Hospital, which looms over the southern end of Hampstead Heath.

The Regent's Canal at Camden Lock

East Heath Lodge 1750 **B1** a
East Heath Road NW3
⊖ Hampstead
These two mid-eighteenth-century houses of plain brick have a surprisingly large common pediment facing south. Further to the west are Heath Lodge and Heath Side, two slightly larger cottages of symmetrical composition with bay windows. The latter is attributed to James Wyatt (1775).

Keats Grove NW3 c1815 **B2** e
⊖ Hampstead, Hampstead Heath
Keats Grove is of a piece with Downshire Hill, although more loosely constructed and even more leafy. The houses, in mixed stucco and yellow brick and with very deep front gardens, give a good picture of the early-nineteenth-century village suburb, designed on aesthetic principles for artists.

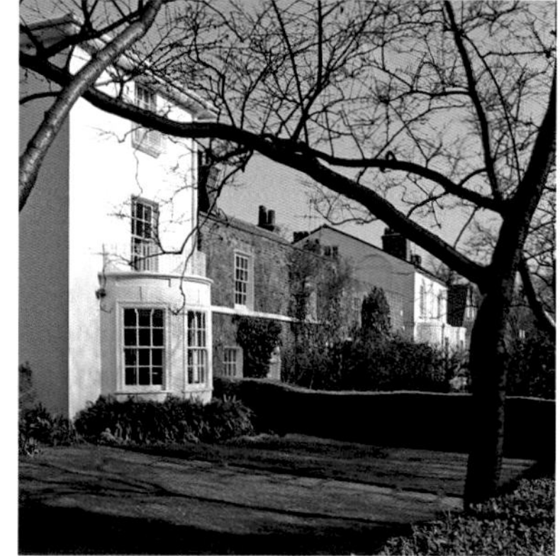

Keats House 1815 **B3** e
Keats Grove NW3
⊖ Hampstead, Hampstead Heath
It is unlikely that this two-storey stuccoed house would have gained entry to this guide without its literary associations: it is not particularly distinguished, and was rescued from destruction in the 1920s only by courtesy of money from the USA. When occupied by John Keats and Fanny Brawne it consisted of two semi-detached houses, converted into one after Keats's death. Decorated with period furniture and wall-coverings, and open to the public, Keats House gives a very good idea of how such houses (many of which still stand in London) were originally equipped and used.

St John 1818 **B4** e
Downshire Hill NW3
S P Cockerell(?)
⊖ Hampstead, Hampstead Heath
This delightful cube-like chapel with white stuccoed walls, portico and cupola, and airy, light interior is one of London's few remaining proprietary estate chapels. Located at the acute corner of Downshire Hill and Keats Grove, it is a reminder in miniature of one of the twin churches of the Piazza del Popolo in Rome.

Grove Terrace c1830 **B5** d
off Highgate Road NW3
⊖ Gospel Oak

An early but typical example of Georgian ribbon development on the roads radiating out of London. Built originally in the open countryside between the villages of Kentish Town and Highgate, Grove Terrace is well set back from Highgate Road and has no overall formal composition.

The Round House 1847 **B6** o
Chalk Farm Road NW1
Stephenson, Dockray and Normanville
⊖ Chalk Farm

The Round House was originally an engine shed serving Euston Station. In the 1950s it was used as a warehouse for Gilbey's Gin, and in the 1960s it became a venue for London's first large hippy gatherings and concerts.

The shed's robust engineering survives. Stalls for the engines are defined by a ring of cast-iron columns; these support both a gallery and the first level of the roof, which stands between them and the massive outer wall of stock brick.

A thorough restoration was started in 1997 (architects John McAslan and Partners), and in 2006, through the energies and benefaction of Torquil Norman, the Roundhouse was once more reopened as an important arts and community centre. The great circular space was always a successful venue for a variety of arts events; the renovation continued this tradition. The addition to the north should, however, have resisted the circular geometry in a concentric arrangement which serves to dilute the original building. This is as though the Pantheon had sponsored circular ripples into the city fabric of Rome.

St Stephen 1869–76 **B7** e
Rosslyn Hill NW3
Samuel Teulon
⊖ Belsize Park

This is one of the most impressive nineteenth-century churches in London. The style is a mixture of thirteenth-century Gothic and Victorian invention, best shown by the massive tower with its capped roof, the ornamental brickwork of the interior, and the square-headed aisle windows. The materials are particularly uncompromising: various tones of Luton brick with granite dressings. In 2008 the building was being restored by Anthony Richardson and Partners.

On the opposite side of Rosslyn Hill, in Lyndhurst Road, is another Victorian masterpiece, the **Congregational Church** (1883–4) by Alfred Waterhouse. The plan is centralized and hexagonal, and the use of materials is unmistakably Waterhouse – hard purple brick and terracotta. Happily, it was converted into a recording and animation studio.

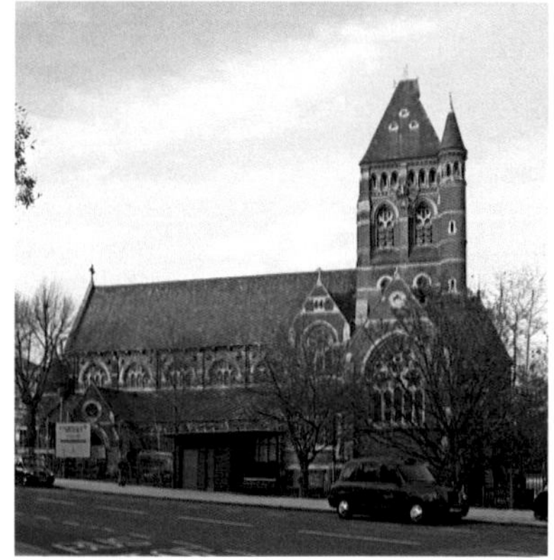

Belsize Park Gardens c1870–85 **B8** i
NW3
⊖ Belsize Park
A long and majestically formal avenue of large Italianate semi-detached villas with informal tree planting. The white stuccoed façades of the closely packed villas have massive and almost identical first-floor bay windows, with small variations only in the detail, though many of the columns and their capitals have now been debased. The consistency of the white paintwork, often a surprise to the visitor, is due to the landlord's covenant, showing the continued influence of the Great Estates. As with many of London's grander houses all of the villas are now in multiple occupancy.

Mall Studios 1872 **B9** k
Tasker Road NW3
Thomas Batterbury
⊖ Belsize Park
A group of 'artisan' type studios which were built originally to be leased to working artists. Inside, the double-height studios with galleries are unexpectedly impressive, as are their generous gardens. Much original detail remains – chimney pots bearing the monogram of the original owners on numbers 3 and 4, east-facing skylights, bull's-eye windows to the west – but the storage balconies in all except number 1 have been converted into an extra bedroom, and the models' changing rooms are now dining alcoves.

From the late 1920s to the beginning of the Second World War Mall Studios were a residence and meeting ground for artists of international repute. In 1927 Barbara Hepworth was a resident of number 7, to be joined by Ben Nicholson in 1931. In 1934 Herbert Read moved into number 3, from where Unit One and Circle magazines were produced, edited by Leslie Martin, Nicholson and Gabo. Henry Moore (of 11a Parkhill Road), Moholy-Nagy and Naum Gabo (of nearby Lawn Road flats B17)and Piet Mondrian (whose time at 60 Parkhill Road is commemorated with a blue plaque) were among the frequent visitors to the Mall.

House 1878 **B10** e
61 Fitzjohn's Avenue NW3
R Norman Shaw
⊖ Hampstead
A broad and generously composed red-brick house, entered from the side in Netherhall Gardens. With its two Dutch gables, high chimneys and projecting apsidal garden room, this house, together with Shaw's Three Gables at 6 Fitzjohn's Avenue (demolished) was the model for the red-brick expansion of Hampstead in the 1880s and 1890s.

Houses c1880 **B11** m
1–9 and 43–73 Eton Avenue NW3
(odd numbers only)
H B Measures
⊖ Swiss Cottage, Belsize Park

In contrast with the white stuccoed Italianate villas of **Belsize Park Gardens** B8, these red-brick buildings use Norman Shaw's Free Style with amazing variety. They all have two bays to the street and square brick gateposts, but beyond this each house develops a different architectural arrangement within the genre – wilfully offset entrances, conical corner windows, major and minor bay windows and side projections. In many of the façades it is possible to detect the features of the human face (the entrance bridge as tongue, the doorway as mouth, the chimney as nose and the oval windows either side as eyes), so that the street becomes a series of opulent Victorians looking out. The backs in contrast are quite ordinary. The magnificent studio at number 69, with leaded lights built into the side elevation, should also be noted. Built originally for single families, the houses are now converted into either flats or institutions. With their elaborate mass-produced ornamentation, they lend themselves as suitable models to those clamouring for greater variety and formal complexity in housing design. Note a further use of the type in Lyndhurst Gardens NW3.

At the eastern end of the avenue, the **Sarum Hall School** is an accomplished work by Allies and Morrison (1995). The humble barn form which the T-shaped building presents to the street is enriched with subtle inflexions, and some of the mannerisms which became a feature of the practice's later work.

Wychcombe Studios c1880 **B12** j
Englands Lane NW3
Thomas D Becket, builder
⊖ Belsize Park

Approached by a narrow, walled drive, this fine group of six studios forms an L-shaped court. They were built by Thomas D Becket (see his terracotta monogram set in the front wall of each studio) on land leased from the Eton College Estate. The high Dutch gables are reminiscent of the contemporary **Stratford Studios** I16 in west London.

Houses 1880s **B13** e
1–21 and 2–6 Hampstead Hill Gardens NW3
Batterbury and Huxley
⊖ Hampstead

A very fine group of well-crafted artistic houses, and in strong contrast to the earlier and more sober stuccoed Greek Revival terraces further down the street to the south (numbers 25–33).

All Hallows 1889 **B14** g
Chancel 1913
Shirlock Road NW3
James Brooks, chancel Giles Gilbert Scott
⊖ Belsize Park
'One of the noblest churches of its date in England' (Pevsner), All Hallows is, however, cramped on its site by later red-brick houses. It is a 'hall church' without a spire; the buttresses supporting the aisles give the west front a 'hunched' look.

House 1890 **B15** n
16 Chalcot Gardens NW3
C F A Voysey
⊖ Belsize Park
An addition to the front of an existing house, built for the illustrator Arthur Rackham. The horizontal windows with leaded lights, the relieving brick arches and stone trim are typical of Voysey. The exaggeratedly steep pitched roof and brickwork are not, as the design had to blend in with the existing house.

Police Station 1896 **B16** l
Holmes Road NW5
R Norman Shaw
⊖ Kentish Town
A simple three-storey yellow-brick building, with restrained baroque touches to the stonework surrounding the two arched entrances. The large archway leads to the court behind (now disused), the minor one being the principal street entrance. Shaw was a major exponent of the baroque revival (1890–1900s) and showed more panache in his later works, notably the **Piccadilly Hotel** K125.

Isokon Flats 1933 **B17** f
Lawn Road NW3
Wells Coates
⊖ Belsize Park

The client, Jack Pritchard, was a pioneer of English modernism who mass-produced furniture, and the flats take their name from his Bristol factory, in which the furniture of Marcel Breuer was already in production. This connection and the contemporary furnishing of Lawn Road are principally responsible for its reputation.

Set physically against the slope of Lawn Road and ideologically against the neighbouring red-brick Edwardian villas, the white-stuccoed Isokon flats were prototype dwellings for the mobile intelligentsia of the 'new society'. The building was planned as a 'collective', or long-stay hotel for single professionals, with its own bar and clubroom (designed by Marcel Breuer but subsequently altered). The social idea derived from Le Corbusier's Pavilion Suisse (1930) in Paris and Moisei Ginzburg's Narkomfin apartments in Moscow (1929). Despite such a pedigree the building ironically conveys the feeling of massive permanence and, notwithstanding its reputation in the history of English modern architecture, is not a very distinguished work. Its intention is best expressed in the *Existenzminimum* planning.

Isokon Trust with the Notting Hill Housing Trusts purchased the building from Camden Council in 1999, following its Grade 1 listing, and it was renovated by Avanti Architects in 2004.

Kent House 1936 **B18** p
Ferdinand Street NW1
Connell, Ward and Lucas
⊖ Chalk Farm

A rare and early example of the new architecture applied to low-income housing. Despite the socialist ideals of much early modern architecture in Europe (notably Brinkman's Spangen Housing, 1922, in Rotterdam, Moisei Ginzburg's Narkomfin apartments, 1929, in Moscow, and Ernst May's Frankfurt housing of the 1930s), pre-war modern architecture in England was principally a middle-class experiment. Kent House consists of two identical buildings (except for an extra storey to the street building), representing a series rather than a static, finite place. With their white-stuccoed walls, metal window frames and exaggerated cantilevered balconies, they come as close as anything in London at the time to the Heroic modern style. The building's appearance was seriously compromised when the balcony balustrades were painted red and their height increased.

Odeon Cinema 1937 **B19** m
Finchley Road NW3
Harry Weedon
⊖ Swiss Cottage
A grand streamlined *moderne* design in well-made red brick, whose shape follows the street lines. The cinema's huge interior has, like most others outside the West End, been subdivided. Its interior architecture is consequently destroyed, and its glamour lost. The fine original lettering of the exterior has been removed and replaced by tawdry shiny metal. Note immediately to the south Regency Lodge, a fine block of flats by Robert Atkinson of 1937. Atkinson is remembered more for his flamboyant Art Deco entrance hall interiors at the **Daily Express Building** L118.

Houses 1940 **B20** e
1–3 Willow Road NW3
Ernö Goldfinger
⊖ Hampstead
Built by Goldfinger for himself and others, this pleasant row of houses looks as if it might be one big villa. The projecting frames round the top-floor windows and the single frame uniting the windows of the first-floor living rooms both became worked-to-death clichés in other hands. Nevertheless, the houses have worn better than most English stucco-modern, perhaps because the imagery is as much Georgian as modern. They were built in spite of the opposition of the local authority, which was overridden by the LCC. In 1994 number 2 Willow Road (Ernö Goldfinger's residence) was bought by the National Trust and its interior can now be visited.

St Anne's Close 1950 **B21** c
Off Highgate West Hill N6
Walter Segal
⊖ Tufnell Park
Approached down a narrow drive off busy Highgate West Hill, this small group of semi-detached houses, designed by the architect who in the 1970s promoted self-build and community architecture, has a simple logic. As a result of the south-facing slope there is an inevitable and clear relationship between the sequence of parking, common front garden, house and private back garden. The large areas of Critall Hope steel glazing to the living rooms on the ground floor with their wide frontages give the houses an impression of an easy-going relationship between inside and outside that is more characteristic of small-town USA than London.

Houses 1956 **B22** b
80–90 South Hill Park NW3
Howell and Amis
⊖ Hampstead, Hampstead Heath
This terrace was designed by the architects for their own occupation when they were in the LCC Architects Department, working on the housing at **Alton West** V12. The houses have very narrow frontages of 3.6m (12ft) (one of Le Corbusier's *Modulor* dimensions), but they are deep. Their sections are designed ambitiously to exploit the site, which slopes down steeply to the ponds on the Heath. Some houses have double-height living rooms with gallery bedrooms, giving them the sort of spatial intricacy which the architects would perhaps have liked to see at Alton West. The taller garden façades, now overgrown with creeper, are more satisfactory than those to the street because they are less utilitarian, but both are good examples of the short-lived English Brutalism.

House 1961 **B23** b
31 South Hill Park NW3
Michael Brawne
⊖ Belsize Park, Hampstead Heath
A narrow-fronted terrace house, designed by the architect for himself. The steep slope of the site allowed an independent flat on the ground floor, while at the rear the first floor bridges an area to reach the garden, which is shared with the neighbouring house. The brick panels and timber screens on the exterior and the open ground-floor plan express the architect's preoccupation with Charles Eames, Japan and the Smithsons – formative influences on the English avant-garde in the late 1950s. The house to the south, while it shares many of the same concerns, is less memorable.

Centre Heights housing, offices and **shops** 1961 **B24** m
Finchley Road NW3
Douglas Stephen and Panos Koulermos
⊖ Swiss Cottage
During the speculative building boom of the early 1960s, when New York's Lever House was universally accepted as the model, this scheme offered a critical alternative. The ground floor is devoted to shops, above which are five floors of offices and five floors of flats and maisonettes approached by galleries. The building, however, has an ambiguous relationship with the street, its concrete mass and rhetorical stair tower making it more a freestanding object than part of a street façade.

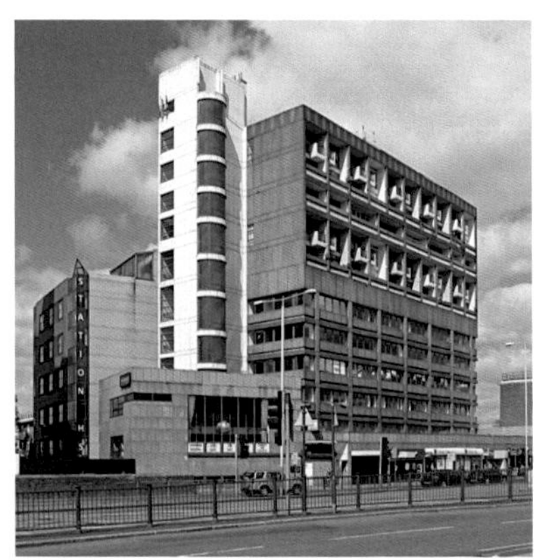

Public library 1964 **B25** m
Avenue Road NW3
Basil Spence, Bonnington and Collins
⊖ Swiss Cottage

The library is all that remains of an ambitious civic centre planned by Spence for the former Borough of Hampstead, abandoned when the Borough of Camden was created in 1965. This included a swimming pool, since demolished and replaced, to the east. Recent development on the whole block has included a new building for the Hampstead Theatre (designed by Bennetts Associates, 2003), a central landscaped area (Gustafson Porter, 2005) overlooked on the north by a hulking addition to the Central School of Speech and Drama (Jesticoe + Whiles, 2005); and sheltered housing and very obtrusive flats for sale on Winchester Road.

The interiors of the library, renovated by John McAslan and Partners in 2003 but with much of its original furniture removed, show some signs of 1960s largesse in well-finished and generous circulation areas; but they also show that it did not occur to the architects of the Welfare State, as it certainly had to the Victorians, that public buildings might be as good as private ones and perhaps even better.

Housing 1967–77 **B26** f
Fleet Road NW5
London Borough of Camden Architects Department; Neave Brown
⊖ Belsize Park

Fleet Road is a definitive example of 'low-rise high-density' design, which was fashionable in the 1960s as a reaction to mixed development (towers, slabs and terraces) and the excesses of high-rise living of the previous decade. In plan it is a series of alleys running parallel to Parkhill Road, supported by the beginnings of an upper-level walkway over Southampton Road (intended to connect with the main redevelopment of Gospel Oak to the east).

The scheme has an ingenious cross-section giving large balconies and communal gardens to all the residents. Without a concierge, however, the exclusive semi-public realm results in the visitor feeling intrusive, and the resident feeling invaded.

House 1968 **B27** b
78 South Hill Park NW3
Brian Housden
⊖ Hampstead, Hampstead Heath

A strange and individual house on a sloping site overlooking the heath. Housden, building for himself and influenced by the Dutch architect van Eyck, made rooms defined by an exposed concrete frame, inset with panels of glass bricks and red-framed windows.

Housing 1973–81 **B28** g
Mansfield Road NW3
London Borough of Camden Architects Department; Gordon Benson and Alan Forsyth
⊖ Gospel Oak
This long street terrace goes some way to repairing the damage inflicted on Mansfield Road by the particularly unfortunate building by Frederick Macmanus and Partners to the west. The first impression is of a 'normal' terrace of houses, but the internal requirements of the section do not allow this. The pavement is gathered into the building as an access gallery at first floor, leaving a curious no-man's land between the building line and the street.

Note the nine terraced houses in Lamble Street (1971), in Oak Village to the south of Mansfield Road. Designed for Camden by Benson and Forsyth, they have a characteristically complex internal arrangement of half levels and simple abstract exteriors. They are united by a continuous attic storey, like **Winscombe Street** R29.

House 1975 **B29** e
49a Downshire Hill NW3
Michael Hopkins
⊖ Hampstead
The house was built initially as both a home and an office, and Hopkins was the first of the exponents of so-called 'high tech' to realize a house from the techniques of warehousing and offices. The understated architecture of this house suggests that buildings do not always need to carry the usual signs (parapet, door, window and so on). Built on a slope, and with virtually no street presence, the two-storey house is entered via a metal bridge at first floor. The street and garden elevations are totally glazed, and the flanks are of stove-enamelled corrugated metal sheet. Despite its modernity this is a nostalgic building, reminiscent both of Charles Eames's house and studio in Santa Monica (1949) and of the English nineteenth-century engineering tradition of glass and iron. It has practical engineering virtues: low cost, speed of construction and flexibility, deriving from its 100mm (4in) square steel columns at 3.6m (12ft) centres and proprietary steel beams. Whether it could be more than a one-off in an urban context remains doubtful.

Note Michael and Charlotte Bunney's tiny end-of-terrace house of 1936 opposite at 13 Downshire Hill, its white stucco and cantilevered 'eyebrow' hinting when built at the presence of the modern in a street of otherwise late-Georgian houses.

Houses 1981 **B30** i
2c and d Belsize Park Gardens NW3
Spence and Webster
⊖ Belsize Park
Two single-storey houses, one originally for each of the architect-partners, are joined round a courtyard, and shelter behind the former garden walls of the grand detached house to the north. They are distant descendants of Mies van der Rohe's court house studies of 1931–40, but are built of very spindly steel and aluminium sections, and lack the originals' free plans.

Television studios 1981–3 **B31** p
Hawley Crescent NW1
Terry Farrell and Co.
⊖ Camden Town

This was a conversion of a former garage. In the long sinuous façade to Hawley Crescent, and in the elaborately decorated interiors, Farrell developed his figurative and anti-modern vocabulary. The problem with this vocabulary was that the real materials of which it was constructed – corrugated metal siding, painted rendering, glazed masonry blocks – carry their own lugubrious messages which often contradict the would-be playfulness of the forms. 'Depression Deco' always appeared tired, and the jokes, at best only one-liners, still fall flat. The giant eggcups used as finials on the elevation to the canal, a reference to the building's original occupants, a breakfast television company, were briefly admired.

Houses 1986–9 **B32** d
Coutts Crescent, 23 St Alban's Road NW5
Chassay Wright Architects
⊖ Kentish Town, Archway

Challenging a suburban street of Betjemanesque inter-war semis, this terrace of eleven large four-storey houses is arranged in a shallow crescent set back behind a walled yard for car-parking. The houses in the crescent are lavishly planned with south-facing terraces, while those at the ends are crowned with double-height 'studio' bedrooms. A wealth of traditional and fashionable influences have been absorbed and successfully synthesized, and the scheme is well detailed and well built.

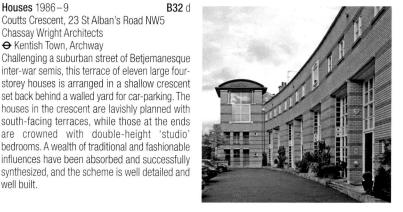

Holloway
continued section R
Sports Ground
Tufnell Park
HM Prison
Kentish Town
continued section B
13
15
12
11
16
10
18
14
17
9
20
Camden Town
continued section G
Freightliner Terminal
a
b
e
f
j
k
m
n

continued section R

continued section D

continued section G

Camden Town (north) ■ Kentish Town ■ Tufnell Park ■ Holloway ■ Barnsbury

Railways criss-cross this part of London: running north–south are the main lines from King's Cross (cut in 1851) and St Pancras (1868), while to the south runs the North London Line, mainly on viaducts. Before the railways there had been only villages and fields, although some of the village high streets had been lined with Georgian ribbon development: it is still possible to see these three- and four-storey houses behind the single-storey shopfronts of Camden and Kentish Town High Streets, in Holloway and Seven Sisters Roads, and in Caledonian Road (where some houses have remained unconverted).

The development of Barnsbury, to the west of fashionable Islington, was begun early in the nineteenth century and completed by 1835. Between the coming of the railways and the beginning of the First World War, the whole of the rest of the section was covered in houses. In 1845 began the building of large semi-detached houses around Camden Square in the south-west, and development then spread north and east along Camden Road, laid out in the 1820s. As a result, the prisons of **Pentonville** C4 and **Holloway** C6, and the **Caledonian cattle market** C6 (all of which had deliberately been placed outside the city), were enclosed by housing.

The eastern part of the section is in the London Borough of Camden, and contains some of that authority's own housing designs of the 1970s, for example **Maiden Lane** C14 on abandoned railway land.

From 2000 onwards the redevelopment of abandoned railway lands was encouraged by official policy. To the north, the **Emirates Stadium**, C22, the new ground for the Arsenal Football Club, built on derelict railway sidings, was a virtual coliseum set in a sea of three-storey terraced houses. The southern boundary of the section became the site of the massive Argent redevelopment on lands north of Kings Cross station, on which construction began in 2008 for a new district of the city and was planned to continue for at least a decade.

Twenty-first-century housing, Hornsey Street N7

Barnsbury c1820 **C1** p
N1
Thomas Cubitt
⊖ Highbury and Islington
Lying between Liverpool Road and Caledonian Road, north of Richmond Avenue, Barnsbury was laid out by Thomas Cubitt before his more famous speculations in Bloomsbury and Belgravia, and is a rather loose composition of suburban open-cornered squares, crescents and streets either side of Thornhill Road.

Barnsbury Square (with the two partial crescents leading off its north-west and south-west corners), **Belitha Villas** and **Richmond Avenue** are the best parts. Although run down, Richmond Avenue has good terraces: sphinxes and miniature obelisks flank the entrances of numbers 46–72. In the north corner of Barnsbury Square is **Mountford Crescent** (c1830), an early pair of two-storey semi-detached villas, stuccoed, bow-fronted and set back from the street in their private garden. After 1830 the semi-detached villa became a popular model for developers, but here late-nineteenth-century terraces have unfortunately destroyed the original image of villas standing in their own leafy gardens. To the west is **Thornhill Square** (c1850), the largest square in Islington, its elliptical composition completed by **Thornhill Crescent**. To the east note **Barnsbury Street** and **Bewdley Street**, where the condition of the houses varies from gentrification to seedy decay.

Mountford Crescent

Thornhill Crescent

Barnsbury Park 1830s **C2** p
N1
⊖ Highbury and Islington
Islington has many continuous late Georgian terraces, and was also the scene of experiments in various forms of housing. The south side of this street is an elegant two-storey terrace, with set-back entrances which give the effect of semi-detached villas.

St James 1837–8 **C3** l
Chillingworth Road N7
Inwood and Clifton
⊖ Holloway Road
The eccentric south façade bears no relation to the main body of the church which is now exposed by demolition on both sides: the asymmetrical composition gives a central flat-pedimented portico with four Ionic demi-columns. The square tower on the west has a circular top decorated with grapes and ears of wheat. In the 1980s the building was converted into flats.

Pentonville Prison 1840–2 **C4** o
Caledonian Road N1
Major Jebb (First Surveyor General of Prisons)
⊖ Caledonian Road
The prison's portico and massive, inclined wall dominate this section of the Caledonian Road. Behind, there are five brick wings radiating from a central control block. The plan is derived from Haviland's famous Eastern Penitentiary in Philadelphia (1829) and is the only surviving example of Bentham's Panopticon prison type in London.

Milner Square 1841–3 **C5** p
N1
Roumieu and Gough
⊖ Angel, Highbury and Islington
With its continuous attic floor this is a particularly European square, entered in the middle of its ends like other small squares in Islington. The houses are of three bays separated by thinly proportioned pilasters, an arrangement which gives the façades exaggerated height.

The Market Tower

One of the original four public houses

Caledonian Market Tower 1855 **C6** j
North Road and Market Road N7
J B Bunning
⊖ Caledonian Road
Only the gaunt white tower, the outer railings and three (of the four) public houses remain of this once famous market; it was designed by the City's architect to accommodate 34,900 sheep, 6,616 bullocks, 1,425 calves and 900 pigs on six hectares (15 acres) of granite paving. The tower housed banks and a telegraph office at its base. The public houses at the corners of the enclosure are tall, robust and Italianate. At **Holloway Prison** (1849–51) on Parkhurst Road, only a fragment of one of the gatehouses remains of Bunning's City of London Prison, demolished in the 1970s complete with its central tower (a parody on Warwick Castle). The reformist intentions of the stellar plan and its attendant castellated architecture may now be outdated, but at least the building looked like a prison. The trouble with the new Holloway is that it resembles a local authority housing scheme with bars over the windows. The demolition of Holloway virtually completes the destruction of works by this eminent architect: his magnificent Coal Exchange was senselessly demolished in 1962 and the Caledonian market buildings were removed in the 1960s.

St Clement 1863–5 **C7** l
Davey Close, south of Bride Street N7
George Gilbert Scott
⊖ Highbury and Islington

'Far less conventional and well bred than most of Scott's work' (Pevsner), this church remained neglected, buried and almost forgotten in a new housing estate. The very tall, expressive, three-bay west front is of stock brick with a bellcote above, and the pitch to the nave roof is exaggeratedly steep. In the early 1990s the church was converted into flats.

Samuel Lewis Buildings 1910 **C8** p
Liverpool Road N1
⊖ Highbury and Islington

A late attempt by a charitable trust to bring high style to its housing: there are elaborate un-English mansarded gables, bay windows and sandstone trim. But the five blocks of flats are too close together for privacy – the spaces between them are mean.

Holloway Estate 1962–9 **C9** f
Parkhurst Road N7
McMorran and Whitby
⊖ Holloway Road

The 128 flats are contained in eight buildings (rather than 'blocks') of three and four storeys forming three simple courtyards with open corners. Their neo-Georgian style (like the buildings in the Inns of Court), with arched public doorways in black brickwork (impervious to graffiti), simple openings and slate roofs, is a sane contribution to public housing. With McMorran's other London buildings – **100 Pall Mall** K167 and **Wood Street police station** L123 – they show that there is still mileage in the classical tradition.

Houses 1964–72 **C10** n
Murray Mews NW1
Team Four, Tom Kay and Richard Gibson
⊖ Camden Town

London mews were built from the seventeenth to the nineteenth century as stables for houses on the principal streets. As traffic and land values have increased the relative calm and cheapness of mews properties has recommended them for residential use. Murray Mews is a good example of this transformation.

On the north side is a terrace of three houses, numbers 15, 17 and 19 (1964) designed by Team Four (Norman Foster, Wendy Foster, Richard Rogers and Su Rogers) before the practice dissolved in 1967. The ground floor is protected from the mews by a solid red-brick wall, and a sloped patent glazed roof provides daylight to the principal living space behind. The houses follow the nineteenth-century studio tradition – a top-lit double-height space surrounded by secondary

15, 17 and 19 Murray Mews

rooms. This is a very appropriate 'mews' type.

Number 22 was designed by Tom Kay (1972). The living accommodation is at first floor, surrounding an entrance court, and on the ground floor are a garage and small office. An ingenious section provides light to the deep plan and the principal rooms look to the rear.

Almost merging with number 22, through the use of the same common stock brick, number 20 is a small house designed by Richard Gibson in 1965. The plan is a simple two-storey atrium and the court is glazed at roof level, supplementing the light to the rooms on either side. Despite their relatively complex interiors, all three houses present a neutral face to the mews.

22 Murray Mews

House 1965 **C11** m
62 Camden Mews NW1
Edward Cullinan
⊖ Camden Town

For many architects London mews have offered the opportunity to realize personal ideas without the larger-scale responsibilities and restrictions of 'housing' schemes. In this case, the thesis was to prove a prototype for later work, notably **Highgrove** T32. Designed by the architect for himself, the plan is simple and hierarchic. The public rooms form a long gallery or *piano nobile* set over a plinth of bedrooms. The garden too is at first-floor level over the garage. The glazed timber screens and overhanging eaves have both elegance and directness. These planning and constructional concerns made the house a place of pilgrimage for students in the late 1960s. Number 66 Camden Square, designed by Peter Bell, is also of interest, and was occupied in 1985.

62 Camden Mews

66 Camden Square

Studio apartments 1968–71 **C12** j
Cliff Road NW1
Georgie Wolton
⊖ Caledonian Road

Two of the first multi-storey groups of studios built in London since the Edwardian era. The building to the north is in the European tradition of six studios paired either side of a central staircase. The exterior is rendered and painted white, and the double-height studios are set back in section as they rise, facing north over the garden. Naum Gabo was a resident of this fine building, a type which is too rare in London.

Next door to the south a four-storey building provides generous single-storey studio apartments. A central core divides the floor plan in half; the studios face the street, and living accommodation looks out over the garden to the rear with fine views of Highgate ridge in the distance. On top is a very beautiful roof garden with exotic vines and waving pampas grass. The elevation to Cliff Road is a painted concrete frame filled in with glass bricks; at one end are up-and-over industrial metal louvred doors (which when open turn the inside space into a balcony). Taken together this building and its neighbour are a valuable contribution to the lapsed London studio tradition.

Flats 1975–80 **C13** e
14 Leighton Crescent NW5
Edward Cullinan Architects
⊖ Kentish Town
Built for the London Borough of Camden, this small block in the middle of the rundown crescent shows the architects grappling with the problem of designing housing without using the clichés of modern architecture. The windows (except for the attic strip under the overhanging roof) are treated as holes in the wall and the wall is decorated with a trellis of balconies and rainwater pipes. While spare and assured in these hands, this format quickly became debased in others.

Maiden Lane Stage 1 1976–81 **C14** n
Agar Grove NW1
⊖ Camden Road
London Borough of Camden;
Gordon Benson and Alan Forsyth
A large enclave of 225 dwellings on former railway land behind Agar Grove, the Maiden Lane estate was designed by the same architects as **Branch Hill** A19 and adopts a similar site organization and materials. The scheme is divided in two by the extension of St Paul's Crescent, either side of which is a public network of footpaths and pedestrian decks. An outer wall of four-storey terraces on plinths protects the housing in both parts from the railway to the south, and encloses small public piazzas and a continuous fabric of two-storey narrow-fronted terraces stepping gently to the west. However, while half of the dwellings look over open space to the west, the rest look out onto their backs.

By 2008 and after years of poor maintenance, plans were being made for the phased demolition of the entire estate.

Housing 1978 **C15** i
5 Caversham Road and
6–10 Gaisford Street NW5
London Borough of Camden;
Colquhoun and Miller
⊖ Kentish Town
Two small infill sites in a late-nineteenth-century block, with large semi-detached villas on one side and terraced housing on the other, have resulted in two extremely successful and sane housing buildings. Refreshingly, they take their inspiration from the existing building types, completing the missing half of a semi-detached villa in Caversham Road and reinterpreting three houses as part of a terrace in Gaisford Street. On both sites, maisonettes are incorporated in the image of the large house or villa. Both buildings are beautifully detailed, the off-white rendering modulated by a series of grooves. Their cool, abstract and modern appearance shows that the adoption of existing types does not inevitably result in pastiche.

Houses 1982, 1989 **C16** m
42 and 44 Rochester Place NW1
David Wild
⊖ CamdenTown

Number 44 is an ambitious house which managed to combine public and private architecture. The two-storey portico and monumental corner column (carefully preserving an existing tree) establish a public scale to the street while, set back within the portico, the glass brick panels, exposed concrete blockwork and glazed screens give the interior a domestic scale. It is a surprise, therefore, that this house was built by the architect for himself, as this usually results in a utilitarian appearance justified by the demands of economy. Number 42 was also designed by David Wild (1989), but built by a general contractor.

Sainsbury's supermarket **C17** m
1988–90
Camden Road NW1
Nicholas Grimshaw and Partners
⊖ Camden Town

The supermarket is part of the larger redevelopment of an irregular triangular site formerly occupied by a bakery. The shopping hall is a single bland volume without columns and with a curved ceiling which follows the line of the arched roof. The supports to the roof at either side are counterbalanced by the weight of the first floors, which contain rooms for staff. These floors are prevented from falling over by the cables which project from the face of the building. The façade to Camden Road fearlessly exhibits the consequences of the structural scheme to produce an uneasy mixture of industrial imagery and street architecture. The rest of the site is occupied by a service yard, a block of workshops to Kentish Town Road and, facing north-east across the Regent's Canal, a terrace of houses faced in what appear to be the recycled parts of aeroplanes.

Studios 1988–90 **C18** m
Cobham Mews, Agar Grove NW1
David Chipperfield Architects
⊖ Camden Town

A contribution to the collection of small buildings of character in the environs of Camden Square, these studios for Chipperfield's practice are arranged in three bays in parallel on a tight triangular site. The language and materials are cool and uncompromisingly modern: rendering, concrete beams, and steel window frames with inset panels of glazed blocks.

School of Architecture and Interior Design 1995 **C19** l
London Metropolitan University
Spring House, 6–40 Holloway Road, N7
Brady Mallallieu
⊖ Holloway Road
The building's four storeys have a definite and characterful presence on the street, thereby extending the influence of the University further south along the Holloway Road. A five-bay arcade of concrete piers support the upper floors, which are clad in panels of yellow stock brick composed asymmetrically with galvanized metal window frames and trim. That this intriguing building houses a London school of architecture is appropriate.

Gormley Studio 2003 **C20** n
Vale Royal, N7
David Chipperfield Architects
⊖ Kings Cross
Artists' studios were often in quiet residential enclaves but this one is in a busy industrial estate. Gormley had failed to find suitable existing premises and briefed the architect to design the space he had been looking for. The result is a fine double-height saw-toothed shed finished in white render. A large functional external yard for the assembly and shipping and receiving of work provides an approach. A pair of galvanized steel staircases on either side of the studio's central door give access to the more private studios above. Ironically, the space reflects the industrial arrangement where management above oversees the shop floor below.

Graduate Centre 2004 **C21** h
London Metropolitan University
Holloway Road N7
Studio Daniel Libeskind
⊖ Holloway Road
For those familiar with Libeskind's Jewish Museum in Berlin this will be a disappointment: not unlike his unbuilt spiral project for the V&A, formal collision has been introduced irrespective of function. This was a façade job to the existing library; the client was looking for a landmark and possibly not noticing that next door the original fourteen-storey polytechnic tower of the 1960s already provided one for the University, which Rick Mather's Technology Tower of 1998 helped to consolidate.

Emirates Stadium 2006 **C22** h
Hornsey Road, Queensland Road N7
HOK Sport, Buro Happold
⊖ Arsenal, Holloway Road
Very few completely new football stadiums were built in London in the second half of the twentieth century. The twenty-first brought two at once: this, the new 60,000-seat home for Arsenal Football Club, the other, and larger, the replacement for the old **Wembley Stadium** T42. While Wembley stands free, rather as Rome's Colosseum does today, the 'Emirates' (named for its airline sponsors) is successfully embedded in the city's streets much as the Roman arena originally was. The integration of architecture (the seating, surrounding rooms and circulation) and engineering is more satisfactory here than at Wembley with its complicated retractable roof.

continued section R

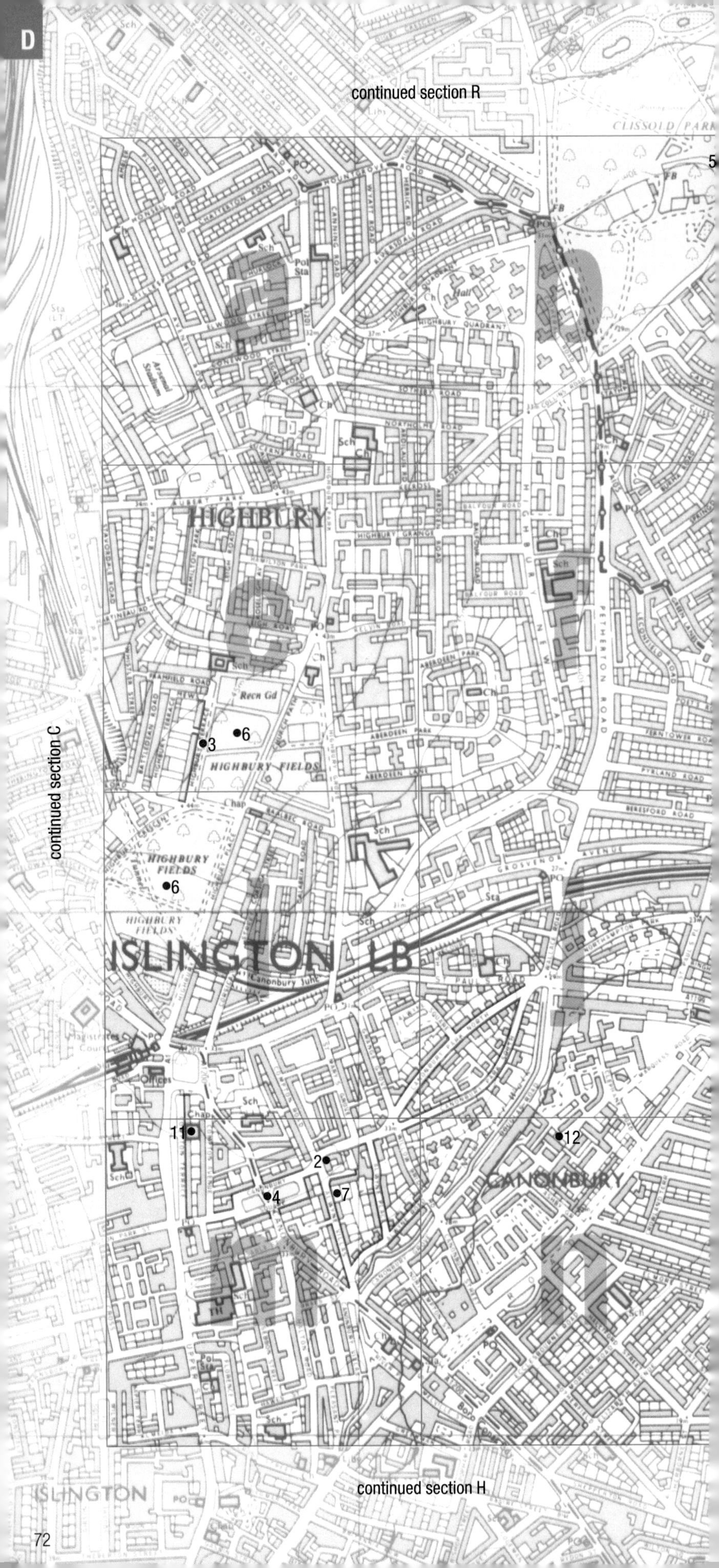
HIGHBURY
HIGHBURY FIELDS
Recn Gd
Arsenal Stadium
ISLINGTON LB
Canonbury Junc
CANONBURY
ISLINGTON
CLISSOLD PARK
3
6
6
11
2
4
7
12
5

continued section C

continued section H

continued section R

continued section U

continued section H

Stoke Newington ■ Highbury ■ Hackney ■ Canonbury ■ De Beauvoir Town ■ Dalston

Two significant engineering works, nearly 2000 years apart, divide this part of London into recognizable areas. Firstly, Ermine Street, the straight Roman road from Lincoln to the City of London, forms a north–south alignment along Stamford Hill (section U), Stoke Newington High Street, Stoke Newington Road and Kingsland Road. Secondly, at right angles to Ermine Street, the North London railway line (c1865) divides the section into its northern and southern parts. Ermine Street and the North London Line have no specific character, but they have proved significant and useful in defining districts.

To the east of Ermine Street and north of the North London Line is Hackney, and to the south-east is Dalston. To the east and west of Kingsland Road are Dalston and De Beauvoir Town – the south-west corner of the borough of Hackney (the majority of which lies in section U). The development of the De Beauvoir Estate in 1840 was the first large-scale building enterprise in Hackney where, unlike its neighbouring developments, the Estate retained close control of the operation, giving it a conspicuous consistency (see **De Beauvoir Square** D8 and its surrounding streets). The urban villa – a semi-detached house in a variety of styles – was by the middle of the nineteenth century the typical form of development. The villa was more versatile than the terraced house, being suitable for both small and large sites. In the massive urbanization of the second half of the nineteenth century, Hackney's development was piecemeal, and its population rose from 120,000 to 370,000 between 1837 and 1901. Redevelopment after severe bombing In the Second World War increased the fragmentary nature of the area.

The area to the west of Ermine Street and north of the railway line was essentially rural until the middle of the nineteenth century. Stoke Newington was a medieval village with the parish church of **Old St Mary** D1 at its centre; its two reservoir ponds and Clissold Park still give the impression of a nineteenth-century suburb. Islington, to the south, was surrounded by the hamlets of Newington Green, Canonbury and Lower and Upper Holloway (see section C). From 1750 this rural picture changed dramatically with the building of the New Road: by 1805 there was a suburban nucleus south of St Paul's Road which was consolidated by the 1850s.

The district now known as Highbury had its origins in the eighteenth-century expansion of Islington along the main roads out of London. It has much late Victorian and early-twentieth-century by-law housing (dwellings conforming to statutory light, ventilation and drainage), light industry, goods yards, and, at its centre, **Highbury Fields** D6, forming a beautiful small park enclosed on two sides by fine eighteenth-century terraces.

Canonbury: The New River

Old St Mary

Old St Mary from 14th century **D1** c
St Mary 1858
Stoke Newington Church Street N16
George Gilbert Scott
⊖ Manor House
Positioned either side of Stoke Newington Church Street, the two churches are an interesting pair: one the church of a medieval village, the other showing the aspirations of an emerging London suburb. Old St Mary is picturesque: the nave is late medieval; the west tower, south aisle and vestry were added in 1560. Barry added the north aisle in 1824 and the timber spire is of 1829. Scott's new church is run-of-the-mill Gothic Revival; extensively damaged in the war, and subsequently repaired.

Canonbury House c1780 **D2** m
Canonbury Place N1
⊖ Highbury and Islington
The house is an elegant two-storey villa built for the developer of the Canonbury House Estate, which filled in the northern triangle between Canonbury Road and the earlier ribbon development of Upper Street. The houses in **Canonbury Place** are of the same date, and are interesting as an early example of the use of stucco.

Highbury Terrace 1789 **D3** e
N5
⊖ Highbury and Islington
A fine Georgian terrace with wide pavements faces the small park of Highbury Fields. The first-floor windows are unusually slender (like **Duncan Terrace** H5 in South Islington), and accentuate its height. The eighteenth-century terraces of Highbury have an ethereal, lost quality, embedded as they now are in dense nineteenth-century artisan housing; they recall the time when Highbury and much of Islington was open country inhabited by the wealthy few.

Canonbury Square 1800 **D4** m
N1
Jacob Leroux (?)
⊖ Highbury and Islington
A completely preserved square of particularly beautiful proportions, distinguished by raised pavements on the south side (reminiscent of Clifton in Bristol), and a public garden at its centre. The houses have tall first-floor windows with arched brickwork. The square is now divided and threatened by heavy traffic on the Canonbury Road. George Orwell lived at number 27b in 1945. To the east note **Canonbury House** D2, Canonbury Place, **Alwyne Villas** D7 and the fine terraces in Compton Road and Canonbury Grove.

Clissold House 1820–30 **D5** b
Clissold Park N16
Joseph Woods
⊖ Manor House
This monumental portico of six Doric columns, superimposed on the three-storey stock-brick villa overlooking Clissold Park, is a memory of Stoke Newington's more affluent and rural past.

Highbury Fields, Highbury Park **D6** e
and **Highbury New Park** 1830, 1850
N5
⊖ Highbury and Islington
Highbury Fields is a pleasant surprise in dense semi-industrial surroundings: a small park with mature plane trees and broad gravel paths, it is nevertheless large enough to absorb normal community activities (a crèche, swimming pool, tennis, five-a-side football, and the occasional travelling circus or fair). The Fields developed with Highbury Park (c1830) and Highbury New Park (c1850). The large Victorian detached villas on its west side, in mixed Italo-Romanesque styles, are now in multiple occupancy, but speak of the district's more affluent past.

Canonbury 1835–45 **D7** m
Alwyne Villas, Alwyne Road, Alwyne Place, Canonbury Park north and south, New River Walk N1
⊖ Highbury and Islington
An early suburb, conveniently near the City, consisting mostly of semi-detached houses of two and three storeys in spare Italianate style, and with a loose and now leafy street pattern. To the south the pleasantly tamed New River (illustration page 74) forms a charming park. Canonbury Park is grander and more regular with good semi-detached houses.

De Beauvoir Square 1838 **D8** o
N1
Roumieu and Gough
⊖ Essex Road
This huge square of 107 by 108m (350 by 350ft) has lost its original east side. With its supportive pattern of streets, it is Georgian in layout, but the architecture of its semi-detached villas is a curious Dutch and Jacobean mixture. The Tudor details of the oriel windows and mullions, the picturesque Dutch gable profiles, and the decorative stonework are a world away from Roumieu and Gough's strangely abstract and classical **Milner Square** C5, of only two years later.

Albion Square 1846–9 **D9** p
E8
J C Loudon
⊖ Essex Road
Semi-detached villas, by celebrated landscape designer Loudon, which according to Pevsner show 'the transition from late classical to the Italianate'. These simple brick boxes with mass-produced stuccoed embellishments were the prototype for the massive house-building boom in Hackney and the other outer boroughs in the second half of the nineteenth century. The urban villa – a grand house occupied by two or more families – lent itself to both small and large sites, and this versatility made it more appropriate than the terraced house for suburban development.

St Matthias 1851 **D10** g
Wordsworth Road,
off Matthias Road N16
W Butterfield
⊖ Dalston Junction
The church, damaged in the Second World War and since restored, is an important early example of Butterfield's emerging elemental Gothic style – note the tall gabled east tower and the steeply pitched roofs over the aisles and nave.

Union Chapel 1888 **D11** m
Compton Terrace N1
Bonella and Paul
⊖ Highbury and Islington
The buildings in which Congregationalists first worshipped were as plain as the religion itself. This huge and wild Victorian Gothic chapel is therefore a surprise, especially as it erupts from the Georgian serenity of Compton Terrace (1806). The savage contrast is tempered by the narrow strip of park which separates both chapel and terrace from Upper Street.

Marquess Road Estate 1970 **D12** n
Essex Road and
St Paul's Road N1
Darbourne and Darke
⊖ Essex Road, Highbury and Islington
The urban vernacular style of this estate goes back to Darbourne and Darke's entry (O14) for the Lillington Gardens competition of 1961, and unfortunately has found widespread official approval as an antidote to the excesses of the tower block. Large sections of London, as at Marquess Road, are consequently being rendered inaccessible and incomprehensible by the construction of dense urban villages. The buildings are of brick with small window openings and slate roofs, but do not fall into the ordinary patterns of the city (street, house, and so on), Instead they coagulate, giving the impression of an extremely large institutional building – the very form they were meant to avoid.

continued section A

continued section T

continued section I

continued section A

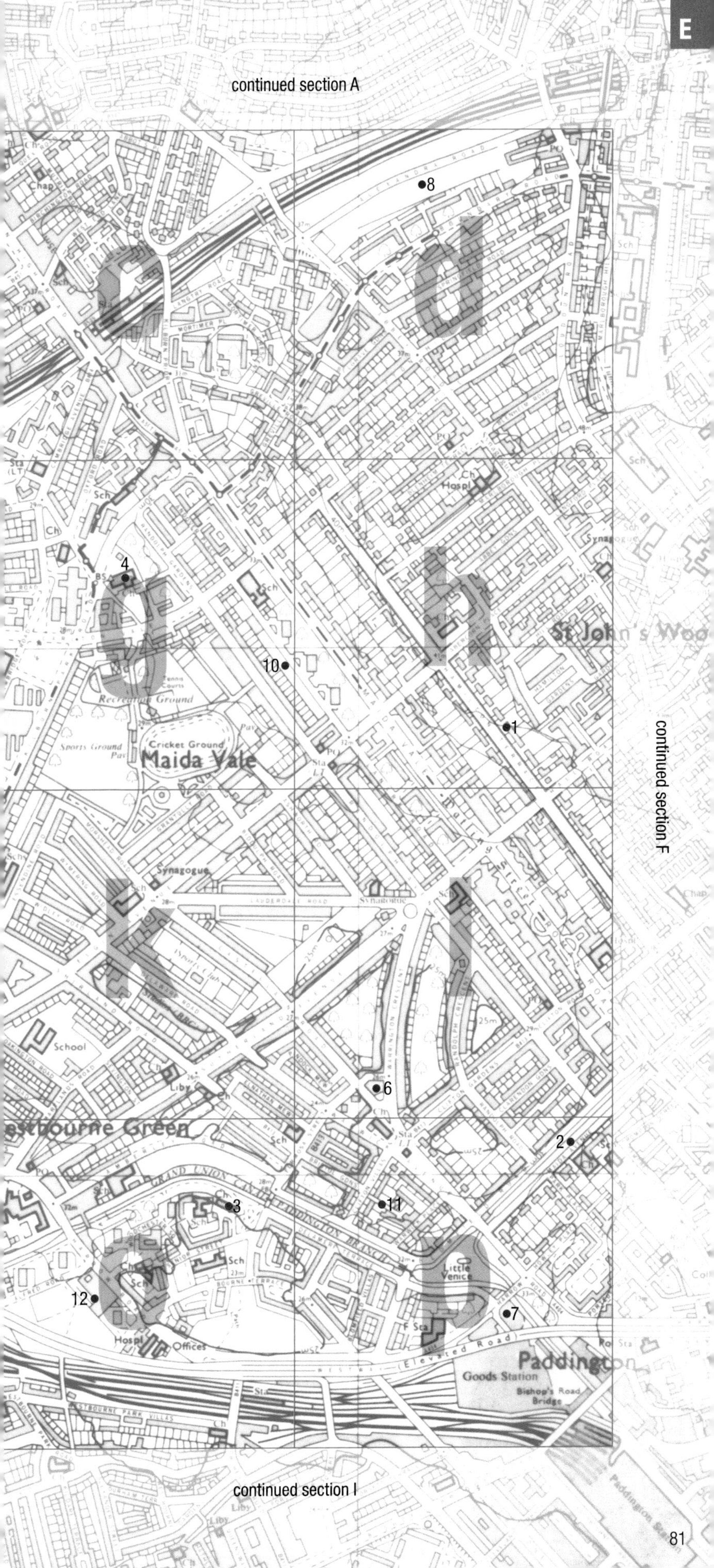

continued section F

continued section I

North Kensington ■ West Kilburn ■ Kensal Rise ■ Kilburn ■ Westbourne Grove ■ Maida Vale ■ St John's Wood (west)

The lines of transport connecting London to the west and north-west dominate this section. Edgware Road (the Roman Watling Street) runs straight north-west to St Albans and on to north Wales; now no longer a national route, it becomes tamed as a high street at Kilburn High Road, where the village of Kilburn used to be. To the south is the Paddington branch of the Grand Union Canal, constructed from 1795. Joined to the national canal network in 1805, it was extended eastwards via Regent's Park to the docks at Limehouse before being made obsolete by the railways. The original terminus of Brunel's Great Western Railway was built from 1832–8 at Paddington, then a village round its green, giving impetus to London's westward growth.

St John's Wood, to the east of Edgware Road, was developed as a suburb in the 1840s: at first villas stood alone in their own plots, later to form handsome streets like **Hamilton Terrace** E1. The suburb, fully developed by the 1850s, was never isolated: from the beginning it was served by buses to the West End and City, and in the 1870s the Metropolitan underground line was extended, further increasing its accessibility.

At the same time Little Venice, the first of the developments west of the Edgware Road, was growing around the junction of the canal with its branch to Paddington Basin. It was followed later in the nineteenth century by the huge areas of two-storey artisans' housing in West Kilburn, Kensal Rise (which had been an eighteenth-century spa) and Kilburn (see for example **Queen's Park Estate** E5).

In the 1960s Westway was built, the urban motorway following the line of the railway and connecting Euston Road (an eighteenth-century bypass) with the A40, the main road to Oxford. Raised on legs, its effect on the neighbourhood through and over which it passed was destructive, and its opening was marked by protests. This road was probably largely responsible for the popular distrust of large-scale engineering schemes, which led to the abandonment of the proposed inner motorway 'box'.

An architecture of free-standing buildings has arisen in the *cordon sanitaire* of Westway beginning first with **Trellick Tower** E9 in the 1970s and then accelerating from 2000 with the redevelopment of the Goods Yards as part of the larger Paddington Basin project (which extends into Section F). This cluster of dismal and uncomfortably dense medium-rise slabs and towers greets those arriving in central London from the west.

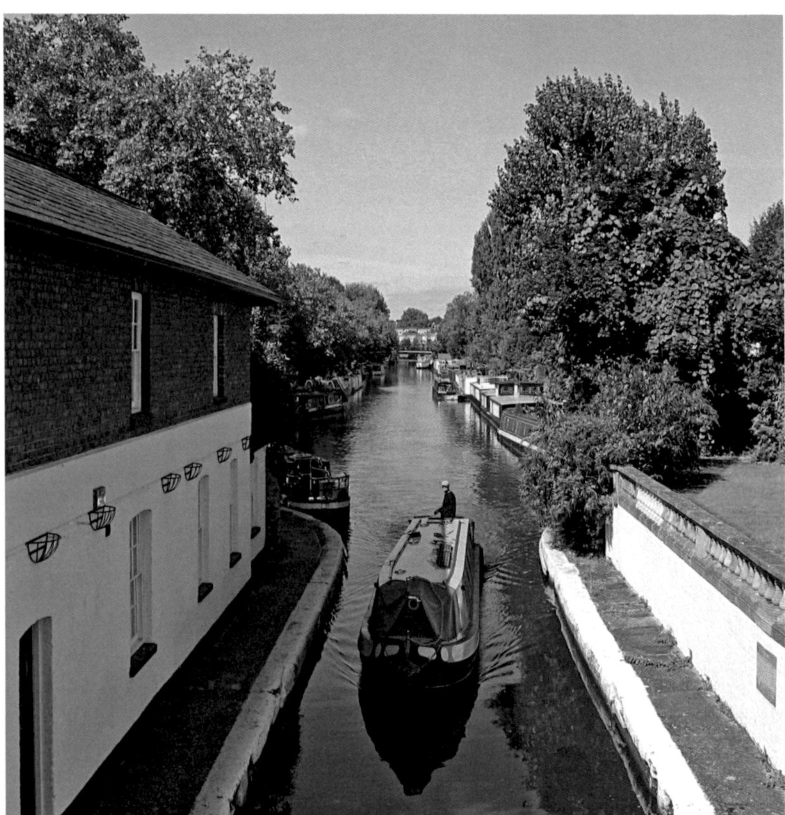

The Regent's Canal at Blomfield Road W9

Hamilton Terrace laid out 1830  **E1** h
St John's Wood NW8
⊖ Maida Vale

A very long (1100m/3600ft), undulating, wide and tree-lined street, Hamilton Terrace developed from the south, first with terraces and later with detached villas, and shows that suburbs did not have to use picturesque forms or curved streets. None of the architecture is particularly good and the success of the whole relies entirely on the width of the street and the limited range of materials: stock brick and stucco. Number 58 (1934), by Francis Lorne of Burnet, Tait and Lorne is the only 'modern' house in the street. Note the bow fronts of the houses in St John's Wood Road, terminating the south end, and the gentlemen's public lavatory at the junction of St John's Wood Road and Maida Vale, a Victorian public convenience (now disappearing as a type) with polished brass handrails to the staircase, white and green glazed wall tiles and pavement lights.

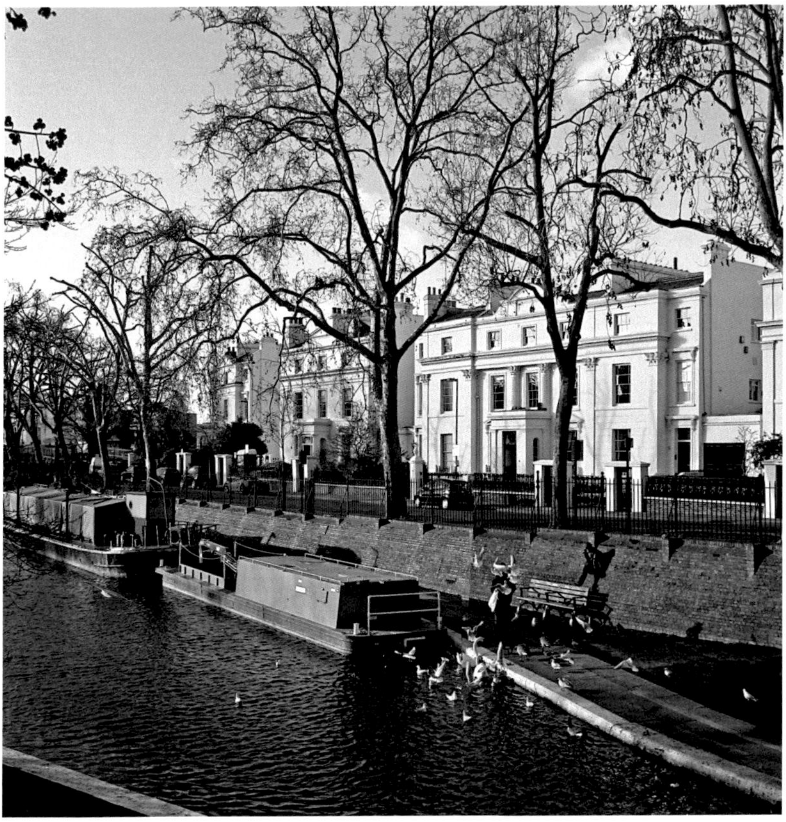

Maida Avenue

Blomfield Road and **Maida Avenue** c1840 **E2** p
W9
⊖ Warwick Avenue

Blomfield Road and Maida Avenue, 'planned' streets on either side of the canal between Warwick Avenue and the Edgware Road, are unique examples (more Dutch than Venetian) of the canal's use as an extra ingredient in a London street. The buildings on either side vary from elegant nineteenth-century semi-detached stuccoed villas and terraced houses to Edwardian mansion flats. The secret of this special place lies in the mature trees forming a canopy to the canal, and the presence of boats and the bridge at either end of the wide space. To the south-west the canal continues and divides at the basin of Little Venice, where, with the visible proximity of both the Westway and more recent building, the magic of Blomfield Road evaporates.

St Mary Magdalene 1868–78 **E3** o
Woodchester Square W2
George Edmund Street
⊖ Royal Oak

One of the finest Gothic Revival churches in London, and a defiant landmark among the banal high-rise towers seen by the motorist from Westway. The exterior is banded with stone and dark brown brick and the tower with its slender spire is positioned asymmetrically.

The interior is also very good: the nave is high, and the theme of brick and stone banding to the external walls recurs, with an astonishingly rich and decorative use of diagonally laid green and pink tiles below dado level. The columns on the north side are separated from the wall to form a screen, and there is a tall clerestory and vaulted ceiling. The crypt, by J N Comper, is notable for its elaborate timber screens, paintings and stained glass.

St Augustine, Kilburn 1870–80 **E4** g
tower 1897–8
Kilburn Park Road NW6
J L Pearson
⊖ Kilburn Park

According to Pevsner, St Augustine's is one of the finest churches of its date in England. It is now surrounded by new housing and roads that have all but destroyed the coherence of the area, which the church used to dominate with its spire 77m (254ft) high. While the sources of its architecture (Early English and Albi Cathedral) are as scholarly as could be expected of a late Victorian building, the forms have an expressionistic baldness.

Queen's Park Estate 1875–83 **E5** a
NW6
Austin, Roland Plumbe
⊖ Queen's Park
Built by the Artisans', Labourers' and General Development Company on land bought from All Souls College, Oxford, this 'improving' estate of 33 hectares (76 acres) provided 2000 houses for 16,000 residents at a cost of £700,000. Although there was no public house and behaviour was firmly regulated, the estate was always successful, the early residents being 'of the regular employed class: railwaymen or police, artisans, small clerks ...' The houses have Gothic details, and there is a 1.6-hectare (4-acre) park.

The Prince Alfred c1880 **E6** l
Formosa Street, Castellain Road
and Warrington Crescent W9
⊖ Warwick Avenue
Formosa Street is a remarkable shopping street, forming a grand but miniature urban block. Its east and west façades, stuccoed blank, have giant Corinthian pilasters; and on the south-west corner is the Prince Alfred pub. The double-height ground-floor screen – a complex series of curves in bevelled, etched and inscribed glass set in a delicate timber frame – is especially fine and surprisingly intact. Inside, there are more screens which originally divided the large single space into four separate bars.

ex **Paddington Maintenance Depot** **E7** p
1966–8
179 Harrow Road W2
Bicknell & Hamilton
⊖ Warwick Avenue, Royal Oak
These two buildings, early examples of motorway architecture – a low garage to the east and offices and workshops to the west – were built on an awkward site near Paddington Station and between the Regent's Canal and the M40 to service British Rail's parcel van fleet. The taller, with its sweeping curves best seen from the motorway, was originally clad in cream mosaic, painted in 2001 when the building was converted for use as headquarters for a fashion company.

Housing, Alexandra Road 1969–79 **E8** d
Abbey Road, Boundary Road
and Loudoun Road NW8
London Borough of Camden Architects
Department; Neave Brown
⊖ Swiss Cottage, South Hampstead
Alexandra Road was probably the last (and the most ambitious) of the large comprehensive redevelopments of the inner city originating in the mid-1950s. The 6.6-hectare (16-acre) site marks the northern boundary of St John's Wood, an area characterized by a loose pattern of nineteenth-century villas, and the development occupies an entire city block with a main-line railway cutting to the north. The planning brief required housing for 1660 people in 520 dwellings with garages, a training centre for mentally handicapped children, a community centre, children's reception centre, a school, and a local park of 1.6 hectares (4 acres).

The site was conceived by the designer as a 'single gesture' and is organized linearly, like a

giant centipede, in open rows of long terraces of varying height. The social buildings are grouped to form its 'head' at the eastern extremity, and its 'legs' are two pedestrian streets extending the length of the site, giving access to the dwellings on either side of the park.

The principal terrace at Alexandra Road demonstrates the correct application of the stepped section: by forming an eight-storey wall to the railway cutting it develops a generous front of sun-filled terraces to the south. The interiors of the flats, like their antecedents at **Winscombe Street** R29 and **Fleet Road** B26, have a generosity of planning and quality in detail that are unrivalled in any post-war local authority housing. The estate was listed Grade 2* in 1993.

Note the remaining fragment of the west elevation of Evans and Shalev's Home for the Physically Handicapped of 1978 on Boundary Road, shockingly semi-cannibalized by a bland double attic.

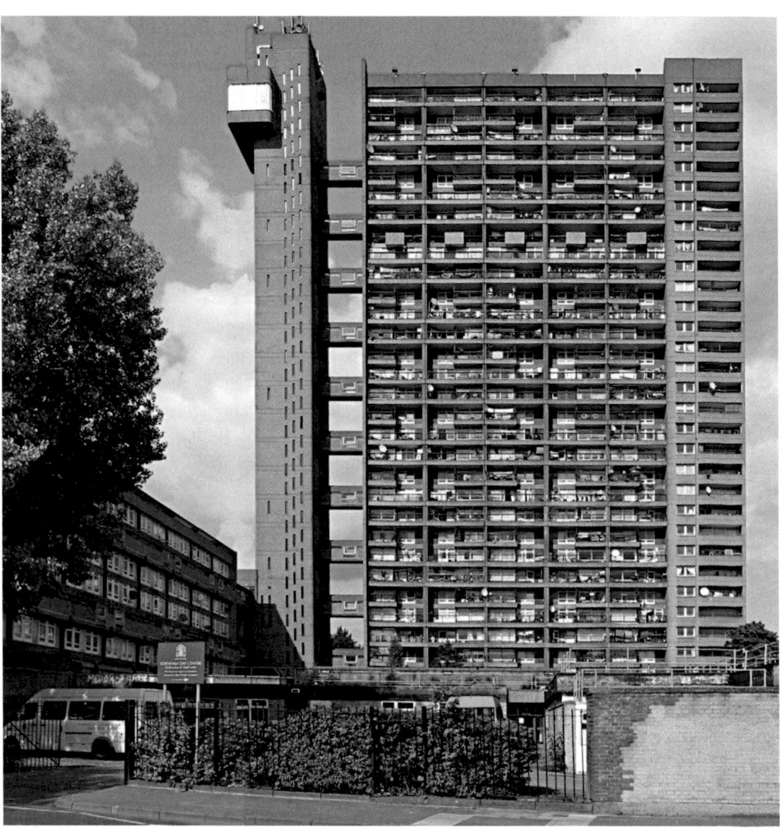

Trellick Tower 1973 **E9** m
Golborne Road W10
Ernö Goldfinger
⊖ Westbourne Park

When built, these were the tallest flats in England. Goldfinger was experimenting both with the 'deck' form, in which one access corridor serves three levels of maisonettes (like Le Corbusier's *Unité d'habitation*, but with the corridor on the outside), and with his own language of the articulated concrete frame. The projection at the top of the separate lift and stair tower houses the gas-fired boiler, below which is a glazed meeting room for tenants. When journalists write of the horrors of tower-block living, the inhabitants of this tower, mostly without children, write back saying how much they like it. If we must have towers (and this now seems doubtful), then this is one of the best.

Housing 1979–82 **E10** g

171–201 Lanark Road W9
Jeremy and Fenella Dixon
Maida Vale

A radical reproach to the urban model of the 1960s which it faces across Lanark Road, this row of what appears to be eight 'villas' actually contains flats. Their form paraphrases the nineteenth-century suburban housing types and street architecture with which Maida Vale was first developed. In the details there is a strong contrast between the 'traditional' forms of the front – deeply overhanging gables and arched windows with stucco surrounds – and the utility of the sides with their metal stairs and the backs with their flush gables.

Shop 1985 **E11** p
Clifton Nurseries, Clifton Villas W9
Jeremy Dixon BDP
Warwick Avenue

Clifton Nurseries have several sites and have been imaginative patrons of small-scale architecture. This small shop, extended from an existing greenhouse, was elaborately wrought using materials which would wear well: the exposed structure is in oak and the whole is covered in a copper roof. The open framework which serves as entrance canopy is also by Dixon.

Westminster Academy 2007 **E12** o
Harrow Road W2
Allford Hall Monahan Morris
with BDP Landscape
Royal Oak

Westminster Academy is the latest in a line of city academies instigated under the Thatcher government, assisted with a gift from David Dangoor, an Iraqi property developer; it provides education for 1175 pupils. The site is on the other side of the tracks of the main line into Paddington station and at eye level with Westway. The architects have exploited this exposed situation with a strong polychromy to identify the building as a billboard – 'You know, the yellow and green one.' The building supposedly challenges comfortably held positions as to appearance and character, although it might be argued that, like the red and yellow of the Shell petrol station next door, this arbitrary graphic branding has hijacked the 'normal' architectural apparatus.

On the inside the branding idea continues. The central atrium is decorated with large-scale slogans – 'Global Citizenship', 'Communication', etc, as well as quotations from international leaders, all in green and yellow. In the shadow of this hip presentation, complete with Charles Eames furniture, is a sensible plan with thoughtful detailing, especially in the much-used lavatories and staircases. If the building is a 'decorated shed' outside, facing the interior of the site it establishes a convincing relationship with the independent and timber-clad sports centre. Well-detailed external spaces lead to a grid of netted basketball courts positioned under and given a 'ceiling' by the long curving concrete soffit of Westway above. Never has this albatross of the 1960s looked so elegant or been used so appropriately.

F

continued section B

continued section E

continued section J

continued section B

continued section G

continued section J

St John's Wood (east) ■ Primrose Hill ■ Regent's Park ■ Marylebone (north) ■ Camden Town (west)

The medieval village of St Mary-le-Bourne (the main street being part of the present Marylebone High Street, and Marylebone Lane, a track meandering through open fields), the small settlement of Camden Town to the north, the mound of Primrose Hill set in open countryside, and the Roman Watling Street (now Edgware Road) were the only developments here until the end of the seventeenth century. Between 1717 and 1817 two important enterprises transformed this rural picture, permanently connecting most of the area to central London.

In 1708 the Duke of Newcastle bought the Marylebone Estate; in 1717 he laid out Cavendish Square and the surrounding streets (see section J), which encouraged continuous residential building within its orderly grid of streets for the rest of the century. **Portland Place** F3 to the east, the grandest street in eighteenth-century London, dates from 1775, and Baker Street to the west was completed shortly before 1800. The northern boundary of the development was the New Road (now Marylebone Road, Euston Road and Pentonville Road), laid out in 1756 as an east–west bypass (London's first) of the West End. By the beginning of the nineteenth century Marylebone Road defined London's northern limits, as Oxford Street had done in the seventeenth century.

In 1812 the Prince Regent commissioned John Nash's plans for **Regent's Park** F5, to be carried out from 1817. An area of heathland in the eighteenth century, Regent's Park is now, thanks to Nash, London's largest and most impressive civic design: in contrast to most of London's civic spaces it is the result of a conscious plan rather than the fortuitous outcome of centuries of change. Included in Nash's plan for Regent's Park was Regent's Canal (see section E), which, apart from being an early example of industrial engineering, adds an unexpected touch of romance to the northern edge of the park. Much of the excavated material was intelligently added to the mound of Primrose Hill.

By 1830 Regent's Park was encouraging the growth (to the west) of St John's Wood, originally the Eyre Estate, which by 1855 was covered with white-stuccoed detached villas, and (to the east) of Camden Town, completed by about 1850. Here, as elsewhere, the railways had a significant effect: the London and Birmingham Railway, which originally terminated at Chalk Farm near the **Round House** B6, was ingeniously extended to Euston in 1836, cut in the seam between Camden Town and Albany Street, to the east of Regent's Park.

In a little under fifty years rough heathland had become an impressive new urban addition to the centre of London, its general form remaining unchanged up to the present. The area south of Marylebone Road has been rebuilt successfully many times, retaining the original layout of streets and squares and small households. But this part of London is scarred by the housing redevelopments of the late 1950s and '60s – the worst being the monstrous Lisson Green Estate to the west of Regent's Park, not much improved by its recladding of the 1990s.

The most conspicuous new development in this section was on Paddington Basin and the Edgware Road immediately north of Paddington Station. Here from 2000 onwards a series of mediocre medium-rise apartment and office buildings were intensively built. They confirmed, however, the commonsensical idea that railway stations as places of interchange might provide appropriate sites for dense development, thereby taking pressure off central London sites.

Giraffe House, London Zoo F28

Broadcasting House F42, Eric Gill's *Prospero and Ariel*

Chandos House 1769–71 **F1** p
Chandos Street W1
Robert Adam
⊖ Oxford Circus
At the same time as he was building the large **Adelphi** K58, Adam was developing a single plot: a serious, plain, four-bay stone-fronted house, its front decorated with a single band of carved waves. It is now owned by the Royal Society of Medicine and its (usually inaccessible) interiors were restored in 2004. The stuccoed mews building decorated with sphinxes, in Duchess Street at the back, was built in the 1920s by Arthur Bolton. See also **20 Portman Square** J12.

Houses 1770s **F2** p
5–15, 18, 20–2 Mansfield Street
W1
Robert Adam
⊖ Oxford Circus
Outside, only the fine and characteristic fan-topped doorways of these big, plain houses suggest their authorship, although the decorated ceilings of the first floors can be glimpsed from the pavement. Lutyens lived and worked at number 13. The street is closed at the north end by a seven-bay composition of a pair of houses: symmetry is achieved by the left-hand house having three bays, and the right four.

Portland Place 1776–80 **F3** p
W1
James Adam
⊖ Oxford Circus, Regent's Park
Started after the **Adelphi** K58, Portland Place is another of the Adams' speculative schemes: a single street, and very wide for its time (34m/110ft), designed as a whole from Foley House at the south end to the New Road (now Marylebone Road) at the north. The uniformity of the street has suffered from much rebuilding, which started with the enormous Langham Hotel built on the site of Foley House in 1864. Twentieth-century building cut some of the delicate pediments in half, and bombing in the Second World War continued the destruction. The only fairly complete section is that between Weymouth Street and New Cavendish Street on the east side, although even here the attics are later additions. The brick house-fronts continue the stylistic innovations of the Adelphi; thin stucco pilasters with sunken panels decorated with honeysuckle support delicate flat pediments. By the 1780s fashion was beginning to turn against the Adams, but this particular decorative scheme continued in popular use for another twenty years. The street was incorporated by Nash in his grand route from Carlton House to Regent's Park, terminating Portland Place with the half-circus of **Park Crescent** F6.

St Mary 1788–91 **F4** m
Paddington Green W2
J Plaw
⊖ Edgware Road

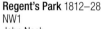

Now set forlornly between the ugly A40 and the rebuilt north side of Paddington Green, St Mary's was restored to its eighteenth-century charm in the 1970s by Erith and Terry. In plan a Greek cross, the design is not of a particular school, although the extensive use inside of the segmental curve places it in the mainstream of the architecture of the end of the century. Quinlan Terry's modest church hall to the west of the church was built in 1981.

Regent's Park 1812–28 **F5**
NW1
John Nash
⊖ Regent's Park, Baker Street, Camden Town

John Nash's name is now automatically associated with his designs for Regent's Park, in its day one of Europe's most original architectural developments. The rough heathlands of Marylebone Park to the north of the New Road (Marylebone Road) were leased to the Duke of Portland for hunting up to the end of the eighteenth century. When the land reverted to the Crown in 1809, John Nash's plans for its transformation into a proper park were immediately accepted.

Nash's original intentions were far more extensive than the actual results. Park Crescent was planned as a giant circus (Europe's largest) to terminate Portland Place; the perimeter of the park was to be lined entirely by terraces; a second grand circus was projected on the site of the Inner Circle, with twenty-six villas scattered among the trees and two crescents at the north end; and the Prince Regent was to have a valhalla, churches and a pavilion. Seen as a whole the scheme was an early garden city of great originality, but a combination of factors, practical and aesthetic, constrained Nash's grand ideas. It was feared that too much building in the centre of the park would spoil the scenery – and in any case the speculative venture had run out of funds. The consequent reduction in building and modification of the grand circus to **Park Crescent** F6 proved to be successful revisions.

The **Zoological Gardens** F28 were laid out in 1827 by Decimus Burton and have been progressively enlarged ever since. The Inner Circle was leased to the Royal Botanic Society in 1839, and the open air theatre was built in 1932.

The people's park, like the museum, is an invention of the nineteenth century. In the seventeenth and eighteenth centuries parks had been the scene of pageants and hunts. Regent's Park, with its scholarly collections of exotic flora and fauna in the botanical and zoological gardens, provided a diverting educational spectacle for the Sunday promenade. At the same time, Nash's idea of the urban terraces looking out over an ideal landscape anticipated the garden city and suburb of the late nineteenth and early twentieth centuries.

Many of the terraces were under threat of demolition following the Second World War to make way for a more profitable use of the land for the Crown Estate. Fortunately, such plans were resisted. However, the same cannot be said of the continued overdevelopment of the lands immediately north of the Marylebone Road. The tower at the Euston Road underpass has always had an unwelcome presence seen from the park, which unfortunate initiatives of the 2000s at the south end of Albany Street will only help to exacerbate.

Cumberland Terrace F25

Park Crescent 1812 **F6** p
Regent's Park W1
John Nash
⊖ Regent's Park, Great Portland Street

The crescent marks the formal entry to Regent's Park from the south. Intended as a circus, which would have been the largest in Europe, it has single-storey colonnades of paired Ionic columns running the length of the two wide quadrants, creating an almost abstract architectural order. The colonnades screen the individuality of the houses' doors and areas, and the window openings above are simple and unembellished, unlike Nash's other terraces. All other architectural features are merely a background to the dominant idea of the colonnade. Despite a radical change of use to offices, and much rebuilding behind the east façade, it keeps alive the theatrical intentions of its designer and is one of the finest architectural set-pieces in London.

In **Park Square East**, to the north, two doors in the middle of the terrace once led to the famous Diorama, designed by Nash and the elder Pugin. Although neglected for many years and stripped of its interior fittings, it was renovated in 1998 and occupied by the Prince of Wales Trust.

St John's Wood Chapel 1813 **F7** f
Park Road NW1
Thomas Hardwick
⊖ St John's Wood

The Ionic portico and turret of St John's successfully close the view to the north up Park Road. The churchyard is particularly fine, although the two-storey brick church hall to the east is unfortunate, especially when compared with Terry's hall for **St Mary, Paddington** F4. Inside, Tuscan columns support glazed galleries, where Ionic columns in turn support the slightly curved ceiling.

St Mary 1813 **F8** o
Marylebone Road NW1
Thomas Hardwick
⊖ Baker Street

In 1770, with the rapid expansion of the parish, plans were proposed for rebuilding St Mary's, but only in 1813 was the new building begun. The grand Corinthian six-column portico looks up York Gate into Regent's Park, thereby extending the spirit of Nash's composition across the New Road (now Marylebone Road). The fine circular tower has a ring of free-standing columns, above which the dome is supported by gilded caryatids, The choir was remodelled by the Victorian 'rogue' architect Thomas Harris in 1885; it gives the east end an uncharacteristic 'high church' and Byzantine effect.

Next door, note Philip Gumuchdjian's splendid basement gymnasium of 2007 for the St Marylebone School, the excavation involving the displacement of one thousand bodies (the architect James Gibbs and painter George Stubbs among them).

Dorset Square c1815 **F9** n
NW1
⊖ Marylebone

Part of the northerly limits of the Portman Estate, Dorset Square is a relatively intact example of the late Georgian style. Rather than being subordinate to the overall composition of the façade, the houses have some individuality. On the east side they have fine cast-iron verandas: the growing use of verandas in the early nineteenth century was an early sign of the influence of colonial lifestyles (particularly eastern) on domestic architecture, which was to flourish in the Regency period a decade later (see houses in **Park Lane** J21).

Macclesfield Bridge c1815, 1874 **F10** f
north gate to Regent's Park
from Prince Albert Road NW8
John Nash
⊖ St John's Wood

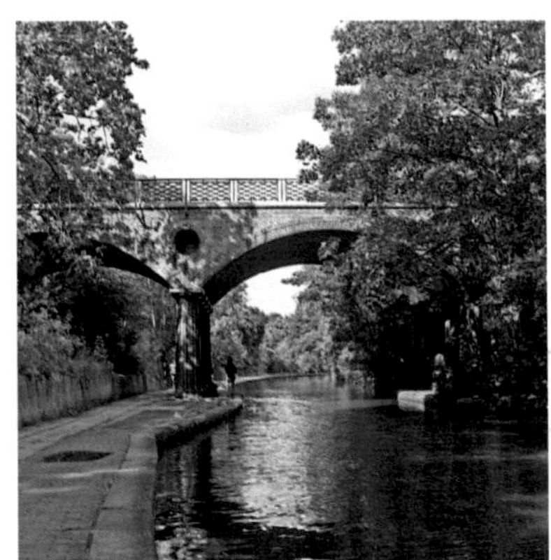

Marking the northern vehicular approach to Regent's Park across the Regent's Canal, this fine bridge has three arched bays: brick vaults are supported on two rows of Doric cast-iron columns. In 1874 an explosion on a barge carrying gunpowder completely destroyed the bridge and it was subsequently rebuilt using the original columns.

The Holme 1818 **F11** k
Inner Circle, Regent's Park NW1
Decimus Burton
⊖ Baker Street

Nash's original plan for Regent's Park had included a large area to be given over to villas; The Holme, **St John's Lodge** F12 and Burton's **Grove House** F17 (now Nuffield Lodge) are all that remain. The Holme is Burton's first building, designed when he was eighteen for his father, Nash's builder. Although the whole is less ambitious than Grove House, the Corinthian portico on the entrance side is impressive.

Viewed from the north across the park, it gives a good idea of the original appearance of the white classical villa standing in its own spacious grounds.

St John's Lodge 1818, 1847, 1890 **F12** g
Inner Circle, Regent's Park NW1
J Raffield, Charles Barry, R Weir Schultz
⊖ Baker Street

Only St John's Lodge, **The Holme** F11 and **Grove House** F17 remain of the eight villas built in Regent's Park. The original house has been much altered – Barry added the projecting wings and a second storey in 1847 – but it has a very fine entrance hall leading to a beautifully enclosed garden, now public and accessible from the Inner Circle. Like The Holme, when viewed from its garden St John's Lodge revives Nash's vision of a very privileged suburb.

Cornwall Terrace 1821–3 **F13** k
Regent's Park NW1
John Nash with Decimus Burton
⊖ Baker Street

Cornwall Terrace was restored in 1980 and had its roof, parapets and chimneys put back properly (unlike Park Crescent F6, where the clean curve of the new roof gives a curiously modern look). It is 171m (560ft) long, and at the north end presents an elegant bay window to the triangular garden; it does not have a strip of garden separating it from the Outer Circle, and consequently seems more 'urban' than the other terraces. The attribution to Burton is strange: he was twenty-one and working in the office of Nash, whose builder was Decimus's father.

Sussex Place 1822 **F14** j
Outer Circle, Regent's Park NW1
John Nash
⊖ Baker Street

It is no surprise that this terrace is contemporary with Nash's Brighton Pavilion (completed in 1823): with its curved end wings, octagonal domes, polygonal bay windows and Corinthian central portico, Sussex Place (198m/650ft in length) is the most eccentric terrace in Regent's Park.

Hanover Terrace and **Hanover Lodge** 1822–3 **F15** j
Outer Circle, Regent's Park NW1
John Nash
⊖ Baker Street

This terrace, 140m (460ft) long, is of simple composition: straight, with three prettily decorated pediments, one at each end and one in the middle, in a not very refined Roman Doric. The only other modelling is the ground-floor arcade, rusticated with segmental arches.

Hanover Lodge, of the same date with additions by Lutyens (1909), marks an entrance to Regent's Park. An island lodge with gates on either side, it is a delightfully simple stuccoed octagon with a tall central chimney and shallow pitched roof. The open loggia on the park side has been closed, and the building is now overshadowed by Gibberd's **Mosque** F56 next door.

All Souls 1822–4 **F16** p
Langham Place W1
John Nash
⊖ Oxford Circus

This is one of Nash's major works, partly because of the intrinsic originality of the design, but principally because it manages to give Regent Street a satisfactory conclusion on a difficult site. Nash used the quadrant to change direction from Lower Regent Street to Regent Street; here he also enlisted the circle as a device to change direction between Upper Regent Street and the existing line of Portland Place. The church's circular portico acts as a pivot, and its rectangular nave is rotated on the north-east axis and thus concealed from the principal views. The conical spire surrounded by a Corinthian peristyle, a diminutive version of the portico below, caused a storm of controversy at the time, prompting the famous cartoon of Nash sitting on his spire. As Summerson observed, 'It is nevertheless a curiously ambiguous design … both modern French and old English'. With the building of **Broadcasting House** F42 in 1931 the church was overwhelmed and much of its town planning importance lost. Inside, the flat coffered ceiling is reminiscent of Wren; it is carried on Corinthian columns, the galleries on chamfered piers. The new glass doors and screen to the entrance are unfortunate. Note the bust of John Nash by the entrance, looking south down Regent Street.

Grove House **F17** f
1822–4
Prince Albert Road NW1
Decimus Burton
⊖ St John's Wood

The purest of the surviving villas in Regent's Park, Grove House is also one of the few remaining examples of the Edwardian 'artist's house'. Burton's designs for the original owner, G B Greenough, were modifed in 1877, and as a result have lost their former strict neo-Palladianism. Grove House was designed to meet the requirements of a cultivated and liberal-minded bachelor, who enjoyed mapping out obscure areas of the globe as much as he enjoyed his weekly soirées at home, and it had the

atmosphere of a small London club.

The four elevations are all different – the most imposing was the south front to the garden, a portico of four Ionic double columns. After Greenough's death the house was extended (1877) by Burton's cousin Henry Marley Burton. The bachelor's villa was transformed into a family house by the addition of windows and bedrooms, and it was bought by the Nuffield Foundation in 1953. See also the **Studio** F37.

Clarence Terrace 1823 **F18** k
Outer Circle, Regent's Park NW1
Decimus Burton
⊖ Baker Street

Burton's invention of three-bay attached screens either side of the central pavilion is the special interest here. They have an arched base, paired columns and a flat entablature, and behind each is a single bow-fronted house. The device anticipates Burton's **Ionic screen** J25 for Hyde Park Corner two years later. Clarence Terrace was insensitively rebuilt and its new back can be seen from Park Road.

St Mary 1823 **F19** n
Wyndham Place W1
Robert Smirke
⊖ Baker Street

The semicircular portico of Ionic columns and the slim round stone tower and cupola of St Mary's have a well-planned, monumental relationship to **Bryanston Square** J19 to the south. The main body of the church to the north is rectangular and built of stock brick, with two-tier windows, and forms part of the adjoining pattern of streets. The interior, with its gallery and the Doric columns supporting the gently curved coffered ceiling, is further evidence of Smirke's successful use of the Greek Revival style.

Smirke's glorious portico now sits on a paved forecourt. Part of this modest urban improvement is Tarrant Place (1989–90) to the west by Quinlan Terry. These eleven houses arranged around a granite cobbled courtyard are a reinterpretation of the traditional mews.

Ulster Terrace and **Ulster Place** **F20** l
1824–5
Outer Circle and Marylebone Road NW1
John Nash
⊖ Regent's Park
Ulster Place is a very plain stuccoed terrace fortunately set back from the torrential traffic of Marylebone Road. Ulster Terrace faces Regent's Park, and is a more ambitious design, though the engaged Ionic columns to the ground floor are distinctly un-grand. The bay windows providing emphasis at the ends are unique in the Nash terraces.

York Terrace, Upper Harley Street and **York Gate** 1824–6 **F21** k
Regent's Park NW1
John Nash
⊖ Regent's Park
This long composition (430m/1410ft) is arranged axially round the York Gate entrance to **Regent's Park** F5, but is not seen to advantage from the park because one looks south into the sun. The two terraces have giant Ionic features in the centres and at the ends, between which runs a Greek Doric colonnade on the ground floor. Between the eastern range and Upper Harley Street is a fine pair of Doric semi-detached houses. York Gate was designed to frame Hardwick's earlier **St Mary, Marylebone** F8 and successfully does so, but the vista is now spoilt by the anachronistic and obtrusive street furniture required to direct traffic into the park: this short street could well be pedestrianized. Between York Terrace and Marylebone Road are the delightful two-storey stuccoed mews houses built for the servants; these are all that remain of Nash's small domestic buildings.

Holy Trinity 1824–8 **F22** l
Marylebone Road NW1
John Soane
⊖ Great Portland Street
Of Soane's three churches built at the same time, Holy Trinity is the least interesting, and much less idiosyncratic than **St Peter Walworth** P1. The shallow Ionic porch here projects, rather than being recessed into the plane of the front, and the tower is less geometrically pure: only the finials to the columns of the first stage show the strangeness characteristic of Soane. See also **St John, Bethnal Green** U19.

Chester Terrace 1825 **F23** h
Regent's Park NW1
John Nash
⊖ Regent's Park
The longest unbroken façade in the park (287m/940ft), Chester Terrace has a complex alternating system of bays (ABCBABCBA), marked periodically by giant Corinthian columns. At either end are projecting wings, connected to the main façade by theatrically thin triumphal arches.

St Katharine's Hospital 1826 **F24** h
Outer Circle, Regent's Park NW1
Ambrose Poynter
⊖ Camden Town
This early example of the Gothic Revival brings further variety to the buildings surrounding Regent's Park. Despite a medieval air the plan is Palladian, with a large central chapel and curved 'collegiate' wings connecting to the domestic quarters. The Royal College of St Katharine was moved to Regent's Park when its original site, next to the Tower of London, was excavated to make way for **St Katharine's Dock** L72.

Cumberland Terrace 1826–7 **F25** h
Regent's Park NW1
John Nash, James Thomson
⊖ Regent's Park
The grandest of Regent's Park's eleven terraces, Cumberland Terrace is 244m (800ft) long and embodies the idea of a palace confronting a 'natural landscape' within the city. The centre block has a temple front: a giant order of ten Corinthian columns capped with a pediment containing exuberant sculptures; on each side of this are symmetrical terraces, terminated by pavilions and detached triumphal Ionic arches. It is the most daring, scenographic and successful terrace in the park.

Gloucester Gate and **Gloucester Lodge** 1827 **F26** d
Regent's Park NW1
John Nash
⊖ Camden Town
The two-storey Lodge is asymmetrically composed: to the right of the central portico of attached Ionic columns is a pavilion of three bays; to the left is a more substantial building which turns the corner into Parkway, and from which the Lodge is entered. Gloucester Gate is the most northerly of Nash's terraces, secluded behind a well-planted garden. The stuccoed façade is modulated by Ionic pilasters, with attached columns to the three projecting bays.

Kent Terrace 1827 **F27** j
Park Road NW1
John Nash
⊖ Baker Street
The only terrace to face outwards from the park, and one of the last to be built. Its long (112m/368ft) and stuccoed façade is usually described as plain and dull, but it would be no bad thing if London had more buildings of this quality and from this period – when, perhaps for the last time, middle-class taste was educated and homogeneous.

Mappin Terraces

The Zoo (Royal Zoological Society Gardens) started 1827 **F28** c
Regent's Park NW1
laid out by Decimus Burton
⊖ Camden Town
The Zoo is the British Museum of live animals and, like that institution, an invention of the early nineteenth century. The private Zoological Society employed Burton to lay out the gardens, and his building work survives only in the restored stock-brick Buffalo and Giraffe Houses (illustration page 90) on the terraces overlooking the Regent's Canal. The layout is a 'campus': the buildings are loosely arranged, with patches of grass and trees in between. There is no structure of blocks like those of a city, but the buildings are too close together for it to be a park.

The Society has patronized many distinguished architects, including Belcher and Joass (the fake mountains of the **Mappin Terraces** of 1914, with the Aquarium underneath); John Burnet's Camel House; Hugh Casson and Neville Conder (the former Elephant House in ribbed concrete 1962–5); Tecton and Lubetkin (**Gorilla House** F43 and **Penguin Pool** F46); and Price, Snowdon and Newby's (**Aviary** F53). As fashions in housing and explaining the animals have changed, and when a lot of the larger species were moved to the wider spaces of Whipsnade, many of the earlier purpose-built houses were altered or lost their purposes.

Park Village East and **West** 1829 **F29** d
Albany Street NW1
John Nash, J Pennethorne
⊖ Camden Town
Nash established a model for the suburban Victorian villa in these two park villages, once separated by a branch of the Regent's Canal (now filled in). With their various styles, these villas were Nash's final contribution to Regent's Park. Park Village East is linear, bounded by the street and the canal; Park Village West is picturesquely arranged along a winding 'country' road. The interiors have been altered, but it is the romantic, classical Tudor and Italianate mixture of the exteriors that is important – cream stucco, projecting eaves, and black lattice pergolas. Such stylistic variety was much imitated by Victorian suburban builders.

Christ Church 1838, altered 1868 **F30** h
Albany Street NW1
J Pennethorne, alterations by W Butterfield
⊖ Great Portland Street
Successfully marking the bend in Albany Street, Christ Church is decidedly understated, despite its classical pretensions. There is no portico, the entrance being marked by two giant pilasters, above which rises a simple thin tower and spire. On the west side are two tall secondary doors, and the north and south façades have high arched windows. The marble floor is by Butterfield, and the glass of one of the south windows is by Rossetti.

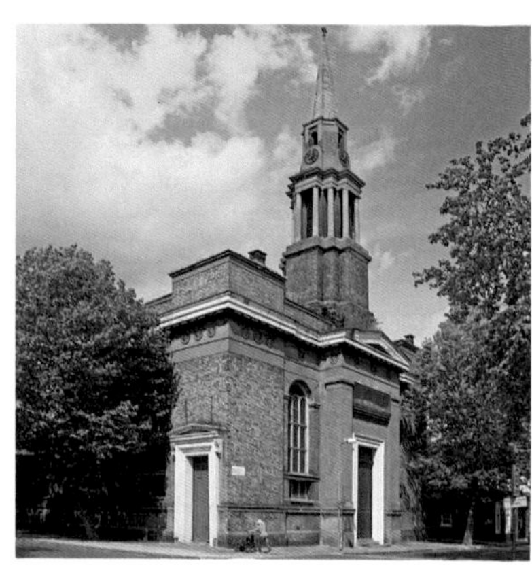

Circular Factory c1860 **F31** d
Oval Road NW1
⊖ Camden Town

Once a famous piano factory (Camden Town specialized in pianos and still does), this magnificent five-storey cylindrical building is a fine example of the Victorian functional tradition.

Primrose Hill Studios 1882 **F32** c
Fitzroy Road NW1
Alfred Healey
⊖ Chalk Farm

Twelve studios occupy the back gardens of Fitzroy Road: by the 1880s the tradition of artists' studios appropriating mews or the ends of gardens was well established. Here, they vary in size and complexity: on the south side of the 9×19m (30×64ft) court are exclusively top-lit studios with minimal living accommodation; on the north side and at the ends are more ambitious 'studio houses' with their own gardens. The combination of two-storey cottages – simple red-brick gables and slate roofs – and the quiet of the surrounding back gardens created the illusion of being in the country. The painters J Waterhouse, R Talbot Kelly, Arthur Rackham, Lord Methuen, Patrick Caulfield and the conductor Henry Wood were residents.

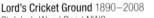

Lord's Cricket Ground 1890–2008 **F33** e
St John's Wood Road NW8
Various architects
⊖ St John's Wood

That the Marylebone Cricket Club (MCC) and the home of world cricket should be almost invisible from the street is more a comment on the particular emergence of the ground on this site than any national concern for understatement. After various and previous locations, the MCC settled here through the energies of Thomas Lord, from whom the ground takes its name. The **Pavilion** of 1890–1 is a particularly fine building with its famous Long Room and rooftop loggias. This set the scene for Lord's being a collection of buildings around a cricket ground (of the village green paradigm) as opposed to a stadium. Up to the mid-1980s Lord's did not have a reputation for commissioning distinguished architecture. This was all to change with the **Mound Stand** (1985–7) by Hopkins and Partners on the south side of the pitch. The lower part of the new work is a remodelling of an earlier open terrace whose arcade in stock brick was extended in a curve to the east. Above this, a new white-painted steel structure supports private boxes and a second cantilevered terrace protected by a white fabric roof suspended from masts.

This was followed by the replacement of Herbert Baker's North Stand of 1930 with the **Grand Stand** by Grimshaw and Partners of 1994–8. Here a structural idea of one central column supporting a balanced cantilevered truss, in turn supporting the various terraces below, is

Pavillion

Mound Stand

an audacious idea but not visually compelling. By way of contrast the **Media Centre** of 1998 by Future Systems was a notable example of MCC patronage. This has become a recognizable symbol for the ground and, given its prominence, reflects the audience for cricket worldwide. It received the Stirling Prize for architecture in 2003. Either side of the Media Centre are the **Compton** and **Edrich Stands** of 1991, also by Michael Hopkins and Partners; neither enhances nor detracts from Lord's. At the nursery end of the ground are the **Indoor School** and various temporary pavilions by David Morley and Associates of 1993–5.

Herzog & de Meuron were appointed in 2008 to draw up plans for the grounds as a whole, in order to increase the capacity of Lord's to meet the competitive demands of the modern game.

Grand Stand

Media Centre

Marylebone Station 1898–9 **F34** n
Melcombe Street NW1
Colonel R W Edis
⊖ Marylebone

Outside the City of London, Marylebone Station is the latest and smallest Victorian terminal. The glass and iron porte cochère spanning Melcombe Street and connecting the station to the former Great Central Hotel opposite is memorable, as is the discretion with which the building fits into the eighteenth-century street pattern of Marylebone. Below right: note at the corner of 28 Dorset Square the exemplary refacing of an existing 1960s office building by John McAslan and Partners, 2006. The minimal palette of limestone retains the original Georgian hierarchy, but with a handsome character reminiscent of Mussolini's EUR outside Rome of 1935.

Arlington House **F35** d
ex **Rowton House** 1905
Arlington Road NW1
H B Measures
⊖ Camden Town

The philanthropy of Lord Rowton provided accommodation for 1000 men in single rooms. The original Rowton House at Mount Pleasant was converted into a hotel, but other hostels still exist at Vauxhall and Whitechapel. The elaborate red-brick detailing to the street façade and the marvellously decorated front door are rare examples of the Free Style. This massive building serves as a reminder that nineteenth-century philanthropy is still alive: the building dominates Arlington Road as strongly as its residents influence the subculture of Camden Town.

House and studio 1907 **F36** e
40 Grove End Road NW8
Lawrence Alma Tadema
⊖ St John's Wood

Alma Tadema directed the work of adapting and enlarging an earlier house on the site into this remarkable house and studio for use as workplace and family home. Although much altered externally, the domed studio and atrium (with fountain) remain intact, as do many of the remarkable Graeco-Egyptian external embellishments reminiscent more of Vienna than St John's Wood. The building is an eminent addition to the late Victorian tradition of artists' studios and houses in St John's Wood. Having become nearly derelict in 1999, at the time of writing a complete restoration was underway.

Entrance and studio above

Studio Nuffield Lodge **F37** f
ex **Grove House** 1908–10
Prince Albert Road NW1
Sidney Tatchel
⊖ St John's Wood

Sigismund Goetze, the painter and penultimate private owner of Decimus Burton's fine **Grove House** F17, converted the stables into a studio for himself. Despite the restrictions imposed by the curved wall, the studio house has two highly distinctive and original exteriors. From Prince Albert Road it is immediately apparent, with tall arched windows and a large pyramidal lantern rooflight (below which is an oval lay light).

From the garden side, the house is picturesque and more of a cottage. The doors and windows, conceived on a domestic scale, are placed at random in its slowly curving stuccoed wall. This is extended, by an attached trabeated screen of Tuscan columns, to the semicircular free-standing greenhouse which forms the back wall.

Royal Academy of Music 1910–11 **F38** k
Marylebone Road NW1
Ernest George
⊖ Regent's Park

A composition of three pavilions in red brick with stone quoins, George's late work might pass as that of Lutyens, who, although younger, had already invented his 'Wrenaissance' style. However, the heavy central pediment and sculpture obviously derive from the nineteenth century or from Michelangelo.

The tunnel vaulted and semi-subterranean concert and recording hall to the west (John McAslan and Partners, 2002) is just visible from Marylebone Road).

Flats 1910–70 **F39** f, b, c
Prince Albert Road NW8
⊖ St John's Wood
With the common ingredients of a south front and a magnificent view across Regent's Park, it is interesting to see how these large apartment buildings either value this relationship or offer alternatives to Nash's original vision.

First, from the east, is **Northgate** (1910), a large Edwardian mansion building occupying a whole block. It is self-centred with no obvious acknowledgement of the park apart from decorative balconies, although its gabled and turreted profile is very impressive from the park. At its east end **104–14 Northgate** (1936), by Mitchell and Bridgwater, is an elegant and restrained modern red-brick building with a central curved bay window addressing the park. The building has seven floors making the same height as the five floors of its neighbour. **Oslo Court** (1938) by Robert Atkinson follows, bounded on either side by Culworth Street and Charlbert Street. This is the first of the 'democratic' versions: within the site depth the building is stepped in plan, to give every apartment a balcony with sun and a view.

Next is **Viceroy Court** (1937) by Marshall and Tweedy: the curved corners and large balconies give this fine building a genuinely European feeling – it could be in Vienna or Berlin.

Two more recent apartment buildings follow: **Imperial Court**, 55–6 Prince Albert Road (1965) and **2 Avenue Road** (c1970). With their exaggerated balconies both conspicuously celebrate the value of outside space; resembling the holiday architecture of the Costa del Sol, they are a retreat from the spirit of the pre-war buildings.

Stockleigh Hall (1937) by Robert Atkinson is the most interesting group of all, arranged around a deep four-storey entrance courtyard framing a collective view to the park. This building and Viceroy Court are very important additions to Regent's Park, showing that the forms of modern architecture are sometimes not incompatible with the existing city.

After the interruption of Primrose Hill, the sequence is concluded by **Albert Court** of 1963–6 at 23 Prince Albert Road by Martin Richmond and Malcolm Higgs (1966), one of the better apartment buildings from this period.

Oslo Court

Viceroy Court

Albert Court

Westminster Council House **F40** n
Marylebone Town Hall 1914–21
and **Public Library** 1939
Marylebone Road NW1
Edwin Cooper
⊖ Baker Street
Two buildings in the classical tradition occupy a block to the north of Georgian Marylebone. They demonstrate how public buildings should be arranged on an important street, and how much mileage there was (and still is) in the classical tradition. The twenty-five year interval between the two shows a good Edwardian architect working in good Portland stone, and stripping down his classical repertoire from the elaborate Wren tower of the earlier building to the smoothness and near-modernity of the later. The two buildings are a reproach to the thin modernity and unfortunate composition of **Marathon House** F51 opposite.

Council House

Rudolph Steiner House **F41** j

1926–37
Park Road NW1
Montague Wheeler
⊖ Baker Street

An example of expressionism, and a fairly tame one. Steiner's dislike of the right-angle shows only in a few curved eyebrows over the irregularly placed windows of the flat ashlar façade. The Anthroposophists clearly had a smaller budget than their rivals, the **Theosophists** (G56).

Broadcasting House 1931, 2003– **F42** p
Portland Place W1
Val Myers and Watson-Hart
MacCormac Jamieson Prichard
⊖ Oxford Circus

The monolithic Portland stone façades, the Georgian proportions of the window openings and the sculptures of Eric Gill (illustration page 90) represent a compromise between deference to the architecture of Nash's Regent Street, and a building style appropriate to the heroic days of national broadcasting. Broadcasting House successfully overcomes an extremely complicated site, and its massive, prow-like, rounded shape gives the building a semi-marine quality. The spirit of the new medium was better expressed inside – Wells Coates, Chermayeff, McGrath and others contributed interiors which have unfortunately not survived. The rigorous requirements for soundproofing, isolation, artificial lighting and air-conditioning of the studios produced further technical innovations in this building, which was to become a potent symbol of national unity in the 1930s and '40s.

Plans by MacCormac Jamieson Prichard for expansion were made in 2003, and these once more opened up the urban design debate about this complex site. The new addition to the east balanced the original building and introduced symmetry and a sense of closure into the composition. This opposed the pivot of Nash's circular portico to **All Soul's** F16 which successfully leads the eye around the corner from Upper Regent's Street into Portland Place. At the time of writing the second stage facing Portland Place was under construction, its original design regrettably but not significantly revised by other architects.

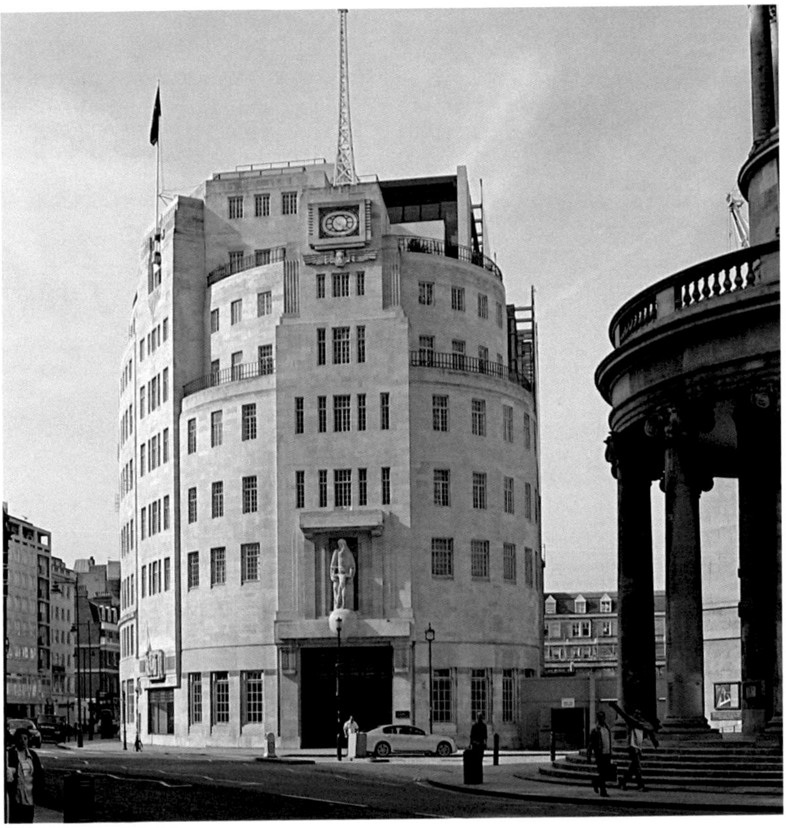

Gorilla House 1932 **F43** c
London Zoo, Prince Albert Road NW1
Lubetkin and Tecton
⊖ Camden Town

Lubetkin's first English building was for apes, not people. In 1932 Tecton was commissioned by Julian Huxley, Director of the Royal Zoological Society, to design a new house to accommodate two Congolese gorillas. It was the first of a series of zoo buildings by Tecton: in the face of widespread human opposition to, and scepticism about, modern architecture, it was the animals of London and Whipsnade Zoos that benefited. The brief for the cylindrical Gorilla House, situated between the Outer Circle and the canal, called for the strictest climatic control. After intensive quasi-scientific research – Tecton's typical method – the cylinder was divided into two halves, the ends of one sealed with an open mesh of caged steel, and those of the other with solid white concrete walls. Within the cylinder was a semi-circular shield which could be rotated to protect the animals from the English winter. The prospect of ape and human viewing each other through Lubetkin's cylinder was not without humour, but in 2008 other primates, the nocturnal aye-ayes, were installed, and the gorillas transferred to a miniature version of Regent's Park. See also the **Penguin Pool** F46.

Royal Institute of British Architects **F44** p
1932–4
66 Portland Place W1
Grey Wornum
⊖ Regent's Park

The winner of a competition, Wornum's design is everything an institute should be: it is clearly not a house, and the large plain features of the Portland stone front establish its importance. Models for buildings of this kind were then scarce (it would have been very strange to have found an example of continental modern among the competition entries). Wornum used those available from Sweden – in particular Asplund's Stockholm Public Library, 1920–8 – especially in the eclectic, complex, and elaborately detailed section and interiors, which incorporate many decorative works of craftsmanship. The building combines the functions of learned institute (library, lecture halls and committee rooms) with those of a club for members. If impressive size and generosity of circulation are a measure of learning, then RIBA members are very knowledgeable, but they are less well served as members of a club (here a subsidiary function), with accommodation which cannot match other London clubs for style. On the ground floor, open to the public, is a good architectural bookshop and a notice board with information about lectures, trips and events. Exhibitions are occasionally staged in the large first-floor rooms.

Houses c1933 **F45** b
1, 3, 4, 6, 8, 10 Wells Rise NW8
Francis Lorne and Tait
⊖ St John's Wood

These stuccoed terrace houses are a fragment of a 1930s modern bourgeois street, stepping down the hill to Regent's Park. The combination of vertical and horizontal elements (the double-height windows to the staircases contrasting with the entrance canopies) is faintly reminiscent of J J P Oud's 'heroic' terraces.

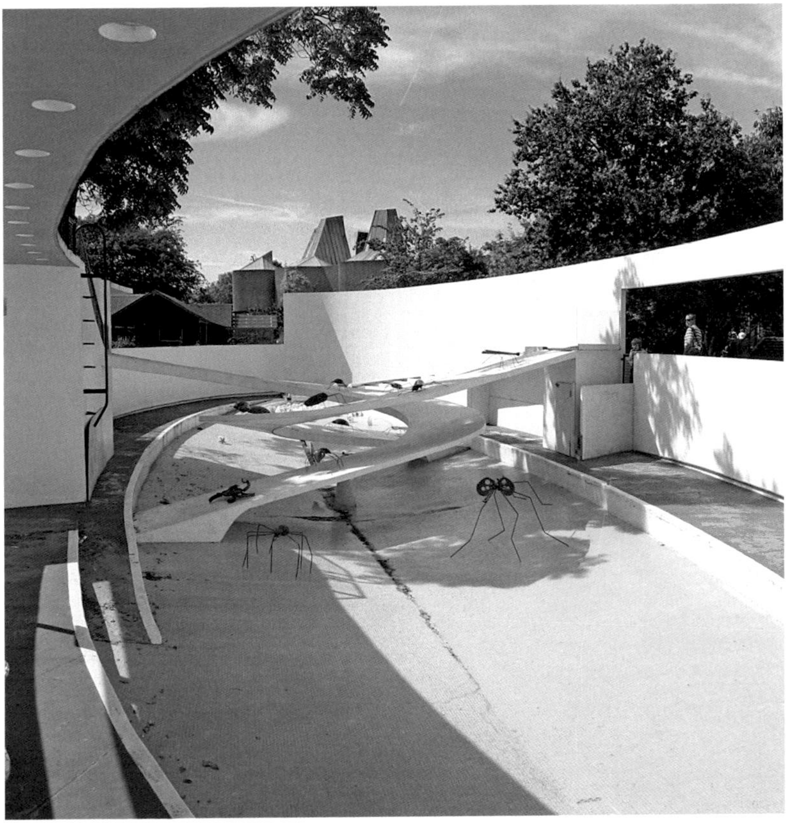

Penguin Pool 1934–5 **F46** g
London Zoo,
Prince Albert Road NW1
Lubetkin and Tecton
⊖ Camden Town

The Penguin Pool, on the park side of the Zoo, managed to combine the principles of modern architecture, the results of behaviourist research, structural virtuosity and humour. It was the result of Lubetkin's collaborations with Ove Arup, the Danish consultant engineer, and Felix Samuely, employed by the general contractor L Kier, and recently arrived from Berlin. The exuberance of the pool's oval plan, narrow spiral ramps, and rendered screen walls was inspired partly by Cubism and partly by Lubetkin's Beaux Arts training. The architects' research shows in the design of the long curved ramps, which encouraged the penguins to promenade or form patient queues, displaying their comic resemblance to English City gents. The floor surfaces vary from slate to rubber to concrete, and were designed to agitate the penguins' feet, thereby (it was hoped) helping to relieve boredom.

Built of unsupported reinforced concrete, the ramps (14m/46ft long, 1.2m/4ft wide and tapering from 150mm/6in to 75mm/3in in section) were technical innovations. See also the **Gorilla House** F43.

The pool was renovated and restored successfully by Avanti architects in 1987, but in 2008, although Grade 1 listed, lay scandalously unused: the penguins had been transferred to a much less distinguished, more conventional pond.

Dorset House 1935 **F47** o
Gloucester Place and
Marylebone Road NW1
T P Bennett with Joseph Emberton
⊖ Baker Street

Dorset House conveys an optimistic 1930s image of modern urban life. Above a two-storey plinth of shops and entrances, the plan of nine storeys of flats is formed by a series of interconnected Ts. Emberton's involvement is immediately noticeable in the elevations – curved corner balconies, green-painted metal balustrades, and mannered structural details. Berkeley Court, another block of mansion flats next-door across Glentworth Street, is of a similar scale with a continuous privet hedge and a roof garden; and across Marylebone Road, **Bickenhall Mansions** (1896) by W H Scrymgeour uses the Free Style of Norman Shaw, with many bay windows and gables all in red brick and terracotta.

The White House 1936 **F48** l
Albany Street NW1
R Atkinson
⊖ Great Portland Street

The White House was built as a number of small service flats, supported by recreational facilities, shopping and restaurants, and displays this period's preoccupation with constructing a 'city within a city' (see also **Dolphin Square** O12). The nine-storey star-shaped plan occupies a whole city block and has two main effects: first, following functionalist principles, the increased area of the façades provides optimum light and ventilation, avoiding the need for light wells; second, it breaks away from the usual continuous street façade, thus isolating itself from the traditional city. The façades of the White House (unlike those of many of its contemporaries) are not white-stuccoed but beautifully made of cream faïence tiles with no sign of deterioration. The corner windows, projecting caves and elegantly detailed handrails further contribute to the building's suave and urbane appearance.

Gilbey's Offices and **Warehouses** 1937 **F49** d
Oval Road and Jamestown Road NW1
Serge Chermayeff
⊖ Camden Town

With its slightly curved plan and top-floor loggia this is a quiet and well-mannered affair when compared to its more recent neighbours. Finished in white stucco, its reinforced concrete frame incorporates technical innovations by Felix Samuely, the consulting engineer; the foundations, for instance, were floated on 100mm (4in) of cork insulation to protect Gilbey's wine stocks from the vibrations of trains in the nearby cutting. The entire building was also air-conditioned to combat the noise and dirt from the railway. The training of engineers of the period was less specialized than it is today, allowing them to be scientific consultants, and more than just calculators. Samuely was particularly concerned with acoustics, services and insulation.

Flats c1955 **F50** d
Regents Park Road NW1
Ernö Goldfinger
⊖ Camden Town

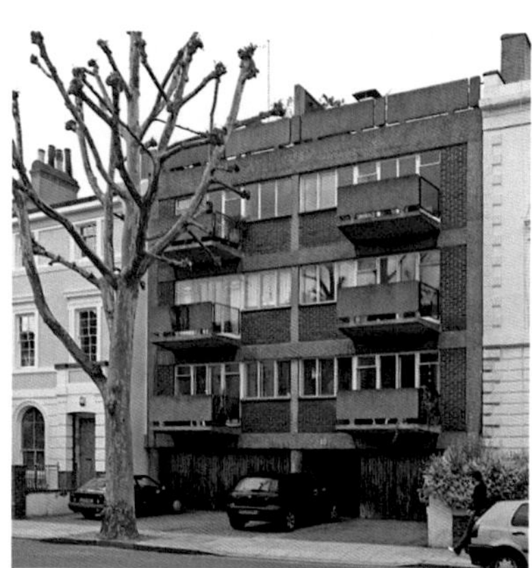

With its cantilevered balconies, fairfaced concrete and plain timber doors, the manner of this four-storey block of flats establishes a strong contrast with its stuccoed and decorated nineteenth-century neighbours. This it does by setting itself back from the building line but aligning the front face of its balconies with it. It comes as close as anything in London to accurately representing the New Brutalist sensibility of the 1950s. It has a strong European pedigree and has weathered extremely well.

Marathon House **F51** n
ex **Castrol House** 1960
174 Marylebone Road NW1
Gollings, Melvin, Ward and Partners
⊖ Baker Street

In the mid-1950s London's fire regulations which had restricted buildings to a height of 30m (100ft) were relaxed; the fifteen storeys of Castrol House took early advantage of this. Superficially resembling New York's Lever House (1952), it was one of London's first 'towers on a podium' and was subsequently widely imitated. Despite our strong criticisms of the form, the curtain wall of Castrol House was at the time elegantly reductive, and its industrial refinement impressive. In 1998 the building was converted into flats and its original curtain walling replaced.

Royal College of Physicians 1960–4 **F52** l
Outer Circle and St Andrew's Place,
Regent's Park NW1
Denys Lasdun and Partners
⊖ Regent's Park

The oppositions of street versus park, brick versus mosaic, transience versus permanence, day-to-day versus ceremonial, and wall versus pavilion, are some of the concerns of this ambitious building. The ceremonial functions of entrance hall, library, dining room and conference room are seen as permanent in their relationship to the park: covered in white mosaic, they form a pavilion on *pilotis*. The day-to-day offices have a transient, terraced form on Albany Street – alternating bands of dark brickwork and windows. The half-submerged lecture theatre, ceremonial but also in dark brickwork, is enigmatically inconsistent.

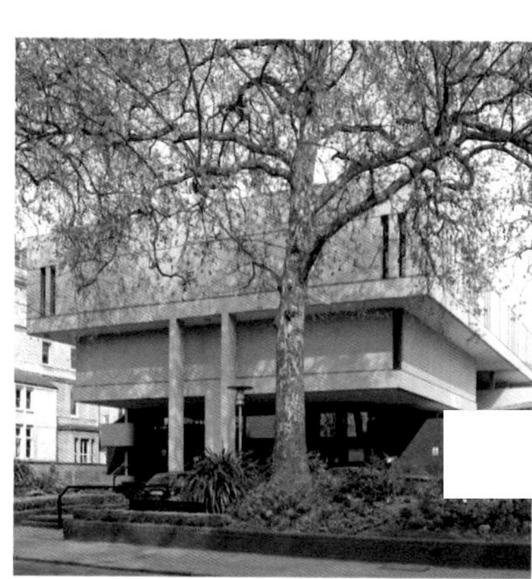

Aviary 1963 **F53** c
London Zoo,
Prince Albert Road NW1
Anthony Armstrong Jones, Cedric Price,
Frank Newby
⊖ CamdenTown

A wide range of Indian and African birds are housed in this large, netted, irregular enclosure. Despite the aviary's experimental 'tensegrity' structure (in the Buckminster Fuller tradition), the tight-angled corners have always seemed hostile to flight; the birds themselves are rendered rather pathetic, like leaves blowing in the wind.

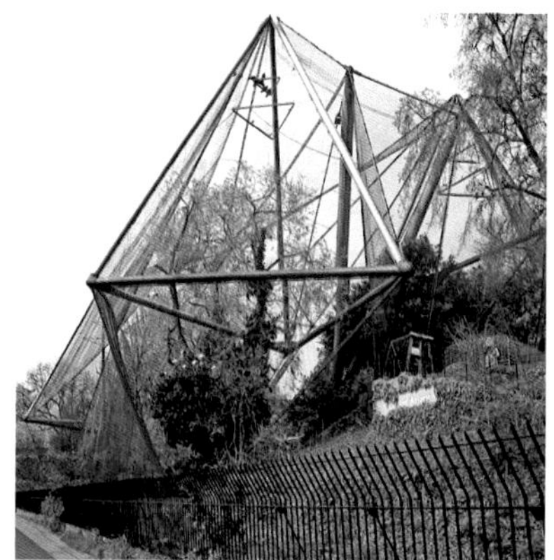

Flats 1964 **F54** d
37 Gloucester Avenue NW1
James Stirling
⊖ Camden Town

Four identically planned floors of flats, built for the London Borough of Camden, are raised on columns above a car park. Only the hard red brick, symmetrical planning, and characteristic entrance ramp suggest that this modest infill, designed to be repeated on either side, is the work of one of England's internationally renowned architects. The living rooms face the garden behind, and their windows are larger than those to the street.

Flats 1970 **F55** j
125 Park Road NW1
Farrell and Grimshaw
⊖ St John's Wood, Baker Street
The signifcance of this slim tower (containing thirty-six one- and two-bedroom flats and four one-bedroom penthouses) lies in the simple idea of building around a single central core, with one internal escape stair ventilated by a shaft. The beneficial results are firstly, that the entire periphery is given to habitable rooms (as opposed to corridors and staircases) and secondly, that the flat plans acquire real flexibility. In appearance the tower is a period piece. The façade banded with corrugated metal and the indifferently inclined patent, glazed penthouse roof are in the 'high tech' fashion of the mid-1960s, and with the passage of time the paucity of these architectural ideas is exposed: metal sidings are characteristic of the factory and not of housing.

Mosque 1978 **F56** j
Park Road and Hanover Gate NW1
Frederick Gibberd and Partners
⊖ Baker Street
The winner of an open competition, Gibberd's scheme was conventionally 'Arabized' between the competition and final designs, and as built has a cardboard thinness and lack of architectural inventiveness in the detail. It will not be remembered in histories, but its minaret and gilded dome make a curious addition to the skyline of Regent's Park, and complement Nash's more sober fantasies.

Housing Marylebone 1984 **F57** n
Ashmill Street NW1
Jeremy and Fenella Dixon
⊖ Edgware Road
This terrace of fourteen tiny two-storey houses set over seven basement flats is built on a very narrow strip of land. The white-stuccoed base sliced by a series of tall staircase windows lends considerable character and a larger scale to the whole. The project is for the same client as the villas at **Lanark Road** E10. In the absence of a local authority housing programme, these dwellings were sold at the bottom end of the market to people on the local authority waiting list.

Offices 1985 **F58** j
Broadley Street NW8
Michael Hopkins and Partners
⊖ Edgware Road, Marylebone
These offices were built to house Michael Hopkins's practice which had outgrown its previous accommodation – the architect's **Studio House** B29 of 1975. The office building follows the same matter-of-fact ethos as the house: low cost, speed of construction and flexibility, but with the added ingredient of a generous double-height volume. Here Hopkins developed further the 'Patera' building system, in which an identical composite metal panel is used for both walls and roof.

Ionic, Veneto and **Gothic Villas** **F59** f
1988–91
Outer Circle, Regent's Park NW1
Quinlan Terry
⊖ Baker Street

As they were built for the Crown Estate Commissioners, it is not surprising that the nouveau-riche and poorly proportioned style of these villas should reflect the preferences of our future monarch. They neither detract from nor significantly enhance the Outer Circle. They do however raise questions of authenticity. When seen next to Gibberd's **Mosque** F56 they become part of a cloying and complacent world of make-believe.

Lisson Gallery 1992 and 1996 **F60** n
52–54 Bell Street, NW1
Tony Fretton Architects
⊖ Edgware Road, Marylebone

The Lisson Gallery has become synonymous with the London avant garde with both its exhibitions and its architecture. The building is north-facing and naturally lit with minimal detail internally and a cool matter-of-fact exterior offering an egalitarian public room for the city. From inside, the windows offer flexible display: work can be presented either against opaque and translucent panels or in relationship to views of the city; there is a good view of the distinguished **Rutherford Secondary Modern School** and its playground by Leonard Manasseh and Partners (1960).

Pavilion 'The Hub' 2005 **F61** g
Regent's Park NW1
David Morley
⊖ Regent's Park, Camden Town

Most of Regent's Park is flat, and large areas are devoted to sport. In the centre of one of these, this pavilion replaced the former ugly and inadequate changing rooms provided in the 1960s. Its form is in the tradition of circular garden ornaments, particularly that of the lookout, such as Schinkel's 'Large Curiosity' (Große Neugierde) at Klein-Glienicke, Potsdam, which also sits on a graded mound. The mound in Regent's Park contains the bulk of the accommodation, the changing rooms, while the lookout serves as a terraced café.

Offices and **Rolling Bridge** **F62** m
2004, 2005
Paddington Basin W2
Richard Rogers & Partners, Heatherwick Studio
⊖ Paddington

Two projects stand out for comment – one large, the other small. The large is a 20,526-square-metre (220,940 sq ft) office building ('Waterside') of 2004 by Richard Rogers and Partners. Here are the servant and served spaces, now a hallmark of this practice, elegantly refined over many years and with its steelwork painted a characteristic mustard yellow. The building is best viewed from Westway where the picturesque profile of its vertically emphasized service towers can be appreciated.

The smaller project is a remarkably inventive 'rolling up' bridge for pedestrians by Thomas Heatherwick (2005). Its eight articulated steel and timber sections span a 12m (40ft) wide inlet of the Basin, and are made to curl by hydraulic rams positioned in the handrail between each section. It is open and is worth a detour into the Basin at noon on Friday (although at the time of writing it was removed for maintenance.)

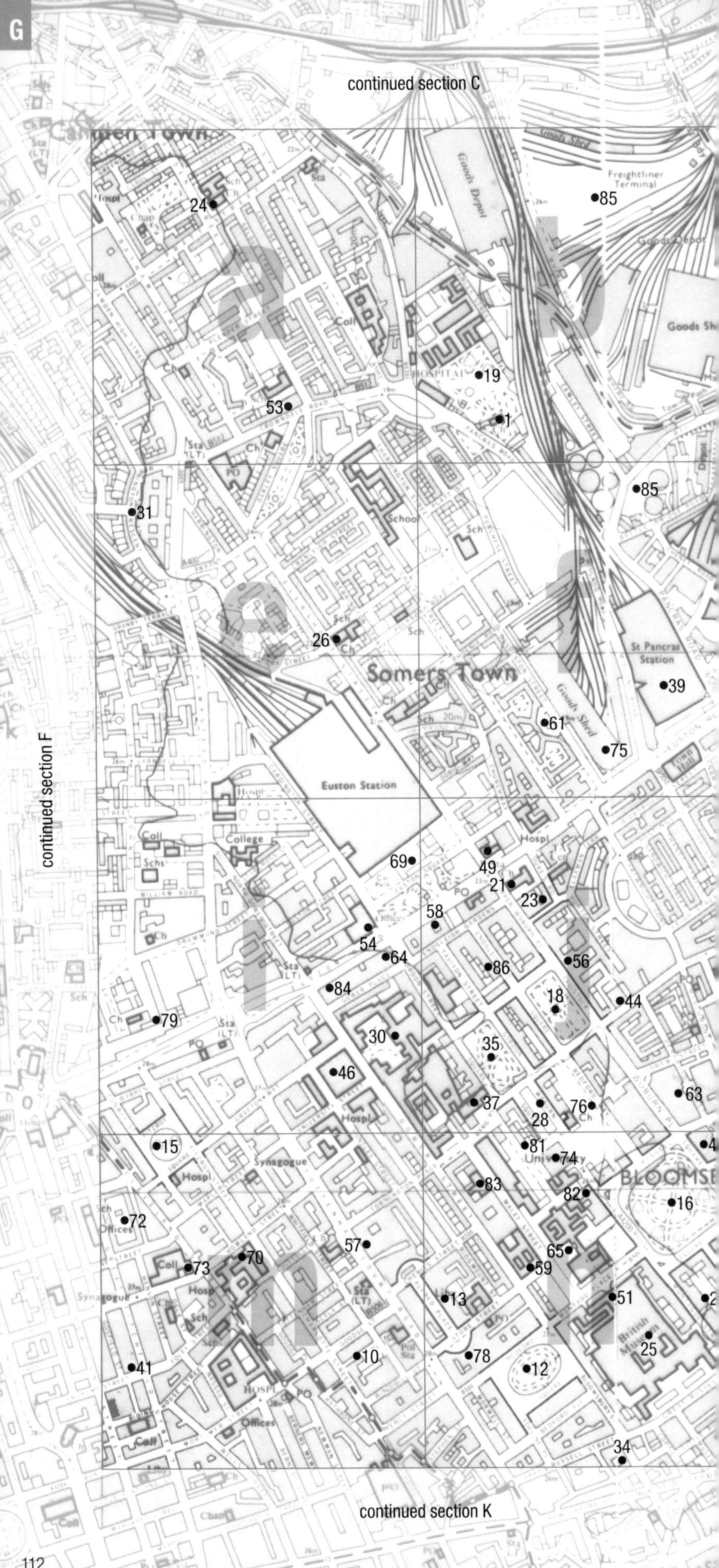
G
continued section C
continued section F
continued section K
Camden Town
Goods Depot
Goods Shed
Freightliner Terminal
Somers Town
Euston Station
St Pancras Station
BLOOMSBURY
British Museum
University
Synagogue
School
College
Hospl
a
b
e
f
i
j
m
n
24
85
19
53
1
31
85
26
39
61
75
69
49
21
23
58
54
64
86
56
18
44
84
79
30
35
46
37
28
76
63
15
81
74
83
82
16
72
57
65
73
70
59
13
51
25
41
10
78
12
34

continued section C

continued section H

continued section K

Camden Town (south) ■ Somers Town ■ King's Cross ■ Islington (south-west) ■ Finsbury ■ Clerkenwell ■ Bloomsbury ■ Holborn

New Road – now Marylebone Road, Euston Road and Pentonville Road – was started in 1756 to connect Bayswater Road with the City while bypassing the West End. It divides this section in half: to the south (and north of the line of the Roman Road, Holborn) lies the eighteenth-century development of Bloomsbury. To the north are the railway termini and Victorian Somers and Camden towns. This neat scheme is upset only by Islington and Barnsbury, which grew north from the City from the seventeenth century onwards.

The earliest remaining building (although much restored) is the Norman church of **Old St Pancras** G1, which still stands in open ground. Ely Place marks the site of the Bishop of Ely's house, whose chapel was **St Etheldreda** G2. Nothing remains of the original fourteenth-century foundation of Gray's Inn, the most northerly of the three Inns of Court which lay to the west of the City, beyond its boundaries.

The first urban developments north of Holborn were Bloomsbury Square (1660) and Red Lion Square (1684), both now much changed. Over the next forty years, the land to the north was built over, giving us the fine houses of Queen Square, Great Ormond Street and **Great James Street** G7. In 1742 the Foundling Hospital was built in fields north of Great Ormond Street, and its demolition in the twentieth century left one of the area's largest open spaces, Coram Fields, Brunswick Square and **Mecklenburgh Square** G14. **Bedford Square** G12 to the east was begun in 1775, and remains a magnificent, unscathed example of Georgian planning. The development of Bloomsbury continued over the next fifty years, and was completed by Cubitt. London's first evidence of the Industrial Revolution was the Regent's Canal (1814–20), running at first from Limehouse to Paddington, where it connected to the Grand Union and hence to the national canal network.

In the years of peace after the Napoleonic Wars, the British Museum was founded, to be followed, two years later, in 1827, by the foundation of University College with its new building south of the New Road. Between them, these two institutions transformed the domestic character of Bloomsbury over the next 150 years. At about the same time the development of Barnsbury was beginning, with **Cloudesley Square** G27 (1825) followed by **Lonsdale Square** G33 (1845). In thirty years three major railway termini were built to the north of the New Road: **Euston** G69 in 1836, **King's Cross** G36 in 1851 and **St Pancras** G39 in 1868.

A pall of soot and smoke hung over the early Victorian workers' dwellings of Somers Town and Camden Town, and was dispelled only by the electrification of the railways in the 1960s. The slums of Somers Town became the object of late nineteenth- and early twentieth-century experiments in housing reform.

The twentieth century did not much alter the physical pattern of this part of the city. The biggest single change was the conversion of Bloomsbury from private residences to the campus of the University of London, the most striking evidence of which is Holden's **Senate House** G65 (1932). In the 1930s the socialist Borough of Finsbury, with some of London's poorest and unhealthiest citizens, commissioned from Tecton architecture for a new and more enlightened age: a **Health Centre** G66 and housing at **Collier Street** G68.

From its beginnings in the 1840s, Camden Town was a traditional stopping place for waves of settlers, and since the late 1970s its markets and music scene have ironically made it one of London's principal tourist destinations; it is now twinned with Hollywood. The large city-in-the-park post-Second World War council estates to the west of Euston Station and those to the east at Somers Town left an indelible mark on the area, separating it from the normal patterns of the city. The **British Library** G75 was finally completed in 1998 and, with the redevelopment in 2008 of **St Pancras Station** G39 to accommodate international trains, began to form a recognizable urban place.

After several false starts, plans for the redevelopment of the former railway lands to the north of Kings Cross and St Pancras finally began construction in 2008.

Mary Ward Settlement G44, detail

School of Hygiene and Tropical Medicine G59, detail

Old St Pancras Church **G1** b
11th century
Pancras Road NW1
restored 1848 by Roumieu and Gough
⊖ King's Cross
The chief interest of Old St Pancras is that it is the sole remainder of medieval St Pancras: thirteenth-century fragments can be seen in the Norman doorways (north and south) and a lancet window in the chancel. The churchyard (now a park) contains interesting period monuments, the most remarkable of which is the **Soane Mausoleum** G19.

St Etheldreda c1300 **G2** p
restored 1874
Ely Place EC1
⊖ Chancery Lane
St Etheldreda is almost all interior apart from its façade and east window set back behind the building line of Ely Place. Built as the private chapel of the town house of the Bishops of Ely, it is a single volume of great beauty, dimly lit through the fine stained glass of the east and west windows. The entrance bay from the south is separated by a simple timber screen, and the plain undercroft has nineteenth-century columns. See also **Ely Place** G11.

Houses 1586 **G3** p
restored 1866, 1937
Staple Inn, Holborn EC1
⊖ Chancery Lane
This small group is London's only remaining domestic architecture of the sixteenth century, showing typical (if incorrect) half-timbering, strip windows, gables and overhangs. They are now almost completely rebuilt, and face a street much too wide for them.

Bedford Row WC1 **G4** o
laid out 1680
Nicholas Barbon
⊖ Chancery Lane
Although many of the houses in this sober street, 23m (75ft) wide and 198m (650ft) long, were rebuilt after the Second World War, its form survives. Much of the west side is original, in brown brick with red trim to the flat-headed windows. Note the paired front doors and fine detailing of numbers 12 and 13.

St Andrew Holborn 1684–90 **G5** p
Holborn Viaduct EC4
Christopher Wren
⊖ Farringdon
This church was sumptuously rebuilt after being bombed in the Second World War. The Corinthian architecture starts above the dado of woodwork, which includes the galleries, and the east end is dominated by the huge double-decker Venetian window. Used on Sundays for Coptic services, during the week St Andrew's is a regular City church.

Gray's Inn late 17th century **G6** p
Holborn and
Gray's Inn Road WC1
⊖ Chancery Lane
The Society of Gray's Inn came into existence on this site in the fourteenth century. A curiously public private place, the most northerly of London's Inns of Court is also the easiest to see as a whole (from Theobalds Road across Gray's Inn Fields). With Staple Inn, Lincoln's Inn, the Law Courts and the Temple, Gray's Inn forms an almost continuous band of lawyers' colleges separating the City of Westminster from the City of London. The buildings here are more formally comprehensible than those of the **Temple** K4, but also suffered severe damage in the Second World War. The raw new brickwork and absence of trees give **Gray's Inn Square** (first built 1678–88) a rather blank quality. Originally a cross range (demolished in 1685) divided the square into two courts; on the south side are the hall and chapel. The main approach is from the gatehouse in Holborn via **South Square** (built 1685), where Number 1 is mid-eighteenth century, and all the other houses, destroyed in the war, have been rebuilt to the original plans; Number 10 is by Raymond Erith. In the south-west corner of Gray's Inn Square a passageway leads to **Field Court**, which lacks architectural coherence (number 2 dates from 1780 and its neighbour from 1936) but is open to the spacious gardens, approached through an extremely elegant iron gate (1723).

Field Court

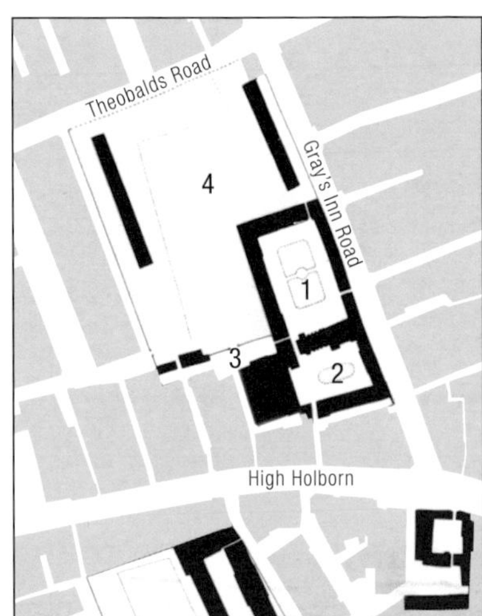

1 Gray's Inn Square
2 South Square
3 Field Court
4 Gray's Inn Gardens

Gray's Inn Gardens

Holborn early 18th century **G7** o
area bounded by
Guilford Street, Southampton Row,
Gray's Inn Road and Theobald's Road WC1
⊖ Russell Square, Chancery Lane

This area formed the eastern edge of the eighteenth-century expansion north of Gray's Inn. At the centre is **Great James Street** (1720–30), the best-preserved, longest and most uniform early eighteenth-century street in London. The houses are built of red brick with segmental arches to the windows, and most have complete bracketed door hoods. To the east is **John Street** (1760) which is also well preserved, with its mews intact.

The street is very wide and leads into **Doughty Street** G17 of the following century. To the west of Great James Street the streets retain their original pattern but are less well preserved. **Lamb's Conduit Street** has the fine nineteenth-century Lamb public house, opposite which **Great Ormond Street** leads into **Queen Square**.

Great James Street

The Italian hospital (founded in 1884, rebuilt in 1900) and the church of St George the Martyr (1723, transformed inside in 1867) are noteworthy.

St George 1716–31 **G8** n
Bloomsbury Way WC1
Nicholas Hawksmoor
⊖ Holborn

The two equal cross-axes common to all Hawksmoor's churches were here used to reconcile the restrictions of a deep, narrow site with the direction of liturgical east. The altar was originally on the short axis (in the semicircular niche on the right of the entrance through the portico), as were entrances through the tower. In 1781 the altar was moved to the northern recess and the northern gallery was removed, but the characteristic flat-ceilinged central space nevertheless maintains the coherence of the interior. The arrangement and nature of the exterior elements are unique: none of Hawksmoor's other churches uses the grand Corinthian portico (for which see **St Martin-in-the-Fields** K40 and **St George, Hanover Square** J6, both built at the same time). The tower, which comes down to the ground, is square, not rectangular, and is crowned with a paraphrase of the Mausoleum of Halicarnassus and a statue of George I. The north façade to Little Russell Street is a wonderfully Roman two-storey arcade over the massive keystones of the crypt windows.

A major programme of conservation and

restoration was begun in 2004 and completed in 2008. The exterior was cleaned and repaired and, controversially, the spirited if alarmingly anatomically correct sculptures of lions and unicorns at the base of the tower's pyramid (which had been removed in one of the frequent bouts of alterations to the church but for which there is clear documentary evidence) were replaced. The interior was re-ordered to restore the original east–west axis and the position of the altar, and the south gallery was repaired and a new northern gallery installed.

Inner Court, Staple Inn 1734 **G9** p
Holborn EC1
⊖ Chancery Lane
Approached through an arched opening in the best-surviving timber façade in London (G3), Inner Court has been extensively renovated over the years. The only buildings to survive the Second World War were the east side (1729–34), with rubbed-brick detailing, and the Hall (1581) with its fine hammerbeam roof. The others were indifferently rebuilt by Maufe (1954–5). Through a small arched opening in the south side is the garden court, and beyond a short cut to Chancery Lane. See also the **Temple** K4.

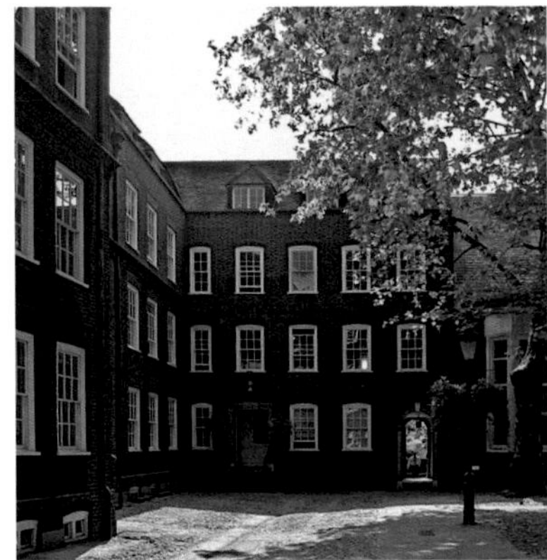

Colville Place 1766 **G10** m
off Charlotte Street W1
⊖ Goodge Street
A rare survival: a small Georgian alley of houses, some with shop fronts, partly and badly rebuilt after damage in the Second World War.

Ely Place 1773 **G11** p
Holborn EC1
Charles Cole and John Gorham
⊖ Chancery Lane
Built on the site of the Bishop of Ely's town house, Ely Place is an almost intact eighteenth-century close of great charm and tranquillity. It retains its delightful miniature lodge, centrally positioned, with working wrought-iron gates to either side. The houses on the east side are very regular with clipped bay trees marking each front door; on the west side Ely Court leads to Hatton Garden, which is also gated. In this passageway is Ye Olde Mitre pub, dating from 1546. See also **St Etheldreda** G2.

Bedford Square c1775 **G12** n
WC1
Thomas Leverton (?)
⊖ Tottenham Court Road

A completely preserved square (162×117m/530×385ft), the next to be developed on the Bedford Estate after Bloomsbury Square of a century earlier. The square is made up of plain four-storey houses in brick, with ornaments in Coade stone. Although the yellow stock brick looks handsome when cleaned, research suggests that the houses may originally have been painted black with the tuck pointing outlined in white. The centre houses on each side are stuccoed, with pediments supported on pilasters, and the end houses on the south side are capped with balustrades. The result is that, in spite of the repetitive front doors, the square can be seen as four palace fronts facing each other. Number 1, at the south-east corner, is in a different style, and was built by Leverton for himself. It has a charming entrance hall and stair.

When the square was built, the streets approaching it were gated, for the exclusive use of residents. Coaches and services were accommodated in the now-demolished mews behind, Owners and tenants of the houses still have keys to the oval garden, which is filled with mature London plane trees – a place of rural magic in one of the densest districts of London, and a vestige of the power of private landlords.

The houses are now used as offices and publishing houses, and numbers 34–6 are occupied by the Architectural Association and its School, where there are frequent exhibitions open to the public. Visit the bar and first-floor front rooms for a good view over the square from a high-ceilinged and elegantly ornamented Georgian living room.

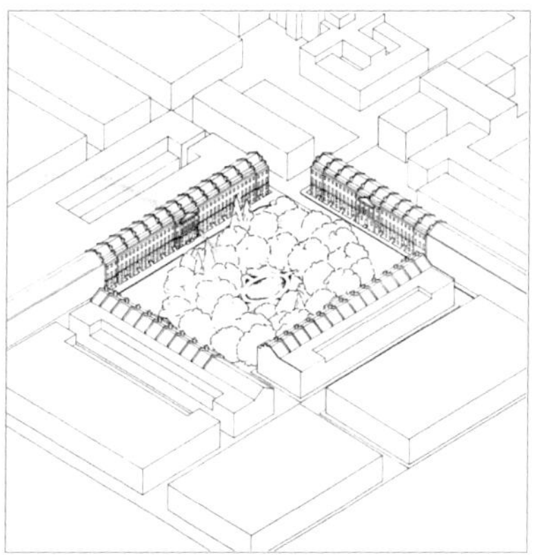

Alfred Place 1790 **G13** n
WC1
George Dance the Younger
⊖ Goodge Street
The buildings of Dance's street schemes have mostly been destroyed and none remain here. His plans, however, are relatively indestructible – here a broad street with a shallow crescent at each end. See also **The Crescent** L60, **Seven Dials** K25, and **Finsbury Square** H18.

Mecklenburgh Square and **Brunswick Square** 1790–1812 **G14** k
WC1
S P Cockerell, Joseph Kay
⊖ Russell Square
The squares, a speculative development by the Governors of the Foundling Hospital on fields either side of the hospital, were planned and supervised by Cockerell. The east side of Mecklenburgh Square by Kay, Cockerel's pupil, is the most complete composition: it follows the example of Adam's **Fitzroy Square** G15, but in brick and stucco, and with fine Greek detailing. With Coram's Fields, the two squares form the largest open space in central London outside the parks (larger than Lincoln's Inn Fields or **Russell Square** G16), but the present division into three prevents this being appreciated.

On the south side of Coram's Fields are the entrance gates and loggias of the Foundling Hospital (1742–52), which once stood in the Fields but was demolished in 1928. The hospital was one of several established around London in the first half of the eighteenth century and, like the others, stood in its own grounds in the fields outside the City.

Mecklenburgh Square: east side

Fitzroy Square 1793–8,1827–35 **G15** m
W1
Robert Adam
⊖ Warren Street
The **Adelphi** K58 had nearly brought the Adams to financial ruin, but in 1789 they undertook a very large speculation on undeveloped farmland owned by Lord Southampton (formerly Fitzroy). This was to be their last.

Fitzroy Square was the focus of the extended layout of new houses which stretched to the New (Euston) Road to the north and Tottenham Court Road to the east. While planned as an entity, funding it proved difficult, and development proceeded slowly. The longer, east side of the square (1793–8) was built in Portland stone as a unified palazzo of large individual houses, the centre pavilion having attached unfluted columns. The shorter, south side was built in 1794, with a central tripartite window. The north and west sides were built in 1827–35 and have stuccoed fronts. While the use of stone in residential building was typical of Bath and Bristol in the eighteenth century it was unusual in London.

In the 1970s, zealous planners excluded cars from the square, leaving it seeming strangely empty. Termed an 'environmental area', it was given miserable street furniture: benches, street lamps, and the inevitable bollards to keep out the traffic. Many blue plaques record former illustrious and artistic residents: Madox Brown, William de Morgan, Roger Fry and Vanessa Bell of the Omega Workshops, Virginia Woolf and George Bernard Shaw.

East side 1793–8

Russell Square laid out 1800 **G16** n
WC1
James Burton, Humphry Repton
⊖ Russell Square
Very few of the houses which enclosed one of London's larger squares – 210×205m (690×673ft) – remain, and those on the south-east and north-west corners are not in their original state. Terracotta ornaments were added as part of the Bedford Estate's attempts to make Georgian Bloomsbury more acceptable to Victorian taste, which found it gloomy, with the windowpanes too small. Gross hotels now line the eastern side, and face the unfinished wing of Holden's **Senate House** G65 on the west. To the north, Lasdun's **Institute of Education** G76 presents its southern end to the square.

Following the restoration of 2002, the garden's paths, lawns and beds were re-arranged as far as possible to Repton's plans, and a new central water-feature installed to replace that of the 1960s. The perimeter railings were replaced to a period pattern (but much higher than the originals), and, to prevent what had become their traditional deviant night-time use, the gardens were made open to the public only in daylight hours.

Doughty Street early 19th century **G17** k
WC1
⊖ Chancery Lane
Doughty Street consists of continuous late Georgian terraces. A few houses have been cleaned, but it is a pity that 'planning' has not prevented some of the brickwork from being painted. Charles Dickens lived at number 48, which is now a small museum. The greenery of Mecklenburgh Square and Gray's Inn conclude the street at either end.

Tavistock Square 1806–26 **G18** j
WC1
Thomas Cubitt
⊖ Euston
Cubitt's west side survives in this 165×110m (540×360ft) Bloomsbury square and his terrace shows the drift towards more individual houses which emerged in the nineteenth-century recipes for the architecture of squares; the numerous pilasters and features both at the ends and in the middle fragment the composition more than uniting it. The other sides of the square were rebuilt in the twentieth century, and the only building of significance is the **British Medical Association Headquarters** G56 on the west side.

The surviving west side

Soane Mausoleum 1816 **G19** b
Old St Pancras Churchyard
Pancras Road NW1
John Soane
⊖ Kings Cross

Although modest in scale, John Soane's tomb for his wife, his son and himself is typically complex. A shallow domed canopy with four pierced pediments surrounded by low stone railings barely contains the cube-shaped monument. The decoration is minimal, and where it occurs (on the capitals and the knobs to the railings) there is no obvious historical reference.

The level of the churchyard is raised above Pancras Road, and in winter, when the trees are bare, the profile of **St Pancras Station** G39 and the large form of Cecil Rhodes House opposite are revealed, creating a touchingly incongruous combination, typical of London.

Lloyd Square 1819 **G20** h
WC1
⊖ King's Cross

The square was laid out as part of the development of the Lloyd Baker Estate, with houses less stylish than their pedimented neighbours in Lloyd Baker Street. Note **Cumberland Gardens** off the north-west corner of the square: a single-sided paved alley (unusual in London) whose houses look across the back gardens of the block.

To the north-east is **Myddleton Square** (1827), a well-preserved, large and regular square, with St Mark's Church by W Chadwell Mylne standing in public gardens at the centre. Off the north-west corner of Myddleton Square is **Claremont Square** which has a reservoir in the middle.

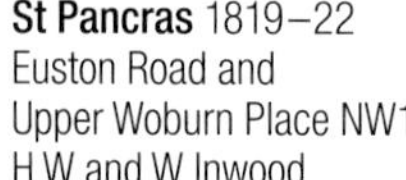

St Pancras 1819–22 **G21** j
Euston Road and
Upper Woburn Place NW1
H W and W Inwood
⊖ Euston

The earliest and probably the finest Greek Revival church in London, St Pancras was built as part of the southern expansion of the borough, superseding the **Old St Pancras Church** G1 on Pancras Road to the north. Following the model of Gibbs's **St Martin-in-the-Fields** K40, the octagonal bell tower (based on the Tower of the Winds in Athens) stands above the giant six-column Ionic portico. Two lower additions to the east, duplications of the portico of the Caryatids of the Erechtheum, confirm the pagan inspiration. After the promise of the exterior the interior is plain and disappointing.

One of the two Caryatid porches

Montague Street and **G22** n
Bedford Place c1820
WC1
James Burton, builder
⊖ Russell Square, Holborn

The houses of the two Georgian streets leading into Russell Square from the south are plain and well proportioned, with rusticated stuccoed ground floors. Bedford Place is perfectly preserved; Montague Street lost its south-west corner with the building of the British Museum, but has intricate cast-iron balconies on the south-east corner.

Woburn Walk and **G23** j
Duke's Road early 1820s
WC1
Thomas Cubitt
⊖ Euston

Cubitt was responsible for the development of the Bedford Estate north and east from Russell Square. His work is distinguishable from the earlier Georgian of the area by its extended use of stucco, and the articulation of the elevations of his squares (for example **Gordon Square** G35 and **Tavistock Square** G18). Here, however, he was working to the tiny scale of a short pedestrian street, one of the few in London designed as a whole. He used a restrained Greek style, the dryness of which was revealed by restoration in the 1960s. The buildings are continued round the corner into Duke's Road, on the east side of which is the entrance to **The Place**, a significant dance school, whose entrance now provides a route connecting to that for students on Flaxman Terrace (architects Allies and Morrison, 2001). The elegant and vertically proportioned new elevation over three floors at night presents the dancers stretching on the staircase in silhouette as a literal advertisement for the institution.

Woburn Walk

All Saints, Camden Town **G24** a
1822–4
Camden Street NW1
W and H W Inwood
⊖ Camden Town

A disappointment for those who have seen the Inwoods' masterpiece, **St Pancras** G21, All Saints was converted into a Greek Orthodox church serving Camden Town's Greek Cypriot settlers. Its interior, while still retaining its original gallery, has been fitted with a screen bearing icons and separating the sanctuary and nave (the iconostasis). The yellow stone exterior and semicircular portico are unaltered.

British Museum 1823–47 **G25** n
Great Russell Street WC1
Robert Smirke and others
⊖ Tottenham Court Road

The nation, to which several connoisseurs had left their collections of art and antiquities in the late eighteenth and early nineteenth centuries, and to which George IV had sold his father's Royal Library, found in Smirke a neoclassical architect whose style matched the new programme of a public museum.

At the time the site was occupied by Montague House, which had served as a disorganized museum since the mid-eighteenth century. Smirke planned a quadrangle extending north from the house, and this plan was carried out in stages. The east side was built first to house George III's library, and this is the most handsome original room in the building, 90m (295ft) long. It is spanned with iron beams clad in concrete, an early use of the material. It was restored in 2004 (architects HOK) and appropriately furnished with an exhibition of the artefacts and ideas of the Enlightenment.

The west and north wings off the quadrangle, for antiquities, were built between 1831 and 1838, and later filled with a remarkable collection of architectural trophies from Rome, Greece and

Asia Minor. (The splendid west wing was redecorated to Smirke's original colour scheme when the Egyptian collection it housed was rearranged in 1980.) It was only in 1842 that Montague House was demolished and the magnificent Ionic colonnade and portico of the façade begun. Smirke probably knew of Schinkel's Ionic colonnade on the front of the Berlin Altesmuseum, built twenty years previously, and both buildings probably derive from Durand's academic project for a museum of 1808. Smirke's quadrangle was filled by his brother, Sidney, who designed the great circular domed Reading Room, finished in 1857. The museum expanded north during the nineteenth century until, with the building of the **Edward VII Galleries** G51 in Montague Place in 1914, it occupied a complete block of 4.6 ha (11.3 acres).

In 1998, the British Library moved to **King's Cross** G75 taking with it its foundation, the books of George III's library. An ambitious Lottery-funded competition-winning scheme to reorder the space vacated was designed by Foster and Partners, and implemented. A new glazed roof, its shallow diagonal arches engineered by Buro Happold, now covers the central courtyard in the centre of which stands the circular Reading Room, and opens up new public routes connecting all four wings of the museum, but leaves the Reading Room marooned in a sea of 'circulation'.

An original Smirke gallery, now the Egyptian Room

The Great Court

St Mary 1824–7 **G26** e
Eversholt Street NW1
W and H W Inwood
⊖ Euston
The symmetrical west front has a centre tower of London stock brick, and the thin cast-iron columns in the interior support vaults. When compared with the stronger Greek Revival style of **St Pancras** G21 and **All Saints, Camden Town** G24, the undeveloped scraped Gothic of this church illustrates the Inwoods' versatility in response to the various desires of their patrons.

Cloudesley Square, Cloudesley Street and **Stonefield Street** 1825 **G27** d
N1
⊖ Angel
A set piece development immediately west of Liverpool Road; the two streets meet with a square at their intersection. The square is entered in the middle of its sides, on the seventeenth-century model, and is exceptional for its wedged corners on the west side and Barry's **Holy Trinity** G29 in the centre.

To the south of Cloudesley Square are Batchelor Street, Cloudesley Road, Barnsbury Street, Cloudesley Place and Bewdley Street, a good pattern of minor streets, relatively untouched except by the local council's environmental area strategies, which rendered them inaccessible to through traffic. The condition of the houses varies from 'gentrification' to seedy decay. The north end of Cloudesley Road, with its wide pavements, is particularly fine.

Cloudesley Square

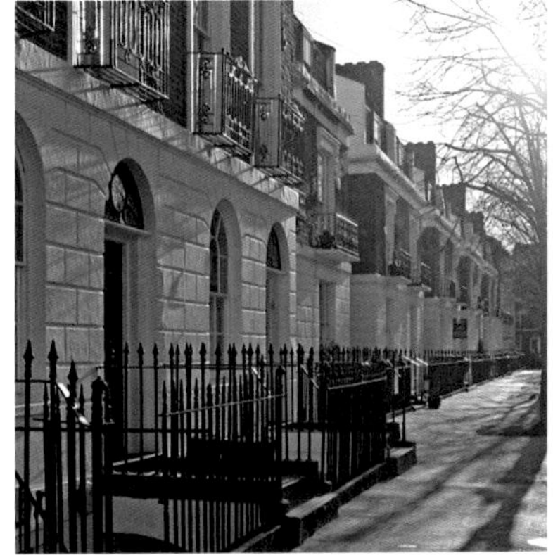

Cloudesley Street

Woburn Square WC1 1825 **G28** j
⊖ Russell Square
This poor relic south of Gordon Square (only the modest terraces on the north-east and south-west sides are original) is included only to catalogue the squares of Bloomsbury. The University of London was the destroyer and Lasdun's **School of Oriental and African Studies** G74 to the south is merely an 'object in space', rather than one of the 'space-defining' elements which originally constituted Bloomsbury.

To the west is the contemporary **Torrington Square**, now a square only in name, with the remains of an original terrace on the north-east corner. The square was to have been included in Holden's grandiose plan for the University, which included the **Senate House** G65.

Holy Trinity 1826–8 **G29** d
Cloudesley Square N1
Charles Barry
⊖ Angel

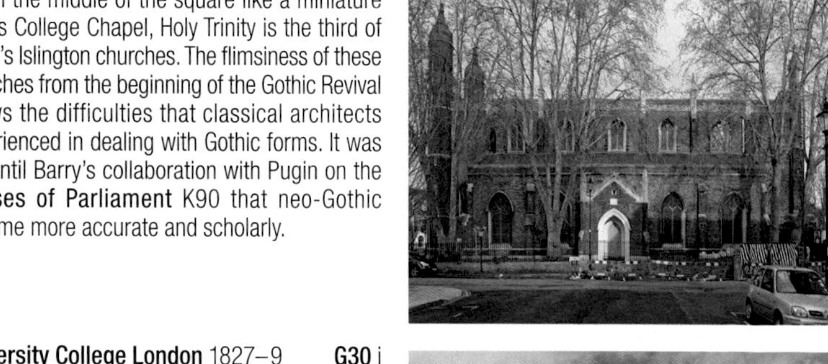

Set in the middle of the square like a miniature King's College Chapel, Holy Trinity is the third of Barry's Islington churches. The flimsiness of these churches from the beginning of the Gothic Revival shows the difficulties that classical architects experienced in dealing with Gothic forms. It was not until Barry's collaboration with Pugin on the **Houses of Parliament** K90 that neo-Gothic became more accurate and scholarly.

University College London 1827–9 **G30** i
Gower Street WC1
William Wilkins, J Gandy Deering
⊖ Euston Square

University College, the founding institution of the present University of London, was established in the early 1820s. Its private sponsors, modelling its constitution and curriculum on current German education practice, were concerned to extend the range of subjects taught at universities; to free university education from the influence of the Church of England; and to extend its franchise to Jews, Roman Catholics and, later, women. So it is appropriate that Wilkins won the competition for the design of the new college's buildings: his radical neoclassical style matched the institution's aims and newness. Here, however, unlike his earlier Downing College, Cambridge (1807), but like his later **National Gallery** K88, he was unable to rise to the occasion: his lofty portico, centrepiece of the design, has always been criticized for having its columns too close together. The interior spaces behind it are also disappointing: the dome seems cramped and the 'cloisters' (largely rebuilt after destruction in the Second World War) are nondescript.

The north and south sides of the quadrangle were built between 1869 and 1881 by Hayter Lewis. The frontage of early-twentieth-century buildings to Gower Street remained unfinished until 1987, when the ends of the two wings were completed in an appropriately elegant classical style, and the two brick lodges were rebuilt, by the Casson Conder Partnership. The opportunity of finally ridding the handsome quadrangle of academics' cars was not taken.

At the time of writing, should funds be found to redevelop the vacant site on Gordon Street to house the Petrie Collections, this would provide UCL with a credible address to the east and with a through route to the Gower Street frontage.

Mornington Crescent c1830 **G31** e
NW1
⊖ Mornington Crescent

One of London's most ambitious crescents suffered two setbacks. Firstly, soon after its construction, the London & Birmingham Railway of 1836 was built immediately behind it, cutting back its gardens and reducing its social status. Secondly in 1926, Carreras built 'the most modern hygienic cigarette factory in the world' in its front garden – one of the two events which provoked the London Squares Act of 1931. The advent of trains at the bottom of the garden encouraged a certain seediness which became popular with the Camden Town Group of painters. Walter Sickert lived and worked at Number 6 from 1905 onwards.

The former **Carreras Factory** designed by M E and O H Collins, 170m (550ft) long, with its Egyptian-style centrepiece and two giant black cats outside, advertising Carreras' most popular brand, was sensitively upgraded and redecorated with the original colours in 1999 by Munkenbeck and Marshall. The west elevation, with its large well-proportioned openings and monumental boiler flue (an Egyptian obelisk), is not as 'abominable' as Nikolaus Pevsner observed in 1952.

Gibson Square and **Theberton Street** 1830–40 **G32** d
N1
⊖ Angel
To the east of Cloudesley Square, Theberton Street leads into Gibson Square, the corner houses of which have giant pilasters.

In the middle of the square is Raymond Erith and Quinlan Terry's **Victoria Line ventilation shaft** (1970), derived appropriately from the Temple of the Four Winds. The building is in brick and stone, its roof netted for ventilation.

Lonsdale Square 1838–45 **G33** d
N1
R C Carpenter
⊖ Highbury and Islington
Carpenter departed from Georgian tradition by giving the houses in the square Tudor styling: the façades have recesses for the entrances, there are gables on the face, and the windows are square or horizontal with stucco surrounds and Tudor 'eyebrows'. He later became a successful if cramped church architect.

Model Dwellings for Families **G34** n
1849
Streatham Street WC1
Henry Roberts
⊖ Tottenham Court Road
The Society for Improving the Condition of the Labouring Classes was one of several set up in the 1840s as a result of progressive agitation, including that of Roberts. Some of the Society's earlier model dwellings were built as two-storey cottages, but this was their first experiment on a dense urban site. The courtyard is lined with open galleries giving access to the flats, which have a living room, kitchen and scullery, and mostly two bedrooms. Construction is fireproof: brick load-bearing walls and arched hollow-brick floors. The galleries are supported by brick piers which span two floors, more in the tradition of the Georgian engineer than the Victorian speculative builder. The top floor is a later addition. It is interesting to consider the direction modern architecture might have taken if this space-defining pattern had been adopted as a housing model, instead of the contemporary Peabody Trust blocks, which were designed as obstinately free-standing objects.

Gordon Square WC1 1850 **G35** j
Thomas Cubitt
⊖ Euston
The last of the Bloomsbury squares to be completed (its gardens were renovated in 2007), Gordon Square shows Cubitt drifting into Victorian fashion. The east side, especially the five-storey section to the south, is more like the contemporary Italianate houses of Kensington. The Tudor-style building on the west side, Dr Williams's Library, was built by Professor Donaldson in 1848 as a hall of residence for the new University College. The rendering of the terrace north of the library is unpainted, which is unusual. See also **University Church of Christ the King** G37.

King's Cross Station 1851–2 **G36** g
Euston Road NW1
Lewis and Joseph Cubitt
⊖ King's Cross
King's Cross was the terminus of the Great Northern Railway, opened in 1850 to accommodate the massive tourist influx to the Great Exhibition. It is a bold engineering building, memorable for its massive brick façade, its great arches indicating the roofs of the train sheds, each spanning 26m (71 ft), and separated by the central clock tower 37m (120ft) high. The bluffness of King's Cross (compared with Scott's romantic **St Pancras** G39 next door) was later severely compromised by insensitive additions to the forecourt. The original cast-iron brackets supporting the arches are still there, but the timber roof construction has been replaced by steel.

In 2008 work was started to remove the clutter between the station and Euston Road, creating a new piazza, and to build a new arrival and booking hall in a semicircular building to the west (architects John McAslan and Partners).

University Church of Christ the King 1853 **G37** j
Gordon Square WC1
Raphael Brandon
⊖ Goodge Street
Originally built for the Catholic Apostolic Church, a sect (often called 'Irvingites') which originated in Scotland in the 1830s, this huge Victorian Gothic church is strangely empty of the accumulated bits and pieces which would normally by now have softened its harshness. The unbuilt steeple was to have been 90m (295ft) high, and would have topped Holden's **Senate House** G65.

Business Design Centre **G38** d
ex **Agricultural Hall** 1861–2
Islington High Street and Liverpool Road N1
F Peck
⊖ Angel
The huge 117×66m (384×217ft) hall, with its central clear span of 46m (150ft) in iron, is set back from Islington High Street, from which it is reached via a giant entrance arch with angle towers. The roof profile can best be seen from Liverpool Road to the west. The building was renovated in 1986 and its generous spaces since used for exhibitions and trade conventions.

St Pancras International 1866–8 **G39** f
Hotel and offices 1868–76
Euston Road NW1
Hotel, George Gilbert Scott;
train shed, W H Barlow and R M Ordish
⊖ King's Cross

This station, originally the terminus of the Midland Railway, was one of the three main-line stations to the north of Euston Road constructed during the 1860s railways boom. Broad Street, Cannon Street, Charing Cross and Victoria were also constructed in this decade, but St Pancras is architecturally the most important. Scott, at the peak of his career and public esteem, was designing the **Foreign Office** K106 at the same time, and his **Albert Memorial** J45 was under construction. Here he could exhibit his masterly synthesis of Gothic motifs, both in the craggy, wilfully picturesque composition (best seen from Pentonville Road), and in the details which partial cleaning has revealed. The complex multi-level planning and circulation is startingly assured. The materials he chose, from the areas served by the Midland Railway – bright red bricks from Nottingham, red and grey granite, and beige stone – demonstrate the Victorians' passion for colourful buildings which would be visible through the smoky atmosphere of the nineteenth-century city, and which would resist the attack of pollution.

The inclusion of that quintessential Victorian building type, the hotel, in the station's accommodation was part of the boom in London hotel building of the 1860s and '70s, to serve an increasingly mobile, international and imperial society. The uninterrupted shed, 210m (689ft) long and 75m (245ft) wide, was extremely ambitious, being for many years the widest span in the world. Its ingenuity lies in concealing the ties necessary to hold the vault together under the platforms.

The straightforward juxtaposition of shed and high-art building worried the Victorians, and can now be seen, as Donald J Olsen suggests, as a direct indication of the schizophrenia of a period obsessed both with the past and its styles (architecture), and with the glamour of technology (engineering).

The building of Euston, St Pancras and King's Cross stations drastically affected the area to their north: for a century it consisted of grimy, soot-infested workers' housing, until the railways started to use electric and diesel trains in the 1950s.

The restoration of Gilbert Scott's hotel, by RHWL and Richard Griffiths, the renovation of Barlow's great train shed, and the new addition to receive the extra length of the Eurostar trains (original design by Foster and Partners) by the Rail Link Engineering team, headed by Alistair Lansley, are exemplary projects. Connected by 23km of tunnel under East London it established improved connections to Europe from the north of England and Scotland. Its façade, a combination of panels of glass brick and transparent glass, has a repetitive nature appropriate to a terminus. It diminished Barlow and Ordish's great train shed and the visibility of its arch without even the decorum of the coupling of two train carriages. But when seen in perspective from the north along either the east or west façades, the two corner towers to Gilbert Scott's façade form fitting conclusions to the overall composition. This is particularly effective where the British Library completes the street section to the west, whereas to the east construction in 2008 was poised to begin on the huge Argent project.

Offices to Euston Road (photograph 2009)

Offices ex **Prudential Assurance** **G40** p
1879, 1899–1906
Alfred and Paul Waterhouse
Holborn EC1
⊖ Chancery Lane

In a city made principally of stock brick, Portland stone and stucco, Waterhouse's vibrant, blazing-red terracotta Gothic palace for Prudential Assurance is a remarkable and rather forbidding exception. Its size is a consequence of the wealth and self-importance gained by insurance in the nineteenth century. The redness may be Waterhouse's whim, but it is more probably the result of Victorian architects' desire for materials which would resist London's polluted atmosphere and could be seen through it. The 1879 scheme at the corner of Brooke Street (rebuilt in 1932) was extended in 1899–1906 to encompass the whole block. The principal Holborn façade is symmetrical, with prefabricated terracotta units, three-storey ranges of lancet windows, a roof profile of gables and spires, and a big central tower crowned by a pyramidal roof. Waterhouse's son Paul finished the building after his father's death in 1905.

Hotel c1885 **G41** m
35 Langham Street W1
⊖ Oxford Circus

The Victorian concern for materials which would not be destroyed by London's polluted air here reaches its absurd and extreme conclusion – the façade of this former clinic is entirely of shiny white glazed brick and looks as if it will last another century.

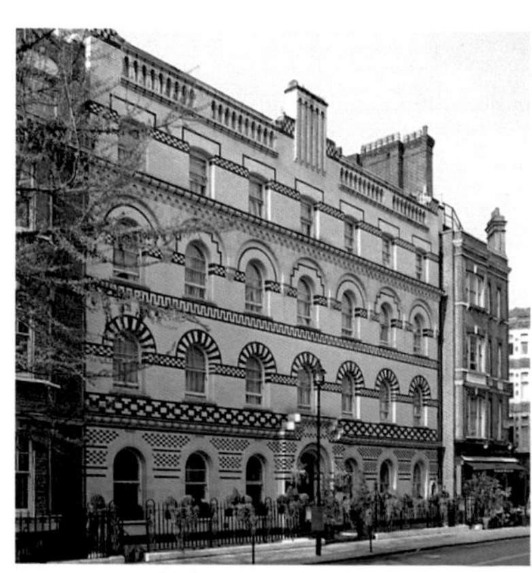

Church of the Holy Redeemer **G42** l
1887
24 Exmouth Market EC1
J D Sedding
⊖ Angel

An unexpected and magnificent asymmetrical composition in a relatively modest street, this church, with a square bell tower standing beside its giant portico, might be described as Lombard Romanesque – all in London stock brick with stone banding. The tower is positioned to be seen in deep perspective from Wilmington Square to the north across Rosebery Avenue. In giant gilt letters 'Christo Liberator' stands triumphantly above the entrance and below is a decorated pediment. Surprisingly the church is Anglican: the result of a remarkable collaboration between an enthusiastic Anglo-Catholic priest and his wealthy patroness. Inside there are more delights, and a surprisingly Wren-like character.

See also J D Sedding's **Holy Trinity** N26.

Rosebery Square 1889–92 **G43** l
Rosebery Avenue EC1
⊖ Chancery Lane
Rosebery Avenue was one of the last Victorian 'improvements', cut through slums north of Clerkenwell Road. Rosebery Square is a pathetic widening of the rows of dreadful walk-up dwellings with which the avenue is lined.

Mary Ward Settlement 1895–8 **G44** j
Tavistock Place WC1
Smith and Brewer
⊖ Russell Square
This is a major work and one of the best examples of the Free Style applied to a public building in the 1890s. Although owing something to Charles Rennie Mackintosh (despite predating his Glasgow School of Art by three years), C H Townsend and Norman Shaw, the language of this building is handled with great sophistication and originality.

The overall composition of the street façade is symmetrical, with local asymmetries to the entrance (reminiscent of Townsend). The tripartite window arrangement is typically Norman Shaw; the stepping windows for the staircases at either end are not. Wedged into the surface of the building is the side door, with projecting canopy and stepped stonework, all very good indeed.

Finsbury Town Hall 1895–9 **G45** l
Rosebery Avenue EC1
G Evans Vaughan
⊖ Chancery Lane
The turn of the century was a period of architectural experiment, and the revived Tudor style used here associates itself ultimately with the glory of Elizabethan England. The Borough of Finsbury lost its identity when London's local government was reorganized in 1965, and its exuberant and wilfully asymmetrical town hall no longer serves the symbolic function it had when built.

ex **University College Hospital** **G46** i
1897–1906
Gower Street WC1
Alfred Waterhouse
⊖ Euston Square, Warren Street
Set in Georgian Bloomsbury and opposite the Greek Revival of Wilkins's University College, Waterhouse's eccentric turrets and spires in red terracotta are a lesson to the 'in keeping with' lobby, which has justified much timid and mediocre building. As with all his London buildings, the sheer virtuosity of the forms and the precision of buildings are overwhelming, The X plan of seven storeys connects the four corners of the square site diagonally. It was an exemplary hospital model in its day, but the triangular spaces left over between the building and the street are problematic. The hospital moved to an extraordinarily feeble new building on Euston Road to the north in 2006, bringing further degradation to the area of the Euston Road Underpass. The old building was converted for use by UCL as a research institute.

Russell Hotel 1898 **G47** n
Russell Square WC1
C Fitzroy Doll
⊖ Russell Square
The construction of this hotel (a characteristically Victorian building type), was the first large incursion into Georgian Bloomsbury. Twice as high as its then domestic neighbours, it is in the uncertain late Victorian style – a confused mixture of eclectic motifs in beige faïence, from which Shaw was able to show a way out in his cooler **Piccadilly Hotel** K125 of only seven years later. See also **Russell Square** G16.

Derby Lodge late 19th century **G48** g
Britannia Street WC1
⊖ King's Cross
A renovated six-storey tenement building with fine iron arches to the staircase landings.

Fire Station 1901–2 **G49** j
Euston Road NW1
LCC Architects Department; W E Riley
⊖ Euston

The English 'Arts and Crafts' Free Style originated in the second half of the nineteenth century in the domestic work of Philip Webb and R Norman Shaw, among others. It was later applied to public buildings: the LCC Architects Department was an influential early advocate of the movement, and this building is one of the best examples. As Gavin Stamp writes, 'The style came to be regarded as essentially utilitarian and informal, suitable for a fire station but not for a bank, excellent for flats but not for a town mansion.' The Eversholt Street elevation should be noted for its complex handling of windows, relieving arches, gables and projections, all in very good red brickwork and Portland stone – a remarkable composition.

Bourne Estate 1901–7 **G50** p
Clerkenwell Road EC1
LCC Architects Department; Owen Fleming
⊖ Chancery Lane

This is the only pre-war LCC estate that approaches **Boundary** H36 and Millbank in size. 3900 people are housed behind the extensive façade to the Clerkenwell Road; from the road the arched openings reveal perspectives through a series of long courtyards. The five-storey tenement blocks are laid out north–south and although the flats have gallery access their living rooms receive maximum sunlight. But compared with the Boundary and Millbank Estates it feels overcrowded, and marks a retreat from the previous Free Style ideals of the young LCC architects. The buildings are also more in the Edwardian grand manner than in the tradition of Shaw or Webb.

Edward VII Galleries 1904–11 **G51** n
British Museum
Montague Place WC1
John Burnet
⊖ Tottenham Court Road

The galleries were built to extend the museum and, continuing the replacement of Bloomsbury's Georgian houses with large institutions, completed the block on which it stands. The composition of the façade, with its flat higher ends framing the Ionic screen, owes as much to Schinkel's Berlin Altesmuseum as to Smirke's south front of this **museum** G25, but it has a specifically Edwardian Beaux Arts flavour: there are straightforward commercial windows between the engaged columns. The lions terminating the balustrade and flanking the entrance are particularly fine. See also **Kodak House** K135.

The first floor gallery

Sicilian Avenue 1905 **G52** o
between Bloomsbury Way and
Southampton Row WC1
W S Worthy
⊖ Holborn

A corner is sliced through with an 8m (27ft) wide pedestrian street separated from the main roads by spindly Ionic screens. The five storeys of offices (originally flats) above the shops are clad in a mixture of bright red brick and white terracotta.

The Italian restaurant was one of the first to provide that rare thing in London, a nice place to sit outside – a fragment of Italy, but with a view of the plane trees of Bloomsbury Square. Sicilian Avenue demonstrates that the means of making a civilized public place removed from traffic can be quite modest, making the 'decks' of the **South Bank** K177 seem unnecessary.

Working Men's College 1905 **G53** a
Crowndale Road NW1
W H Caro
⊖ Mornington Crescent

One of a series of such colleges for the further education of adults, set up under Fabian socialist and self-help auspices. This one sports the full Edwardian apparatus for public buildings, and could be a town hall or library.

The corner building is particularly impressive with its monumental 'head' of mostly blank, gently curved brickwork addressing Crowndale Road, and the 'body' immediately behind, of many classroom windows facing Camden Street.

Department of Health and Social Security ex **London, Edinburgh and Glasgow Assurance** 1907 **G54** i
Euston Road and Melton Street NW1
E Beresford Pite
⊖ Euston

Pite started his career as assistant to John Belcher, who combined a commitment to the Arts and Crafts movement with his own fine baroque style, and Pite's early work followed that of his master. This strange concoction of archaic and classical Greek motifs departs wildly from the earlier baroque. The remarkable tiled entrance hall is in a strange style of its own.

Central School of Arts and Crafts **G55** o
1907–9
Southampton Row WC1
LCC Architects Department;
W E Riley with A Halcrow Verstage
⊖ Holborn

Although normally attributed to Lethaby (who as Principal of the Central School was influential on the design and consultant for the specification), this is another example of the formal variety of buildings produced by the LCC under the direction and supervision of W E Riley. The massive stone façade has segmental arches in shallow relief and, almost as an afterthought, a curious domed entry system on the corner. Lethaby's preoccupation with symbolism emerges in some of the circular decorative details.

British Medical Association **G56** j
ex **Theosophical Society Headquarters** 1911–13, 1922–9
Tavistock Square and Burton Street WC1
Edwin Lutyens, completed by C Wontner Smith
⊖ Euston, Russell Square

The Burton Street range is all that Lutyens built for the Theosophical Society (of which his wife was a founder member) before work was stopped by the First World War. Its façade, of brick with stone dressings, is truly monumental: a plinth of open arches supports a *piano nobile* four storeys high and with very large, simple window openings. After the war the building was taken over by the BMA, and the equally grand brick façade to Tavistock Square was added by Wontner Smith.

East elevation to Burton Street

Façade to Tavistock Square

Heal's 1916 **G57** m
196 Tottenham Court Road W1
Smith and Brewer
⊖ Goodge Street

The firm founded by Ambrose Heal was distinguished for promoting the functional qualities of vernacular furniture – the large-scale craft workshops of Heal's kept the Arts and Crafts Movement alive and were a rebuke to the cheap revivals in the other furniture stores on Tottenham Court Road. As Le Corbusier wrote in *Vers une architecture*, 'The existing plan of the dwelling … is conceived as a furniture store. This scheme of things, favourable enough to the trade of Tottenham Court Road, is of ill omen for Society.' The store's façade aptly expressed its owner's sober, functional and craft-based preoccupations. The stone casings to the steel frame running the full height of the store are separated by decorative blue spandrels depicting the tools of the trade; note also the elegantly crafted internal staircase. The later extension to the north did not have the original's quality.

Friends' House 1925–7 **G58** j
Euston Square NW1
H Lidbetter
⊖ Euston
The range of buildings on the south side of Euston Square, from Gordon Street to Woburn Place, including Friends' House, used to show how the neo-Georgian style – red brick with stone dressings for important features – could successfully be used for most urban building types, including the religious. Friends' House provides a meeting place and offices for Quakers. The main rooms are in the middle, with rings of offices round light wells on either side.

School of Hygiene and Tropical Medicine 1926–8 **G59** n
University of London
Gower Street and Keppel Street WC1
Morely Horder and Vernon Rees
⊖ Goodge Street
With its 'stripped classical' Portland stone façade, this building works well as an example of neutral town planning. In one direction it maintains the continuity of Gower Street; in the other direction, with Keppel Street as its central axis, it anticipates the Beaux Arts composition of Holden's massive **Senate House** G65. The gold insects and other fauna decorating the balconies and the gilded metal street names are interesting details.

Charles Rowan House 1928–30 **G60** l
Merlin Street, Wilmington Street WC1
Gilbert Mackenzie Trench
⊖ Farringdon, Angel
Ninety-six flats for the families of policemen are arranged in a courtyard from which stairs provide access. The surprising severity of the red-brick elevations to the surrounding streets, noted at the time of their building, arises from the placing of the chimneys sideways on the external walls and capping these with water tank enclosures to form towers. The result suggests an awareness of some contemporary Dutch and German developments.

Levita, Chamberlain and **Walker Houses** 1928 **G61** f
Chalton Street, Phoenix Road and Ossulton Street W1
G Topham Forrest
⊖ Euston
A palatial set piece of local authority housing, combining formal street façades, arched entrances to internal courts, and diminutive avenues of trees. Although at the time of writing in need of some repair, the scheme might not have seemed out of place in a benevolent Socialist mid-European state.

Offices **G62** o
ex **W S Crawford Limited** 1930
233 High Holborn WC1
Frederick Etchells and Welch
⊖ Holborn

It is appropriate that Crawford's, one of London's most progressive advertising agencies in the 1920s, should have commissioned one of the earliest examples of the 'new architecture' for their offices. The building handles the corner site traditionally and its use of materials is both urbane and sensuous. Unlike its more abstract rendered contemporaries, the building has a polished black marble ground floor or plinth, above which are alternating bands of white stucco and continuous windows. The windows are subdivided by structural mullions with chromium steel cover-strips (see Mies van der Rohe's Barcelona pavilion of 1929). As a result of its external detail, the building has weathered extremely well.

This was unfortunately Etchells's only building of consequence in London. His reputation as a pioneer of modernism is attributable more to his translation into English of Le Corbusier's *Vers une architecture* and his association with Vorticism.

Offices **G63** j
ex **Daimler Car Hire Garage** 1931
Herbrand Street WC1
Wallis Gilbert and Partners
⊖ Russell Square

In this quiet back street there rises unexpectedly a baroque 1930s façade. What was once a palace for the motor car (when compared with today's more utilitarian equivalent), with ramps contained in cylindrical forms complete with striped rendering, and horizontal windows, has knowingly been converted into advertising offices.

Wellcome Building 1931 **G64** i
Euston Road NW1
Septimus Warwick
⊖ Euston Square, Euston

A well-mannered, late example of classicism, used appropriately for an institution. Originally of four storeys, the building has been spoilt by the later addition of two attics. The Wellcome Foundation is an offshoot of the drug company, and the building houses a small museum.

See also Warwick's **Brixton Town Hall** W9, and the **Wellcome Trust**'s newer building to the west G84.

Senate House University of London **G65** n
started 1932
Malet Street and Montague Place WC1
Charles Holden
⊖ Tottenham Court Road

Soon after Holden's **London Transport** building K146 was finished, he was employed by the University to make a plan for its new administrative centre in Bloomsbury. In line with Store Street Holden proposed, as a landmark for London, a tower from which a high spine block would have extended north as far as Torrington Place. At right angles to this block, lower wings would have run to the streets bounding the site to the east and west. In the event, work was interrupted by the Second World War, and neither the northern extension of the scheme nor Holden's design for a ceremonial hall on the west side of Russell Square was built.

The elaborately modelled tower houses many different functions, and its structure allows for changing the internal arrangements; even the steel-beamed floors were designed to be moved up or down. The style is Holden's late stripped classical, here so stripped that the only horizontal mouldings remaining are those of the parapets and balustrade-cappings. Holden was particularly concerned to control the weathering of Portland stone and although the buildings have been cleaned several times since their completion, his skill in anticipating the inevitable effects of pollution and weather is clearly visible. The ceremonial interiors are splendid, using travertine for floors and wall panelling, and have excellent examples of light-fittings (for which Holden had gained practice from his **Underground stations** R24, T24).

Entrance Hall

Finsbury Health Centre 1938 **G66** l
Pine Street EC1
Lubetkin and Tecton
⊖ Angel

With the approach of the Second World War this building was to be Tecton's last in the optimistic spirit of the 'new architecture' of the 1930s. The health centre, partly indebted to that at **Peckham** X10, was a pioneering idea of the time. This project, for a slum clearance area of Finsbury, was the first to coincide with Tecton's declared socialist ideals. Its symmetrical two-storey H-plan, withdrawn from the existing street pattern, is reminiscent of the public buildings Le Corbusier projected for the continuous parklands of the *Ville Radieuse*. When the centre was built it stood as a shining white rebuke to the decayed area of Finsbury, but it is important for a less obvious reason. Its symmetrical plan and the baroque exuberance of its entrance sequence reaffirm the autonomy of architecture: they are not dictated by the programme (that is, form does not follow function) but show instead the inevitable presence of 'historical' or Beaux Arts planning techniques in pioneer works.

Research Building **G67** h
ex **Metropolitan Water Board** 1938
Rosebery Avenue EC1
Howard Robertson
⊖ Angel

A grandiose curved arrangement on a prominent site, but a disappointment from the only architect since Durand to attempt a book describing the art of 'composition'. He later designed the South Bank's **Shell Centre** K166.

Priory Green Estate 1938–52 **G68** g
Collier Street N1
Tecton: Skinner, Bailey and Lubetkin
⊖ King's Cross

Although planned and started before the Second World War, the Priory Green Estate was postponed and subsequently revised. The 269 flats occupy 3.5 hectares (8.7 acres) and unlike the later **Hallfield Estate** I27 follow the alignment of the original street pattern. They form two eight-storey set-back formations, with four identical four-storey blocks adjacent. The site was converted into a fenced and gated estate by the Peabody Trust (Avanti Architects 2000).

Note also **Bevin Court**, in Holford Place south of Pentonville Road, built by Tecton in 1953. Named after Ernest Bevin, this seven-storey block of flats is triangular in plan, access to its wings gained via a much-photographed circular staircase. The façades have alternating panels of brick and pre-cast concrete.

To the south, in Killick Street, is **Stuart Mills House** of c1937, a six-storey block of flats designed by Joseph Emberton. It is a reminder that even the 'heroes' of the 1930s were capable of indifferent designs when called upon to produce low-cost housing.

Euston Station and **offices** **G69** i
1960–80
Euston Road NW1
British Rail Architects Department
and R Seifert and Partners
⊖ Euston

Philip Hardwick's great Euston Arch (1836–40) was senselessly demolished by British Rail in 1961, together with the other front buildings. The reason given was that it would get in the way of the station 'improvements', and the extra platform lengths which were required. However, following the demolition of the arch the track lengths were not increased, leaving the site untouched.

The new station hall (1965) by British Rail and Seifert's offices (1979–80) were a particularly glib and depressing replacement. Unlike Hardwick's arch they fail to convey any sense of arrival or departure. Various initiatives to improve the sordid open space between the station and offices were failures, and at the time of writing plans were being considered for the redevelopment of the whole site including the reconstruction of the station.

London Telecom Tower 1963–6 **G70** m
Howland Street W1
Architects Section of the Ministry of Works
⊖ Warren Street

This structure was one of a series dotted across the country, linking the large cities in the UK by microwave transmission of telephone and other signals. When completed, it was widely admired as an example of pure, 'innocent' engineering; why this was, given its poorly proportioned and clumsily detailed curtain wall, is not now clear. At 174m (580ft) high, it was the tallest building in London until the **National Westminster Tower** L130 was finished in 1981. The observation gallery was a good place from which to appreciate London's loose structure (compared with Paris or New York), but was closed after an explosion.

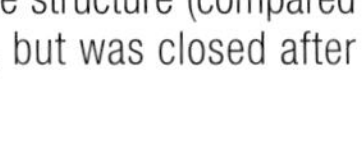

Brunswick Centre 1965–73 **G71** k
Brunswick Square and Guilford Street WC1
Patrick Hodgkinson (design),
Bickerdyke Allen (construction)
⊖ Russell Square

The original design resulted from Hodgkinson's long, complex and spirited inquiry (starting in the early 1960s under Leslie Martin in Cambridge) into high-density, low-rise alternatives to the universal prescription of high-rise towers for inner-city areas. Like much British housing of the 1960s, the Brunswick Centre as built was for a time considered a heroic failure. Despite frequent changes of client before the building was finished, it was still just possible to detect some of the early passion for an 'ideal' city block.

The two parallel buildings of flats follow the existing street pattern and face each other across a raised internal plaza. The extruded nature of the stepped section, with its monumental back-of-stadium effect on its surroundings, especially on Marchmont Street, and the emptiness of the central plaza, were some of the design's problems.

These were addressed in the thorough renovation completed in 2006 (architects Levitt

Bernstein, consultant Patrick Hodgkinson). The central 'street' was narrowed, repaved and provided with new furniture and canopies; the concrete was repaired and painted cream (as originally intended); the windows re-glazed, and the whole was rebranded 'The Brunswick'.

Housing and showrooms 1966–71 **G72** m
Clipstone Street W1
Frederick Macmanus and Partners, designed by Michael Gold
courtyard landscape by Michael Ellison
⊖ Great Portland Street

Housing for 800 people, in a six-storey ring with basement car-parking below, stands apart from a two-storey triangular block of showrooms. The housing is a fortuitous illustration of Leslie Martin's theories of the usefulness of building along the edges of sites to produce high densities, here about 720 people to the hectare. The buildings are reticently styled: the painted concrete frame shows on the outside, but on the inside the courtyard has continuous projecting balconies; its excellent planting and trees are now mature. The comprehensive crude re-windowing of the 1990s destroyed the façades' original elegance but not the soundness of the planning proposal.

College of Engineering and Science 1970 **G73** m
Polytechnic of Central London
Clipstone Street W1
Lyons Israel and Ellis
⊖ Great Portland Street

This building shows a mixture of influences. The towers housing offices and laboratories are separated from smaller attendant towers housing services (stairs, ducts, lifts and so on), recalling the 'served' and 'servant' spaces of Louis Kahn. The patent glazing, cantilevered lecture theatres, and external gantries and boiler flues pay homage to the celebrated Leicester University engineering laboratories (1964) designed by Stirling and Gowan (one-time assistants in the firm of Lyons Israel and Ellis). While the industrial and constructivist imagery may be appropriate to an engineering faculty and a red-brick university campus, the same forms are incongruous in the eighteenth-century layout of streets and squares of London. However, the entrance hall with flying galleries is quite spectacular.

School of Oriental and African Studies 1973 **G74** n
University of London
Woburn Square WC1
Denys Lasdun and Partners
⊖ Russell Square

The school comprises teaching rooms arranged around a double-height roof-lit library. Built in concrete and clad in white precast concrete panels which seem to have been designed for a Mediterranean climate, the building disregards the pattern of streets and squares that characterizes what remains of Georgian Bloomsbury. It suggests only a future pattern of isolated and unrelated objects – a still life.

British Library 1974–1998 **G75** f
Euston Road NW1
Colin St John Wilson with
Property Services Agency
⊖ King's Cross

George IV sold his father's library to the British Museum and the circular reading room of 1857 remained the symbolic core of the library for over 100 years. After various schemes to provide a replacement on sites to the south of the Museum were abandoned, the large site of a former potato market next to St Pancras station was chosen. Although the new building took a quarter of a century to construct and cost nearly £500m, of the accommodation originally intended only about half was built: a second phase was planned on the remainder of the site to the north.

Two libraries, humanities to the west and science to the north, are accommodated in broad wings placed at the edges of the site and well back from the noise and dirt of Euston Road. In the space between these, the lofty entrance hall rises up from a modest single-storey vestibule to a carefully day-lit space six storeys high. It is dominated by the rehoused George III Library in its grey glass enclosure. The books themselves are kept in up to five basements and transported to the reading rooms by sophisticated machinery. The eastern wing is extended towards the Euston Road to house a conference centre and partly enclose the large fussily decorated courtyard that provides an approach to the building and a refuge for smokers.

The finishes of well-laid red brick, travertine, oak and bronze are lavish. The users of the libraries appreciated the new luxury, and the mechanized book handling worked surprisingly efficiently. The public is less well served in the new galleries designed to show off some of the collection's 'treasures', and while for the first time these are properly displayed and lit, their uncertain setting has the ambience of a Bond Street jewellery store.

In 2007 the library's Centre for Conservation, designed by Long & Kentish, was added to the north.

Institute of Education 1975–9 **G76** j
University of London
Bedford Way WC1
Denys Lasdun and Partners
⊖ Euston Square, Russell Square

Contemporary with Lasdun's **National Theatre** K178, the Institute provides offices, classrooms and lecture rooms. One side of Bedford Way, to which it presents a suave continuous curtain wall 236m (770ft) long, is punctuated by aggressive triangular features in concrete. The treatment at ground level is unsatisfactory and although aligning itself to the pavement the project is 'anti-street'. The side away from the street was planned to grow by receiving a series of stepped wings. Only one was built, extending towards Lasdun's **School of Oriental and African Studies** G74.

ITN offices 1987–90 **G77** l
200 Gray's Inn Road WC1
Foster Associates
⊖ Farringdon

These offices were originally a speculation but since their completion were mainly occupied by Independent Television News. The accommodation is arranged around a full-height and roof-lit atrium. To the street, and consolidating it, the office floors present their sheer skin: an energy-efficient 'neutralizing wall' of two planes of widely separated glass. Below this at pavement level the generous entrance is recessed behind painted concrete columns.

Imagination offices and **Gallery** 1990 **G78** n
Alfred Place, Store Street WC1
Ron Herron and Associates
⊖ Goodge Street
The provocative roofscape of fabric domes seen from Bedford Square is the only external expression of this project. An inauspicious light well has been transformed into an atrium of extraordinary qualities. The combination of heavy masonry walls, light steel, and inventively designed bridges spanning the brilliant white interior, topped by the tented roof structure, produces a spatial effect of remarkable luminosity. When there are public exhibitions it is possible to appreciate this central space from the rooftop gallery.

Offices 1991–2008 **G79** i
Regent's Place NW1
Sheppard Robson Architects
⊖ Warren Street, Great Portland Street
Just as the retention of 'historic' façades has become a familiar compromise for many London developments, so the opposite tendency of providing new façades to existing buildings might be seen as less conservative and more didactic (see also **Orion House** K168). Here we have one of the more successful attempts, which went some way to moderating the miseries of this section of Euston Road. Further redevelopment of the whole block is planned (to a master plan by Sheppard Robson).

To the north, 1 Regent's Place was designed by Arup Associates and completed in 1998. Six floors of offices are arranged within a square plan around an atrium 38m (125ft) square whose floor accommodates a single trading floor. Lifts, stairs and services are placed at the outside corners of the square and clad in alarmingly polychrome Belgian limestone while between these span energy-conscious fully glazed walls.

The earlier dull slab facing Euston Road was replaced by offices that did nothing for Euston Road except to add to the bulky buildings lining the canyon of the underpass. The curious garden created in 1998 between this building and the Euston Tower was intelligently designed and provided some relief from the traffic.

Sadler's Wells Theatre 1998 **G80** h
Rosebery Avenue EC1
RHWL with Nicholas Hare Architects
⊖ Angel
The rebuilt Sadler's Wells Theatre, replacing that of Frank Matcham & Co built in 1931, provided a new auditorium and a much-improved presence on Rosebery Avenue. The street façade, designed by Nicholas Hare Architects, is formed by a three-storey brick screen in which a tall window exhibits the audience ascending the principal staircase to their seats; the working theatre was the responsibility of Renton Howard Wood Levin. This was London's first completed cultural project funded by the National Lottery.

The Clore Centre 1998 **G81** n
Torrington Square WC1
Stanton Williams
⊖ Euston

In the intervening period since Lasdun's various diagrammatic assertions on the University of London in the mid-1970s, concerns for context and conservation have resulted in more conciliatory buildings. The Clore Management Centre is a clear example of the emerging détente (see also **Brunei Gallery** G82). Here a Georgian terrace is concluded with the traditional base, *piano nobile* and attic storey, but in this case, instead of windows set in the load-bearing masonry wall we have large areas of glazing.

Brunei Gallery for Islamic Art 1998 **G82** n
School of Oriental and African Studies
University of London
Russell Square WC1
Nicholas Hare
⊖ Russell Square

The various sites left over from Holden's incompletely realized plan for the **University of London** G65 were after 1945 slowly occupied. Those to the north of Senate House broadly followed Holden's massing although in poorer materials; others like Lasdun's **SOAS** G74 ignored it completely and were designed as free-standing objects.

Hare's design for this intricate brief combining a public gallery, teaching and lecture theatre responded both to the strong east–west axis north of Senate House that marked the northern extent of Holden's work and to its frontage to nearby Russell Square. The offices are housed in a carefully contextual four-storey building to the east while the more 'representational' elements, including the entrance, are on the north-west corner, all without Islamic pastiche. The wing that returns south from this entrance, however, has a roof garden to an Islamic design.

Royal Academy of Dramatic Art **G83** n
2001
62–64 Gower Street/Malet Street WC1
Avery Associates
⊖ Goodge Street, Warren Street

The bulge in the otherwise quiet Malet Street frontage suggests a dense occupation within. The Royal Academy of Dramatic Art (RADA) now has two entrances, one institutional and existing from Gower Street, the other for public performances and new from Malet Street. Two teaching theatres (the Vanburgh and the Gielgud) have been skilfully shoehorned into the space between, separated by a dramatic vertical slot of space reaching for the sky. This is an exemplary essay in working within the dimensional limitations of height and building frontage, a typical challenge on central London sites.

Wellcome Foundation Offices **G84** i
2004
Euston Road NW1
Hopkins Architects
⊖ Euston Square, Euston, Warren Street

With the Foundation's **museum** G64 together with their new offices, the Wellcome Foundation now occupies an entire urban block addressing the frontage of Euston Road, from Gordon Street to Gower Street. The new building houses offices in an eight-storey glazed wall with a dramatic south-facing atrium, setting down to five storeys facing Gower Place behind. This is now a familiar Hopkins *parti* – see **Evelina Children's Hospital** K192. The building is beautifully detailed and is a rebuke to the crass commercialism across the street that makes up the architectural banality of the Warren Street intersection (which the celebrated American architect Frank Gehry found of interest). In the atrium and partly visible from the street is the Heatherwick Studio's remarkable 30m (100ft) tall hanging sculpture *Bleigiessen*: 142,000 dichroic glass spheres suspended on 27,000 high-tensile steel cables.

King's Cross railway lands redevelopment 2004– **G85** b, f
NW1, N1
Various architects
⊖ King's Cross St Pancras

The contract to construct the high-speed rail link from St Pancras to the Channel Tunnel transferred about 27 hectatres (67 acres) of land formerly occupied by the railway sidings north of King's Cross and St Pancras stations to the builders of the new line. For this land the planning application of 2004, one of Europe's largest, proposed about 750,000 square metres (8m sq ft) of dense mixed development, offices, shops and housing, arranged around tree-lined streets and squares.

The first development begun was the conversion of the Granary, a former wheat store and the largest remaining historic building on the site, into a new home for the University of the Arts (incorporating Central St Martin's College), together with some retail and office development. Work started in 2008 to designs by architects Stanton Williams. This will overlook the largest open space on the site, facing south over the Regent's Canal. The largest gasworks in London, opened in 1824 by the Imperial Gas, Light and Coke Company, was based at the southern end of the site, but by 2004 only one of its tall cylindrical gas-holders was left standing. It was planned to renovate and reuse this and some of the others which had been dismantled.

The Granary

School of Slavonic and East European Studies 2005 **G86** j
UCL
Taviton Street WC1
Short and Associates
⊖ Euston

The expression of windows to processional staircases either side of the front door gives this building an unexpected grand scale like a palazzo. The balanced composition is further emphasized by arched and gated service entrances and tall fully glazed regular attic windows topped by an exaggerated cornice all in good brickwork and with inventive stone details. The plan is elegantly compact with a semicircular ring of offices over five floors. A central full-height light well relates all floors to the entrance, and confirms the symmetry of the whole, and the prominent chimneys for ventilation are an expression of the building's 'sustainable' agenda. Its character is not normal to London but, true to its brief, it would not be out of place in Zagreb.

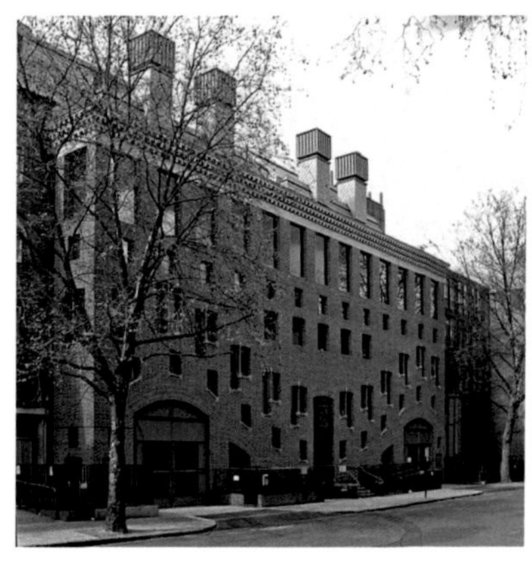

Gazzano House, housing and shop 2005 **G87** l
167–9 Farringdon Road WC2
Amin Taha
⊖ Farringdon

This six-storey block, a replacement for the more modest building formerly on the site, provided new premises for Gazzano's delicatessen on the ground floor with flats above. The exterior has fashionable irregularly placed windows and is clad in shingles of Cor-Ten steel (also used earlier at John Winter's **house** R30), which develops a weatherproof rusty surface and in this district rich in 'buildings of character', why not? The treatment falters only where the tiles meet the pavement.

Gagosian Gallery 2005 **G88** g
4–24 Britannia St WC1
Caruso St John
⊖ King's Cross St Pancras

The location of commercial art galleries is crucial to their success. Here a New York- and Los Angeles-based gallery found in gritty but fast-gentrifying King's Cross suitable former light-industrial premises for a large new gallery for the temporary exhibitions of their wares. The architects have provided a 30m (100ft) long suite of connected large rooms with 'industrial' floors, smooth white walls, exquisitely detailed lighting and rooflights, and near-invisible arrangements for air-conditioning.

Kings Place 2008 **G89** c
York Way N1
Dixon Jones
⊖ King's Cross

As opposed to the privatization of city land, a characteristic of most commercial building, the developer here invited the public to share his enthusiasms for music, art, eating and urban renewal. The semi-derelict Battlebridge Basin and the Regent's Canal were transformed into places of public promenade. The 90×70m (295×230ft) site, while providing accommodation for 30,000 square metres (322,900sq ft) of office space, also houses unexpectedly on the ground floor and below a 420-seat concert hall and a full rehearsal hall, as well as art galleries and restaurants.

Externally the building proposes contrasting elevational strategies. Facing the basin and canal with its surviving nineteenth-century warehouses, the building is composed of discreet and separate stone-clad volumes, with a rotunda at the north-east corner forming a pivot between basin and canal. The west and south frontages, on the other hand, facing the heavy traffic of York Way and the railway tracks into King's Cross, adopt a different approach. Here, a triple-glazed six-storey-high screen is introduced with a gently undulating outer layer of glass. This, with its arcaded ground floor, when seen in perspective along York Way, gives a strong visual identity to the offices above.

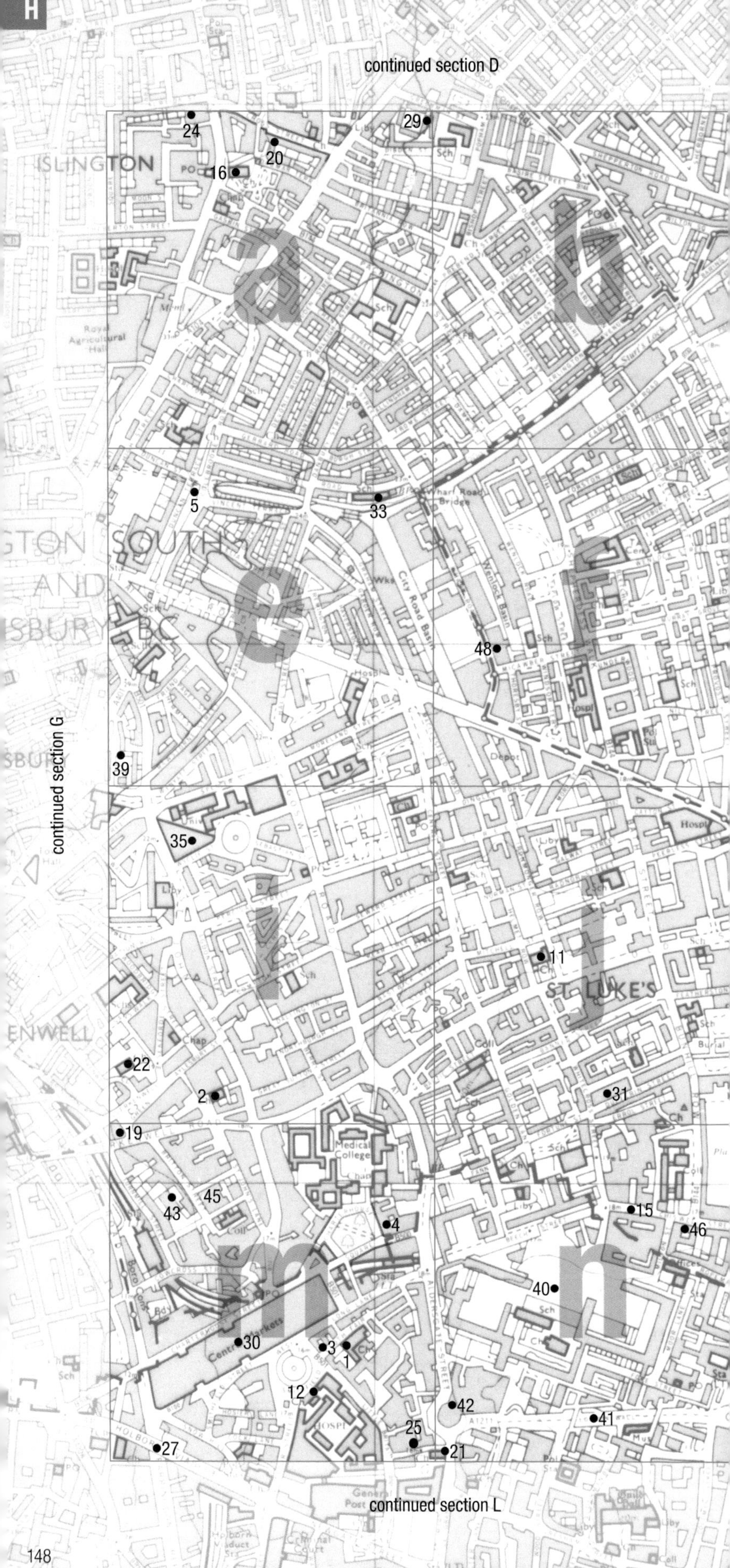
H
continued section D
ISLINGTON
a
b
e
f
i
j
m
n
24
20
29
16
5
33
48
39
35
11
ST LUKE'S
22
2
31
19
43
45
4
15
46
40
30
3
1
12
42
41
25
21
27
City Road Basin
Wenlock Basin
Wharf Road Bridge
Royal Agricultural Hall
Medical College
Central Markets
General Post Office
continued section G
continued section L

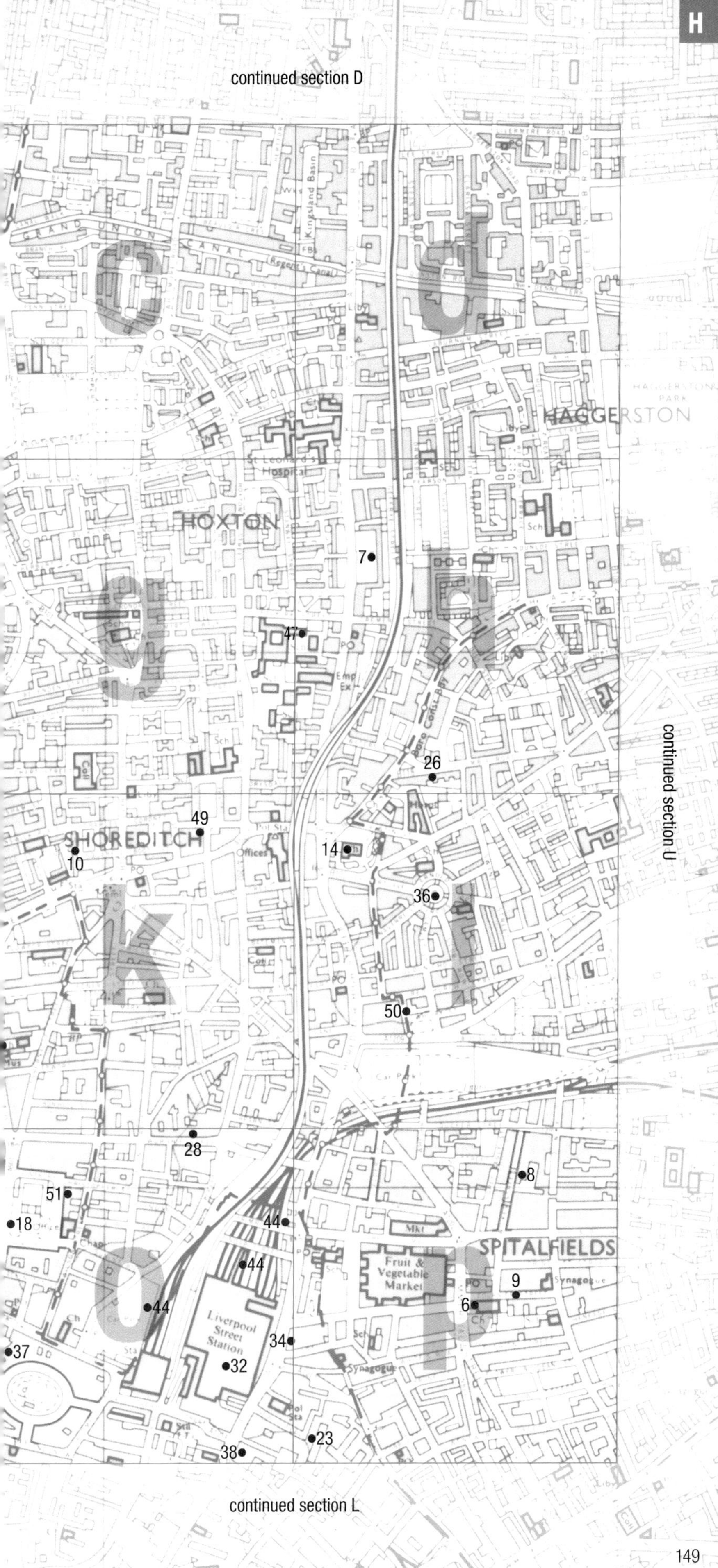
continued section D
HAGGERSTON
HOXTON
SHOREDITCH
SPITALFIELDS
St Leonard's Hospital
Liverpool Street Station
Fruit & Vegetable Market
Kingsland Basin
GRAND UNION CANAL
(Regent's Canal)
continued section U
continued section L

Finsbury ■ Shoreditch ■ Spitalfields ■ Islington

The historic boroughs of Shoreditch and Finsbury to the north and the hamlet of Spitalfields to the east were among the first outer districts of London to merge with the medieval City. It is ironic that the most historic areas of London should, as a result of continuous development, be the most confusing and architecturally disappointing, and nowhere is this more true than in the areas adjacent to the City.

Shoreditch today has no architectural links with its medieval and Elizabethan past, its earliest buildings dating from the late seventeenth century. Hoxton Square, where no original houses now remain, was laid out shortly after 1683 in an attempt to emulate developments to the west, and acquired for the district a reputation for genteel living. Many almshouses were built in the eighteenth century, but only the **Geffrye Museum** (Ironmongers' Almshouses) H7 survives, built in 1715 on Kingsland Road, the borough's boundary with the country. In the nineteenth century the population of Shoreditch rose abruptly, indicating a rise in trade and a corresponding decline in gentility. The area is still characterized by warehouses, offices and workshops, and retains the timber and furniture trades which started here in the nineteenth century. Badly bombed in the Second World War, Shoreditch has been reconstructed in a piecemeal fashion, and in the 1990s started to be occupied by artists, gentrifiers and galleries such as the **White Cube** H49 in Hoxton Square.

Spitalfields was a silk-weaving area, settled by French Huguenots exiled largely as a result of the revocation of the Edict of Nantes (1685), and was one of the nine hamlets in the parish of Stepney. Some silk weavers' houses – identifiable by large windows to the upper storey to light the looms – survive near the dominant **Christ Church** H6 and near the **Bethnal Green Museum** U22. By the late eighteenth century Spitalfields had developed, like Shoreditch, into a desirable residential area. Evidence of this more salubrious past remains in the many early-eighteenth century houses in Spital Square, Folgate Street, Elder Street, **Fournier Street** H9 and **Wilkes Street** H8 immediately north and east of Spitalfields Market. By the nineteenth century, however, Spitalfields had followed the East End's general pattern of industrialization. In the 1980s, many of London's railway stations and markets were redeveloped. Broad Street Station was demolished for part of the new **Broadgate** H44 and **Liverpool Street Station** H32 was surrounded by new offices in an extension of the same scheme. The market at Spitalfields closed in 1991, but after various contested proposals and counterproposals for its comprehensive redevelopment, the site was replanned with new large offices (Foster and Partners) to the west and the original market buildings restored.

Sixteenth-century Finsbury, next to the City but outside its jurisdiction, was (like Southwark, section L) popular for theatres – Sadler's Music House started in 1685. In the early seventeenth century it attracted religious and nonconformist groups. However, nothing remains today of this romantic past, with the exception of the Charterhouse, Finsbury's only surviving medieval monument. The urban development of Clerkenwell and Finsbury was encouraged by reconstruction after the Great Fire of 1666: **Charterhouse Square** H4 dates from about 1700, and **Finsbury Square** H18 was laid out by the younger Dance in 1777 in an attempt to emulate the development of the great estates to the west. Unfortunately no houses remained after the Blitz. Finsbury Circus, laid out to the south in 1815, retains only the plan of the younger Dance's original proposal: its mediocre twentieth-century transformation is now complete with the exception of **Lutyens House** H37. Standing on the fringes of London, a traditional location for hospitals, Finsbury acquired two in the same year, 1751: St Luke's and the Lying-In Hospital.

Islington, to the north, had remained a village, but by the beginning of the nineteenth century it too was becoming absorbed in London's growth. Expansion to the north and west was accelerated by two important engineering works, the New Road (1770) and the Regent's Canal (1814–20). Both were concerned with the practical matter of bypassing the congested centre of London, to facilitate the passage of goods from the expanding West End to the City and finally to the Docks. At the same time they bridged the historic divide between the cities of London and Westminster (see section K).

Old Spitalfields Market, 1887

Broadgate Circle H44

St Bartholomew the Great 1123 **H1** m
restored by Aston Webb 1880–1900
West Smithfield EC1
⊖ Farringdon

In 1123 the Augustinian Priory and Hospital of St Bartholomew the Great were founded. The present church is the remains of the Priory, whose precinct lay to the south. The nave was demolished, leaving a T-shaped arrangement, and the apsidal east end was completely rebuilt in the late nineteenth century. Nevertheless, St Bartholomew's is London's only surviving monastic church from the twelfth century, and its only example of large-scale Norman work – for the small scale see the Chapel of St John in the **Tower of London** L4. The (rebuilt) half-timbered gatehouse in Little Britain marks the position of the original entrance to the nave.

St John 1721 **H2** i
crypt 1140 and 1180, gate 1504
St John's Square EC1
⊖ Farringdon

Only the crypt remains of the twelfth-century priory church of the order of St John of Jerusalem, its rib vaulting showing that the church had the circular nave then customary. The massive vaulted gate from St John's Lane (restored by John Oldred Scott in 1903) suggests the size of the original priory which, although it was damaged during the Peasants' Revolt in 1381, survived until the dissolution of the monasteries during the reign of Henry VIII. The present church is eighteenth century, unexceptional and understated, and stands behind a fine red-brick wall with rubbed brick detail. In the wall is a memorial gateway to the Doewra family leading to a small garden. Prior Doewra rebuilt the priory in 1504.

Houses mid-17th century **H3** m
41–2 Cloth Fair EC1
⊖ Barbican

The timber houses destroyed by the Great Fire were replaced in brick. These houses escaped the Fire, and their timber construction gives an idea of what early-seventeenth-century London was like. On a corner site, adjacent to the typically narrow alleys of Cloth Court and Rising Sun Court, they have four two-storey timber bay windows capped by pediments. Numbers 39–45 Cloth Fair are owned by the Landmark Trust.

Houses c1700 **H4** m
4–5 Charterhouse Square EC1
⊖ Barbican

Standing in one of London's few remaining gated squares, these houses are more severe than their contemporaries at **Queen Anne's Gate** K31 and numbers 1 and 2 **Laurence Pountney Hill** L49. The doorcases are later.

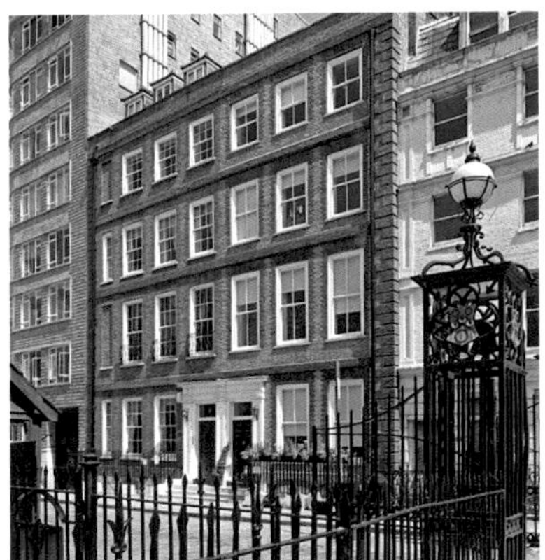

Colebrooke Row and **H5** e
Duncan Terrace c1710 and 1786
N1
⊖ Angel

The pride of eighteenth-century residential Islington, these two long terraces faced each other originally across the New River: a garden now follows the course of the culverted river. Duncan Terrace, on the west side, is a sequence of impressive façades, regular but for the interruption of the massive church of St John the Evangelist (1843) which Pugin described as 'the most original combination of modern deformity that has been erected for some time past'. The raised pavements accommodating the slope either side of **Charlton Place** are particularly good. Charlton Place itself is a little street of Georgian cottages made special by the shallow curve on the south side, its uncertain stepped cornice line following the slope of the street towards the New River.

To the east of Colebrooke Row are Cruden Street, Chantry Street, Queen's Head Street and St Peter's Street, a triangular area of small-scale streets best appreciated as part of an extended Islington walk.

Christ Church 1714–29 **H6** p
Commercial Street E1
Nicholas Hawksmoor
⊖ Aldgate East, Liverpool Street

Of Hawksmoor's six London churches this is the most magnificent. The composition of the church demonstrates Hawksmoor's characteristic abruptness: the very plain rectangular box of the nave is surmounted at its west end by a broad tower of three stages topped by a steeple more gothic than classical.

It was savagely altered in 1850 by Ewan Christian (better known as the architect of the **National Portrait Gallery** K118), who removed the galleries, blocked in the windows at the corners of the central space, and lowered the main windows.

After years of neglect it was restored in 2006 to its pre-1850 condition, using the original building documents where possible. The restoration revealed the most complex and sumptuous of Hawksmoor's interiors. The central space with its flat ceiling is lit by a clerestory, and flanked by aisles. These are roofed with elliptical barrel vaults carried on a raised Composite order (see also Wren's **St James, Piccadilly** K21). This order is also used for the screens across the east and west ends. The Venetian window at the east end may show the growing influence of the Palladians, or it may be a rhyme with the arched pediment of the huge Tuscan entrance portico, repeated in the wide main stage of the tower.

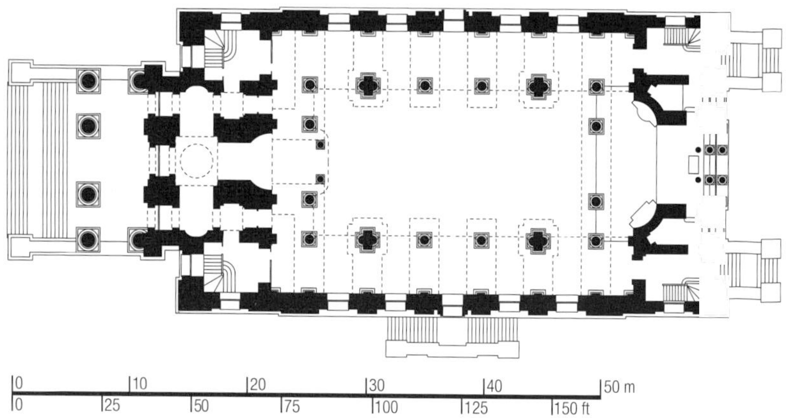

Geffrye Museum **H7** h
ex **Ironmongers' Almshouses** 1715
Kingsland Road E9
⊖ Old Street

A two-storey group of fourteen almshouses forms three sides of a generous courtyard; in the centre is a chapel, approached by a formal avenue of lime trees (planted in 1719) from the gated entrance with fine lampholders on Kingsland Road. A statue of Robert Geffrye, the benefactor, stands benignly in a recess above the entrance.

In 1910–14 W E Riley of the LCC converted the almshouses into a museum now housing exhibits of historical domestic interiors and furnishings: by removing the first floors, stairs and much of the party walls he produced a long sequence of small galleries.

Branson Coates designed the new twentieth-century galleries and café, added in 1998 to the southern end of the existing buildings.

Houses 1721 **H8** p
Wilkes Street E1
⊖ Shoreditch

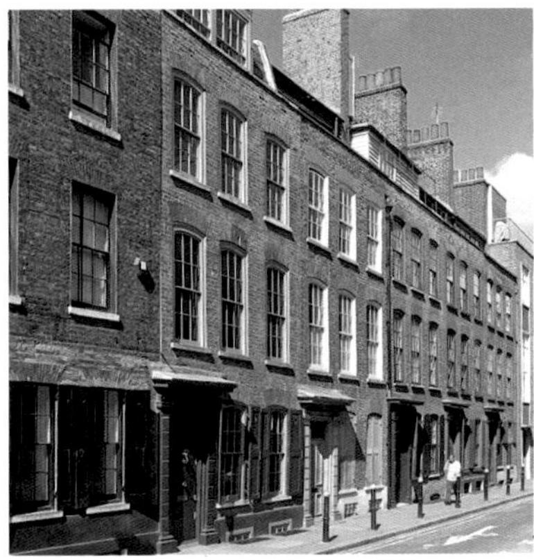

In this street are good and atypical examples of Spitalfields' surviving eighteenth-century housing stock. Number 1 has tall windows in the roof to illuminate work at the loom: number 2 has a generous frontage, although the house inside is cramped and only one room deep; and the wooden doorcase to number 11 is one of the few surviving examples in London.

Fournier Street 1722–8 **H9** p
Spitalfields E1
⊖ Aldgate East

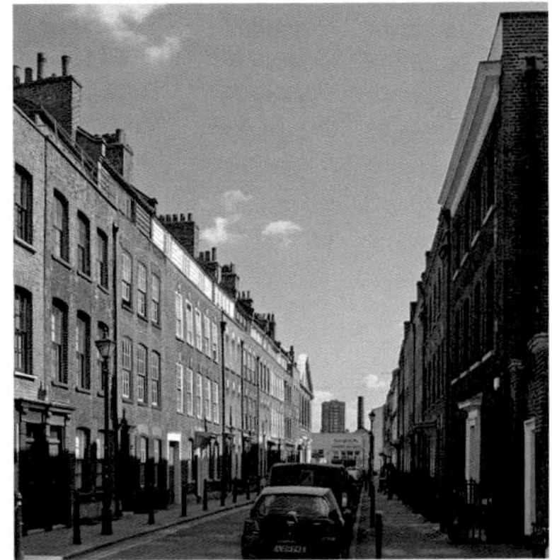

Running alongside **Christ Church** H6, this is the least damaged and most renovated of the several surviving early-eighteenth-century streets in the district. The four-bay rectory of Christ Church on the south side is by Hawksmoor.

House c1725 **H10** k
16 Charles Square N1
⊖ Old Street

The only original house in the square, this was refurbished in 1980: it has five bays, a good doorcase, and rather unfortunate painted keystones to the windows.

St Luke 1727–33 **H11** j
Old Street EC1
Nicholas Hawksmoor and John James
⊖ Old Street

This and the demolished St John, Horsleydown formed a pair of late Commissioners' churches. The bizarre fluted obelisk steeple is attributed to Hawksmoor, who had a reputation for strange tower terminals; in 1730 he had proposed a similar but unfluted design for **St Giles-in-the-Fields** K45. James was also architect of **St George, Hanover Square** J6.

In 2003 the shell of the near-derelict church was roofed and the nave converted into a performance and rehearsal space for the London Symphony Orchestra, architects Levitt Bernstein.

St Bartholomew's Hospital **H12** m
1730–59,1834
West Smithfield EC1
James Gibbs, Philip Hardwick
⊖ Barbican, St Paul's

With its long history of adaptation and its formal entrance sequence, St Bartholomew's resembles other English institutions, particularly the Inns of Court and the colleges of Oxford and Cambridge. The first buildings dated from 1123, but the earliest surviving are the fifteenth-century tower and vestry of the hospital church, St Bartholomew-the-Less. The octagonal body of the church was added in 1823 by Philip Hardwick, to plans by George Dance the Younger. It now forms the north-east side of the hospital's first courtyard, entered through the boundary wall to West Smithfield. Over the entrance is the magnificent but eccentrically tall gatehouse, entirely rebuilt by Hardwick in 1834. A Venetian gateway leads from here to the principal courtyard. The Gibbs court was originally four detached stone buildings, spare and Palladian in detail, with a fountain and large plane trees at the centre. In summer the trees form a canopy, and the combination of water and shade encourages patients and visitors to use the space as a grand salon. The statues and urns which once stood on the parapets and the big arches connecting the open corners have unfortunately disappeared. In 1934–5 Lancaster, Lucas and Lodge replaced the south side with the George V building, a dull and uninspired copy of the original. The three surviving Gibbs buildings (re-cased by Hardwick in 1856) were London's earliest large-scale examples of the use of Bath stone. The most interesting interiors are the main staircase and the great hall, both good secular examples of English baroque.

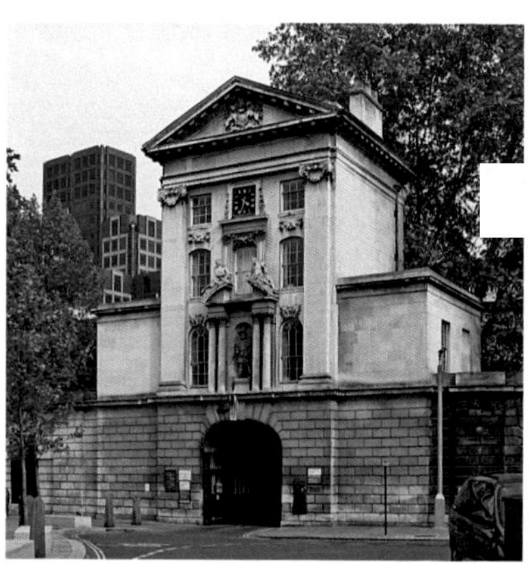

Note, to the west, across West Smithfield, **Haberdashers' Hall** by Michael Hopkins and Partners of 2002 embedded in the block and with no street frontage.

Honourable Artillery Company **H13** j
1735,1828,1857
City Road and Bunhill Row EC1
Jennings (?)
⊖ Moorgate

The HQ building (1735) is a large five-bay house of London stock brick, with a parapet decorated with cannonballs instead of the customary urns. Originally it was freestanding, and faced Artillery Grounds to the south (now a cricket field). In 1828 a wing was added to the house, and in 1857 the barrack buildings on City Road were built, in an appropriate castellated fortress style. To the west, on Bunhill Row, is 21–9 Artillery Row, a four storey early-nineteenth century terrace, and a further extension of the Artillery Company. The original house is now almost totally concealed, and the best view of it is from Finsbury Street across the playing fields to the south.

View from Finsbury Street

St Leonard 1736–40 **H14** l
Shoreditch High Street E1
George Dance the Elder
⊖ Liverpool Street, Old Street

Since at least the twelfth century a church has existed at the junction of the two main Roman roads north out of the City, now Kingsland Road and Old Street. The present St Leonard's, while as grand as one of Hawksmoor's, is not a Commissioners' church but was built to replace the one which collapsed in 1713. The outside is notable for its multi-staged and obelisk-finished steeple nearly 60m (200ft) tall and its fine Tuscan portico, both in Portland stone and arranged like Gibbs' **St Martin-in-the-Fields** K40. The interior is very plain and emptier than it should be: the galleries, which were supported by the Tuscan arcade between nave and aisles, have been removed. It is St Leonard's 'Bells of Shoreditch' that are mentioned in the nursery rhyme *Oranges and Lemons*.

ex **Whitbread's Brewery** from 1749 **H15** n
Chiswell Street EC1
⊖ Moorgate

This famous English brewery, closed in 1976, straddled Chiswell Street. The eighteenth-century buildings, on the south side, form an internal courtyard which was restored for conferences and entertainments. To the north of the archway is the original house, a fine early-eighteenth-century building in the carved brick 'artisan' style with a canopied door and arched window above. Of the early brewing buildings only the Porter Tun Room of 1774 survives, 49m (160ft) square, and with a magnificent timber-truss roof. The south yard has a ramped and colonnaded entrance (previously an exit for barrels), also very well restored.

St Mary 1751–4 **H16** a
Upper Street N1
Launcelot Dowbiggin
⊖ Angel

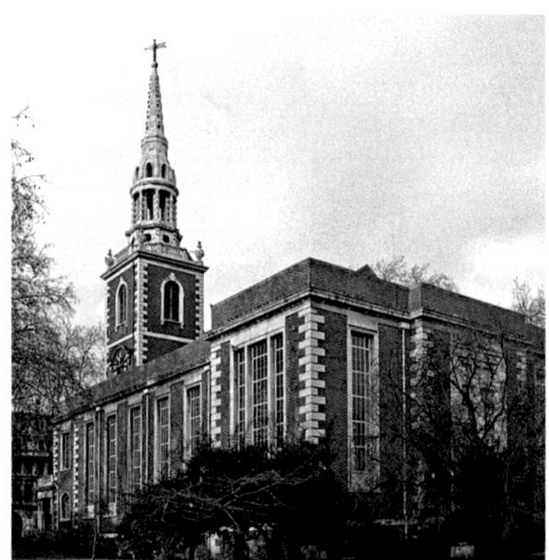

Set back behind a line of plane trees, St Mary's is a curious architectural hotchpotch. The rather fine steeple is all that remains of the original church: the under-scaled porch was added in 1903; and the remainder, including the nave, was destroyed in the Second World War and replaced by a stripped classical design.

Wesley's Chapel 1777 **H17** k
and **House** 1770
47 City Road EC2
⊖ Old Street

The architecture of Methodism? No: the chapel is a straightforward late Georgian design for a public building, in brick, altered in the 1890s when the present porch was added. John Wesley, the founder of Methodism, lived in the house (now a museum) and is buried in the churchyard.

Opposite the Chapel on the west side of City Road lies the tranquillity of Bunhill Fields, since 1365 a burial ground for dissidents, whose tombs include those of Daniel Defoe and William Blake.

Finsbury Square EC2 **H18** o
laid out 1777
George Dance the Younger
⊖ Moorgate
As with his other schemes, all the original houses of Dance's only large square have been destroyed. Even the central space has been humiliated by an ugly underground car park and poorly designed and maintained landscaping (proprietor London Borough of Islington). See also **Alfred Place** G13 and **America Square** L60.

Clerkenwell Conference Centre **H19** m
ex **Middlesex Sessions House**
1779–82
Clerkenwell Green EC1
Thomas Rogers
⊖ Farringdon
An early example of a court house, carried out in a very late Palladian style, commanding what remains of Clerkenwell's village green.

Cross Street c1780 **H20** a
N1
⊖ Angel
Sloping gently from Upper Street, the pavement and carriageway at the east end of Cross Street are separated in a manner more characteristic of Bristol and Bath than of London. The dilapidated houses on the south side are mostly late eighteenth century, and the doorways of numbers 33 and 35 are imitations of the Adams's **Adelphi** K58, as John Summerson noted.

St Botolph 1788–9 **H21** n
Aldersgate Street EC1
Nathaniel Wright
⊖ Barbican
A stuccoed and very rural-feeling parish church with a pleasant interior containing the original woodwork to gallery and organ.

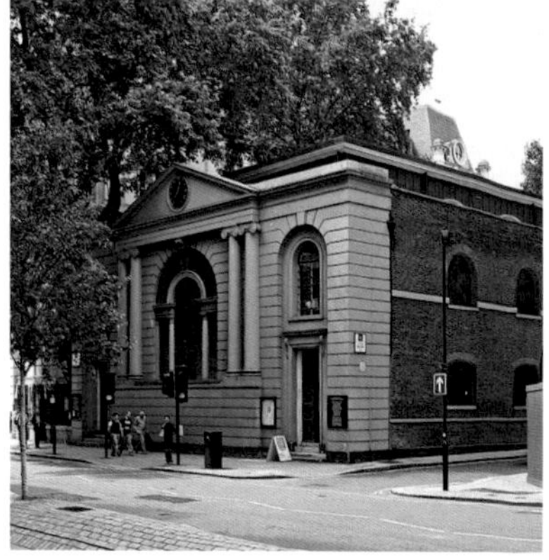

St James 1788–92 **H22** i
Clerkenwell Close, Clerkenwell Green EC1
James Carr
⊖ Farringdon
A typical London church in the tradition of Wren, Hawksmoor and Gibbs, St James stands on prominent ground at the north end of Clerkenwell Close. Its square stone tower, fine obelisk-like spire and entrance gate close the view from the Green up Clerkenwell Close. The stock brick exterior to the remainder is consistent but unexceptional. The interior has a curved west end and a gallery with two fine staircases, approached unexpectedly from rooms either side of the tower.

Warehouses **H23** p
ex **East India Company** 1798–1820
New Street, off Bishopsgate EC2
W Jupp, Henry Holland
⊖ Liverpool Street
Only the façade of these grand warehouses remains after their internal rebuilding as offices. They have lost the workman-like character which remains in the earlier Bengal Warehouses (1764) on the south side of the street.

Almeida Theatre **H24** a
ex **Literary Institute** 1837
Almeida Street N1
Roumieu and Gough
⇌ Essex Road
A good example of a secular public building of the period in the inevitable Greek Revival style with which both learning and religion were associated. After an undistinguished history it was restored for use as a 300-seat theatre in 1980; the back- and front-of-house were extended in 2001–2. The architects for both were Burrell Foley Fisher.

Warehouse 1858 **H25** m
12 Little Britain EC1
T Young and Son
⊖ St Paul's
Little Britain was spared from the westward extension of the dual carriageway, London Wall. Most of the commercial buildings have less charm than number 12, with its arcades on free-standing columns and Florentine cornice.

Model Dwellings 1860–2 **H26** h
Columbia Road E2
H A Darbishire
⊖ Shoreditch, Old Street

Baroness Burdett-Coutts was one of the aristocratic agitators behind the Metropolitan Association for Improving the Dwellings of the Industrial Classes, set up in 1852 as a rival to the Society for Improving the Condition of the Laboring Classes, which had started building in 1845 and commissioned the **Streatham Street flats** G34 using Henry Roberts as architect. Coutts's favourite architect was Darbishire, who later provided the dreadful model for the freestanding 'Peabody' blocks of flats in **Greenman Street** H29. However, these continuous four- and five-storey blocks with open staircases and short access galleries are along a street, and originally formed part of an ambitious plan which included the famous Columbia Market (demolished). They have been modernized, with stairs and bathrooms added on the south side.

Again with Darbishire, the Baroness built houses for her staff at **Holly Village** R11 in Highgate – the smarter end of London.

Holborn Viaduct 1863–9 **H27** m
EC1
William Heywood, engineer
⊖ Farringdon, St Paul's

The Victorians' concern with making London's traffic circulation efficient concentrated on improving the connection between the Cities of London and Westminster. The main route – Fleet Street and the Strand – had become hopelessly congested, and two bypass schemes were instituted: to the south, the **Embankment** K104, to the north the improvement of the line of the old Roman road between Marble Arch and the Post Office, north of St Paul's. Holborn Viaduct and the cutting of New Oxford Street were important links in the latter. The viaduct spans the valley of the Fleet River which runs, culverted, under Farringdon Street.

It is notable for its integration of engineering and architecture (see also **Waterloo Bridge** K160), evident in the decorative use of the cast iron beams which comprise the main span, and in the tastefully Italianate 'houses' at its abutments (only those on the south remain), which actually contain the staircases connecting Farringdon Street and High Holborn. Fine art is represented in the improving statues on the parapets.

Shops and houses 1863 **H28** o
91–101 Worship Street EC2
Philip Webb
⊖ Old Street

Work by the architect who designed the **Red House** X8 for William Morris is unexpected in commercial Shoreditch, and the style of Webb's short terrace actually resembles the high street of a quiet country town. The buttressed facade divides the terrace into six bays, and the ground-floor shops have a continuous shallow pitched roof, behind which the remaining floors are set back. There are two arched windows to the first floor, the second floor has three extremely small square apertures, and the roof has high dormers. At the eastern end of the terrace is a drinking fountain.

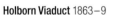

Housing for Peabody Trust 1865 **H29** a
Greenman Street N1
H A Darbishire
⇌ Essex Road
The Peabody Trust built large numbers of 'improving' sanitary housing schemes to many designs, and it is surprising how many survive. This is one of the nastiest: four five-storey blocks (called 'Block A', 'Block B', etc) face each other round a tarmac square. The scant Italianate styling does nothing to lessen the prison-like effect of the deeply recessed windows. Contrast with the nearby refurbished **Theberton Street** G32.

Smithfield Market 1866 **H30** m
Farringdon Street, Charterhouse Street and Smithfield Street EC1
Horace Jones
⊖ Barbican
Smithfield is London's principal wholesale meat market, located on the site of a horse and cattle market dating back to 1200. Unlike Covent Garden (London's main fruit, flower and vegetable wholesale market, which was moved ignominiously to the 'industrial zone' of Nine Elms) and Billingsgate fish market (now on the Isle of Dogs), Smithfield is still active as a traditional city market, complete with arcaded avenues of meat stores. The market buildings are impressively straightforward and typically mid-Victorian in scale; the four massive trading halls are organized around Grand Avenue, East Poultry Avenue and West Poultry Avenue, all lit from above by linear glazed lanterns. The exterior, of red brick with stone dressings, has domed corner turrets.

To the west, the new market hall (1962–3) by T P Bennett lost the arcaded quality of the original, but instead has a massive concrete central dome.

Peabody Trust Dwellings 1870 **H31** j
Chequer Street, Dufferin Street, Whitecross Street and Roscoe Street EC1
⊖ Old Street
'Tough' and 'grim' are the adjectives generally applied to these six-storey tenement buildings – a standard philanthropic housing recipe. Although the buildings provide little in the way of light and air, they nevertheless form identifiable streets with proper addresses. The recent swing of the philanthropic housing pendulum means that residents suffer from a surfeit of light and air at the expense of isolation from the city.

Liverpool Street Station **H32** o
1874–5, extended 1891–4
Hotel 1884, altered 1901
EC2
E Wilson, extension by W N Asbee;
hotel originally Charles Barry,
but altered by R Edis
⊖ Liverpool Street

One of the last major stations to be built in London (only Marylebone was to follow), Liverpool Street consolidated the pattern of rail termini which persists today. It served as the metropolitan terminus for what was to become the Great Eastern Railway, and more locally for trains which put the north-eastern suburbs – Enfield, Stamford Hill, Tottenham and Edmonton – within easy commuting distance of the City.

The buildings are not particularly fine – the Gothic is more restrained than that of St Pancras. In the 1980s, as a result of the massive **Broadgate Development** H44, the station was partly rebuilt and significantly renovated. Like other redevelopments of the capital's railway stations – see **Charing Cross** K102, **Cannon Street** L81 – the original building was diminished in character.

Note the renovation to the Great Eastern Hotel by the Manser Practice of 2000 with its impressive new atrium drawing together the various parts of the original hotel.

Hanover School 1876, 1932 **H33** e
Noel Road N1
⊖ Angel

This architecturally sophisticated early primary school is shoehorned into a narrow linear site between the tight residential street dimensions of Noel Road to the north and the expansiveness of the City Road Basin to the south. The single aspect plan provides south-facing classrooms with generous windows and balconies giving magical and unexpectedly long views to the activities of the Basin and to the towers of the city of London beyond. The corridors are expressed to the street behind double-height brick arcading leading to staircases and entrances at either end – an example of gender differences supporting symmetry in school design. Commonsensically the playground is on the roof, also with magnificent views behind its netted enclosure, an arrangement that present legislation would forbid. Note the treads and risers of the staircases are expressed in applied stone as functional decoration to the façade. As a result of subsidence in 1932 the school partly fell into the canal and was subsequently rebuilt.

Bishopsgate Institute 1894 **H34** o
Bishopsgate EC2
C H Townsend
⊖ Liverpool Street

The beige faïence façade is a mixture of Victorian and proto-art nouveau motifs. The composition is symmetrical: a large round arch for the entrance is recessed between narrow towers. The art nouveau decoration of this conventional scheme is rare in London: there are flat trees on the towers, and under the steep roof between the towers is a fine panel of lettering. See also Townsend's **Whitechapel Art Gallery** L98 and **Horniman Museum** X9.

City University College Building **H35** i
ex **Northampton Institute** 1896
St John Street, Spencer Street and Northampton Square EC1
Edward Mountford
⊖ Angel

This massive and ambitious building by one of the principal architects of the Edwardian baroque revival (see also Mountford's **Old Bailey** L99 and Battersea Town Hall) responds successfully to a demanding site – the acute corner of Spencer and St John Streets to the north of Northampton Square. The resolution of this corner is a tour de force – turret, cupola and walls interlock with the big curved gable of the hall behind. The front to St John Street is asymmetrical and very grand, and the central entrance tower (reminiscent more of Townsend than of the baroque) is topped with massive brick- and stone-striped drums surmounted by a shallow dome. Unlike newer City University buildings to the east, the Institute has a direct formal relationship with Northampton Square, but note by way of contrast across St John's Street the cool minimalism of the **School of Social Sciences** (Stanton Williams 2004).

Boundary Street Estate 1897–1900 **H36** I
Arnold Circus E2
LCC Architects Department;
Owen Fleming
⊖ Shoreditch
The first and probably the best of many large housing estates designed by the LCC at the turn of the century is also the least well known. The scheme, which replaced the infamous 'Jago' slum immediately east of Shoreditch Parish Church, is a series of streets radiating from Arnold Circus. The buildings are five-storey tenements and their architecture reflects the designers' taste for the work of Street, Shaw and Philip Webb: high gables, good-quality brickwork and, around Arnold Circus, bands of yellow brick to give the façades greater elaboration. 5524 people were rehoused at a density of 200 people per acre, with all the support facilities of shops, surgery, school and so on. This estate, despite its conspicuous neglect, is a very fine example of urban design. It supports the claim that the output of the early LCC is to be counted among the highest achievements of the Arts and Crafts movement in English architecture.

Britannic House **H37** O
ex **Lutyens House** 1924–7, 1987–9
Moorgate and Finsbury Circus EC2
Edwin Lutyens
Peter Inskip and Peter Jenkins Architects
⊖ Moorgate
Only the oval plan remains of George Dance the Younger and William Montague's Finsbury Circus (1815), once part of an ambitious extension to the City including **Finsbury Square** H18 to the north. On the north-west side is Britannic House, Lutyens's first large London building. The classical repertoire is stretched to seven storeys, to form a magnificent curved frontage to the circus. A rusticated base supports two rusticated floors; above these is a three-storey Corinthian screen of attached columns – a pity he did not design the whole circus.

The renovation of the 1980s introduced an impressively large-scale semicircular atrium to increase the penetration of natural light to an otherwise deep and dark office. This was a good example of the contemporary approach, based on discontinuity and surprise, to the appropriation of dormant space in City office buildings. The circular void brings to mind, albeit in modern dress, Vignola's rotunda at the Palazzo Farnese at Caprarola, one of the inspirations for the original building.

Stone House 1927 **H38** O
136 Bishopsgate EC2
Richardson and Gill
⊖ Liverpool Street
A large, handsome corner building: the ornate curved metalwork above the double-storey plinth refers to art nouveau, while the generous curved corner with large and simple openings anticipates later commercial street architecture.

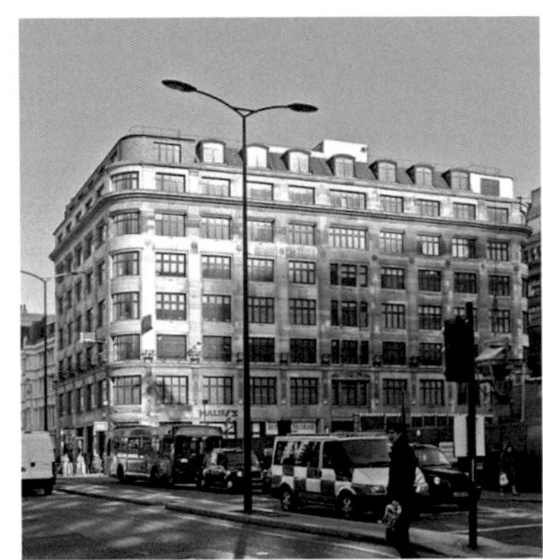

Spa Green Estate 1950 **H39** e
Rosebery Avenue and
St John Street EC1
Lubetkin and Tecton
⊖ Angel

Three slabs run north south: two straight ones of eight storeys with, between them, a sinuous one of four storeys. In this housing for Finsbury Borough Council, Lubetkin and Tecton were unable to adopt Le Corbusier's ruthless social programme – the self-contained housing unit – and, in spite of their politics, their housing done after 1945 shows no clear idea of what a partly reconstructed city should be like. The obsessive pattern-making of the façades is as arbitrary as the arrangement of the blocks – both are examples of the practice's decline from the clarity of **Highpoint 1** R27 into busy formalism. In 2008 a very successful renovation project was completed. The original polychromy was restored and the brick and tiled façades repaired, the result a rebuke to those London boroughs to whom 'improvement' means insulated over-cladding and new, crude plastic or aluminium windows.

Barbican Estate 1959–79 **H40** n
bounded by London Wall,
Beech Street and Moorgate EC2 and
Aldersgate Street EC1
Chamberlin, Powell and Bon
⊖ Barbican, St Paul's, Moorgate

That the area of the City most devastated by the Second World War should be developed into a new quarter of 24 hectares (60 acres) comprising 2113 flats for 6500 people is indicative of the good intentions of post-war socialism. That the forms for this memorial should be 125m (412ft) high towers loosely mixed with slab buildings (the tallest residential buildings in Europe when planned and the only high-density housing models available in the late 1950s) is the predictable outcome. Whatever the merits of the restored St Giles church with its new churchyard, the excavated Roman wall, the generous landscaping and the Arts Centre, these do not ameliorate the emptiness of the Barbican and its severance from the rest of the City. It has become, however, a highly sought-after address, offering what Cedric Price described as 'well-serviced anonymity'.

Successive managements of the Arts and Conference centre (completed in 1981) have worried about its confusing circulation, the decoration of its foyers and public spaces, and commissioned several improvement schemes, the latest of which was designed by AHMM in 2007.

London Wall 1963–91 **H41** n
between St Martin-le-Grand
and Moorgate EC2
City of London Planning Department;
various architects
⊖ Moorgate, Liverpool Street

London Wall was part of a huge redevelopment area in the City, much of which had been bombed in the Second World War. To the north is the residential part, the **Barbican** H40, and to the south the 'Barbican Commercial Fringe', originally devoted to six office buildings, regularly arranged on either side of a new road, part of an intended new bypass north of the City.

With hindsight, London Wall can be regarded either as a plausible idea let down in its realization by poor architecture, or as a proposal so bizarre and problematical as to be incapable of success. The six office buildings of similar format were placed on two-storey podia in a staggered arrangement, not at right angles to the road but parallel to Moorgate to the east. The roofs of the podia, when connected with bridges across

Looking east from St Martin-le-Grand

roads, were supposed to provide a new traffic-free 'ground level'. It was intended that this format should be extended to most new buildings in the City and some, such as the **Commercial Union building** L125, still bear the evidence of the subsequently mostly abandoned scheme. The difficulties were first, that the English climate made life on the podia unpleasant for a large part of the year; second, that few architects have been able to relate a building to its podium successfully; third, that a main entrance to a building was impossible to design (witness the **Museum of London**'s H42 unsatisfactory arrangements); fourth, that the street was destroyed, even for the motorist; and fifth, that there never was the slightest chance that a substantial portion of the City could have been rebuilt in this way. Barbican and London Wall remain islands approached by inadequate flights of stairs.

Only forty years after the completion of London Wall, and in the waves of speculation which overtook London in the late 1980s, some of the office buildings were rebuilt, drastically altering what later appears to be the modest scale of the original scheme. The huge Alban House, by Terry Farrell and Co., contributed a muddled form and bridged the road, destroying the original pattern and offering nothing in return but sheer bulk.

Museum of London 1975 **H42** n
London Wall EC2
Powell and Moya
⊖ Barbican, St Paul's
The Museum of London is sited inaccessibly at one corner of a traffic intersection and is approached at an upper level by bridges. Its banal and utilitarian architecture is completely inadequate. Don't be put off. The museum contains an extraordinary fund of material on London's history and social life from prehistoric times to the present, though this deserves better housing. See also **London Wall** H41.

Offices and flats 1976–9 **H43** m
24 Britton Street EC1
YRM Partnership with
Fitzroy Robinson and Partners
⊖ Farringdon
On a steeply sloping backlands site next to a small former churchyard, the three-storey office building sits on a two-storey podium, the roof of which forms a courtyard at the level of Britton Street. The frame of the building is covered with well-made aluminium panels originally finished in scarlet paint. The six-storey block of flats and shops facing the street was built behind the reconstructed façade of a former gin distillery, designed by E W Mountford about 1900.

Broadgate 1984–6 **H44** o
Finsbury Pavement EC2
Arup Associates
Broadgate stage 1 1984–88
between Sun Street, Finsbury Avenue, South Place/Eldon Street and west of Liverpool Street Station
Arup Associates
Broadgate stage 2 1988–91
between Bishopsgate and Appold Street,
Skidmore Owings and Merrill
⊖ Liverpool Street
Two contiguous and ambitious schemes on the northern edge of the City and extending its commercial value, by two of the few London developers who patronized good architecture: Greycoat and Rosehaugh Stanhope.

Broadgate Circle

For the Finsbury Pavement buildings and the first stage of Broadgate, Arup Associates ignored the models of the city as a machine and instead revived the urban forms last used in the 1950s. 150,000 square metres (1,615,000sq ft) of office buildings of modest height are effortlessly connected with the existing city. They are informally arranged to compose two new linked squares, one empty, the other filled with an elaborate terraced circular feature containing shops and with a skating rink at its centre. These outdoor spaces are finished with fine materials previously only seen in Europe and North America (compare for example the **Barbican** H40 and **London Wall** H41). The offices are entered through semi-public atriums whose glazed roofs are the pretext for virtuoso displays of engineering. The outsides of the buildings became successively more mannered through the various phases: the earlier façades of Finsbury Pavement are in metal with refined sunbreakers, while those of Arup's Broadgate attempt a more decorative treatment with implausible 'curtains' of fretted granite.

To the north and east of Liverpool Street Station the second stage of Broadgate, by SOM, while following the same urban model, introduces a new and overbearing scale, particularly in the very long fourteen-storey block to Bishopsgate – whose vacuous architecture does little to disguise its bulk. 'Exchange Square', built on a deck over the railway tracks and facing south, provides, however, a well-landscaped retreat from the noise and density of its immediate surroundings.

House 1987 **H45** m
44 Britton Street EC1
CZWG Architects (Campbell, Zogolovitch, Wilkinson and Gough)
⊖ Farringdon

This is an improbable part of London for a highly individual house, planned on four floors with a studio in its pitched roof. The yashmak of diagonal screens, the lintels of concrete logs, and the grading of the exterior brickwork from dark to light are just some of the building's eccentric elevational devices.

Offices 1987–90 **H46** n
1 Moor Lane, Chiswell Street EC1
Denys Lasdun, Peter Softley and Associates
⊖ Moorgate

An impressive but enigmatic speculative office building in a style completely unprecedented and unexpected in Lasdun and Softley's work. The building is one of a contemporary series developed along Chiswell Street and fully occupies the block on which it stands. It is clad entirely in two layers of glass, the outer one green and frameless with patch fixings, the inner one framed and visible only at night. The lower parts of the exterior are sheer, but the glass on the upper storeys is thrown into a wildly picturesque and faceted silhouette with corner towers, the whole suggesting the forms of defence. It is surmounted by an enormous pitched roof which spans the atrium, around which the offices are disposed.

In 2007 the original entrances on the north-east and south-east corners were blocked up and a conventional new one inserted in the Chiswell Street frontage.

Hackney Community College **H47** h
1991
Falkirk Street, N1
Hampshire County Council Architects Department, Colin Stansfield-Smith, Perkings and Ogden
⊖ Old Street

As local authority architects' departments were being shut down unceremoniously across the country following Thatcher's moratorium on building the welfare state, at Hampshire in the 1980s, through the energies of Stansfield-Smith, the state educational programme was kept alive. This large community college in Hackney serving 14,000 students was the beneficiary of this resistance and continued expertise. Ironically, security was a key issue for this community initiative. Whilst managing to maintain a series of active frontages to the surrounding streets, like a contemporary monastery, the outer perimeter protects a large and informally landscaped central courtyard, separated from the world outside. The construction of brick, laminated timber arcades, and stretched fabric give the buildings an appropriately institutional expression.

Victoria Miro Gallery 2006 **H48** f
16 Wharf Road N1
Claudio Silvestrin
⊖ Old Street
In a cumulative fashion the gallery has skilfully renovated space in an existing furniture warehouse over a period of six years. Don't be put off by a relatively uneventful ground floor reception, which leads into the interior of the site and the discovery of the canal's Wenlock Basin. From here a dramatically narrow diagonal staircase leads up through three floors to a place of vantage overlooking the entrance on Wharf Road. Then a series of splendid lofty galleries provide a sequence concluding in an exaggerated cantilevered balcony with an opportunity to view floating objects in the basin below. The public sequence follows the letter Z in section, creating surprising and magical events at each change of direction with a great economy of effort.

White Cube Gallery 2002 **H49** k
Hoxton Square N1
Mike Rundell
⊖ Old Street
Hoxton Square and the White Cube have become synonymous with this part of London as an artistic enclave. The minimal two-storey addition on the routine red-brick Edwardian base is audacious, but it is a disappointment that this houses offices and conference facilities and not a gallery. See also the White Cube Gallery in Mason's Yard, St James's, where it occupies a converted redundant electricity substation.

Houses and **flats** **H50** l
Dirty House, Chance Street E1
David Adjaye Associates 2002
Houses, 13–17 Chance Street E1
Stephen Taylor 2006
Flats, 41 Old Nichol Street E2
Maccreanor Lavington 2005
⊖ Old Street
As gaps in the mews and byways of North London gave opportunities for architects such as **Cullinan** C11, **Wild** C16, **Hopkins** B29, and **Foster and Rogers** C10 to build houses either for themselves or friends, over the last decade similar possibilities have arisen in east London. To the east of Shoreditch High Street three projects are noteworthy.

The **Dirty House**, unlike the artist's studio that provided a background to the production of art, is a studio house which is itself a work of art and radically distinct from its neighbours. A fully glazed living pavilion sits on top of an enigmatic two-storey cube. This is a conversion of a 1930s warehouse now coated in anti-graffiti black paint, with windows fitted with mirror glass. Two double-height studios occupy the interior. There is, however, a particular drama to the exaggerated cantilever of the pavilion's roof seen hovering above the black cube. It is particularly effective at night.

Dirty House

Three small houses, 13, 15 and 17 Chance Street, successfully reinvestigated the possibilities of living in 4m (13ft) wide frontages, a perennial

London housing topic – see for example Howell's 1956 3.6m (12ft) wide terraced **houses** B22.

At Old Nicol Street, Maccreanor Lavington designed a new four-storey block of **flats** and a **studio** adjoining and sharing a staircase with an existing warehouse. The façade of timber and glass is as carefully proportioned and built as would be expected from the architects responsible for one of the earliest contributions to the redevelopment of Shoreditch, the multifunctional Lux building on the south-west corner of Hoxton Square, completed in 1997.

Houses in Chance Street

Offices 2003 **H51** o
30 Finsbury Square EC2
Eric Parry Architects
⊖ Moorgate

This is a paradoxical building. A first impression is that, within its acceptance of conventional urban design guidelines, it appears unusual. On the one hand the building wears the same sober city suit of Portland stone as its neighbours and conforms obediently both to the building line and to Islington's 30m (100ft) height limit. On the other hand the almost universal structural convention of placing load upon load has been put aside in favour of structural transfer. Added to this, the introduction of the picturesque in the ad hoc arrangement of the piers sets the building against existing conventions. On closer examination it is noted that the piers are audaciously load-bearing masonry and that they act as a *brise soleil* to the fully glazed façade behind. This is a remarkable achievement, creating a counterpoint between the regular rhythm of the stainless-steel mullions and the syncopation of the stone piers in the foreground. As a pictorial device this introduces a metaphor of geological strata into the London street, which creates a problem in identifying the front door. In less capable hands these ideas have degenerated into cliché.

The Broadgate Tower **H52** o
and **201 Bishopsgate** 2008
EC2
SOM (Chicago)
⊖ Moorgate

Possibly the final buildings on the Broadgate site H44, these were when built the largest speculative development ever carried out in the City and provided 76,000 square metres (822,000sq ft) of office space on a difficult site spanning the main-line railway tracks of Liverpool Street station. They are impressive only for their size and bulk, and will perhaps come to represent the 'Livingstone Years', when any development tall and 'global' enough gained his active support, much as **Centre Point** K175 came to stand for the LCC's policy of placing high buildings at important road intersections with little regard for the consequences at ground level.

View from Spitalfields

The 'galleria' between the two buildings (September 2008)

continued section E

continued section T

continued section M

Paddington
continued section E
c
d
Bayswater
g
h
continued section J
Round Pond
KENSINGTON GARDENS
k
l
Kensington
o
p
KENSINGTON AND CHELSEA LB
continued section M
25
27
21
30
29
4
6
31
2
6
10
11
19
22
13
24
18
16

Notting Hill ■ Ladbroke Grove ■ Bayswater ■ Holland Park ■ Kensington ■ Kensington Gardens

The first developments here were royal and aristocratic: Henry VIII enclosed Hyde Park, including what is now Kensington Gardens, for hunting grounds; in 1600 **Holland House** I1 was started as a country manor and estate (now Holland Park); and **Kensington Palace** I2 was enlarged for William and Mary in the 1690s.

The westward development of the area was a nineteenth-century enterprise, and illustrates the changes in housing layouts in the period. In the 1820s Orme Square, north of Kensington Palace, was laid out as a simple and traditional rectangle open to the south. But the most important contribution to Victorian ideas of town planning was the **Ladbroke Estate** I7, started in 1840: in contrast to contemporary Pimlico, houses were laid out on sloping ground in a loose and picturesque way, using Italianate styling. Both the pattern and the style became very influential.

In the 1840s and '50s Bayswater was laid out north of Hyde Park. The model was Georgian, based on squares, but the houses were huge, Italianate and very un-Georgian – all are now hotels or subdivided into flats. At the same time, Kensington Palace Gardens was developed, with opulent and very large detached houses and lavish planting of trees. These private mansions (now occupied mainly by embassies and consulates) are perhaps London's nearest equivalent to Beverly Hills.

To the west, the streets north of Holland Park were laid out and lined with sumptuous Italianate terraces, still with their own mews, and later in the century the streets on either side of Addison Road became the site of more adventurous experiments, for example houses by Norman Shaw and Halsey Ricardo (I14 and I20).

In 1863, London's first underground railway was opened, from Bishop's Bridge Road near Paddington to Farringdon. Its successor, the Circle Line, runs partially in an open cutting along the western edge of the section.

The museums were established in the 1850s (see section J), and South Kensington's long streets of Italianate houses (Queen's Gate and Queen's Gate Terrace, for example) followed in the 1860s and '70s. The stuccoed homogeneity of these large houses (subdivided soon after they were built and probably always too big for their intended occupants) was disrupted only by the later red brick of Norman Shaw (see I13).

By the end of the nineteenth century Kensington High Street was a fashionable shopping street and a rival to the West End. Its commercial heyday was in the 1920s and '30s, and it has good examples of department store buildings of the period, from the modernistic **Barkers** I19 to the art deco **Derry and Toms** I22.

Unlike most London Boroughs, the Royal Borough of Kensington and Chelsea took the lead in improving the quality of public space. In 2003 Kensington High Street was cleansed of the traffic engineer's absent-minded obsession with traffic lanes and the squalor of low-grade materials and it was admirably reordered, repaved and refurnished to the highest European standards.

Kensington Palace

Holland House 1606–7 **I1** j
Holland Park W14
⊖ High Street Kensington
The ruined Holland House is the only remaining example in central London of an E-plan Jacobean manor. The front court was south-facing and graced with a loggia, and the house is set in its own large and pretty grounds – the first park west of Kensington Gardens. The west wing has been rebuilt as a youth hostel. For a complete Jacobean house see **Chariton House** U1.

The Orangery

Kensington Palace 1661–1702 **I2** k
W8
Christopher Wren, Nicholas Hawksmoor, William Kent, Thomas Ripley(?)
⊖ High Street Kensington
In 1689 the bronchitic William III withdrew from Whitehall Palace to the purer air of Kensington. There he bought Nottingham House (built for the Earl of Nottingham in 1661) as his permanent residence. The king did not, however, bestow any royal magnificence on Kensington, unlike Hampton Court. Pevsner observes, 'never did any powerful monarch of the age ... build a less ostentatious palace [But if] the social and political implications of the building are considered, this sensible, domestic, one is tempted to say democratic, structure assumes a new meaning, even if not a higher architectural value'.

Kensington Palace is the result of a series of pragmatic additions, begun with William III and continued by George I, producing a disjointed overall composition grouped around three courtyards. Wren's south and east façades have some monumental ambition, but the remainder, built entirely of brick with rubbed-brick detailing, resembles almshouses more than a royal palace. The interiors by Wren (c1690) and William Kent (1723–7) are correspondingly simple. The grandest addition is the King's Gallery (1695–6); this and the Orangery (1704–5), are attributed by Kerry Downes to Hawksmoor. The fine brick exterior and austere white interiors of the Orangery link the design with those at Easton Neston, Northamptonshire, and Blenheim, Oxfordshire.

Edwardes Square 1811–20 I3 n
W8
⊖ High Street Kensington
A modest late Georgian square, Edwardes Square derives its name from William Edwardes, the second Lord Kensington, who leased land from the Holland House Estate. It has the quality of a large back garden formed by the back walls of Earls Terrace to the north, a medley of nondescript buildings to the south, and two consistent terraces to the east and west. The Tuscan garden house or temple is particularly delightful.

Houses 1823–4 I4 h
3–5 Porchester Terrace W2
J C Loudon
⊖ Queensway, Lancaster Gate
This apparently detached villa (designed by Loudon, the famous landscape architect) is an example of the well-established English tradition of domestic architectural illusion. With the symmetry of the central domed conservatory, side verandas and dummy windows masking the party walls, Loudon ingeniously concealed the pair of semi-detached houses within (one of which he lived in). During repairs in 1972 later Victorian additions to the sides of the house were removed, revealing the clarity of the original design.

Norland Square 1837–46 I5 i
and **Royal Crescent**
St James's Gardens, Addison Avenue and Queensdale Road W11
Robert Cantwell
⊖ Holland Park
Royal Crescent's regular four-storey stuccoed façade with cylindrical turrets, Norland Square's shallow bow fronts, St James's Gardens' stone-faced connected pavilions, and Addison Avenue's generous dimensions and plane trees are all conveniently connected by Queensdale Road and Princedale Road. This combination of urban types – crescent, gardens, avenue and square – could have been a useful model for the reconstruction of London after the comprehensive disasters of the 1960s.

Royal Crescent

Kensington Palace Gardens 1843 I6 g
W8
laid out by James Pennethorne
⊖ High Street Kensington
Private roads with lodge gates at either end were common in the eighteenth and nineteenth centuries: this street of opulent villas in spacious gardens is a rare and anachronistic survival. It was laid out on the site of the kitchen gardens of **Kensington Palace** I2, and between 1844 and 1870 the following architects contributed: entrance lodges and numbers 18–19, Wyatt and Brandon; number 8a, Owen Jones; number 15, Knowles; numbers 12 and 18, Banks and Barry; number 12a, Decimus Burton, Sydney Smirke and James Murray; number 13, C F Richardson. At the south end of the road is Palace Green, where in 1868 Philip Webb built **number 1** I10 for the Earl of Carlisle. Number 2 is the neo-Georgian house Thackeray designed for himself (1861).

Ladbroke Square

Lansdowne Road

Elgin Crescent: the gardens

Ladbroke Road

Ladbroke Estate started c1850 I7 f
bounded by Kensington Park Road, Clarendon Road, Cornwall Crescent and Holland Park Avenue W11
Thomas Allom
⊖ Notting Hill Gate, Holland Park, Ladbroke Grove

The Italianate houses of the Ladbroke Estate are large, but lack architectural distinction. However, the estate was one of the most important contributions to early Victorian suburban planning. Since (like the later **Bedford Park** T17) it was such an influential and much-copied model, its virtues are easy to overlook. Its early success was due both to its site – on a healthy breezy hill as opposed to the contemporary development on Belgravia's drained swamp – and to its informal, fairly low-density layout. The north–south axis of the Estate is **Ladbroke Grove**, a wide street which rises over the hill and passes beside the very large **Ladbroke Square** on the site of Ladbroke's racecourse, the Hippodrome. The Ladbroke coat of arms can still be seen on the iron gates leading into the square from **Kensington Park Gardens**. Individual houses on the south side are large and stuccoed.

To the north of the square are **Lansdowne Crescent**, **Elgin Crescent** and **Clarendon Road**. The houses range from semi-detached villas to groups of four, and follow the curves of the crescents to make very pleasant streets. The remarkable communal gardens contained by the houses are one of the most congenial arrangements in London: in a sense the traditional London square has been inverted, as access to the gardens (exclusive to the residents) is through each dwelling's private back garden.

29½ Lansdowne Crescent, by Jeremy Lever (1973), ingeniously fills a left-over wedge with a 3m (10ft) frontage to the street in an existing crescent. Its stuccoed front, bay window and simple openings unite it with its neighbours without recourse to period pastiche.

Lansdowne House c1860 **I8** e
8e Lansdowne Road W11
H Flockhart
⊖ Holland Park

A multi-storey group of studios, rare in London, but more familiar in Paris and Brussels. The tall composition of stock brick, with stone detailing, turreted corners, north-facing studio windows, and the seventh floor set back to form a pediment, is an unexpected urban addition to the leafy Arcadia of Lansdowne Road. Charles Ricketts, Charles Shannon and Glyn Philpot were among artist residents here.

Leighton House 1865–79 **I9** n
12 Holland Park Road W14
George Aitchison
⊖ High Street Kensington

Leighton House was the home and studio of Lord Leighton (1830–96), one of the most successful and fashionable painters of his generation. Now open as a museum, it displays some of his paintings and houses his collection of drawings. The classical exterior was very unusual for the time (Webb's Gothic studio for Val Prinsep was next door) and was like an Italianate villa, reflecting the style of Leighton's own paintings. The richly coloured interiors – red walls and black woodwork – imitated a Venetian palazzo.

In 1877 Aitchison added the Arab Hall, based on the hall of the twelfth-century Moslem Palace of La Zisa at Palermo, to display Leighton's collection of Saracenic tiles. William de Morgan designed new tilework, Boehm carved the capitals, and the mosaic frieze is by Walter Crane. The house established Aitchison as a master of decoration. Note also the window with a sliding, mirrored shutter, positioned above a fireplace (the flue ingeniously concealed by an S bend) and looking out to the garden on the ground floor. The back door for the models, the generous promenades for the clients, and the luxurious studios are a reminder of the successful artist's social position in the mid-Victorian era.

House 1868–70 **I10** k
1 Palace Green,
Kensington Palace Gardens W8
Philip Webb
⊖ High Street Kensington

Built for the Hon. George Howard (later ninth Earl of Carlisle), this is Webb's most important town house. The original design was turned down by the Commissioners (headed by the architect James Pennethorne) because of the absence of stone as a relief to the brick façade, and Webb finally conceded some stonework in the elevation. The tall red-brick building has an exceptionally deep plan and an asymmetrical front with a pointed pediment to the porch, a three-storey bay window to the right and open battlements above. In the side elevation is a tall arched niche with a staircase leading to the garden; either side of the niche are modulated chimney breasts. The combination of tall Queen Anne-style windows and pointed arches considerably predates Norman Shaw's use of them, but it has been said that Webb subscribed more to the rational principles of Pugin than to the artistic and empirical methods of Shaw. Gavin Stamp observes that 'many of Webb's buildings have a certain awkwardness which was proof of his Gothic revival and puritanical conscience'.

St Mary Abbots 1869–72 **I11** k
Kensington High Street and
Kensington Church Street W8
George Gilbert Scott
⊖ High Street Kensington
In this church Scott was designing in Gothic while his classicist **Foreign Office** K106 was being built. It is a dull design in Early English style, with a very tall spire 85m (278ft) high.

Linley Sambourne House **I12** n
c.1870
18 Stafford Terrace W8
⊖ High Street Kensington
The house of illustrator Linley Sambourne (1844–1910), with interiors preserved much as he left them. They give a rare opportunity to see how the interior of an otherwise characteristic Kensington house was furnished by an 'artistic' owner.

The house was bought by the GLC in 1980, and was subsequently managed by the Royal Borough of Kensington and Chelsea and opened to the public.

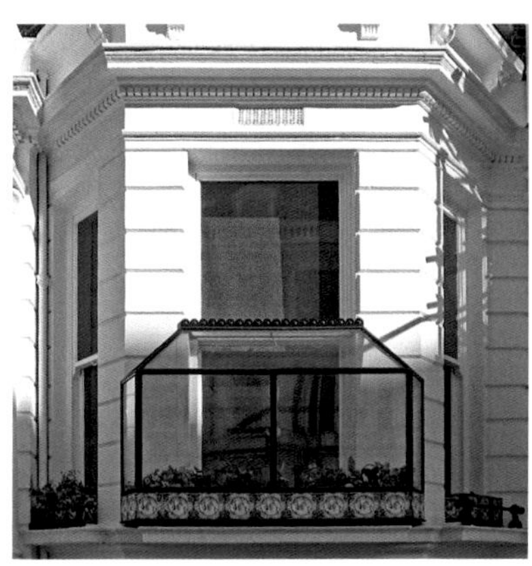

Bay window of the ground floor

House 1875 **I13** p
196 Queen's Gate SW7
R Norman Shaw
⊖ High Street Kensington
A characteristically asymmetrical composition of superimposed Dutch pilasters, early Renaissance decoration, and Shaw's by then typical window motif. The result is a complex arrangement of projecting balconies and local symmetries, built in red brick with terracotta decorative panels. With 180 Queen's Gate (demolished in the early 1960s) this house set the style – which became known as 'Pont Street Dutch' – for speculative developments in Kensington up to the end of the century.

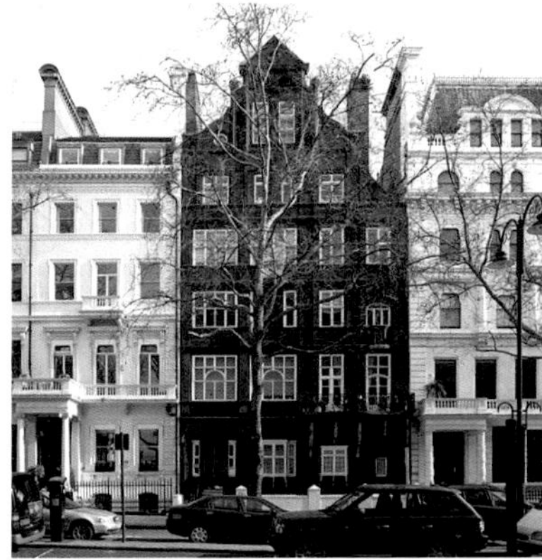

Studio house 1875–6 **I14** n
8 Melbury Road W14
R Norman Shaw
⊖ High Street Kensington
Built for the painter Marcus Stone, this is the Queen Anne style at its most fluent and memorable – contemporary with Shaw's own house at **6 Ellerdale Road** A11 and the **Swan House** N21. The composition of the ground floor is asymmetrical, with narrow vertical windows, above which three symmetrical oriel windows are cut through the cornice. At the same time, across the road at **number 31** and obscured by trees, Shaw designed another studio house for the painter Luke Fildes. It is less notable and has been considerably altered.

Tower House 1876–81 **I15** n
29 Melbury Road W14
William Burges
⊖ High Street Kensington

Built by Burges (a convinced Gothicist) for himself, the Tower House contrasts with the new Queen Anne style of its contemporary neighbours (numbers 8 and 31) by R Norman Shaw. The exterior, of massive and picturesque brickwork, with the corner dominated by a circular staircase tower topped by a conical roof, shows all Burges's preoccupations with medieval castles and the theoretical work of Viollet-le-Duc. But the magic of the house is in the inaccessible interiors, as described by Gavin Stamp: 'All the rooms tell a story. The dining room was meant to convey an idea of Chaucer's House of Fame; the library, with its birds painted by H Stacy Marks, has an elaborate castellated stone chimneypiece illustrating the dispersal of the parts of speech ... A staircase window illustrates the storming of the castle of love. Burges finished his own bedroom so that he could imagine himself – when in an opiate haze – at the bottom of the sea.'

Stratford Studios c1880 **I16** o
off Stratford Road W8
⊖ High Street Kensington

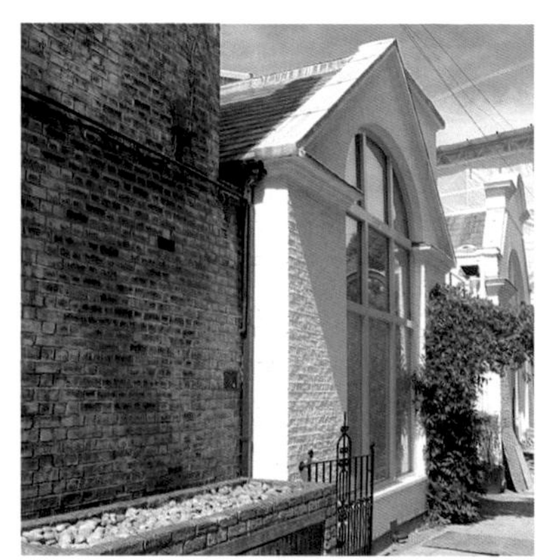

A gated, miniature close of ten high, Dutch-gabled studios: a reminder of the area's artistic tradition, given impetus by the Great Exhibition of 1851. The buildings have now been gentrified and converted into family houses, although their original use is unmistakable.

Studios 1882 **I17** j
77–9 Bedford Gardens W8
R Stark Wilkinson
⊖ Notting Hill Gate

In the 'suburban' context of the early-nineteenth-century villas and cottages of Bedford Gardens, this five-storey group of eleven artists' studios is exceptional for its 'urban' scale: as the foundation stone records, the building is 39m (128ft) deep (north south) and 11m (34ft) wide. The working studios are approached by a public central staircase around a generous well, daylit by a large glass lantern above. The street façade is formed by north-facing studio windows, set back in section between robust red-brick piers.

House 1887–9 **I18** p
170 Queen's Gate SW7
R Norman Shaw
⊖ South Kensington

The elongated windows to either side of the central bay are the only clues to the authorship of this large and restrained classical house: 170 Queen's Gate is the bridge between the free composition characteristic of Shaw's earlier designs and the baroque revival of his later works.

Barkers Department Store **I19** k
1904–38
Kensington High Street W8
Bernard George 1937–8
⊖ High Street Kensington
George's façade and remodelling of Barkers store (previously designed by John Barker, 1904, and Reginald Blomfeld, 1912–13) completed its long building history. Barkers and **Derry and Toms** I22 next door gave London a fragmentary art deco commercial frontage, a reminder that England during this period was less innovative than at the turn of the century and was reverting to her previous role as a sympathetic receiver of European ideas – in this case the jazz modern of Paris in the later 1920s.

Debenham House 1905–7 **I20** i
8 Addison Road W14
Halsey Ricardo
⊖ High Street Kensington
This masterpiece of coloured ceramic architecture was originally designed for Ernest Debenham, whose department store in Wigmore Street was faced in white tiles. The exterior of the house is remarkable in that all the surfaces are in Burmantoft's Staffordshire bricks and Doulton's tiles – even the capitals, cornices and medallions are moulded and glazed. The white tiles delineate the two-storey superimposed arcade, attic and chimneys; the panels of blue and green glazed bricks echo the colours of the sky and the trees in the garden, giving the house an ethereal, transparent quality. Ricardo was a member of the Art Workers' Guild, and many of the interior furnishings were executed by his friends – the peacock-blue tiles by William de Morgan's firm, plaster ceilings by Gimson, timber staircase by William Aumonier, and lead rainwater heads by the Birmingham Guild. The house is occupied by the Richmond Fellowship, and has been used as an 'exotic' set for numerous feature films.

Whiteleys Department Store **I21** c
1908–12, 1989
Queensway W2
Belcher and Joass, Building Design Partnership
⊖ Queensway, Bayswater
The old conflict between the shopkeeper's desire for large areas of glass and the architect's wish to produce large buildings with strong bases was partly resolved at Whiteleys by the use of metal (rather than stone) facings to the intermediate floors. Daniel Burnham's contemporary contribution to **Selfridges** J61 is more vigorous and single-minded by comparison. Had Hitler's invasion of England succeeded, Whiteleys might have achieved a kind of celebrity, for it is said that the Führer was particularly fond of it and wished to make it his HQ.

After its closure in 1981, the store was ambitiously renovated, transforming the staid Edwardian interior into a North American shopping mall 'experience', complete with ramped auto drop off at the rear.

Department Store **I22** o
ex **Derry and Toms** 1933
Marks and Spencer and
British Home Stores
Kensington High Street W8
Bernard George
⊖ High Street Kensington
A large dull rectangle by the designer of the much more exuberant **Barkers** I19 to the east. Examples of the splendid *moderne* internal fittings, a lift car and its doors from the store are in the Museum of London. The store was famous for its roof garden, which, though restored, is now part of the nightclub which occupies the top floor and so is not open to the public.

Flats c1933 **I23** e
65 Ladbroke Grove W11
E Maxwell Fry
⊖ Ladbroke Grove
The five-storey façade, comprising access galleries and an asymmetrically positioned lift and stair shaft, is now mostly hidden by dense and mature trees. The combination of materials – yellow stock brick, steel tube and mesh balustrading, and blue-tiled dados – is very well handled. The ramped approach to the semi-basement for cars, a motorized 'area' in very tight dimensions, is also ingeniously planned. The flats follow the same programme as **Lawn Road** B17, but with more architectural ability: the well-serviced anonymity of Le Corbusier's *machine à habiter*. See also **Kensal House** T29.

A little to the north, on the corner of Lansdowne Road, the five-storey block of flats clad in Portland stone is by John Pawson (2004).

Flats 1938 **I24** p
10 Palace Gate W8
Wells Coates
⊖ Gloucester Road

These flats, together with those at **Lawn Road** B17, are Coates's most important extant London works. He used an ambitiously complex section on a difficult narrow site. Three floors of service rooms, bedrooms and access galleries are set against two floors of living rooms (compare the similar arrangement at Norman Shaw's **Albert Hall Mansions** J51, of 1886).

Coates handled the exterior with more style than his contemporaries, using direct quotations from Le Corbusier's Pavillon Suisse in Paris. The small facing panels of reconstituted stone were used as permanent shuttering to the reinforced concrete frame.

House 1938 **I25** c
32 Newton Road W2
Denys Lasdun
⊖ Bayswater

Set among mid-Victorian semis, Lasdun's incredibly early work on his own account (he was twenty-four) is more influenced by Le Corbusier than by the work of his first employer, Wells Coates. However, its interior does not have the dynamic spatial complexity of its apparent model, the Maison Cook in Paris.

Houses 1951–2 **I26** j
15, 17 and 19 Aubrey Walk W8
Raymond Erith
⊖ Holland Park

In this very modest short terrace in an area whose property values have since become extremely immodest, Erith demonstrated his complete, but expected, disregard for the then-fashionable clichés of English domestic design. Its beautifully laid brickwork weathered and matured after fifty years, the façade to the street still shocks by its apparent paucity of windows. The invisible south elevation, to the gardens, has more, together with Regency verandas. The scheme was noted by supporters of modern architecture: Ian Nairn admiringly described it as the work of 'somebody who is living a century and a half out of phase'. See also Erith's **Jack Straw's Castle** R28.

Hallfield Housing Estate 1951–9 **I27** d
Bishop's Bridge Road W2
Tecton, Drake and Lasdun
⊖ Westbourne Park, Queensway

One of the early large and comprehensive post-war redevelopments, which should have been an early warning to the subsequent well-intentioned bureaucratic appetite for such excesses. Although bearing superficial resemblances to **Highpoint 2** R27, and carrying watered-down quotations from Le Corbusier's Ville Radieuse, the fifteen large slabs and attendant social buildings can either be seen in hindsight as a contribution to 'collage city' or a permanent scar on a fine nineteenth-century district of London. They show the last use of Tecton and Lasdun's elevational composition – at last it was seen to be merely arbitrary pattern-making as a device to relieve the mass of the buildings.

The **Hallfield primary school** (1951–4), with a ramped entrance from Inverness Terrace is also by Lasdun. The two-storey building is linear and curved in plan, with vertical *brises soleil* to protect its south-facing classrooms. In 2001–5 the school was extended: more classrooms and a nursery school which tactfully extended the circulation pattern were added, designed by Caruso St John.

Flats, The Mount 1961–4 **I28** j
Bedford Gardens and
Campden Hill Road W8
Douglas Stephen and Partners
⊖ Notting Hill Gate

This four-storey block was one of the first in a line of eclectic reworkings of European modernism (especially the work of Giuseppe Terragni and the Italian Rationalists) from the office of Douglas Stephen. After the Second World War such work had been beyond the pale, stigmatized by Fascism. The flats represented an early reaction to the whimsy and provincialism of the Festival of Britain era.

Maisonettes 1964 **I29** h
13–16 Craven Hill Gardens W2
Douglas Stephen and Partners,
Associate Architect Kenneth Frampton
⊖ Queensway

The Mount I28 and this much larger block marked the transition of Stephen's practice from a craggy to a smoother manner. The arrangement derived from the LCC's 'scissors' section: the forty-eight dwellings cross above and below the central access corridors in half-levels, so allowing all the living rooms to face the street, and all the bedrooms, each with a balcony, to face the garden at the back. The corridors are reached via stairs and lift at the north end; the disadvantage of this format is that the entrance lobby is only as large as the landings above. The façades are sober and smart, even if their subdivision suggests a hostel or an office building, but the concrete, originally exposed, was subsequently painted.

Across the road note the dummy façade of 20 Leinster Gardens, concealing the gap in the terrace caused by the Circle Line.

Phillips West 2 1976 **I30** c
10 Salem Road W2
Campbell, Zogolovitch, Wilkinson and Gough
⊖ Queensway, Bayswater

A conversion of a two-storey warehouse into a flamboyantly styled mixed-use building. The combination of pink-painted brickwork, grey window frames and sensuously curved dark blue metalwork to the balconies and principal entrances indicated the emerging architectural dandyism of the mid-1970s. The auction rooms are on the ground floor and offices above. Seven duplex apartments enclose a remarkable enclosed court on the second floor, reached by a lift with a pantiled 'hat'. An arcade, also with a pantiled roof, surrounds a miniature tropical jungle.

Kensington Place restaurant **I31** g

1987
205 Kensington Church St W8
Tess and Julyan Wickham
⊖ Notting Hill Gate

A splendid single space lit by 'industrial' windows the length of the façade to the street and entered through a superbly minimalist revolving door. Inside, the most elaborate feature is the ceiling, which is nearly outclassed by the colourful mural occupying the whole of the north wall. A pioneering and surviving conjunction of good architecture and good food.

Flower Shop, **Public Lavatory** and **Clock** 1993 **I32** b
Colville Rd, Westbourne Grove, W11
CZWG Architects
⊖ Westbourne Grove, Notting Hill Gate

As opposed to the utilitarian Portakabin, this small, likeable triangular pavilion celebrates with wit the combination of these three human necessities. This it does with turquoise glazed bricks, a projecting polycarbonate glazed canopy and a big clock.

J

continued section F

continued section I

CITY OF WESTMINSTER

KENSINGTON GARDENS

The Serpentine

Knightsbridge

Imperial College

Brompton

40
80
19
31
31
2
79
45
77
51
48
74
46
50
39
57
20
73
62
60
81
59
70
55
63
44
53
41
49

continued section N

continued section F

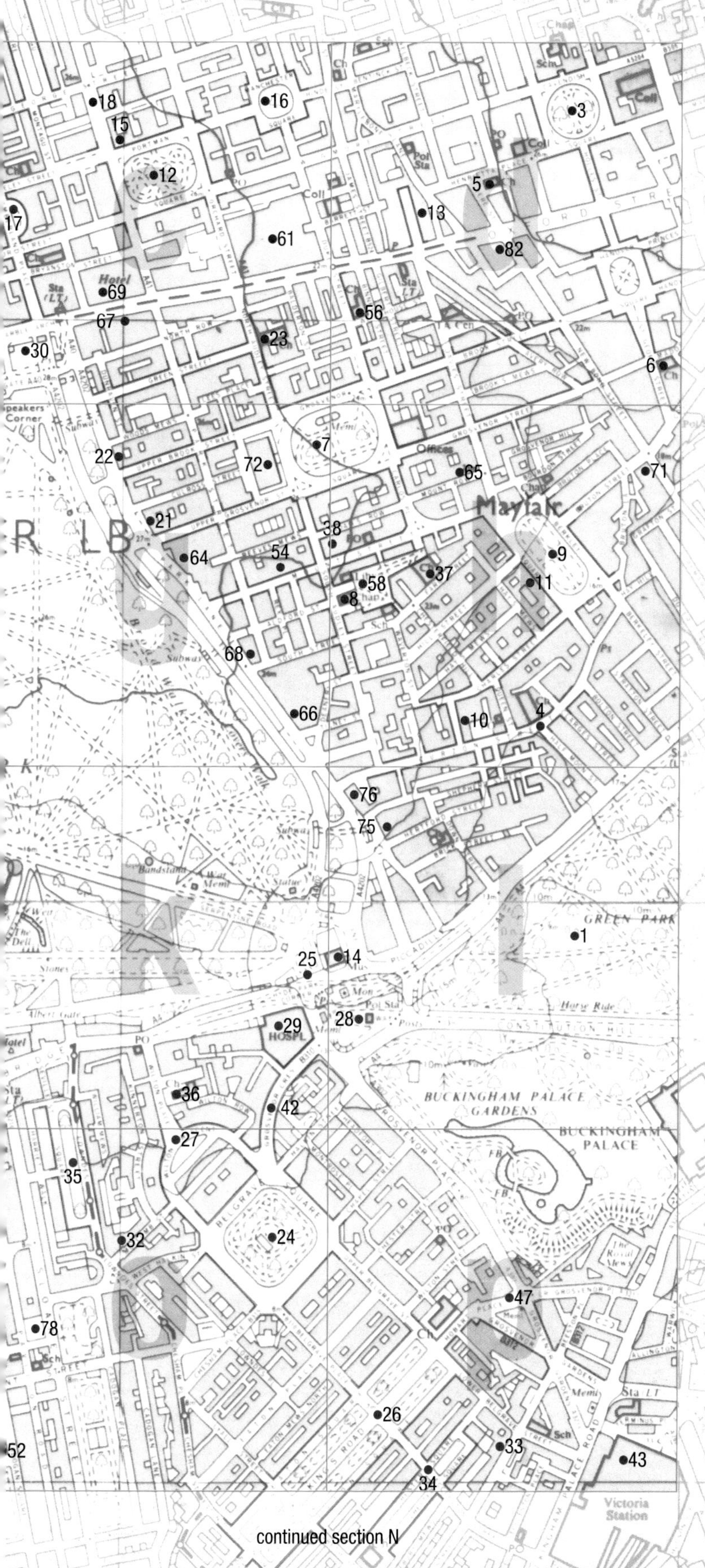

continued section K

continued section N

Belgravia

Marylebone (south) ■ Paddington ■ Mayfair ■ Knightsbridge ■ Belgravia ■ Imperial College ■ Hyde Park ■ Green Park

At the beginning of the seventeenth century the West End of London was open countryside, with two small rivers (the Westbourne and Tyburn), two Roman roads (now Edgware Road and Oxford Street), the medieval villages of Paddington and St Mary-le-Bourne, various manors standing in their own estates, and the royal hunting ground of Hyde Park.

The rivers now run in underground culverts and are no longer visible. The Westbourne (later dammed to form the Serpentine in Hyde Park) was bridged at Knight's Bridge, on the approaches to St James's Palace. The Tyburn Brook, to the east, gave its name to Tyburn Hill (now Marble Arch) in the north-east corner of Hyde Park, which until the end of the eighteenth century was London's place of public execution.

By the mid-seventeenth century the City of Westminster was contained to the north by Lincoln's Inn and to the south and east by the Thames and its marshy ground. Although the king's initiative was significant in expansion to the west, most of the building was the result of the aristocracy's development of their estates. **Green Park** J1 and **St James's Park** K9 were first enclosed by Henry VIII as hunting grounds for St James's Palace. By the mid-eighteenth century they had become fashionable for promenades and for the new large and noble houses along the north and east edges, notably **Spencer House** K51 and **Buckingham House** K76.

Hyde Park J2 had been abbey land until it too was enclosed by Henry VIII as a deer park. In the eighteenth century its area was reduced by the formation of Kensington Gardens (see section I), and in 1730 the Serpentine was created. Rotten Row, the period's other large-scale feature, derives its name from *Route du Roi*, the king's route from St James's Palace to Kensington Palace.

Mayfair's early-eighteenth-century development was given impetus by Lord Burlington, who built up the streets behind his house on Piccadilly. The square, with its supporting network of streets, was the format for development: Hanover Square, **Grosvenor Square** J7 and **Berkeley Square** J9. In 1720 New Bond Street was started as an extension of Old Bond Street.

The Tyburn Brook (now South Molton Street and Avery Row) runs like a fault line through Mayfair. The marshes on its banks were never developed by the Great Estates, and were thus available for less salubrious building and for service trades to the estates. By the mid-eighteenth century the urbanization of Mayfair was complete.

In 1708 the Duke of Newcastle bought the Marylebone Estate to the north of Oxford Street (then Tyburn Road, the processional route to the place of public execution). In 1717, in relatively open countryside, he laid out **Cavendish Square** J3 and the surrounding streets. His daughter

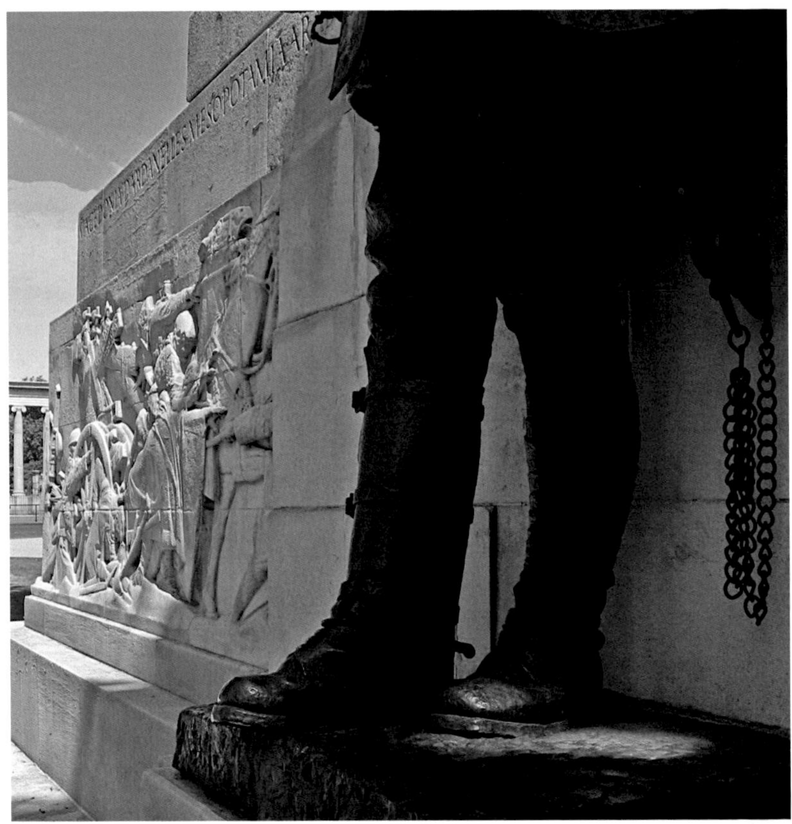

Royal Artillery Monument 1921–5, Hyde Park Corner, C Sargeant Jagger, detail

Lady Margaret Cavendish married the second Duke of Portland, and the estate remained in the hands of the Portlands until 1879, when it passed to Lord Howard de Walden, to whose family it still belongs.

There is evidence of earlier building to the north and south of Hyde Park, but it was not until the nineteenth century that the areas of Belgravia to the south and Tyburnia to the north were developed: further stages in the western extension of London under the agency of the Great Estates. The builder Thomas Cubitt was to Belgravia what his contemporary Nash was to Regent's Park. In 1810 Belgravia – then the Grosvenor Estate – was mostly open fields. With its free composition of large-scale stuccoed crescents (**Wilton** J27), squares (**Belgrave** J24) and avenues (**Eaton Square** J26), Belgravia was completed by 1825, and remains one of London's most architecturally impressive districts (see section N).

Until 1820 Paddington was still a village. In 1825 part of the Bishop of London's estate, the triangular area enclosed by Praed Street to the north, Edgware Road to the east, and Bayswater Road to the south (later known as Tyburnia), was developed to the plans of S P Cockerell, surveyor to the Bishop. Although much rebuilt since 1945, Tyburnia, with Bloomsbury and Belgravia, is one of London's finest early-nineteenth-century planned districts, combining English squares and crescents with wide European avenues (see Sussex Gardens and Westbourne Terrace J31).

By the mid-nineteenth century the Industrial Revolution – particularly the advent of the railways – had caused the further expansion of London. **Paddington Station** J40, the terminus of the Great Western Railway, was begun in 1850, and the rapid growth of Paddington and the areas to the west (see section I) in the 1840s and '50s can be directly attributed to the railway. A population of 6500 in 1831 had by 1881 increased to 100,000.

Following the Great Exhibition of 1851, plans were drawn up for the area now known as the Imperial College campus, south of Hyde Park. This agglomeration of cultural and educational institutions is compressed into the area from the **Albert Memorial** J45 in the north to the **Victoria and Albert Museum** J41 in the south, and from Exhibition Road in the east to Queen's Gate in the west. The museum and technical institution were inventions of the nineteenth century, and this dense area represents the Victorian passion for cataloguing and analysing the world.

As a result of no single estate bordering Hyde Park's perimeter, land speculation has intensified. This progress began tentatively with Lutyens's four belvederes on the **Grosvenor House Hotel** J64, before getting into full stride by the 1960s with the towers of the **London Hilton** J75, Royal Lancaster Hotel, the **Household Cavalry Barracks** J77, etc. At the beginning of the twenty-first century this appetite for speculation showed no sign of abating. In 2007 Bowater House (1961), with its underpass into Hyde Park, was demolished to make way for Rogers Stirk Harbour's apartments at No.1 Hyde Park. With this development the land values in this part of London reached exaggerated new heights.

Hyde Park Corner, *Achilles*, Richard Westmacott 1822

Grosvenor Square J7, statue of F D Roosevelt

The Fountains, Italian Gardens, Hyde Park J2

Royal Geographical Society J48, detail

Green Park 16th century **J1**
SW1
⊖ Green Park
With **St James's Park** K9, Green Park was part of Henry VIII's hunting grounds. It was never subsequently developed and remains a large patch of grass with many plane trees, some of them arranged in an avenue from the Queen Victoria Memorial in front of Buckingham Palace to a pair of fine eighteenth-century gates onto Piccadilly. Two sides of the park provide 'good addresses', commercial on the north and residential on the east (see **Spencer House** K51 and Lasdun's **flats** K170).

Hyde Park 16th century onwards **J2**
W2, SW1, SW7
⊖ Hyde Park Corner, Marble Arch, Knightsbridge, Lancaster Gate
Originally one of Henry VIII's hunting grounds, enclosed by him and stocked with deer, Hyde Park with Kensington Gardens is London's largest park, about 250 hectares (600 acres) in area. It has been open to the public since the mid-seventeenth century, but 'improvements' were not carried out until 1730, when the Serpentine was formed by damming the Westbourne River. Throughout the eighteenth century the park remained the 'natural' western edge of London, which began properly at Hyde Park Corner. Only in the early nineteenth century, after the building of Belgravia and Pimlico, did development spread beyond it to Kensington, Bayswater and Notting Hill. The park became ringed with the five- and six-storey terraces which, until the hotel- and barrack-building boom of the 1950s and '60s, successfully maintained the fiction of 'the country in the town', for their roofs were lower than mature plane trees. The wonderful distant view of the Houses of Parliament from Rennie's elegant masonry bridge (1826) across the Serpentine was tragically destroyed by the erection of government offices in Petty France (designed by Basil Spence) in the 1970s. To the north of the bridge is the Magazine, a little stock-brick pavilion with a Doric colonnade, remodelled by the young Decimus Burton in 1825. He also designed (at the age of twenty-one) Grosvenor Gate, Stanhope Gate and Cumberland Lodge, and his work culminated in the grand entrance to the park, the **Screen** J25 and **Arch** J28, at Hyde Park Corner.

The park was the site of Paxton's Crystal Palace for the 1851 Great Exhibition, which stood south of the Serpentine opposite Kensington Road. Its royal sponsor is commemorated in the **Albert Memorial** J45 in Kensington Gardens on the other side of the Ring. Hyde Park has had a richer social history than the other London parks, and has seen the passing of many fashions. In the early nineteenth century it was a favoured place for rioting, but its activities now are generally more sedate: oratory at Speakers' Corner in the north-east near Marble Arch, horse-riding along the sanded Rotten Row, American baseball, and concerts.

In the 2000s, the park was provided with two initiatives: the permanent and unfortunate memorial fountain to Diana Princess of Wales just south of the swimming enclosure; and the temporary garden pavilions at the **Serpentine Gallery** J79, which under the direction of Julia Peyton Jones became a splendid addition to London's summer calendar.

Lodge to Burton's Screen J25

Cavendish Square 1717 **J3** d
W1
John Prince
⊖ Oxford Circus

The first square to be built on the Marylebone Estate north of Oxford Street, Cavendish Square established both the pattern of surrounding streets and their monuments and a planned relationship with Hanover Square, the other side of Oxford Street. Many of the mature trees in the middle of the square were uprooted in the 1960s to make way for an underground car park.

Two magnificent stone-faced houses (circa 1770) on either side of a triumphal arch form the south-facing centerpiece. To the west are houses of a similar date. To the east, the illusion of historical continuity is represented by the terrace of 2008 by Rolfe Judd that mirrors and replicates the original. The unexceptional John Lewis department store (1939) on the south side is by Slater, Moberly and Uren.

Curzon Street c1720 **J4** h
W1
⊖ Hyde Park Corner, Green Park

Shepherd Market

Enough Georgian terraced houses remain here – numbers 21–3, 28–30, 47 and 48 – to recall Curzon Street's elegant eighteenth-century origins. Number 30 (1771–2) was designed by Robert Adam, and has a magnificent first floor and entrance hall. The most distinguished building is **Crewe House** (c1730) further to the east: built by Edward Shepherd, it is a rare example of the large detached mansion set back from the street behind a generous garden. Its white-stuccoed classical façade, with seven bays and a central pediment, was added in 1813; when floodlit at night it is unexpected and surreal. Opposite is the **Curzon Cinem**a (1963) by John Burnet, Tait and Partners. For those who remember the restrained and stylish Dutch modern façade and mysterious dark blue velvet interior (with double seats) of the original cinema of 1933, its replacement by the same architects is unfortunate.

In 1735 Shepherd laid out **Shepherd Market** just to the south, a development of small shops to serve the grand residences of Piccadilly which retains its eighteenth-century scale.

St Peter 1721–4 **J5** d
W1
Vere Street
James Gibbs
⊖ Oxford Circus

The charming church of St Peter was built as a chapel for Cavendish Square; it sits confidently on its island site. The small double cupola tower is well proportioned with the simple rectangle of the body of the church, built in the brick tradition started by Wren. The plan, with a broad nave, is also indebted to Wren. Summerson noted, however, that its interior – the curved ceiling, giant columns, and decorative plasterwork (now altered) – look forward to Gibbs's more important work at **St Martin-in-the-Fields** K40.

St George, Hanover Square 1721–4 **J6** d
W1
John James
⊖ Oxford Circus

At St George's, a Commissioners' church, James first introduced the portico to the west front of a London church. It was soon to be followed by **St George, Bloomsbury** G8 and **St Martin-in-the-Fields** K40, but only here does the portico span the level pavement. James's solution to the difficult problem of adding a tower to a Roman temple is not as stylish as Gibbs's. The side elevation to Maddox Street is much more robust than those of James's later churches, which by comparison seem thin and poverty-stricken. The interior arrangement loosely follows Wren's **St James, Piccadilly** K21, but was restored by Arthur Blomfield in 1894. See also **St Luke, Old Street** H11.

Grosvenor Estate 1720–5 **J7** g
Grosvenor Square, Upper Brook Street, Brook Street, Upper Grosvenor Street, Grosvenor Street, North Audley Street, South Audley Street, Carlos Place, Carlos Street and Duke Street, W1
⊖ Marble Arch

At the beginning of the eighteenth century the Grosvenor Estate was agricultural land bounded by Oxford Street, Park Lane and, to the east, the Tyburn Brook. Grosvenor Square, laid out in 1720, followed the initiative of Hanover Square and was twice its size. The streets listed above were part of this ambitious development and all date from about 1725. With Brook Street and Carlos Place making connections to Hanover Square and Berkeley Square respectively, the principal urban network of Mayfair was established.

These houses are original, although many have been refaced: Upper Brook Street, numbers 35–6; Brook Street, numbers 25 (residence of Handel), 41, 43, 66–76 (residence of Colen Campbell, editor of *Vitruvius Britannicus* and architect of the original south side of Grosvenor Square), and 86; Upper Grosvenor Street, number 48; Grosvenor Street, numbers 16 and 34; North Audley Street, numbers 11 and 12, refaced about 1820, but with one of the finest Georgian interiors in London.

Grosvenor Square, north side

33 Upper Brook Street, Robert Taylor's first London town house (c1765 – the second was **Ely House** K60), is a grand affair in brick, occupying two standard house frontages. The placing of the front door in the middle of the three bays is unusual. The ground floor arches are particularly elaborate: instead of Palladian rustication, Taylor used a complicated layering of recessed arches, the main ones supported on Tuscan columns.

Grosvenor Chapel 1739 **J8** h
South Audley Street W1
Benjamin Timbrell
⊖ Marble Arch

Built to serve the newly developed Grosvenor Square to the north, this little chapel is the work of builders and craftsmen rather than architects. Seen down Aldford Street from Park Lane, it appears to have been transported from New England. The Ionic screen in the otherwise original interior is by Ninian Comper. Behind the chapel are **Mount Street Gardens** J58.

Note, immediately to the south at 17–20 South Audley Street buildings by Ernest George and Peto of 1876, which occupy a small urban block all in fine and inventive brickwork for Thomas Goode. The sequence of top-lit galleries provides an anachronistic display of expensive household goods.

Berkeley Square started 1739 **J9** h
W1
⊖ Green Park

Berkeley Square was never conceived as an architectural entity: the east side (known as Berkeley Row) was built first and the west side followed in 1745. Today the houses on the west side and the magnificent plane trees, over 200 years old, are the square's main points of interest. Of the houses, **number 44** J11 by William Kent is the *pièce de résistance*. Numbers 45 and 46 are original, dating from 1744, and have especially good rusticated stonework and wrought-iron railings. Number 47 is a good example of imitation Italian Renaissance (1891); numbers 49–51 have particularly fine lamp-holders; and number 52 has two bays to Charles Street and a pedimented Ionic doorway to the square.

Chesterfield Street c1740 **J10** h
W1
⊖ Green Park

Remarkable for its complete and regular Georgian terraces (though number 10 is slightly later and has different details), Chesterfield Street terminates in the contemporary **Charles Street**, also remarkably intact and richly decorated.

44 Berkeley Square 1744–5 **J11** h
W1
⊖ Green Park
William Kent
Built for Lord Burlington's cousin, Lady Isabella Finch, this has been called the finest terrace house in London. The exterior is modest, the only clues to the palatial arrangements inside being the pediments to the first-floor windows and a large rusticated surround to the front door. The principal staircase and drawing room are among the grandest and most technically ingenious of any eighteenth-century private house in London. See also **Berkeley Square** J9.

Portman Square laid out 1761 **J12** c
W1
⊖ Marble Arch
A regular square 170×143m (560×470ft) in which no ordinary houses remain. On the north side, numbers 20 and 21 are two grand Adam **houses** J15. The huge and very undistinguished Churchill Hotel on the west side extinguished the other remaining eighteenth-century houses.

Stratford Place c1770 **J13** d
off Oxford Street W1
⊖ Bond Street
An almost complete eighteenth-century close, offering welcome relief from the bustle of Oxford Street. The north end is concluded by **Derby House** (1773), a stone-faced classical mansion by R Edwin in the style of Adam: the view of its dignified Ionic pilasters and central pediment is a reminder that Oxford Street was once a relatively calm spot on the northern edge of London.

Apsley House (Wellington Museum) **J14** l
1771–8, 1828–9
Hyde Park Corner SW1
Robert Adam, Benjamin and Philip Wyatt
⊖ Hyde Park Corner
By the end of the 1820s, Apsley House (postal address Number 1, London) formed part of an extraordinary group of neoclassical monuments on the edge of Hyde Park: **St George's Hospital** J29 (1827–8), the **Screen** J25 (1825) and the **Arch** J28 (1825). Built by Adam for Baron Apsley, it was originally a much smaller brick building; in 1828 Benjamin and Philip Wyatt transformed and enlarged it for the Duke of Wellington, facing it in stone, and adding the Corinthian portico and the west side extension. Much of Adam remains in the interior, however, notably the semicircular staircase, the drawing room with its eastern apse, and the portico room. The Wyatts' principal contribution to the interior is the Waterloo Gallery, which houses many trophies from a grateful

nation – the most impresssive is Canova's 3.4m (11ft) statue of Napoleon as a near-naked hero holding out a golden victory emblem. The house is now open to the public as the Wellington Museum.

Apsley House is now marooned in the midst of the Hyde Park Corner traffic intersection, and the former neoclassical ensemble has been all but destroyed. In the 1960s the adjoining buildings on the east side were demolished for road widening, and the exposed flank was refaced with a copy of the Wyatts' west extension.

Houses 1775–7 **J15** c
20 and 21 Portman Square W1
Home House, number 20, Robert Adam; number 21, James Adam
⊖ Marble Arch
Home House and **Chandos House** F1 are the only remaining great houses in London designed by Robert Adam. Here he was able to develop both the planning of a continuous sequence of rooms, differentiated by function, shape and style, and his delicate, flat, linear decoration which he started at Syon. Summerson proposed that the Music Room represents the summit of this development. The top floors of both houses are later additions.

Manchester Square laid out 1776 **J16** c
W1
⊖ Marble Arch
The form of this square, with three streets entering at the mid-points of the sides (rather than at the corners, as at the contemporary **Bedford Square** G12), is a throwback to the seventeenth-century form (for example **St James's Square** K18). The south and east sides are complete, with grand houses but no attempt at composition. The square was developed by the Duke of Manchester, who built himself a commanding but dull free-standing house on the north side. In 1882 the house was altered to its present form by Richard Wallace, whose collection of paintings, objects and armour it now contains. A scheme of expansion and improvement, including providing a new glazed roof to the courtyard, designed by Rick Mather architects, was completed in 2000.

Great Cumberland Place 1789 **J17** c
W1
⊖ Marble Arch
A circus was originally planned in the middle of Great Cumberland Place, but while the crescent on the east side was built in 1789, the opposite side followed the straight line of the road. As part of the planned composition of the Portman Estate the road was extended northwards (1810–15), creating the oblong **Bryanston Square** J19 and terminating in Wyndham Place at Smirke's **St Mary's** F19. The lampholders and railings are among the best in London.

Gloucester Place **J18** c
late 18th and early 19th centuries
W1, NW1
⊖ Baker Street

It was this sort of street, 1.4km (1 mile) long, that confirmed the Victorians in their belief that Georgian architecture was rigid and boring. This street of grand houses escaped their recipe for improvement (the insertion of red brick), which can be seen in Harley and Wimpole Streets. It remains remarkably intact, with the only interruption at Marylebone Road.

Bryanston Square and **Montagu Square** 1811 **J19** b
W1
Joseph Parkinson, Albert Richardson
⊖ Baker Street, Marble Arch

Bryanston Square, the westerly extension of the Portman Estate, forms part of an axial composition from the older Great Cumberland Place in the south to Smirke's fine church in **Wyndham Place** F19 to the north. Parkinson's original houses remain on the east side and at all four corners. The square was designed as two grand palaces with stuccoed end pavilions and giant Ionic columns confronting each other, but this image was impaired by Albert Richardson's replacement of the houses in the centre section of the west side with a particularly bleak affair, consisting of a neo-Georgian façade to a large apartment building. To the east is Montagu Square, a companion to Bryanston Square, with shallow bay windows to the houses.

Stirling Street and **Trevor Square** 1818 **J20** n
Montpelier Square and **Montpelier Place** 1837
SW7
⊖ Knightsbridge

A small collection of Regency houses, which look more appropriate to the seaside than to their site between busy Brompton Road and Knightsbridge.

Montpelier Place

Houses 1820s **J21** g
91–9 Park Lane W1
⊖ Marble Arch

The only complete collection of individually designed and built terrace houses remaining on Park Lane, these have the Regency bow windows and fine cast-iron verandas which used to be characteristic of the street.

Dudley House 1824–7 **J22** g
100 Park Lane W1
William Atkinson
⊖ Marble Arch

Park Lane was originally lined with many aristocrats' detached houses built along the edge of the Grosvenor Estate. Dudley House, small but pretentious with an Ionic colonnade and first-floor glazed iron loggia, is the only one left.

St Mark 1824–8 **J23** c
North Audley Street W1
J P Gandy Deering
⊖ Marble Arch

The very fine tall Greek portico, with two Ionic columns, a straight entablature without pediment and an elegant octagonal lantern behind, is best appreciated from Green Street opposite. The interior was 'Normanized' by Arthur Blomfield in 1878 and is of no special interest. The whole church is in need of repair.

Belgrave Square 1825 **J24** o
SW1
Thomas Cubitt
⊖ Hyde Park Corner

The diagonal approaches, marked by four corner mansions, are Belgrave Square's distinguishing feature. It is also large, nearly 4 hectares (10 acres), and grand – its name synonymous with the high society of the area as a whole. All the terraces are of four storeys with the attic set back behind the cornice, but Cubitt, in collaboration with the architect George Basevi, was determined to break the uniformity of the Georgian square. The entrances are individual, and the elevations employ various different motifs. The houses in the corners are by various architects: the north-west by Robert Smirke (1830), the south-west by H E Kendall (1826), the south-east by Philip Hardwick (1842) and the north-east by George Basevi (c1840).

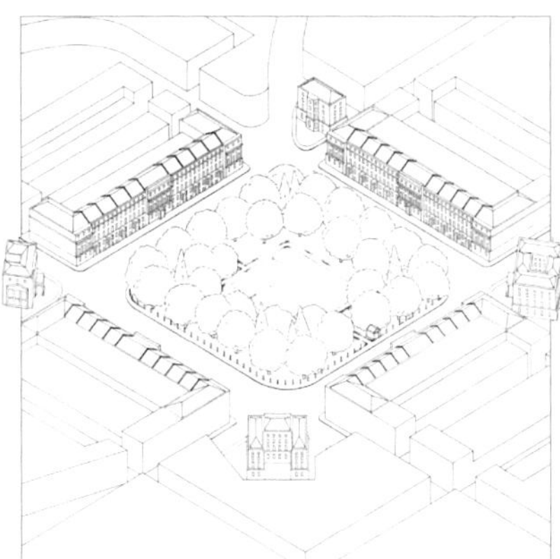

Screen 1825 **J25** k
Hyde Park Corner SW1
Decimus Burton
⊖ Hyde Park Corner

Hyde Park Corner was always regarded as the important entrance to London from the west, and a number of schemes for improving it were proposed during the eighteenth century. We are lucky in that the present arrangement is the consequence of the building boom in the years following the battle of Waterloo: nowhere else in London is there a group of buildings of such great distinction of this period. It is, however, characteristically English that this important place should be called merely a 'Corner' – perhaps it was this name which allowed the traffic engineers of the 1950s to rape it so shamelessly. The Screen and **Arch** J28 are the culmination of Burton's work in Hyde Park, for before them he had designed many of the lodges. The combination of delicacy and correctness in the Ionic Screen is perhaps a happy consequence of Burton's youth – he was twenty-five when designing them. The busy Greek sculpture on the attic above the central arch is by John Henning junior, who with his father carried out the magnificent frieze on Burton's **Athenaeum** K80.

Eaton Square 1826–53 **J26** p
SW1
Thomas Cubitt
⊖ Victoria, Sloane Square

One of the grandest architectural set pieces in London (originally the formal beginning of the route from St James's Palace to Hampton Court), Eaton Square is more of a triumphal way than a typical square. King's Road forms its central axis from Hobart Place in the east to Sloane Square in the west, and parallel streets on either side (like a European boulevard) serve the generously composed and varied terraces (see also **Tyburnia** J31). The north side was developed by Thomas Cubitt, the south side by Seth Smith (1825–30). At the north east corner of the square is Henry Hakewill's church of St Peter (1824–7), a standard Greek Revival work with a giant portico of six Ionic columns. Fire gutted the building in the 1980s, and destroyed Arthur Blomfield's unfortunate Norman interior of 1872.

Wilton Crescent 1827 **J27** o
SW1
Seth Smith
⊖ Hyde Park Corner

Approached via Hyde Park and Wilton Place to the north, Wiiton Crescent is a typical nineteenth-century device to give the visitor a grand introduction to the estate. However, where Nash's **Park Crescent** F6 has a view of Regent's Park, here the south side is blocked by buildings, which confuse the entrance to Belgrave Square. The north side was refaced with stone by Balfour and Turner in the early twentieth century. The stuccoed fronts and giant pilasters of the south side are typical of Belgravia.

Wellington Arch 1827–30 **J28** l
Hyde Park Corner SW1
Decimus Burton
⊖ Hyde Park Corner
The Arch was built as a northern gate to the grounds of Buckingham Palace, and originally stood opposite and to the south of Burton's **Screen** J25, where its solidity and Corinthian order complemented the delicacy and openness of the Ionic Screen. In this position, it formed an orthogonal composition with the other buildings of the 1820s (**St George's Hospital** J29 and the portico of **Apsley House** J14) which, before Belgravia was built, marked the entrance to London from the west. The Arch was moved to its present position at the head of Constitution Hill in 1883. In 1912 the Quadriga – Adrian Jones's magnificent imperial bronze depicts *Peace descending on the Chariot of War* – replaced the original statue of the Duke of Wellington. Since the reconstruction of Hyde Park Corner as one of the biggest and busiest traffic roundabouts in Europe in the late 1950s the setting of the Arch has been less than satisfactory.

Note immediately to the east on Constitution Hill the **Memorial Gates**: four curiously large 'colonial' gateposts of 2002 by Liam O'Connor. Their position appears to be arbitrary and their purpose somewhat belated (to commemorate those Commonwealth men and women who died in two world wars).

St George's Hospital 1827–9 **J29** k
now the **Lanesborough Hotel**
Hyde Park Corner SW1
William Wilkins
⊖ Hyde Park Corner
While the London hospital is largely an eighteenth-century building type, several were built or rebuilt in the years of peace following Waterloo. St George's was founded in 1719 and Wilkins's building replaces that of 1732–4. The Greek stucccoed façade to Hyde Park Corner has a central porch of square columns, with two side wings curiously divided into two bays by a central pilaster. The top floor is a later addition. There are some good Grecian interiors. The hospital was enlarged in the mid-nineteenth century, but closed in 1980. It was subsequently redeveloped as a hotel and Wilkins's façades were restored.

Marble Arch 1828 **J30** c
Oxford Street and Park Lane W1
John Nash
⊖ Marble Arch

Marble Arch was designed to stand in front of (its material in contrast to) the Bath stone façade of Nash's Buckingham Palace, but was moved when the Palace was extended after Nash's death. It is based on the three-arched Roman model and like this was intended to have more sculptured decoration than it now sports. A statue of Victory was to be placed on top, but this was replaced by one of George IV, which eventually found its place in Trafalgar Square. While it suits the delicacy of the design, marble is a poor material to use outdoors in London and vulnerable to frost and acid. Its miserable setting in the middle of a poorly designed traffic roundabout is unforgivable.

Tyburnia 1828–35 **J31** b
Connaught Square,
Connaught Street, Kendal Street,
Hyde Park Square, Sussex Gardens,
Westbourne Terrace,
Sussex Square, Hyde Park Street, W2
S P Cockerell and George Gutch
⊖ Paddington, Edgware Road

The special interest here lies in the combination of the established eighteenth-century patterns of domestic streets and squares (stuccoed after Nash) and the larger-scale European-style avenues such as Sussex Gardens and Westbourne Terrace (tree-lined, with service streets on either side, separated by strips of green). In the eighteenth century squares were never seen as through-routes, and were often gated and exclusive to their residents.

Westbourne Terrace

Pantechnicon 1830 **J32** o
Motcomb Street SW1
Seth Smith
⊖ Knightsbridge

An extraordinarily large Doric façade to a warehouse, formerly Sotheby's Belgravia auction rooms.

ex **Pimlico Literary Institute** **J33** p
1830
22 Ebury Street SW1
J P Gandy Deering
⊖ Victoria

The Institute, now converted into flats, uses a Greek Doric propylaeum format set in a stuccoed street frontage. The towers at the sides rise higher than the portico – not a satisfactory arrangement – but make a tastefully modelled secular public building, as good as any of Nash's similar, contemporary works.

Chester Square 1835 **J34** p
SW1
Thomas Cubitt
⊖ Victoria
Although Chester Square, very long and thin, is divided by the traffic of Eccleston Street, it is the most intimate of Belgravia's squares, with differing details in the frontages.

Lowndes Square laid out in 1836 **J35** o
SW1
⊖ Knightsbridge
The few houses on the east and south sides (by Lewis Cubitt, 1841) are all that remain of the original. In 1931 Messrs Joseph completely redeveloped the west side of the square with large red-brick blocks of flats. Despite their inconsistencies with the earlier houses – double-storey rustication and greater overall height, for example – these stripped classical buildings are impressive.

St Paul 1840–3 **J36** k
Wilton Place SW1
Thomas Cundy III
⊖ Hyde Park Corner
One of the dignified churches of the Grosvenor Estate. The castellated west tower is open at the ground floor, forming a grand porch. Inside, the three galleries are supported by fine cast-iron columns, and the construction of the timber roof is exposed.

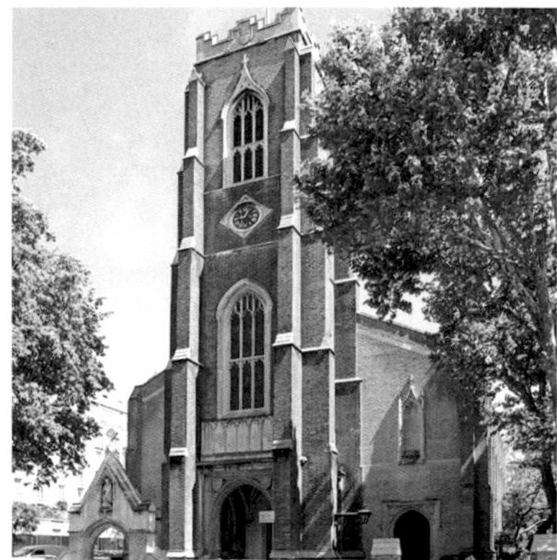

Church of the Immaculate Conception 1844–9 **J37** h
Farm Street W1
J J Scoles, high altar by Augustus Welby Pugin
⊖ Bond Street, Green Park
A remarkably beautiful and unexpectedly large Gothic interior is to be discovered behind the Immaculate Conception's unexceptional street façade. The nave and aisles are of eight bays, with red granite columns and tall clerestory windows; the east window and the porch and rose windows at the west are supposedly inspired by Carlisle Cathedral. The ceiling, white with a spare red geometric pattern, is quite ethereal. The church has two later outer aisles: to the right by Henry Chilton (1878) and to the left by W H Romaine Walker (1898–1903). The buttressing to the nave subdivides both into independent polygonal chapels. There is a secondary entrance from the north (from **Mount Street Gardens** J58) ingeniously positioned between the chancel and the chapel – a short cut for those who know.

Houses 1845 **J38** g
1–2, 26–32, 64–9 South Audley Street W1
⊖ Hyde Park Corner
The street's architecture is a mixture of calm Georgian remains (see numbers 71 and 72) and the wilder Victorian insertions listed above. The ensemble is characteristic of Mayfair, and is held together by the right-angled street grid of the Grosvenor Estate, laid out in the eighteenth century.

All Saints 1846–9 **J39** n
Ennismore Gardens SW7
L Vullliamy; front by C H Townsend 1892
⊖ Knightsbridge, South Kensington
A rare, early example in England of a copy of a primitive Christian basilica (they were more common in Germany), All Saints is decorated in Arts and Crafts sgraffito by Heywood Sumner, and has surprisingly secular stained glass. It is now the Cathedral of the Dormition of the Mother of God and All Saints of the Russian Orthodox Church.

Paddington Station 1850–4 **J40** a
Eastbourne Terrace and
Praed Street W2
Isambard Kingdom Brunel,
Matthew Digby Wyatt, Owen Jones
⊖ Paddington

The hotel marking the south front to Paddington Station is an earlier and separate building by Philip Hardwick, and established the railways' tradition of putting hotel fronts to the large engineering sheds behind (see **St Pancras** G39, **Charing Cross** K102 and so on). The station is the work of Brunel, the engineer of the Great Western Railway: Wyatt and Jones added the architectural decorations. It had three parallel sheds (the fourth was added in the twentieth century), with roofs of wrought iron and glass and columns of cast iron). Originally the inner platforms were reached by retractable drawbridges, as there was no concourse at the south end, and the station-master's lookout was behind a second-floor oriel window on platform 1.

The interior was renovated and refreshed in 1999 by Grimshaw architects and now forms a fitting place of arrival for those travelling on the Paddington Express from Heathrow.

Externally the east side of the station is very impressive, like a long, curved whale's back, the front or head visible from London Street to the south. To the east, in London Street, are P G Culverhouse's **Great Western Railway Offices** (1933), a delightful and rare example of a *moderne* office building.

Victoria and Albert Museum **J41** m
ex **South Kensington Museum**
1856–1909
Cromwell Road SW7
Captain Francis Fowke, Godfrey Sykes and others, main quadrangle 1856–84; Aston Webb, Cromwell Road entrance range 1899–1909
⊖ South Kensington

The Victoria and Albert Museum was promoted by Prince Albert to improve the technical and art education of designers and manufacturers, at a time when Britain was beginning to lose her industrial supremacy to other European countries. The extensive collections of ceramics, furniture, tapestries and other *objets d'art* from around the world were assembled by the museum's energetic first director, Henry Cole. Cole profoundly distrusted architects, preferring to commission engineers and decorative artists for the buildings: it is this combination that gives the first galleries for South Kensington Museum their distinctive style.

Until Webb's Cromwell Road façade was built (1899–1909) the museum presented an extremely utilitarian appearance to the public. Known disparagingly as the 'Brompton Boilers' because of their cast-iron structures and corrugated-iron facings, the buildings were dismantled and moved to form the Bethnal Green Museum (now the **Museum of Childhood** U22) in 1867. The earliest surviving gallery is the Sheepshanks (1857–8) by Fowke. North of this are the Vernon and Turner Galleries (1858–9), east of these are North and South Courts (1861–2), and to the south is the great East Court (1868–73) by Lieutenant Colonel Scott. All the courts were 'engineered' utilitarian iron structures, decorated later by artists including Moody and Leighton. Even the main quadrangle, the principal architectural space, was built in stages as part of the museum's slow growth. It is a good example of the South Kensington style of terracotta, red brick and mosaic. First was the West Side (1862–3), then the North (1864–6) with an arcaded loggia designed by Sykes, mosaic lunettes by Townroe, terracotta detail by Gamble and the great bronze doors designed by Sykes and modelled by Gamble and Townroe. The South Side remained open until 1879, when it was filled by the Art Library range. The East Side was formed by the 'backs' of the Sheepshanks and Vernon and Turner Galleries until 1901, when Aston Webb faced them by reproducing the west side.

There are some very remarkable interiors on the north side of the main quadrangle. The New Refreshment Room (1866) and the Grill Room (1865–73) are both splendid examples of the use of glazed ceramic tiles. The Green Dining Room (1866–9), designed by William Morris's firm, was his first major secular commission. The stained-glass window is by Edward Burne-Jones.

In 1891 Aston Webb won the competition to complete the principal Cromwell Road façade. The design is exceptional for its pomp and mixture of historical motifs, and the interiors of the entrance hall are very tall and impressive in their oversized way. As the capital of the British Empire, London was thought to require such grand civic gestures.

The Royal Institute of British Architects' drawing collection was rehoused at the museum in 2004, when the Architecture Gallery (architects Gareth Hoskins) was also opened. This displays drawings, models, photographs and architectural fragments.

In 2001 following new access regulations, a skilful combination of ramps and steps was installed to the Cromwell Road entrance to the designs of Pringle Richards Sharratt.

Grosvenor Crescent 1860 **J42** k
SW1
Seth Smith, Thomas Cubitt
⊖ Hyde Park Corner

Beginning with the fine Greek Revival façades of Wilkins's **St George's Hospital** J29 on Hyde Park Corner, Grosvenor Crescent is the diagonal approach to Belgrave Square from the north east. The north side, by Seth Smith, is a fine continuously curving elevation. Cubitt's south side, consisting of individual houses, is more fragmentary.

Victoria Station 1862 **J43** p
partiallly rebuilt 1898–1908
Victoria Street SW1
J Fowler
Grosvenor Hotel 1860
Buckingham Palace Road SW1
J T Knowles
⊖ Victoria

Victoria Station was run originally by two railway companies, which had no connection until 1923. To the east are two fine vaulted iron and glass structures, built by J Fowler for the London, Chatham and Dover Railway Station (now platforms 1–8). To the west is the London, Brighton and South Coast Railway station (platforms 9–17), which was entirely rebuilt in 1898–1908. The railway line was built on the course of the Grosvenor Canal, which allowed access to the Thames; the Southern Railway Companies were thus enabled to build the first railway crossing of the Thames in central London. Romantic associations with journeys on the *Flèche d'Or* to distant European capitals have inevitably now been subsumed by the station's over-use in the service of Gatwick Airport.

The Grosvenor Hotel, although not the first station hotel in London, was one of the first examples of the French 'Second Empire' style. The large-scale design, an elaborately decorated large rectangle of brick and stone, expresses the confidence of the railway age. On the first and top storeys, between the arched windows, are medallions with portraits of Queen Victoria, Prince Albert and Lord Palmerston, among others. At either end of the curved and dormered roof are four French pavilions. The Grosvenor Hotel proved to be an influential building (see the Langham Hotel, Portland Place, by Giles and Murray) and as Summerson writes, 'is one of the representative monuments of Victorian London'.

Henry Cole Building **J44** m
ex **Huxley Building** 1863–73
Exhibition Road SW7
Lieutenant General Scott
⊖ South Kensington

The Henry Cole Building, the work of an inspired amateur architect, was first occupied by the School of Naval Architects, then the Science School, followed by the Imperial College of Science, and was then absorbed into the Victoria and Albert Museum. The building is truly monumental: seven central bays are flanked by pedimented corner pavilions and topped by a continuous loggia. To the left an arched gateway leads through to the (original) Royal College of Art, its name and the Imperial College of Science's inscribed in the stonework above. The exterior is extensively decorated with terracotta panels ornamented in Minton majolica.

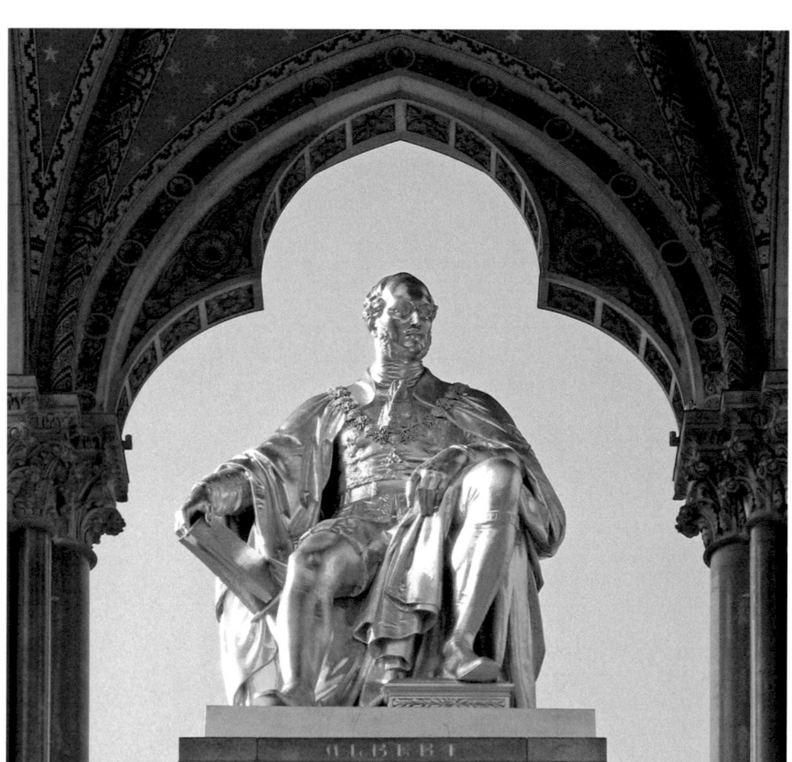

Albert Memorial 1863–75 **J45** i
Kensington Gardens,
Kensington Gore SW7
George Gilbert Scott
⊖ Knightsbridge

That the Prince Consort should be commemorated by a monumental interpretation of a medieval shrine, normally associated with the relics of saints, is typical of High Victorian idealism. Scott's idea was 'to erect a kind of ciborium ... on the principle of the ancient shrines', encrusted with precious metals and enamel.

The 53m (175ft) high memorial has a Gothic spire decorated with angels, and a 4.2m (14ft) high seated bronze statue of Prince Albert forming the apex to a remarkable pyramid of sculpted figures representing the ideals, aspirations and achievements of the Victorian age. In the four projecting corners, groups of marble figures symbolize the Imperial colonies and the four corners of the globe: Asia (by J H Foley), Europe (Patrick MacDowell), America (John Bell) and Africa (William Theed). Below, figures at the corners represent Agriculture (W Calder Marshall), Manufacture (Henry Weekes), Commerce (Thomas Thornycroft) and Engineering (John Lawlor). Between them is a continuous frieze of painters, poets, composers, architects and sculptors. The poets, musicians and painters are by H H Armstead, the rest by J B Philip. All this stands on a massive granite plinth of twenty-four steps.

The memorial has provoked hostility and affection, but has finally gained acceptance as a relic of the age it so accurately portrays. So many artists and craftsmen were involved that it is as much a memorial to the Arts and Crafts movement as it is to Albert. It is best seen either at close quarters, or from the east (the site of the original Crystal Palace) framed by the majestic avenue of London plane trees. It was completely restored in 1994–8.

Royal Albert Hall 1867–7 **J46** m
Kensington Gore SW7
Captain Francis Fowke,
carried out by General H Y D Scott
⊖ Knightsbridge, High Street Kensington

The vast elliptical Albert Hall holds 8000 within its approximately 225m (735ft) circumference. Together with Norman Shaw's **Albert Hall Mansions** J51, George Gilbert Scott's **Albert Memorial** J45, and in spite of the Royal College of Art (1962), whose chief virtue is to expose the beautiful end wall of the Royal College of Organists, the Albert Hall forms one of the best Victorian set-piece designs in London. The central axis runs from the front steps of the **Natural History Museum** J49 on Cromwell Road through Queen's Tower to the Imperial College campus. The simple domed brick cylinder and terracotta decoration has been attributed to the influence of the architect Gottfried Semper, a political refugee befriended by Prince Albert. The frieze, running the full circumference and depicting *The Triumph of Arts and Letters*, is a particularly fine work by Armitage, Pickersgull, Marks and Poynter. The interior of the Hall has three tiers of boxes, including the balcony and the gallery above. The dome is of iron and glass.

In 1995–2004, the back-of-house areas were comprehensively upgraded by Building Design Partnership with a revised entrance sequence from Prince Consort Road to the south.

Grosvenor Gardens 1870 **J47** p
SW1
Thomas Cundy III
⊖ Victoria

Grosvenor Gardens and Grosvenor Place were laid out as a north-western extension of Victoria Street to Hyde Park Corner. The Grosvenor Estate seems to have started its experiments with French styles at about this time (and continues to do so – see **Grosvenor Square** J7). For Grosvenor Gardens it introduced not only the clothing of a French apartment building, but also the *maison meublée* of about 200 rooms to be let off in various numbers to form apartments. There was a restaurant on the ground floor to serve both residents and public. The social experiment has long been discontinued, and the building is now used as offices.

Royal Geographical Society **J48** i
ex **Lowther Lodge** 1873–5
Kensington Gore and Exhibition Road SW7
R Norman Shaw
⊖ Knightsbridge, High Street Kensington

With its skilfully asymmetrical elevations and masterful brickwork, Lowther Lodge is a *tour de force* of the Queen Anne style. When the house was built (for William Lowther MP) Kensington was almost fully developed, although the adjacent sites were still empty. Unlike Shaw's other (more urban) London houses, this seems to be a country mansion encroached on by the town. The Hyde Park front is set back behind an entrance court with the stable wing to the east. The façade of fine brickwork has no stone dressings, and the pediments, gables, pilasters, massive chimneys and exaggerated cornices are made from 50mm (2in) cut brickwork. The external details are reminiscent more of Shaw's partner Nesfield's Lodge at Kew (T16) than of his own contemporary work in **Queen's Gate** I13 and **Melbury Road** I14. Following Lowther's death in 1912, the house was bought by the Royal Geographical Society. In 1928–30 an inoffensive lecture hall was added by Kennedy and Nightingale on the site of the stables at the corner of Kensington Gore and Exhibition Road. The statues of Shackleton and Livingstone, also on the corner facing Exhibition Road and Kensington Gore, are by C Sargeant Jagger (1932).

In 2004 an extension was completed by Studio Downie and provided a new entrance from Exhibition Road. This helps to consolidate the proposed role of Exhibition Road as a cultural promenade from South Kensington to Hyde Park.

Natural History Museum 1873–81 **J49** m

Cromwell Road SW7
Alfred Waterhouse
⊖ South Kensington

The first public building in London by this eminent Victorian architect, the Natural History Museum dominates the Cromwell Road, and its glazed terracotta slabs in the Romanesque style were new to the city's streets. When compared with neighbouring buildings (notably Aston Webb's loosely composed front to the **Victoria and Albert Museum** J41) the Natural History Museum has a breathtaking tough consistency. It has beautiful and varied zoological decoration along its 206m (675ft) frontage. Inside the huge entrance hall, the monumental staircase, steel-and-glass roof and large exhibition halls are particularly impressive. The Department of the Environment's pretentious extension of 1977 at the south-east corner is deplorable. It is unfortunate that the museum has adopted the current clichés of contemporary museum display in many of its principal exhibition halls; the visitor is distracted from the exhibits by over-diagrammatic and populist presentation.

In 2008 the **Darwin Centre** Phase 2 by C F Møller Architects formed a new garden façade for the Museum facing Queens Gate. Enclosed by hermetically sealed glazed eight-storey façades is a 'cocoon' containing storage and workplaces for scientists which can be overlooked by the public.

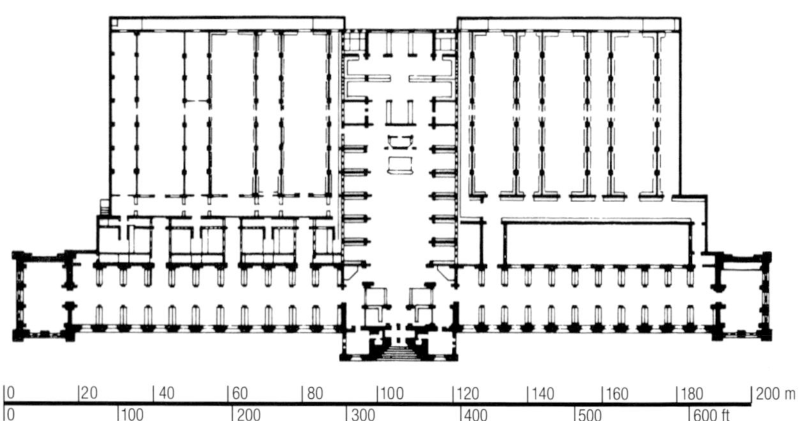

Royal College of Organists 1875 **J50** m
Kensington Gore SW7
H H Cole
⊖ South Kensington

A strangely eclectic four-storey, three-bay building, whose effect derives more from its decoration in cream, maroon and pale-blue sgraffito by F W Moody than from its form. The College's decorative frieze of musicians curiously contains no organ. H H Cole was a soldier in the Royal Engineers, like so many of the designers of the buildings erected round the Albert Hall.

Albert Hall Mansions 1879–86 **J51** i
Kensington Gore SW7
R Norman Shaw
⊖ High Street Kensington, Knightsbridge
In their sheer mass and scale these buildings are reminiscent of a fragment of a European city: their swirling shapes contain the **Albert Hall** J46 and offer a grand façade to Kensington Gardens. Shaw had studied the French apartment type before taking this new departure, which influenced flat development in Kensington up to 1910.The double-storey plinth (supporting the main storeys with twice repeated double arches) and the tall Dutch gables above show Shaw's inventive use of the Queen Anne style.

House 1879 **J52** o
4 Cadogan Square SW1
George Edmund Street
⊖ Knightsbridge
Grandly occupying a corner, Street's house makes few concessions to the prevailing 'Pont Street Dutch' – only the use of red brick and perhaps the restrained window arrangements. His Gothic is given full rein in the magnificently asymmetrical porch to the front door. See also Norman Shaw's houses, numbers 60a, 62, 68 and 72 (N25) and J J Stevenson's numbers 63–73 (N24).

The London Oratory 1880–93 **J53** n
Brompton Road SW3
Herbert Gribble; house by J J Scoles
⊖ South Kensington
The Oratory was the first large new Roman Catholic church to be built in London after the Reformation. Its building was the culmination of the influence of the Oxford Movement which set up branches of St Philip Neri's Oratorians at Birmingham and London in 1845, when John Henry Newman and Frederick Faber became Catholics. Rather as Islam is associated today with a particular style, so Gribble's huge church, chosen in competition by Alfred Waterhouse, is studiedly Roman, using a domed nave (each dome with a central rooflight) to which vaulted side chapels are attached. The vaults and domes are in concrete (see also **Westminster Cathedral** K120). The Roman atmosphere is enhanced by the skilful recycling of genuine Italian ornaments and statues, but the seven-branched candlesticks are by Burges. The painting of Saints Thomas More and John Fisher in St Wilfred's Chapel is by Rex Whistler.

Mount Street c1885 **J54** g
W1
Ernest George
⊖ Bond Street, Hyde Park Corner
The most complete and lavishly decorated red-terracotta-tiled street in London, largely by Ernest George, though numbers 125–9 by W H Powell (1889) and J T Smith's numbers 118–21 (1886) are the most astonishingly ornate examples. The Connaught Hotel (one of the best in London) is by Isaacs and Florence (1901). From Carlos Place the street is more regular; numbers 87–102, three-storeyed and gabled, are by A T Bolton (1893). On the south side of Mount Street are the two gated entrances to **Mount Street Gardens** J58.

Imperial Institute Tower **J55** m
1887–93
Imperial Institute Road SW7
Thomas Edward Colllcutt
⊖ South Kensington

The tallest marker on the (invisible) axis extending south from the Albert Hall to the Natural History Museum, this 85m (280ft) tall tower (now surrounded by the redevelopment of Imperial College) is all that remains of the building erected after the 1886 Colonial Exhibition. Collcutt's striped style is more restrained here than in his contemporary **Palace Theatre** K117.

Ukrainian Catholic Cathedral of the Holy Family in Exile **J56** d
ex **King's Weigh House Chapel**
1889–91
Duke Street W1
Alfred Waterhouse
⊖ Bond Street

Waterhouse's style and materials are unmistakable – a curious mixture of Gothic and Romanesque in brick and buff terracotta tiles. The Duke Street façade is asymmetrical, with a tall tower on the south-west corner. Inside, the principal space is oval, with an impressive gallery carried on iron piers encased in terracotta.

Albert Court c1890 **J57** m
Prince Consort Road SW7
Frederick Hemings, R J Worley
⊖ South Kensington

With Norman Shaw's **Albert Hall Mansions** J51, Albert Court follows the line of the Albert Hall establishing around it a ring of civic space (which unfortunately was not continued by the Royal College of Art to the west). The curved façades are a memory of the crescents which previously formed the north boundary to the Royal Horticultural Gardens of 1862. The large brick seven-storey building is exceptional for its long entrance corridor (90×7m/296×23ft) connecting it with the steps from Prince Consort Road to the Albert Hall: this impressive internal street is furnished with large fireplaces, postboxes, grandfather clocks and minstrel galleries, and is lit by light-wells. The façade to Prince Consort Road is remarkable for its corner turrets and three storeys of columned loggias.

Mount Street Gardens c1890 **J58** h
ex **St George's Gardens**
entrances on South Audley Street, Mount Street and South Street W1
⊖ Hyde Park Corner

A beautiful, meticulously maintained, irregularly shaped secret garden, walled in by the backs of mansion flats and by **Grosvenor Chapel** J8 and Liddon House to the west. For those who know, it is a tranquil place to sit in the middle of Mayfair; all the benches face south, and the enormous 200-year-old plane trees give it a leafy ceiling in summer. The bronze fountain is by Ernest George (1892).

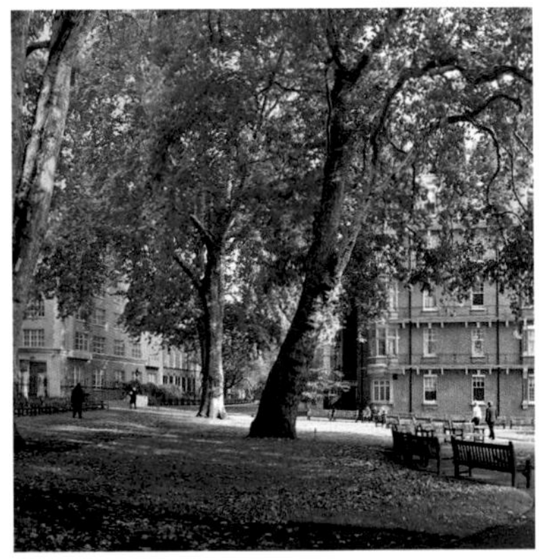

Houses 1891–2 **J59** n
14–16 Hans Road SW3
C F A Voysey
House 1894
12 Hans Road SW3
A H Mackmurdo
⊖ Knightsbridge

These houses by Voysey are among his earliest works in London, contemporary with his **Studio Houses** T19 and T20, in **Bedford Park** T17. They distinguish themselves from the verticality of their Dutch surroundings by the emphatic horizontals of their grouped windows and their squat, smooth porches. Mackmurdo's house is less radical: it displays a mixture of Queen Anne-style motifs, with others, like the oriel windows, derived from Norman Shaw.

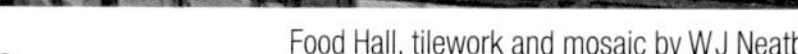

Food Hall, tilework and mosaic by W J Neatby

Harrods Department Store **J60** n
1901–15
Brompton Road SW3
Stevens and Munt
⊖ Knightsbridge

Under scaffolding, 2008

Although they are architecturally and technically less adventurous than their continental equivalents of the same period – Samaritaine in Paris and Messel's Wertheim store in Berlin – the London department stores are impressive for their sheer size and Edwardian splendour. From its modest beginnings in 1849 as a small grocer's shop, Harrods expanded vigorously to become the largest store in Europe. It now occupies a whole city block of 1.8 hectares (4.5 acres), with over 5.5 hectares (13.5 acres) of sales space on its five floors – the 214 departments and staff of 4000 seeming to justify the store's motto, *omnia, omnibus, ubique* (everything for everyone, everywhere). With its eight public entrances, sixty-six window displays and complex internal organization of lifts and escalators, it seems like a miniature city within the city. Inside, the Food Halls are a *tour de force*: the mosaic friezes and tilework (designed by W J Neatby) combine magnificently with the sensuous display of food. Recalling Harrods' original trade, they are an oblique memorial to the energies of Henry and Charles Harrod. The gentlemen's hairdressers in the basement and the ladies' lavatories on the first floor are unexpectedly fine art deco designs. The exterior is made with red terracotta tiles of small-scale decorative relief (also by Neatby), and is impressive when adorned with its festive lighting at Christmas.

Selfridges Department Store **J61** c
1907–28
Oxford Street W1
R F Atkinson with Daniel Burnham;
supervised by John Burnet
⊖ Marble Arch
The design and building of Selfridges, London's grandest shop façade, has a complex history. Although R F Atkinson is credited with the design, there are significant contributions by Daniel Burnham of Chicago (with Francis Swales), the internal steel frame is attributed to Albert Miller, and the first stages of construction (the east section) were supervised by John Burnet. The massive and richly decorated Ionic columns of the façade are set forward from the three intermediate floors, which are concealed by metal panels. The store follows the nineteenth-century tendency for a single building to occupy a whole city block, and this extraordinary temple of the retail business was promoted with Edwardian zeal by Mr Gordon Selfridge. As commercial street architecture it has a generosity of scale which has remained unmatched.

See also opposite Joseph Emberton's **shop**, the former 'His Master's Voice', of 1939. The panel of glass blocks set in the black granite rectangle is all that remains of the original composition.

Royal School of Mines **J62** m
1909–13
Prince Consort Road SW7
Aston Webb
⊖ South Kensington
The last of Webb's three buildings in Kensington – the earlier ones are the **Victoria and Albert Museum** J41 and Imperial College – carried out in hard white stone during the Edwardian classical revival, suggests that he was losing his touch. The monumental central semicircular niche with sculptures is impressive but cramped.

Science Museum 1913 **J63** m
Exhibition Road SW7
Office of Works; Richard Allison
⊖ South Kensington
Allison used the department store as the model for the inside of his building, and the Edwardian office building (those in **Kingsway** K132 for example) for the outside. The combination works well, and the generous circulation spaces using well-finished, practical materials accommodate the flocks of mainly young visitors easily. The roof-lit central well is good for the display of large engines, and the surrounding open galleries used also to be naturally lit. Fashion now requires that exhibits are best looked at under artificial light, if not in near-darkness.

The Wellcome wing, displaying contemporary technology (much of the display constantly out of

action) and including an IMAX cinema was added to the west in 2000, architects MacCormac Jamieson Prichard.

Note the **Dana Centre** at 165 Queensgate of 2005 also by MacCormac Jamieson Pritchard, and part of the Science Museum, occupying a conventional house depth but, unlike a house, presenting formal façades to both front and back.

Grosvenor House Hotel 1926–8 **J64** g
Park Lane W1
Wimperis, Simpson and Guthrie; consultant Edwin Lutyens
⊖ Marble Arch
Built on the site of Lord Grosvenor's early-nineteenth-century house, this was one of the first in a series of grand hotels on Hyde Park. Although very large, it avoids the conspicuous bulk or height of its successors such as the **Hilton** J75 and the Royal Lancaster. The 478 bedrooms and 160 flats are contained in four closely packed blocks at an angle to Park Lane. Lutyens, who designed only the elevations, marked the ends of these blocks with square roof pavilions or belvederes which are very impressive when seen from the park, riding above the trees. The massive, abstract base, the disappearing pilasters, and the quadrant screen of giant Corinthian columns to the first-floor terrace, are his further contributions to this urbane building. R D Russell's interiors of 1955–61 have, predictably, been replaced by ubiquitous international chic.

Tudor House 1929–31 **J65** h
6–10 Mount Row W1
Frederick Etchells
⊖ Green Park, Bond Street
These curious Tudor-ish offices confirm the Etchells enigma and John Betjeman's comment that, 'Etchells was a craftsman who enjoyed making things with his hands ... an artist first and an architect *faute de mieux*.' As the architect of **Crawford's** G62 and translator of Le Corbusier's *Vers une architecture*, Etchells also showed that modern architecture was for most English architects at the time a style like any other, to be used when appropriate. The rear court has notable decorative plasterwork in the form of trees.

Dorchester Hotel 1930 **J66** g
Park Lane W1
W Curtis Green
⊖ Green Park
In its time the Dorchester was thought very modern. Owen Williams designed the structure, but resigned from the job when there were objections to his plans for covering the frame. London lost a potentially modernist hotel on the park, but it is still the best building on Park Lane. It fills the block to the pavement line, and the convexity to the south is just enough to mark the entrance. The exterior, faced in faïence, is well mannered and decorated in the *moderne* style.

Department Store **J67** c
ex **British Industries House**
and **Hereford House**
1931–3
200 Oxford Street W1
Messrs Joseph; Edwin Lutyens
(designer Francis Cashmore)
⊖ Marble Arch
Lutyens was one of the last great architects in England to do 'styling': here he designed the exterior proportions and decoration of a very large part of a block. Viewing the successful if bland results, both here and at the **Grosvenor House Hotel** J64, one must regret that the practice has gone out of fashion.

Aldford House 1932 **J68** g
Park Lane W1
Val Myers and Watson Hart;
Edwin Lutyens, consultant for elevations
⊖ Hyde Park Corner, Marble Arch
Lutyens and Val Myers were the principal contributors to the appearance of Park Lane in the 1920s and '30s. The superimposition of a scraped classical façade on a utilitarian plan was not unusual at the time, and it was also quite usual for the designer of the façade to be a celebrated architect whereas the internal organization of the building was delegated to those less well known (see Lutyens's façades to the department store (J67) and **Grosvenor House Hotel** J64, and Myers's 80 Park Lane and Fountain House). The façade has broad bands of stone and red brick, capped at either end by pavilions with stone pediments of a scale appropriate to Park Lane.

Under scaffolding at the time of writing

Thistle Marble Arch Hotel 1932–3 **J69** c
Oxford Street and Bryanston Street W1
John Burnet, Tait and Partners;
designed by Francis Lorne
⊖ Marble Arch
This hotel is an excellent example of how Beaux Arts planning round light-wells, smart streamlined Dutch styling, and the influence of Mendelsohn enable a very large building occupying a whole block to be assimilated into the structure of the city and the surrounding buildings. From Oxford Street one sees only shops, as the hotel entrance is at the back in Bryanston Street.

Flats c1935 **J70** m
59–63 Princes Gate SW7
Adie, Button and Partners
⊖ South Kensington
An example of the language and tradition of London's nineteenth-century white-stuccoed terraces applied to an early twentieth-century block of flats. It is set back from the pavement by a traditional area, and the top two of its nine floors are further set back to form an attic. The rendered façade acknowledges its neighbours' rusticated ground and first floors – its bands align with the transoms of the metal window frames; and, appropriately, the basement car park is entered from the mews. The waffle slabs and cantilevered balconies and corners were characteristic of this fine building's period.

Time & Life Building 1952 **J71** h
New Bond Street and Bruton Street W1
M Rosenauer
⊖ Bond Street, Green Park

The London Time & Life Building, unlike its stridently commercial New York counterpart, is well mannered and unexceptional: a Portland stone façade sitting on a marble plinth. Many contemporary artists and designers contributed to its decoration, coordinated by Hugh Casson and Misha Black: the frieze panels are by Henry Moore, sculpture by Geoffrey Clarke. The building combines with the Westbury Hotel opposite (in the same style) to make something like a fragment of a mid-European socialist city.

United States Embassy 1956–9 **J72** g
Grosvenor Square W1
Eero Saarinen and Associates, with Yorke Rosenberg and Mardall
⊖ Bond Street

Compared with the clean-cut certainties of Saarinen's earlier General Motors' Detroit headquarters, the Embassy is by contrast muddled. It is shorter than the sides of the square it attempts to command, and the residual spaces were only later filled by plane trees. The exterior's fussy, non-structural Portland stone facings are supported on a ground-floor structure of diagonal beams; its appearance and flimsy 'gilded' aluminium trim suggest a department store rather than the dignity appropriate to an Embassy. In 2008 the building was put up for sale.

Hall of residence Imperial College 1960–3 **J73** m
Princes Gardens SW7
Richard Sheppard, Robson and Partners
⊖ South Kensington

This building is all that remains of an ambitious scheme for redeveloping the whole of Princes Gardens; that on the south side was demolished in 2005 and replaced by a more 'gentrified' version. The northerly one, however, has a scale like the remaining houses on the square. The style is an accomplished late English 'brutalism'.

Royal College of Art 1962–73 **J74** m
Kensington Gore SW7
H T Cadbury Brown, Hugh Casson
⊖ South Kensington

One of several educational institutions established in Kensington after the 1851 Exhibition under the patronage of Prince Albert, the College was intended to train designers for British industry, but soon outgrew its original accommodation. The functions of the new building – workshops, hall and library – were arranged in three linked wings round a courtyard. Seen from the park, the massing was intended to complement the huge **Albert Hall Mansions** J51 to the east, and the seven-storey workshop block succeeds. Close to, however, the detailing of the tall block's glazing is fussy and that of the squat Gulbenkian Hall, facing the Albert Hall, crude. In the late 1980s the conversion of three large houses in Queen's Gate and a new building in Jay Mews finally provided space for some departments that had never been housed in the main building (architects Colquhoun and Miller).

London Hilton 1963 **J75** l
Park Lane W1
Lewis Solomon Kaye
⊖ Hyde Park Corner
This was an early and unwelcome arrival of 'Manhattanism'. The chief attraction of the view from the rooftop restaurant and bar, one of the earliest in London, is that this particularly inept building is for once absent from the skyline (as Victor Hugo remarked of the Eiffel Tower).

Offices ex **Playboy Club** 1963–5 **J76** l
45 Park Lane W1
Cotton Ballard and Blow, with Walter Gropius, Llewelyn Davies and Weeks
⊖ Hyde Park Corner
Gropius always advocated teamwork, but it is ironic that the founder of the Bauhaus should collaborate with the least distinguished speculator architects of the decade (see what they did to Notting Hill) and with the planners of Milton Keynes to design the Bunny Club's premises. The banal precast concrete façades with their feeble rounded corner were a disappointment to those weaned on the suggestion, further subverted by his Pan Am building in New York, that Gropius was one of the masters of modern architecture.

Household Cavalry Barracks **J77** j
1967–9
South Carriage Drive, Hyde Park SW1
Basil Spence and Partners
⊖ Knightsbridge
These barracks replaced the outworn but unobtrusive four-storey red-brick Victorian buildings previously on the site. It is not clear why living accommodation for soldiers should have been allowed to spoil 400 years of Crown and public investment in Hyde Park: until the late 1950s, it was still possible to stand in the middle of the park and, not seeing any buildings, to pretend one had left the city. First the **Hilton Hotel** J75, and then the Barracks' tower destroyed this illusion. (Spence's later government office building at Petty France seriously interfered with the wonderful long view of the Palace of Westminster from the Serpentine's bridge.) The loose arrangement of red-brick buildings, strung out from the foot of the tower along Knightsbridge, contributes nothing to the street or the park.

Danish Embassy 1977 **J78** o
55 Sloane Street SW1
Arne Jacobsen; Dissing + Weitling
⊖ Knightsbridge
A strange work by Denmark's best-known international architect and his only built work in London. Jacobsen's style was distinguished by an extreme delicacy and refinement of the parts, and those of this building are treated as individual exercises in product design. Facing Sloane Street are four floors of offices behind aluminium panels, above which, set back, are two floors of offices and flats clad in flush dark-brown curtain walling. The building is inoffensive but has little to do either with London or with its immediate context – Jacobsen's better work is to be found at Oxford.

Serpentine Gallery **J79** i
ex **Serpentine Tea Pavilion** 1998
Kensington Gardens SW1
J Grey West Chief Architect to HM Office of Works
John Miller and Partners
⊖ Lancaster Gate

This charming pavilion in the park was built in 1934 as a tea room. It has since acquired a reputation as a gallery for contemporary art. In 1998 it was sensitively renovated with particularly fine new gallery lighting to the designs of John Miller and Partners. The unexpectedly grand central gallery was treated minimally in a style expected of contemporary art galleries. The relationship of the galleries to the parkland was maintained.

Hampden Gurney School 2002 **J80** b
Nutford Place, W1
BDP
⊖ Edgware Road, Marble Arch

An area characterized by casinos, hotels and Lebanese street life is not the most obvious site for one of London's best recently built primary schools. Its vertical arrangements echo earlier LCC Board schools and Bijvoet and Duiker's canonical open-air school in Amsterdam of 1932. The school's former site was redeveloped to finance the new building and provide its very dense surrounding housing. The new plan exhibits four stacked play-gardens at the corner. Its simple expression of a concrete frame and glazed screens is a welcome relief from the ingratiating polychromy of many newer school buildings.

Tanaka Business School 2003 **J81** m
New Faculty Building
Imperial College 2004
Exhibition Road, SW7
Foster and Partners
⊖ South Kensington

The Tanaka Building proclaimed the entrance from Exhibition Road that the college had long lacked. The portico of four-storey-high slender white steel columns provided entrances both to the college and the Business School. These lead the visitor to Dalby Court and thence to a diagonal ramp which cuts through the new faculty building to connect Exhibition Road and Queen's Lawn, the formal heart of the college. The simple four-storey faculty building with its blue cladding panels and bright orange columns was a departure for the Foster office and an attempt to humanize an otherwise corporate office building. Both buildings form part of Foster and Partners' masterplan for Imperial College as a whole.

Shop and offices 2004 **J82** d
Oxford Street, W1
Allies & Morrison
⊖ Bond Street

Since Daniel Burnham's **Selfridges** J61 and Joseph Emberton's HMV nearby, Oxford Street has neglected its patronage of architecture. It is therefore an agreeable surprise to discover Allies & Morrison's fine retail palazzo holding its own amongst the dross of the contemporary shopping strip and skilfully turning the corner into New Bond Street. The offsets and asymmetries forming the generous openings over four floors introduce the idea of multi-level display, a concept more typical of Tokyo than London.

continued section G

continued section J

continued section O

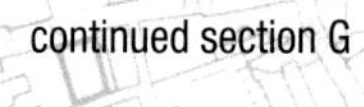

continued section G

continued section L

continued section O

Westminster ■ St James's ■ Soho ■ St Giles ■ Strand ■ Covent Garden ■ Lincoln's Inn ■ Temple ■ Lambeth ■ South Bank

The line of the Roman road from London to the west, now Oxford Street, forms the upper boundary of this area, but there is little evidence that the Romans occupied the flat marshy area which was to become the administrative hub of the British Empire, and which, as Westminster, is now the royal, religious, legislative and administrative centre of the United Kingdom. The first Abbey was one of many founded outside the City and owned the land up to the City boundary. It was probably established in the tenth century, but acquired importance only when it was rebuilt in 1065 by Edward the Confessor. Edward's successor William Rufus confirmed the royal presence by building **Westminster Hall** K5 nearby in 1097–9. The twin poles of the cities of London and Westminster have existed side by side for 900 years, and for 800 years the slow growth of links between them shaped the development of London. First the **Temple** K4 was built alongside the Thames in the twelfth century, followed in the thirteenth by a hospital near Charing Cross. In 1245 Henry III began the Gothic rebuilding of the **Abbey** K2, a work continued through the following 300 years, finishing with the **Chapel of Henry VII** K8 in 1512.

The present large-scale planning of Westminster is the result of Henry VIII's ambitious activities. He enclosed St James's Park, Green Park and Hyde Park as a chain of royal hunting grounds; he dissolved the monasteries and confiscated their land, making the Abbey's strip north of the Thames ripe for development; he established the Palace of Westminster as England's administrative centre, and started work on **St James's Palace** K10. Under the Tudor dynasty and with the beginnings of imperial exploration, England prospered, and London began to expand. By 1600 there were houses as far north as St Giles, and in the century up to 1605 the population quadrupled to 225,000.

At the beginning of the seventeenth century, the architecture of the Renaissance reached London in the person of Inigo Jones, whose white buildings (the **Banqueting House** K12, **Queen's Chapel** K13 and **St Paul, Covent Garden** K15) made the Tudor brick muddle look provincial and old-fashioned. London's growth was now the result of two methods of development: aristocrats speculated with land from their own estates (as at Covent Garden), while builders bought land and built speculative houses (as at Lincoln's Inn).

Westminster survived the Great Fire of 1666 undamaged, and the century also saw the consolidation of the pattern of streets and squares south of Oxford Street. The gridiron pattern of St James's was laid out in the 1660s, and with the completion of Wren's **St James, Piccadilly** K21 north of **St James's Square** K18 in 1684 it was fully established as a district. Soho followed in the 1680s and '90s, growing round **Golden Square** K20 and **Soho Square** K24,

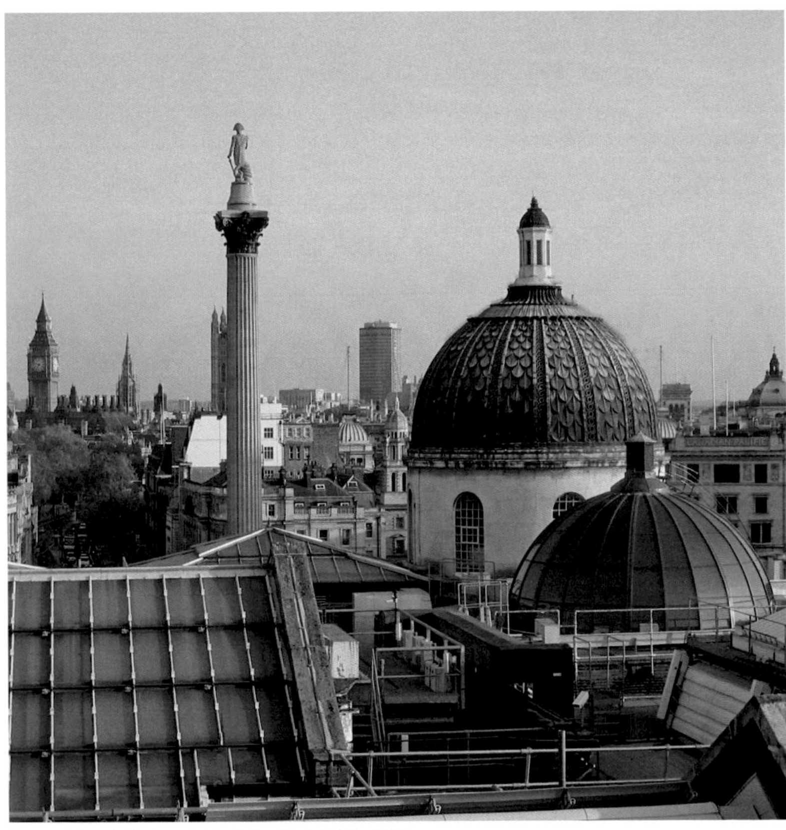

View south from the Restaurant of the National Portrait Gallery K118

which now give little sense of their original spacious style.

North of the aristocrats' mansions of Piccadilly, speculative development continued to the end of the century, with the laying out of **Berkeley Square** J9, Albemarle Street, and Thomas Bond's Bond Street.

A century after Jones's assault on Tudor disorder, Lord Burlington, from his headquarters in Piccadilly, launched his attack on the seventeenth century's debasement of Jones's correctness. In 1715–17 he had **Burlington House** K36 remodelled and to the north he laid out streets where his protégés could build. Houses were now built south of Westminster Abbey around **Smith Square** K38 and Archer's **St John** K35: many remain, their doll's house plainness a contrast to the pomp with which Mayfair was being developed.

At the same time a wave of churches, all of architectural significance, were being built to serve these new districts: **St George, Hanover Square** J6, introduced the pavement portico to Mayfair; Gibbs's **St Mary-le-Strand** K34 brought Rome to the royal route from Westminster to St Paul's, and **St Martin-in-the-Fields** K40 solved the Anglican problem of combining temple and steeple. Whitehall's government offices were now rebuilt to suit their functions (the Admiralty in 1722–6, for instance, and Kent's **Horse Guards** K50). Westminster Bridge joined Westminster to Lambeth and the south in 1749. Whitehall nearly lost its administrative supremacy when **Somerset House** K62 was built between the Strand and the river (to house a large number of government departments); the Adams' contemporary **Adelphi** K58, also on the river, formed a private speculative counterpart.

The introduction of Greek taste to London can be dated exactly to James Stuart's exquisite house at **15 St James's Square** K56, but Greek and second-generation Palladian architecture (exemplified by Robert Taylor's **houses** J7, K60, and his magnificently dour **Stone Buildings** K61 at Lincoln's Inn) were able to coexist.

The building activities of the Prince Regent, Nash's patron, mark the years of peace after the Battle of Waterloo (1815), providing in Regent Street the first north–south axis to connect London's three main east–west routes (Oxford Street, Piccadilly and the Strand). Nash rebuilt **Buckingham Palace** K76, planned **Trafalgar Square** K70 and, with Repton, restyled St James's Park. Just before his death he built **Carlton House Terrace** K77 as the magnificent southern end to his north–south route.

The 1820s and '30s saw the peak of the classical taste, coinciding with the invention of new building types, from barracks to gentlemen's clubs. In the **Travellers' Club** K82, Barry introduced his Italianate, which provided one of the routine styles for the rest of the century. In 1834 the Old Palace of Westminster burnt down and the Gothic Revival was launched with Barry and Pugin's competition-winning design (K90) for its replacement.

The reforming conscience of the Victorians showed itself in concern for hygiene; sewers were built to prevent cholera, slums were cleared by building roads through them, and the displaced poor were rehoused by charitable trusts. **Shaftesbury Avenue** K108, **Charing Cross Road** K115, New Oxford Street and **Victoria Street** K95 were all cut through and redeveloped, giving the West End its present pattern. Victorian efficiency and engineering zeal is exemplified in the **Embankment** K104 (designed to bypass the congested Strand), then the single most ambitious engineering work ever undertaken in the capital. It combined a wide road, a finely detailed retaining wall, a large sewer, and a tunnel for the underground railway. By the beginning of the twentieth century the last of the metropolitan improvements was finished, as Kingsway and **Aldwych** K132 provided sites for commercial palaces and a subway for trams.

The royal route was upgraded by the construction of **Admiralty Arch** K129 and the **Queen Victoria Memorial** K121 and Buckingham Palace was given a new front in time for George V's coronation in 1911; at least part of the capital now had architecture appropriate to the centre of a huge and prosperous empire.

Westminster escaped devastation in the Second World War, and plans were made (notably by Forshaw and Abercrombie in their County of London Plan, 1943) for grand post-war rebuilding – but in the exhaustion that followed nothing came of them.

After the 1970s high buildings were successfully discouraged in Westminster, much of the area included in this section, and the **London Eye** K187 remains the only exception. Unlike the grand projects of Paris where new buildings for arts institutions were promoted, the principal initiatives in London were in the conversion of existing institutions, most notably at the **Royal Opera House** K99, the **Royal Academy** K36 and the **National Portrait Gallery** K118.

Lambeth and the South Bank

Lambeth Palace K3 stood alone on the South Bank until houses and factories were built in the mid-eighteenth century. In 1769 the works for Coade stone (to provide the architectural ornaments for Bloomsbury) were set up on the future site of County Hall, and **St Thomas's Hospital** K174 was established in the 1860s. In 1951 the land at the southern end of Waterloo Bridge, where the river bends sharply, was used for the attempt at national cheering-up, the Festival of Britain. The **Royal Festival Hall** K163, the most distinguished of the Festival buildings, was the only permanent one and it is still one of the few good modern buildings in London.

The unsatisfactory aspects of the cultural ghetto established next door with the building of the **Hayward Gallery** and **Queen Elizabeth Hall** K177 and the **National Theatre** K178 were addressed by the masterplan prepared by Rick Mather Architects, which was fitfully implemented. However, these buildings established the beginnings of a very popular riverside promenade which extends along much of the South Bank between Vauxhall and Tower bridges.

Temple Church **K1** d
c1160–85, c1220–40,
19th and 20th century
Inner Temple EC4
Robert Smirke 1825, E Blore 1841–3,
Walter H Godfrey 1948–58
⊖ Temple

A Norman and Gothic church, extensively renovated in the nineteenth century. The tradition of the circular nave derives from the Church of the Holy Sepulchre, Jerusalem, and two other examples survive in English parish churches: Holy Sepulchre, Cambridge, and Holy Sepulchre, Northampton. The building as a whole is one of the earliest in London to be built according to strict Gothic principles – the triforium with its small marble columns is worth noting, as are the piers surrounding the circular nave, 18m (59ft) in diameter. The nave and porch date from about 1160. Below the chancel is the Undercroft (c1170) and to the south the underground Chapel of St Anne (thirteenth century). The present chancel (1220–40) was an enlargement of the original and, with very fine marble piers and capitals and high lancet windows, is one of the best thirteenth-century examples in England.

The church was restored by Smirke in the nineteenth century and was further renovated following extensive damage in the Second World War.

Westminster Abbey **K2** n
from 1245
Parliament Square SW1
⊖ Westminster

The Abbey and **Westminster Hall** K5 across the road were to become the nucleus of the City of Westminster, 3km (2 miles) upstream from the site of the (Roman) City of London. While Roman remains have been found at Westminster, the first building of which evidence exists is the abbey built by Edward the Confessor (1042–66) on the site of an earlier one. A Norman church was built between 1110 and 1150, but this was demolished under Henry III's huge building programme, and a new church started in 1245. It is this church with its later nave which we see today. The chancel, transepts and crossing, and the first five bays of the nave, were built between 1245 and 1260. The polygonal apse with its radiating chapels originally forming a chevet (the first of its kind in Britain), its tall (31m/103ft high) nave (the highest of all England's Gothic churches), and its lavish decorations are all of French derivation and reflect Henry III's interest in the

French court. The architect, Henry of Reynes, may have been French.

For a hundred years the abbey church had a Gothic east end and a Norman nave, and it was only in 1375 that the Norman work was demolished. The master mason for the new nave was Henry Yevele, who instead of building in the current Decorated style, modestly built in keeping with the earlier work. The nave was completed in the 1390s, when the west window, much altered since, was done in Perpendicular style. The last significant additions to the Abbey were the **Chapel of Henry VII** K8 and Hawksmoor's **West Towers** K48.

The Abbey's continued existence is the result of its role as the religious centre for coronations, royal weddings and burials; for a time it acted as Treasury, and Parliament sat in the Chapter House. Its appearance has changed drastically. When completed, the interior was painted white, the carved decoration picked out in bright colours and gilded, the windows filled with stained glass; there was a delicate screen across the chancel, quite unlike the present massive one which supports the organ, and the place was as yet empty of 700 years' accumulation of monuments, about which critics including Pugin and William Morris were to complain.

The Abbey was built of soft Reigate stone, and the exterior has been refaced several times. Wren was surveyor for a time; he made unrealized designs for completing the crossing, but it was his pupil Hawksmoor who completed the exterior with his West Towers started in 1735.

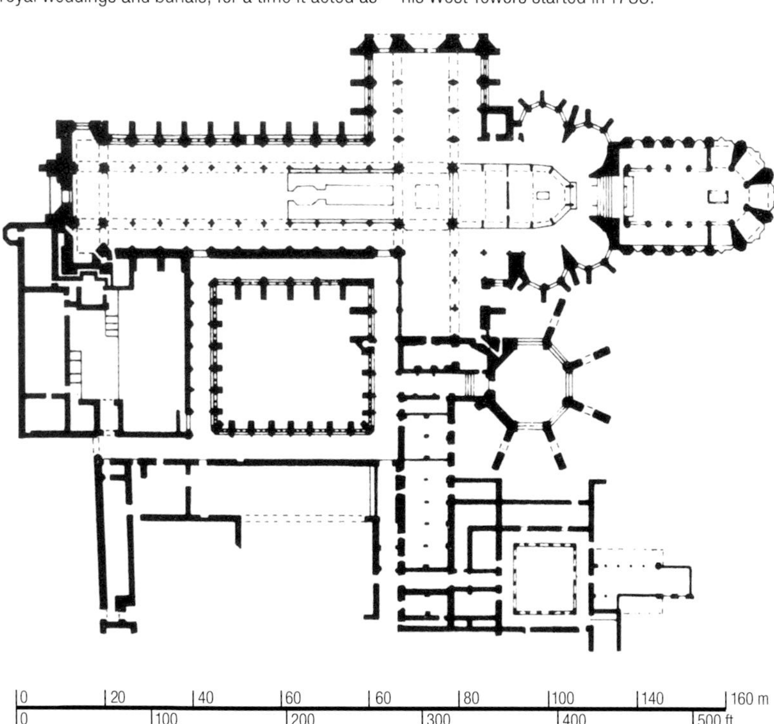

Lambeth Palace **K3** o
1297, 1495, 1660, 1829
Lambeth Palace Road SE1
⊖ Vauxhall

The fine medieval, Tudor and Jacobean buildings of Lambeth Palace have been the official residence of the Archbishop of Canterbury for seven centuries. Before the building of the Albert Embankment, with its bridges and traffic roundabouts, the Palace was approached from the river (boats were moored on the site of the pier now used as a café); it must then have seemed considerably more impressive than it does today.

Immediately to the north of the tower of **St Mary** K96 is the red-brick gatehouse, known as Morton's Tower, built by Archbishop Morton in about 1495. On either side of the gateway are five-storey brick wings; inside, on the south side of the cloisters, is the Hall, rebuilt by Archbishop Juxon in about 1660–3, and the Palace's finest building. The magnificent hammerbeam roof was restored after damage in the Second World War. The Chapel, which probably dates from about 1230, was also gutted in the war.

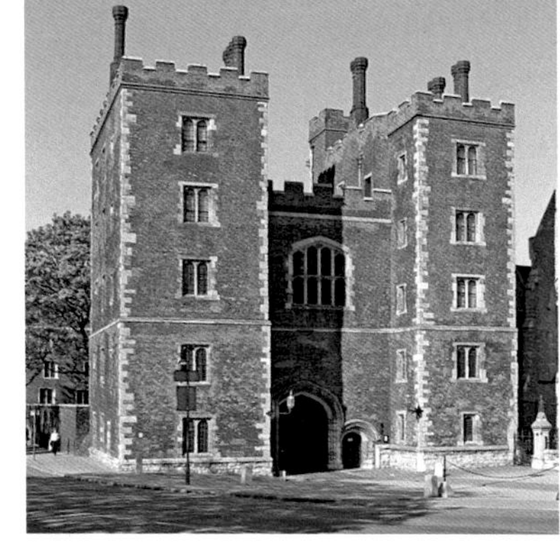

The neo-Jacobean extensions to the north and east of the Hall, incorporating the cloisters and partly medieval guardroom, are by E Blore (1829–33); they give the Palace an unfortunate lugubrious quality. The extensive Archbishop's Park, to the east, is now open to the public.

King's Bench Walk

Southern gate to Middle Temple Lane

The Temple **K4** d
c1350 and c1500 onwards
Fleet Street and Victoria Embankment
⊖ Temple

With its many gated and controlled entrances, the Temple is an exclusive English institution dating back to the fourteenth century, when it was leased to students of law by the Order of St John. At the Dissolution the Temple reverted to the Crown, and Templar lands on the west side of the Fleet became the site of Henry VIII's Bridewell Palace. In 1608 the Temple was leased by James I to the Benches of the Inner and Middle Temple. Its position, midway between the merchants' City of London and the royal City of Westminster, is no coincidence.

There is now no visible distinction between the Middle Temple (to the west) and the Inner Temple (to the east), and the buildings are linked by a labyrinth of passageways and courts almost as complex as the legal system they encompass. There was much destruction in the Second World War, and many buildings have been either renovated or replaced. A leisurely walk is the best way to appreciate the area.

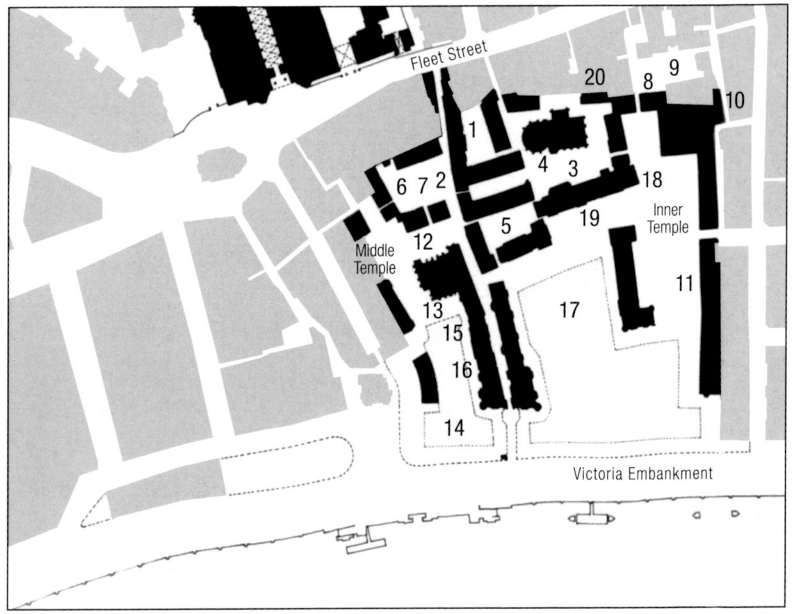

1 Hare Court
2 Pump Court
3 Church Court
4 Temple Court
5 Elm Court
6 Essex Court
7 Brick Court
8 Mitre Court
9 Sergeant's Inn
10 Niblett Hall
11 King's Bench Walk
12 Fountain Court
13 Middle Temple Hall
14 Middle Temple Garden
15 Middle Temple Treasury
16 Middle Temple Library
17 Inner Temple Garden
18 Inner Temple Library
19 Inner Temple Hall
20 Master's House

Westminster Hall 1394–1402 **K5** n
St Margaret Street,
Parliament Square SW1
Henry Yevele, mason; Hugh Herland, carpenter
⊖ Westminster

The Hall replaced that built in 1097 by William Rufus, while the Tower was being finished at the other end of London; only some eleventh- and twelfth-century masonry survives of the original. Richard II's rebuilding involved the construction of a spectacular hammerbeam roof with massive timbers; restored after fires and bombings, it survives as London's earliest example of this kind of roof. All the openings in the extremely thick walls have been altered from the original. See also **Eltham Palace** X1 and **Guildhall** L8.

Photograph 1982

Gatehouse to Chancery Lane

Lincoln's Inn Hall

Lincoln's Inn c1400 **K6** d
WC2
⊖ Chancery Lane

Lincoln's Inn, between Street's **Law Courts** K107 and Lincoln's Inn Fields, is one of London's three districts now devoted to the law (the others are the **Temple** K4 and **Gray's Inn** G6). The original nucleus of the district was a Dominican friary (1221–76), later the Earl of Lincoln's house, which in the fourteenth century became a hostel for lawyers. The lawyers' offices are now in a number of buildings of all ages, loosely arranged around four connected spaces, forming a delightfully picturesque ensemble like the colleges of Oxford or Cambridge.

The **Gatehouse** (1518) has massive doors in a central, four-centred arch. Much of the red brickwork patterned with blue diapers is original, as are the doors, but the windows were inserted in the seventeenth century. It leads to the east court and **Old Buildings** beyond, a collection of picturesque and turreted brick houses of the early sixteenth and seventeenth centuries. The north side of the courtyard is formed by the stone **Chapel** (1619–23), from the curious period in English architecture when late Perpendicular Gothic coexisted with continental classical imports (usually Tuscan, as here, until Inigo Jones showed how to do the other orders). Note the unusual vaulted ground floor.

The **Old Hall** (1492), bay windowed and buttressed, was the living room of the original residential community of lawyers. Its interior furnishings are of the seventeenth century. The thirteenth-century arch between the Hall and the Chapel is reset from the original hall. See also New Square and Taylor's extraordinary **Stone Buildings** K61.

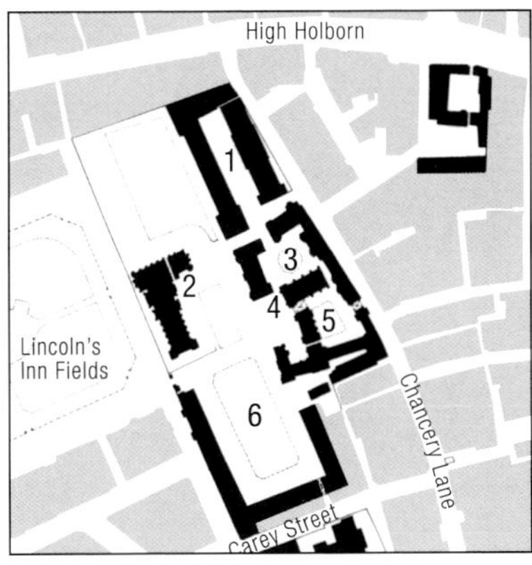

1 Stone Buildings
2 Lincoln's Inn Hall
3 Old Square
4 Chapel
5 Old Buildings
6 New Square

St Margaret, Westminster **K7** n
founded 1120–40, rebuilt 1480–1523
Parliament Square SW1
⊖ Westminster

The ‘parish church’ of the House of Commons since the seventeenth century, St Margaret's is dwarfed by neighbouring Westminster Hall and Westminster Abbey. The church is a strange mixture of late Perpendicular Gothic and eighteenth-century Gothick. The nave and aisles, although restored in the eighteenth and nineteenth centuries, are original. In 1735–7 John James rebuilt the tower in the Gothick style of William Kent, and in 1758 Kenton House added an apse, which was altered by S P Cockerell in 1799–1802. The degree to which this small church has been renovated and extended over the years (the interior was restored by Giles Gilbert Scott in 1877, for instance) and the lavish inventory of its fittings befit its national status and prominent site in Parliament Square. Samuel Pepys and John Milton are among those who have been married here.

Henry VII's Chapel **K8** n
Westminster Abbey
1503–12
Parliament Square SW1
Robert Vertue(?)
⊖ Westminster

While Bramante was designing the first centralized Renaissance plan for St Peter's in Rome, England's last Tudor kings, Henry VII and Henry VIII, built King's College Chapel, Cambridge, the Chapel of St George at Windsor, and this, London's finest complete late Perpendicular chapel. Widely spaced piers support the extraordinary fan-vaulted, cusped and pierced vault and define the nave, returning at the east end to make an apse in the shape of half a hexagon. Very large windows span between them so that the interior is like a brightly lit cage, combining practical and elegant engineering with a taste for intense, busy decoration. Most of the original extensive statuary has survived, although it has lost its bright colour. On the outside the buttresses supporting the vault are exposed, but are pierced and carved to reduce their structural effect. The outer piers, carrying the load from the buttresses, are folded, panelled and crowned with playful turrets which carry gilded weathervanes.

St James's Park SW1 **K9** i, j
from 16th century
⊖ Charing Cross, Westminster, St James's Park
Like so many of central London's parks, St James's was originally Crown land, enclosed by Henry VIII as hunting grounds for St James's Palace. It was remodelled in French style under Charles II, with a straight, tree-lined canal and the first setting out of the Mall, and opened to the public. The park's present picturesque arrangement dates from Nash's work of 1828; he converted the canal into an irregular lake which, like that of Regent's Park, is now a sanctuary for resident and visiting wildfowl.

Note the café and restaurant, **Inn the Park** (Hopkins Architects 2004), pictured above, positioned close to the lake with splendid views across it towards the **London Eye** K187 in the distance. From one direction it is a timber pavilion, from the other part of the landscape.

St James's Palace 1530s **K10** i
Cleveland Row, Marlborough Gate SW1
⊖ Green Park
The Palace is another of Henry VIII's building projects – he was the monarch who shaped more than any other the future pattern of central London, even more than Nash's patron, George IV. The original palace had four courts, and while fire and rebuilding have now reduced these to two, the outdoor Tudor work is all visible from the street, most notably the toy-like gateway to Cleveland Row. The state rooms, which face south and can be seen over the wall to the Mall, were rebuilt in 1703, possibly by Wren.

Gough Square and **K11** d
alleys **Hind Court**, **Bolt Court**
and **St Dunstan's Court**
17th century
off Fleet Street EC4
⊖ Blackfriars
A remarkable network of pedestrian alleys winding between modest three- and four-storey buildings; the most notable of these is the seventeenth-century house in which Dr Johnson lived from 1748–59.

Banqueting House 1619 **K12** j
Whitehall SW1
Inigo Jones
⊖ Westminster

Jones's first work, the **Queen's House** U2 at Greenwich, stood alone. Three years later the Banqueting House started James I's ambitious plan for the rebuilding of Whitehall: when first built, it stood among a medieval and Elizabethan jumble of small-scale buildings. Its startling newness in this setting is unimaginable today, when the surrounding buildings are faced in the same fine Portland stone. Jones is credited with having introduced the material to London and first used it here for the lower storey, perhaps in imitation of the white stone with which Palladio's urban palaces were covered. The building is a box with two levels: the lower a crypt for the king's less formal parties, the upper a sumptuous room for masques and banquets. This is one of London's great seventeenth-century rooms, a double cube 17×34×17m (55×110×55ft) with a flat ceiling. The room's only features are the gallery, the fine Ionic porch to the entrance and the decoration of two orders – Ionic below, Corinthian above, as on the outside. The panelled ceiling was painted by Rubens in 1634–6 and, like the decoration in Palladio's buildings, appears today to have a robust gaiety which the architecture denies.

The exterior owes much to Vicenza, but perhaps in Jones's hand English versions of Palladio were becoming more correct than those of the master. Its crispness is due in part to John Soane's refacing of 1829.

Queen's Chapel 1623–7 **K13** i
Marlborough Road SW1
Inigo Jones
⊖ Green Park, St James's Park

The chapel was built for James I's wife Queen Anne, and belongs to St James's Palace – Marlborough Road was cut later through to the Mall. With the **Queen's House** U2 at Greenwich, and the **Banqueting House** K12, it is part of Jones's success in dragging English architecture into the (Italian) sixteenth century, and a marvellously pure work. The interior is a double-cube volume, the coffered ceiling a segmental tunnel vault, and the whole is lit from a full-width Venetian window (the first in England) at the east end. The exterior has the same primitive quality as **St Paul, Covert Garden** K15, the front having a simple pediment over stucco walls reinforced with Portland stone quoins.

Covent Garden Piazza 1631 **K14** c
WC2
Inigo Jones
⊖ Covent Garden

Covent Garden is one of London's more romantic districts, associated with the opera, Pygmalion, and (until 1974) London's principal fruit and vegetable wholesale market. Architecturally it is significant because the piazza was London's first real square, built under the patronage of one of the Great Estates which reshaped London in the following 250 years.

The land was formerly a convent garden, belonging to Westminster Abbey. After Henry VIII's confiscation of all land belonging to the monasteries in 1552, Covent Garden was given to the first Earl of Bedford. The idea of a residential square is attributed to the fourth Earl, who in 1631 commissioned Inigo Jones to produce plans. Bedford apparently knew the Place Royale in Paris (the present Place des Vosges) built by Henri IV twenty years earlier. However, Inigo Jones's proposal was classical, unlike the Place Royale, and its origins were Italian (as the name 'Piazza' suggests). The square of individual houses behind the continuous classical façade was very successful, at first inhabited by the highest society in London. The façades are like the walls of a big public room, governed by the large temple of **St Paul** K15. In 1671 the Earl obtained the right to hold a daily vegetable market, and by the end of the century the square was no longer a respectable residential area. The arcades, however, remained so popular that the word piazza came to be associated with them rather than with the square itself.

The central market building (K81) of 1831 was lovingly restored, but its demolition and the restoration of the Piazza, which has kept its original proportions through several rebuildings, might have been better. With the redevelopment of the **Royal Opera House** K99 (1983–1999) the blighted north-east corner of the market square was finally reconstructed.

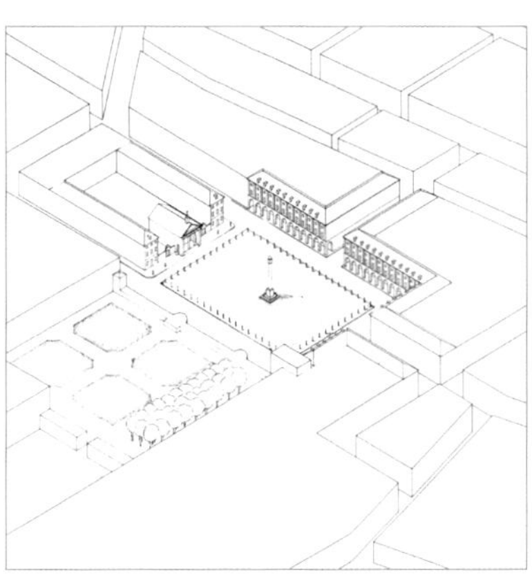

St Paul, Covent Garden 1631–8 **K15** g
Covent Garden Piazza WC2
Inigo Jones
⊖ Covent Garden

The monumental portico to this Etruscan temple, with projecting timber beams supporting the pediment and eaves, constitutes the headpiece – a shelter and meeting place – to Jones's original **Covent Garden Piazza** K14. It is not the main door to the church of St Paul: this is through Inigo Place off Bedford Street to the west. Whether Jones intended this deceit (following Scamozzi's idealized illustrations of urban Etruscan temples), or whether, as contemporary evidence suggests, the church was planned originally with the altar at the west end and was revised following ecclesiastical objections, is not clear. In any event Jones's famous saying, 'You shall have the handsomest barn in England', is vindicated by this revision and by the building's further modifications over the years. In 1795 a fire gutted the interior, and in his restoration Thomas Hardwick omitted to replace the side galleries and on the exterior substituted stone for the original brick facing. It was later re-restored in brick by Henry Clutton.

Lindsey House 1640 **K16** c
59–60 Lincoln's Inn Fields WC2
Inigo Jones(?)
⊖ Holborn

Following the initiative of **Covent Garden Piazza** K14, Lincoln's Inn Fields were London's first garden square, laid out by William Newton in 1640. By 1658 there were houses established on three sides; the fourth side (east) had already been appropriated by Lincoln's Inn. The central garden is now a public place with tennis courts and a café.

Lindsey House is the earliest town house in London to use a giant order on a rusticated base, and is the only remaining example of the type developed in Lincoln's Inn Fields in the early 1600s. This type was to be used for at least two centuries (see also **Bedford Square** G12), and was repeated in stone a century later at numbers 57–8, but in Palladian taste. The building is of brick, which was originally exposed but later stuccoed. It is in the style of Jones, but the authorship is disputed.

The Mall 1660 and 1906 **K17** i
SW1
Le Nôtre(?) and Aston Webb
⊖ Charing Cross

Surprisingly, the processional route from Trafalgar Square to Buckingham Palace is only a century old, and its history is a typical example of English empiricism. The earlier traditions of private land ownership and the power of the great London estates impeded the development of royal triumphal routes, but by the end of the nineteenth century their absence was becoming a national embarrassment to the world's largest capital. The original alignment of the Mall was part of Charles II's plan for **St James's Park** K9 and its avenues, laid out in 1660 and attributed to Louis XIV's great landscape gardener, Le Nôtre. Nash's **Carlton House Terrace** K77 was the only building with a planned, formal façade to the park; the remaining buildings along the north edge (Marlborough House, Schomberg House, St James's Palace and Lancaster House) all have an informal, modest relationship with it.

Until 1900 a narrow and unimportant street called Spring Gardens separated St James's Park from Trafalgar Square. It was here that Aston Webb's magnificent **Admiralty Arch** K129 brilliantly reconciled the shift of axis from the Mall to the Strand. With his less than magnificent façade to **Buckingham Palace** K76 and **Rond Point** K121 to the west, the capital's principal processional route was established with minimum disruption.

The Sultan's elephant visits the Mall 2006

St James's Square **K18** e
started 1665
SW1
⊖ Piccadilly Circus
London's most regular seventeenth-century square – which, unlike those of eighteenth-century Bloomsbury, is actually square, with streets connecting the centre of each side (except the south). The north–south axis is on the line of Wren's **St James, Piccadilly** K21, and the east–west axis was later extended by Nash to his **Theatre Royal, Haymarket** K85. The streets and squares of this period were designed as settings for fashionable perambulation; here, the views from the square are stopped by either monuments or churches, while services are provided by a labyrinth of mews and alleys at the back. Unlike its contemporaries (**Soho Square** K24 and Red Lion Square) St James's Square has remained very fashionable.

Whereas the north side of the square is mostly intact with original houses, the south-west corner was disastrously redeveloped in the 1960s. See also **houses** K42, K47, K56 and K136.

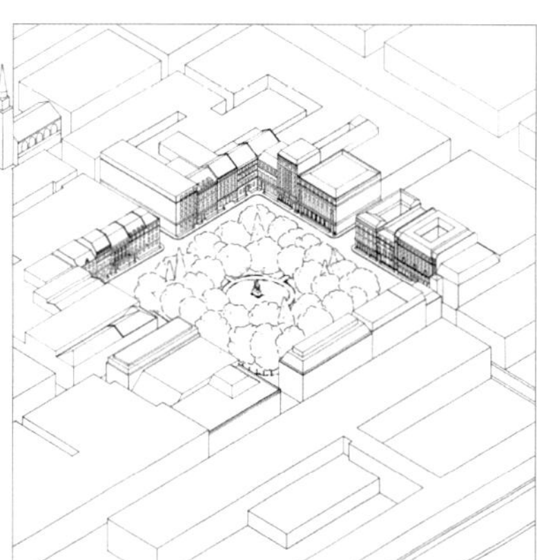

Leicester Square 1670 **K19** f
WC2
⊖ Leicester Square
One of London's earliest squares, laid out by the Earl of Leicester on ground known as Leicester Fields to the south of Leicester House. The square now represents the heart of London's West End, and its buildings, which have been renewed continuously, are mediocre; the Odeon (1937), with a *moderne* black tower, is the most memorable.

Golden Square 1673 **K20** e
W1
⊖ Piccadilly Circus
Golden Square was not completely built-up until the early eighteenth century. Except for numbers 11 and 21, which are original, the buildings are mostly of the twentieth century, large and undistinguished. The 'Cotswold' walls to its raised and redesigned garden (1952) are particularly feeble. At the centre is a diminutive statue of George II in Roman costume by John Nost, erected in 1753.

St James, Piccadilly 1676–84 **K21** e
Piccadilly and Jermyn Street SW1
Christopher Wren
⊖ Piccadilly Circus
Designed to hold 2000 people, St James is one of Wren's best-known and most influential works. It was built in connection with Lord St Albans's contemporary scheme for the development of the St James's area, and the tower and general siting of the church were intended to 'stop the view' from St James's Square, when seen in perspective along Duke of York Street. The rows of five two-tiered windows on the north and south elevations express the practical rectangular plan. Although this suited the Anglican liturgy, it indicated Wren's retreat from his earlier, and more idealistic, centralized plans. Largely as a result of its economy, it was taken up by Gibbs (see **St Martin-in-the-Fields** K40), and through his influence was copied in many British colonies (Harrison's Christ Church, Boston, USA, of 1723, and Richard Munday's Trinity Church, Newport, USA, of 1725–6, for example). The brick exterior is restrained, with its simple stone detailing and square tower added by Wren's office in 1700; a new spire was completed in 1968 by Albert Richardson, who also designed the clergy house on Piccadilly to the east. The church was badly damaged in the war and restored in 1947–54; a further restoration was in progress in 2008.

St Clement Danes 1680 **K22** d
Strand WC2
Christopher Wren, tower by Gibbs 1719–20
⊖ Temple
Wren's church recased some of the masonry of its predecessor, but it illustrates a stage in his development of the section of the two-storey church, which achieved its definition in **St James, Piccadilly** K21. In this development the columns supporting the vault and side galleries were progressively raised on plinths above the fixed pews of the nave. Unique among his churches, the aisles of St Clement's return at the east end in semicircles. The upper stages of the tower were added by Gibbs, in a style owing more to the Italian baroque (which he used in his earlier **St Mary-le-Strand** K34 further west along the Strand) than to his predecessor Wren or to his contemporaries, the Palladians. The church was bombed in the Second World War, and was rebuilt as a memorial to the Royal Air Force.

Houses 1680–1766 **K23** j
10, 11 and 12 Downing Street
SW1
⊖ Westminster

That the official residences of the Prime Minister and the Chancellor should be unremarkable houses in a nondescript cul-de-sac might be a fine example of English understatement. That the Georgian London house can perform such a function and acquire symbolic importance carries a still-unlearned lesson for today's architects. The houses, all interconnecting, have been continually altered over three centuries: William Kent and Soane were among those who refitted rooms, Kenton Couse refaced them in 1766, and Raymond Erith repaired the exterior and did some interior remodelling in 1962–4.

Soho Square and **Greek Street** **K24** b
laid out 1681
W1
⊖ Tottenham Court Road

Started at about the same time, Soho's two squares (the other is **Golden Square** K20) have both since been almost completely transformed. Soho Square often seems gloomy but the shade of its mature plane trees is welcome in the summer. There are two churches – **St Patrick** K119 and the French Protestant church on the north side – and a few early houses. Some regret the changes of scale since the square's setting-out, but some admire its present diversity, as the Victorians who contributed most to the change would have done. The statue under the plane trees in the centre is of Charles II by Cibber and was originally flanked by personifications of English rivers which were transferred in the 1870s to **Grims Dyke** Q3.

Number 1 Greek Street (the House of St Barnabas for destitute women) turns the corner into Soho Square. Built in 1746, it is the most distinguished building in the street and has very fine interiors. The exterior is restrained, with large, simple window openings. Two obelisks stand either side of the doorway, added by Richard Beckford MP after he bought the house in 1754; by the mid-eighteenth century these and stone-consoled doorcases and had become fashionable. Numbers 50 (1736) and 48 (1741–2) are also noteworthy.

Seven Dials laid out 1690 **K25** b
WC2
Thomas Neale
⊖ Leicester Square

A few houses survive of this early and, for London, rare example of French street planning. The layout consists of a rectangle bordered by Shelton Street, Neal Street and Tower Street, and the later Shaftesbury Avenue, crossed at right angles by Mercer Street and Shorts Gardens and diagonally by Earlham and Monmouth Streets. In the 1980s the crossing was consolidated by undistinguished rebuilding on the western corners and substantial work on the many late-seventeenth- and early-eighteenth-century houses of the **Comyn Ching Triangle** K180. Finally, a replica by Whitfield Partners of the column which originally stood at its centre was erected, complete with new sundials.

New Square c1690 **K26** d
Lincoln's Inn WC2
Henry Serle
⊖ Chancery Lane
This remarkably well-preserved early 'square' (actually a north facing U-shape) was built between Carey Street, to which it is connected by an arched passage, and Lincoln's Inn. It has always been occupied by lawyers, originally as flats, now as offices, their names painted on boards at the feet of the staircases. The ensemble represents an important stage in the development of the London square. There is no private open space (gardens, back yards or mews) and on the west the houses back directly onto the pavement of Serle Street. This arrangement is characteristic of the colleges of Oxford and Cambridge (perhaps one of the origins of the London square) and it suits the present semi-collegiate habits of the legal profession.

Schomberg House c1698 **K27** i
Pall Mall SW1
⊖ Charing Cross
Built for the German Duke of Schomberg, this is a rare surviving example of a house of the period which is not in the routine terrace format. Schomberg House is built of the customary brown brick with red trim, but has tall windows of Dutch proportions (abandoned by the eighteenth century, but revived by the Shavians), and decoration derived from contemporary French sources. The central porch with caryatids is later.

St Anne, Soho **K28** b
Late 17th century, tower 1801–3, 1991
Wardour Street W1
S P Cockerell; the Westwood Practice
⊖ Leicester Square
The outer walls and tower are all that survived the Second World War. The nave, which remained a car park for over forty years, was replaced by two wings of residential building in 1991. The yellow brick tower of the church has at its apex an eccentrically bulbous form from which bulge four clock faces. The garden, raised above street level on the west side, is an unexpectedly tranquil place.

Savile Row laid out early 18th century **K29** e
W1
⊖ Piccadilly Circus
Laid out soon after **Burlington House** K36 was built, the streets north of the house were inhabited by many of Burlington's circle. William Kent lived in Savile Row, of which numbers 3–17 are the only originals to survive. The street is now known as the centre of London's bespoke tailoring trade, whose activities can be viewed from the pavements – the tailors work near the basement windows lit from the 'areas' typical of Georgian London. See also **Old Burlington Street** K43. Number 33, at the north-east end of the street, is an office building that replaced the former headquarters of English Heritage (Eric Parry Architects 2009).

Greycoat Hospital 1701 **K30** m
Greycoat Place SW1
⊖ Victoria, St James's Park
An example of the philanthropic provision of education (see also the near contemporary **Blewcoat School** K32 in Caxton Street). Following extensive damage in the war, the charming centre section, with its lantern and wings, was rebuilt in twentieth-century Queen Anne style. The miniature buildings are a reminder of the scale of early eighteenth-century London. Note the two wooden statues of charity children.

Queen Anne's Gate and **Old Queen Street** started 1704 **K31** j
SW1
⊖ StJames's Park
The best and most complete street of regular houses of its date in London. In 1704 Queen Square was developed in an L-shape, entered from Broadway and with a gate into St James's Park. Although the widths of the houses vary, they are all regular in design and built in brown brick with stone bands marking the division of the storeys. The decoration is pre-pattern book, as can be seen from the intricate carved rustic foliage surrounding the doorways, and the pendants, arches and frieze (see numbers 17, 19, 23 and 25 and opposite numbers 26, 28 and 30). In the south-east corner of the square stands a statue of Queen Anne, to the east of which the character of the street changes, becoming more uniform (owing to the emergence of pattern books). On the south side numbers 5–13 (1773–5) have doorways marked by Doric pilasters carrying pediments with open architraves. On the north side numbers 14–24, of the same date, have magnificent bow windows facing the park. Also of the same date is 34 Old Queen Street, the narrow eastward continuation of Queen Anne's Gate. Numbers 9–11 Old Queen Street are earlier and more modestly detailed.

Blewcoat School 1709 **K32** m
23 Caxton Street SW1
⊖ St James's Park
A marooned relic, this tiny elegant brick schoolhouse was built as a charitable act by a brewer. It is one of the earliest examples of this building type extant in London. Now, stranded among new offices, it is a reminder of the minuscule scale of the early-eighteenth-century city. The school is owned by the National Trust.

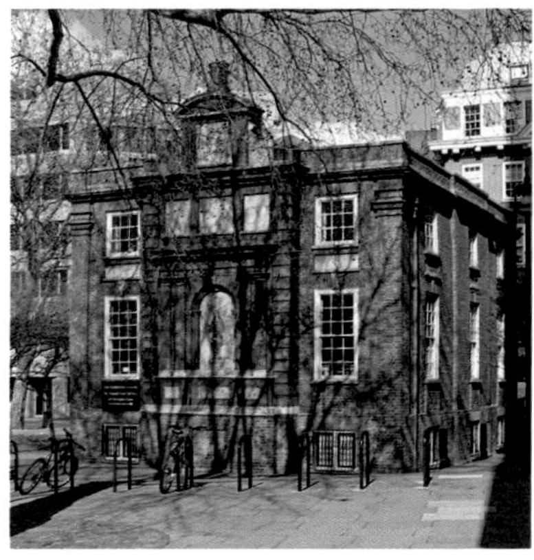

Marlborough House **K33** i
1709–11, 1861–3
Pall Mall SW1
Christopher Wren, James Pennethorne
⊖ Green Park
In gratitude for his victories against the Dutch and the French, Queen Anne commissioned Vanbrugh and Hawksmoor to build the first Duke of Marlborough a monumental palace at Blenheim, and Wren to build his London residence on the Mall. Wren's Marlborough House has been much altered: in the nineteenth century the original house, with thirteen bays to the south front, was extended by two extra floors and further stables and outbuildings added to the east. To the north of the main entrance court is a fine red-brick screen of arched recesses and pediments. In 1861–3 the north side of the original house was almost totally concealed by a range of rooms with a deep porch, added by Pennethorne for the Prince of Wales.

St Mary-le-Strand 1714–17 **K34** c
Strand and Aldwych WC2
James Gibbs
⊖ Temple
Though twenty years his junior, Gibbs was Hawksmoor's working contemporary, and from 1713–15 acted as his fellow surveyor to the Commissioners' fifty new churches. His architectural training had been in Rome, unlike Hawksmoor's, and the body of this delicate little church is clearly derived from Mannerist models – the porch from Cortona's Santa Maria della Pace. The tower, not part of the original design, owes more to Wren. Gibbs quickly changed his style after this early effort and produced Palladian designs more likely to appeal to the Whigs in power. The original setting, cramped between houses, was destroyed in the Edwardian 'Improvements' to Kingsway and Aldwych, and the church is now stranded on a large traffic island. See also **St Martin-in-the-Fields** K40.

St John 1714–28 **K35** n
Smith Square SW1
Thomas Archer
⊖ Westminster

Built at the same time as the square which it still dominates, this church marks an extreme of baroque London: its design owes as much to Rome as to Wren. Externally, the plan appears to be a Greek cross, but the north and south 'transepts', marked by wild fractured pediments, are porticoes to the entrances. The interior is rectangular, the east and west ends having huge Venetian windows. Burned in 1758 and bombed in 1941, the church was rebuilt as a concert hall. The four corner towers – drums with circular entablatures over the corner columns, topped by pineapples – have been much criticized; we like them. See also Archer's **St Paul, Deptford** U7.

Sackler Galleries, Foster Associates 1991

Burlington House **K36** e
refaced and remodelled 1715–17;
extended and remodelled 19th century
Piccadillly W1
Colen Campbell and others
⊖ Piccadilly Circus

Richard Boyle, third Earl of Burlington (1694–1753), first visited Italy at the age of twenty, and on his return immediately employed Colen Campbell to remodel the façade of the family house in Piccadilly. Gibbs, who had been working on curved colonnades (demolished in 1728) connecting the house to the street, was sacked. Campbell became the first member of Burlington's circle of artists; William Kent, at first as painter, and the sculptor Rysbrack were to follow. In 1715 Campbell had begun to publish *Vitruvius Britannicus*, his illustrated descriptions of British 'regular buildings' – those showing the direct influence of Antiquity, Inigo Jones, or Palladio. Leoni's English translation of Palladio's *Quattro Libri* was published in the same year. The remodelling of the first Earl's seventeenth-century house was therefore the beginning of Burlington's successful campaign to shift English architecture from the pragmatic baroque of the Wren school towards a more correct Italian (ancient Roman and sixteenth-century Vicentine) – a style judged appropriate to George I's new Hanoverian dynasty. Campbell's two-storey façade was based on Palladio's Palazzo Porto Colleoni in Vicenza, but with details from Jones. It was in Portland stone, of seven bays with a rusticated ground floor, an Ionic order above, and Venetian windows in the projecting wings at either end. Behind it Burlington created on the first floor an enfilade of

'Great Rooms' which, while they have been greatly changed over time, provide an idea of what taste and money could commission.

The radical, cool elegance of the original design can now be appreciated only in drawings of the period, for at the beginning of the nineteenth century a series of remodellings was started, and in 1867 the building became the Royal Academy's headquarters. The interior was then converted by Robert Smirke, who also added the present top storey with its statues of artists. The arched building fronting Piccadilly was added in 1873 by Banks and Barry. A more recent addition, the new Sackler Galleries by Foster Associates, of 1991, provided three top-lit vaulted rooms at roof level. They are reached by a new glass lift and stair set in what had become a light-well. The result is a masterly synthesis of space and fine modern detailing which is effortlessly juxtaposed against the classical masonry.

The modest fountains in the forecourt, installed in 2003, emulated the successful ones at **Somerset House** K62.

Arcade 1716–17 **K37** i
Stable Yard, St James's Palace SW1
Nicholas Hawksmoor
⊖ Green Park
One of Hawksmoor's few surviving secular buildings, this little arcade in stock brick, with a stone trim and turrets at the corners, was ruined in 1980 by the Department of the Environment's crude restoration. The inside was gutted, and the exterior pointing in modern mortar clumsily smudged. In 2008 Stable Yard was inaccessible inside a 'security' enclave.

Smith Square, **Lord North Street** and **Cowley Street** c1720 **K38** n
SW1
⊖ Westminster
Dominated by Archer's magnificent church (K35), Smith Square takes its name from James Smith, who developed the square and streets around. The south and east sides were damaged in the Second World War and unfortunately redeveloped as twelve-storey offices, which have destroyed the relationship between the church and the square. With the exception of numbers 1 and 2, rebuilt after the war, the north side is original, as are the ironwork and lampholders. Numbers 6–9 are almost identical to each other and date from 1726, and 36 is by Lutyens in his neo-Georgian style. On the north-west corner of the square the house (1930) by Oliver Hill is also neo-Georgian. Lord North Street and Cowley Street are almost complete early Georgian streets, like rows of doll's houses in brown brick with red-brick dressings to windows and arches.

Houses c1720 **K39** d
14–15 Tooks Court,
off Cursitor Street EC4
⊖ Chancery Lane
Two unexpectedly grand small houses, both of three storeys and three bays with segmental window heads of rubbed brick. The grand elements are the three-storey Ionic pilasters in antis, marking the party walls, and the ornate rubbed- and carved-brick cornice to number 15 (known as Dickens' House), which also retains its original mansard roof.

St Martin-in-the-Fields 1721–6 **K40** f
Trafalgar Square WC2
James Gibbs
⊖ Charing Cross

Gibbs's synthesis of influences from Rome, Wren and Palladio here produced a type which has had widespread and continuing influence in the English-speaking world. The interior scheme was derived from Wren, but improved on its models – the giant order is raised on pedestals and the galleries firmly relegated. The exquisite plasterwork of the ceiling is by the Italian craftsmen Artari and Bagutti. Outside, Gibbs provided the definitive model for the relationships between the tower and the steeple and the portico. In his introduction to the exterior of the round-headed window edged with dies (to be known as 'Gibbs surrounds'), and of the coupled columns at the corners, he considerably extended the architectural repertoire for the sides and backs of churches. Because of its position, St Martin's is one of the few London churches that still gives the Italian feeling of being used: the steps are good for resting on and the portico provides shelter from the rain.

Major works, both new and of restoration, were completed in 2008. The church was repaired and cleaned inside and out, and the new works, designed by architects Eric Parry, included a large extension to the north at basement level, reached by a new circular entrance pavilion above. The railings of the churchyard were moved south to create a generous pedestrian connection between St Martin's Place and Adelaide Street and a setting for the new pavilion.

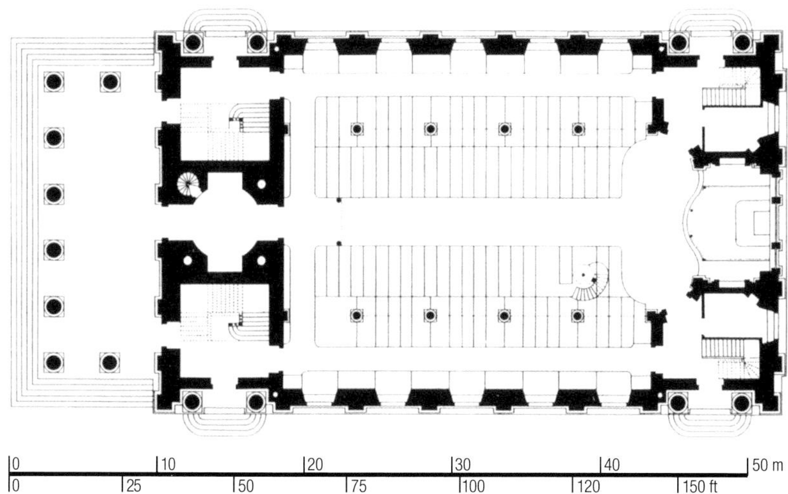

College, Westminster School **K41** n
1722–30
Little Dean's Yard SW1
Lord Burlington
⊖ Westminster
Gutted in the Second World War and much altered – the ground-floor arcade has been glazed in and the first-floor windows, originally blank, have been opened up – Burlington's only surviving early work in London nevertheless shows his fastidious interpretation of his models: Palladio, via Scamozzi and Inigo Jones. The flat, fifteen-bay stone façade is proportioned 4:1, but the rainwater pipes make this difficult to read.

House 1726–8 **K42** e
4 St James's Square SW1
Edward Shepherd
⊖ Piccadilly Circus
The five-bay elevation to the square is strangely horizontal, a consequence of the deep band of brickwork above the first-floor windows. The delicate balance of vertical and horizontal which was later to mark Georgian compositions is here absent.

Old Burlington Street **K43** e
started c1730
W1
⊖ Piccadilly Circus
Almost completely rebuilt, and now a pleasant mixture of styles and uses, the architectural interest of the area north of Burlington House is now one of association rather than of buildings. Burlington laid out the streets up to Clifford Street, and many of the artists he worked with or patronized (Colen Campbell and William Kent, for example) took or built houses in them. Numbers 31 and 32 are original, with a fine lampholder and ironwork to the doorway of number 31, but the stucco surrounds to the windows look heavy and Victorian. See also **Savile Row** K29.

Pickering Place 1731 **K44** i
off St James's Street SW1
⊖ Green Park
A surprising tiny enclave of houses arranged round a paved court, reached down a timber-lined passage from St James's Street: it would be more at home in a cathedral town than in the centre of London.

St Giles-in-the-Fields 1731–3 **K45** b
St Giles High Street WC2
Henry Flitcroft
⊖ Tottenham Court Road

The church is a standard eighteenth-century galleried box for preaching and being preached at. Its interior arrangement follows the model of Wren's **St James, Piccadilly** K21, and its vault that of Gibbs's **St Martin-in-the-Fields** K40. Flitcroft was a clerk in the Office of Works which Wren had left in 1719, and Gibbs's designs had been published in 1728.

The original wooden model stands in a niche in the vestibule under the tower, and Flitcroft's name is carved above the west door under the pediment. The arch outside the west door was built in 1800, incorporating a sooty wood carving of the Resurrection of the Dead (1687).

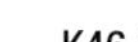

Treasury Building **K46** j
1733–6, 1824–7, 1844
Whitehall SW1
William Kent; John Soane, Charles Barry
⊖ Westminster

The symmetrical flanking wings and pavilions of Kent's original design unfortunately were never built, but the central building has great Palladian elegance. The façade is curiously mannered and vertical, with overall stone rustication and a diminutive portico of four Ionic columns on the second floor. Inside there are three rooms of note on the first floor, two facing north and the third to the west. Their design – unusually for Kent – is very simple: restrained plaster panelling to the ceilings, and simple coves and marble fireplaces. The building overlooks Horse Guards Parade and can also be reached from Treasury Green via Treasury Passage.

In 1824–7 Soane built a new Board of Trade and Privy Council facing Whitehall. The building proved too small, and was dismantled in 1844, to be replaced by Charles Barry's new Treasury, incorporating Soane's columns and frieze. Fortunately the interior still has Soane's remarkable entrance halls from Downing Street and Whitehall. The modest relief of Barry's façade is typically early Victorian, showing the insecurity of Victorian neoclassicism in the face of neo-Gothic's growing popularity. It has far less authority than Soane's designs for the same building two decades earlier.

Houses 1734 **K47** e
9, 10 and 11 St James's Square SW1
Henry Flitcroft
⊖ Green Park

Flitcroft was one of Lord Burlington's circle, so it was appropriate that he should use the Palladian style for these large houses, whose spare, refined façades make the earlier **number 4** K42 look clumsy by comparison.

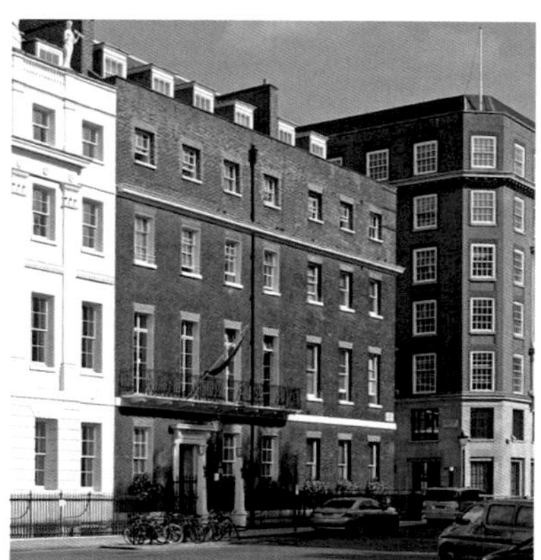

West Towers  **K48** n
Westminster Abbey 1735–45
The Sanctuary SW1
Nicholas Hawksmoor
⊖ Westminster

As Surveyor of the **Abbey** K2, Hawksmoor completed its West Towers which had remained as stumps since the 15th century. His last public work before he died in 1745 is one of the two examples of his Gothick style in London (see also **St Michael Cornhill** L9). The flatness of the corner buttresses, their interruption by broad string courses, and the oval arch over the clock betray the towers' eighteenth-century, rather than medieval, origins.

Houses 1736 and 1740–55 **K49** e
16 and 22 Arlington Street SW1
James Gibbs and William Kent
⊖ Green Park

Number 16 has a plain brick elevation to Green Park. It is now part of the Overseas Club, entered from Park Place, but the main entrance used to be through the big arch at the end of Arlington Street. Number 22, Wimbourne House, has been partly obscured by a new seven-storey office building, and Kent's interiors are inaccessible. Its interest lies in the unusual plan: it has two large rooms of similar size with bay windows facing the park; and, on the entrance side, a vaulted passage along the north side of the filled-in court connects the front door to the street.

The Horse Guards 1745–55 **K50** j
Whitehall SW1
William Kent, John Vardy
⊖ Charing Cross, Westminster

Built by John Vardy after Kent's death in 1748, this building demonstrates the dryness of English Palladianism when not in Burlington's hands. Its picturesque composition is built up from arched openings housing either Venetian or pedimented windows, both set in rusticated masonry entirely without columns or pilasters. The façade to the Parade, through the arch from Whitehall, with the backs of Downing Street to the south and the Admiralty to the north, now forms an impressive background for pageantry like Trooping the Colour. On the Whitehall side, the Horse Guard is changed twice a day.

Spencer House 1752–4 **K51** i
27 St James's Place SW1
John Vardy; altered by Robert Taylor 1772 and Henry Holland c1785
⊖ Green Park

This fine double-fronted mansion built for the Earl of Spencer is strictly Palladian. The entrance faces the confines of St James's Place, and a rhetorical façade gives onto the open spaces of Green Park. Of the two façades the elevation to the park is more memorable and public, having a rusticated ground floor and an upper floor of seven bays separated by engaged Tuscan columns, with a five-bay pediment.

In 1759–66, and contemporary with the publication of the first volume of his and Revett's *Antiquities of Athens* (1762), James Stuart decorated and designed furniture for several rooms. The entrance hall, with rounded corners and plaster ceiling, and the staircase, with Ionic pilasters and a tunnel vault, by Robert Taylor of about 1772, are especially fine. Henry Holland remodelled the rooms to the west of the entrance in 1785. In 1991 a restoration of the whole house was completed. This included the decoration and furnishing of nine of the state rooms by David Mlinaric and these can be visited.

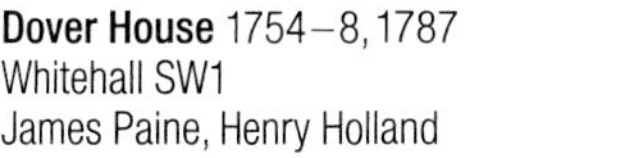

Dover House 1754–8, 1787 **K52** j
Whitehall SW1
James Paine, Henry Holland
⊖ Charing Cross

The original house was built as a private residence by James Paine, one of the most prolific Palladian architects. When the Duke of York bought the house in 1787 he appointed Henry Holland to add new façades, with the result that the courtyard was filled in, and of the original only the inner block now remains. With this transformation of the façade Holland gave Whitehall its finest architecture (excepting Inigo Jones's **Banqueting House** K12), modest in scale and very un-English. The Greek Ionic portico flanked by attached columns and the rusticated wall strongly resemble the French *hôtel particulier* of the early eighteenth century.

House 1756–60 **K53** n
6–7 Old Palace Yard SW1
John Vardy
⊖ Westminster
Portland stone, Palladian, and now stranded out of context.

Admiralty Screen 1759–61 **K54** j
Whitehall SW1
Robert Adam
⊖ Charing Cross

In 1758, after returning from Rome and a visit to Diocletian's Palace at Spalato, Adam set up in private practice, and his first work, at the age of thirty-one, was a public one. The screen hides the courtyard of Thomas Ripley's earlier feeble Admiralty (1722–6) from Whitehall. The seriousness of its correct Roman Doric order anticipates none of Adam's departure from Palladianism towards a new delicacy, which is so evident in the screens at **Osterley** T10 and **Syon** T9. Decoration is restricted to the seahorses on top of the piers flanking the central arch, and to the sculptured pediments of the astylar end pavilions.

To the south of the Admiralty is S P Cockerell's Admiralty House (1786–8), which has good but inaccessible interiors and presents only its side to Whitehall. To the west, Leaming and Leaming's building of 1894–5 provided an unappealing façade to the north side of Horse Guards Parade.

Shop c1760–70 **K55** f
ex **Fribourg and Treyer**
34 Haymarket SW1
⊖ Piccadilly Circus

A rare surviving example of a mid-eighteenth-century shop front. The house dates from about 1760 and the shop front and its elegant internal screen were added about ten years later.

Lichfield House 1764–6 **K56** e
15 St James's Square SW1
James 'Athenian' Stuart,
interiors Samuel Wyatt, 1791–4
⊖ Piccadilly Circus

James Stuart visited Greece with Nicholas Revett in 1751–3, surveyed the ancient monuments, and in 1762 began publishing the results as *The Antiquities of Athens*. Built shortly afterwards, this suave stone façade capped with a single pediment uses exclusively Greek motifs. The capitals of the Ionic giant order are exact copies of those of the Erechtheum.

Boodles Club 1765 **K57** e
28 St James's Street W1
John Crunden
⊖ Green Park

The London club is an eighteenth-century invention, with its origins in the coffee houses and inns of the previous century. Boodles – named after the original proprietor – is one of the earliest and best examples of the type. Designed in the style of Robert Adam, it is the only building in London attributed to Crunden. The fine yellow-brick façade to St James's Street, with a central arched Venetian window and flanking porches, represents the main 'upper room' of the club. The interior, partly remodelled by Papworth, is also good. The Smithsons' buildings for **The Economist** K176 next door drew Boodles into their composition of small towers on a raised podium, and the new, faceted bay window was built onto the club's newly exposed south wall as a gesture of continuity.

Engraving c1770

The Adelphi 1768–74 **K58** g
Adelphi Terrace: John Adam,
Adam and Robert Streets WC2
James, John and Robert Adam
⊖ Charing Cross

Only a few fragments remain of one of eighteenth-century London's most ambitious and important urban designs, but these are of such high quality that its history is given here. In 1768, the Adams became developers: they leased land between the Strand and the Thames, where they built a quay and high set-back vaults for warehousing. On the roofs of the vault they raised four streets, two parallel to the river and two at right angles. Set back from the edge of the platform, a terrace of eleven four-storey brick houses faced the river, closed by the projection of the terraces in Robert and Adam Streets. The centres and ends of the terraces projected slightly, and were decorated in the new style with flat, horizontal bands of stucco, and pilasters with sunken panels of delicate honeysuckle strands. These can be seen in 1–3 Robert Street, all that remains of the composition to the Thames. Even better is 7 Adam Street where, because the dark brick has not been cleaned, the pale stucco carries both the Adams's prettiness and their strange, sometimes chill, archaeological neoclassicism. Fragments of the scheme also remain on either side of this last house and at 4–6 John Street, next to the Royal Society of Arts building. This has a stone façade (a serious Ionic order and pediment) and some good original interiors, particularly the library.

Offices, Collcutt and Hamp 1936–8

The Adelphi was derided by the contemporary architectural establishment, headed by William Chambers, but liked by the artistic (for example Garrick, who in 1772 moved in). The houses did not sell and the Adams were saved from bankruptcy only by disposing of them by lottery. Chambers went on in the same decade to design **Somerset House** K62, using the Adelphi's format, and the Adams to speculate again at **Portland Place** F3.

In 1872 many of the houses were stuccoed, and in 1936 the central block was demolished for the present offices. An LCC blue plaque on 9 Robert Street records that 'eminent writers and artists lived here'. The street names, given by the brothers themselves, record their achievement. 'Adelphi' is the Greek for 'brothers'.

Albany 1770–4, 1803–4 **K59** e
Piccadilly and
Burlington Gardens W1
William Chambers, Henry Holland
⊖ Piccadilly Circus

Built for Lord Melbourne and originally known as Melbourne House, Albany has two approaches, one from Piccadilly and the other from Burlington Gardens, and is the product of two architects of the golden age of the eighteenth century. Seen from Piccadilly through a formal gateway, the house is set behind a forecourt, on either side of which is a two-storey nine-bay building. The principal façade is of seven bays with a projecting three-bay pediment. The general arrangement of the house is like a Parisian *hôtel particulier*, or miniature palace in the town, but here the square openings in a brick façade are relatively restrained.

Albany's most original feature is towards the back where, instead of the garden of the Parisian *hôtel*, there is an elongated court. In 1803 Henry Holland converted the house itself into apartments and built two parallel rows of apartments approached by a covered way. The buildings are stuccoed, with segmentally arched windows, and the elevation to Burlington Gardens is of one-storey lodges either side of the fine entrance gate, also by Holland. One of the lodges is still a florist's for the residents; the other, formerly a cigar shop, is now a gallery.

House 1772 **K60** e
37 Dover Street W1
Robert Taylor
⊖ Green Park

Set between two lower stuccoed houses, the tall house built by the Bishop of Ely for himself looks as authentically Vicentine as a work from a second-generation Palladian architect should. The very high first floor alters the expected balance of solid and void in the façade, emphasizing the flatness against which the precise architectural features are placed. The central medallion between the first and second floors bears the Bishop's coat of arms. The interiors are much altered.

Stone Buildings 1774–80 **K61** d
Chancery Lane and Lincoln's Inn WC2
Robert Taylor, Philip Hardwick (additions in 1842)
⊖ Chancery Lane

One of the best examples of Palladianism in a public building in London, built entirely of Portland store, with a two-storey rusticated base, above which are two plain storeys topped by a cornice and open balustrade. The west front to Lincoln's Inn Gardens is impressively restrained, and the ends are articulated by projecting pedimented pavilions with giant Corinthian columns. The internal court (91×18m/300×60ft) has two entrances from Chancery Lane: a gate, and a concealed pedestrian passage in the north-east corner. The centre of the east side is stone-faced, while the ranges either side are of brick, giving the court a lopsided emphasis. The offices' moated entrances, complete with cast-iron lamp-holders, are particularly fine.

Somerset House **K62** g
1776–86, 1830–5, 1856
Strand, Lancaster Place and
Victoria Embankment WC2
William Chambers, Robert Smirke,
James Pennethorne
⊖ Temple

Somerset House – purpose-built offices for several government departments – offered the challenge to William Chambers of designing the greatest English public building since the **Royal Naval Hospital** U3. Several factors made his task difficult: firstly, the need to demolish the Protector Somerset's house (1547–72) with its fine chapel (1630–5) by Inigo Jones and the magnificent riverside gallery by John Webb; secondly, the recent achievement of Robert Adam's **Adelphi** K58 upstream (Chambers was openly Adam's rival); and finally Chambers's lack of experience in the grand tradition of monumental design. His work prior to Somerset House had been concerned with smaller-scale domestic buildings for the nobility. The Strand block and the central court were begun in 1776 and completed in 1780 and 1786 respectively. The Strand façade occupies only a third of the total site width and seems like a gatehouse to the large interior court behind. The triple-arched gateway to the court is particularly fine, and reminiscent of Le Vau's entry to the Louvre.

Apart from its sheer size, 106×95m (350×310ft), with equal emphasis on three sides and central Corinthian pavilions, the court is more like a grand square for domestic residence than a *cour d'honneur* for principal administrative offices. By London standards the river front is extremely long (244m/800ft), including Smirke's extension to the east for King's College and the western extension by Pennethorne. Like the Adams's Adelphi it has the repetitive imagery of a grand and dignified housing scheme. The building stood originally on large arches rising out of the river, between which Chambers positioned water gates, thereby linking the separate pavilions in the façade. When the **Victoria Embankment** K104 was built the building's main relationship to the river was lost.

Most of the sculpture in Somerset House was drawn by Cipriani and carved by Carlini, Wilton and Bacon, friends of Chambers. Inside there are a number of excellent rooms, whose ceilings and fireplaces (inspired by Louis XV ornamentalism) are among the finest of Chambers's decorations.

Winter skating in the courtyard

In 1990 London University's Courtauld Institute moved to Somerset House. The Courtauld Gallery is open to the public and incorporates fine Impressionist paintings housed in the refurbished suite of rooms above the wing facing the Strand. The most splendid of these, the 'Great Room' with its huge lantern, was first used to display paintings by the Royal Academy in 1780. The display of the 15th–18th century collection on the first floor was completed in 1998.

In 1997 plans were adopted to transform Somerset House into an arts centre. Firstly, the central courtyard was cleared of car-parking and it was repaved to a scheme by Donald Insall and Partners. Dixon Jones were commissioned in 1998 to prepare a masterplan. This proposed a connection to Waterloo Bridge to form a new pedestrian route along the South Terrace, through Somerset House and King's College and beyond to the Inns of Court to the north. In 2000, as part of the masterplan, a fountain of 55 jets of water was introduced into the central court, transforming it into one of London's most dramatic public rooms. With the fountains turned off, the courtyard has also provided a venue for seasonal attractions: concerts and theatre in the summer and ice skating and Christmas festivals in the winter.

Brooks's Club 1777–8 **K63** e
St James's Street SW1
Henry Holland
⊖ Green Park

Holland's work is less elaborate and more scholarly than that of his rival, Adam. The white-brick façade to Brooks's, with its giant Corinthian pilasters and cornice, is scraped of any embroidery or illusion and decidedly anti-Adam. The interior is similarly restrained, the remodelled stone staircase leading, under a glass dome, to two superb rooms on the first floor and the subscription room with a coved ceiling and Venetian window. Next door, in the room with the second Venetian window, are busts of Fox and Pitt (by Nollekens), a reminder of Holland's successful association with members of the Whig hierarchy, and particularly Charles James Fox, whose career coincided with his own.

White's Club 1787–8 **K64** e
37–8 St James's Street SW1
James Wyatt
⊖ Green Park

The most memorable feature of Lockyer's façade to this famous club, added in 1852, is the large, round-headed central window. The banded rustication in the upper floor and oval relief panels in the garlands show French influence.

Theatre Royal 1810–12 **K65** c
porch 1821, colonnade 1831
Drury Lane WC2
Benjamin Wyatt and others
⊖ Covent Garden

The London theatres of the eighteenth century regularly burned down – the present Theatre Royal is the fourth on the site. Its large brick box is decorated with classical low relief. The porch and Ionic colonnade were added ten years after Wyatt's building, and their present painting scheme might be improved. The interior public spaces are a rarity in London theatres: spacious, large, and with their original early-nineteenth-century decoration.

Imperial War Museum **K66** p
1812–15, 1839, 1989
Lambeth Road SE1
J Lewis, Sydney Smirke, Arup Associates
⊖ Lambeth North, Elephant & Castle

Ironically this building was originally the Royal Bethlehem Hospital for the Care of the Insane, or 'Bedlam', until the institution moved to Shirley in 1931. The Ionic portico and dome were added in 1838 by Sidney Smirke, the younger brother of Robert. The Imperial War Museum was established by an Act of Parliament in 1920 and was to remain a rather lugubrious affair until its successful renovation by Arup Associates in 1989. Built within the old courtyard, the new top-lit exhibition hall forms a dramatic spectacle for the arriving visitor of suspended aeroplanes and other

large objects. This space also forms a focus for the four new exhibition levels that surround it. The diagonal latticed barrel-vault roof is supported by a light steel structure and contrasts convincingly with the restored heavy masonry walls of the original hospital.

If some relief is required from the display of military achievements, the museum also contains the second-largest collection of twentieth-century British art in the country (some 10,000 works). This extensive collection of war artists like Stanley Spencer, Augustus John, Paul Nash, Wyndham Lewis and Eric Kennington makes a compelling and poetic statement against war.

The Breakfast Room

Sir John Soane's Museum **K67** c
1812–34
13 Lincoln's Inn Fields WC2; 12 (1792–4) and 14 (1823–4) Lincoln's Inn Fields WC2
John Soane
⊖ Holborn

A brief account of these three houses is necessary in order to understand the layout of the Museum at number 13. Number 12 was built first by Soane for himself and includes a particularly fine (restored) breakfast room with a star-shaped ceiling. Number 14 was built and sold off immediately by Soane. The back half was retained, however, to be incorporated into the principal house at number 13.

The present museum was the residence, studio and private museum of Soane until his death in 1837. It houses his collection of antiquities, architectural fragments, paintings and books left to the nation in his will. It is a complex and highly personal building and within its standard London house dimensions the eclectic, experimental, whimsical and, above all, illusionist preoccupations of its designer are immediately apparent: Soane was not as straight a neoclassicist as is commonly believed. The Museum also has more than 30,000 architectural drawings, some (designs for Tudor and Jacobean houses) by John Thorpe, others by Robert Adam, and a collection of etchings by Soane's contemporaries, including Piranesi. The house is lovingly and authentically maintained, to the extent that you feel that Soane has just retired for the moment.

In 2008 the newly restored number 14 was opened as the Adam Study Centre and new spaces for educational activities.

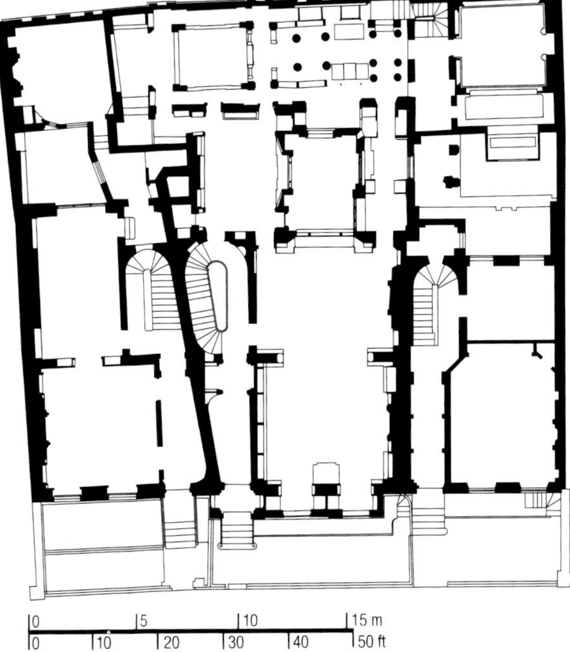

Plan of the three houses in 1837

Burlington Arcade 1810–12 **K68** e
between Piccadilly and
Burlington Gardens W1
Samuel Ware
⊖ Green Park

This arcade, built on a narrow strip of the garden of Burlington House in the years after Waterloo, is the archetype of London's arcades, and one of the few to have remained fashionable over the years. Copied from earlier continental models (as was Nash's near contemporary **Royal Opera Arcade** K69) it has a glass roof and very small, delicately detailed shops. The gross façades at the ends were added by E Beresford Pite in 1911.

Royal Opera Arcade 1816–18 **K69** f
connecting Charles II Street and
Pall Mall SW1
John Nash and G S Repton
⊖ Piccadilly Circus

This beautiful and modestly scaled arcade is one of London's earliest (following the French invention of the type at the end of the eighteenth century) and was once part of Nash's grand Royal Opera House on the Haymarket, which burned down In 1867. Because it was next to the opera, which needed secondary entrances, the arcade had shops on the west side only – in this it was unique. The perspective from either end conceals this imbalance: it is achieved by a series of simple vaulted bays with glass domes, which contain the bow-fronted shops. The gentle slope of the ground is also absorbed by minute adjustments between the bays.

Trafalgar Square started 1820 **K70** f
WC2 and SW1
⊖ Charing Cross

Nash suggested that a square should be made where the east–west route between Buckingham Palace and St Paul's crossed the top of Whitehall; he also proposed that the north–south route should be extended to the British Museum. But he designed only the east side, the West Strand Improvements (K84), behind **St Martin-in-the-Fields** K40. The rest of the buildings which enclose this far from satisfactory space were built over the following century. Smirke's Royal College of Physicians (now **Canada House** K74), on the west side, was built of Bath stone in 1824–7, and was followed by William Wilkins's timid **National Gallery** K88 on the north side. Barry's granite terrace, steps and pools were built in 1840. The Corinthian column supporting Nelson's statue was designed by William Railton and erected in 1842. The lions by Edwin Landseer and the reliefs were finished in 1867.

Nash's proposed route north from the square was eventually built as **Charing Cross Road** K115, to the west of St Martin's Lane. On the south side, the two huge Victorian former hotels by F and H Furness have been converted for use as offices. The magnificent view down Whitehall is framed by these and, on the south-west side, by George Aitchison's Royal Bank of Scotland (1885). Herbert Baker's **South Africa House** K158 filled in the east side of the square in 1935, and Lutyens's **fountains** K159 were added in 1939. On the south-east corner with Northumberland Avenue, the rebuilding of the late Victorian Grand Buildings was finished in 1990, the result of an architectural competition held in 1985 which was won, in a spectacular failure of patronage, by a design which proposed this replica of what already occupied the site.

The most recent addition to the Square was the ingratiating **Sainsbury Wing** K182 of the National Gallery in the north-west corner. The rearrangement of the traffic circulation, the pedestrianization of the square's north side and the steps in front of the National Gallery were completed in 2003, architects Foster and Partners.

Suffolk Street and **Suffolk Place** **K71** f
1820
SW1
John Nash and others
⊖ Charing Cross
Nash's great 'Improvement' from Carlton House to Regent's Park was a strip of development which included not only the buildings along the route but also some of the side streets. These two are all that remain to give an indication of their quality. The north side of Suffolk Place and numbers 7–11 Suffolk Street are by Nash, and the style is Greek for all but number 7, which is in Roman Doric. All are stuccoed and have fine iron balconies. Numbers 18 and 19 are the back of the **Theatre Royal** K85.

St John 1822–4 **K72** l

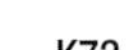

Waterloo Road SE1
F O Bedford
⊖ Waterloo
One of many 'Waterloo churches' built by the Church Commissioners to commemorate the battle. The Greek portico and three-stage tower with an obelisk-like spire form a dignified landmark at what is now a major traffic intersection. The church was restored as the 'Festival Church' in 1951, when its interior was remodelled.

Richmond Terrace 1822–5 **K73** j
Whitehall SW1
Henry Harrison
⊖ Westminster
A strange domestic relic in the now pompous setting of Whitehall, formerly threatened with demolition by the grandiose plans of Leslie Martin for the redevelopment of the area in the 1960s. The rebuilding of the interiors of this stone-and-brick terrace was finally begun in 1982. The jazzy neo-Perpendicular entrance from Whitehall (pictured above) was added in 1987 by William Whitfield and Partners. The building is occupied by the Department of Health.

Canada House **K74** f
ex **Union Club** and
Royal College of Physicians
1824–7
Trafalgar Square WC2
Robert Smirke
⊖ Charing Cross

With this block, Smirke successfully resolved the triangular wedge formed by Pall Mall and Nash's plan for **Trafalgar Square** K70 (1820). When built it was a dignified composition in Bath stone, with a recessed portico to the square and projecting porticoes to the side streets north and south. Only the building for the Royal College of Physicians remains unchanged, following the disastrous conversion and extension of the upper parts. Its particularly fine interiors, notably the staircase and library, remain intact.

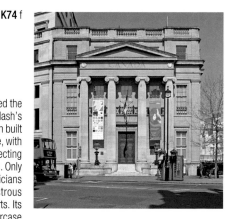

Lancaster House 1825–9 **K75** i
Stable Yard Road SW1
Benjamin Wyatt
⊖ Green Park

Robert Smirke's foundations for this house for the Duke of York had already been built when Wyatt replaced him. Smirke returned to the job after Wyatt's death, adding the attic in 1841. The grand exterior (with three Corinthian porticoes) is in the fashionable Bath stone of the 1820s (see also Nash's **Buckingham Palace** K76 and **Apsley House** J14). The interior has a central hall and stair by Barry (1843) and is occasionally open to the public during the summer. The house is now used as a government conference centre.

The Royal Mews

Buckingham Palace 1825–1913 **K76** i
The Mall SW1
John Nash 1825 30, Edward Blore 1830–47, Aston Webb 1912–13
⊖ St James's Park, Green Park

As Pevsner observed, 'Buckingham Palace is in two ways supremely English. Firstly, it was not originally intended as the monarch's official London residence: its faltering development over the years demonstrates a typically English empiricism. Secondly, the present building (despite Webb's *rond point* and radiating avenues) conveys the image of a large and rather stiff country house set in its own parkland, so the English delight in the country house and a humanized countryside triumphs in the Royal palace.' The Palace takes its name from Buckingham House, a country house on the same site, built in 1715 by John Sheffield, Duke of Buckingham. In 1762 it was bought by George III and became known as 'The Queen's Palace' but remained a country house until the Prince Regent became George IV in 1820. The absence of an appropriate permanent residence for royalty was beginning to prove a national embarrassment, and the elderly John Nash was commissioned to transform Buckingham House into a royal palace. Despite great expenditure and Nash's involvement, the result retained much of its country-house origins. Of Nash's work, the west façade facing the garden is relatively intact. The large bow window at the centre is the only concession to a rather pedestrian elevation of Bath stone. The east front was formed by a grand deep forecourt, entered by the **Marble Arch** J30, which in 1847 was built over by Edward Blore in order to provide extra accommodation for Queen Victoria and Prince Albert. Nash's north and south ranges, both modified by Blore, are of little architectural interest.

With **Admiralty Arch** K129, the **Queen Victoria Memorial** K121 and Webb's new façade (completed, astonishingly, in three months, in time for George V's coronation) London finally, in 1913, acquired a royal processional route. Webb's neoclassical front is in fact a recasing of Blore's east façade of 1847 – it remains a feeble and run-of-the-mill pastiche, and the design is popular more for what it represents than for any architectural merit. However, the work is significant as a conclusion to the Mall. See also the **Queen's Gallery** K191.

The unexpected treasure of Buckingham Palace is to be found to the south-west, facing Buckingham Palace Road – the **Royal Mews**, entered through a giant archway with magnificent Roman columns on either side. The clock tower above was added in 1824. Inside, the Riding House (1764) has a fine acanthus frieze and a pediment depicting Hercules and the Thracian Horses, both commissioned by Pennethorne from William Theed junior in 1859.

Carlton House Terrace 1827–32 **K77** f
SW1
John Nash
⊖ Charing Cross

The terraces were built on the site of Carlton House, George IV's residence before the building of Buckingham Palace, and were Nash's last design before his death in 1835. They consist of two very long ranges, each of 140m (460ft), mounted on platforms overlooking the Mall, and framing the magnificent granite **Duke of York's Steps** K86. While they exhibit some eccentricities, such as the two-storey attics at the ends, the buildings have always received more favourable architectural criticism than Nash's other large-scale works. The squat Doric columns of the platforms are made of cast iron, an early use of the material for decoration. The buildings now house a variety of professional and artistic bodies, including the Institute of Contemporary Arts. Numbers 7–9 contain the only London work of Albert Speer, the interiors of the pre-war German Embassy. At the southern end stands 4 Carlton House Gardens, by Reginald Blomfield – unfortunately it is built in stone, and out of scale with the terraces.

Institute of Directors **K78** f
ex **United Services Club**
1827, 1842
Pall Mall and Waterloo Place SW1
John Nash, Decimus Burton
⊖ Charing Cross

Nash planned two clubs to face each other across Waterloo Place. Decimus Burton designed the **Athenaeum** K80 and although Nash designed the United Services, Burton was commissioned in 1842 to remodel his work. It is this later design which we now see: Victorian Italianate, mixing orders (but still using Roman Doric for the porch), and laboured in comparison with the lucid Athenaeum opposite. The grand internal arrangements are splendid but can only be visited by members.

Waterloo Place c1828 **K79** f
W1
John Nash
⊖ Piccadilly Circus

The beginning of Nash's triumphal way from Carlton House Terrace to Regent's Park, Waterloo Place is one of the most impressive pieces of town planning in London. Following the demolition of Carlton House, Carlton House Terrace was built with at its centre the **Duke of York's column** K86 and a broad flight of steps down to St James's Park. The simple and symmetrical composition of Waterloo Place is formed by the back of Carlton House Terrace (an extraordinary change in scale from the monumental front addressing St James's Park), the **Institute of Directors** K78 and the **Athenaeum** K80 on the intersection with Pall Mall, which form two pavilions. The space, used mainly for car-parking, is a candidate for tactful reordering and proper surfacing.

Pallas Athene, E H Baily 1830

The Athenaeum 1828–30 **K80** f
Pall Mall and Waterloo Place SW1
Decimus Burton
⊖ Piccadilly Circus

This elegant stuccoed block, with its large-scale porch of paired Doric columns to Waterloo Place, is one of the most distinguished buildings of the classical revival in London and has similarities with the contemporary work of Schinkel in Berlin. It has a first-floor continuous balcony on finely detailed brackets, a large gilded figure of Pallas Athene by Baily above the porch, a paraphrase of the Parthenon's Panathenaic frieze by James Henning above the main windows, and a cornice and balustrade. Much of the furniture was also designed by Burton. The unfortunate attic storey was added in 1899. See also Burton's **Grove House** F17.

The Market Covent Garden **K81** c
1828–31
WC2
Charles Fowler; restored 1975–80 by GLC Architects Department, Historic Buildings Division, B Ashley Barker, Surveyor of Historic Buildings
⊖ Covent Garden

The Earl of Bedford, having commissioned Inigo Jones's **Piazza** K14, exploited his invention by starting a market there in 1671. This grew, until 200 years later it was rehoused in these buildings. In 1974 the market was moved out to a new site at Nine Elms, and following the defeat of a proposal to demolish and comprehensively redevelop the area and run a motorway east–west through it, the Greater London Council lovingly cleaned and restored Fowler's building and the surrounding cobbled streets and pavements. It was reopened in 1980 for use as high-rent shops and restaurants.

The building has three routes running east–west: an elegant central arcade is flanked by two large market halls, roofed with iron arches in the 1880s and '90s and lit with patent glazing. The whole is surrounded by a delicate Tuscan colonnade of Aberdeen granite monoliths, with little square pavilions at the corners, also faced in granite. The upper parts are of sandstone.

The sculptures on the gable ends of the central arcade are by R W Sievier; above the entrances on the cross axis are the Bedford arms and motto, *Che sara sara*.

Travellers' Club 1829–32 **K82** f
Pall Mall SW1
Charles Barry
⊖ Charing Cross

The Travellers' Club stands between Burton's **Athenaeum** K80 and Barry's later **Reform Club** K91. Together, these clubs make a collection of neoclassical buildings of a quality to equal Schinkel's Berlin or von Klenze's Munich. Like those architects, Barry was to extend his repertoire from strict ancient classical models to include Italianate and, later, Gothic. The plan is that of a cortile, the plain stuccoed façade that of a palazzo.

King's College 1829–35 **K83** c
Strand WC2
Robert Smirke
⊖ Aldwych

Founded as the Church of England's answer to the establishment of the non-religious University College (although both are now part of London University), King's forms the final eastern section of Chambers's plan for the river frontage of **Somerset House** K62. Although contemporary with his early work on the **British Museum** G25, King's shows none of Smirke's usual elegant restraint, appearing merely dull. The smallness of the original gateway from the Strand to the narrow courtyard provided the young Pugin with ammunition for an unfavourable comparison with the medieval colleges of Oxford and Cambridge.

West Strand Improvements 1830 **K84** f
Adelaide Street WC2
John Nash
⊖ Charing Cross
Immediately behind **St Martin-in-the Fields** K40, the triangular block enclosed by Adelaide Street, King William Street and the Strand is known as Nash's West Strand Improvements. The pepper pots at the corners and the stuccoed façades are characteristic of Nash, but the block was refurbished by Frederick Gibberd for the expanded premises of Coutts Bank, whose set-back, fully glazed elevation interrupts the stucco façade to the Strand. See also the former **Charing Cross Hospital** K87.

Theatre Royal 1831 **K85** f
Haymarket SW1
John Nash
⊖ Piccadilly Circus
The Theatre Royal and the houses behind it in **Suffolk Street** K71 are surviving fragments of Nash's ambitious triumphal way from Carlton House Terrace to Regent's Park. The theatre has a grand portico of six Corinthian columns built over the pavement, and above that a row of nine decorated circular windows. Facing the end of Charles II Street and closing St James's Square to the west, the portico is particularly monumental when viewed down Haymarket from the north. The interior has been altered significantly, but much of the stage machinery is original.

Duke of York's Column 1831–4 **K86** f
Waterloo Place W1
Benjamin Wyatt
⊖ Piccadilly Circus
The Duke of York's Column marks the southern end of Nash's triumphal way from **Carlton House Terrace** K77 to Regent's Park. Set in **Waterloo Place** K79 above an impressive flight of steps down to St James's Park, it dominates one of the most dramatic spaces in London. Wyatt's memorial is a giant Tuscan column, containing a spiral staircase and carrying above its capital a dome bearing Westmacott's statue of the Duke of York, surrounded by a square balcony.

Police Station **K87** f
ex **Charing Cross Hospital**
1831–4
Agar Street and William IV Street WC2
Decimus Burton, altered by J Thompson 1877
⊖ Charing Cross
Part of Nash's plan for the west Strand, this hospital (one of several built and rebuilt in this decade) has now ended its useful life, and the institution moved to Fulham. The architecture – decent stuccoed Corinthian for the rounded corner, Doric for the entrance – was adapted to accommodate the police station in 1994.

National Gallery 1832–8 **K88** f
Trafalgar Square W1
William Wilkins
⊖ Charing Cross

Buildings appropriate to grand processional routes or very large public spaces are not as common in London as in other European cities. Its architects have often failed to rise to the occasion, either because they were more used to domestic building (see Chambers's **Somerset House** K62) or because their nerve failed, like Wilkins's here. As a climax to Nash's newly formed **Trafalgar Square** K70, Wilkins's façade is inadequate. It is, as Summerson wrote, 'divided into no fewer than thirteen sections, six on either side of the central portico. Unfortunately all the subsidiary sections have approximately equal value, and the two sorts of pavilions are so similar in height that one is inclined to evaluate them as alternative suggestions rather than complementary parts of a single design.'

The rich interiors are mainly by E M Barry (1867–76) and the central hall is by J Taylor (1885). The gallery holds one of the world's greatest collections of paintings: begun in 1832 with thirty-eight pictures bought by the government, it now comprises forty-six rooms covering the development of European painting from the mid-thirteenth century to the French Impressionists. The fine collection of Renaissance paintings is now displayed in the **Sainsbury Wing** K182 of 1990.

In 1998 a masterplan was prepared by Dixon Jones to improve facilities and disabled access for visitors, and to respond to the pedestrianization of the north side of the Square. The portico entrance was enhanced and the new Paul Getty entrance at ground level provided a much-needed new foyer, leading to the new Annenberg Court.

Wellington Barracks 1833 **K89** m
Birdcage Walk SW1
Philip Hardwick
⊖ St James's Park

All European capitals built barracks at about this time: we are fortunate that such good neoclassical taste then reigned. This 120m (394ft) and pleasantly dull three-storey building, fronting its parade ground, has small accents of Greek Doric ornamentation. It was reconstructed in 1979–82, and now looks particularly good when floodlit.

Houses of Parliament 1835–60 **K90** o
Palace of Westminster SW1
Charles Barry, Augustus Welby Pugin
⊖ Westminster

Approached from Westminster Bridge to the east, the profile of the Houses of Parliament is immediately familiar, culminating with the clock tower containing Big Ben, 98m (320ft) high, in the north and the taller Victoria Tower, 103m (336ft), in the south. Approached from the west, the group of buildings known as the Palace of Westminster is a confusion of styles, including the authentic Gothic of **Westminster Hall** K5, and the excellent neo-Gothic of the Houses of Parliament.

The present Parliament building is on the site of Edward the Confessor's original Royal Palace of Westminster, but in 1834 a fire destroyed everything but Westminster Hall, the Law Courts to the west and the Cloister of St Stephen. The following year it was decided to build new and enlarged Houses of Parliament on the same site, and a competition was announced for a building in either Gothic or Tudor style. The Houses of Parliament, with their exuberant neo-Gothic interiors, are the result of the collaboration of two architects, Barry for the general arrangements and Pugin for the meticulously detailed Gothic design. Their appearance prompted Pugin's famous comment from a boat on the Thames, 'All Grecian, sir; Tudor details on a classic body.'

The buildings have a simple axial plan, the principal rooms being arranged along a north–south spine in a progression befitting the hierarchical nature of British society (House of Commons, Commons Lobby, Central Lobby, Lords Lobby, House of Lords, Princes Chamber and Royal Gallery).

If the grand and eloquent exterior can be attributed principally to Barry, the details of the interiors were exclusively Pugin's. From the public entrance, the visitor proceeds up a flight of stairs to the great octagonal lobby; in front lie the reception rooms, to the left the House of Commons and to the right the House of Lords. The interior of the House of Commons was completely redesigned and rebuilt by Giles Gilbert Scott after bombing in the Second World War. Fortunately the House of Lords remains intact, and its very rich decoration is Pugin's London masterpiece. The mural paintings in the Palace of Westminster should also be noted: the most impressive is *The Death of Nelson* and the *Meeting of Wellington and Blücher* by Daniel Maclise in the Royal Gallery. As a result of the fresco technique many of the other patriotic murals are in a poor state of repair.

The principal dates of building activity were as follows: the river wall was started in 1837, and the building in 1840; the House of Lords was opened in 1847 and the other main buildings in 1852; the clock tower housing Big Ben (the bell) was completed in 1858 and the Victoria Tower in 1860, the year of Barry's death. E M Barry, his son, supervised the final stages.

It is sad that architects involved in large-scale public works are often inadequately appreciated and badly paid: Barry and Pugin were no exception. Pugin died in Bedlam (the Bethlehem Hospital for the Care of the Insane) in 1852, the year of the official opening of the Houses of Parliament, and Barry died worn out by the worry of his massive undertaking.

Reform Club 1841 **K91** f
Pall Mall SW1
Charles Barry
⊖ Piccadilly Circus, Charing Cross
The successor to Barry's **Travellers' Club** K82, next door to the east, the Reform is a grand two-storey palazzo in smooth Portland stone ashlar, raised half a storey above the pavement. Inside, the main rooms are grouped round a glazed, cloistered courtyard. It was cleaned and restored in 2007 when the decayed roofing was replaced by startling orange pantiles.

Offices **K92** i
ex **Conservative Club** 1843
74 St James's Street SW1
George Basevi and Sydney Smirke
⊖ Green Park
A grand Italianate effort which shows how quickly neoclassicism became pompous and decorated; the contrast between the **Athenaeum** K80 and **United Services** K78 is another example. Basevi seems to have been better at laying out houses, as in **Pelham Crescent** N11.

All Saints 1849–59 **K93** a
Margaret Street W1
William Butterfeld
⊖ Oxford Circus
A remarkable early High Victorian design to the programme of the Cambridge Camden Society, a reform group determined to reinstate the Liturgy and its equipment in the Church of England. Two houses for clergy and choir school frame a small courtyard and expose the south wall of the church, with its very un-English tower and steeple. The lofty and highly decorated interior was an inspiration for the artists and architects of Arts and Crafts movement. The altarpiece is by William Dyce. See also **St Augustine, Queen's Gate** N19.

Warehouses c1850 **K94** b
Neal Street, Earlham Street and Shelton Street WC2
⊖ Covent Garden

At the beginning of the 1970s the whole of the Covent Garden area was under threat of demolition and redevelopment, but was saved by a successful campaign by local residents. The Earlham Street warehouse, used for storage first by a brewer and then by a paper manufacturer, is particularly impressive for its fine mid-Victorian brickwork (like that of the Docks) and simple segmental-arched windows. Used as shops and offices, with the other nearby warehouses, it was the focus for the renewal of the Covent Garden area.

Victoria Street laid out 1850s **K95** m
SW1
⊖ St James's Park, Victoria

Victoria Street was one of the series of nineteenth-century 'improvements' to alleviate traffic congestion, remove slums, and develop land by speculation. This street connected the southern end of Whitehall to the top end of Vauxhall Bridge Road, and swept through notorious slums round Tothill Street. Its line was later extended north through **Grosvenor Gardens** J47 to Hyde Park Corner. Most of the original regular six-storey Italianate shops, offices and 'mansion' flats were destroyed in the twentieth century and redeveloped as a catalogue of half-baked architectural fashions. **New Scotland Yard** K173 and the development in front of Westminster Cathedral partly restored the Victorian cornice line.

St Mary-at-Lambeth **K96** o
nave 1851–2
Lambeth Road SE1
P C Hardwick
⊖ Lambeth North

Hardwick rebuilt the nave in an unremarkable Decorated Gothic style to match the existing fourteenth-century tower. The church is associated with the Tradescants, father and son, gardeners to Charles I, who travelled abroad collecting plants and who are buried in the churchyard. The building now houses the Garden Museum and its interior was reordered by Dow Jones architects in 2008.

ex **Public Record Office** **K97** d
1851–66 and 1891–6
Chancery Lane WC2
James Pennethorne, John Taylor
⊖ Chancery Lane

Pennethorne was architect and surveyor to the Office of Works, but the Victorian state built few public buildings. Pennethorne's functional Gothic design for the archive faces Fetter Lane, and Taylor's later extension is to Chancery Lane. In 1997 most public records were moved to a new site at Kew, and this building was converted for use by King's College London for its Maughan Library.

Swiss Protestant Church 1853 **K98** b
Endell Street WC2
George Vulliamy
⊖ Covent Garden

Strangely, the Swiss Protestants did not demand the Gothic that the period required for English Protestants. Instead they were provided with this very late, clumsy Palladian.

Bow Street façades

View north from Covent Garden Piazza

Royal Opera House **K99** c
1857–8, 1982, 2000
Bow Street WC2
E M Barry; Gollins Melvin Ward; Dixon Jones BDP
⊖ Covent Garden

The casual siting of important institutions was not unusual in London at this time (see also the **British Museum** G25) but it has been said that the Royal Opera House was built in a Covent Garden back street because of public disapproval of the theatre. Garnier's near-contemporary Paris Opera, on its prominent site, offers a pertinent contrast. The building replaced Robert Smirke's neoclassical theatre (1809) burnt down in 1856, and was completed in six months. Compared with the Paris Opera this is not an imaginative building in either plan or style. Barry's giant Corinthian six-column portico above the rusticated ground floor conveys an image of great size with none of his father's invention. Behind the portico is a long frieze by Flaxman showing Tragedy and Comedy; this and the statues in the niches either side of the front are from Smirke's original theatre. The auditorium, however, is very good indeed. Despite its size, it manages to maintain the intimacy of the theatre and a festive atmosphere; a giant shallow saucer dome (an idea borrowed from Soane) unifies the space, and the balcony fronts are richly decorated with gilded angels and garlands. At the same time Barry also built the Floral Hall next door, for selling flowers to opera-goers. It occupied the site of Smirke's auditorium, which ran parallel to Bow Street (as opposed to Barry's, which is at right angles to it). The westerly expansion of 1982 extended the back-of-house accommodation to James Street; and Gollins Melvin Ward, by replicating a further five bays of Barry's façade, successfully completed the Floral Street frontage.

In 1990 planning permission was granted for the total redevelopment of the Royal Opera House to the designs of Dixon Jones BDP. This ambitious project reconstructed the entire city block formed by Covent Garden Piazza, Russell Street, Bow Street, Floral Street and James Street. It included a home for the Royal Ballet, a new fly tower, a modernized stage and extensive front-of-house facilities centred on the reconstruction of Barry's Floral Hall. The north and east sides of the Piazza gained an arcade of shops.

Threading through all the technical requirements of the theatre, the public foyers take the form of a promenade. From the arcading of the Covent Garden Piazza, a new route makes a connection to Bow Street, from which stairs lead up to the Floral Hall. From here, escalators give access to the amphitheatre foyers and the open loggia overlooking the square. The sequence is full of surprises, as well as serving the important purpose of moderating the social hierarchy of the Opera House.

The **Bridge of Aspiration** (Wilkinson Eyre architects 2003) across Floral Street, is a part-opaque, part-glazed, twisting sculptural structure which links the Royal Ballet School to the Royal Opera House.

Westminster Bridge 1862 **K100** k
SW1 and SE1
Thomas Page
⊖ Westminster
An unremarkable, modest design replacing that of a century earlier, Westminster Bridge predates the development of the **Embankment** K104 by two years. With **Waterloo Bridge** K160 and **Blackfriars Bridge** L85, it is one of the trio which provide Thames crossings for routes north through Lambeth from the Elephant and Castle. While it seems too wide, it does give good views of the **Houses of Parliament** K90.

Hungerford Bridge 1863 **K101** g
WC2 and SE1
John Hawkshaw
⊖ Embankment
The bridge and Charing Cross Station were both built during the spate of terminus construction in the 1860s: until then trains serving London's south-eastern suburbs and Kent had terminated at London Bridge. The trussed iron bridge (replacing a footbridge by Brunel of the 1840s) was the only one in central London which combined train and pedestrian crossings. The views from it towards the City and Waterloo Bridge were spectacular, and the noise and rattle of the trains added a metropolitan spice.

The bridge was transformed in 2002 with over-engineered pedestrian bridges on either side, to designs by Lifschutz Davidson (who resigned from the 'design-and-build' contract). Its materials, crude detailing and lighting are entirely inappropriate for its prominent metropolitan setting especially when compared with, for example, those of the contemporary **Millennium Footbridge** L143.

Charing Cross Station and **Hotel** **K102** f
1863–4
Strand WC2
John Hawkshaw (station), E M Barry (hotel)
⊖ Charing Cross
Charing Cross Station is another example of the architect using the railway hotel as the decorated front to the engineer's utilitarian train shed. The present station was built on the site of Hungerford Market and its massive railway bridge required the demolition of Brunel's Hungerford suspension footbridge (1841–5). Barry's hotel façade to the Strand, richly decorated with mixed Renaissance motifs, has been altered by the addition of two upper storeys; it was reputedly one of the first façades in England to use reconstituted stone. The **Eleanor Cross**, a stone spire In the station's

forecourt designed by Barry and carved by T Earp, is near the site of the last of the thirteen crosses built by Edward I along the processional route from Nottinghamshire to Westminster Abbey for the funeral of his queen. It is also the point from which all distances to London are measured. The station was transformed by the later building over the platforms (K181).

Garrick Club 1864 **K103** f
15 Garrick Street WC2
Frederick Marrable
⊖ Leicester Square

The club was founded in 1831 as a place where 'actors and men of education and refinement might meet on equal terms', away from St James's but near the West End's many theatres. They met at first in a hotel and only after twenty-five years commissioned this building. Marrable is best known as the first architect to the Metropolitan Board of Works, from 1856, where his duties included the laying out of streets including Garrick Street itself. He resigned his post in 1861 and went on to design the club, his only extant notable building. Its gigantic Italianate façade was finished in cement rendering which immediately weathered badly but was only cleaned in 2005; it conceals equally gigantic suites of members' rooms – regrettably inaccessible, although the grand staircase may be glimpsed through the front door.

Victoria Embankment **K104** k, g, h
1864–70
SW1, WC2 and EC4
Joseph Bazalgette
⊖ Westminster, Embankment, Temple, Blackfriars

Extending in a gentle curve from the **Houses of Parliament** K90 and **Westminster Bridge** K100 in the south-west to **Blackfriars BrIdge** L85 in the north-east, the Victoria Embankment is a large-scale metropolitan 'Improvement'. It was also central London's first formal public Thames frontage. The Embankment forms a particularly memorable sense of arrival in central London from the east.

In the most ambitious engineering scheme ever seen in London, a complex section was constructed simultaneously to contain a road bypass for the hopeless congestion of the Strand, an embankment as a defence against the disease-carrying Thames mud, a new trunk sewer, and an underground railway. Above ground, the Victoria Embankment is memorable for its street furniture, bridges, granite wall and monuments, rather than for particular buildings. The cast-iron lamp standards by Timothy Butler (1870), with dolphins twined around the columns, and the iron benches decorated with camels and sphinxes, are particularly good. The many monuments randomly commemorate British imperialism and national heroes: for example, Boadicea by Thomas Thornycroft (1850), the Gilbert Memorial by George Frampton (1914), and a bronze of Isambard Kingdom Brunel by Marochetti (c1877) appropriately commemorating the great Victorian engineer.

Hungerford Bridge K101 (1863) was contemporary with the Embankment, and replaced Brunel's elegant suspension bridge (1841–5), while **Waterloo Bridge** K160 (1939–45) by Giles Gilbert Scott replaced Rennie's famous classical bridge.

Cleopatra's Needle, dating from 1500BC, is London's oldest outdoor architecture, imported in 1877 from Egypt. The heroic operation of shipping and erecting its 177 tonnes (180 tons) of pink Aswan granite is well described in a display at the Museum of London. Since the obelisk's original function was to celebrate the sun, it seems wan under our skies. Its twin is in Central Park, New York. The Victorian sphinxes are by George Vulliamy.

Royal Academy Offices 1866–9 **K105** e
ex **University of London**
Burlington Gardens W1
James Pennethorne
⊖ Piccadilly Circus

Whereas the Italianate style was successfully incorporated into English domestic architecture, its monumental equivalent in public buildings always looks lifeless (see Scott's contemporary **Government Offices** K106, and the additions to **Burlington House** K36). Pennethorne had started as a correct neoclassical architect, but his attempt here to do cheerful *cinquecento*, with worthy statuary (spot the intellectual), merely looks crowded. The building was used for a time as the home of the 'Museum of Mankind' – the British Museum's ethnographic collections. In 2008 the Royal Academy commissioned David Chipperfield, an Academician, to produce plans for its own use.

Foreign Office, the staircase

Home Office and **Foreign Office** 1868–73 **K106** j
Whitehall SW1
George Gilbert Scott
⊖ Westminster

Scott had publicly proposed Gothic as the only style appropriate for all buildings, and was proving his faith at **St Pancras Station** G39. However, the 'Battle of the Styles' (Gothic versus classical, inaugurated by Pugin's *Contrasts*, 1836) seems here to have become a personal battle between Scott and Lord Palmerston, his patron. Scott made two designs before the present Italianate one was accepted. The very large five-storey building, planned around five courtyards, is symmetrical, save for the picturesque excursion with two corner towers on the elevation facing the park. The elevations are erudite but (in spite of their extensive sculpture) quite unlikeable, except when seen from across the park.

Immediately to the south are the very large **New Government Offices** linked to the Home Office by an arch. The building in English baroque style terminates Parliament Street and provides a uniform façade to the north side of Parliament Square. Built in 1898–1912 to the designs of John Brydon and completed by Henry Tanner, its offices are planned around a circular courtyard and, much in the manner of **County Hall** K137, many light-wells. Its basement facing the Park was used in the Second World War as Churchill's 'War Rooms', and these are presented as a museum to the designs of Casson Mann.

Royal Courts of Justice 1874–82 **K107** d
Strand WC2
George Edmund Street
⊖ Chancery Lane

The last great Gothic public building in London, known by its detractors as 'the grave of modern Gothic', although the Great Hall and the Strand façade are triumphs in anyone's terms. The competition announced in 1866 to replace Kent and Soane's old Law Courts at Westminster was a farce, with an abortive change of site to the new Embankment at the last moment. Although the style was not specified, it was assumed to be Gothic, and the well-known Gothic revival architects entered. In the event the architect judges put E M Barry first and George Gilbert Scott second; the lawyers put Scott first and Waterhouse second. Street and Scott were then recommended as joint architects, and when Scott resigned in 1868 Street was made sole architect. In the centre of the building is the Great Hall, one of the most authoritative examples of English thirteenth-century Gothic revival, 70m (230ft) long, 15m (48ft) wide and 25m (82ft) high. With its ecclesiastical associations, it is suitably awe-inspiring for innocent and guilty alike. It also connects Lincoln's Inn to the Temple, thus completing the continuous walk which we have called **Legal London**, from Gray's Inn Fields to the Temple on the Embankment (see page 478).

The Strand façade is a *tour de force*. The apparent symmetry of the plan is modified by the employment of repeating and overlapping elements, principally the bays of turrets and the position of the east tower. It has been said that Street intentionally put his staircases on the exterior to enliven the elevation. Street died in 1881, just before the completion of the Great Hall. Like others employed on large public commissions, he was worn out by the Herculean task, made no easier by constant demands for economy and the growing critical reaction against the Gothic Revival. A monument to Street by Armstead was placed against the east side of the Hall in 1886: holding a pair of metal dividers, he is seated above a frieze of artists and craftsmen (this is not without irony, for Street could never delegate work).

Shaftesbury Avenue 1877–86 **K108** b
W1 and WC2
⊖ Leicester Square, Piccadilly Circus
Shaftesbury Avenue connects Piccadilly Circus in the south-west to New Oxford Street. Like the contemporary **Charing Cross Road** K115, it was one of the series of 'Improvements', starting with New Oxford Street and Holborn Viaduct, which cut through slum areas in order to move their inhabitants elsewhere and improve the circulation of traffic. Now it is a street of theatres, and many of the buildings date from its original setting-out: see Collcutt's **Palace Theatre** K117 and the Shaftesbury, ex French, Hospital in red terracotta by Thomas Verity (1899). The theatre built most recently was the Savile, by T P Bennett in 1931, with its Thespian frieze by Gilbert Bayes. It is now a cinema.

Royal Arcade 1879 **K109** e
connecting 28 Old Bond Street
to 12 Albemarle Street W1
⊖ Green Park

London's most elegant surviving High Victorian arcade, the Royal Arcade was built to form a direct shopping perambulation between the fashionable Brown's Hotel and Bond Street. It was originally called simply 'The Arcade' (see the entrance pediment) but was ennobled in 1882 as a result of its royal patronage – Queen Victoria bought her riding skirts and wool from H W Brettel's. The arcade is 40m (132ft) long with nine shops on either side. Each shop has a bay through the full height of the building; the bays are then separated by arches with an open pediment above, and the glass roof runs the full length of the arcade. The balance between decoration and structural elements is perfectly controlled, as is the play of light and shadow. The glass of the shop fronts is rounded at the corners, and the window frames, painted black with columns of gold piping, give the sense of a black reflective plinth to the lighter structures above painted an unfortunate orange. The street façade is reminiscent of **Burlington Arcade** K68; the four columns were originally crowned with urns. The proportions of the entrances have been ruined, however, by a new shop front.

James Smith and Sons c1880 **K110** b
53 New Oxford Street WC1
⊖ Tottenham Court Road

An intact nineteenth-century shop front, retaining its highly graphic Victorian typography. Increased sales of umbrellas in the nineteenth century coincided with the popular introduction of window-shopping and promenades.

The Red Lion c1880 **K111** e
Duke of York Street SW1
⊖ Piccadilly Circus

One of the finest surviving and busiest small Victorian pubs in London: the intimate interior of cut, bevelled and mirrored glass set in dark mahogany frames is magical.

Flats 1882 **K112** i
1 and 2 St James's Street SW1
R Norman Shaw
⊖ Green Park
Built at the peak of Shaw's influential and much-copied brick and gabled style, this block of flats successfully turns the corner of Pall Mall and St James's Street. See also Shaw's later number 88 opposite (K123).

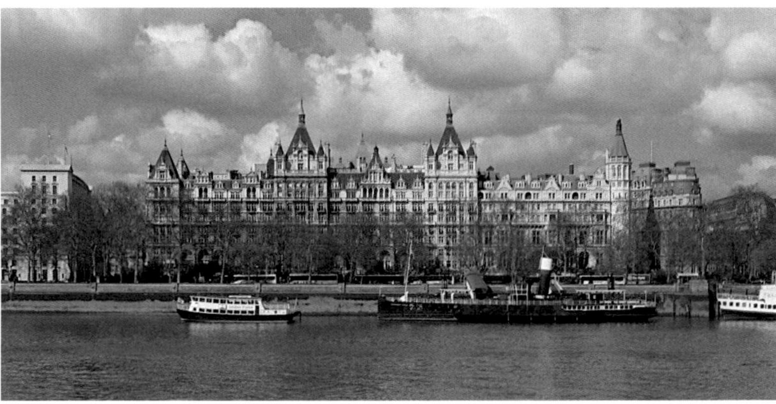

Whitehall Court 1884 **K113** k
SW1
Thomas Archer and A Green
⊖ Westminster, Embankment
The construction of this huge block of flats was one of the first to take advantage of the completion in 1870 of the **Victoria Embankment** K104 to produce salubrious building sites next to the Thames, and while its size anticipated later developments, its style was never repeated on such a grand scale. It was one of the first buildings in London to use lifts to reach its nine regular floors and two attics. The style of its façades, roofs and motifs is relentlessly French Renaissance, successful enough, as an unbelieving Pevsner wrote, 'to make Chambord green with envy'. Its manically profiled skyline is best seen in the long views from the opposite shore of the Thames, or looking from the end of the lake in St James's Park. Adjoining the building to the north and with its own more Gothic tower on the corner is the former National Liberal Club by Alfred Waterhouse.

ex **New Scotland Yard** **K114** k
1886–90 south wing 1906
Victoria Embankment SW1
R Norman Shaw
⊖ Westminster
The first of these very large offices was built when Shaw's style was turning away from the domestic and towards the baroque of his contemporaries. In Scotland Yard he incorporated the round corner tower of the Scottish castle, and the later south wing has a Scottish tower on one corner and a baroque gable on the other. The stone base surmounted by stripes of red brick and stone, and the grandly punctuated skyline, set off the procession of large buildings of character – best viewed from the South Bank – which continues along the Embankment to Blackfriars Bridge.

Charing Cross Road 1887 **K115** b
WC2
⊖ Tottenham Court Road, Leicester Square
Charing Cross Road is a Victorian 'Improvement' and companion of Shaftesbury Avenue, which crosses it at Cambridge Circus. It was the outcome of fifty years of discussion, started by Nash, of a north–south route which would clear some of the slums of east Soho. (Nash had proposed a route to the east joining Trafalgar Square to the British Museum.) Like Shaftesbury Avenue, it is now also a street of theatres, none of them architecturally noteworthy, bookshops, and a surprisingly large number of dwellings.

Number 109 is the former **St Martin's School of Art** (1937–9), a good, large building of a type now usually consigned to island sites in the suburbs, designed for the LCC by E P Wheeler.

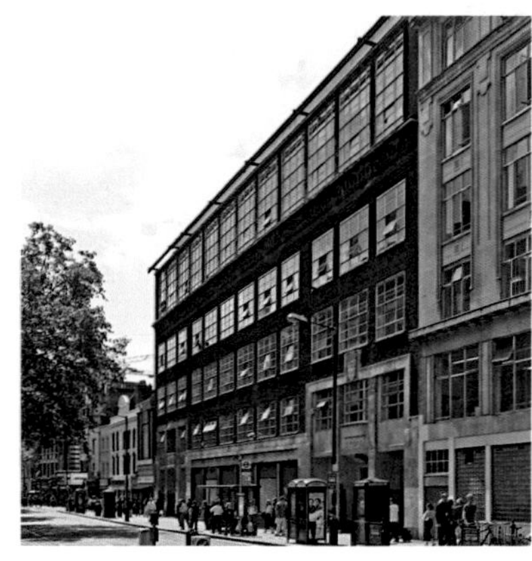

Savoy Hotel 1889 and 1903–4 **K116** g
Strand and Victoria Embankment WC2
A H Mackmurdo, Thomas Collcutt
⊖ Charing Cross
The Savoy has two buildings: that on the Strand is by Collcutt in his very mixed style (see also his **Palace Theatre** K117), unified here by the exclusive use of white-glazed terracotta. Mackmurdo's bedroom wing overlooking the Thames looks curiously commercial – it might be a Chicago office building of the period – and lacks any art nouveau features.

In 1929 the entrance court to the Strand was restyled by Easton and Robertson, who introduced the stylish art deco stainless steel fascia. Some of Basil Ionides's interiors of the same time survive.

Palace Theatre 1890 **K117** b
Cambridge Circus WC2
Thomas Collcutt
⊖ Leicester Square
This huge theatre (none larger has since been built in London) was originally constructed as an opera house for the impresario D'Oyly Carte. The grand exterior is in Colcutt's mixed and striped style, mingling bands of red brick and impervious cream faïence to disturbing effect, made even more pungent by the thorough cleaning and refurbishment of the 1980s.

National Portrait Gallery **K118** f
1890–5, 1994–2000
St Martin's Place WC2
Ewan Christian, Dixon Jones
⊖ Charing Cross Road
The main building is in the Italian Renaissance style, with round-headed windows. Its plan, strung out along a very extended frontage with an unused service yard at its centre, was never ideal. The entrance is undistinguished and confusingly abuts what appears to be a continuation of the National Gallery, also designed by Christian.

In 1994, under the guidance of the then director Charles Saumarez Smith, a masterplan was prepared by Dixon Jones. Two key moves were proposed. First, that the optimizing of the service yard made possible by a 'deal' with the

National Gallery would provide the missing centre of gravity for the institution. Second, that the introduction of an escalator would allow greater accessibility to the collections on the floors above. The resulting Ondaatje Wing provided greatly improved visitor facilities, a new Tudor Gallery and rooftop restaurant with one of the best views in London. From here can be seen many of the institutions in which those celebrated in the gallery made their reputations. When the National Portrait Gallery was opened to the public in 1896 it had 12,000 visitors a year. By 2008 this figure had increased to just under two million, reflecting its growing popularity as a Pantheon of national figures, dead and alive.

Entrance to the Ondaatje Wing 2000

St Patrick 1891–3 **K119** b
Soho Square W1
Kely and Birchall
⊖ Tottenham Court Road
Italian on the inside, red-brick Italianate on the outside, St Patrick's is one of the many churches in Soho which have served various waves of settlers. The elevation to Sutton Row and the modelling of the apse are all in fine red brickwork. Note also the terracotta French Protestant Church in the north-west corner of the Square.

Westminster Cathedral, Archbishop's House and **Clergy House** **K120** m
1895–1903
Victoria Street SW1
John Francis Bentley
⊖ Victoria
A convert to Roman Catholicism, Bentley had done most of his church work In Gothic, but was asked by Cardinal Vaughan to build the new Roman Catholic Cathedral in Byzantine style, perhaps to avoid stylistic competition with the Abbey. He accordingly visited Italy, Greece and Constantinople, and designed quite the best modern church in London, in a mixture of Byzantine and Romanesque styles. The plan has a three-bay nave, each bay covered with a concrete dome, a crossing marked by a raised dome and transepts, and a semicircular apse, all held together by bridges supported on delicate Ravennesque columns. Bentley's designs for the marble and mosaic cladding to the stock brick structure have been only half carried out, but the result is impressive.

For a suggestion of how it might look were the money ever to be found to finish it, see the Lady Chapel with its gold mosaic. The fine Stations of the Cross, mounted on the main piers of the nave, were carved by Eric Gill and done during the First World War (see also his later sculpture for **Broadcasting House** F42).

The exterior, with its off-centre tower, is less startling than the interior but is well done, and the redevelopment of Victoria Street in the 1970s allowed for a small piazza in front of the narthex, whose decoration could then be seen properly for the first time.

Queen Victoria Memorial **K121** i
and **Rond Point** 1901–13
opposite Buckingham Palace SW1
Astor Webb and Thomas Brock
⊖ Green Park, St James's Park

In 1901, Webb and the sculptor Brock won a limited competition for the design of the Memorial. Over the next ten years, Webb laid out the Mall and designed **Admiralty Arch** K129 and the new front for **Buckingham Palace** K76, which was completed in time for George V's coronation in 1911. Webb's original design for the *rond point*, the symbolic hub of the Empire, had elaborate colonnades. As built, it is more modest, with formal gardens as the settings for Brock's Victoria Memorial, a gilded statue of Victory surrounded by allegorical groups. The monument stands on a marble base circled by solid granite paving.

Law Society Library 1902 **K122** d
Chancery Lane and Carey Street WC2
H Percy Adams, designed by Charles Holden
⊖ Chancery Lane

Holden was twenty-seven and working in Adams's office when this first example of his stripped classicism was built. The horizontal lines of the cornice and window heads are continued from L Vulliamy's offices next door, but the Venetian windows in a crude Tuscan order arranged symmetrically across the corner are Holden's own. This could be seen as a stage in his one-man evolution of English modernism, which had started with his training with C R Ashbee, and was to finish with his **Underground Stations** R24, T24 and **Senate House** G65.

Offices 1903 **K123** i
88 St James's Street SW1
R Norman Shaw with Ernest Newton
⊖ Green Park

This building, which closes the west end of Pall Mall – Wilkins's **National Gallery** K88 slews across the eastern end – is in Shaw's late stone baroque style, but with one large, symmetrical and very un-baroque gable. See also Shaw's earlier 1 and 2 **Pall Mall** K112 opposite.

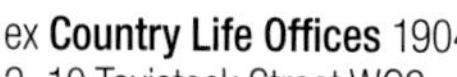

ex **Country Life Offices** 1904 **K124** g
2–10 Tavistock Street WC2
Edwin Lutyens
⊖ Covent Garden

This was Lutyens's first building in London, a large house or small palace in a transitional style. It is a mixture of what was later to become his complete domestic 'Wrenaissance' and of the current Edwardian baroque. Those who like complexity and contradiction will be charmed by the window caught inside the segmental entrance pediment.

Le Meridien ex **Piccadilly Hotel** **K125** e
1905–8
Piccadilly W1
R Norman Shaw
⊖ Piccadilly Circus

A contemporary of the **Ritz Hotel** K127, Shaw's last big building is in his late heavy baroque style. It was the only part built of his larger scheme for the redevelopment of Piccadilly Circus and the southern side of Nash's quadrant (see Blomfeld's **County Fire Office** K138). The bedrooms are recessed from Piccadilly behind a screen of triple-height Ionic columns, but this arrangement has been muddled by the later addition of the glazed restaurant on the terrace. The composition is framed at the west end by a floridly pedimented gable, intended to be one of a symmetrical pair. The Ionic columns on the curved Regent Street façade are engaged.

Methodist Central Hall 1905–11 **K126** n
Storey's Gate SW1
Lanchester and Rickards
⊖ St James's Park

A huge hall for Methodist assemblies (although much used for secular meetings), sited appropriately near other national religious buildings, but built in a sumptuous, worldly style inappropriate to nonconformism. While other Edwardian architects were ransacking Wren for their baroque, Lanchester and Rickards used French and German models. The result is what might be, in Pevsner's words, 'a substantially built Kursaal' or a casino. See also their Third Church of Christ Scientist, Curzon Street.

Ritz Hotel 1906 **K127** e
Piccadilly W1
Mewès and Davis
⊖ Green Park

This was the first steel-framed building in London. It has a redundant self-supporting skin of Norwegian granite on the ground floor and of Portland stone above. Note the very French two-storey roof. The grand arcade to Piccadilly (modelled, like Nash's plan for Regent Street, on Percier and Fontaine's rue de Rivoli in Paris) is the finest in London, where its scale and detailing have never been bettered. For a treat, and to relish the Edwardian elegance which the Ritz celebrated, take afternoon tea in the Winter Garden.

One Aldwych 1906–7 **K128** c
south-west corner of Aldwych WC2
Mewès and Davis
⊖ Aldwych, Temple

The Norwegian granite facings to this suave Parisian façade conceal one of London's earliest steel-frame structures. This is one of many examples by these architects of the 'French' manner which they had introduced to Edwardian London with the **Ritz Hotel** K127. Built to house the *Morning Post* newspaper, in 1998 it was converted into a hotel appropriately befitting its style and its location. The prow of the building looks directly south and over Waterloo Bridge, a fact that the renovation of its ground floor failed to recognize.

Admiralty Arch 1906–11 **K129** f
between the Mall and Trafalgar Square SW1
Aston Webb
⊖ Charing Cross
The Arch terminates the grand axis leading from **Buckingham Palace** K76 and Webb's **Queen Victoria Memorial** K121 (completed in the same year), and skilfully negotiates the obtuse angle formed by the axes of the Mall and the Strand. Constructed in Portland stone, it has a giant Corinthian order with heavy, characteristically Edwardian, classical decorative motifs, especially in the huge attic. The Latin inscription, Edward VII's tribute to his mother, is unique in London in its size and length. The completion of the Arch accomplished the transformation of the Mall, from its beginnings in the 1660s when it was laid out with St James's Park, to its current role as the first part of the royal route from Buckingham Palace to St Paul's Cathedral.

Zimbabwe House **K130** g
originally the
British Medical Association 1907–8
429 Strand WC2
Charles Holden
⊖ Charing Cross
Holden is remembered principally for his services to London Transport and the stripped classicism of his **Senate House** G65, but the earlier buildings were more inventive within the same genre. With its complex system of narrow bays, 429 Strand suggested an alternative to the Free Style of the Arts and Crafts – here an example of Free Style classicism. The ground and first two floors (built in Cornish granite) use a remarkable number of classical devices, the blank and restrained detail to the entrance from Agar Street being particularly impressive. The mutilated and melted figures between the second-floor windows are by Jacob Epstein, who was a friend of Holden. This was his first major commission in England, and caused a scandal at the opening of the building, resulting in the disfigurement of the naked figures.

Royal Automobile Club 1908–11 **K131** i
Pall Mall SW1
Mewès and Davis with E Keynes Purchase
⊖ Green Park
With a current membership of 11,000, the RAC is much bigger than the earlier clubs in the district (such as the **Reform** K91 and **Boodles** K57): an opulent Edwardian celebration of the advent of the motor car, and an expression of the cosmopolitan character of Edward VII's London. Mewès was a Frenchman and, apart from his earlier **Ritz Hotel** K127, most of his other commissions were for the fashionable *demi-monde* who frequented the spas of Le Touquet and Deauville. The Portland stone façade to Pall Mall is large-scale and unexceptional, but it conceals the large double-height oval entrance hall leading to the grand club rooms, both in the Louis XVI style. The principal interest of the building, however, is below ground. Because of its modern steel and concrete construction, the basement houses extensive spaces, which are now used as squash courts, Turkish baths, a solarium and a swimming pool. The latter, a long green rectangle carved out of the marble floor, is truly spectacular. Its Doric columns are faced in fish-scale mosaic which is matched in the pattern of the large window panes (lit from a two-storey area). The whole shows a degree of Edwardian luxury and hedonism not to be found in contemporary chlorinated public baths.

Kingsway and **Aldwych** **K132** c
opened 1909
WC2
various architects
⊖ Holborn

Kingsway was the last of the series of streets – the first was Nash's Regent Street – which wiped away slums and low-rent areas by driving new thoroughfares through them, usually on the seam between neighbouring estates: Kingsway is on the boundary between the Bedford Estate to the west and Lincoln's Inn Fields to the east. The street is 30m (100ft) wide, and mostly lined with unebullient Edwardian commercial buildings, from which the **Gallaher Building** K135 by Burnet and Tait, the former **Holy Trinity Church** K134, and **Bush House** K145 stand out.

In an early example of multi-level engineering, a subway for trams was built under the street: it left the surface at the north end (in Southampton Row where the ramp can still be seen) and travelled south the full length of Kingsway, emerging at the Embankment under the abutment of **Waterloo Bridge** K160. In 1961 the southern end was converted to take ordinary traffic, bypassing the Aldwych.

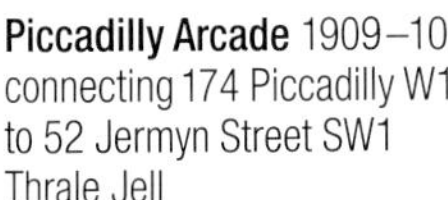

Piccadilly Arcade 1909–10 **K133** e
connecting 174 Piccadilly W1
to 52 Jermyn Street SW1
Thrale Jell
⊖ Green Park, Piccadilly Circus

London's last real arcade, Piccadilly Arcade was built (a century later) as an extension to **Burlington Arcade** K68. Unlike its predecessor it is not an independent piece, but more of a passageway under a building, lined by shops and insufficiently lit by occasional circular roof-lights. It is more like the arcades at entrances to the London Underground. However, the glazed bow-fronted shops (twenty-six in all) were extremely elegant, stepping gently and almost imperceptibly down the slope to Jermyn Street. Seen in perspective the little steel balconies act as 'capitals' to the 'columns' of the shop windows. Number 5 is occupied by Sims and Reed, booksellers specializing in rare books on art and architecture.

See also **Princes Arcade** a few doors to the east which has no roof-lighting whatever: the type is reduced to a mere passage.

ex Holy Trinity 1910–12 **K134** c
Kingsway WC2
Belcher and Joass
⊖ Holborn

The church's beautiful and unexpected stone façade devoid of conventional classical detail describes a shallow concave curve facing Kingsway. Pevsner attributes this Roman baroque manner to Pietro da Cortona's Santa Maria della Pace; the influence of Nicholas Hawksmoor's English baroque is also important. Its simple interior was incorporated into the supermarket to the north in the 1990s.

Gallaher Building **K135** c
ex **Kodak House** 1911
65 Kingsway WC2
John Burnet
⊖ Holborn

Most of the architecture of **Kingsway** K132 was provided by Trehearne and Norman. Burnet's classicism (see also the contemporary **Edward VII Galleries** G51) was here stripped, leaving a free-standing six-storey commercial office building. It is elegantly articulated, with a base, middle and cornice in fine materials: Portland stone and decorated bronze. The standard architectural histories describe this building as proto-modern. This is not helpful, for its traditions are much older, and its successors are more like the Smithsons' **Economist Building** K176 than the continental modern of the 1930s.

Offices 1911 **K136** e
No 7 St James's Square SW3
Edwin Lutyens
⊖ Piccadilly

This is one of the last really large-scale private houses built in London before the First World War. The building would have been familiar to those who attended the Royal Fine Arts Commission hearings up to the mid-1990s, particularly the impressive sequence from the front door to the principal rooms overlooking the square on the first floor, rooms in which Norman St John-Stevas held court. The red-brick elevation is very tall and well proportioned and sits quietly within the almost historically intact north side of the Square.

ex **County Hall** 1911–22 and 1931–3 **K137** k
east end of Westminster Bridge SE1
Ralph Knott
⊖ Westminster, Waterloo

Knott won the competition for the design of the administrative headquarters for the London County Council (formed in 1889) at the age of thirty, but he did not live to see the building completed. Its main characteristic is its enormous size: it occupies a rectangle of two hectares (5 acres) and the main façade to the river is 223m (730ft) long. Like any thick Edwardian office building it is planned round a series of white-glazed tiled light-wells, with the important rooms, the Council Chamber and the Members' suites, in the middle.

These are marked on the river side by the segmental niche (not a portico or pediment), which, within Knott's already out-of-date baroque, is the only original feature of the design. This is as it should be, as the entrance is on the side away from the river on Belvedere Road. An integral part of the design was the start of the embankment of the south side of the river at this point, and Londoners gained a well-engineered granite traffic-free walk next to the Thames, as well as an all-too-large symbol of their local government. Sixty years later the walk was extended.

County Hall was last inhabited by London's elected city-wide strategic authority, the Greater London Council. This institution was abolished in 1985 since when the building has been occupied commercially in the service of the ever-popular **London Eye** K187 and a hotel.

County Fire Office and **Department Store** **K138** e
ex **Swan and Edgar** 1913–30
north and west sides Piccadilly Circus W1
Exteriors by Reginald Blomfield
⊖ Piccadilly Circus

The destruction of Nash's great work began in 1848, when the colonnades were removed from his Quadrant. It continued with the rebuilding of the Swan and Edgar block (including Shaw's **Piccadilly Hotel** K125) and continued up Regent Street over the next thirty years. Blomfield, using the new French (rather than English) baroque style, had the grace to repeat Nash's County Fire Office dome to close the view up Lower Regent Street. It is perhaps a pity that Blomfield's grandiose plan was not realized round the north and east sides, but the circus's present irregular shape is wonderfully characteristic of London, and Blomfield's stiff façades might not easily have accommodated illuminated advertising signs.

Note the **Regent's Palace Hotel** of 1915 next door with its remarkable art deco basement interiors by Oliver Barnard of 1935. At the time of writing the building is being significantly redeveloped and these will be retained.

Oxford Circus 1913–28 **K139** a
W1
Henry Tanner
⊖ Oxford Circus

The demolition of Nash's Regent Street continued with the rebuilding of the western side of Piccadilly Circus by Shaw (**Piccadilly Hotel** K125) and Blomfield (**Swan and Edgar** K138) from 1905. Tanner redesigned Oxford Circus, where stucco was felt to be inappropriate to the intersection of London's two most important shopping streets. His façades are neat if uninspired, and now frame a hopeless confusion of traffic and people.

The Cenotaph 1919–20 **K140** j
Whitehall SW1
Edwin Lutyens
⊖ Westminster

In 1917 Lutyens was among those established architects asked by the Imperial War Graves Commission to advise on the design of memorials to the dead in both Britain and France: his pre-war work in India at New Delhi had already made him the country's 'imperial' architect *par excellence*. The Cenotaph was the national memorial, first erected in temporary form in 1919. The design was felt to be so appropriate that it was rebuilt in stone by November 1920, when the tomb of the Unknown Soldier was established in Westminster Abbey.

Lutyens's design commemorates the dead without Christian imagery, using instead purely architectural means, classically derived and of extreme delicacy and refinement: very slightly inclined planes and minute articulations of the Portland stone courses. The monument is the centrepiece of the national rituals of Armistice Day on 11 November.

Westmorland House 1920–5 **K141** e
117–27 Regent Street W1
John Burnet, Thomas Tait
⊖ Piccadilly Circus

Interrupted by the First World War, the rebuilding of Nash's Regent Street and Quadrant continued in earnest in the 1920s. Immediately north of Blomfield's contemporary Quadrant, Burnet and Tait contributed Westmorland House, their first post-war commission. Their contemporary designs (for example **Adelaide House** L110) suggest that although the firm could work in several styles at once, their buildings nevertheless have in common end pavilions enclosing a plain range, the centre of which is scarcely emphasized. This was the same scheme as Burnet's pre-war **Edward VII Galleries** G51, and one which later proved very popular for the fronts of factories (for example the **Hoover factory** T25). The style of Westmorland House is continental stripped classical. The corners are rounded, accommodating the acute corner at Vigo Street, decorated with columns, and crowned with copper-covered domes reminiscent of the work of Vienna's Otto Wagner; they frame six column-free storeys of shops and offices, topped with a cornice.

ex **Midland Bank** 1922 **K142** e
196a Piccadilly W1
Edwin Lutyens
⊖ Piccadilly Circus

A charming confection in red brick and Portland stone, owing as much to Verona's Sanmicheli as to Wren, but a fitting neighbour for **St James's Church** K21. The bank left and its interior was occupied by a gallery.

National Westminster Bank

ex Barclays Bank

National Westminster Bank **K143** e
1922–3
63–5 Piccadilly W1
ex **Barclays Bank** 1926
157–60 Piccadilly W1
W Curtis Green
⊖ Green Park

Only four years separate Curtis Green's designs for these two large bank branches, yet they are remarkably different. The elevations of the National Westminster on the corner of Piccadilly and Albemarle Street are original, lively compositions. There are arches on the ground floor, more arches spanning the upper floors, and at the top, under the green slate roof, a loggia of two storeys behind slender Ionic columns.

The former Barclays Bank, on the south side of Piccadilly (at the corner of Arlington Street) is by contrast heavy and conventional. The large arches on the ground floor, decorated with magnificent ironwork, support a giant Corinthian order with coupled columns. This motif later became one of the clichés of bank design: see for example Edwin Cooper's National Westminster (formerly National Provincial) Bank, Poultry (L116). The magnificent former banking hall was successfully transformed into a fashionable brasserie 'The Wolseley'.

Liberty Department Store **K144** a
1924, 1926
Great Marlborough Street and
218 Regent Street W1
E T and E S Hall
⊖ Oxford Circus

Before the First World War, Liberty was among the advanced proponents and sellers of art nouveau, but their first post-war store changed direction towards selling a regressive 'Tudor' dream. The store is a perfect example of the type developed in Paris (for example Samaritaine): a central roof-lit well is surrounded by galleries over the edges of which merchandise is displayed. The Tudor style is carried through consistently, producing a building of great character, with hand-made roof tiles, leaded lights, and linen-fold panelled lift doors. The timbers are of oak recycled from two nineteenth-century battleships. In contrast to the earlier Tudor-style building, the former Liberty on Regent Street by the same architects (1926) is neoclassical, with a massive concave screen of columns above the rectangular base at street level, topped with an impressive group of figures flanking Britannia. Note the observant figures looking over the parapet.

Bush House 1925–35 **K145** c
Aldwych WC2
Hemle and Corbett
⊖ Holborn

Kingsway K132 was opened in 1905, but lining it and Aldwych with buildings took many years. The architects here were American, and there is certainly no other street termination in London to compare with Bush House's vulgar but grand exedra and the heap of masonry on top of it, which bring a welcome flourish of American Corinthian to London. It looks very good floodlit: the effect is pagan. The building is the home of the BBC's World Service.

Night by Jacob Epstein

Broadway House 1927–9 **K146** n
55 Broadway SW1
Charles Holden
⊖ St James's Park
When built, the new headquarters of London Transport was one of the capital's tallest (53m/175ft) and most 'modern' buildings, but it is now difficult to be very enthusiastic. The composition is similar to Holden's later **Senate House** G65, but here the cruciform tower and wings sit on a low two-storey podium, seriously damaging the integrity of the Broadway and Petty France street façades. The end of one wing, however, marks the entrance and dominates the corner appropriately. The sculptures (art for those of the travelling masses who notice it) are by Jacob Epstein (Day and Night), Eric Gill, Henry Moore and others.

Freemasons Hall 1927–33 **K147** c
Great Queen Street WC2
Ashley and Newman
⊖ Holborn

A very large building with assembly rooms and offices addresses the corner to Wild Street with a magnificent door and tower: its Edwardian confidence was already twenty years out of fashion. See also **Port of London Authority** L102.

ex **Daily Telegraph Building** 1928 **K148** d
135 Fleet Street EC4
Elcock and Sutcliffe, with Tait
⊖ Blackfriars

It is ironic that the conservative *Daily Telegraph* should have provided itself with this modernistic delight. Only three years later, the populist *Daily Express* occupied Owen Williams's orthodox modern palace (L118) in the same street. London has so few examples of jazz modern that this one should be relished for its façade and entrance hall. The *Daily Telegraph* moved its printing works and offices to the Isle of Dogs in 1989, leaving their Fleet Street headquarters for development. A huge extension designed by Kohn Pedersen Fox was built on the north of the site. The expensive detailing and many setbacks cannot disguise its enormous bulk.

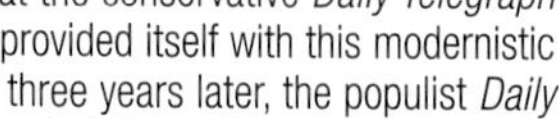

Offices and Showroom 1928–29 **K149** f
120 Pall Mall
Edwin Lutyens
⊖ Piccadilly

From the second floor to the roof the building exhibits a conventional tripartite bay topped by a pedimented attic. However, below is a surprising and contrasting asymmetrical composition of a small front door set beside a giant arch representing a vaulted hall within, originally designed to exhibit baths and luxury sanitary appliances for Crane Bennett Ltd. Here we find Lutyens at the height of his powers following his return from India, introducing the 'Delhi order' to the capital. The building is directly contemporary with Le Corbusier's Villa Savoye at Poissy.

Palladium House **K150** a
ex **Ideal House** 1928
Great Marlborough Street and Argyll Street W1
Raymond Hood, Gordon Jeeves
⊖ Oxford Circus

Palladium House is a notable exception to the lamentably unimaginative architecture which, justified by morality, theory or expediency, is all too common in England. The American architect, Raymond Hood, had won first prize with a neo-Gothic design in the famous Chicago Tribune Building competition of 1923. Later, in the 1930s, his designs for the Daily News Building acquired him a reputation as one of the pioneer architects of the New York skyscraper.

The severity of the sheer, polished, black granite cube with simple window openings is tempered by an Egyptian cornice, the slightly battered inclination of the walls, decorative floral tiles, and a piping of inlaid gilt. The whole combines the suave urbanity of 1930s New York with a nostalgia for the florid decoration of the 1925 Paris Exhibition.

Bank and flats 1929 **K151** i
67–8 Pall Mall SW1
Edwin Lutyens with
W H Romaine Walker and Jenkins
⊖ Green Park

A corner building to Marlborough Gate, incorporating a bank on the ground floor and flats above. As with many of his London buildings, Lutyens was responsible only for the design of the elevations. The windows on each floor are different (not unlike his **Reuters and Press Association Headquarters** L119), showing 'how to get up a building without repeating yourself'.

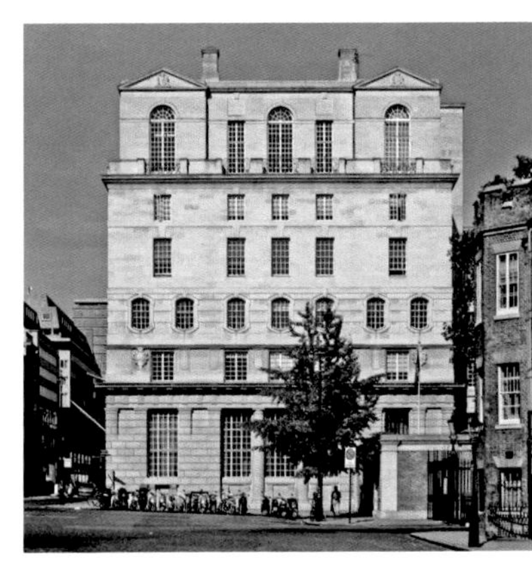

New Victoria Theatre 1929–30 **K152** m
Wilton Road SW1
E Walmsley Lewis
⊖ Victoria

This very large theatre has fronts to both Vauxhall Bridge Road and Wilton Road. Both confidently exhibit, for the first time in London, the continental *moderne* styling of alternate horizontal bands of windows and striped spandrels. The style is developed in the splendidly decorated garish interiors.

Hotel ex **YWCA Hostel** 1930–2 **K153** b
16 Great Russell Street WC1
Edwin Lutyens
⊖ Tottenham Court Road

One of Lutyens's later works, the hostel was planned as a doughnut round very mean light-wells, producing unpleasant interiors. Outside, it uses the domestic neo-Georgian language of red brick with Portland stone dressings: very dead-pan. The Post Office successfully used exactly the same style for telephone exchanges.

Shell Mex House 1931 **K154** g
Strand and Victoria Embankment WC2
Messrs Joseph
⊖ Embankment, Charing Cross

Shell Mex House, occupying an entire block from the Strand to the Embankment, was originally the Cecil Hotel, which with 800 bedrooms was the largest hotel in Europe when it was opened in 1886. The riverside façade, characterized by the giant and eccentric clock face, was remodelled in 1931. Looking like a giant mantelpiece ornament, or the top of a much taller building, it is positively suave (almost a New Yorker) when compared with the lugubrious tower (K166) which Howard Robertson built across the river for the same company.

St Margaret's House 1932 **K155** a
Wells Street W1
Albert Richardson and C. Lorett Gill
⊖ Oxford Circus

With its large, vaulted, copper-clad roof, high dormer windows and stripped severe three-storey-high stone piers, this is as close as Albert Richardson came to abandoning classical detail. Seen in deep perspective from Margaret Street to the west the building has a strong presence and it appears to anticipate the forms of Aldo Rossi of half a century later.

Ministry of Defence 1935 60 **K156** j
Whitehall SW1
E. Vincent Harris
⊖ Westminster, Embankment

The majority of the government buildings on Whitehall have their entrances facing that street. This very large office block of eight storeys, however, presents the broad stone flanks of its ranges to Whitehall and the Embankment, and the entrances face the streets to south and north. Its building was interrupted by the Second World War, and its *retardataire* style outraged serious modernists like Pevsner who, writing in 1957, disliked the Georgian window proportions and called it 'a monument of tiredness and distrust'. Fifty years on, its virtues can be appreciated, especially those of the pavilions which crown the ends of the cross-wings and which animate its skyline when seen from the South Bank. Since it would clearly make a good and enviably sited hotel, it is surprising that it was not sold off in the 1980s.

In the garden between the building and the Embankment are the conserved fragments of the ruins of the Tudor Whitehall Palace and Queen Mary's Steps, the terrace designed by Wren that provided access to the Thames.

Waterstones **K157** e
ex **Simpson's Department Store** 1935
Piccadilly W1
Joseph Emberion
⊖ Piccadilly Circus

One of the great pioneering works of 'heroic' store design, Simpson's was the result of collaboration between Emberton, the engineer Felix Samuely and the designer Laszlo Moholy-Nagy. The façade to Piccadilly, with horizontal strip windows and a canopy to the top storey, is reminiscent of heroic European modernism (particularly Eric Mendelsohn's Hirpich Fur Store in Berlin, 1924) rather than the decorative *moderne* style of much British shop design in this period. The structure of Simpson's followed Samuely's first all-welded-steel frame in England, for Mendelsohn's De La Warr Pavilion, Bexhill (1934). The welded-steel structure with massive vierendeel girders above the first floor was thought by the LCC to be too unconventional, and modifications were required. The detailing of the external metalwork and the illumination of the façade (incorporating the sign) at night are particularly impressive.

Unlike the 'warehouse' planning of most department stores, Simpson's was arranged like a large house, with a sequence of rooms. As a result the interiors have been subject to relatively little change over the years. These 'rooms' and the central staircase have a spaciousness and generosity which are emphasized by the luxurious use of materials: glass lifts, travertine floors and walls, and the original rugs. The ground floor can be used as a shortcut from Piccadilly to Jermyn Street, and the top-floor café now gives unexpected views south over St James's Square. The two penthouse storeys, added in the 1960s by the Architects' Co-Partnership, remain unfortunate.

The large floor plates of offices of the building immediately to the west (Robert Adam Architects 2008) are concealed behind 'classical' façades considerably less assured than those of their predecessors further along Piccadilly: Lutyens's and Curtis Green's **banks** K142, K143, or Mewès and Davis's **Ritz Hotel** K127.

South Africa House 1935 **K158** f
Trafalgar Square WC2
Herbert Baker
⊖ Charing Cross

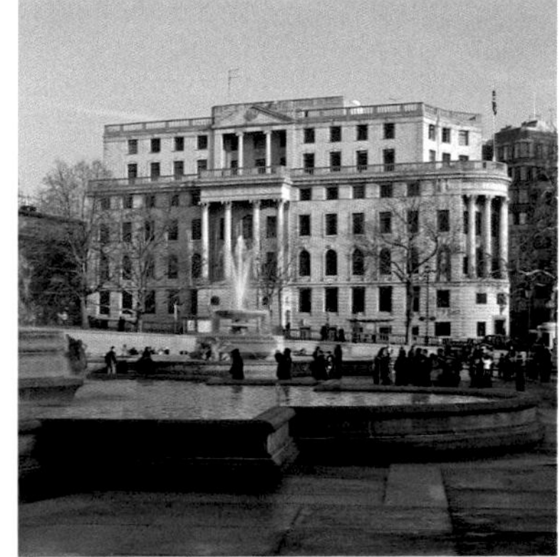

The last imperial addition to Trafalgar Square shows the prolific Baker not quite rising to the occasion. The massing of his large white building provides, with Wilkins's unsatisfactory **National Gallery** K88, another sound edge to help hold the square together, but the rhyming of his new porticoes with that of St Martin's is too obvious.

Fountains 1939 **K159** f
Trafalgar Square WC2 and SW1
Edwin Lutyens
⊖ Charing Cross

The pools were part of the original furniture of the square, designed to restrict the amount of open space available for crowds. Their two fountains, memorials to Admirals Jellicoe and Beatty, are Lutyens's very elegant last London work, and mark the end of the imperial works by other designers which started with **Kingsway** K132, the **Queen Victoria Memorial** K121, and **Admiralty Arch** K129. Each fountain's assembly of circular mouldings and profiles, some probably of Indian derivation, sits on a base like a huge hexagonal nut. The edges of the pools are large blocks of granite – now polished by millions of visitors – set in a splendid pavement of granite slabs. Public furniture, now usually designed by engineers, has never since achieved such excellence (compare with the pedestrianized **Leicester Square** K19).

Nearby: another fountain designed by Lutyens, the Obelisk fountain, now against the south wall of the **Citadel** K161.

Waterloo Bridge 1939–45 **K160** g
WC2 and SE1
Giles Gilbert Scott
⊖ Waterloo
The view from the bridge is one of London's best: a good place from which to get one's bearings in the city – upstream to the **Houses of Parliament** K90 on the right, and the **Royal Festival Hall** K163 on the left, downstream to **Somerset House** K62 on the left and the **National Theatre** K178 on the right. The Embankment sweeps round to the towers of the City (now a poor imitation of, say, Frankfurt or Pittsburgh) which rear over St Paul's. From the bridge, London still looks surprisingly like a white city: many of the buildings in sight are built of or covered in Portland stone.

The present bridge, which replaces that designed in the Greek style by Rennie, has five spans of 76m (250ft). Built in concrete, it is clad in Portland stone which has weathered to a beautiful crusty white, exposing some of the fossils of which it is composed. The abutments and details are elegantly and tactfully designed: note particularly the junction with the Duchy of Lancaster building of 1930–2 on the north-east side, and the steps next to Somerset House on the north-west. The bridge was the last big engineering structure in London to be integrated successfully into the fabric of the city, enhancing rather than destroying its surroundings. See also **Holborn Viaduct** H27.

The Citadel 1940 **K161** j
The Mall SW1
W A Forsyth
⊖ Charing Cross
A curiously expressionist and enigmatic mass on the north-west corner of Horse Guards Parade, the Citadel is one of the few remains in London of the architecture of the Second World War. The building contains approaches to a subterranean shelter, six floors below, for the country's leaders during the Blitz, and the observation slits were for gun emplacements with the Mall as their arc of fire. The massive compressed pebble and flint walls are formed into black and beige strips, and the building is now almost totally concealed by Virginia creeper, resembling in summer a large work of topiary.

Parliament Square 1945–60 **K162** j
SW1
Ministry of Works
⊖ Westminster
Laid out originally by Barry, but now not so much a square as a lawn surrounded by statues of parliamentarians and national heroes, this is insufficiently defined by ordinary buildings to warrant being called a square. The thunderous, dangerous traffic makes it hard to contemplate the **Palace of Westminster** K90, **St Margaret's** K7 and the **Abbey** K2. The government buildings on the north side (1898–1912) are by John McKean Brydon, completed after his early death by Henry Tanner. The **Middlesex Guildhall** (1905) on the west side is by Gibson and Russell, and in 2008 was being converted into premises for the Supreme Court.

Royal Festival Hall 1951 **K163** k
extended 1962, altered 2007
South Bank SE1
LCC Architects Department; Robert Matthew, Leslie Martin, Edwin Williams and Peter Moro
⊖ Waterloo, or Embankment and walk over Hungerford Bridge

The large 2600-seat concert hall was what emerged from earlier grandiose plans for a 'cultural centre', and the only permanent building of those erected in 1951 for the Festival of Britain. London acquired a modern acoustically designed hall to replace the Queen's Hall (destroyed in the Second World War) and to supersede the **Albert Hall** J46, with its huge capacity and uncertain acoustics. For Londoners this building was an introduction to the marvels of Modern Architecture, used confidently and consistently in a non-utilitarian public building. The 'egg' of the auditorium nests high in a forest of columns, among galleries and huge glazed screens, recalling Le Corbusier's unbuilt Palace of the Soviets. The scale and detailing of the interiors are just right for what passes for social display in England.

Fifty years on, it is possible to relish the decoration of the Hall itself (the curly fronts to the boxes, the obsessive use of enclosing frames), and to admire its excellent lighting. The Hall's foyers and landings suffered over the years from unsuitable additions and alterations, but in the 1990s a programme of partial restoration was undertaken (architects Allies and Morrison), although much of the original colour scheme was then not reinstated. The exterior, clad largely in Portland stone, had already lost much of its decorative character when the building was extended and recased in the 1960s.

A major work of 'transformation' was completed in 2007, architects Allies and Morrison. The surrounding terraces were truncated and those that remained tidied up or restyled, the exterior and lobbies were cleaned and repaired, and, in the quest for better acoustics and the ability to stage musicals, the hall itself drastically altered and some of its important original features destroyed.

Eastern ground-level entrance

Offices and showrooms 1953–8 **K164** e
45–6 Albemarle Street W1
Ernö Goldfinger
⊖ Green Park

This six-storey office building with a four-bay structural frame and projecting two-bay oriel windows on the third and fifth floors has a European toughness, unlike its post-Festival of Britain contemporaries. It derives from the work of Auguste Perret in whose atelier Goldfinger spent a year of his apprenticeship in 1924. Goldfinger later used the same approach less successfully in his massive Elephant and Castle **offices** L124.

Congress House 1953–60 **K165** b
Great Russell Street WC1
David du R Aberdeen
⊖ Tottenham Court Road

Aberdeen's winning entry in the competition for the Trade Union Congress is stylistically a lone voice of pre-war modernism. Maintaining the continuity of the street while at the same time giving expression to its role as a public building, it is a rare and stylish instance of the language of modern architecture successfully rebuilding the city within its own traditions. The extensive use of bronze window frames and large areas of plate glass, marble and mosaic gives the building durability and an appropriately monumental air. However, the central court, with its Pietà by Jacob Epstein proves to be more of a light-well than the grand memorial public space anticipated from the street. The statue over the entrance canopy is by Bernard Meadows.

Shell Centre Offices 1953–62 **K166** k
Belvedere Road, South Bank SE1
Howard Robertson
⊖ Waterloo

In their plans for the post-war reconstruction of the South Bank between Westminster and Southwark bridges, Abercrombie and Forshaw had proposed a crescent of large office buildings set back and separated from the Thames by a zone of recreational and cultural functions. The first (and last) development within this plan was this composition of office buildings for the oil company: two eleven-storey slabs following the street lines, and a twenty-seven-storey tower facing the Thames and the same company's earlier building (K154) on the north bank.

Robertson, American-born but educated in England, had in London previously designed the **Royal Horticultural Society Hall** O9 (1935) and the Metropolitan Water Board's **Research Building** G67 of 1938. He was also co-credited with Le Corbusier, Oscar Niemeyer and others for the design of the United Nations Headquarters in New York of 1947–53. Little of that international glamour, however, was displayed on the South Bank: the slabs (with extra storeys added when those to the east were converted into flats) are well made but dull, and the tower, its plan form a mystery, is extremely feeble. Its top-floor loggia was designed as a public viewpoint but was closed very soon after it opened. None of the buildings has anything to offer the street at ground level and the efforts at 'landscaping' the left-over spaces were, and remain, paltry.

Offices 1956–8 **K167** e
100 Pall Mall SW1
D Armstrong Smith and Donald McMorran
⊖ Piccadilly Circus

After the Second World War, when classical forms had became associated with totalitarianism, the Swedish modern style was generally adopted in England as the 'architecture of democracy'. For this reason McMorran's London buildings (see also Wood Street **Police Station** L123 and the extension to the **Central Criminal Court** L99) are particularly interesting.

In this ambitious building, which replaced Sydney Smirke's **Carlton Club** (1847), a number of overlapping influences can be detected. The general proportions of the six storeys are neo-Georgian; the window openings, apparently carved out of a giant cube of Portland stone with occasional segmental arches, recall the Italian Rationalists of the late 1930s; the symmetrical roof pavilions refer back to Lutyens (see **Aldford House** J68); and the thick teak window frames and spindly ironwork of the street railings are of the Festival of Britain era.

Orion House **K168** b
ex **Thorn House** 1957–9
Upper St Martin's Lane WC2
Basil Spence and Partners, designed by Andrew Renton; renovated by Renton Howard Wood Levin 1988–90
⊖ Leicester Square

After only twenty years many of the office buildings of the 1960s were found to be unsatisfactory, having been built to standards lower than those subsequently required for easy letting. Some were demolished and rebuilt. Others, like Thorn House, were stripped, refitted and re-cased. The original composition had been, with **New Zealand House** K171, one of London's earliest efforts at the tower on a podium format: a low, two-storey podium on St Martin's Lane appeared to pass independently through the base of the tower. In the alterations, the amount of accommodation on the site was increased, an undistinguished street frontage was restored to St Martin's Lane, and the original curiously tentative architecture of the slab was replaced by bland metal panelling with pink-painted window frames, with a new projecting services stack at the back. Originally placed on the east side of the building, the spiky sculpture on the north side of the slab is by Geoffrey Clarke.

National Theatre Studio **K169** l
ex **Old Vic Theatre Workshop** 1958
83–101 The Cut SE1
Lyons Israel and Ellis, designed by John Miller
⊖ Waterloo

A very early example of English Brutalism – the style is here used appropriately for a semi-industrial building, with a large double-height scene-painting workshop on top. The building was restored and converted for use by the National Theatre in 2008, by architects Haworth Tompkins, when its original external raw concrete was repaired but painted and lost much of its essential character.

Flats 1958–60 **K170** i
26 St James's Place SW1
Denys Lasdun
⊖ Green Park

The first architecturally respectable luxury flats to be built in London after 1945, this small eight-storey block, on a very privileged site next to Vardy's **Spencer House** K51 and overlooking Green Park, signalled Lasdun's later preoccupation with horizontal banding. Here the bands mark the floor levels, establish a grand scale, and demonstrate the split-level section: three storeys of smaller rooms to the north are set against two floors of generously high-ceilinged living rooms on the corner overlooking the park. The arrangement is like those of Wells Coates's Palace Gate **flats** I24 and Tecton's **Highpoint 2** R27 (Lasdun had worked for both), and was probably derived from Le Corbusier's work. The block is memorable for its use of impervious materials: granite facings for the horizontal bands, and bronze for the heavy window frames – both, as the Victorians knew, well suited to London's atmosphere.

New Zealand House 1960 **K171** f
Haymarket and Pall Mall SW1
Robert Matthew, Johnson Marshall
⊖ Charing Cross

This is London's archetype of the slab-on-a-podium form of redevelopment, derived from Le Corbusier and from Skidmore Owings and Merrill's Lever House in New York. Although it was a good example of its kind, it nevertheless now seems more destructive than constructive, and remains isolated in a predominantly eighteenth- and nineteenth-century part of London. The podium breaks Haymarket's cornice line at an important corner where it would be better consolidated, and the tower acquires an unwarranted importance in views, especially from Trafalgar Square.

It was one of the first fully air-conditioned office buildings in London, and this was exploited in the design by using large sheets of glass. Subsequent appreciation of the strength of the sun led to extensive screening measures, and the elevations now consist of opaque, grubby-looking pleated curtains separated by thin horizontal strips of stone. See also the **Royal Opera Arcade** K69, which was restored when New Zealand House was built.

Offices 1960 **K172** d
Greystoke Place EC4
YRM Architects and Planners
⊖ Chancery Lane

YRM built these offices for their own occupation, but the firm subsequently moved to **Britton Street** H43. The style is an intermediate stage between their routine European modern and the full embrace of the Chicago style. The white tiles (used here as they were by the Victorians on restricted city sites) were employed extensively in YRM's late '60s buildings, for example Warwick University.

New Scotland Yard 1962–6 **K173** n
Victoria Street and Broadway SW1
Chapman Taylor Partners,
façades designed by Adrian Gale
⊖ St James's Park

As a part of the general redevelopment of Victoria Street started in the late 1950s, these offices were built speculatively and only later occupied by the Metropolitan Police. The two slabs occupy a triangular site. The lower one on Victoria Street continues the street line, though with a completely unsatisfactory blind ground floor; however, the arrangement of the rear block creates nasty pockets of residual space which are useful only for parking police vehicles. Given these reservations about the composition, the granite and aluminium façades are smart and the planning rational, and both show evidence of well-digested Chicago examples.

St Thomas's Hospital **K174** o
started 1963
Lambeth Palace Road SE1
Yorke Rosenberg Mardall
⊖ Westminster

Established in Southwark 800 years ago, the hospital was moved to this site in the 1860s. Of the nineteenth-century hospital, built to Florence Nightingale's specification in the Italianate hygienic style, only the southernmost wards remain. The rest has been rebuilt, most of it to YRM's master plan. This proposed an open 'campus' layout of rectangular buildings at right angles to each other, and parallel to the **Houses of Parliament** K90 opposite, and to YRM's Beckett House on the other side of Lambeth Palace Road. A sizeable part of London thereby acquired the sort of grid which exists in Mayfair and in many North American cities. YRM here employed the tile style both for the huge cubic ward block and for the linear nurses' homes on the north-east corner of the site.

Good views of the Houses of Parliament can be had from the public walk along the Thames in front of the hospital.

Centre Point 1963–7 **K175** b
101 New Oxford Street WC1
Richard Seifert and Partners
⊖ Tottenham Court Road

The position of Centre Point marks St Giles Circus, conforming to a fashion and an LCC planning policy in the early 1960s for placing tall buildings at principal traffic intersections. The elephantine structure allows a bridge of first-floor accommodation to span the newly formed roundabout; the pathetic pond and fountains which further inconvenienced the pedestrian on the already inadequate pavements were only some of the building's many drawbacks. The 121m (398ft) tower of thirty-five storeys remained empty for over a decade. Land speculation has been central to the development of London since the seventeenth century, and the private development of the Great Estates endowed the city with much of its character. However, when private speculation is not moderated, it contains within itself the seeds of destruction. Centre Point was then London's most conspicuous example.

The Economist Building 1964 **K176** e
25 St James's Street SW1
Alison and Peter Smithson
⊖ Green Park

Offices for *The Economist* newspaper, a bank and flats are each housed in separate buildings on a slightly raised plaza. The architects' aims were to make a composition compatible with the scale of St James's Street; to provide public open space and through views, possibly beginning a wider network of pedestrian routes; and to tidy up the backs or 'inside' of the block. The buildings' reinforced-concrete frames are clad with roach-bed Portland stone; window frames and water-channelling trim are of aluminium painted light grey. The exposed flank wall of **Boodles Club** K57 is faced in yellow stock brick, and its new bay window in precast concrete is painted to match the rest of the Club's stucco.

The design is remarkable for having largely achieved the architects' aims: its approach to the rebuilding of a vulnerable part of the city was intelligent and it successfully extended the idea of a building standing free in its plaza. The group treats St James's Street civilly and, even if the tower is too tall, the effect of this is far less damaging than that produced by the directional slabs which had been the model for this kind of development (see **New Zealand House** K171). The architects controlled the weathering of Portland stone, thus preventing the formation of the black and white 'moustaches' which ruin the appearance of other modern stone-clad London buildings without classical ledges and copings.

The buildings were refurbished by Skidmore Owings Merrill in 1990, when the glazed lobby to the tower was enlarged and conventionally Americanized, and the inconsequential glazed canopy added.

Queen Elizabeth Hall, Purcell Room and **Hayward Gallery** **K177** g
1967
South Bark SE1
LCC/GLC Architects Department; Hubert Bennett and Jack Whittle; designed by Warren Chalk, Dennis Crompton and Ron Herron; job architect Norman Engelback
⊖ Waterloo

These buildings and their terraced surroundings were designed at the height of two fashions: first, for creating the 'multi-level city', and second, for making buildings look like something else (here comparisons were made with landscapes, and the craggy Mappin Terraces at the **Zoo** F28). The raised pedestrian decks and bridges seemed both inconvenient and irrelevant on this quiet site, with no through-traffic from which pedestrians might need protection. The decks were windy, offering no shelter from the weather, and were difficult for the frail or disabled to negotiate. Neither they, nor the buildings' other forms, marked or indicated the entrances for the intending visitor: there were no 'front doors'. The ground on which the buildings stand was degraded to a shabby undercroft, used mainly by skateboarders and rollerskaters. The construction – of exposed rough-shuttered reinforced concrete with some areas of exposed aggregate concrete cladding panels – weathered badly and suffered from a scandalous lack of maintenance.

The concert hall, seating just over 1000, is an ugly room: more concrete, no decoration, and unsympathetic lighting. The Purcell Room, for recitals, seats 368. The lobby common to both halls works badly, and shuffling queues always form at the entrances to the auditoria. This is particularly strange, as part of the rationale of 'organic' architecture of this sort is that each space or form should be tailored specifically to suit its function. The Hayward Gallery, designed for temporary and travelling exhibitions, has five galleries of different shapes and lighting methods.

Always criticized for their brutality and remote from the later model of the white box, in the hands of skilled exhibition designers they have proved remarkably versatile. In a misguided attempt at 'gentrification', the equally brutal entrance was remodelled in 2003 (architects Haworth Tompkins).

The South Bank Board, present management of these buildings and of the **Royal Festival Hall** K163, wishing to remedy some of the inconveniences and to speculate on the value of the site, in 1987 commissioned an improvement scheme from Terry Farrell and Partners, and a subsequent design from the Richard Rogers Partnership, who proposed covering the buildings with a 'glass wave'. This was abandoned in 1998, and this pungent and unloved reminder of a very particular period in London's architecture remains with all its faults.

The roundabout at the southern end of Waterloo Bridge, which for a time became notorious as 'Cardboard City', shelter to about 1000 of London's homeless, was cleared in 1999 to provide a site for a circular IMAX cinema designed by Avery Associates. Its glazing shelters a large advertising billboard.

National Theatre 1967–77 **K178** h
South Bank SE1
Denys Lasdun and Partners
⊖ Waterloo

The National Theatre's opening was the culmination of a long campaign, by George Bernard Shaw among others, to establish such an institution. Many sites were considered, and Lasdun's first commission was for a building between the Royal Festival Hall and County Hall. The present building contains three separate auditoria: the Olivier, with an open stage and seating 1160; the Lyttelton, a smaller conventional proscenium 890-seater theatre; and, with its own separate entrance at the back, the Cottesloe, a black-painted 'studio' with flexible seating, for experimental productions. The Olivier is a huge success, perhaps at its best with epic productions and a full house: the combination of the audience's proximity to the acting and the very sophisticated stage machinery and lighting is unique.

In plan, the main axis of the Olivier is set at forty-five degrees to that of the Lyttelton. This, together with the insistent but broken-up horizontal layers which Lasdun wrapped around the theatres, provides a series of highly differentiated foyers and terraces, with good views both of each other and across the Thames to Somerset House. A programme of 'modernization' was completed in 1998 (architects Stanton Williams). Conducted without reference to the original architect, this provided new lighting and fittings to the interior, and a new entrance opening off a remodelled paved space between the theatre and the river. The entrance and its relationship to the reinvigorated riverside

walk remains problematic. Exterior coloured lighting was installed and finally gave some purpose to the large areas of concrete at night.

Immediately to the east of the Royal National Theatre is the former **IBM Central London Marketing Centre** of 1978–84. It housed offices, suites for conferences and seminars, and computers, and was also designed by Denys Lasdun, Peter Softley and Partners. The architectural language is similar to that of the National Theatre, with strong continuous horizontals, of concrete panels precast rather than cast *in situ*.

Queen Elizabeth II Conference Centre 1979–86 **K179** n
Broad Sanctuary SW1
Powell Moya and Partners
⊖ St James's Park

The site opposite Westminster Abbey had been empty for forty years. Proposals for a purpose-built official conference centre here originated in Leslie Martin's plan of the 1960s for the redevelopment of Whitehall: conferences had previously been held in, for example, **Lancaster House** K75. The present building provides four large conference rooms on the third floor: these are signalled on the outside by the projecting glazed foyers visibly hanging from beams. Below this floor is accommodation for the press, and above it, recessed, a further conference room and offices. The external composition is additive – it has no strong corners or edges – although it respects its neighbours in height, it is undistinguished and unclear as to whether it is background or monument, a problem which did not concern its more confident neighbours.

Comyn Ching Triangle **K180** b
started 1984
between Monmouth Street,
Mercer Street and Shelton Street WC2
conversion by Terry Farrell and Partners
⊖ Leicester Square

Named after the firm of architectural ironmongers who had occupied much of the site, this block of late seventeenth- and early eighteenth-century houses which forms an important part of the area of **Seven Dials** K25 might have been demolished had the more grandiose plans for Covent Garden been realized. It was, however, spared, and Farrell tactfully consolidated the original work, supplied a taller new building in inoffensive pastiche to each of the three corners, and opened up the interior of the block for public use.

Charing Cross Station and **offices** **K181** g
1990
Strand WC2
Terry Farrell and Partners
⊖ Charing Cross

The overbuilding of **Charing Cross Station** K102 presented a dilemma. On the one hand the project continued the unfortunate fashion for dismantling London's fine nineteenth-century railway sheds and replacing them with commercial offices built over the existing platforms, thus sacrificing the public realm for private profit. On the other hand, unlike London's other railway termini, Charing Cross is double-fronted and was therefore a special case. Although oversized and formally diagrammatic when viewed from Waterloo Bridge, Farrell's building contributed a new and monumental profile to the Embankment.

Sainsbury Wing 1990 **K182** f
National Gallery
Trafalgar Square W1
Venturi, Rauch, Scott Brown;
executive architects Shepherd Robson and Partners
⊖ Charing Cross

After all the controversy surrounding earlier competitions for this site Venturi's building was a rather pedestrian affair. As an addition to Trafalgar Square it is not unlike the replacement of Grand Buildings diagonally opposite, also the subject of a controversial competition in 1985, the winner of which was a replica of the previous building to occupy the site. It neither threatens nor directly enhances the square, and is most prominent in the rather casual display of its roof-lights. The discontinuous treatment of the various elevations was a well-tried 'postmodern' reaction to the varying importance of city streets. The result is not altogether successful: a part-decorated and part-melted classical billboard.

Inside, the galleries compensate to some extent for the failings of the exterior. The enfilade grid of lofty rooms (inspired in section by Soane's **Dulwich Picture Gallery** W3) forms an appropriate permanent home for the Gallery's magnificent collection of Italian and Northern European paintings of 1260–1510, including such masterpieces as Uccello's *Battle of San Romano* and Jan van Eyck's *Arnolfini Portrait*. The muted greys of the galleries complement the gilded detail of the works.

ex **Waterloo International Terminal** **K183** l
1993
Waterloo Station SE1
Nicholas Grimshaw and Partners
⊖ Waterloo

Its role as a gateway for high-speed trains to and from the continent was replaced in 2008 by **St Pancras International** G39. This glazed snake of a terminus with its eccentric roof structure and 400m (1320ft) long platforms was a worthy successor to the Victorian tradition and marked the moment of arrival and departure with suitable confidence. Abandoned and unmaintained at the time of writing, its platforms were to be incorporated with those of Waterloo Station.

Portcullis House 1993–2000 **K184** k
Bridge Street SW1
Michael Hopkins & Partners
⊖ Westminster

Various schemes for parliamentary offices were considered but none built on this prominent site formerly occupied by undistinguished buildings. The present building provides six floors of offices for Members of Parliament, and is arranged around an atrium at first-floor level over ground-floor shops and basement underground station. It is an expensive building (designed to last for at least 100 years), with lavish finishes to its mainly precast concrete structural components: sandstone, and bronze window frames and sunshades. The steeply pitched roof echoes that of Norman Shaw's **New Scotland Yard** K114 to the north, and its prominent, rhetorical ventilation ducts recalled for some the 'dark satanic mills' of industrial England.

When completed it received a mixed reception – Deyan Sudjic remarked that it represented 'the half-closed eye' school of design, referring to the conflation of the verticality of Barry's Houses of Parliament with Shaw's pitched roofs. However, despite its functionalist obsession in the detail, in the wider context of the river frontage this is a well-mannered building, a complement to the Houses of Parliament.

See **Westminster Underground station** of 2001 immediately below, also by Hopkins, the walls of its escalator box following the perimeter of the offices above. Instead of mildly fictitious narratives about the underworld like some other Jubilee Line stations (the mausoleum of Southwark and the Big Blue of North Greenwich) there is the drama and pure engineering of the escalators which thread their way between the monumental columns supporting the box.

Channel 4 Television Headquarters **K185** n
1994
Horseferry Road SW1
Richard Rogers Partnership
⊖ St James's Park
Channel 4 moved premises from Charlotte Street to Victoria following a limited competition in 1990. This building, unlike the same architects' **Lloyd's** L129, observes the boundaries of the site. The plan is diagonally symmetrical, with two wings either side of an animated entrance sequence and a further two residential wings (by Lyons Sleeman and Hoare) enclosing a central garden. If the plan is conventional, its realization as a building is highly theatrical, befitting its media client.

Offices and **flats** 1999 **K186** i
Stirling Square SW1
Stirling and Wilford
⊖ Piccadilly
A posthumous and commemorative work, this mixed-use building of offices and flats was completed seven years after the death of Stirling and appropriately named after him. When compared to his other posthumous work at **Number 1 Poultry** L140 this building is quiet in manner, cool even, taking its place discreetly among neoclassical neighbours. It is in the 'dense pack' genre, biaxially symmetrical in plan, interlocking in section, topped by rustic pergolas and grounded by a vigorously striped base. At both the east and west end is an angular bay window supported by a central column and surmounted by circular and grand balconies. These portals are the building's most obvious signature. It is especially convincing when seen obliquely from St James's Square across Pall Mall. Here the stepped assemblage of forms that make up its inventive portico are at ease with and form a background to McMorran's **100 Pall Mall** K167 and Barry's **Reform Club** K91.

London Eye 2000 **K187** k
Jubilee Gardens, Belverdere Road SE1
Marks Barfield, Arup Associates
⊖ Waterloo
Following its completion, no structure divided public opinion more vociferously: for some it was an upstart on the London skyline and for others an appropriately dramatic and gestural recognition of the millennium. Sponsored partly by its architects, the wheel was built as a temporary celebration of the year 2000 but, following its subsequent sponsorship by British Airways, it remained at least until the time of writing. Unlike all the various well-intentioned masterplans for the South Bank since its opening in 1951, the London Eye has proved to be more popular and has drawn more people to this area of London.

Its structure is that of a spoked bicycle wheel 135m in diameter, its axle cantilevered out over the Thames from a single A-frame. Its continuous motion takes 35 minutes to complete a full revolution. Each of its observation 'pods' holds twenty-five people and is kept level by rotating in cylindrical bearings. The components came from five countries of the EU, the doubly curved glass of the pods from the Venetian island of Murano.

As a result of its location on the bend of the river the structure is oriented north–south and the views from the 32 capsules are as unexpected as they are spectacular.

London School of Economics **K188** c
2001
John Watkins Place WC2
⊖ Holborn

There are two notable projects related to the LSE: one interior, the conversion of an existing building into the principal library by Foster and Associates of 1993; the other external, concerning improvements to the adjoining streets by MacCormac Jamieson and Prichard.

The library is a large conversion (20,000 square metres/215,300 square feet) of an existing bookstore. Central to the plan is a splendid and generously dimensioned stepped spiral ramp giving daylight and focus to the library as a whole. Certainly this form has recurred in the work of the practice (see **City Hall** L146) but this is its most successful application. Not unlike its celebrated inspiration – Frank Lloyd Wright's Guggenheim Museum in New York – it gives a large and complex building a space of orientation, giving identity to the whole.

In the somewhat confusing collection of small streets and semi-public courtyards that forms the LSE campus at the south-east corner of Lincoln's Inn Fields, a series of modest and successful interventions have helped to clarify the public realm – places for students to sit, to meet and to enter significant parts of the institution.

Housing 2001 **K189** h
Upper Ground SE1
Haworth Tompkins
⊖ Waterloo

This is the fourth phase of the Coin Street Community Builders' ambitious masterplan for this area of the South Bank. Earlier phases included Bernie Spain Gardens, Lifschutz Davidson's row houses and tower of 1994, as well as their refurbishment of the Oxo Tower. This is the most prototypical and urban of the developments. Here we have a perimeter block comprising 59 dwellings, arranged along the lines of the **Ladbroke Estate** I7, four-storey terraced houses with private gardens leading to a communal space at the centre of the block as a refuge from the city. The elevations employ a deliberate strategy of fronts and backs – to the street, well-proportioned, simple brick façades in contrast to those facing the interior of the site, a mixture of timber cladding, *brises soleil* and an abundance of projecting metal balconies.

Offices Broadwick House 2002 **K190** a
17 Broadwick Street W1
Richard Rogers and Partners
⊖ Piccadilly Circus

This relatively small but distinguished office building (4000 square metres/43,000 square feet) in its compressed way carries many of the signatures of the Rogers practice – servant and served spaces clearly separated and all realized in fine detail in support of an uncompromising modernity in a historic setting. This it achieved with a four-storey cube of offices raised on *pilotis* above a stylish Chinese restaurant and tea room, topped with a flamboyant arched roof containing a magnificent double-height studio. The result is a welcome contribution to a characterful area of London contaminated in recent years by a cloying obedience to conservation.

Queen's Gallery 2002 **K191** m
John Simpson and Partners
Buckingham Palace Road SW1
⊖ Victoria
For the Queen's Golden Jubilee, a competition was held for a new building to replace the earlier, cramped gallery of the 1960s and to conserve and display some of the very large Royal Collection of art and objects which extends from drawings by Leonardo da Vinci to *bric-à-brac* from Britain's colonial period. The result is a mélange of erudite classical references built in Bath and Portland stone and approached via a diminutive portico leading to an entrance hall whose decoration attempts an allegory of British Art. The galleries themselves are ingeniously fitted to the very restricted site but are so relentlessly decorated that, with the exception of that for the drawings, they tend to overwhelm the exhibits. There are more than enough architectural ideas here to decorate several Las Vegas hotels.

Evelina Children's Hospital 2005 **K192** o
Lambeth Palace Road SE1
Hopkins Architects
⊖ Lambeth North
A single building amalgamated all St Thomas's facilities for the treatment of children nearly literally under one roof. The wards with their 140 beds are in the seven-storey wing to the north and overlook broad terraces giving onto an atrium with a fully glazed but shaded roof. Treatment and other rooms are in the wing to the south. The design is composed in the Hopkins' offices characteristic 'functionalist' manner – functions are identified and housed in discrete building elements and placed together, the whole exterior then clad only in very orange terracotta panels, and glass. See also the **Wellcome Building** G84.

City Literary Institute 2007 **K193** c
Keeley Street WC2
Allies and Morrison
⊖ Holborn
If only more urban buildings could observe city conventions with such decorum as this addition to the 'City Lit'. The building completes the six-storey wall to Keeley Street and as a result, bestows some dignity on Seifert's circular office building of the 1960s next door. The generalized buff-brick enclosure provides a ground for the skilful handling of offsets, slots, linings, arcading, and asymmetries that we have now come to expect from the practice.

Young Vic 2007 **K194** l
The Cut SE1
Howarth Tompkins
Upper Ground SE1
⊖ Waterloo
Instead of the conventional discontinuity between the street and entrance foyer, here the intention is that the bar and its terraces form part of the street, promoting an informal relationship to the auditorium. As with the practice's renovation of the Royal Court Theatre in Sloane Square, there is a no-nonsense attitude to construction detail, although the image of the theatre has been subsumed by its social agenda.

continued section H

continued section K

continued section P

continued section H

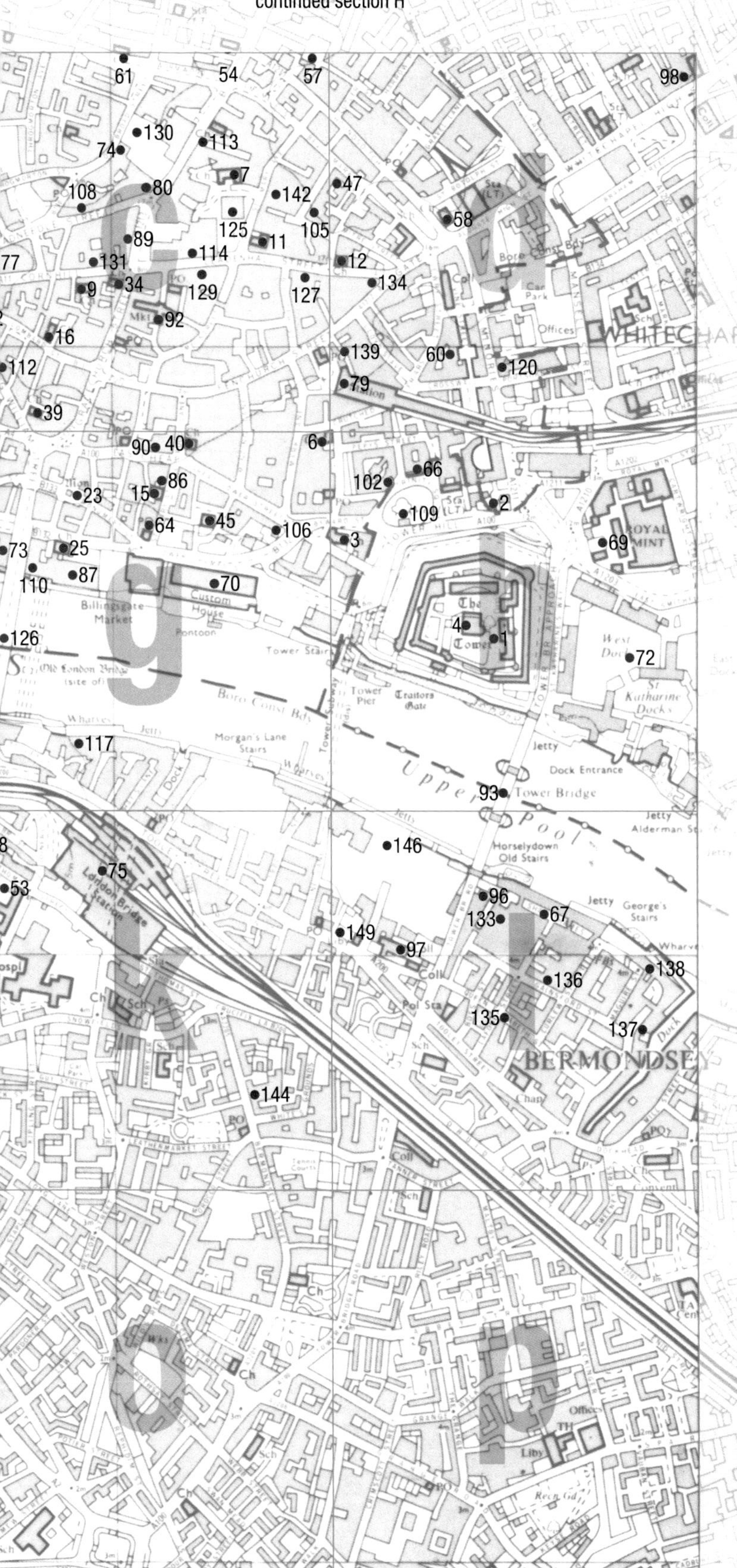

continued section U

continued section P

City of London ■ Whitechapel (south) ■ Borough ■ Bermondsey

The Thames, from Blackfriars Bridge in the west to Tower Bridge in the east, is a convenient north–south dividing line for this area. Embedded in the north is the historic City of London, and to the south are the Borough and Bermondsey. The Roman wall, built at the beginning of the third century AD, stretched from the Tower of London to Blackfriars, enclosing a total area of 134 hectares (330 acres). The smallness of this area was to encourage early settlements outside the wall, and the City quickly became scattered rather than concentrated in form. Watling Street, Ermine Street, London Bridge (the only permanent crossing until 1729) and the great wall are the Romans' legacy to London: their other buildings have disappeared, and are now the study of archaeologists.

Following the Romans' withdrawal in the fifth century, the Saxons invaded, but very little remains of anything that they might have built in London. The Norman city has all but vanished under later rebuilding, the **White Tower** L4 and **St Bartholomew the Great** H1 being conspicuous exceptions.

By the early thirteenth century Royal Charters had established London's independence by granting the trading privileges still enjoyed by the City, and the markets of Eastcheap, Leadenhall, Billingsgate and Smithfield were established within its dense fabric. Urban medieval London imposed its patterns on manorial London: inns and religious foundations are now buried in urban blocks, indicated only by a gate and an alley.

By the middle of the seventeenth century London was an extraordinarily dense and labyrinthine timber-built city, an easy prey to the Great Plague of 1665 (killing at least 100,000 inhabitants) and the Great Fire the next year, which laid waste to 136 hectares (336 acres) and destroyed 13,200 houses (virtually all the City's domestic buildings). London as a brick city emerged from this time. Plans for the total reconstruction of the City were immediately put forward by Christopher Wren, Robert Hooke and Richard Newcourt. Despite these ambitious proposals, inspired by the regular grids and *ronds points* of the continental city, pressing needs for housing and business premises meant that London's reconstruction actually took place on its medieval foundations.

This pattern still remains, giving the modern City its special feel of being a City within the city. When the Great Estates to the west were developed into coherent new sections of London (Bloomsbury, Belgravia and so on) the City stubbornly resisted. The small patterns of land ownership established by guilds, trading companies and parks were permanently to frustrate any large-scale reordering.

The most impressive and significant architectural remains of the seventeenth and early eighteenth centuries are Wren's City churches, built after the Great Fire, of which only 23 of the original 51 remain (19 were destroyed in the Second World War). In 1672 Wren also began the designs for rebuilding **St Paul's Cathedral** L28, which was complete by 1711.

At the turn of the century a few squares, crescents and some fine houses on a par with the more elegant developments in the West End were introduced (**Devonshire Square** L57 and the Minories). The most important single building of this period was the **Mansion House** L56 (the official residence of the Lord Mayor, designed by George Dance the Elder). In 1760 the City gates were demolished and the houses removed from London Bridge under the supervision of George Dance the Younger, architect to the Corporation. In the eighteenth and early nineteenth centuries the City gained a hospital (James Gibbs's St Bartholomew's) and a bank (the Bank of England, designed by George Sampson).

As part of the metropolitan improvements carried out at the beginning of the nineteenth century, Southwark Bridge was built in 1815 and in 1823–31 London Bridge was rebuilt. In 1830 King William Street was cut through to connect the new bridge with the Bank of England, and in 1841 the **Royal Exchange** L77 was built to mark the Bank crossing and to celebrate the new focal point of the City. In 1801 the City had a population of 128,000, but by 1881 it had fallen to 50,000 (by 1951 there were only 5000 residents following the Second World War).

The railways made an early appearance, connecting the commercial and trading centre with the expanding suburbs: **London Bridge Station** L75, in Bermondsey, was London's first railway station. Next was **Fenchurch Street** L79, to the north of the Tower of London, built in 1836 to serve the London and Blackwall Railway; **Cannon Street** L81 and Blackfriars Stations followed in 1865 and 1880, providing more bridges across the Thames to connect the City to the expanding southern suburbs; and Liverpool Street Station (1870) made nationwide connections to the north and east. In 1863 the first Underground line opened from Paddington to Farringdon. There were now six railway stations within the boundaries of the Roman city wall.

The contemporary City gives few visible clues to its rich and complex past, apart from some distinguished Victorian office buildings, Wren's City churches, and fragments of the medieval pattern of courts and alleys. Before the Great Fire (1666) London had been destroyed by invading armies several times; since then its architecture has suffered one great misfortune and two disasters. The misfortune was that none of the plans put forward for rebuilding after the Great Fire could be fully realized; the disasters were, first, Second World War bombing and, second, the completely inept efforts at reconstruction which ensued (the Holden Holford plan for St Paul's Precinct is outstanding in this respect). In the 1960s and '70s the City acquired a skyline of ugly towers and slabs at variance with the medieval pattern of streets from which they rise.

Two debates dominated building in the City of London after 1990 – the first concerned the setting of St Paul's Cathedral and the second, the siting of tall office buildings. These debates reflected the tension between two opposed groups: on the one hand, that a city like London is essentially space-containing and horizontal – as favoured by the Prince of Wales – and on the other the pursuit of 'object' or 'iconic' buildings reflecting the high-rise of the North American city as supported by the Lords Foster and Rogers.

There was a mixed reception to Foster's Swiss Re (the Gherkin) and with the active support of Ken Livingstone (London's then mayor), other tall buildings with equally disingenuous nicknames were anticipated – the 'Shard' at London Bridge by Renzo Piano, the 'Cheese Grater' by Richard Rogers, and Rafael Viñoly's 'Walkie Talkie'. The protracted debate on Paternoster Square north of St Paul's in the 1980s between the supporters of the Prince of Wales and the 'moderns' resulted in a stalemate. The final scheme, under the direction of William Whitfield, proved a disappointment.

The City viewed from City Hall to the south

South of the river

The history of Southwark, across the Thames to the south, is inextricably bound up with the City of London. With the bend of the river to the west, the area forms the hinge point between the cities of Westminster and London, and as a result was the focal point of roads converging on London from the south and south-east (including the Roman Watling Street). It also formed a bridgehead for London Bridge, the sole Thames crossing until the eighteenth century. The evidence of its colourful past as a place of theatres, inns and bear-baiting rings, and of the less colourful history of its prisons, has all but disappeared. However, the borough possesses the most important medieval monument south of the river apart from Lambeth Palace: the Augustinian Priory of St Mary Overie (now **Southwark Cathedral** L5), founded in 1106, and with much remaining thirteenth- and fourteenth-century work.

By the middle of the eighteenth century Southwark was bounded by Bankside along the river and by Borough High Street from London Bridge. The possibilities of its position between Westminster and the City were opened up with the building of Westminster Bridge (1739–50) and Blackfriars Bridge (1760–9). George Dance the Younger, Clerk of Works to the City, realized this potential with his masterplan of 1769, which extended the line of Blackfriars Bridge due south in a wide avenue to meet the road from Westminster Bridge at the *rond point* of St George's Circus. Dance's was the boldest plan to be carried out in eighteenth-century London and opened up more land for development: St George's Road and the New Kent Road quickly followed and by 1815 Great Dover Street had been cut through to the east. Southwark Street (1864) and Tower Bridge Road (1900) followed Haussmann's example in Paris, cutting through decayed and congested areas. Dance's work and the improvements of the nineteenth century are now only lines on the ground: Southwark was badly bombed in the Second World War, and its rebuilt housing gave little care to making good streets – a familiar and depressing spectacle. To the east lies Bermondsey (the north-west corner of which falls in this section, the remainder in section U). The northern limits were densely built over by 1750, but the only relics of its medieval past are fragments of a gatehouse to the Priory. Bermondsey suffered the same fate as Southwark during and after the Second World War: unfortunately the well-intentioned post-war local authority housing policies have damaged parts of London even more permanently and extensively than the Blitz.

Through the conversion of **Tate Modern** L121, the building of the **Globe Theatre** L141, and the popularity of Borough Market this previously inactive frontage to the Thames, with its connections east to Shad Thames and west to the South Bank, has been transformed. These various attractions consolidated what was started in 1951 at the Festival of Britain and also reinstated the tradition of the south side of the river as a place of popular entertainment. As Abercrombie and Forshaw had proposed in 1944, it finally became possible to walk alongside the Thames between Lambeth Bridge and Bermondsey, encountering hardly any traffic.

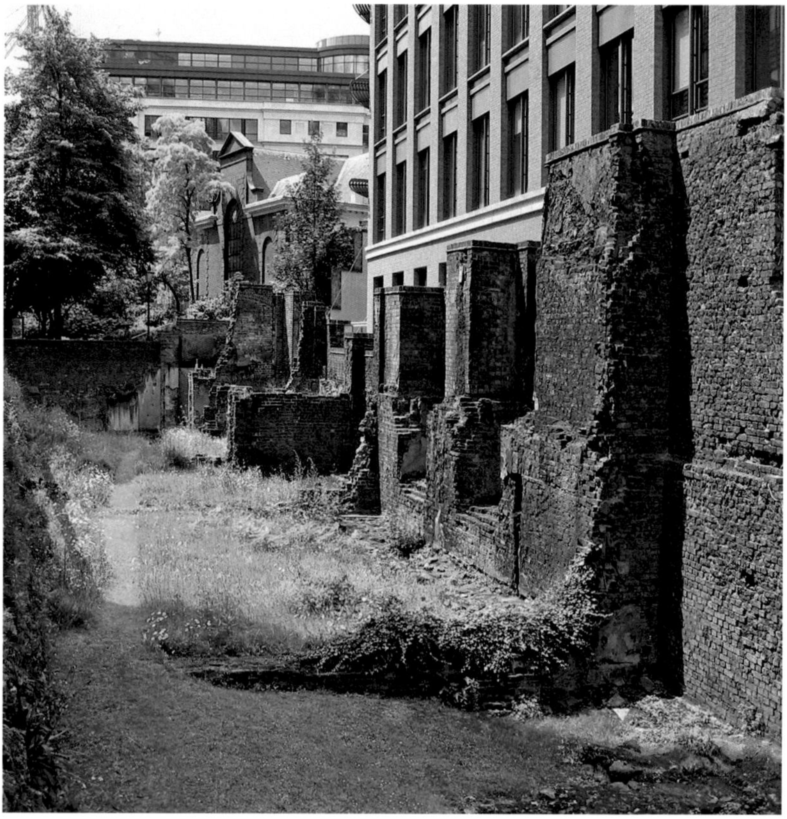

Roman wall at Foster Lane

Roman Wall 3rd and 4th centuries **L1** h
Tower of London, Tower Hill EC3
⊖ Tower Hill
The early-third-century Roman wall terminated at the Thames where the Tower now stands. A short stretch with part of a mid-fourth-century bastion is visible to the east of the White Tower. See also **Barbican** H40.

Roman Wall 3rd and 4th centuries **L2** h
Trinity Square EC3
⊖ Tower Hill
One of the largest fragments of the wall still visible, over 7m (24ft) high. On it can be seen the courses of flat red Roman brick separating and binding layers of masonry rubble. Above these is the ashlar facing of medieval rebuilding. Illustration page 10.

All Hallows-by-the-Tower **L3** h
founded 675
Byward Street EC3
⊖ Tower Hill, Tower Gateway
Only fragments remain of the original seventh-century church constructed over the remnants of a Roman building; the nave walls are from the fourteenth and fifteenth centuries, the rest from then until the present day. It was gutted in the Second World War and completely rebuilt and re-dedicated in 1957. The new design by Seely and Paget included anachronistic new vaults in concrete to the nave and aisles. At the same time the spire was added to the tower, which had in turn been reconstructed by Pearson in the late nineteenth century.

The White Tower, plan of 3rd floor

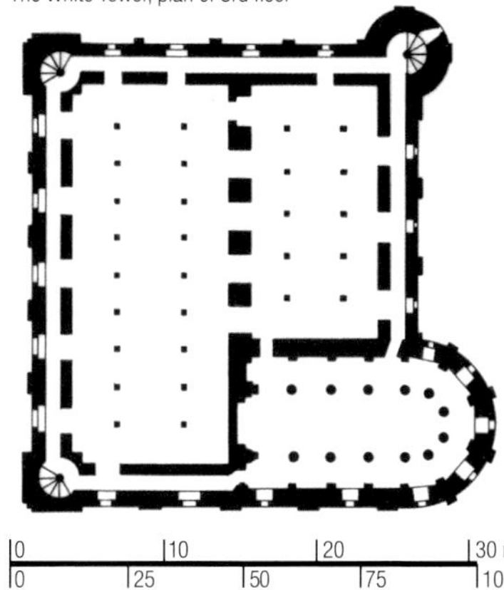

Tower of London 11th century **L4** h
Tower of London, Tower Hill EC3
⊖ Tower Hill
The Tower was begun by William the Conqueror twelve years after his invasion of England in 1066: the White Tower stood alone when finished in 1097, and was a defence against attacks from the continent via the Thames estuary. While much altered (the corner cupolas which give the Tower its toy-like silhouette were added in the fourteenth century), it remains one of the most important examples of Norman military architecture in the country. Built of Caen stone (like Canterbury Cathedral) with walls 3.7m (12ft) thick at the base, the keep's square plan is divided into three rooms on each floor; the rooms have been converted to more ceremonial uses over 900 years, and the lower floors now display parts of the Royal Armouries collection.

The inner curtain wall was started under Henry III and completed under Edward I, who began work on the outer wall. The two large circular bastions on the north of this outer wall were remodelled by Henry VIII. Much of this original work survives in spite of four centuries of alterations and additions. The Chapel of St John is London's Norman church masterpiece – tiny, but massive and primitive, yet with more than adequate lighting through its two arcades.

For many years the approach to the Tower from the west had remained squalid and inadequate. In 2005, a comprehensive landscape proposal designed by Stanton Williams transformed this situation and provided a single, monumentally wide ramp connecting Tower Hill to the Thames Path and framed by the facilities for visitors to London's most popular tourist attraction.

Southwark Cathedral 1106 **L5** f
Borough High Street SE1
⊖ London Bridge
Once the Augustinian Priory of St Mary Overie, founded in 1106, this subdued Gothic church became a cathedral in 1905 and is one of the few tangible reminders of Southwark's Norman and medieval past. Today it is marooned and almost engulfed by the upper-level railway tracks from Cannon Street to London Bridge.

In the thirteenth century the Priory burned down and in 1303 it was declared a ruin, and the dates of some of its original parts are therefore in doubt, but from the fourteenth century the general arrangement is well documented. There were significant renovations in the nineteenth century: in 1822 the tower and retrochoir were restored, and in 1838 the nave was demolished and rebuilt, to be further replaced by Arthur Blomfield's nave of 1890–7. A rather feeble imitation of the existing thirteenth-century chancel, this detracts significantly from the whole. Pevsner observed that the building's Gothic style and details are part French and part English: the proportions of the chancel are English, but the arcaded first-floor wall passage was found only in cathedrals like Chartres and Reims. The capitals are puritanically undecorated, but the vaulting shafts are taken to the ground in the French manner. The clerestory is typically English with an exclusive use of lancet windows, while the vaults of the aisles, chancel and retrochoir are quadripartite, following French precedent. The dates of the individual parts of the building are

equally varied: the crossing tower is fourteenth century in its lower stages, early fifteenth century in the top two stages, and the parapet and pinnacles date from 1689. The north and west walls of the north transept are Norman, while the south transept is exclusively fourteenth century. The elaborate south window is nineteenth century. The interior of the Harvard Memorial Chapel, east of the north transept, dates from 1907, while the walls are of the twelfth century.

To the west, between the railway and the river, lies an area of nineteenth-century warehouses, still suggesting London is a working port. On Clink Street (site of the famous prison) is an unexpected fourteenth-century rose window in a free-standing wall – all that remains of the Bishop of Winchester's medieval palace.

St Olave 15th century **L6** g
Hart Street and Seething Lane EC3
⊖ Tower Hill
One of the City's few remaining Gothic parish churches, St Olave's is best approached through the churchyard from Seething Lane. The gateway, of 1658, has a pediment decorated with skulls and bones. The nave and aisles, of three bays, have quatrefoil piers of Purbeck marble: it has been suggested that much of the building material was reused from the original thirteenth-century church. The interior was gutted in the Second World War and rebuilt by E B Glanfield. However, many of the original furnishings were saved, notably the pulpit, communion rail, main door, and the panelling and stucco ceiling of the vestry.

St Helen, Bishopsgate **L7** c
started 15th century
Great St Helen's EC3
⊖ Liverpool Street
St Helen's is the largest medieval London church to have survived both the Great Fire and Second World War. A convent church was added to the earlier parish church, their two naves standing side by side (in what looks like an early and knowing example of duality) and finishing in a common west front with two doors. The northern nave was for the nuns, the southern for the laity, and they were originally separated by a screen. The bulk of the interior is of the fifteenth century, with some seventeenth-century work – the south door dates from 1633 – and nineteenth-century rearrangement by J L Pearson. The church was damaged by the bombs in 1992–3 and subsequently restored and reordered by Quinlan and Francis Terry. There is an extensive collection of monumental brasses from 1470 on, and some very fine Elizabethan and Jacobean tombs, the gaudiest of which is that of the Spencers (1609).

The Guildhall

The Guildhall Art Gallery (Richard Gilbert Scott 1999)

Guildhall 1411–40 **L8** b
front 1788–9
Guildhall Yard EC2
John Croxton, front by George Dance the Younger
⊖ Bank
Built only a few years after Westminster Hall, the Guildhall, while more extensively altered, still retains its medieval outlines. It is the City's largest secular room and, with the Mansion House, is still used for formal civic occasions. The roof is modern, but the eighteenth-century front to the Yard is an extraordinary and delicate mixture of Greek, Gothic and Indian (the cusped windows) motifs.

St Michael Cornhill 1421 **L9** c
rebuilt 1670–2, 1715–22, 1856–60
Cornhill EC3
Christopher Wren, Nicholas Hawksmoor, George Gilbert Scott
⊖ Bank

The lower parts of the tower to the original church, built in 1421, survived the Great Fire. Following Wren's rebuilding of the nave, his office rebuilt the rest of the tower to Nicholas Hawskmoor's Gothic design (1715–22). In 1856–60 Scott added the north entrance porch and the Venetian tracery to the windows, best viewed from the former churchyard to the south.

Like **St Peter's** L34, St Michael's is connected by its side passage to a complex system of medieval alleys behind, a pattern which characterized most of the City up to this century; note Bengal Court, only 1m (3ft) wide.

Holy Sepulchre without Newgate **L10** a
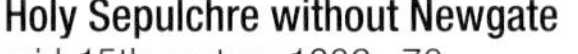
mid-15th century, 1666–70
Holborn Viaduct EC1
⊖ Chancery Lane

The church was considerably rebuilt in 1666–70 following the Great Fire, but the fine west tower belongs to the fifteenth century and is a proud reminder of the Gothic parish church, first mentioned in the twelfth century. The interior has seven bays and is surprisingly spacious, with no division between the nave and chancel.

St Andrew Undershaft 1520–32 **L11** c
Leadenhall Street and St Mary Axe EC3
⊖ Bank

Though dull and much restored, St Andrew's is remarkable for being one of the few medieval churches to have survived both the Great Fire and the bombs of the Second World War, even to the seventeenth-century stained glass of the west windows. However, any atmosphere it might have had is now dispelled by its use as a centre for the Christian teaching and training of business people and the young.

St Katharine Cree 1628–31 **L12** d
tower 1504
Leadenhall Street EC3
⊖ Aldgate

Saved from the Great Fire, St Katharine's is an important survival from a transitional period in English architecture. Its interior has a vaulted plaster ceiling with bosses at the intersections, but this is supported on arches carried on the very primitive-looking Tuscan order of nave columns. The church was restored in 1962 when the aisles were closed off. The cupola was added to the tower in the eighteenth century.

Dean's Court 1670 **L13** a
Deanery, St Paul's Churchyard EC4
Christopher Wren(?)
⊖ St Paul's

With its very large windows and slightly incompetent-looking decoration the house looks more Dutch than English, and is an important domestic survival from the post-Fire seventeenth century. The attribution to Wren is dubious. No longer the Dean's house, it has been restored and developed as luxury offices.

St Vedast alias Foster 1670–3 **L14** b
tower 1697
Foster Lane EC2
Christopher Wren
⊖ St Paul's

The attraction of this church is the tower – late Wren, with the last memory of English Gothic and its steeples gone. The baroque is Italian, at least for the upper stages where convexity, concavity and transparency are combined. The interior is a plain flat-ceilinged box.

St Mary-at-Hill 1670–6 **L15** g
St Mary-at-Hill EC3
Christopher Wren
⊖ Monument

The façade to the street is best ignored; St Mary's is reached through the narrow doorway of **Peek House** L86, and across a typical tiny paved City courtyard in the centre of the block. The interior is one of Wren's most extreme centralized compositions: a central dome, supported at the four corners by Corinthian columns, from which four 'transepts' emerge. A fire in 1988 destroyed the roof and much of the woodwork, including the original reredos and pulpit.

St Edmund the King 1670–9 **L16** c
Lombard Street EC3
Christopher Wren(?), Robert Hooke(?)
⊖ Bank

The vertical street façade (of three bays with arched windows incorporating the octagonal lantern) and the curved sides to the short, black spire are the main points of interest in this church. The interior, reorganized by Butterfield in 1864, has some excellent woodwork and panelling.

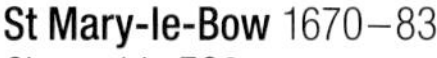

St Mary-le-Bow 1670–83 **L17** b
Cheapside EC2
Christopher Wren
⊖ St Paul's

St Mary's is distinguished by its magnificent tower and steeple. The tower was set forward from the body of the church and separated from it by a lobby to dominate the huddled houses of Cheapside, but it is now isolated. The plain upper stages contrast with the elaborate doorway recessed into a rusticated opening.

The interior, restored since bombing, is now gentrified: the trim modern pulpit and harshly coloured modern glass have reduced the plain white and gold of the architecture to calendar prettiness. In the crypt, however, some original Norman columns can still be seen.

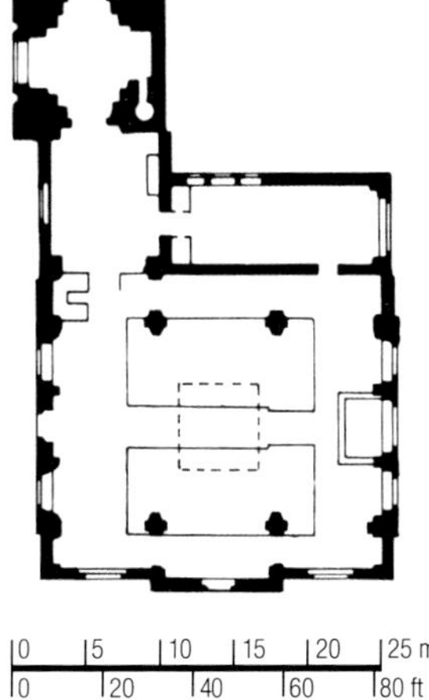

St Bride 1670–84, tower 1701–3 **L18** a
Bride Street, off Fleet Street EC4
Christopher Wren
⊖ Blackfriars

St Bride is one of the grander churches of Wren's series after the Great Fire of 1666. It nestles in its small yard, entirely surrounded by former newspaper offices: a plain box of a nave, to which is attached the tallest of all Wren's steeples – 68m (226ft) high. His fully fledged baroque starts at the foot of the west door with a segmental pediment, which is repeated across the full width of the second stage. Above this starts the succession of octagonal arcades, pulled out 'like a telescope', as Pevsner said, and surmounted by a vestigial steeple.

Inside, the five-bay nave and aisles are separated by the Tuscan arcade which supports the tunnel-vault ceiling. The woodwork is not original but restored after bombing and although the original galleries were not replaced, a good sense is conveyed of the original seventeenth-century church where the wooden fittings were independent of the brick or stone shell of the architecture. Note the permanent exhibition in the crypt.

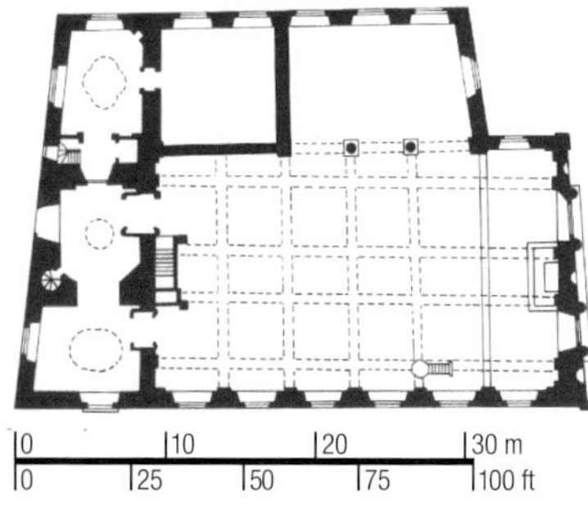

St Lawrence Jewry 1670–87 **L19** b
Gresham Street EC2
Christopher Wren
⊖ St Paul's
A big church, whose uninterrupted nave is separated from a small screened chapel (all restored after bombing, when coloured modern glass was inserted). The magnificent Corinthian east front, facing the entrance of Guildhall Yard, is related to Wren's model design for **St Paul's Cathedral** L28. The plain projecting tower at the east end has a fine lead-covered baroque steeple.

Innholders Hall c1670 **L20** f
façade 1886
College Street EC4
J Douglass Mathews
⊖ Cannon Street
The façade's interest lies in the early-eighteenth-century doorway, with a decorated scroll pediment and coat of arms. The hall was badly damaged in the Second World War and uninterestingly restored in 1950.

Vintners Hall **L21** f
1671, 1870, 1909–10
Upper Thames Street EC4
Edward Jarman and others
⊖ Mansion House
The original brick hall, marked by a nineteenth-century Coade stone statue, can be seen in Vintners Place. The squat front which shields it from Upper Thames Street is of the late nineteenth and early twentieth centuries.

College of Arms 1671–7 **L22** a
Queen Victoria Street EC4
⊖ St Paul's
The design of the College of Arms was the responsibility of a master bricklayer, not an architect, and the result is a good example of the 'artisan style' (see also **Cromwell House** R4). The simple brick façade forms three sides of a shallow open court, closed to Queen Victoria Street by magnificent black and gilded iron gates, transferred to the College in 1956 from Goodrich Court, Hertfordshire. The first floor has an external stone gallery, from which the view to the river – with Wren's St Benet's in the foreground – is a vignette of seventeenth-century London.

Sculptured panel on the west side of the pedestal

Monument 1671–7 **L23** g
Pudding Lane EC3
Christopher Wren, Robert Hooke
⊖ Monument

The site of the outbreak of the Great Fire of 1666 is marked by this robust Roman Doric column 62m (202ft) high. Of fine white Portland stone, it stands on a square pedestal, on which the wings of the City's griffins act as acroteria at the corners. Wren's original design was decorated with gilded flames and crowned with a statue – replaced by Robert Hooke with the present spiky ball. One can climb to the top, and while the panorama is not particularly spectacular, it does afford a rare aerial view of the City. The grand, busy allegorical sculpture on the base is by C G Cibber and shows Charles II trampling on Envy and bringing help and freedom to the burned City. He is accompanied by the female figures of Science, Nature and Architecture, who carries square and compasses.

For a vivid description of the Fire based on Samuel Pepys's account see the 'Fire Experience' at the **Museum of London** H42.

St Nicholas Cole Abbey 1671–7 **L24** b
Queen Victoria Street EC4
Christopher Wren
⊖ St Paul's

Wren's church, which replaced the original dating back to 1144 and destroyed in the Great Fire, was itself burnt out in the Second World War. Unfortunately, the restoration by Arthur Bailey is undistinguished, and the approaches fell victim to 'traffic improvements' and pedestrian precinct planning of the mid-1950s.

St Magnus 1671–85 **L25** g
tower 1705
Lower Thames Street EC3
Christopher Wren
⊖ Monument

Now in an extraordinary position almost underneath London Bridge, St Magnus has one of Wren's more conventional plans. Aisles flank a straight nave, whose tunnel vaulting – punctuated by oval windows – is supported by Ionic colonnades. The original reredos and west gallery, restored in the 1920s, are among the best surviving. The exterior was cleaned and partly refaced in 1980–1.

St Stephen Walbrook 1672–7 **L26** b
spire 1717
Walbrook EC4
Christopher Wren
⊖ Bank, Cannon Street

The site of St Stephen's is typically dense and irregular. The tower and spire look up to the **Mansion House** L56 from the corner of Walbrook, and the main body of the church and its small garden were buried in the interior of the block, with a narrow passageway on one side. The entrance is by a stairway leading from Walbrook into an apsidal lobby, from which the church appears, ambiguously, to be a longitudinal space with a centralized plan. St Stephen's demonstrated better than his later churches Wren's preoccupation with centralized plans (a means of providing a closer connection between the service and the congregation) as opposed to the traditional longitudinal east–west orientation. Simultaneously, he was working on the same combination of nave, aisles and transepts with a central dome space at St Paul's Cathedral.

The beautiful coffered dome is carried on eight arches and free-standing columns, giving the sense of a building within a building. Four arches determine the nave, chancel and transepts, and another arch is thrown across each corner; the resulting half-groin vaults, each supported on a column, describe a triangular space. This aspect of the design is very much in the spirit of St Paul's.

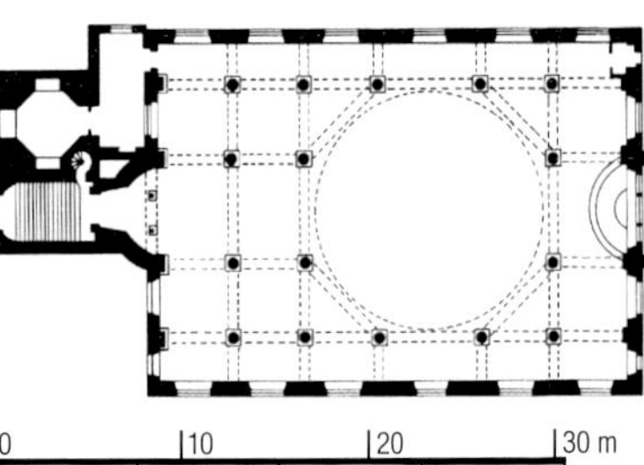

The church was restored 1978–87 when the central circular altar, sculpted in travertine by Henry Moore, was installed.

St James Garlickhithe 1674–87 **L27** f
steeple 1713
Garlick Hill EC4
Christopher Wren
⊖ Mansion House

St James, one of Wren's more accessible works, is a contemporary of **St Stephen Walbrook** L26; the brightly lit interior shows Wren exploring the theme of centrality versus the east–west liturgical axis (which later exercised Hawksmoor). Centrality wins in the open central bay of the nave, but the liturgical axis is emphasized by the window at the east end, unfortunately now obscured. There is much good original woodwork in the interior, which is one of the few among Wren's churches to have retained some of the atmosphere of late-seventeenth-century Protestantism. The spire is one of Wren's more delicate baroque inventions, marking the entrance through the pedimented door.

St Paul's Cathedral 1675–1711 **L28** a
Ludgate Hill EC4
Christopher Wren
⊖ St Paul's (the best approach is on foot from Ludgate Circus)

The present building replaces the Norman and Gothic cathedral destroyed in the Great Fire of 1666. The previous building was itself a replacement of one destroyed by fire in 1087. The pre-Fire building had fallen into decay, having lost its pointed spire in 1561, and in 1634 Inigo Jones refaced some of the walls and added a giant portico to the west end. After Jones's death, but before the Fire, Wren was appointed to report on the fabric. He suggested recasing the nave 'after a good Roman Manner'.

In 1669 Wren, aged thirty-seven, was appointed Surveyor-General. He produced two designs, the first a domed Greek cross (the enormous model of which is in the Library, visits by arrangement). The second, an elongated plan with a spire over a domed crossing, received royal approval in 1675. The foundation stone was laid at the east end on 21 June 1675, and the building finished in 1711, when Wren was seventy-nine.

The design is an arrangement of four volumes: the nave and choir of medieval section (nave with two lower aisles, the nave vaulting supported by flying buttresses), the transepts, the dome and crossing, and the west end. Externally, all the lower parts are clothed with a two-storey screen, the upper storey is blind, and the two storeys are carried across the west front in a double portico which can be read as two superimposed temple fronts. The relief in the pediment, including a pyramid, shows the Conversion of St Paul. Two very complex towers flank the portico. The dome above the drum is constructed in three parts: an inner dome of brick, an intermediate cone of brick, and an outer casing of wood, without ribs, covered in lead. The clear separation of drum and dome is made by a projecting ring of attached columns, of which every fourth one engages a structural pier.

A comprehensive cleaning programme was completed in 2007, and the interior, in cream and white is one of the coolest in Europe (try to see it without too many other visitors). A single Corinthian order supports ribs and saucer domes; the only original decorations are the frescoes in the dome by John Thornhill (see also the **Painted Hall, Greenwich** U3) done in 1716–19. The baroque complications at the crossing arise from making the dome as wide as nave and aisles combined; where the aisles pierce the piers supporting the drum, they are spanned by segmental arches.

Climb the dome, walk round the Whispering Gallery and climb to the lantern, ball and cross, for a fine view of the Cathedral and of the City, largely and ineptly rebuilt since 1945. The crypt (entrance from the outside), although utilitarian and architecturally unremarkable, contains many tombs and monuments, among which is that of Wren himself (*lector, si monumentum requiris, circumspice*) as well as those of British celebrities from Horatio Nelson to Ivor Novello. The Cathedral is floodlit up to midnight during the summer: from the south the symmetrical composition is then clearly evident.

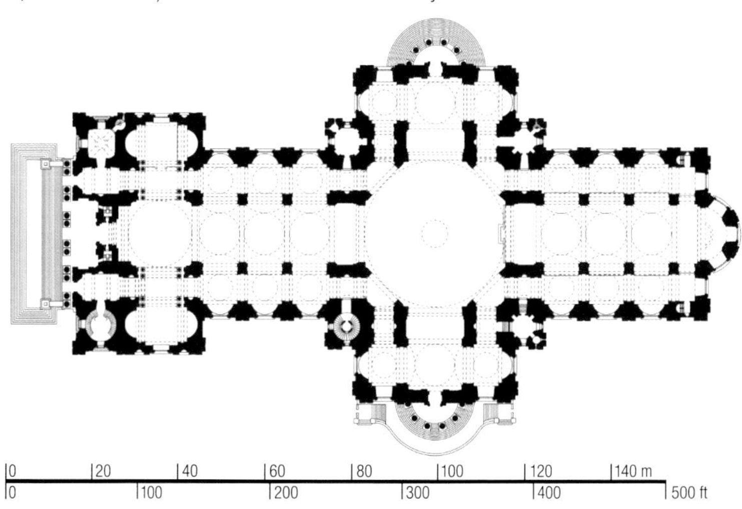

The George Inn started 1676 **L29** j
71 Borough High Street SE1
⊖ London Bridge
The George is London's only remaining working example of the inn type, predecessor of both the motel and the theatre (although it is now missing the northern side of the galleried courtyard). The interiors, their style now more of the eighteenth century than of the seventeenth, still provide a plausible impression of an inn's hospitality; generations of brewers' improvements have been accomplished discreetly. It is owned by the National Trust.

St Anne and St Agnes 1677–80 **L30** b
Gresham Street EC2
Christopher Wren, restored by Braddock and Martin Smith 1966
⊖ St Paul's
First mentioned in about 1200, rebuilt by Wren following the Great Fire, and very well restored after the Blitz, St Anne and St Agnes has one of Wren's purest centralized plans. The exterior is of pink brick, the three bays, with arched windows and a central 'Dutch' pediment, accurately expressing the interior volume. The tower and end bay are rendered and the curiously squat spire was added in 1714. The interior space, deriving from the early Christian plan of a Greek cross, is very fine indeed. In the centre is a large dome supported on four columns; the arms are vaulted and at the corners are four smaller domes. The Lutherans, the present occupants, keep the church locked most of the time; otherwise it would (and should) be better known.

St Benet, Paul's Wharf 1677–83 **L31** a
Upper Thames Street EC4
Christopher Wren
⊖ Blackfriars, Mansion House
Replacing an earlier church (c1111) St Benet's is a delightfully simple brick cube of red and blue chequerwork with a hipped roof, and garlands above the three windows on the west and south sides. The tower has a simple short lead spire on a lead dome. Like many of Wren's churches, it now stands marooned by municipal open space 'improvements' of the worst kind. The interior is lit by large, clear windows.

Christ Church 1677–87 **L32** a
Newgate Street EC1
Christopher Wren
⊖ St Paul's
All that remains is the tower, one of the most elegant in London. It is in three stages: the bell stage is crowned by segmental pediments; the next stage is recessed with a free-standing colonnade and above this is a miniature spire topped with a vase. The tower is best seen as the conclusion to an avenue of trees in the garden to the west.

St Martin 1677–87 **L33** a
Ludgate Hill EC4
Christopher Wren
⊖ Blackfriars, St Paul's
Wren here used one of his centralized plans, a cross inside a square (see also **St Anne and St Agnes** L30 and **St Mary at Hill** L15). The cross is defined by columns which support two intersecting barrel vaults. There were originally wooden galleries in three of the arms of the cross but now only that on the west remains supporting the organ. The symmetrical street façade has the entrance under the tower.

St Peter upon Cornhill 1677–87 **L34** c
Cornhill, via St Peter's Alley
and Gracechurch Street EC3
Christopher Wren
⊖ Bank
As its extended address implies, this church is buried in a labyrinth of medieval passageways and courtyards. The most comprehensive view of it is from the churchyard to the south: a stuccoed exterior with a simple brick tower capped by an obelisk on a dome. From Gracechurch Street to the east, the façade is impressively Palladian: the ground floor has five uniform arched windows separated by pilasters, and the upper floor has one arched and two semicircular windows, completed by a pediment and two curved side pieces.

Gateways c1680 **L35** b
21–22a College Hill EC4
⊖ Cannon Street
A typical piece of historical transformation on a small scale. These two magnificent late-seventeenth-century stone gateways, both with broken and richly decorated pediments, were originally part of Whittington's College, which itself was part of **St Michael Paternoster Royal** L43 on College Street. With their bull's eye windows they form a symmetrical group. Behind number 21 is a delightful small courtyard.

St Augustine 1680–3 **L36** b
Watling Street EC4
Christopher Wren
⊖ St Paul's, Mansion House
The tower, all that remains of the church after the Blitz, has been incorporated into the post-war Choir School of the Cathedral. It is not one of Wren's more exuberant designs, and only the graceful steeple suggests his hand.

St Mary Abchurch 1681–6 **L37** c
Abchurch Lane EC4
Christopher Wren
⊖ Bank, Monument

If this modest church were more accessible it would be better known; hidden away down Abchurch Lane, the church faces a tiny square, its former graveyard. The restrained exterior has three bayed south and east elevations, in brick with stone dressings, and a tower in the north west corner. The interior is a surprise and deeply impressive: the dome, supported by eight arches, stands free of the outer walls and suggests great spaciousness in a very small building. It was painted by William Snow in 1708–14, and the superbly designed altarpiece is by Grinling Gibbons.

St Mary Aldermary 1682 **L38** b
Queen Victoria Street EC4
Christopher Wren(?)
⊖ Blackfriars

This is a Gothic copy, possibly by Wren, of the sixteenth- and seventeenth-century church destroyed in the Fire. The problem of whether it is correct or a pastiche still exercises art historians. The details – the fan vaulting and pinnacled spire – can be matched in earlier English Perpendicular churches, but our guess is that the design is a free reinterpretation. The strange bald tower looks like an essay in Perpendicular Expressionism. The setting of the church is not its original one; Queen Victoria Street was cut through the City in 1867–71 as a Victorian 'Improvement', an extension of the Embankment's east–west traffic route.

St Clement Eastcheap 1683–7 **L39** c
Clements Lane and
King William Street EC4
Christopher Wren
⊖ Bank, Monument

A simple little church, with a pedimented and stuccoed exterior, and exposed brickwork in the top parts of the tower. The interior is equally plain; the south aisle was much altered by Butterfield (1870–89) and has since been further modified.

St Margaret Pattens 1684–9 **L40** g
Eastcheap EC3
Christopher Wren
⊖ Monument

There are two noteworthy features to this otherwise plain church: the entrance, flanked by a good early-nineteenth-century house and shop, and the tower, set back from Eastcheap and crowned with a tall, spiky, and very un-baroque spire. The interior has good original joinery, including the excellent churchwardens' pews, dated 1686.

St Andrew-by-the-Wardrobe **L41** a
1685–95
Queen Victoria Street EC4
Christopher Wren
⊖ Blackfriars
A brick church, its interior now largely without character. It was rebuilt after bombing, when the aisles under the galleries were enclosed behind panelling. For contrast, see **St James Garlickhithe** L27, an un-bombed church which has retained both its parish church flavour and some of the strange rigour of English Protestantism.

St Margaret Lothbury 1686–90 **L42** b
Lothbury EC2
Christopher Wren
⊖ Bank
The present church (the original dated from about 1200) has a simple, nearly rectangular plan, with the tower rising in the south-west corner. The delicate lead spire of the square and undecorated tower is an obelisk on a domed base. Particularly interesting are the furnishings, many of which originate from St Olave Jewry.

St Michael Paternoster Royal **L43** b
1686–94
College Street EC4
Christopher Wren
⊖ Cannon Street, Mansion House
The old church of St Michael, which dated back to 1219 and in which Dick Whittington established a college before his death, was destroyed in the Great Fire. Wren's replacement – one of his last City churches – was further damaged in the Second World War and restored by E Davies. The spire, surmounted by a delicately recessed and transparent octagonal lantern in three stages, is particularly fine and was completed in 1713. The church itself is a plain brick parallelogram with a stone-faced front executed by Wren's master mason, Edward Strong. The renovated interior is of no great interest apart from a pulpit attributed to Grinling Gibbons.

St Mary Somerset 1686–95 **L44** b
Upper Thames Street EC4
Christopher Wren
⊖ Blackfriars
The body of the church was demolished in 1871. The plain tower which remains finds itself in a sad little garden typical of the City's absent-minded suburban approach to the design of many of its outdoor spaces.

St Dunstan in the East 1697 **L45** g
St Dunstan's Hill EC3
Christopher Wren
⊖ Monument
Only Wren's tower remains after bombing – the body of the church had in any case been rebuilt in 1817. The four-stage tower is seventeenth-century Gothic, distinguishable from the real thing in its occasional continuous horizontals – compare with Hawskmoor's **West Towers** K48 at Westminster Abbey.

The Anchor and houses **L46** f
early 18th century
1, 49, 50 and 52 Bankside SE1
⊖ London Bridge
These surprising fragments are all that remain of eighteenth-century Bankside. The Anchor pub, number 1, and its setting against the abutment of Cannon Street railway bridge are picturesque, but the inside has been redone in all-purpose brewer's Dickensian. Number 49, 'Cardinal's Wharf', is the house on which a confident plaque claims (although there is no evidence) that Wren lived in it while designing St Paul's on the opposite side of the river. Numbers 50–2, Provost's Lodgings, were restored after being gutted in the Second World War.

Spanish and Portuguese Synagogue **L47** d
1700–1
Bevis Marks EC3
Joseph Avis
⊖ Aldgate
A routine Georgian place of worship, indistinguishable from contemporary buildings of other religions. Built by a Quaker master builder, this early and well-preserved synagogue, complete with many contemporary furnishings, is now a unique survival.

Chapter House **L48** k
Southwark Cathedral
1702–3
St Thomas Street SE1
⊖ London Bridge
The now redundant church of St Thomas was the nucleus of the original St Thomas's Hospital, before it moved to its present site in 1868. The operating theatre installed in the roof of the church in 1821 can be visited. In the eighteenth century the group was extended with a terrace of houses (numbers 11–15), and set back from the line of St Thomas Street.

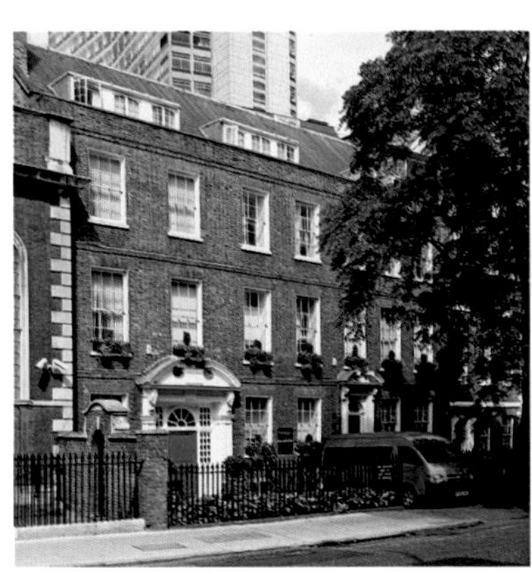

Houses 1703, rebuilt 1976 **L49** f
1–2 Laurence Pountney Hill EC4
⊖ Monument
These grand houses and the small street in which they stand convey very well the red-brick, domestic matrix of the rebuilt City, within which stood Wren's white churches and Cathedral. They are sumptuously but innocently decorated, the work of master builders rather than architects, See also **Queen Anne's Gate** K31 of the same date.

Wardrobe Place c1710 **L50** a
off Carter Lane EC4
⊖ Blackfriars, St Paul's
This contained and tranquil close is a good surviving example of the medieval City's pattern of courts. Of the buildings, numbers 3–5 date from about 1710 and the remainder are more recent. The name derives from the Great Wardrobe, or royal storehouse, moved here from the **Tower** L4 in the fourteenth century and destroyed in the Great Fire of 1666.

Chapter House **L51** a
St Paul's Cathedral
1712–14
St Paul's Churchyard EC4
⊖ St Paul's
The Chapter House was gutted in the Second World War and was subsequently restored. A modest cube-like building of seven bays, with quoins at the corners and angles of the central three bays, it has been incorporated into the redevelopment of Paternoster Square to its north.

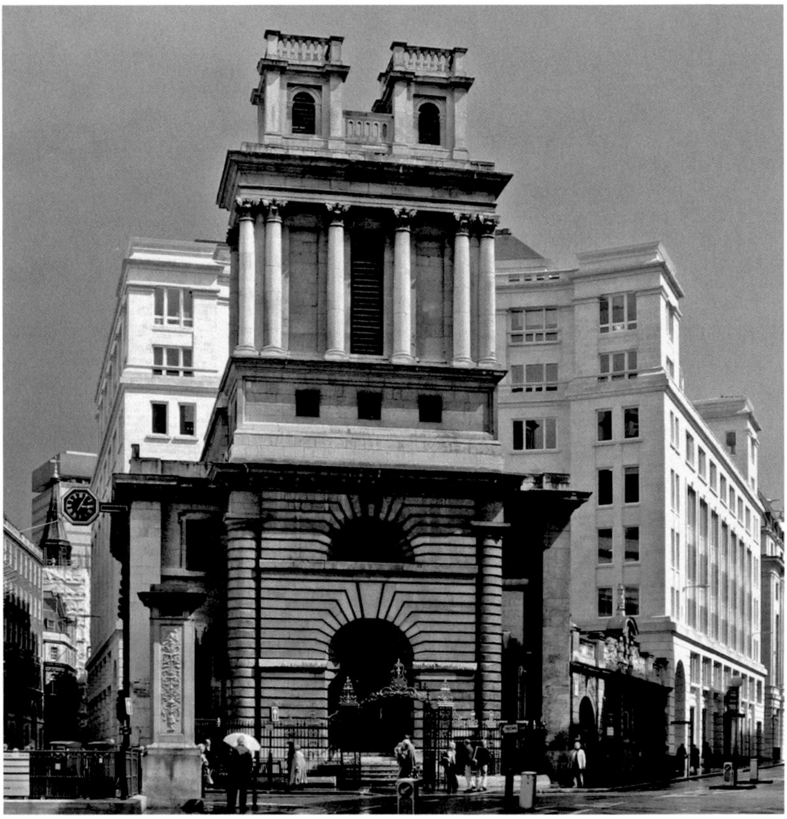

St Mary Woolnoth 1716–27 **L52** c
Lombard Street and
King Wiliam Street EC4
Nicholas Hawksmoor
⊖ Bank

The nave of this exquisite composition is a cubic volume with clusters of Corinthian columns inset from its corners. The columns support a clerestory which supplies light through huge semicircular windows. In Butterfield's alterations of 1875–6 galleries previously occupying the north and south sides were dismantled and the woodwork placed against the walls. The exterior is quite different from those of Hawksmoor's other churches: the 'tower' has become so broad as to occupy almost the full width of the west front. Hawksmoor's rustication and the intensely decorated blind niches of the north façade seem more Mannerist than either antique or baroque. The church was cleaned in 1980, but its sand colour will probably gradually return to black and white.

Guy's Hospital 1722–80 **L53** k
St Thomas Street SE1
Richard Jupp
⊖ London Bridge

Guy's Hospital was founded by Thomas Guy to deal with the overcrowding at St Thomas's Hospital across the street. The original building (1722) forms a magnificent *cour d'honneur,* set back behind iron gates and railings, presided over by a statue of the founder and infested by parked cars. In 1774 the centre bay was improved by Jupp in the Palladian manner, and the ground floor is rusticated and arcaded, as were the wings originally. The eighteenth-century courts beyond are unexceptional (although an alcove from the London Bridge of 1758–62 is preserved in one of them), as are the extensive additions from the nineteenth and twentieth centuries.

To the east of the court and as part of the hospital's wider plan to reorder and tidy up its entire estate, the Heatherwick Studio designed a system of bulging woven-metal tiles as a screen for the main boiler house.

St Botolph 1725–9 **L54** c
Bishopsgate EC2
James Gold, George Dance the Elder
⊖ Liverpool Street
A workmanlike, uninspired design which has been much altered and added to (the interior in 1821 and 1878). Notice the Parish Hall with its touching wooden statues of charity children.

St George Southwark 1734–6 **L55** j
Borough High Street SE1
John Price
⊖ Borough
A grand but provincial-looking affair, St George's has a plain nave, a solid tower and a giant, if squashed, open segmental pediment to the west end. The tower and spire are almost completely solid: they have none of the baroque playfulness of the contemporary **St Giles-in-the-Fields** K45.

Mansion House 1739–52 **L56** b
Mansion House Place EC4
George Dance the Elder
⊖ Bank
Official residence of the Lord Mayor of London, the building presents a porticoed front and side, Palladian as the date would suggest, but both ungainly and provincial. The original unlikely double attics have been reduced in height. The allegorical sculpture in the pediment of 1744 is by the young Robert Taylor, and shows London defeating Envy and bringing Plenty. The building's main interest lies in its axially arranged sequence of state rooms, altered many times. These were originally entered via a vestibule from the portico. The sequence ends in the extraordinary Egyptian Hall, a Vitruvian idea which interested Palladio and was revived by Burlington.

Devonshire Square c1740 **L57** c
EC2
⊖ Liverpool Street
Only just a square – the open south side provides a view of the City at its most unprepossessing. The earliest remaining houses are numbers 12 and 13, both of four bays, in the north-east corner. On the east side is part of the New Street **Warehouse** H23, refurbished as offices in 1982.

St Botolph 1741–4 **L58** d
Aldgate EC3
George Dance the Elder
⊖ Aldgate
Built while Dance was constructing the **Mansion House** L56, this church suffers from the same clumsiness. The Venetian windows are merely the tired remnants of earlier Palladianism; the interior is remarkable for Bentley's 1889 redecoration, especially the ceiling and very bold balustrade.

Hopton Almshouses 1752 **L59** e
Hopton Street SE1
⊖ Blackfriars
A bizarre survival, this group of little houses now faces one of the large clearing banks' computer centres. The houses are grouped in U-shapes round three sides of a square courtyard, at the end of which is the double-height pedimented committee room.

The Crescent, America Square and Vine Street 1760–70 **L60** d
EC3
George Dance the Younger
⊖ Tower Hill
Of the original scheme planned by Dance – from north to south, a square, a crescent and a circus – only a small group of five-storey houses in the crescent remains, numbers 7 and 8 in stock brick, and number 9 in brick with red dressings. See also **Seven Dials** K25 and **Alfred Place** G13.

All Hallows 1765–7 **L61** c
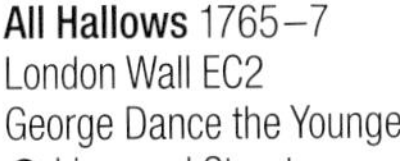
London Wall EC2
George Dance the Younger
⊖ Liverpool Street
Dance was twenty-four when he designed this, his London masterpiece. It combines rudimentary forms (the tunnel vault lit by three semicircular windows on each side and the segmental apse) with spare linear decoration like that of the Adams. The engaged Ionic columns carry only a frieze, before supporting the springing of the vaults to the windows. (Dance's pupil Soane later extended the use of primitive forms and developed the use of arches unsupported by impost mouldings.) Bomb damage and road widening have removed the church's original huddled setting to reveal its brick flanks, which, refaced after bomb damage, now have a rationalist severity.

Opposite, on the south side of the street, are the headquarters of **Deutsche Bank** (Swanke Hayden Connell 1999) whose elegantly restrained façades of Lussac limestone respectfully follow the gentle curve of the street.

Skinners' Hall 1770–90 **L62** f
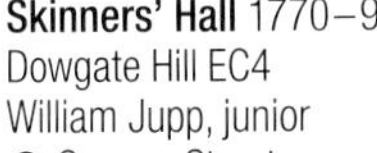
Dowgate Hill EC4
William Jupp, junior
⊖ Cannon Street
One of three surviving Livery Companies' halls in Dowgate Hill, Skinners' Hall is (typically) set back from the street. The five-bay façade is reminiscent of designs by the Adam brothers in **Portland Place** F3, and the Coade stone pediment above the two-storey pilasters was modelled by John Bacon in 1770. The arched passage in the left hand bay leads to a delightful small court, beyond which is the Hall (c1670). Rebuilt in 1850, it is decorated with paintings depicting the history of the skinners and the fur trade from the Middle Ages to the end of the seventeenth century. The court room (c1670) has fine detailed woodwork.

Frederick's Place 1776 **L63** b

off Old Jewry EC2
Adam Brothers
⊖ Bank
An unexpected close of relatively intact Georgian houses, Frederick's Place was a speculative venture by the Adam brothers. Although the individual houses are not particularly special, they have some good external details, and the formal composition of the space is a relief from the ugly and anarchic surroundings of the contemporary City.

Watermen's Hall 1778–80 **L64** g
St Mary at Hill EC3
William Blackburn
⊖ Monument
A sober stone Ionic front to the headquarters of the Honourable Company of Watermen, originally the oarsmen of boat traffic on the Thames.

West Square laid out 1791 **L65** m
SE11
⊖ Elephant and Castle
A regular but incomplete square of grand houses comparable with those of the near-contemporary **Highbury** D3 or **Canonbury** D4, but with irregular entrance streets. The north-west corner was demolished in the mid-1940s but the square as a whole was saved to become one of the many South London enclaves of gentrification.

Trinity House front 1792–4 **L66** h
Tower Hill EC3
Samuel Wyatt
⊖ Tower Hill
Next to and crushed by Cooper's Port of London Authority building (L102), Trinity House is the headquarters of the corporation which organizes and regulates the country's harbour pilots and lighthouses. It has a robust Ionic façade, and some good interiors, both restored by Albert Richardson after war damage.

Warehouses 19th century **L67** l
Shad Thames SE1
reconstruction Conran Roche
⊖ Tower Hill, London Bridge
The reconstruction in the 1980s of the magnificent warehouses on both sides of Shad Thames and of the bridges connecting them obliterated the decayed charm of the narrow street, but was as well done as possible and as archaeologically correct as modern building codes allow. The ground floors of the buildings were converted for restaurants, shops and small offices, and the upper parts into flats.

Life Association of Scotland **L68** a
ex **Bridewell Hospital Offices**
c1805
14 New Bridge Street EC2
James Lewis
⊖ Blackfriars
Bridewell was one of Henry VIII's many palaces, and from the late sixteenth century was used as a prison. It was demolished in 1863, but these offices remain, their chaste architecture – a very giant pilastered order supporting a pediment, all in good ashlar – giving no hint of their former functions.

ex **Royal Mint** 1807–9 **L69** h
Mansell Street E1
Robert Smirke
⊖ Tower Hill
In 1809 the Mint was moved from the neighbouring Tower of London to this dull if dignified classical stone factory. Smirke completed work already in hand by James Johnson, and only the two lodges are his own. In 1986–9 the Mint was 'decentralized' to Wales, and the buildings were renovated as offices by Sheppard Robson, who also designed the overexcited paraphrase of the Lloyd's building to the south.

Custom House 1813–17 **L70** g
river façade 1825
Lower Thames Street EC3
David Laing, river façade Robert Smirke
⊖ Tower Hill
Laing's undistinguished building was much improved by the rebuilding after its collapse of the 148m (488ft) river façade. Behind Smirke's porticoed Portland stone elevation is the Long Room with a magnificent carved ceiling and Tuscan pilasters.

In front is part of the Riverside Walk, offering a rare opportunity to access the north side of the Thames which otherwise is, and has always been, generally appropriated by commercial interests in the City.

Holy Trinity 1823–4 **L71** n
Trinity Church Square SE1
F O Bedford
⊖ Borough
One of the innovations in urban form in the early nineteenth century was the placing of objects, usually churches, in the middle of squares which the earlier Georgians would have left empty. Here is a very successful example: a regular square of houses with two closed corners and Bedford's church set to the south. The north face of the church, acting as the south side of the square, was given monumental width by placing the Corinthian entrance portico alongside the nave, and putting the tower above it. Although this arrangement is wildly unorthodox, there are parallels: for instance, in the original arrangement of Hawksmoor's **St George, Bloomsbury** G8. Holy Trinity shows the church architects of this period re-exploring the classical repertoire, finding still new combinations. See also Porden's **St Matthew, Brixton** W5.

St Katharine's Dock 1828 **L72** h
E1
Thomas Telford, Philip Hardwick and others

The location and small size of these two docks suggest a medieval origin. They are, however, a late addition to the series of docks built further east at the beginning of the nineteenth century on the site of the former St Katharine's Hospital (which moved to new premises in **Regent's Park**, F24). The docks, laid out by Thomas Telford, were badly bombed in the Second World War and subsequently redeveloped as offices; between them, only the building with the tower, designed by Philip Hardwick, remains of the original fabric. At quay level it has arches supported on cast-iron columns and was renovated and converted into shops and flats (1972–4). To the south, the very obtrusive, very brown Tower Hotel on the Thames was by Renton Howard Wood (1970–3).

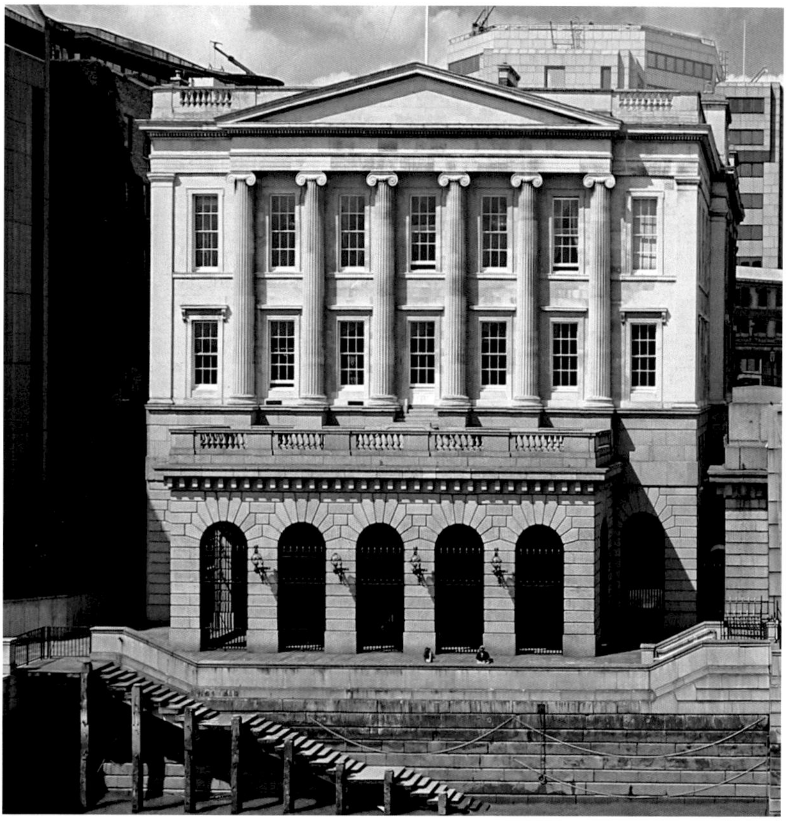

Fishmongers' Hall 1831–4 **L73** g
London Bridge Approach EC4
Henry Roberts
⊖ Monument

Henry Roberts was a pupil of Smirke who later became architect to the Society for Improving the Condition of the Labouring Classes (see **Streatham Street** G34). This competition-winning design, however, is in impeccable Greek Revival style with two elevations of very high standard – with interiors to match – for a City Company. The elevation to the river is very grand, especially when seen from the river walk passing under London Bridge. It is reminiscent of the work of the Palladians a century earlier: only the battered surrounds to the windows show evidence of Stuart and Revett's Greek researches. The entrance front of the Approach is quite different: it could happily find itself in Berlin (note the flat square pilasters at the corners).

City Club 1833–4 **L74** c
restored 1980
19 Old Broad Street EC2
Philip Hardwick
⊖ Liverpool Street

Following the destruction of his slightly later **Euston Arch** G69, only this club remains as an indication of the quality of Hardwick's work. The style is more plain Italianate than neoclassical. The interiors of the ground and first floors were restored in 1980, after the building was saved from being engulfed by the neighbouring development of the National Westminster Bank's offices.

London Bridge Station 1836–51 **L75** k
SE1
George Smith and Henry Roberts; Samuel Beazley
⊖ London Bridge

London Bridge Station is the earliest railway terminus in London, but approached by road it appears to be one of the most recent. The public concourse has been 'comprehensively redeveloped' in a mindless speculators' recipe of a twenty-storey tower and supermarket-type low building. The original building lies behind, and the simple elegance of the fine and slender cast-iron trusses (painted white) over the platforms to the right is a rebuke to the crass and lurid space frames of the concourse outside.

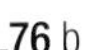

Dyer's Hall 1839–40 **L76** b
10 Dowgate Hill EC4
Charles Dyer
⊖ Cannon Street

The entrance, set asymmetrically in the classical brick and stucco façade, leads to a long and beautiful glass-vaulted corridor. At the end is the dignified committee room, whose principal feature, apart from its fine embossed art nouveau wallpaper, is the curved east wall with a magnificent window.

Royal Exchange 1841–4 **L77** c
Threadneedle Street and Cornhill EC3
William Tite, war memorials Aston Webb
⊖ Bank

The original Exchange was burnt down in 1838, and the competition for a replacement was even more ludicrous than most nineteenth-century competitions: the designs of C R Cockerell (one the most distinguished early-nineteenth-century classical architects) were widely regarded as far superior to Tite's, and in a subsequent muddle London lost a truly remarkable and monumental building. The massive Corinthian portico, with Roman lettering and sculpture in the pediment by Westmacott the Younger, dominates the space between Baker's **Bank of England** L107 and Dance's **Mansion House** L56. At the east end is a baroque spire, reminiscent of a City church. The interior arcaded courtyard accommodates offices; until 1880 it was open to the sky, like a large external room.

Offices 1850 **L78** b
20 King Street EC2
Sancton Wood
⊖ Bank
Built originally for an insurance company, this corner building is important in the nineteenth-century development of a style appropriate for commercial premises. Sancton Wood is better known for his railway stations (Shoreditch, for example, now replaced) but here he uses the language of the palazzo, extending it in three ways: firstly, by opening up the ground floor, using Tuscan columns to support segmental arches; secondly, in putting the upper-floor windows so close that they begin to take over the wall surface; and thirdly, in attempting to find motifs to treat the important corner. In the last he cannot be said to have been successful, but was saved by his own Italianate cornice, which unites the two street façades. The skimpy attic, added in the 1980s, is deplorable.

Fenchurch Street Station **L79** d
1853, 1881–3
EC3
George Berkeley, engineer
⊖ Tower Hill
Fenchurch Street was originally the terminus of the London and Blackwall Railway and the first terminus of the North London Railway, which now stops at Broad Street. It was the completion of this line to Willesden junction which put the Victorian suburb developments of Hackney, Highgate and even Kilburn within commuting distance of the City. The station is undistinguished architecturally, but the form is clever: the bow-arched shape of the elevated train-shed roof is continued over the Italianate brick offices at the front, where it forms a pediment.

National Westminster Bank **L80** c
ex **National Provincial Bank** 1865
15 Bishopsgate EC2
John Gibson
⊖ Liverpool Street
We may smile at the earnest pretension of Victorian bankers, but there were few architectural models for the new institution of the branch bank, and finding an appropriate image was important. They were well served by Gibson, who designed many banks across England. This richly decorated single-storey Corinthian pavilion, ornamented with sky-puncturing statuary and 'improving' panels (showing Industry, Agriculture, Education and so on), has survived. It was thoroughly refurbished in 1981.

Cannon Street Station 1865–6 **L81** f
Cannon Street EC4
J Hawkshaw and J W Barry, engineers
Cannon Street
Two splendid triumphal towers on the river, and the massive flank walls of stock brick, are all that remain of the original station built for the South Eastern Railway. The overall roof has been removed, as has E M Barry's hotel front. They were replaced by substandard curtain-walled offices and shops by John Poulson (1961).

Central Buildings **L82** j
ex **Hop Exchange** 1866
Southwark Street SE1
R H Moore
⊖ London Bridge
Few of London's great Victorian exchanges survive, and this one does so only through its use as a warehouse and offices, and through its fortunate position on a site as yet resistible to developers. It is an important survival, largely for the iron columns on the face and an internal iron structure which supports the galleries running round the central, glass-roofed exchange space.

Offices 1866 **L83** b
103 Cannon Street EC4
Frederick Jameson
⊖ Cannon Street
This inventive mid-Victorian street façade of four bays, with arched Venetian windows retreating in size to the top, is exceptional in contrast with the mediocrity of its recent neighbours. This is now a familiar story in the City, where relatively ordinary Victorian buildings have acquired architectural status by virtue of their increasing rarity.

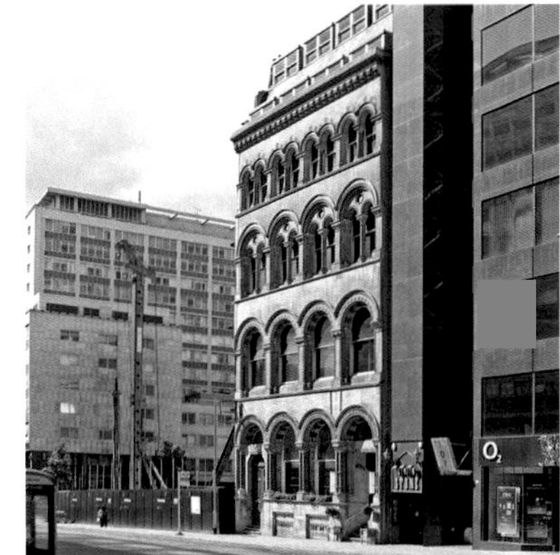

Albert Buildings 1869 **L84** b
Queen Victoria Street EC4
Frederick J Ward
⊖ Bank
One of the few buildings remaining of those that originally lined the newly created 'Improvement' of Queen Victoria Street, this recently restored speculative office block has pretensions to French Gothic art. Like Bucklersbury to the north it is an excellent example of the form of the Victorian City, devoted to commerce.

Blackfriars Bridge 1869 **L85** e
EC4 and SE1
James Cubitt
⊖ Blackfriars
Until Westminster Bridge was built in 1738, London Bridge was the only river crossing. The original Blackfriars Bridge followed in 1760–9, opening the way for the nineteenth-century development of Southwark. As a result of the sharp bend in the river at King's Reach the two bridges and their approach roads form a triangle, with the cities of London and Westminster at the northern and western points: a further connection between London's financial and administrative centres was thus established. The present bridge is a successful combination of architecture – the piers with granite columns, and engineering – the wrought-iron arches.

Peek House 1873 **L86** g
6–7 St Mary-at-Hill EC3
Ernest George and Vaughan
⊖ Monument
While visitors are looking for the entrance to the church of **St Mary at Hill** L15, they might admire this mannered High Victorian façade, cleaned in 1981. It is an extraordinarily 'artistic' composition, using very carefully placed decorated openings in what seems to remain an almost solid wall. The entrance to the church is through the open arch to the small court beyond.

Offices ex **Billingsgate Market** **L87** g
1875, 1990
Lower Thames Street EC3
Horace Jones; Richard Rogers and Partners
⊖ Monument
Since the time of the Roman occupation there had been a fish market on the site of Billingsgate, a tradition broken when the market moved to the Isle of Dogs in 1982. Behind the arcaded ground floor, where once were two large halls filled with the bustle and noise of the market, there is now the silence of unoccupied space dedicated to another market. The well-designed *Bürolandschaft* of Richard Rogers's dealing floors hardly compensates for the lost drama of Billingsgate porters carrying fish in towers of baskets on their heads, now remembered only in the weathervanes of gilded fish on the roof pavilions.

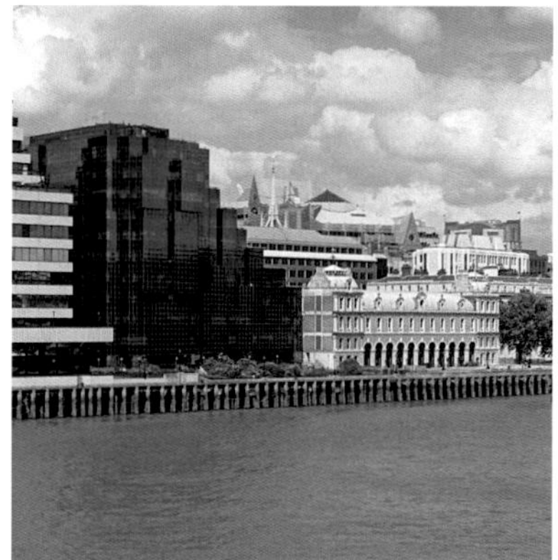

Youth Hostel **L88** a
ex **St Paul's Choir School** 1875
36 Carter Lane EC4
F C Penrose
⊖ St Paul's

The Venetian windows and continuous panels of Renaissance sgraffito decoration of the former choir school are in what Pevsner called the South Kensington style. The highly decorated façade recalls the **Royal College of Organists** J50 of the same date.

Royal Bank of Scotland 1877 **L89** c
3–5 Bishopsgate EC2
Thomas Chatfield Clarke
⊖ Bank, Liverpool Street

A classical façade is successfully reconciled with an extensive commercial frontage in this fine building. From the outside, the former banking hall on the ground floor is clearly visible through large windows set between substantial Ionic columns (the base). The two storeys of offices above are separated by Corinthian pilasters (the *piano nobile*), and topped by the principal cornice and dormer windows (the attic). The façade is of Portland stone, while the rest of the structure is wrought iron.

Shops and offices 1877 **L90** g
33–5 Eastcheap EC3
R L Roumieu
⊖ Monument

An extraordinary survival: Gothic elements are used for a secular building in an expressionist manner more appropriate to high religious fervour than to the trade and banking of the City, which earlier in the century had found its style in Italianate palaces. The building has worn as well as its designer must have intended.

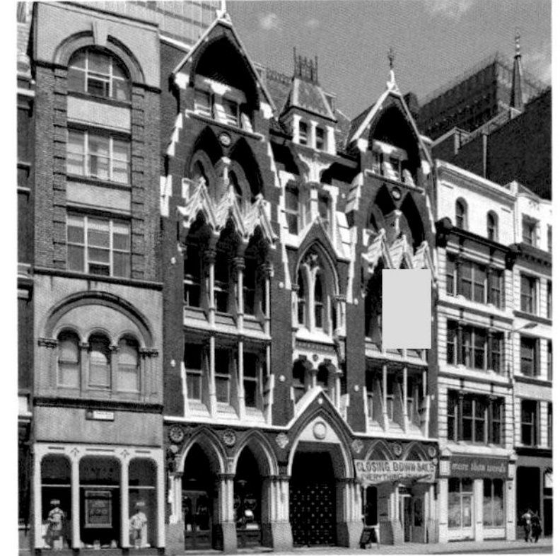

Minor Canons' House 1879 **L91** a
Amen Court EC4
Ewan Christian
⊖ St Paul's

The court is a mixture of architecture, the earliest being fragments of Roman wall tucked away behind the shrubbery at the far end. To the south, and facing the back of St Martin's, Ludgate Hill, is a short row of modest seventeenth-century houses equipped with later torch-snuffers. To the north, Christian's Canons' residence is in a watered-down Shavian style. The whole quiet ensemble is a remarkable survival. Ewan Christian is better known as the architect of the **National Portrait Gallery** K118.

Leadenhall Market 1881 **L92** c
Gracechurch Street EC3
Horace Jones
⊖ Bank
The market is on the site of the large basilica of Roman London, and there has been a poultry market here since the fourteenth century. The present design has an iron and glazed roof which transforms the street into a dramatic and lofty arcade and gives access to the centre of a tight City block, surrounded by institutions like Lloyd's Exchange.

Tower Bridge 1886–94 **L93** h
E1 and SE1
J Wolfe Barry, engineer; Horace Jones
⊖ Tower Hill
One of the most potent tourist images of London, Tower Bridge is, like most great British traditions, a Victorian invention. There are two levels: the lower one which still opens to allow for the passage of tall ships, and the upper one for pedestrians. Architecture (Horace Jones was City Architect) and engineering are integrated in the massive steel-framed stone-clad towers. These house the lifting machinery (originally steam driven, now electric) and the stairs to the upper levels. The bridge was restored in 1982.

Institute of Chartered Accountants **L94** b
1889–93
Great Swan Alley, off Moorgate EC2
John Belcher
⊖ Moorgate
Twenty years on from the High Gothic of the demolished No 1 Poultry, Belcher fully developed his extraordinary free English baroque style in this building. Belcher was a founder of the Art Workers' Guild, and felt that this loose baroque afforded the best opportunity for the incorporation of sculpture. Here it is by Thornycroft and Stevenson, with that on the first-floor string-course and above the door drifting towards art nouveau (ladies turning into leaves). It is surprising that this building is not better known among those who try to reinvent and then distort the classical language – Belcher has almost certainly done it already, even to the keystones.

The Black Friar 1875, 1904 **L95** a
Queen Victoria Street EC4
H Fuller Clark
⊖ Blackfriars
An unexpected survival – a full Arts and Crafts pub, its finely built stone exterior suggesting an important house. The exceptional interior, clad in stripes of green and white marble, exhibits a jolly religiosity very different from the touristic picture of the Victorian pub or gin palace; this was presumably for the City gent rather than the labouring classes.

Courage's Brewery 1891 **L96** l
Shad Thames SE1
⊖ Tower Hill
From the river the distinctive profile of the brewery and its cupola and galleries forms a picturesque group with **Tower Bridge** L93. From the interior of Shad Thames the brewery and other warehouses are very Piranesian, with various bridges spanning the narrow, canyon-like street at different levels. The buildings were mostly rebuilt after a fire in 1891 and were converted into flats in the 1980s.

St Olave's Grammar School 1893 **L97** l
Tooley Street SE1
E W Mountford
⊖ London Bridge
Brick with stone trimmings, the so-called Hampton Court style, was the usual treatment for Victorian institutions. The red brick and white stone dressings are astonishingly fresh-looking in this school building by the architect of the **Central Criminal Court** L99 and the **Northampton Institute** H35. The hall, with a high Georgian lantern, forms the centre of the composition. The school was founded in 1561, and a statue of Elizabeth I from the original building is preserved in the gymnasium.

Whitechapel Art Gallery **L98** d
ex **East London Art Gallery**
1897–9
Whitechapel Road E1
C H Townsend
⊖ Aldgate East

Its façade featuring square corner towers, high strip windows and a massive asymmetrically placed arched doorway in a windowless wall, Townsend's East London Art Gallery marks a decisive break with tradition. An active member of the Art Workers' Guild and follower of the American architect H H Richardson, Townsend (with Lethaby, Shaw, Ashbee and others) was a prime exponent of the English Arts and Crafts style at the turn of the century. The building's monumental mass has characteristic Arts and Crafts foliage decoration, but a great mosaic designed for the central panel by Walter Crane was never executed owing to lack of funds.

The gallery was completely and beautifully refurbished to designs by Colquhoun and Miller in 1984, when the upper gallery was reopened and new accommodation including a restaurant was built at the back. In 2008, work started on the conversion of the former library to the east to provide further gallery space and other accommodation. The architects were Robbrecht en Daem, Witherford Watson Mann, and Richard Griffiths.

Central Criminal Court 1900–7 **L99** a
Old Bailey EC4
E W Mountford
⊖ St Paul's

Mountford, ransacking Wren's baroque for motifs, produced an appropriately grand Edwardian composition on the site of Dance's famous Newgate Prison. The courts are tightly planned on the first floor. The statue of justice on top of the Greenwich-inspired dome (U3) has become famous from countless scenes in films. The extension to the south is by McMorran and Whitby, 1972.

St Anne's Vestry Hall 1905 **L100** a
Church Entry, off Carter Lane EC4
Banister Fletcher and Sons
⊖ Blackfriars
Carter Lane survives between Ludgate Hill and Queen Victoria Street, its seventeenth- and eighteenth-century scale in strong contrast with that of the nineteenth- and twentieth-century commercial development in which it is embedded. The hall is in a typical City passage off the lane, its tiny façade a gem of baroque from the firm which brought us *A History of Architecture by the Comparative Method*, first published in 1896.

Thames House 1911 **L101** f
Queen Street and Upper Thames Street EC4
Collcutt and Hamp
⊖ Mansion House
It would be easy to overlook the virtues of these cheerful Edwardian baroque offices were it not for the post-war reconstruction of Upper Thames Street. Street. This destroyed the street's form, especially the corners at which this building excels, without offering satisfactory alternatives.

ex **Port of London Authority** 1912 **L102** h
10 Trinity Square EC3
Edwin Cooper
⊖ Tower Hill
A fitting monument to the London Docks as the Edwardian mercantile world's capital, Cooper's building dominates Trinity Square just as its giant expressive tower still dominates the approach across Tower Bridge. The building occupies a city block, with a vast circular hall 34m (110ft) in diameter and 20m (67ft) high. The winning entry in a competition, it was criticized at the time for its extravagant architecture: colossal columns, domes, towers, and groups of sculpture. (Cooper's later classicism for **Marylebone Town Hall** F40 was greatly simplified.)

Southwark Bridge 1912–21 **L103** f
EC4 and SE1
Ernest George, architect and Basil Mott, engineer
⊖ Cannon Street
The replacement of the earlier bridge of three spans designed by John Rennie in 1819 is unremarkable: five bays of steel arches supported on granite piers.

Blackfriars House 1913 **L104** a
New Bridge Street EC4
F W Troup
⊖ Blackfriars
The fine pioneering design of these offices (now a hotel) has been spoilt by the insertion of modern aluminium windows. However, the unblemished and delicately decorated white faïence facing and the proportions of frame to opening are both admirable, reminiscent of Otto Wagner's Vienna and of Chicago. See also the Gallaher Building, Kingsway (K135).

National Employers' House **L105** c
ex **Holland House** 1914
1–4 and 32 Bury Street EC3
H P Berlage
⊖ Liverpool Street
This decorative and idiosyncratic City office building was commissioned by a Dutch shipping company, and marks a departure by Berlage, the eminent Dutch architect, from the style of his Amsterdam Exchange (1896–1903). On its complex City site, with two frontages at the corner of Bury Street, the design considers the architectural possibilities of the steel frame. The structural steel mullions are closely spaced at 1.3m (4ft 6in) and clad in greenish glazed tiles. They sit on a polished black granite plinth, which also forms surrounds to the principal entrances and rises the full height of the building at each end, forming five-storey pilasters. Seen in perspective, the mullions give the illusion of a solid masonry wall. The ornamental detail of the spandrel panels, the faceted connections between the mullions and the plinth, and Joseph Mendès da Costa's large, stylized nautical sculpture on the building's acute corner are some of Berlage's devices to temper the geometric tendencies of the steel frame. The later extension to the east, supposedly built in the spirit of the original but without its inventive detail, shows a depressing lack of self-confidence: here the frame is not an end in itself but only one of the means to architectural expression.

Christ's Hospital Offices 1915 **L106** g
26 Great Tower Street EC3
Reginald Blomfield
A good example of 'Wrenaissance' from someone other than Lutyens, who coined the term: calm, restrained, and with excellently crafted brickwork.

Soane's screen to Threadneedle Street

Bank of England 1921–37 **L107** b
Threadeedle Street EC2
Herbert Baker
⊖ Bank

In the early eighteenth century the Bank was housed on this site in the mansion of one of its founders. The wonderful banking halls built by Soane between 1788 and 1808 were additions to this house. The bulk of Soane's work was scandalously demolished to make way for Baker's huge enlargement of the Bank's offices, and only the screen walls to the surrounding streets remain. Although Baker, with Lutyens, was entrusted with the imperial work in New Delhi, this design, like most of his London work (for example **South Africa House** K158), lacks distinction and in no way compensates for the loss of Soane's masterpiece.

In 1988, when the Bank converted part of its accommodation to a museum (entered from Bartholomew Lane), some of Baker's work was undone and Soane's original Stock Office of 1793 was recreated. Although brand new, this now provides an impression of the spatial novelty, the manipulation of light and elemental styling of Soane's work. Baker's dull rotunda houses another part of the museum.

National Westminster Bank **L108** c
1922–31 extended 1936
51 Threadneedie Street EC2
Mewès and Davis
⊖ Bank

Here Mewès and Davis digressed from their customary French style. The handling of the softly curved frontage of Threadneedle Street is a knowing reworking of Peruzzi's Palazzo Massimi in Rome (1535). However, the plan lacks the elegant internal displacements of the original.

Mercantile Marine Memorial **L109** h
1922–52
Trinity Square EC3
Edwin Lutyens; additions by E Maufe 1952
⊖ Tower Hill

Maufe's work is of no interest, but Lutyens's memorial shows him operating in two modes. The first is the 'representational' Tuscan barrel-vaulted temple below, where the piers are covered in panels of bronze, imitating ashlar and bearing the names of the dead. The second is above, in the extraordinary abstract arrangement of white oblongs topped by a low drum in the middle of the Portland stone roof.

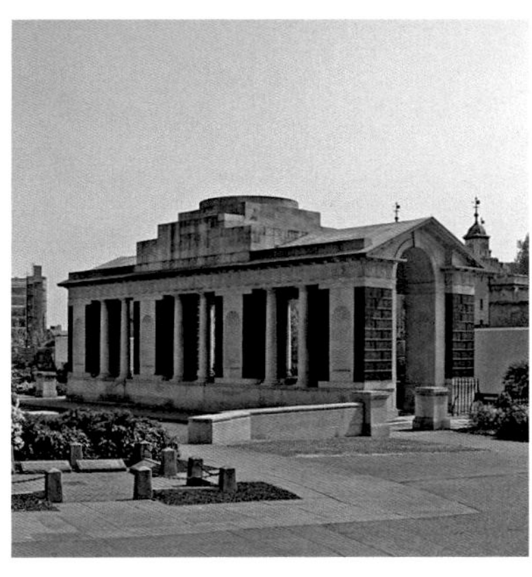

Adelaide House 1924–5 **L110** g
King William Street EC4
John Burnet, Tait and Partners
⊖ Monument

Adelaide House and **Fishmongers' Hall** L73 opposite form the bridgehead to London Bridge, which ambitiously spans Lower Thames Street. Although it was one of the earliest City office buildings to abandon the classical style, some style was still felt necessary and the Egyptian was adopted. Gavin Stamp noted that 'Egyptian was fashionable in the 1920s by virtue of being exotic and excessively monumental'. The building is notable for its massive curved cornices, the regularity of its vertical system of bays, and the four exaggeratedly squat black marble Doric columns at the entrance (the only lapse into the classical).

ex **Midland Bank Head Office** **L111** b
1924–39
Poultry and Princes Street EC3
Edwin Lutyens;
executive architects Gotch and Saunders
⊖ Bank

Lutyens started this, his biggest building in England, at the height of his career. All his experience in the use of classicism shows in the way he composed and inflected the surfaces of the massive building: note for example the re-entrant corners of the fifteen-bay elevation to Poultry, and the way in which the two axes extending from Poultry and Princes Street are united on the skyline by the shallow dome. Despite its bulk, the building does no damage to the delicate structure of the tight City streets. The grand public ground-floor interiors, clad in black and white marble, were magnificent and worth inspecting.

London Life Association 1925–7 **L112** c
King William Street EC4
W Curtis Green
⊖ Bank, Monument
A monumental palazzo façade with a screen of recessed columns in the centre, all in stone, gives the intended image of permanence and reliability.

Hasilwood House **L113** c
ex **Hudson's Bay House** 1928
52–68 Bishopsgate and St Helen's Place EC2
Mewès and Davis
⊖ Liverpool Street
The massive symmetrical stone façade with a mansard roof has a central double-height gateway supported by Tuscan columns. This leads to St Helen's Place, in plan a typical City close, angled to the line of Bishopsgate. In section, however, it is seven storeys high: the close is really more of a *cour d'honneur* with another 'French' façade by Mewès and Davis at the end. This is an exemplary type for the City of London, and a rebuke to the tower forms that have generally replaced it.

ex **Midland Bank** 1929 **L114** c
140–4 Leadenhall Street EC3
Edwin Lutyens, Whinney and A Hall
⊖ Bank
Completed while Lutyens's Midland Bank headquarters (L111) was still being built, this branch of the same bank shows him working with a straightforward street infill façade. One of the neighbouring buildings was subsequently removed, revealing the elaborate towers above an otherwise strangely flat and cramped façade, in which the seven bays of the office floors are supported on five bays of grand arches at street level. Also revealed is the utilitarian back of the building: white glazed brick and big 'factory' windows.

Unilever House 1930–1 **L115** a
New Bridge Street and
Victoria Embankment EC4
J Lomax Simpson with John Burnet, Tait and Lorne
⊖ Blackfriars
The last independent work by Burnet before the practice went modern, Unilever House is a massive baroque urban design, marking the emerging conflict between the use of historical styles (including the classical) and the need for more spacious buildings. The stone quadrant, with a huge rusticated base and giant screen of columns above seems to anticipate an extension of the same scale along New Bridge Street and the Embankment, making Unilever House a fragment of a much larger scheme. The sculpted groups at either end are by William Read Dick. Note also the splendid art deco interiors renovated by Theo Crosby in 1982.

National Westminster Bank **L116** b
ex **National Provincial Bank**
1930–2
Poultry and Princes Street EC2
Edwin Cooper
⊖ Bank
Cooper, faced with the challenge of building next to Lutyens's magnificent bank in Poultry (L111), successfully negotiated the Princes Street corner – one of the City's most important street crossings; note the giant recessed columns and the busy and inscrutable sculptural group interrupting the parapet.

Hay's Wharf and **St Olave House** **L117** g
1931–2
Tooley Street SE1
H S Goodhart Rendel
⊖ London Bridge
The warehouse fronting the river and St Olave House, the office building facing Tooley Street, are gems of lively *moderne*. The buildings stand on columns to allow access for traffic to the river, and their composition contrasts the vertical lift tower against the horizontal projecting 'bulkhead' bronze-framed windows. The steel frame is clad in Portland stone, and both buildings are decorated inside and out with jazz modern works of art. The river façade boasts sculptured panels by Frank Dobson, and the splendid big triangular sectioned wooden letters of the name. The buildings are listed, and were spared in the redevelopment of the river front between London Bridge and Tower Bridge.

ex **Daily Express Building** 1932 **L118** a
Fleet Street EC4
Ellis Clarke and Atkinson with
Owen Williams
⊖ Chancery Lane

In the middle of London's former newspaper-land, this building is a glazed envelope of black and transparent glass (with curved corners), through which the printing presses in the basement could be seen. The rails for the cleaning gantry form a cornice, as in Williams's warehouse (1934) for J Sainsbury in Southwark (now demolished). The top three floors retreat behind the gantry to allow daylight to reach the street and adjacent buildings. Owen Williams remains probably the most original and enigmatic architect-engineer of his generation.

Ronald Atkinson's entrance hall with its elaborate metal decoration is a fabulous *moderne* extravaganza. To left and right are metal relief wall sculptures depicting colonial enterprise past and present. The central approach to the beautiful cantilevered staircase is in the spirit of the entrance to Cleopatra's tomb, complete with chromium twisted snakes as handrails. The lighting is incorporated in metallic stalactites suspended from the ceiling. With the removal of the interiors of the Strand Place Hotel to the Victoria and Albert Museum, the Daily Express entrance hall is now almost unique as a working art deco interior.

In 1989, as part of the general exodus of newspapers from Fleet Street, the *Daily Express* moved to new offices on the south side of Blackfriars Bridge. In 2000 the building was thoroughly renovated as part of the agreement to build a large office building to the north, architects KPF.

Reuters and Press Association Headquarters 1935 **L119** a
85 Fleet Street EC4
Edwin Lutyens with Smee and Houchin
⊖ Chancery Lane

Lutyens's handling of the Reuters site and of the architectural masses and complex geometrics of the building is characteristically masterful. Immediately next to Wren's beautiful **St Bride's** L18, its L-shaped plan acts as a backdrop to the church. The west door of St Bride's is ingeniously linked to Salisbury Square by a double-height vaulted passageway (St Bride's Avenue) through the centre of the building – a modest but thoughtful addition to the labyrinth of passages and courts of this historic area of London.

The building's steel frame is clad in Portland

stone – the upper walls are battered and the windows decrease in width vertically. The independent roof pavilion is another typical Lutyens device – a concave-fronted structure crowned by a large drum. Above, when seen from the dome of St Paul's, its two towers form a symmetrical composition with the spire of St Bride's at its centre. The double-height entrance hall gives the impression of having been carved out of solid marble – its approach is crowned by a deep and massive circular window with a bronze figure of Fame at the centre. The series of long, low window openings, with shallow reveals and standard metal window frames, is as close as Lutyens comes to 'modern' in this, his last commercial building in London.

Detail of entrance with figure of *Fame*

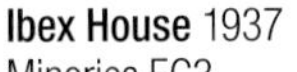

Ibex House 1937 **L120** d
Minories EC3
Fuller, Hall and Foulsham
⊖ Tower Hill
A spirited, large, horizontal office building clad in beige faïence with nicely rounded corners. The unbroken stretch of continuous strip windows (21m/70ft) was when built the longest in London.

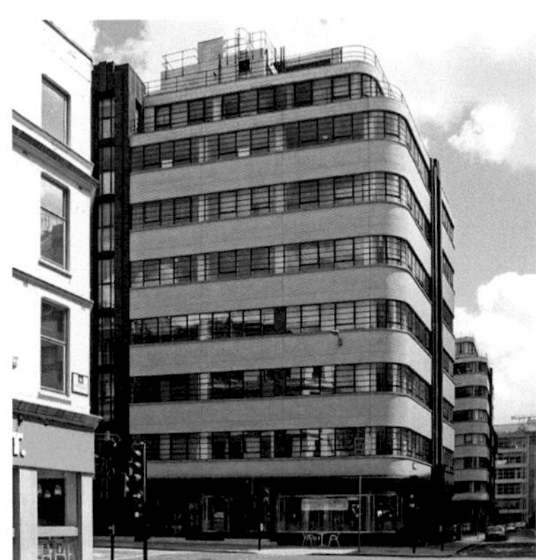

The Turbine Hall

Tate Modern 1994–2000 **L121** e
ex **Bankside Power Station** 1955
Bankside SE1
Giles Gilbert Scott; Herzog & de Meuron
⊖ London Bridge
The transformation of Scott's Bankside Power Station of 1955 into Tate Modern follows what appeared to be London's policy of renovation as opposed to the new buildings of Paris's *grand projets*. Although for some this represented a loss of nerve, it characterized the majority of London's millennium cultural projects. Contemporary art is by definition subversive and any institutionalizing of it with a new building can be problematic. Following a much-publicized limited competition in 1992 Herzog and de Meuron emerged the clear winners. Their scheme established an intelligent dialogue with the existing building – for example, seen from the outside, the long rooftop horizontal light-box contrasting with Scott's monumental chimney forms a billboard and from inside a place to view London's less than wonderful skyline opposite. The drama of the entrance ramp running the full width of the vast Turbine Hall forms a very impressive entrance lobby overlooked by a series of well-crafted light-boxes; the animation of the escalators floor to floor gives the circulation a compressed energy and a real sense of occasion, as the five million annual visitors testify. The building's relationship to St Paul's across the river was consolidated with the pedestrian bridge (L143), completed in 2000.

Note, immediately to the west of the gallery's entrance, **Bankside Lofts**, 130 flats converted and augmented from former industrial buildings by developers Manhattan Lofts (CZWG architects 1998).

Bracken House **L122** b
ex **Financial Times building**
1956–9, 1988–90
Cannon Street, Friday Street
and Distaff Lane EC4
Albert Richardson;
Michael Hopkins and Partners
⊖ Mansion House

Richardson's original building and its reconstruction of the 1980s gain mutually from their conjunction. The seven-storey wings to Cannon Street and Queen Victoria Street were retained but the two-storey octagonal central hall was replaced by a seven-storey circular atrium to provide more offices. The glass and steel crenellations of Hopkins's new perimeter sit convincingly between the original heavy wings.

Richardson was usually associated with neo-Georgian; his work here is less easily categorized. A plinth of red sandstone is surmounted by four-storey piers of dark-red brickwork and topped by an attic cornice of copper set back on miniature glass-brick piers: a combination of a classical formula with Milanese Liberty detail, but the entrance canopies always seemed overdesigned. The new elevations, by contrast, do not distinguish so emphatically between bottom, middle and top; each floor is equal, and transparency is emphasised. There are echoes here of Peckham's **Pioneer Health Centre** X10 of 1934–6 and Oriel Chambers in Liverpool of 1864.

Police Station 1962–6 **L123** b
Wood Street EC2
Donald McMorran and George Whitby
⊖ Moorgate

Historically, this important building offered a reworking of classicism during one of its most neglected periods. The square plan of three storeys surrounding a courtyard, with a twelve-storey campanile of offices to one side, makes a very strong composition. Its cool and abstracted forms connect with Lutyens's later City buildings, and stand out from the surrounding later banal designs. Among its formal inventions are the screen walls marking the basement entrance and the two large rusticated chimneys projecting through the pitched roof. However, some of the details are notably un-classical: there are no parapets to the pediments, and the lack of sills to the windows has resulted in streaking of the stonework. The 'abstract' pattern-making of the ground-floor rustication and the 'Swedish' window frames suggest the post Festival of Britain era.

Note on the west side of Wood Street an interesting comparison of two office buildings completed in 2000. At number 100 Foster and Partners provided two façades: to the street a chequerboard, to the court behind one of leaning glazing – a homage to James Stirling? At number 88, an investment bank commissioned purpose-designed premises from the Richard Rogers Partnership. This shows the practice's mature characteristic composition of 'served and servant spaces'. The details are refined – the ground floor and entrance are particular well handled.

Flats ex **Department of Health and Social Security Offices** 1963 **L124** m
Newington Causeway SE1
Ernö Goldfinger
⊖ Elephant and Castle

Following Abercrombie's planning proposals, one of the methods of 'improving' London from 1945 on was to enlarge traffic intersections. The left-over spaces round the new engineering works were then available for 'comprehensive' redevelopment (usually, as here, with results inferior to those envisaged by Abercrombie). These offices were built as part of that process. There are two seven-storey blocks, which enclose a third block of thirteen storeys, a small piazza and a cinema. Goldfinger's concern for modelling is well demonstrated in the apparently arbitrary setting in and out of the façades, and in the use of the exposed concrete of the frame, painted an unsatisfactory cream when the buildings were converted into flats in 1998.

Offices **L125** c
ex **Commercial Union Assurance**
1968–9
Leadenhall Street and
St Mary Axe EC3
Gollins Melvin Ward Partnership
⊖ Aldgate

Two free-standing buildings, one continuing the Leadenhall Street frontage, the other taller and set back from the street, originally addressed a large piazza. The Leadenhall Street building was demolished in 2007. The sureness of style and the technology of Commercial Union tower (its floors are suspended from cantilevers from the central core) easily match those of its models in the United States, particularly those in Chicago. But it is doubtful whether the open space is appropriate among the tight streets and narrow alleys of the City, and whether, if it is offered in contrast to these, it is done sufficiently well. The tall and formerly open first floor of the tower and the elaborate stairs leading to it are remnants of a largely abandoned planning requirement which proposed an alternative and continuous system of first-floor pedestrian circulation throughout the City (see the **Barbican** H40 and **London Wall** H41).

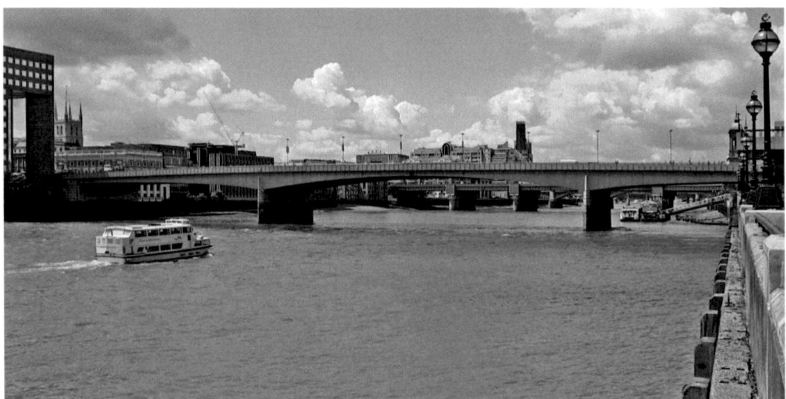

London Bridge 1968–72 **L126** g
EC4 and SE1
Harold King (engineer) and Robert Bellinger
⊖ London Bridge

As the first Thames crossing, London Bridge has a long and rich history going back to the first century and has been rebuilt many times. Debate about the original position of the Roman crossing was resolved in 1981, when remains of its abutments were found under **Billingsgate Market** L87. The narrow picturesque houses of the famous inhabited medieval bridge (about 1200) were removed when it was widened in 1758–62. Fragments of the replacement by Robert Taylor and George Dance the Younger can be seen in **Guy's Hospital** L53 and Victoria Park. The bridge was rebuilt by Rennie (1823–31) and can now be seen crossing Lake Havasu, Arizona, where it has been since 1971. The present bridge is the least distinguished structure in this long history.

Offices 1973 **L127** c
36–8 Leadenhall Street EC3
YRM Architects and Planners
⊖ Aldgate

The tradition of good proportions and fine materials which seemed to have died with Lutyens is revived (via the Chicago School) in this excellent commercial building. The deceptively simple frame, covered with travertine as a change from Portland stone, is a reproach to the oriels, bizarre facing bricks and absurd mansards which were then the City's going style.

Bush Lane House 1976 **L128** b
80 Cannon Street EC4
Arup Associates
⊖ Cannon Street

An extraordinarily complicated little office building, and the only example in London of a tubular stainless-steel diagonal external structure, filled with water as fire protection. The ground floor, originally a void, was subsequently filled with shops.

Lloyd's 1978–86 **L129** c
Leadenhall Street EC3
Richard Rogers and Partners
⊖ Bank, Monument

The present Lloyd's stands on the site previously occupied by Edwin Cooper's neo-Roman building of 1928. Despite its agitated profile and earlier celebrity, Lloyd's is a simple rectangle in plan. It reverses the conventional core arrangement for offices: lifts, fire stairs and lavatories were moved outside the exterior wall in order to make way for a dramatic twelve-storey-high barrel-vaulted atrium at the centre. This arrangement of 'servant and served' spaces is a tribute to Louis Kahn (Richards Laboratories, University of Pennsylvania 1961) and more distantly to medieval castles.

Although some find the appropriateness of such a defensive idea for a city building is questionable, for others this is one of the most important buildings of the twentieth century, courageously keeping faith with modern architecture. That it was commissioned by one of Britain's more conservative institutions is doubly remarkable. The detailing of the exterior is magnificently obsessive and contributes to the overall impression of a remarkable stainless-steel sculpture, which is particularly dramatic when floodlit. In the context of the limp contemporary architectural debate in Britain, Lloyd's continues to stand as a heroic and magnificently fallible building.

Tower 42 **L130** c
ex **National Westminster Tower**
1981
5 Old Broad Street EC2
Richard Seifert and Partners
⊖ Bank
The tower is 183m (600ft) high and was, when built, Britain's tallest building. It was later joined by others to form an untidy and expanding cluster.

Offices 1983 **L131** c
68 Cornhill EC3
Rolfe Judd; design by Richard Dickinson
⊖ Bank
Despite the acknowledged importance of considered new façades for repairing gaps in the street wall, there have been few good examples since earlier in the century. Here is a well-composed and substantial façade in Portland stone on a granite base which sits well between its older neighbours. This is achieved without imitation or pastiche and, to quote Lutyens's phrase, the architect knows in this instance 'how to get up a building without repeating himself'. See the corner offices of 1989 at 62–64 Cornhill, also by Rolfe Judd.

Offices 1985 **L132** b
Queen Street EC4
Terry Farrell and Co
⊖ Mansion House
A speculative office block in the form of a small palazzo makes good decorated street architecture. The height of seven storeys is successfully disguised with setbacks, and exuberance is confined to the attic, where the keystones and curved shapes first popularized by Michael Graves are celebrated. See also Farrell's **offices** L134.

Horselydown Square 1986–91 **L133** l
Gainsford Street, Copper Row, Horselydown Lane, Shad Thames SE1
Wickham and Associates
⊖ London Bridge, Tower Hill
This mixed development of 76 flats with offices and shops on the ground floor forms a pedestrian close diagonally opposite the drama of Tower Bridge. Stylistically the development is a joker in the pack of the well-mannered rehabilitation of Butler's Wharf to the north. The project challenges comfortable ideas of housing typology. The five- and seven-storey façades are both complex and picturesque recalling the European new town in general and the Dutch contribution in particular.

Offices 1987 **L134** d
69 Leadenhall Street,
95–7 Fenchurch Street EC3
Terry Farrell and Co
⊖ Aldgate

The most comprehensive homage in London to Michael Graves's style of the 1970s, these offices successfully fill out their triangular site on the prominent corner of Leadenhall and Fenchurch Streets. The cladding, a mixture of granite, stainless steel and painted aluminium, is well and expensively detailed, and its variations are designed to emphasize the traditional horizontal division of base, middle and top.

The Circle 1987–9 **L135** l
Queen Elizabeth Street SE1
CZWG Architects (Campbell, Zogolovitch, Wilkinson and Gough) with executive architects RKD (Robinson Keefe and Devane)
⊖ London Bridge, Tower Hill

This project provides 302 flats, eight office suites, twelve shops, one restaurant and a swimming pool/health club. In plan it maintains a conventional relationship to the street, with a circular forecourt to serve the entrance halls to the flats. In its vertical surface, however, the scheme is less conventional. The circular forecourt is finished in deep-blue glazed bricks, and with its owl-like profile to the parapet, its diagonal window mullions and its stepped balconies, the project takes on a curiously menacing quality. By contrast the street elevations are built in London stock bricks, with an undulating parapet and louvred balustrades to the balconies which appear to be supported by brackets of pine logs.

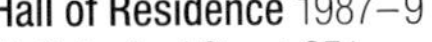

Hall of Residence 1987–9 **L136** l
11 Gainsford Street SE1
Conran Roche
⊖ London Bridge, Tower Hill

Part of the redevelopment of the former industrial area between Shad Thames and Tooley Street, these study bedrooms are for students at the London School of Economics. They are arranged as four 'houses' marked by front doors and central balconies, and are notable for their simple street architecture in brick, and good finishes.

Shop and offices 1987–91 **L137** l
24 Shad Thames SE1
Michael Hopkins and Partners
with David Mellor Design
⊖ London Bridge, Tower Hill

A small building with frontages both to Shad Thames and to the dock beyond provided a headquarters for the designer David Mellor. Although as utilitarian as the warehouses it replaced, the building fits beautifully into the site and the street. Its detailing is robust, and parts of it, including the lead panelling to the flanks and the shuttering to the carefully made concrete frame, were made by the client. The Chicago-esque office building immediately to the south, **Saffron Wharf**, finished in 1990, was designed by Conran Roche.

Design Museum 1989 **L138** l
Butler's Wharf Shad Thames SE1
Conran Roche
⊖ London Bridge, Tower Hill

First impressions of a new '1930s' building are misleading, as the Design Museum is the result of an extensive renovation and transformation of an undistinguished warehouse. As a result the building is architecturally inconsequential, and regrettably its 'cool' stuccoed surfaces cracked as quickly as those of the 1930s buildings that inspired it. The Museum is more important, however, for what it represents, for two reasons: firstly it provided much-needed public focus for part of the emerging 'Docklands' community; and secondly, as a museum of twentieth-century design it filled a conspicuous gap in the otherwise broad range of London's museums. Inside there is an atmosphere of quiet decorum. The galleries on the top two floors work well, and their calm manner is further enhanced by the exhibition display system by Stanton Williams. The Blueprint Café provides well designed-food and makes good use of the building's extensive balconies overlooking the Thames.

Directly to the south of the Museum is the **Clove building**, refurbished by Allies and Morrison in 1987, containing flats, offices and shops. This was another transformation of an existing warehouse using the language of 1930s modernism. However, in this case the black window frames and 'heroic' projecting balconies contrast more convincingly with the white stucco.

Lloyd's Register 1993–2000 **L139** d
71 Fenchurch Street EC3
Rogers Stirk Harbour and Partners
⊖ Tower Hill

Lloyd's Register of Shipping owes its name to the same coffee house as **Lloyd's of London** L129 but is a different organization, originating in the first register of merchant shipping of 1764. Skilfully shoehorned into a constricted site, two linked fourteen-floor slabs of office are fronted by a third that overlooks a new irregular public space in front of Fenchurch Street Station. The whole is carried out in the Rogers practice's late, mature style: the different functions are clearly displayed in different structures, the whole exhibiting a hierarchy of arcticulated parts quite different from the undifferentiated scale-less expanses of catalogue glazing elements with which its contemporaries were clad.

No 1 Poultry 1994–8 **L140** b
Poultry and Queen Victoria Street EC2
James Stirling and Michael Wilford
⊖ Bank

This was the outcome of the developer Peter Palumbo's attempts over twenty five years, and two public enquiries to redevelop this site, including one plan by Mies van der Rohe for a rectangular tower presiding over a new piazza. But like Belcher's earlier building here, Stirling and Wilford's building extends to the edges of the triangular site and presents an equally striking 'prow' to the important road junction facing the Bank of England. Its plan, though, is far from solid, and contains a deep open courtyard, now hexagonal, now circular, which provides a short-cut for pedestrians and another entrance to Bank Underground station. Coq d'Argent, the restaurant on the roof, looks out over a surreal garden. The exterior of the building and the publicly accessible parts of the interior are modelled and decorated in a profusion of the obsessive forms and motifs pungently characteristic of Stirling's late and posthumous work. At this important intersection Stirling took his place in a small pantheon of English architects: Lutyens (L111), Soane (L107) Hawksmoor (L52), Dance (L56) and Wren (L26).

Globe Theatre 1995 **L141** f
Pentagram Design
⊖ London Bridge

The recreation of the 1599 theatre where Shakespeare's plays were performed further consolidated the cultural promenade from the South Bank to Tower Bridge. Here the real oak timbers, stucco and thatched roof are straightforwardly used and avoid the trap of sentimentality. As in Elizabethan times, some members of the audience can stand stoically in the open-air pit for performances.

Offices ex **Swiss Re** 1997–2004 **L142** c
30 St Mary Axe EC3
Foster and Partners
⊖ Bank, Aldgate

In 1992 a bomb exploded in St Mary Axe and ruined the Baltic Exchange, a Grade II listed building that had housed the last Edwardian trading floor in London. The global reinsurance business Swiss Re bought the site, and retained Fosters to design their new London headquarters to replace their dispersed locations in the City by a single building at the centre of the world's insurance business.

City planners required the building be lower than the nearby **Tower 42** L130 (formerly the NatWest building), and its c50,000 square meters (c. 500,000 sq ft) of office space are provided in forty floors of circular plan. In the battle of the styles for making office buildings more distinct from one another, Swiss Re introduced a soft curvilinear profile and was immediately distinguishable (not unlike the dome of St Paul's Cathedral) from the rectangular universe of its neighbours.

The floor plates span between the central core and the triangulated structure at the perimeter and each floor is cut by six voids (which play a part in the sophisticated natural ventilation scheme). These spiral round the perimeter and their dark glazing provides scale to the exterior and gives the elevation its woven appearance, reminiscent of Argyle socks.

It was claimed that the circular plan and very idiosyncratic bulging profile would reduce the speed of wind around the building and reduce its effects at ground level, but it is at ground level that the building is most disappointing: a cramped entrance hall looks out over a series of left-over spaces fenced from the surrounding pavements by 'security' coffers of granite-covered concrete. If the building has no foreground this is compensated above by a dramatic room at the top. From this great domed room (no longer the preserve of plant rooms), masters of the world's financial capital can view the river progressing gently eastwards to the sea and to the west the arrival and departure of flights at Heathrow. The entire territory of London appears to be at their feet.

The building was awarded the 2004 RIBA Stirling Prize, and rapidly nicknamed the 'Gherkin' by London's cabbies, entering the short list of prominent buildings including 'Big Ben' that are identified with London.

Millennium Footbridge 2002 **L143** e
Foster and Partners, Arup, Anthony Caro
⊖ St Paul's, London Bridge

London's most recent, and its sole pedestrian-only, bridge (350m/1150ft long) forms a direct connection between the two tourist hotspots of St Paul's Cathedral and Tate Modern. It was closed soon after its opening as a result of the lack of stability of its innovative suspension structure, in which the primary supporting cables are located mainly *below* the pedestrian deck. What had been hailed as a special collaboration between architect, artist and engineer was then entitled 'the wobbly bridge' and responsibility for it focused exclusively on the engineer. Despite this inauspicious beginning and its structural revisions, this is a handsome addition to the Thames.

Fashion and Textile Museum L144 k
2001
83 Bermondsey Street SE1
Legorreta+Legorreta;
executive architect Alan Camp Architects
⊖ London Bridge
This rare example of a new private museum was the initiative of the fashion designer Zandra Rhodes. Like **Sir John Soane's Museum** K67 it houses both the sponsor's studio and workrooms and exhibitions space. It occupies a converted former warehouse extended upwards to include flats for sale on the top floors. The first European work of their Mexican architect, both exterior and interior rely largely for their architectural effects on extensive areas of brightly coloured (but not very smooth) rendering which reflect the sponsor's taste. These saturated colours, appropriate to tropical climates, seem less shocking than they should in the usually softer light of Bermondsey.

Merrill Lynch 2001–4 L145 a
2 King Edward St EC1
Swanke Hayden Connell Architects
Designed by David Walker
⊖ St Pauls
The architecture of Ivy League values is represented in this almost invisible but very large office building of 80,000 square metres (860,000 square feet). Whereas many London commercial practices have looked to the north American office building as a model, there is evidence that some American architects have been looking in the other direction – John Soane's Bank of England as a source of inspiration as opposed to New York's Chase Manhattan Bank. Here at Merrill Lynch architecture successfully integrates very large floor plates (now a convention of the contemporary city office building) into the city's fabric. This is achieved by breaking the volume into mangeable pieces and also incorporating existing buildings. Wren's bombed-out Christ Church is reclaimed as an urban garden. The manner of the project is conservative, stable, well proportioned and an admirable exemplar for London.

City Hall 2002 L146 l
London Bridge SE1
Foster & Partners
⊖ London Bridge
The headquarters for London's mayor is superficially reminiscent of Foster's Reichstag Building in Berlin. However, it has an uneasy relationship to an overscaled pedestrian plaza, and not unlike a game of French boules, the large glazed cylindrical blob gives the impression of having just come temporarily to rest. Much has been made of the building's glazed 'transparency' as an appropriate metaphor for the new authority. This is clearly expressed by the position of the assembly chamber at the centre of the building and defined by a glazed ramp from which the electors can see their representatives at work. For security reasons this literal idea of democracy has been closed to the public.

85 Southwark Street

The 'Blue Fin Building'

Offices 2003 **L147** i
85 Southwark Street, SE1
Allies and Morrison
⊖ London Bridge, Southwark

Built as the architect's own office, the fully glazed ground floor skilfully integrates a café, a public right of way and a changing exhibition of the practice's work. On the three studio floors above, there is a deliberate and successful contrast between the refined glazed street façade and the exposed concrete of the walls, columns and ceilings in the building's interior. The street façade is topped by a blank storey-height panel behind which is a communal south-facing terrace. This reverses the predictable section forming a particularly successful street elevation.

Across Southwark Street, however, the same architects designed a single very large, very dense development of three differently styled buildings and two new (but private) streets replaced the previous two functionally and architecturally inadequate office buildings from the 1950s. It is to the developer's credit that the newer development with an area of 111,500 square metres (1.2 million square feet) is not mono-functional like the older, but provides shops and restaurants on the ground floors. The developer's desire to 'bring a much-needed heart to Southwark' is redundant: Southwark already has several 'hearts', including, for example, the nearby conjunction of **Southwark Cathedral** L5 and the very popular Borough Market. What is provided on the north side of the street is more like a liver – the largest organ in the body.

Temple Bar relocated and restored

Paternoster Square

Paternoster Square 2004 **L148** a
EC4
Whitfield & Partners (masterplan),
Sidell Gibson, MacCormac Jamieson Prichard,
Allies & Morrison, Sheppard Robson,
Eric Parry Architects
⊖ St Paul's

Over two decades the area immediately north of St Paul's Cathedral, (which had been completely wiped out during the Second World War and absent-mindedly redeveloped to plans by William Holford soon after), had been the subject of intense debate about the future form and character of the city. The pendulum has swung from the modern to the traditional, from competitions in the mid-1980s involving proposals from Stirling, Foster, Isosaki and others, to those aligned to the opinion of the Prince of Wales.

A decade later, the masterplan of William Whitfield produced something between these extremes: not the tight pattern of streets as proposed by Wren soon after the Great Fire of 1666, or that immediately prior to 1940 when the city fabric was seen in contrast to the monumental setting of the cathedral. Instead we have a fictitious new 'square' (but not deriving from the tradition of the originally residential London square), sufficiently close to the cathedral to be in competition with it. Here, a number of architects have been involved to present a sense of variety. Interestingly, those who have used brick have established a clear distinction between fabric and monument (stone). Paternoster House by Whitfield & Partners has an appropriate sense of the archaic about it, reminiscent of the work of Louis Kahn. The other stone-clad office buildings, on the other hand, appear shrill, competitive with St Paul's and at odds with the imposition of a double-order arcade, required by the master plan. The historical fiction is completed by a tall enigmatic Corinthian column in the centre of the square (possibly commemorating the destruction of the Blitz?) and the displacement of the original seventeenth-century Temple Bar gate forming a threshold between the new square and Cathedral Close.

The reality is that a very large chunk of the city has been privatized, pedestrianized and policed. It is only accessible to those with an enthusiasm for 'hobbling over the cobblestones' – as the late Cedric Price might have predicted.

Unicorn Theatre 2006 **L149** I
Tooley Street SE1
Keith Williams Architects
⊖ London Bridge
This permanent home for a one-time children's touring theatre company is appropriately sited south of the river with its theatre traditions. There is a welcoming directness about the fully glazed foyer and its access to the workshop theatre on the ground floor and above to the principal auditorium. The various volumes are clearly expressed – particularly at night, when the building comes alive.

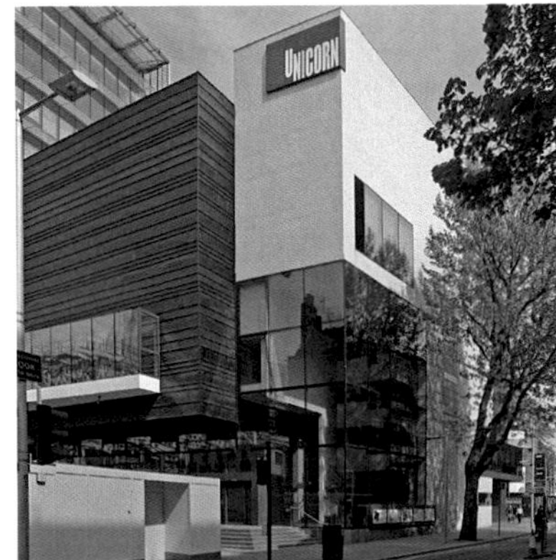

Offices, Palestra 2006 **L150** i
Blackfriars Road SE1
SMC Alsop
⊖ Southwark
With the emergence of large floor plates, a relaxation of daylight requirements, and the pressure of market forces, the contemporary office building becomes subject to the architect's will to form and can adopt virtually any shape. In the case of the Palestra building we find Alsop's artistic preoccupation with the levitating rectangle once more in evidence, a *parti* that informed a **library** U52 at Peckham, an art school in Toronto, and now a very bulky office building in Southwark. The critic Ken Powell has observed that Palestra was a 'slightly intimidating addition to the Southwark cityscape … confirming Alsop's ability to transform urban icons into works of art' – given that it was mostly let to the London Development Agency (LDA), one might reflect that 'brother you ain't seen nothing yet!'

continued section I

5

4

3

continued section T

continued section W

continued section I

continued section N

continued section W

West Kensington ■ Fulham ■ Parson's Green ■ Earl's Court ■ West Brompton ■ South Kensington (west)

Old Brompton Road, winding like a lane, runs from west to east passing through the mid-Victorian developments of South Kensington (**The Boltons** M2 in stucco, for example, and Bolton Gardens in red brick). To its north, Cromwell Road, once a genteel street of mansions, carries thunderous traffic to and from Heathrow Airport and South Wales. **Brompton Cemetery** M1, one of the series of cemeteries built outside the city in the mid-nineteenth century, now lies alongside the District Underground line. Parallel to the railway is Earl's Court Road, now colourfully devoted to the needs of the district's mainly transient population.

There are two huge exhibition halls: **Olympia** M5 to the north, built in the 1880s, and Earl's Court, 1937. Since the building of the National Exhibition Centre at Birmingham, both have tried to find new roles, Olympia as a conference centre and retail furniture warehouse, and Earl's Court as a venue for rock concerts.

To the south of the District Line lie Fulham and West Kensington, huge tracts of late-nineteenth-century two-storey housing for workers. Dull but still serviceable, these houses are preferable both to Peabody dwellings and to their municipal successors, high-rise flats.

Lots Road Power Station, opened 1905, supplied electricity for London Underground and trams until closed in 2001

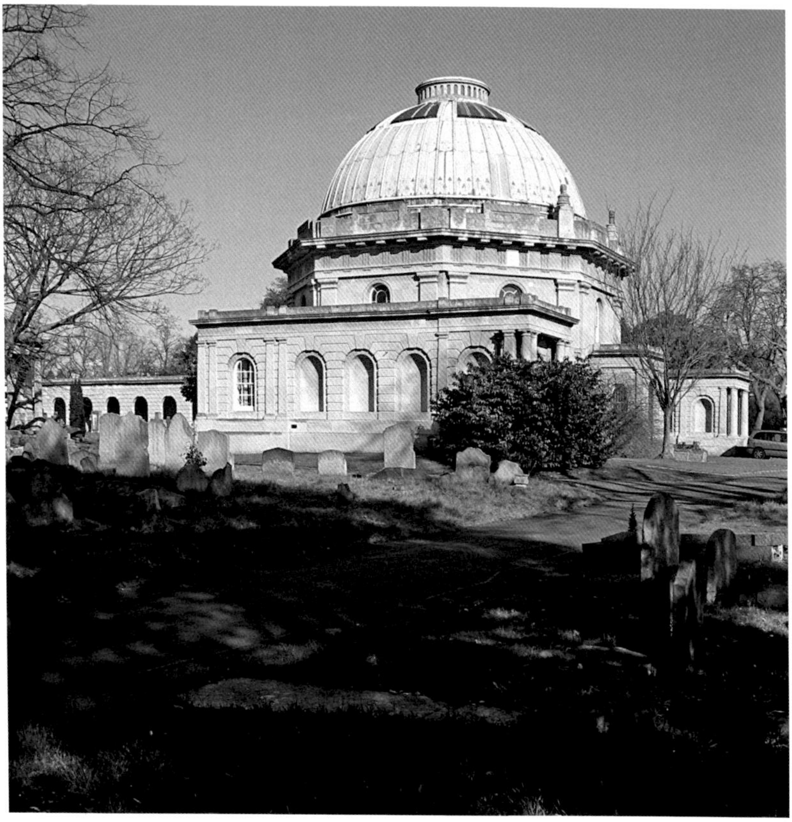

Brompton Cemetery 1840 **M1** g

Old Brompton Road and
Fulham Road SW10
⊖ West Brompton

Founded in 1831 as the West of London and Westminster Cemetery and consecrated in 1840, Brompton Cemetery is one of the earliest of the seven large cemeteries initiated by the period of Sanitary Reform in the 1820s. Unlike the more romantic **Highgate** R9, which was built on the southerly slopes of the north London ridge, Brompton Cemetery is large and rectangular, planned symmetrically on flat ground. The principal architectural feature is at the south end: the domed octagonal Anglican chapel with its extensive and impressive arcading. The mausolea are a mixture of late Gothic and Egyptian, with humorous touches such as the upturned skiff to commemorate Coombes, the champion rower, and the large lion with a portrait of John Jackson, the famous boxer.

The Catacombs

The Boltons 1850–60 **M2** h
SW10
⊖ Gloucester Road

A unique form in the westward expansion of London between the Fulham and Old Roads, the Boltons has very big semi-detached stuccoed villas arranged around a mandala-shaped garden. The Italianate details are of a coarseness characteristic of the time. The church in the middle is by George Godwin, 1850.

St Paul's Studios c1870 **M3** a
135–49 Talgarth Road W14
⊖ Barons Court
This terrace of eight ornate studio houses used to look north across their own quiet residential street to the massive ranges of Waterhouse's equally ornate St Paul's School (1881–5). Sadly, the school was demolished in 1970, the traffic has increased on Talgarth Road, now London's principal western exit, and the studios show signs of deterioration. There are two house types forming a system of pairs at entrance level: one doorway is arched and frontal, and the other is approached diagonally. Both have seats in the doorway (like Baillie Scott's work) for waiting clients or models, and on each side there is a bay window of lead lights. The double-height studio windows are magnificent, and beside them are tall narrow windows for the removal of finished canvases.

Pembroke Studios 1890 **M4** b
Pembroke Gardens W8
⊖ West Kensington
The group of thirteen studios in two rows, to the south-west of **Edwardes Square** I3, is approached through a single-arched entrance (like almshouses), and focuses on a long, rectangular garden. The glazed studios face north and the supporting rooms south, giving the façades an asymmetrical composition. Unlike the more affluent studios of fashionable portrait painters (see **Leighton House** I9) Pembroke Studios are a modest conversion of an existing mews, given continued impetus and patronage by the Great Exhibition of 1851.

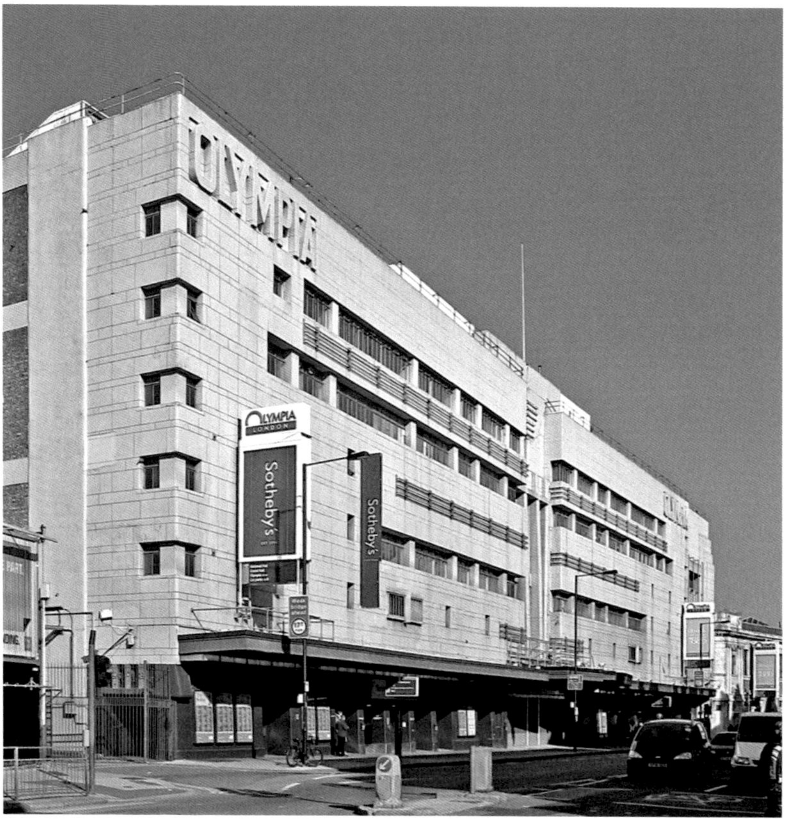

Olympia Exhibition Hall **M5** a 
façade 1930
Hammersmith Road W14
Joseph Emberton
⊖ Olympia, Earl's Court
The distinguished entrance elevation, with deep window reveals and cast lettering, forms a façade to the original exhibition hall (1884) which lies behind. Although the appearance is of white-painted concrete, the construction is of brick and steel. The four-storey garage (1937) in Maclise Road to the north is also by Emberton.

Bousfield School 1955 **M6** h
Old Brompton Road
and Boltons SW10
Chamberlin, Powell and Bon
⊖ Gloucester Road
The school and the housing estate, as types, were the architectural manifestos of post-war socialism. In housing, **Alton East Estate** V10 signified the triumph of 'people's detailing', and Bousfield is its equivalent in school buildings. There is intentionally no overall coherence of plan. The details – spindly steelwork, randomly placed coloured spandrel panels, a water-jump (instead of a fence) to the main entrance, an external amphitheatre, and viewing slots in the extensive boundary walls – confirm the 'democratic' intent. However, rather than standing in the espace et verdure of the *Ville Radieuse*, Bousfield School sits ambiguously in a large garden of the fashionable Boltons.

N
continued section J
continued section M
continued section W
British Museum
Victoria & Albert Museum
Brompton
h Kensington
a
b
e
f
i
j
m
n
19
11
29
39
38
18
15
32
34
14
6
28
5
5
1
20
23
36
41
37
4
St Luke's Church
Chelsea
Cadogan Pier
Albert Bridge (Suspension)
Battersea Bridge
RIVER THAMES
Kensington Boro Wharf
Durham Wharf
Chelsea Wharf
Cremorne Wharf
Flour Mills
Bus Depot
Albert Bridge Road
Reach
Battersea

continued section J

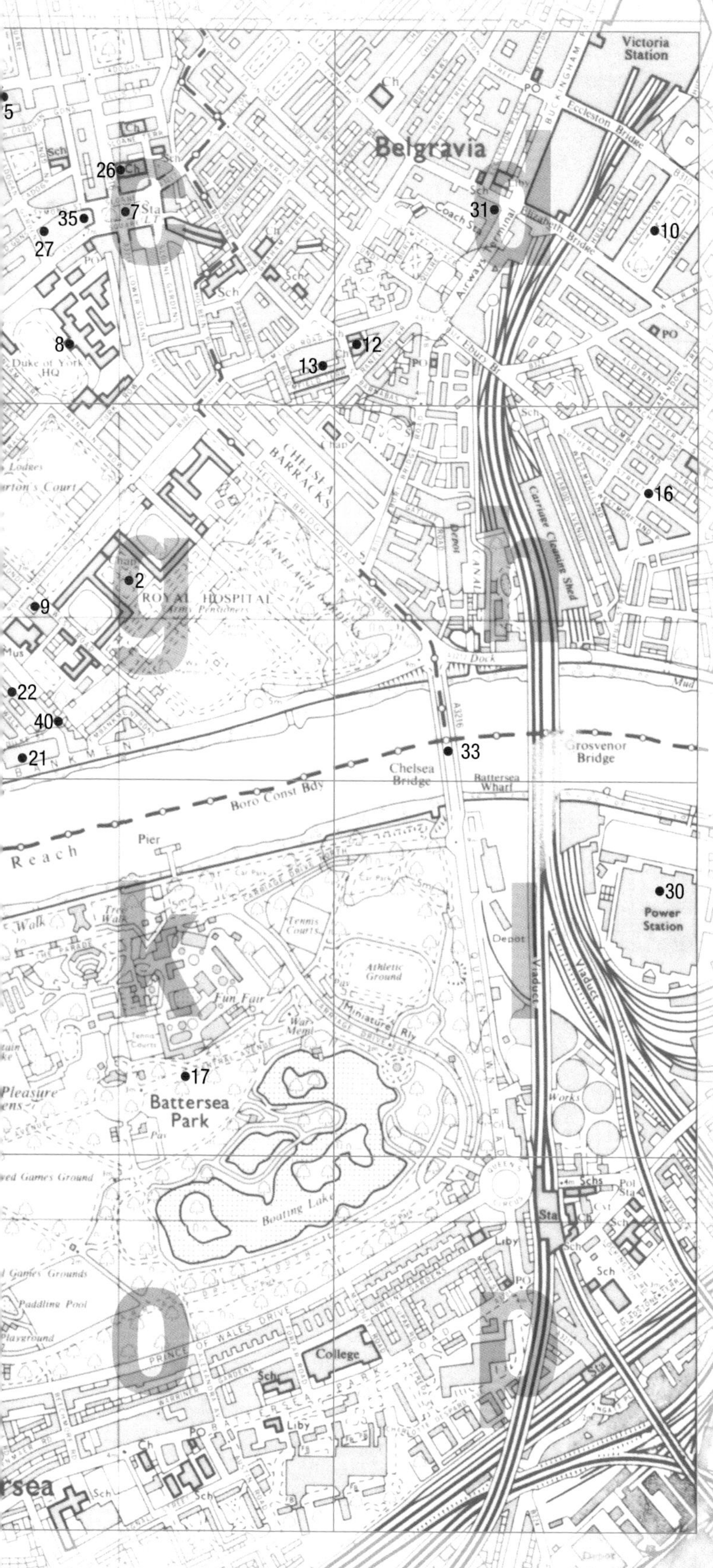

continued section O

continued section W

Battersea ■ Chelsea ■ West Pimlico ■ South Belgravia ■ South Kensington (east)

The Thames – from Chelsea Reach in the west to the contemporary Chelsea Bridge in the east – separates Chelsea in the north from Battersea in the south. It was not until the second half of the nineteenth century that the north and south were linked by permanent bridges – Albert Bridge (1873) and Battersea Bridge (1890): as a result their early development was quite separate, despite their geographical proximity.

Chelsea was a riverside fishing village until the late eighteenth century: Old Church Street and King's Road were its high streets, and it was separated from the City of London by open countryside, The **Royal Hospital** N2, founded in 1681, was the nearest building of consequence, and was itself built outside the City for the treatment and convalescence of war veterans. Wren's palatial building of 1689 was to have been part of a grand axial relationship with Kensington Palace to the north-west – connected by a royal avenue set in open countryside. **Royal Avenue** N3 was all that was ever constructed of this ambitious scheme (in 1692–4), reaching only as far as King's Road.

The eighteenth-century expansion of Chelsea took the form of piecemeal developments of brick terrace housing close to the parish church. With Henry Holland's development of Hans Place in 1777 the village became less concentric in plan, and began to be drawn into the western expansion of the City of Westminster initiated by developments in Mayfair (see section J). This took the form of spontaneous and progressive overlays. First to be built were the streets and squares either side of King's Road, at the beginning of the nineteenth century; then from the north came the encroaching stucco terraces of South Kensington (for example **Pelham Crescent** N11 and the tall red-brick houses of the Cadogan Estate, in a style loosely termed 'Pont Street Dutch' (**Cadogan Square** N25, for example); and finally, by the turn of the century, the eighteenth-century houses of Cheyne Walk, Tite Street and New Chelsea Embankment were replaced by architects of the Arts and Crafts movement, such as Norman Shaw and CR Ashbee. London's westerly expansion in this period consolidated Old Brompton Road, Fulham Road and King's Road: the three radial routes converging from the west on the City of Westminster.

To the east of the Royal Hospital, and now divided by the main-line rail link from the south to Victoria Station, is the western section of Pimlico (see also section O). Like Battersea to the south, Pimlico was an area of market gardens at the beginning of the nineteenth century; but it was rapidly developed by Thomas Cubitt as an extension of his enterprise in Belgravia (see section J). By the middle of the century it had a consistent pattern of stuccoed streets, terraces and squares, for example **Eccleston Square** and **Warwick Square** N10.

Unlike Chelsea, the medieval village of Battersea is now hardly decipherable. In Elizabethan times a marsh wall was built along the Thames, forming an embankment to the south, and the reclaimed marshland was used for market gardening. As there was no bridge across the Thames to it, Battersea enjoyed a relatively remote and agrarian existence until the advent of the railway lines in the 1830s. In 1838 the Southampton Railway opened its London depot at Nine Elms and in 1845 Battersea Station (later called Clapham Junction) was built. With the building of Grosvenor Bridge and Victoria Station in 1862, a permanent connection with central London was finally established.

Albert Bridge (1873), Battersea Bridge (1890) and Chelsea Bridge (1934) were constructed surprisingly late, as was Battersea's chief monument, **Battersea Power Station** N30, completed in 1955. Probably as a result of its remoteness from the western expansion of London in the eighteenth and nineteenth centuries, Battersea is architecturally almost unendowed. Because of the presence of Chelsea Embankment and Battersea Park, between 1985 and 2005 this stretch of the Thames was spared the worst excesses of mindless riverside developments that were inflicted on the areas east of Battersea Power Station.

Albert Bridge N20

Housing, World's End (Eric Lyons & HT Cadbury-Brown 1967–77)

Lindsey House c1674 **N1** i
95–100 Cheyne Walk SW3
⊖ Sloane Square, then bus down King's Road
A large comfortable country residence, defended by its boundary walls from the menace of the twentieth-century traffic outside, Lindsey House is the only surviving house of its date and scale in Chelsea. Originally it was a simple, three-storey house of eleven bays, with a pedimented centre and two corner pavilions. In 1775 it was divided into separate dwellings. The engineers Marc Isambard Brunel and his more famous son, Isambard Kingdom, both lived in Lindsey House, and Whistler lived in number 96 from 1866–79. The gardens to numbers 99 and 100 were remodelled to designs by Lutyens.

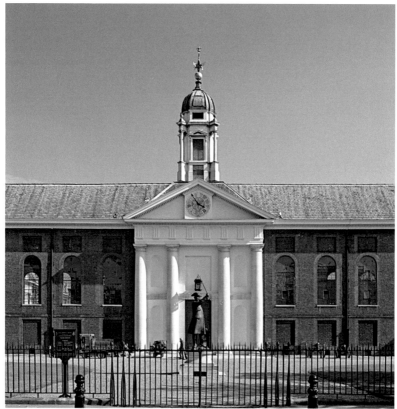

Royal Hospital 1681–91 **N2** g
Royal Hospital Road SW3
Christopher Wren, Nicholas Hawksmoor, John Vanbrugh
⊖ Sloane Square
The hospital was established to house army veterans, imitating Louis XIV's building of Les Invalides. It gave Wren one of his largest secular jobs, and while the planning is that of the traditional closed squares of Oxford colleges, the courts are open, the largest looking outwards to the river. The style, in brick, is more Dutch than French, although each façade is equipped with a triple-height Tuscan portico or centrepiece in stone. Those on the wings are freer, with broken pediments. The hall and chapel are incorporated in the main east–west wing, and share with a modern ease the same roofline as the four-storey ward wings – only the taller arched windows distinguish the special rooms inside. The hall is gaunt, the chapel very grand. In introducing an institution and inventing a style for it, Charles II and Wren provided a model for institutional and collegiate architecture which has proved workable for three centuries in all the English-speaking countries. See also Soane's **Stables** N9. The large new Infirmary on the north-east corner of the site was under construction in 2008, architect Quinlan Terry.

Note, to the west and accessed off Royal Hospital Road, the Chelsea Physic Garden of 1673, hidden behind high walls next to the river: London's oldest surviving apothecaries' garden.

Royal Avenue 1692–4 **N3** f
SW3
⊖ Sloane Square
The Royal Avenue, planted with four rows of plane trees and connecting Wren's **Royal Hospital** N2 to King's Road, is all that was built of William III's more ambitious triumphal way to connect the Hospital with **Kensington Palace** I2. Such dynastic assertion was possible on the agrarian land from Bushy Park to **Hampton Court** V1, but was to be largely frustrated in London. The contemporary Avenue, with its gravel surface lined by nineteenth-century terraces, now forms one of the series of open-ended squares along the King's Road.

Old Battersea House 1699 **N4** m
Westbridge Road SW11
⇄ Clapham Junction
A reminder that Battersea was once a village along the banks of the Thames, with a history predating the now conspicuous presence of industry. Set behind a high wall, the house has nine bays, a hipped roof and a pedimented door.

Cheyne Walk c1700–1880 **N5** i, j
SW3
⊖ Sloane Square, then bus down King's Road
From **Lindsey House** N1 in the west to the beginning of Chelsea Embankment in the east, Cheyne Walk was the focus of the quiet riverside village of eighteenth-century Chelsea. It now boasts 300 years of the finest domestic architecture, and a long list of famous artistic residents.

The most continuous surviving stretch of eighteenth-century buildings is between Oakley Street and the beginning of Royal Hospital Road. In section it rises in layers from the river to the front of the houses making an excellent model for building alongside rivers: the houses are separated from the river by a row of common gardens 6m (20ft) wide, a pavement planted with plane trees and, finally, their own walled and gated gardens. Many of the gates have fine decorated gateposts and ironwork.

From east to west, numbers 3–6 are examples of the original early Georgian style dating from about 1717, characterized by their segmental-headed windows. The painter William Dyce and the novelist George Eliot lived in number 2. Numbers 7–12 (particularly number 9) are in Shaw's style of the 1880s, and numbers 15 and 16, the Queen's House or Tudor House, are further survivors of the early Georgian period. The Queen's House is the largest in the terrace and is well preserved, apart from the nineteenth-century bay window rammed into the centre bay. The ironwork to the entrance court is excellent. Dante Gabriel Rossetti, A C Swinburne and George Meredith were among those who lived here. Numbers 19–26 form a fairly complete terrace, built in 1760 on the site of Henry VII's manor house (demolished in 1753). To the other side of Oakley Street the buildings are less distinguished, apart from C R Ashbee's remarkable group at numbers 38–9 (N28), and numbers 95–100 (**Lindsey House**) N1.

Houses started 1708 **N6** j
16–34 Cheyne Row SW3
⊖ Sloane Square and bus down King's Road
Contemporary with **Queen Anne's Gate** K31 but much altered, this terrace retains only numbers 26 and 34 in a nearly original state. Thomas Carlyle lived in number 24, now owned by the National Trust and maintained as a domestic museum in Carlyle's memory. The collections of furniture and memorabilia (not all belonging to the Carlyles) give the visitor the feel of a nineteenth-century writer's house. The garden is delightful.

Sloane Square laid out 1780 **N7** c
SW1
Henry Holland(?)
⊖ Sloane Square
This square is now surrounded by undistinguished commercial buildings, with the notable exception of the **Peter Jones Department Store** N35 of 1936. Nevertheless the ensemble is coherent, showing how resilient the format of the London square can be. At night the plane trees in the central paved space are decorated with coloured fairy lights. A proposal of 2007 to revise the traffic circulation was resisted by local residents.

Saatchi Gallery **N8** c
ex **Duke of York's Headquarters** 1801
King's Road SW3
J Saunders
⊖ Sloane Square
Originally the Royal Military Asylum for the Children of Soldiers' Widows and later used as a barracks, the long and dignified façade of these buildings, of stock brick with a central Tuscan portico of stone and Palladian curved screens at either end, is best appreciated from Cheltenham Terrace. The central block, the former drill hall, was converted in 2008 to designs by architects AHMM to accommodate the Charles Saatchi art collection.

Stables, Royal Hospital 1814 **N9** g
Royal Hospital Road SW3
John Soane
⊖ Sloane Square
Soane was surveyor to the **Royal Hospital** N2 from 1807. The stables exhibit many of the features of the originality of his work. The large yellow stock-brick wall is modulated entirely with arches, with up to four layers of recesses; there are no mouldings, except for the thin Portland stone plinth, and no decoration other than the octagonal chimneys with their 'toadstools' at the corners. Soane also designed the house (now much altered) on the other side of the hospital's axis, east along Royal Hospital Road, and a primitive garden pavilion in the grounds to the east.

Eccleston Square 1835 **N10** d
SW1
Thomas Cubitt
⊖ Victoria
Before the intervention of Victoria Station, Pimlico and Belgravia were less separate than they are today, though the stuccoed façades in Pimlico are more uniform. Nineteenth-century squares generally differed from those of the two previous centuries in accepting through-traffic as an inevitable ingredient of the plan. The large houses of Eccleston Square, now subdivided into either flats or bed and breakfast establishments, are a reminder of a more opulent past (Winston Churchill lived temporarily at no. 33). **Warwick Square** (1843) next door is also by Cubitt and is almost identical.

Pelham Place and **Pelham Crescent** c1840 **N11** a
SW3
George Basevi
⊖ South Kensington
Pelham Place and Crescent form an ingenious planning set-piece in the triangle formed by Pelham Street, Fulham Road and Onslow Square. The houses are regular, three-storeyed, with an attic and basement, and (in Pelham Place) individual, almost suburban, front gardens. The Crescent is large in plan, 149m (491ft) in diameter, with houses of the same type except for the projecting porches (note the open niche device to the balconies). Despite the generosity of the plan, the result is domestic.

St Barnabas 1847–50 **N12** d
St Barnabas Street, Pimlico
SW1
Thomas Cundy III;
schools and house by William Butterfield
⊖ Sloane Square
Although this was a pioneering Anglo-Catholic church, and is still 'High', much of the original decoration of the tall interior was removed in various refits. The grand exterior composition remains, all of Kentish ragstone. Cundy was surveyor to the Grosvenor Estate and this church is one of his best works and also one of the finest of the period. Butterfield's charming clergy house, less brutal than his usual style, has pointed windows set flush in the stone on either side of the artistic chimney.

Bloomfield Terrace c1850 **N13** c

SW1

⊖ Sloane Square

A complete street of simply decorated semi-detached houses, mostly now joined up, with a little importance added to number 39 by Oliver Hill (1930).

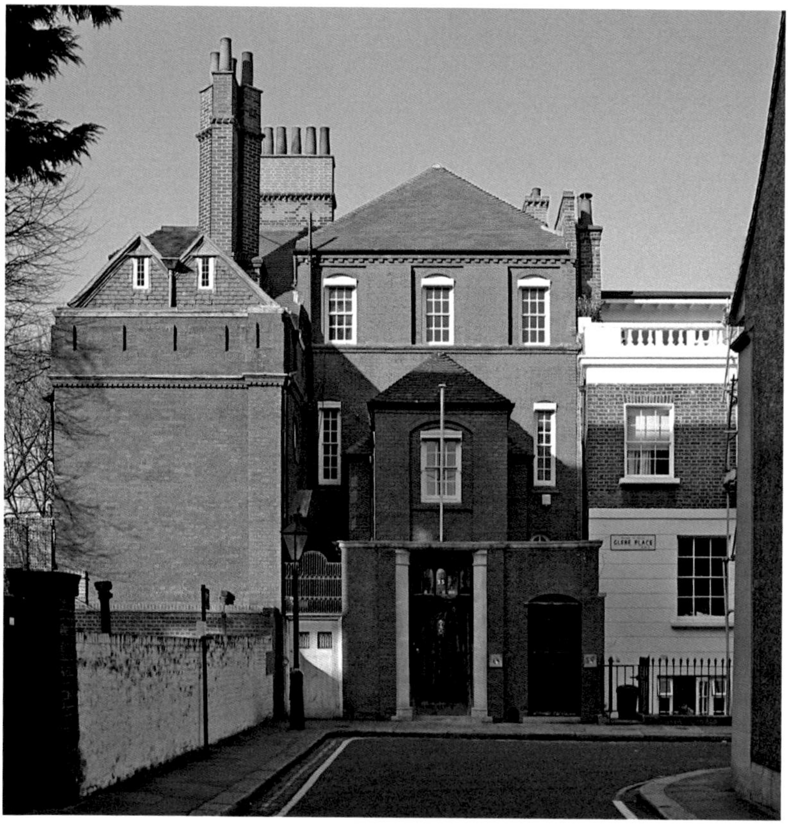

Number 35

Glebe Place c1850 **N14** f

SW3

⊖ Sloane Square, then bus down King's Road

Chelsea was an artists' colony in the nineteenth century, as is apparent in Glebe Place, whose east and south sides consist almost exclusively of nineteenth-century studios. Numbers 66–70 form a symmetrical terrace; numbers 60–1, Glebe Studios, are in red brick with two glazed, north-facing lantern studios projecting above the eaves. Numbers 53–8 make another symmetrical group of two pavilions in blank red brick with Norman Shaw chimneys. Number 48 was Charles Rennie Mackintosh's studio house during the last years of his life. The land behind numbers 43 and 44 is almost totally built over by studios – numbers 1 and 2 Hans Studios were reputedly used by the suffragette movement for their meetings. Many of the studios are still used by artists. Number 35 (1869), by Philip Webb, is an early experiment in the Queen Anne domestic style, using red brick instead of the Georgians' yellow or the Gothicists' stone or terracotta, and wooden windows.

Numbers 66–70

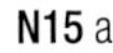

Sidney Close c1850 **N15** a
off Fulham Road SW3
built by Smith Charities
⊖ South Kensington

These fifteen magnificent studios between Onslow Square and Fulham Road were built on the original mews by Henry Smith, a local landowner, for artists involved in the Great Exhibition of 1851. There are two entrances from Fulham Road: the one to the west (under number 74 Fulham Road) is formal, for visitors and models; to the east is the working entrance, giving direct access to all studios from Sidney Mews. The studios are planned linearly either side of a generous and top-lit vaulted corridor 3m x 61m (10ft x 200ft) entered from Sidney Close. The cross-section is asymmetrical, with two storeys to the north and three to the south, so that all the studios receive north light. Sargent and Sandra Blow were residents, and it is said that Baroness Orczy wrote *The Scarlet Pimpernel* in number 10.

West Pimlico c1850 **N16** h
Cambridge Street,
Sutherland Street, Alderney Street,
Westmorland Street, Winchester Street,
Cumberland Street and Gloucester
Street SW1
⊖ Pimlico

A triangular area of late nineteenth-century housing in west Pimlico bounded by St George's Drive to the east, Lupus Street to the south, and Clarendon Street to the west. It is remarkable for its regular and uncharacteristically small urban blocks, generous streets and decent building: a salutary contrast to the more recent **Churchill Gardens** O13.

Battersea Park 1853–8 **N17**
Albert Bridge Road SW11 and
Queenstown Road SW8
Sir James Pennethorne and John Gibson
⇄ Battersea Park, Queenstown Road, Battersea

Following the lead of Victoria Park, Hackney (also by Pennethorne), Battersea Park is London's second significant Victorian park. Its long and protracted conception was frustrated by grudging government support, and the park is more exceptional for its Victorian engineering than for its landscape design. The level had to be raised above the low-lying marshlands of Battersea and a new embankment built: this was achieved with the spoil from the recently excavated London Docks (transported up the river by barge) and additional earth from Thomas Cubitt's development of the surrounding roads (Albert Bridge Road and Prince of Wales Drive).

The serpentine lake and paths (8.5km/5 miles in extent) and the central avenue (12×800m/40ft × half a mile) were by now standard park ingredients. John Gibson (the gardener of Victoria Park) was responsible for the detailed distribution of the 40,000 trees and 45,000 shrubs within the framework of Pennethorne's plan. Battersea Park was a serious contender for the site of the Great Exhibition (1851) and also for Sir Edward Watkin's abortive counterpart to the Eiffel Tower eventually started at Wembley in the 1890s. A century later it became the Festival of Britain pleasure gardens (1951). Today it remains a strange and uncertain mixture of Victorian pleasure ground and Festival of Britain whimsy, with sculpture by Henry Moore, but its frontage to the Thames remains its principal and unique asset.

The grand Edwardian red-brick mansion blocks forming the park's southern boundary are to be noted.

Onslow Square 1860 **N18** a
SW7
⊖ South Kensington
From London's last great square-building phase, Onslow Square is representative of the area between Old Brompton and Fulham Roads, to the west of Basevi's earlier **Pelham Place** and **Crescent** N11. The square is fine, but the houses are enormous and grossly Italianate, and were probably always too large for the single-family occupation intended by their builders. The numerous Lutyens family (Edwin, his parents, and twelve siblings) lived in number 16 and managed to fill it.

St Augustine 1870–7 **N19** a
Queen's Gate SW7
William Butterfield
⊖ South Kensington
In the twenty years between his **All Saints, Margaret Street** K93 and this church, Butterfield lost none of his obsession with colour: every part of the simple interior of St Augustine's is brightly patterned and decorated. The restoration of 1970 removed the whitewash applied in 1928, when the reredos covering the west window was erected. With its multicoloured and diaper-patterned brickwork, the façade is in violent contrast to the Italianate stucco of the rest of Queen's Gate.

Albert Bridge 1873 **N20** j
SW3 and SW11
R M Ordish
⊖ Sloane Square
Albert Bridge connects Chelsea and Battersea and was the first river crossing to incorporate suspended central and side spans – other single-span suspension bridges had been built earlier, for example Brunel's Hungerford Bridge, now demolished. It is a straightforward engineering design with just enough architectural decoration on the piers and spandrels to be delightful: it is spoilt only by its undignified later central support. At night there is a marvellous view of the illuminated bridge from Oakley Street.

Swan House 1876 **N21** g 
17 Chelsea Embankment SW3
R Norman Shaw
⊖ Sloane Square

The finest Queen Anne Revival domestic building in London, Shaw's Swan House has three first-floor caged and fully glazed oriel windows. Above these the second floor projects with three high narrow oriel windows, alternating with flat, narrow Queen Anne windows. The effect is remarkably original, light and graceful.

Houses 1878–9 **N22** g
44 and 46 Tite Street SW3
Edward Godwin
⊖ Sloane Square

As the rue Malet Stevens in Paris commemorates the studio apartment production of Michel Malet Stevens in the 1930s, so Tite Street might have been called Godwin Street by the end of the 1880s. In the event the street was (ironically) named after the odious Sir Wiliam Tite, architect and chairman of the Metropolitan Board of Works – responsible for censoring Godwin's many designs for the street.

Numbers 4, 5 and 6 Chelsea Embankment (1876–8), on the corner of Tite Street, and numbers 44 and 46 Tite Street, are what remain of Godwin's many houses for its emerging avant-garde artistic community. They probably survived as a result of their relatively conventional Queen Anne style. Number 46, known as the Tower House, is distinguished by its multi-storey studio windows. Number 44 was designed for Frank Miles, one of the prominent Aesthetic Movement artists. The design was initially rejected by the Metropolitan Board of Works for being too radical, and its scraped and abstracted forms in white brickwork were revised to give the high gabled elevation of the present building. Godwin was one of the most original architects of his generation, responsible for encouraging the emergence of a new, 'modern' English architecture, free of historical styles.

Battersea Bridge 1886–90 **N23** i
SW3 and SW11
Joseph Bazalgette
⊖ Sloane Square and bus

This bridge replaced the former toll-bridge demolished by the Metropolitan Board of Works and replaced by the current one designed by the Board's engineer Joseph Bazalgette in workmanlike style: five wrought-iron and steel arches are supported on granite piers and cutwaters. The facing arches are connected to their inner neighbours of smaller radius by scalloped, suavely profiled facias.

Houses 1886 **N24** c
63–73 Cadogan Square SW1
J J Stevenson
⊖ Knightsbridge, Sloane Square
Stevenson, the leading light of the Queen Anne Revival, was here trying the impossible: to design a terrace of houses while drawing attention to their individuality. As a result the façades are a mess of motifs.

Houses 1887 **N25** c
60a, 62, 68 and 72 Cadogan Square SW1
R Norman Shaw
⊖ Knightsbridge, Sloane Square
These four houses in 'Pont Street Dutch' style show Shaw working happily in the mode which he and Webb had helped to make fashionable: red brick, gables, white-painted sashes, and occasional leaded lights. The façades are always carefully asymmetrical and 'artistic' compared with the more routine development of the rest of the square. See also Street's **4 Cadogan Square** J52.

Holy Trinity 1888–90 **N26** c
Sloane Street SW1
J D Sedding
⊖ Sloane Square
London's Arts and Crafts church *par excellence*. It was bombed in the Second World War and the vault over the nave destroyed, but it remains a treasure-house of decoration in a mixture of Italian and Gothic styles. The stained glass of the east windows was made by Morris and Company to designs by Burne-Jones; the altar rails, the grille behind the altar in the north aisle and the railings to Sloane Street are by Henry Wilson; and the woodwork of the chancel is by Harry Bates. Other work is by Nelson Dawson, F W Pomeroy and Bainbridge Reynolds.

Studio house 1893–4 **N27** c
25 Cadogan Gardens SW1
A H Mackmurdo
⊖ Sloane Square
This corner studio house, in the Anglo-Dutch tradition established by Norman Shaw, was designed for the artist Mortimer Mempes. Its principal interest lies in the windows, which are used to indicate the relative importance of the two façades. The three richly decorated double-height oriel windows on the principal façade are replaced on the side elevation by flat, recessed windows of identical dimensions.

Houses 1904 **N28** j
38–9 Cheyne Walk SW3
C R Ashbee
⊖ Sloane Square, then bus down King's Road
Charles Robert Ashbee was one of the more important architects working around 1900. Apart from his active involvement in the Arts and Crafts movement, he was also influential in the creation of the *Survey of London*. Of the eight houses he designed for Cheyne Walk only two remain. Of the two, 39 was only a speculative development, but 38 was built as a studio house for the artist C L Christran. The studio occupies the top two floors behind the gabled façade with a porthole window, the gable adjusting to buildings of different height on either side. The tall windows to the lower floors, and the street railings of black ironwork with ornamental gold balls (no doubt made at Ashbee's Guild of Handicraft), help to make this a particularly fine example of Arts and Crafts work.

Michelin building 1905–11 **N29** b
91 Fulham Road SW3
F Espinasse; rebuilding and restoration by Conran Roche, YRM 1984–8
⊖ South Kensington
An exuberant and delightful freak of a building, faced in white faïence, decorated with tyres and celebrating the pleasures and early history of motoring in a series of panels on the ground floor. Nothing in the brief flowering of 'post-modernism' could match it for style, verve and craftsmanship.

The building was completely overhauled in 1984–8 when the illuminated corner turrets in the forms of stacks of tyres were restored, two more set-back office floors were added, and part of the less distinguished side to Sloane Avenue was replaced with the sleek glass skin of the Conran Shop.

Battersea Power Station 1929–55 **N30** l
Queenstown Road and
Battersea Park Road SW8
Halliday and Agate with Giles Gilbert Scott;
S L Pearce, engineer
⇌ Battersea Park

Battersea Power Station was a symbol of 1930s industrial power and progress. It occupies a 6 hectare (15 acre) site and was built in two stages.

The first stage began in 1929 to the designs of the engineer S L Pearce and quickly ran into controversy. It was completed in 1935 by the London Power Company. The second stage was commissioned in 1944, completed in 1955. The architectural background is complex and Scott, as consultant architect to the exterior, was called in to improve on the 'pedestrian brick elevations'. Scott made his final design in 1931 and even then the result was a compromise: he had preferred square-section chimneys to the final fluted columns. Until its closure in 1983, the station provided heating for the **Churchill Gardens Housing Estate** O13 on the north bank. There have since been various unsuccessful initiatives for its reuse. At the time of writing, the building is semi-derelict and no firm plans for its future are in place.

Victoria Coach Station 1931–2 **N31** d
Buckingham Palace Road SW1
Wallis Gilbert and Partners
⊖ Victoria

London's only *moderne* transport terminal. The new style suited the up-to-date function, but the arrangement follows the nineteenth-century pattern: 'architecture', including the cheerfully decorated traditional tower at the corner, encloses and provides a façade to the 'engineering' of the coach shed.

Just opposite is another transport building, the former **Imperial Airways Terminal** of 1939 by A Lakeman, undergoing restoration in 2008. It represented flying in its symmetrical outstretched wings echoed in those of the splendid sculpture by E R Broadbent over the entrance.

Houses 1934 **N32** e
40 and 41 Chelsea Square SW3
Oliver Hill
⊖ South Kensington
Hill was capable of doing quite serious modern architecture (for example the post-war **Newbury Park bus station** S3), but these houses, white stucco in a square of neo-Georgian brick terraces, are in a fey and imaginary neo-Georgian style. The surrounding houses by Darcy Braddell are well mannered, with only the occasional green pantiles to betray their actual date (1930).

Chelsea Bridge 1934 **N33** h
SW1 and SW8
G Topham Forrest and E P Wheeler
⇌ Battersea Park
This fine suspension bridge replaced the original of 1858 and, like **Albert Bridge** N20, its night-time illumination is spectacular.

Houses 1936 **N34** e
64 Old Church Street SW3
Mendelsohn and Chermayeff
66 Old Church Street SW3
Walter Gropius and Maxwell Fry
⊖ Sloane Square
Gropius and Mendelsohn were émigrés from Germany, and this pair of houses, together with the contemporary **Highpoint 1** R27, seemed to bring authentic continental modernism to London for the first time. They are not, however, among their architects' better work – Fry and Gropius's Impington Village College, Cambridgeshire, is much more assured. Originally stuccoed, they were refaced by Crosby Fletcher Forbes in 1968, with a conservatory later added by Foster and Partners.

64 Old Church Street

Peter Jones Department Store **N35** c
1936–8
Sloane Square SW1
W Crabtree with Slater, Moberly and C H Reilly as consultants
⊖ Sloane Square

One of the finest buildings of the decade and a rare example of a modern (semi-engineering) building solving the complex problem of relating both to existing street and square frontages, and to a corner. It was clearly influenced by Eric Mendelsohn's Schocken store (1927) and Columbus House (1931), Berlin. Although it was not London's first curtain wall, the façade remains one of its finest examples. Its secret lies in the glazing bars, which adjust to the gentle curve of King's Road, avoiding any sense of mechanical repetition. The continuous and apparently unsupported ground-floor display windows were elegant as well as technically innovative; the top floor is set back, like an ocean liner. The interior had a large glazed spiral staircase and triple-height spaces, maintaining the pleasurable promenade and fantasy elements of shopping. In 2004 John McAslan and Partners completed William Crabtree's original vision for the store, interrupted by the Second World War, and in the 1960s compromised by an inadequate addition. Floor levels were rationalized and a splendid seven-storey atrium created, which visually connects all floors making this an exemplar of rehabilitation.

Offices and flats 1990 **N36** j
Hester Road SW11
Foster Associates
⊖ Sloane Square ⇌ Clapham Junction

Another example of a practice building its offices (see Hopkins's Broadley Street **offices** F58, and Richard Rogers's riverside **offices** T35). Although in all these instances the obvious message might be self-promotion, they also express a private utopia. When seen from across the river this eight-storey matter-of-fact glass-clad building is conspicuously positioned between Battersea and Albert Bridges. On closer examination it conveys a nostalgia for the 'medium cool' forms of the 1960s, with occasional more distant references to Owen Williams in the window-cleaning 'cornices'. The layered sectional composition of residential penthouses above five floors of flats above two floors of studios, connected by a grand staircase to the entrance lodge and courtyard, proposes a self-contained world. See also Foster's later **Albion Riverside** N41 to the west.

Montevetro 1994–9 **N37** m
112 Battersea Church Road SW11
Richard Rogers Partnership
⊖ Fulham Broadway

This block of 100 flats is an example of the increasing density of building adjacent to the river, demonstrating the reversal of the role of the Thames as a working river to its new role as a place of public amenity. This position has been advocated by Richard Rogers since his exhibition at the Royal Academy in 1986. On the one hand the stepped section of the building has been explained to conservationists as a device to bring the building down to the scale of the neighbouring and beautiful Grade I listed St Mary's Church. On the other hand it more accurately recalls student schemes of the late 1950s and early 1960s with its preoccupation with orientation, view and otherness.

Joseph 1997 **N38** b
74 Sloane Avenue SW3
David Chipperfield Architects
⊖ South Kensington

Two ingredients make this reworking of an existing building noteworthy. Firstly, on the outside, a mesh screen of chain mail has been laid over the second-floor windows giving them an abstract appearance, thereby concentrating attention on the merchandise behind the large plate-glass windows on the floor below. Secondly, on the inside, a memorable white free-standing spiral staircase connects the two levels of retail, with the white ribbon of its balustrade acting graphically as a sign of connection between the floors.

Note opposite, at 60 Sloane Avenue, an exemplary 'new-meets-old' assemblage by YRM and Stanton Williams of 1994.

House 2001 **N39** b
Mossop Street, SW3
Michael Gold Architects
⊖ South Kensington

Designed by the architect for himself and his large family, this house tests the qualities of urban habitation under extreme site conditions. The resulting five bays over four floors have an unexpected Georgian generosity, not unlike a doll's house, with a magnificent barrel-vaulted kitchen and family room on the top floor with views over Chelsea. A lift and a mature tree planted in front furnish additional life-enhancing ingredients. At night the fifteen windows with their tiny lights glow, communicating the pleasure of habitation.

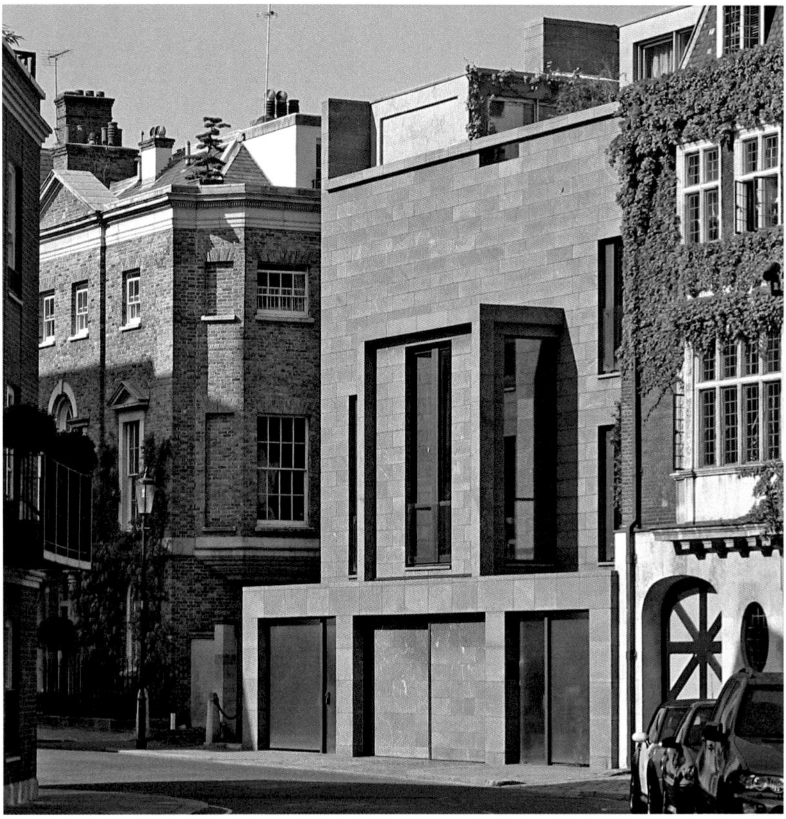

Red House 2001 **N40** g
Tite Street SW3
Tony Fretton Architects,
interiors with Studio Mark Pimlott
⊖ Sloane Square
Chelsea had early in its development become associated with an artistic milieu and in the 1870s Tite Street became the location for a number of highly wrought studio houses for artists, notably those by Edward Godwin (N22). This generously scaled house, designed for an art collector and his family, is clearly associated with that tradition, but distinguishes itself from ingratiating images of domesticity in its severe rectangularity and exotic fine materials: red limestone cladding and bronze window frames.

Albion Riverside 2003 **N41** i
Hester Road SW11
Foster and Partners
⊖ Sloane Square ⇄ Clapham Junction
The helmet-like form of this apartment building is, with the same architects' Swiss Re **offices** L142 and **City Hall** L146, a departure from the practice's earlier and rationalist language next door (N36) for its own offices. Instead of the cool rectangle there is a more sensuous geometry containing 190 flats in a curvilinear court facing the river. The building is a revival of the spirit of **Dolphin Square** O12, with its swimming pool, health club, shops, restaurant, and the collective terrace facing the river. To the south, the shared surface of the approach both to the car-parking and the affordable housing is a paradigm of site planning, from which the resident hardly needs to go anywhere. The building's relationship to the Thames path is less satisfactory.

continued section K

continued section N

continued section W

continued section K

continued section P

continued section W

Westminster (south) ■ Pimlico ■ Nine Elms ■ South Lambeth ■ Vauxhall ■ Kennington

North of the River

Until 1816, with the construction of Vauxhall Bridge and the octagonal penitentiary on the former swamp now occupied by the Tate Gallery, only the northern part of this section had been built on. There were good houses round Smith Square and slums round Vincent Square. The slums were the target for nineteenth-century reformers, religious and social (Baroness Burdett-Coutts, for example, was a benefactor to the poor and built churches such St Stephen with St John, Rochester Row). The twentieth century continued the process: the Millbank Estate by the LCC's young architects provided an alternative housing model to the Italianate barracks of the Peabody Trust; and in the 1920s Lutyens was employed to lay out the large area of slum-clearance housing on either side of **Page Street** O10. An unfortunate result of a century of improvement is the architectural incoherence of the district: even the huge **Vincent Square** O1 seems inconsequential.

To the south of Vauxhall Bridge Road lies the large residential area of Pimlico, developed from 1835 on flat marshy land which had been used for market gardens and the pleasure gardens of Ranelagh. Thomas Cubitt, the builder of Belgravia, laid it out as streets and squares on two grids, one parallel to Belgrave Road, the other parallel to the river. The grids meet at Lupus Street, giving rise to wide, splayed junctions unusual in London. The houses are in a reduced version of the Italianate stucco of Belgravia. The squares are large; and **St George's Square** O2, the last to be built, with one end open to the river, is enormous. The twentieth-century **Dolphin Square** O12 remains England's answer to the *unité d'habitation*, and **Churchill Gardens** O13, part of the post-war redevelopment of the area south of Lupus Street, demonstrates the architecture of the Welfare State.

Millbank Estate, LCC Architects Department, 1897–1902

Second Royal Horticultural Society Hall, 1923–8

South of the River

This flat area is marked by routes running south-west to north-east: first the Roman road (now Clapham Road), and most recently the London and South Western Railway, which terminated originally at Nine Elms and extended to its present terminus at Waterloo (section K) in 1848. The eighteenth century left only ribbons of fine Georgian houses, for example along Kennington Road. During the Industrial Revolution factories were set up along the Thames to serve the city north of the river: glassworks, potteries and mills. The area became the home of the desperately poor, but nevertheless did not attract the attention of the Victorian improvers, with the exception of the brave speculation of Lansdowne Gardens, the establishment of the Oval cricket ground in 1846, and the construction of Henry Roberts's exhibition houses for the poor on the edge of Kennington Park. The twentieth century's slum-clearance programme has left Lambeth and Kennington in a state of urban incoherence from which they may never recover.

In 1974 Covent Garden Market was moved to a new building at Nine Elms, encouraging the commercial redevelopment of the riverside west of Vauxhall Bridge. Because of the Victorian embankment the north bank of the Thames was saved from speculative development, but between 1995 and 2005 the south side of the river proved to be vulnerable to the worst kind. Here, from **Battersea Power Station** N30 in the west, to Vauxhall Cross in the east, a valuable opportunity to incorporate this neglected part of London into the life of the city was lost, an opportunity the Victorians in general, and Joseph Bazalgette in particular, might have seized.

Vincent Square c1780 **01** a
SW1
⊖ Pimlico, Victoria
Surrounded by a medley of buildings, this is now more of a large open space than a characteristic London square. The garden is currently used as playing fields by Westminster School and is large enough for a cricket pitch. Numbers 84, 85 and the detached 86 are all that remain of the original houses. The square accommodates the headquarters of the Royal Horticultural Society. In the north corner is the **Westminster Technical College** (1893) by Blashill, with a particularly fine extension (1937–52) by H S Goodhart-Rendel. The great width of the square gives prominence to the high-rise buildings, notably **Hide Tower**, 64m (212ft) high, by Stillman and Eastwick Field (1957–62).

St George's Square 1844 **02** e
SW1
⊖ Pimlico
A fitting end to a Belgravia and Pimlico promenade, beginning at Wilton Place, immediately south of Hyde Park: this deep, rectangular riverside square, its south side giving the bay-windowed houses long diagonal views of the river. St George's Square is appropriate for its site, and a model from which neighbouring **Churchill Gardens** O13 could have profited. The Perseverance pub at the north-east corner dates from 1840, the rest of the houses from 1850.

At the north end is **St Saviour** (1863–4) by Thomas Cundy III. This neo-Gothic church's traditional east–west alignment creates an ambiguous relationship with the orientation of the classical square. Its major features – the west front, spire and east window – face the sides of the square, ignoring its formal north–south axis.

Cottages 1851 **03** h
Kennington Park Road SE1
Henry Roberts
⊖ Oval
Now serving as the lodge for Kennington Park, these little Tudor-style flats (two dwellings on each floor) were re-erected after being shown at the 1851 Great Exhibition as examples of reformist housing. With their multi-coloured brickwork and feeble decoration they lack the robustness of Roberts's earlier work (for example the Streatham Street **flats** G34).

St James-the-Less, Parish Hall and **Infant School** 1860–1 **04** a
Vauxhall Bridge Road SW1
George Edmund Street
⊖ Pimlico

One of the best Victorian Gothic churches in London, St James-the-Less is now ignominiously embedded in the Lillington Gardens housing estate (O14). The composition of church, hall and school is elemental and formally excellent, with the detached tower marking the entrance from Vauxhall Bridge Road. All the buildings are in red brick with black-brick enrichment. The interior of the church, with three wide bays on broad circular columns, is spatially generous and richly decorated with black brick and red and yellow diagonal wall tiles. The fresco above the chancel arch is by G F Watts.

The Duveen Galleries, 1937

Tate Gallery now **Tate Britain** **05** b
1897–2000
Millbank SW1
Sidney Smith 1897; additions W H Romaine-Walker 1909; new sculpture gallery J Russell Pope 1937; extension J Llewelyn Davies, Weeks, Forestier-Walker & Bor 1971–9; John Miller and Partners 1990–2000
⊖ Pimlico

The Tate has a dual and consolidated presence in London: British art at Millbank and contemporary international art at **Bankside** L121, connected by river launch ('Tate to Tate') from a modern pier (Marks Barfield 2004).

Millbank, on which the Tate Britain now stands, was in the nineteenth century the site of Jeremy Bentham's massive model penitentiary (1812–21) which covered 7 hectares (18 acres). Its octagonal plan can still be traced in the street pattern around the present gallery.

The Tate might appear from the outside to have been conceived integrally but in fact there have been six additions. It is surprising that the impressive central cupola and sculpture galleries were contributed by the Tate's second patron, Lord Duveen, as late as 1937.

Stirling and Wilford's ambitious plans for museums of New Art and Sculpture (now moved to **Bankside** L121) were abandoned and a major reconstruction to the designs of John Miller and Partners was started in 1998 at the north-west quadrant of the Gallery. These galleries provided additional space for British art and for temporary exhibitions. John Miller and Partners also designed the Nomura Gallery and bookshop.

The gardens and the ramped approach to the new public entrance at basement level to the south are by Allies and Morrison, 2000.

ex **Belgrave Hospital for Children** **06** l
1900–3
Clapham Road SW9
H Percy Adams, designed by Charles Holden
⊖ Oval

Holden was twenty-five when he designed this, his first executed building. He had worked for C R Ashbee for a year, and the hospital combines a rational plan with simple Arts and Crafts details such as the fine panel of lettering over the front door. His taste for pyramidal massing is exhibited in both the corner towers and the high stepped and pointed gable of the entrance.

Vauxhall Bridge 1906 **07** f
SW1 and SE1
Maurice Fitzmaurice, W E Riley
⊖ Vauxhall, Pimlico

The wide five-span bridge gives good views downstream towards the Palace of Westminster and the City beyond; the south is unfortunately marred by the grotesquely oversized traffic arrangements of Vauxhall Cross. The piers are decorated with big statues of the Arts and Sciences by F W Pomeroy and Alfred Drury. *Architecture* faces upstream and carries a model of St Paul's Cathedral.

Courtenay Square 1914 **08** h
SE11
Adshead and Ramsay
⊖ Oval

Part of a slum clearance scheme on the Duchy of Cornwall Estate, Courtenay Square, together with houses in Courtenay Street and Cardigan Street and the Old Tenants' Hostel (1913–14) in Newburn Street, is a fragment of a model estate. The two-storey terraced houses follow the Regency model, built in stock bricks with timber-trellis porches. They remain a salutary and convincingly modest example of how to reconstruct a city within its own traditions, without recourse to the mindless pursuit of new types.

First Royal Horticultural Society Hall 1904

Royal Horticultural Society Hall **09** a
(1904) 1923–8
Vincent Square SW1
Easton and Robertson
⊖ Pimlico, St James's Park
This supplemented the earlier, smaller and delicately roofed hall on the corner of Vincent Square by E J Stebbs of 1904. The roof of the later, larger exhibition hall (illustrated page 370) introduced to England the reinforced concrete catenary-shaped arches already in use on the continent. The hall is lit for its full length by stepped-back patent glazing between the arches.

Housing 1928–30 **010** b
Page Street and Vincent Street
SW1
Edwin Lutyens
⊖ Pimlico
Designed for the LCC while Lutyens was continuing his brilliant work for the **Midland Bank** L111, L114, this scheme suggests that the master of classicism was, unlike other twentieth-century architects, not at a loss with public housing. Blocks of flats are arranged round courts at right angles to the street, with access galleries on the inside faces, the outsides covered in an audacious chequerboard pattern of alternating windows and brick and stucco panels. Facing the street between the blocks are shops in the form of classical pavilions.

Lambeth Bridge 1932 **011** c
SW1 and SE1
LCC Architects Department;
G Topham Forrest
and Reginald Blomfield
⊖ Westminster
The bridge has five spans, its shallow steel arches springing from massive masonry bases topped by obelisks supporting lamps, with further pairs of giant obelisks topped by pineapples at each end. It replaced the original bridge of 1862 and forms part of an ambitious composition completed by the broad granite staircase leading to the riverside gardens and the monumental Thames House (1931) on the north bank; this was one of the last urban designs for London as an imperial capital.

Flats, Dolphin Square 1937 **012** e
Grosvenor Road SW1
Gordon Jeeves
⊖ Pimlico
On this 3.1 hectare (7.6 acre) site, 1236 corridor-access flats are arranged in a ring around a central garden. In the middle there is a sports building with courts for tennis and squash, a public restaurant, refurbished in the *moderne* style of the 1930s, and an underground car park for 200 cars. The style is a dull neo-Georgian for the base and upper storeys, with a modern striped top floor. The proposed landing stage for tenants on the cleared waterfront was never built. Dolphin Square is more dense than **Churchill Gardens** 013 along Grosvenor Road, but while only twenty-five years separate their design, the two schemes make a telling urban contrast: one the space-making 'block', the other isolated slabs standing on lawns.

Churchill Gardens Estate **013** e
1946–62
Grosvenor Road, Lupus Street
and Claverton Street SW1
Poweli and Moya
⊖ Pimlico
Approached via the particularly fine nineteenth-century terraces and squares of Victoria and Pimlico, Churchill Gardens suggests a totally new form of urban life. This particularly massive and bleak housing estate is one of London's first significant post-war comprehensive redevelopments. The open competition for the design was won by its young architects, Powell and Moya, when they were still in their final year at the Architectural Association school, and the scheme has always been praised as exemplary. Pevsner, for example, wrote, 'The aesthetic significance of Churchill Gardens is that even now, after twenty-five years, it has remained one of the best estates of this type.' If the type referred to is Le Corbusier's *Ville Radieuse*, the thirty-six blocks built in four sections have always seemed too close together, conveying an image of overcrowding rather than the *espace, verdure et soleil* (space, greenery and sun) of its continental inspiration. Estates like Churchill Gardens have been justified as the result of high densities, but this is a popular myth. For example, **Dolphin Square** 012 is about three times the density of Churchill Gardens.

Lillington Gardens Estate **014** a
1961–71
Vauxhall Bridge Road SW1
Darbourne and Darke
⊖ Victoria, Pimlico
The first appearance of what was later termed loosely 'the new vernacular', Lillington Gardens Estate occupies the area between Vauxhall Bridge Road, Charlwood Street and Tachbrook Street. One of the largest comprehensive redevelopments of the decade, the planning brief required housing for 2000 people, pubs, surgeries, a community hall and a library. The development was planned in three phases, the first the subject of an open competition in 1961. This large, romantic and complex red-brick building, with 'streets in the air', cantilevered balconies, irregular profile and ample external planting, offered a popular and expressive alternative to the drab post-war tradition of mixed development.

This established for its architects a popular reputation. Phases two and three proved less exceptional and expressed a more rigorous economic housing climate.

Millbank Tower **015** b
ex **Vickers Tower** 1963
Ronald Ward and Partners
⊖ Westminster, Vauxhall
At the time of its completion – when tower building was fashionable – this thirty-two-storey tower, marking the bend of the river between Vauxhall and Lambeth and dwarfing the **Tate** O5 next door, received popular approval. With hindsight it is clear that there were certain preferred positions for towers in the city: a) as a focus at large-scale traffic intersections, notably Seifert's **Centre Point** K175 and Goldfinger's **Elephant and Castle** L124; b) at the edge of a park (after Le Corbusier's *Ville Radieuse*), as at **Roehampton** V12 and the new hotels and barracks surrounding Hyde Park; and c) at the edge of water (after Mies van der Rohe's Lakeshore Drive apartments in Chicago), as at Millbank. The preferred architecture was a shiny glass envelope; but the Millbank Tower's irregular plan form stands awkwardly on its podium, and its great mass has no positive order, either vertically or horizontally. It is not surprising that the profile of London, constructed from such disparate and arbitrary sets of references, should have begun to degenerate so rapidly during the 1960s.

Clore Gallery 1979–85 **016** b
Tate Gallery, Millbank SW1
Stirling and Wilford
⊖ Pimlico

The Clore Gallery largely realized the architect's intentions. These were firstly that the building might be read as a garden pavilion attached to a large house, an impression reinforced by the pergola, lily pond and general informality of the entrance sequence (designed with Janet Jack of BDP); and secondly that the façades might be seen as heterogeneous, thereby deferring to the various adjacent buildings. The empty entrance pediment and string courses refer to the classical parent building and the free-style composition of the corner refers to the Queen Alexandra Military Hospital.

Inside, as in other museums by Stirling and Wilford, (notably the Staatsgalerie in Stuttgart), the eventful promenade to the galleries contrasts with the conventional enfilade of the galleries themselves. The main stair leads away from the galleries in a compressed top-lit space. The visitor is then presented with a large window acting as a proscenium to the works beyond. The eight principal top-lit galleries were designed to restore some of the liveliness of natural light while meeting the requirements of conservation.

Lambeth Community Care Centre **017** d
1985
Monkton Street SE11
Edward Cullinan Architects
⊖ Kennington

The familiar paradigm of house and garden is used to draw together an ambitious social and medical programme. The building combines a day-care centre with physio- and occupational therapy, dentistry and social work as well as short-stay accommodation for twenty patients. This building reasserts the role of modern architecture as an agent in social innovation and change. The inclusive and democratic nature of Cullinan's architecture is here a key to the building's success, which stands as a rebuke to the alienating tendencies of hospitals.

MI6 1993 **018** g
Albert Embankment SE1
Terry Farrell and Co
⊖ Pimlico

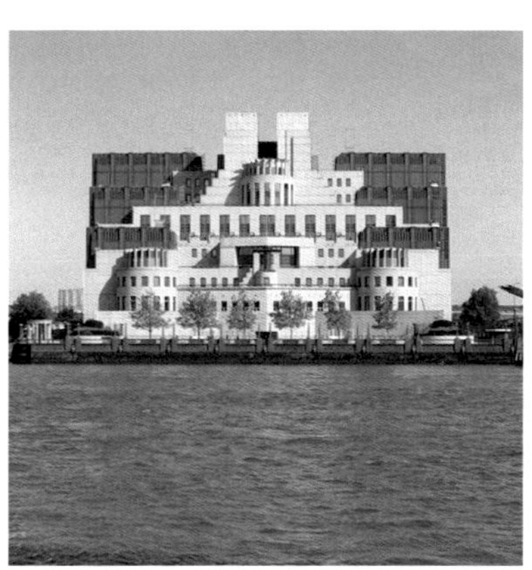

The horticulture on its terraces does not disguise the fact that this is another South Bank office building, but it does serve to advertise that this is the headquarters of MI6, Britain's counter-intelligence agency. Why hanging gardens and a certain 1930s palatial New Yorker appearance should be the 'style for the job' will remain as much of a mystery as the activities of its occupants. Originally intended to shock, when compared with subsequent developments upstream, it appears a model of quiet good taste.

continued section L
NEWINGTON
a
b
e
f
1
i
j
m
n
Kennington Park
MYATT'S FIELDS
CAMBE
continued section 0
continued section W

continued section L

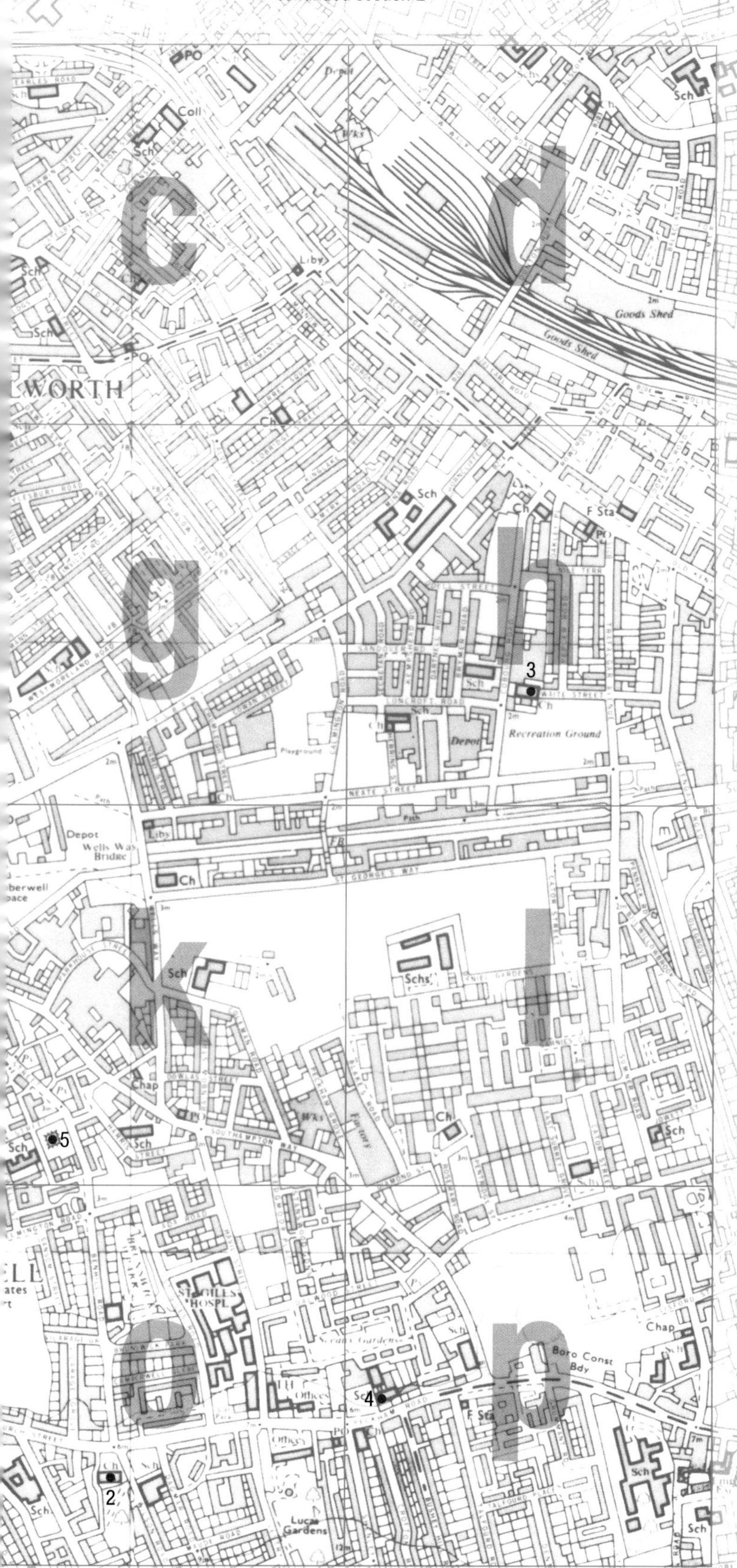

continued section U

continued section W

Camberwell ■ Kennington ■ Walworth

The earliest construction in this area is the Old Kent Road, following the line of the Roman Watling Street, which ran from Southwark and London Bridge to the north-west of England. To the south the majority of the area was open countryside until the late eighteenth century, with the village of Camberwell separated from the nearby villages of Peckham and Dulwich by fields which supplied produce to the markets of London. There is now very little evidence of these village nuclei.

The urban development of the area took place in the second half of the nineteenth century, with a framework formed by the Old Kent Road, Walworth Road, Peckham Road and Camberwell New Road. When the Surrey Canal was built to the east in 1807–9 it passed through open fields. The Camberwell New Road, laid out from 1815, connected the village of Camberwell north to Kennington and then to Westminster. As in much of nineteenth-century suburban London, ribbons of speculatively built brick terraces followed, leaving between them empty areas which were developed later.

In the twentieth century, as a result of heavy bombing in the Second World War, the LCC and subsequently the London Borough of Southwark replaced much of this nineteenth-century housing stock. The resulting urban picture is sad – at best a piecemeal catalogue of local authority housing fashions. The most unfortunate developments are to be found south of the Elephant and Castle: the Heygate Estate and the Aylesbury Estate, north of Peckham Road.

St Peter Walworth 1823–5 **P1** f
Liverpool Grove SE17
John Soane
⊖ Elephant and Castle

The best of Soane's churches in London, St Peter's is a compendium of the architect's concerns: geometry, layered and detached planes, and the invention of extensions of the classical language. The flat front has an Ionic portico recessed by exactly the depth of the columns. These support a frieze with incised Greek key decoration running the full width of the façade. The two-stage tower which rises from a plinth the width of the portico is extremely elongated in contrast to the horizontality of the front. The arched windows to the sides of the portico show the same two layers – a motif continued down the flanks of the church. At the back there is a very dense plastic composition of arched windows and brick arches. The interior, while now decorated in unappetizing colours, shows Soane's use of thin screens to define the adjoining spaces. The chancel is marked by two full-width segmental arches, echoing another that defines the organ loft at the west end, and these are joined to the galleries by round-arched moulding-free screens. See also **Marylebone Road** F22 and **Bethnal Green** U19.

St Giles 1844 **P2** o
Camberwell Church Street SE5
George Gilbert Scott; west front Arthur Blomfield
⇄ Denmark Hill
Because it was so copied – few English towns are without their St Giles – the strength of Scott's innovatory design is not evident today. It embodies the prescriptions of those campaigners for Anglican correctness, the Camden Society – considerable length (47m/ 153ft) and use of the Gothic style. Scott won the competition for the design and with the £14,500 insurance money from the fire which destroyed the old church, was able to erect this very large replacement. The style is roughly English Gothic but with continental details, all well built in Kentish ragstone.

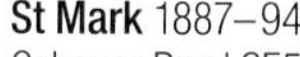

St Mark 1887–94 **P3** h
Cobourg Road SE5
R Norman Shaw
⊖ Elephant and Castle, then bus
Not a very good church, and now a mosque, but a relief perhaps from the Kentish ragstone or papery ashlar of the standard product of the period: strictly for Shaw completists.

Camberwell School of Arts and Crafts and South London Art Gallery **P4** p
1896–8
Peckham Road SE5
Maurice B Adams
⇄ Peckham Rye
Fussy 'Jacobethan' and baroque in red brick, stone and slate.

Brunswick Park Junior School **P5** k
1958–61
Bantry Street and
Picton Street SE5
Stirling and Gowan
⊖ Oval, then bus to Camberwell Green
In this small school building there are many stylistic references to Stirling and Gowan's regrettably unbuilt competition entry for Churchill College, Cambridge (1958). This is its microcosm, and despite its almost complete physical neglect, and buried in the particularly bleak housing estate, it has worn very well architecturally. The modest school hall, like Churchill College, uses a square plan divided into four smaller equal squares. Three, rotated at 90° to each other, are steeply roofed with exposed trusses; the chimney completes the fourth corner. The walls are of white brickwork with occasional red-brick banding, and the building is connected to the ground by large grassy banks extending its geometry. The decorative brick details considerably predated their fashionable use by the 'post-modernists'.

Carey Street WC2

Red telephone boxes 1926, 1935
Everywhere
Giles Gilbert Scott

In 1923 the Royal Fine Arts Commission organized a limited competition for a standard public telephone box. This was won by Scott with his design, the K2, pictured left. Scott originally proposed that its exterior be painted silver with greeny-blue on the inside, but the Post Office decided on red, to match their postboxes. The box, constructed of robust prefabricated cast-iron parts, was designed as a very small garden pavilion, its large windows subdivided by Georgian glazing bars. Scott, a trustee of Sir John Soane's Museum, might well have derived the domed roof of the box (whose form conveniently sheds rain and rubbish) from the ceiling of Soane's **Breakfast Room** K67. In 1935, and to commemorate George V's silver jubilee, Scott was commissioned to revise his design. He produced the 'K6' model, pictured right; this was smaller, with *moderne* windows and a flatter dome.

When the Post Office was privatized in 1984, the earlier models were abandoned and replaced with various less robust modern designs. British Telecom threatened to remove all the older versions, but were prevented by some London boroughs such as Westminster, who listed them, and here they remain, like red buses: cheerful, indispensable anachronisms in the London street scene.

Outer London

Sections Q–X

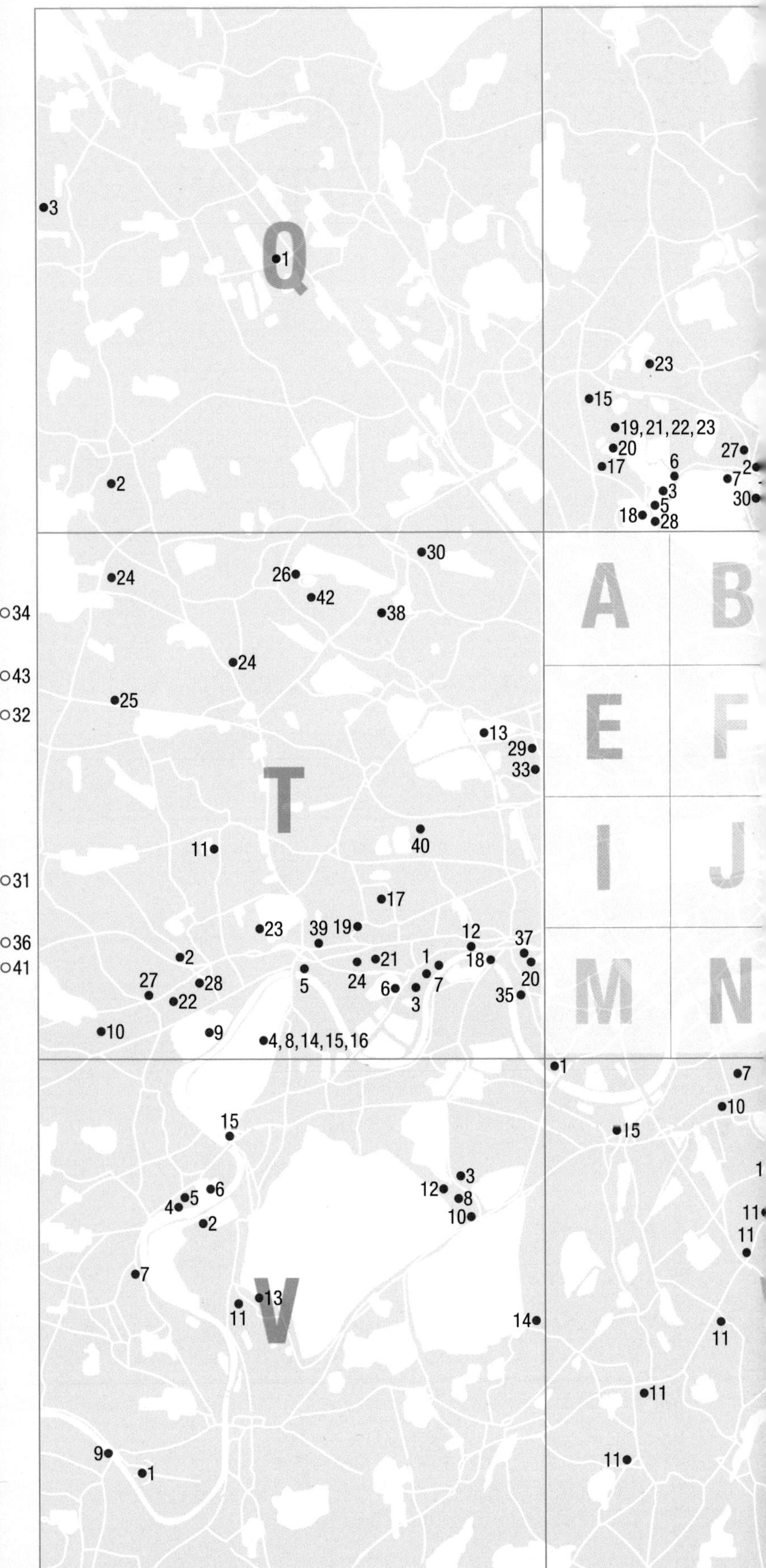

Q
T
V
A
B
E
F
I
J
M
N
3
1
2
23
15
19, 21, 22, 23
20
17
6
27
2
7
3
30
5
18
28
30
24
26
42
38
○34
24
○43
○32
25
13
29
33
40
11
○31
17
○36
○41
23
39
19
12
37
2
21
1
18
24
27
28
5
7
20
6
3
35
22
10
9
4, 8, 14, 15, 16
1
7
10
15
15
3
12
8
5
6
4
2
10
11
11
7
13
11
14
11
11
11
9
1
11

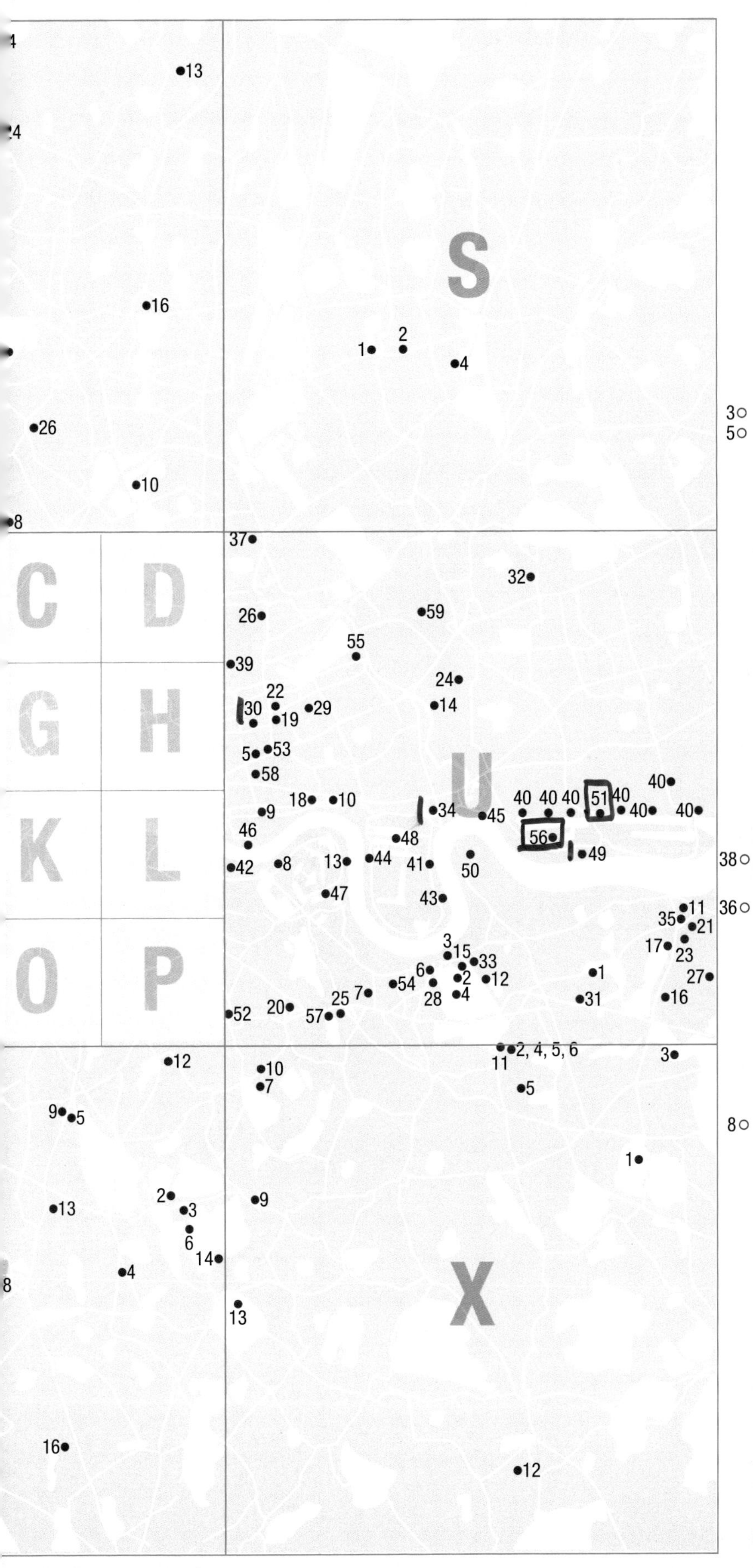
S
U
X
C
D
G
H
K
L
O
P

Outer London, north-west

This section's villages and the small town of Harrow are still discernible, though now engulfed in the suburban development between the wars, which stops at the Green Belt running in an arc from Harrow Weald in the west to Totteridge Park in the east. The land rises from the plain of the Thames, and the low hills are dominated by the spire of Harrow's parish church, St Mary. Transport routes divide up the area: the Roman Watling Street runs straight from Marble Arch to St Albans, bending at Brockley Hill and Elstree. The nineteenth-century railway builders followed its track north from St Pancras. Britain's second motorway, the M1, built in the 1950s, follows the railway before turning north-west for Birmingham.

Most of the villages had a sprinkling of Georgian additions to their High Streets (see, for example, Stanmore's Broadway) but it was the extension of the underground railway after the First World War which led to the suburbanization of the entire area. To the south, the Metropolitan Line runs through Northwick Park and Harrow to Amersham in Buckinghamshire; the Bakerloo Line follows the main line via Harrow and Wealdstone to Watford, the Jubilee Line to Stanmore; and the Northern Line connects both the West End and the City to Edgware and Mill Hill. These routes were the single cause and means of London's expansion between the wars. The name 'Metroland', lovingly revived by John Betjeman, was coined to describe the suburbs springing up around the new lines, and London Transport helped the developers sell their product with posters illustrating seductively the new life they offered. High fares for commuters may by now have dulled the promise, but the pattern of large areas of outer London – now so suitable for those with cars – was established by its public transport.

The section has few architectural gems, although **Harrow School** Q2 has character, and the huge sheds of Elstree Studios, all that remains of Britain's film industry established in the 1930s at Borehamwood, are now used mostly to make Hollywood blockbusters.

The Old School Q2

St Lawrence rebuilt 1715 Q1
Whitchurch Lane, Edgware HA8
⊖ Canons Park
The Duke of Chandos, Paymaster-General to the Duke of Marlborough, lived nearby in the now-demolished Canons, and was responsible for rebuilding and decorating the interior of this parish church. It is a unique, if failed, attempt to bring Roman baroque to London: the interior is painted all over (by Laguerre), like the attached Chandos mausoleum.

New Chapel

Vaughan Library

Harrow School c1818–1921 Q2
Harrow-on-the-Hill HA1
C R Cockerell, Charles Foster Hayward, George Gilbert Scott, William Burges, Basil Champneys, Herbert Baker and others
⊖ Harrow-on-the-Hill
The public school was a nineteenth-century invention, given impetus by the needs of Empire: although founded in 1571, most of the school's buildings date from 1845–84, the period of its greatest expansion. The school grew in a linear fashion along the High Street following the ridge of the hill, the tallest point in London at 114m (375ft). This produces an extremely agreeable integration between 'town and gown' with unexpected long views between buildings across London.

Most of the buildings were designed by Hayward but a number of eminent architects designed others. Scott's flint and stone New Chapel in his Decorated Gothic style anticipated **St Mary Abbots** I11. The Vaughan Library, also in Scott's Gothic style, is built in brick. The Speech Room (1874–7) by Burges, the most formally ambitious building at Harrow (see also his **Tower House** I15), has a Greek theatre plan and arcaded façade. In contrast, the Butler Museum (1884–6) by Champneys is in the late-Victorian Queen Anne style, with high Dutch gables, oriel windows and skilful asymmetries. The open stair running the height of the building is particularly good. A pleasant surprise is the miniature version of Michelangelo's Piazza del Campidoglio in Rome in the stepped ramp, terraces and staircases which skilfully negotiate the hilly terrain leading from the High Street to Herbert Baker's classical War Memorial building (1921) and beyond to St Mary (1042), one of London's earliest parish churches battlemented by Gilbert Scott in 1850.

Grims Dyke 1870–2 Q3
Wealdwood Road, Harrow HA7
R Norman Shaw
⊖ Harrow and Wealdstone
Near the Saxon earthwork after which it is named, this excellent example of Shaw's Domestic Revival shows two typical features of his 'Old English' style: the asymmetrical plan and the Great Hall. It was built for a painter, and was later occupied by W S Gilbert (of Gilbert and Sullivan). In the garden are the statues of English river gods from **Soho Square** K24.

Outer London, north

Highgate Village and the hamlet of North End, the earliest surviving developments in this area, were quite separate from London until the late nineteenth century. From the sixteenth century Highgate was a favourite spot for the wealthy to build their country retreats: **Kenwood** R7 is the most conspicuous example. The Grove and **Pond Square** R2 are among the best surviving seventeenth- and eighteenth-century village nuclei in London, as Waterlow Park and **Highgate Cemetery** R9 are the most characteristically Victorian examples of their type.

For the rest, the urban development is exclusively twentieth-century, consisting typically of the speculative dormitory suburbs of the inter-war years. This northerly expansion of London was given added impetus by the extension of the Northern Line Underground. At the beginning of the twentieth century Golders Green was a country crossroads with signposts to London; its rapid development began in 1906 with the arrival of the Northern Line, as did Hendon's in 1926.

Apart from isolated parks and buildings – for example Repton's Trent Park in Enfield or Charles Holden's **Arnos Grove Station** R24 at Southgate – the suburbs of north London are architecturally uninteresting. There are two key exceptions: the first is **Hampstead Garden Suburb** R19, founded in 1906 by Dame Henrietta Barnett, and laid out in 1907–15 by Raymond Unwin, with significant contributions from Edwin Lutyens and Baillie Scott. The second, in contrast, is a heroic fragment of Le Corbusier's *Ville Radieuse*: Berthold Lubetkin and Tecton's **Highpoint 1 and 2** R27 of the late 1930s.

Piccadilly Line Underground stations R24: Southgate

Lauderdale House 1580 **R1**
Highgate Hill N19
⊖ Archway
Built for John Maitland, Earl of Lauderdale, a City merchant, on the traditional exit route from London up Highgate Hill, Lauderdale House had a part in the rich social history of the Restoration – it is believed that Nell Gwynne and her baby son by Charles II were residents in 1670.

The story of its renovation is as complex as its social history. Of the sixteenth-century house only the masonry and south-east room remain; two notable eighteenth-century features are the lantern on the seventeenth-century staircase, and the entrance hall with a fine recess and Corinthian columns; the exterior is late Georgian, plastered and rather modest. In 1889 the house with its 12 hectares (29 acres) of grounds was given to the LCC by Sidney Waterlow. A fire gutted it in 1963, but it is now enjoyed by the public as a tearoom and small cultural centre. The magnificent first-floor gallery remains to be restored.

Pond Square

The Grove

Highgate 17th and 18th century **R2**
N6
⊖ Highgate
Highgate Village is on top of Highgate Hill, and its earliest houses are round the Grove to the west, and in Pond Square to the east. These loose spaces are joined by South Grove, with grander detached houses. The High Street has a pleasant collection of modest Georgian shops. In spite of the torrents of rush-hour traffic it is still possible to see **The Grove**, a marvellous group of houses, as a seventeenth-century village well outside London: they overlook a small green, and have most uncharacteristic gravelled sidewalks sheltered by trees. Numbers 1 and 2, of the late seventeenth century, have a cornice but no parapet, and the sash-window frames are flush with the outside. Number 5 has a fine Doric porch, number 6 a good iron gate, and Coleridge lived at number 3.

South Grove number 17, Old Hall, is a generous four-bay house of the 1690s. Opposite stands an extraordinary survival: numbers 25 and 26, two tiny pantiled cottages for the servants of the grander houses like Moreton House, number 14, and Church House, number 10, both of five bays and three storeys. The stuccoed Literary Institute was founded in 1839.

Numbers 1–6 **Pond Square** are a noteworthy group of tiny cottages.

In the **High Street** numbers 17–21, 23 and 42 are good and well-preserved eighteenth-century houses.

More Georgian houses are to be found at West Hill (45–7) and on Highgate Hill (106–8).

Wyldes Farm 17th century **R3**
North End NW3
⊖ Golders Green, Hampstead
The only surviving farmhouse in Hampstead, Wyldes Farm sits in its own fenced grounds, having lost its farmland to the Heath extension between **North End** R5 and the **Garden Suburb** R19. Its residents have not always been farmers, however: John Linnell the painter lived here from 1792 to 1882, with William Blake a frequent visitor. Raymond Unwin, the architect and planner of Hampstead Garden Suburb, also lived at Wyldes and was responsible for converting the large barn into living quarters.

Cromwell House 1637–40 **R4**
104 Highgate Hill N6
⊖ Archway
Cromwell House was built for Richard Springwell, and is one of the few remaining large houses in London of its date. It is an example of what Summerson calls the 'artisan style', built as a joint production by skilled craftsmen (probably co-ordinated by the bricklayer) without the controlling influence of an architect. The street façade, with its richly moulded cornices, carved *in situ* at first- and second-floor levels, is a *tour de force* by the bricklayer-contractor. The regularity of the seven window bays is a testament to the growing influence of Inigo Jones. A range of dormer windows and a central cupola complete the top of the house. Inside, the staircase is the earliest in London to have a handrail formed by pierced decorative panels instead of balustrades. Later the staircase would have terminated at the *piano nobile* but here it rises the full height of the building. The house was considerably restored in 1865 by Thomas Harris and is now occupied by a missionary society. (For the artisan style see also **College of Arms** L22.)

North End c1700 **R5**
NW3
⊖ Golders Green, Hampstead
Like the **Vale of Health** A9, North End is a surviving hamlet which can still be appreciated as an entity, although Golders Green encroaches on it via North End Road. The Old Bull and Bush pub, **Wyldes Farm** R3, Byron Cottage, and the site of the residence of Pitt the Elder in 1776 are its oldest remaining features. As a hamlet, North End is best appreciated when approached along the bridle paths from Golders Hill Park to the west, or from the Sandy Heath to the north and east.

The Spaniards 18th century **R6**
Spaniards Road NW3
⊖ Hampstead
A group of 'country' buildings halfway to Highgate along Spaniards Road: on one side the whitewashed public house and its outbuildings, and on the other side a small lodge, once a toll-house. The interior of the pub, with its sequence of small rooms, is a fairly well-preserved example of an eighteenth-century coaching inn.

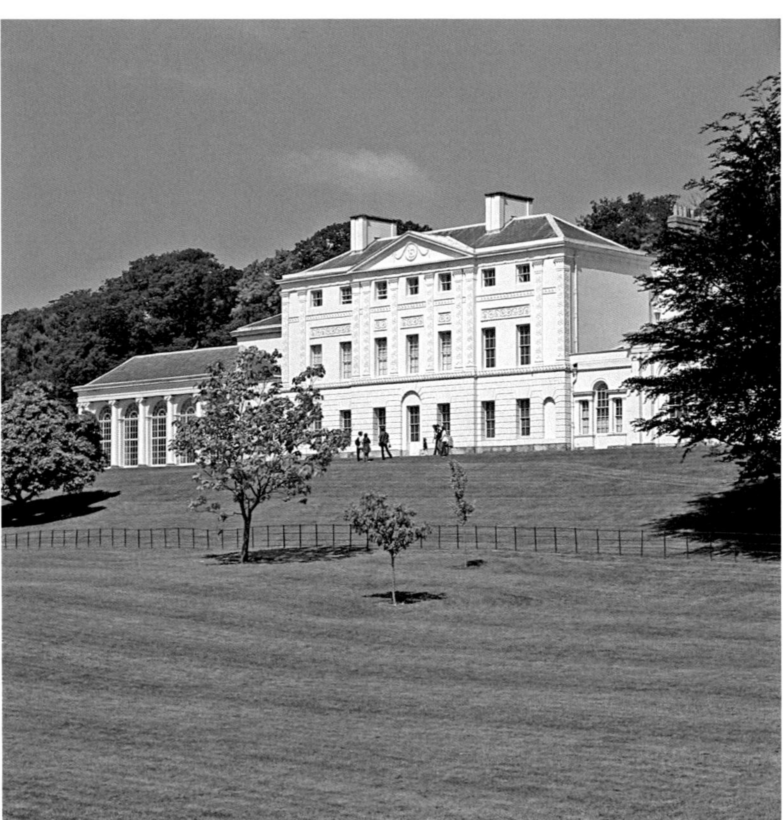

Kenwood House R7
1754, 1764–9, 1793–6
Hampstead Lane NW3
Robert Adam
⊖ Hampstead, then walk across the Heath; or bus to Highgate

Built at the beginning of the seventeenth century, the house was acquired by the first Earl of Mansfield in 1754 and remodelled as a holiday retreat by Adam in 1764, and is the first example of Adam's mature style applied to an exterior. In 1780 it became a permanent residence.

The Hampstead–Highgate road ran much closer to the house in 1754, and it was the Earl who in 1793 set the public road back to its present line, allowing the house to stand free in its park. The house is now approached by two serpentine drives through dense woodlands, from which the grand Adam entrance front with its full-height portico and pediment is suddenly revealed. The white-brick wings are by George Saunders (1793–6).

In contrast with the closed north approach the south front lies open to extensive parkland. The long classical facade confronting a contrived but 'natural' world is quintessential of English house and park design in the eighteenth century. It has been suggested that Humphry Repton was perhaps consulted by the architect, because the serpentine drives and the gardens next to the house are characteristic of his work. The sham bridge at the east end of the lakes was introduced by the first Earl.

The symmetrical arrangement of the south front was prompted by the existing orangery on the left, suggesting the building of the library on the right to balance it. Adam refronted the centre block and raised it a storey with slim pilasters of his own invention. Much of Adam's enriched original stucco has disappeared with time, and the capitals and principal mouldings were restored in 1955–9.

Of the interiors, the sequence from the hall to the main staircase and the marble hall (on the first floor) is all by Adam. It culminates in the library, perhaps one of the finest extant Adam rooms. Although much of the original Adam furniture has been removed, Kenwood has a very fine collection of paintings, contributed by Lord Iveagh when he bought the house in 1925. The second Earl of Iveagh opened the house to the public in 1928 and it is now run by English Heritage. Very loud concerts are given by the lake on summer evenings.

St John the Evangelist 1826 **R8**
Holloway Road N19
Charles Barry
⊖ Archway

One of a pair of nearly identical churches (the other is St Paul's, Balls Pond Road), this undistinguished work is in thin Perpendicular Gothic. Barry is famous as the designer of the **Travellers' Club** K82 and the **Houses of Parliament** K90. This church should be compared with the contemporary and much better work of Bedford and the Inwoods, for example **St John, Waterloo Road** K72 and **St Pancras** G21.

Highgate Cemetery started 1838 **R9**
Swains Lane N6
Stephen Geary, J B Bunning and J Oldred Scott
⊖ Archway

Cedar of Lebanon Catacombs and Beer Mausoleum. Photo 1980

The British cemetery is a product of the great period of sanitary reform that began in 1820. By the beginning of the nineteenth century the rapid growth of population had made the reform of burials long overdue, and seven commercial cemeteries were laid out around London, including **Kensal Green** T13 (1833), **Brompton** M1 (1831), **Nunhead** X7 (1840) and Tower Hamlets (1841). Laid out in the tradition of eighteenth-century landscape gardening, Highgate Old Cemetery epitomizes the High Victorian preoccupation with death and its drama. In 1838 Stephen Geary (owner and architect of the London Cemetery Company) planned the first Highgate Cemetery to the west of Swains Lane. (Ironically, Geary is also reputed to be the architect of London's earliest gin palaces.)

As a result of its architecture, its ingenious layout of paths and magnificent views over London, it soon became popular, and favourable comparisons were made with Père Lachaise, built outside Paris in 1804. In 1854 the cemetery was extended to the east of Swains Lane and now contains approximately 51,000 graves with about 166,000 burials. Geary wanted the architecture of Highgate to be a mixture of Gothic and Egyptian (the latter was fashionable in mortuary art in the early nineteenth century). Two chapels were provided at the entrance to the west cemetery, and both were in use up to 1956. Their details – stairs set in octagonal buttresses, coloured glass set directly into the masonry, and superimposed bays of lancet windows – show the originality of Geary's architecture. The bier at the southern end displays ingenuity *par excellence*, with a hydraulic system to lower the coffins through a deep tunnel under Swains Lane to the new cemetery to the east. To the west an arcaded retaining wall forms a large, curved assembly area for mourners and a turning point for hearses. Up the hill to the north are the Egyptian Avenue and the Cedar of Lebanon Catacombs, formed around a tree from the original estate. The site planning uses the levels skilfully in a series of circuitously connecting paths. In the northern part of the cemetery, abutting the churchyard of St Michael's, are the Gothic Catacombs (1842), attributed to J B Bunning, who relieved Geary as surveyor to the London Cemetery Company in 1839. At the north of the Lebanon Circle is the mausoleum to Julius Beer, the most ambitious architectural work in the cemetery, designed by J Oldred Scott. The magnificent stepped pyramidal roof, derived from the tomb of the Greek King Mausolus at Halicarnassus, is two storeys high.

Among a host of eminent Victorians interred at Highgate are George Eliot, Dante Gabriel Rossetti, Michael Faraday, Henry Crabb Robinson, Carl Rosa, John Galsworthy, Herbert Spencer and Karl Marx.

Waterworks Pumping Station **R10**
1854–6
Green Lanes N16
W Chadwell Myne
⊖ Manor House
One of London's most remarkable working follies, its muscular and castellated forms lend credence to the claim that it pumps a million gallons of water a day to Crouch Hill and Maiden Lane. At one corner of the 'castle keep' is a large, angled tower. At the opposite corner is a turret with a conical top. The buttressing to the keep is exaggerated, and the chimney is a very tall polygonal tower.

Holly Village 1865 **R11**
Swains Lane N6
H A Darbishire
⊖ Archway
Perhaps the most whimsical architecture in this book, this group of highly wrought and decorated houses was erected by Baroness Burdett-Coutts. As campaigner and benefactor of the East End poor she was also responsible with Darbishire for Bethnal Green's Columbia Market (now demolished) and for the first of the Peabody Trust's five-storey housing blocks (H26). At Holly Village, a group of eight buildings placed about a green, Darbishire was in rustic mood to provide fitting dwellings for the Baroness's servants. He allowed his lust for detail to exercise itself on every feature: even the apparently symmetrical gatehouse's bay windows are different.

Alexandra Palace 1875 **R12**
Alexandra Park N10
J Johnson
⇌ Alexandra Palace
An attempt to build a north London equivalent of Sydenham's Crystal Palace, Alexandra Palace (named after the Princess of Wales) was ill-fated. Despite its concert hall for 14,000 people and one of the largest organs in the world, its large, melancholy spaces have never caught the imagination as a 'people's palace'. It was totally gutted by fire a few days after it opened and completely rebuilt the same year. The central section was again destroyed by fire in 1980 and was rebuilt and reopened in 1988.

Brooklyn 1886–7 **R13**
8 Private Road, Enfield EN1
A H Mackmurdo and H P Horne
⇄ Bush Hill Park
A surprisingly modern house for its time. The flat roof, very restrained classical detail, and the six bays of the ground floor suggest an early pioneering work of modern architecture, and the design may also be seen as 'an idiosyncratic interpretation of neoclassicism' (Gavin Stamp). It is more like Edward Godwin's work (before its revision) in **Tite Street** N22 than Mackmurdo's later **25 Cadogan Gardens** N27.

Archway 1900 **R14**
Hornsey Lane and Archway Road N6
Alexander Binnie
⊖ Archway
Archway Road was cut through in the nineteenth century in order to bypass Highgate Hill. The original Archway bridge spanning the cutting was by John Nash; the replacement is a fine cast-iron construction, and apart from its view of the City (a reminder that north London is built on a ridge), also serves as a symbolic gate to it, and a boundary of nineteenth-century London.

Shops and **Flats** 1900 **R15**
Temple Fortune, Hampstead Garden Suburb NW11
Barry Parker and Raymond Unwin, designed by A J Penty
⊖ Golders Green
Two almost identical large blocks of red-brick flats, with shops on the ground floor, stand either side of the junction of Finchley Road and Hampstead Way, acting as a pavilioned western gateway to **Hampstead Garden Suburb** R19. The flats are approached along timber-arcaded galleries from the staircase pavilions at either end. The large pitched roofs with dormer windows are particularly inventive.

White Hart Lane Estate **R16**
1904–12, 1921–8
Risley Avenue N 17
LCC Architects Department; W E Riley (1904–12) and G Topham Forrest (1921–8)
⊖ Wood Green
This estate was the largest cottage development undertaken by the LCC (71 hectares/177 acres) before the First World War. The first stage (1904–12) was laid out in parallel rows of two-storey cottages between Lordship Lane and Risley Avenue, with the Arcadian square of Tower Garden (turfed for tennis and bowls) at the centre. The architects complied as far as possible with the highest ideals of the Garden City movement. The inventive detailing of porches and the two-storey projecting bays were attempts to relieve the flat street frontage – features recommended by Parker and Unwin, who designed **Hampstead Garden Suburb** R19. The second stage, north of

Risley Avenue, was completed after the war. Its curvilinear streets mark a romantic development in suburban layout.

Golders Green Crematorium R17
1905–38
Hoop Lane NW11
Ernest George and Yates
⊖ Golders Green

Henry Thompson, Professor of Clinical Surgery at University College Hospital from 1865 to 1875, founded the secular Cremation Society whose reforming agitation eventually led to the legislation allowing cremation as an alternative to burial. The society constructed Golders Green Crematorium, and the group of chapels in good red-brick Romanesque make it a handsome place from which to depart. Beyond them is a very large unmown meadow for the scattering of ashes, overlooked by Lutyens's very original domed **Philipson Mausoleum** (1914).

Philipson Mausoleum

Pergola 1906–25 R18
West Heath, off North End Way NW3
Thomas Hayton Mawson
⊖ Hampstead, Golders Green

The cliché 'hidden treasure' is here true; apart from Hampstead residents, very few Londoners are aware of this absurdly ambitious yet magical incursion into the plausible wildness of the Heath. It is not signposted, and is best approached off North End Way from the south.

The millionaire William Lever, soap magnate and later Lord Leverhulme, bought the substantial house 'The Hill' on North End Way in 1904. He employed the distinguished landscape architect Mawson to design the gardens to the west, and spoil from the construction of the Northern Line was used to provide a level terrace extending from the house. The retaining wall where the terrace met the wild Heath was crowned with a pergola in easy-going Edwardian classical style. This hugs the site's perimeter, zigzagging in a series of L-shapes, and culminates to the north in a Lutyens-esque pavilion with a pyramidal roof (1925) overlooking a rectangular pond surrounded by a hedge.

In 1960 the LCC bought the pergola and opened it to the public; it was restored by the Corporation of London in the early 1990s.

The Institute

Hampstead Garden Suburb **R19**
started 1906
NW11
Parker and Unwin, Edwin Lutyens,
Baillie Scott and others
⊖ Golders Green

Founded largely as a result of the reformist zeal of Dame Henrietta Barnett, Hampstead Garden Suburb was an attempt to realize a fragment of Ebenezer Howard's grand prescription for London in his influential book *Tomorrow* (1898). Howard pointed to the Garden City as the solution to all our economic and social ills, an argument that was to be misunderstood by the suburban and new town lobby in England and abroad in the twentieth century. Raymond Unwin deepened the misunderstanding with his book *Nothing Gained by Overcrowding* (1918), and Howard's prophecy does not find its embodiment in Hampstead Garden Suburb.

Parker and Unwin were appointed as planners of the new suburb as a result of their successful plans for Letchworth a few years earlier. Unwin remained in charge from 1907–15. The original sections were the west fringe of the Hampstead Heath extension on both sides of Hampstead Way and Wellgarth Road; this land, owned by the original trust, is approximately 128 hectares (317 acres) and constitutes the Garden Suburb proper. It has expanded over the years to 324 hectares (800 acres) and is now less easily identified demographically or architecturally.

The layout is a mixture of residential closes and gently curving principal roads, lined with well-established privet hedges and flowering cherry trees, with a secondary pattern of pedestrian paths. All houses have private gardens divided by the ever-present hedges and are free-standing, semi-detached or terraced, either in country vernacular styles or in Lutyens's new Georgian (see for example **Erskine Hill** R21). The zoned density of eight houses to the acre (about twenty houses to the hectare) and the absence of other uses gives the Garden Suburb the impression of being a gated community. Only in the central square can any urbanity be detected, and this was mainly Lutyens's responsibility. However, many distinguished domestic architects have made contributions to the Suburb – among them Baillie Scott (**Waterlow Court** R20), Curtis Green, Guy Dawber and Geoffrey Lucas.

The tendency for the Suburb to devolve into a one-class area (as opposed to its original mixed social idealism), the absence of commercial uses as a result of the zoning, and the difficulty of public transport in serving such low densities, have justified the now familiar criticisms of Hampstead Garden Suburb and, by extension, of Unwin's misappropriation of the Garden City ideal.

Waterlow Court 1908–9 **R20**
Heath Close, off Hampstead Way NW11
M H Baillie Scott
⊖ Golders Green

Of all Baillie Scott's enlightened designs for multiple housing groups in the Suburb this was the only one to be built. It was designed to contain fifty flats for single working women. Within the general 'Arcadian' context of **Hampstead Garden Suburb** R19 the fully enclosed courtyard of Waterlow Court is quite surreal. The court as a type normally suggests an oasis of calm in a hostile world, and in this case it is approached by a timber-covered way at the end of the leafy close. Inside the two-storey court the white-painted brickwork, arcades with fine semicircular arches on all four sides, and central pavilion with a bellcote opposite the entrance give the impression of a Spanish colonial college somewhere in rural California. The 'back garden' is approached through the corners of the court, and its potting sheds and orderly flower beds call to mind the world of Beatrix Potter.

Houses 1908–10 **R21**
Erskine Hill, Hampstead Garden Suburb NW11
Edwin Lutyens
⊖ Golders Green

Only the west is by Lutyens but both sides form a symmetrical composition treated in Lutyens's magnificent 'Wrenaissance' style, in grey brick with some stone, and white-painted wood windows. The balance between motifs from high architecture and those from domestic, like the dormers, is exquisite. For the essence of the Suburb (R19), walk down Erskine Hill, turn right along Temple Fortune Hill, apparently a cul-de-sac. Go to the end where, leaving the town behind, you are in the country. No, it is Big Wood, a now-enclosed fragment of ancient forest – but what an illusion!

St Jude and **Parsonage** 1909-14 **R22**
Free Church and **Manse** c1910
Institute 1909–20s
Central Square, Hampstead Garden Suburb NW11
Edwin Lutyens
⊖ Golders Green

St Jude

It fell to Lutyens to give Unwin and Baillie Scott's domestic matrix its symbolic non-commercial centre. This group of buildings, set inside a loosely defined square of low two-storey houses on the highest part of the Suburb, is probably one of the most recent examples of successful town planning in London. Lutyens was forty when work started, and, while his earlier 'Wrenaissance' style was already developed (see his houses in Erskine Hill R21), these buildings incorporated new motifs and ideas.

In the most important position, on the main axis, is the Institute, built of small grey bricks with red dressings and stone trim. It is so successful a pastiche of a late-seventeenth-century public building that the magnificent courtyard which terminates the axis looks more Colonial American than English. To the south of the square, to one side of the axis, lies St Jude, which has one of the best and most accessible Lutyens interiors in London. It has a three-bay tunnel-vaulted nave, a domed crossing, and an apsed end. The arches and piers are of red brick, the piers meeting the floor with characteristic curved splays. The bizarre consequences of bringing an Arts and Crafts roof through brick classical arches and introducing square-headed dormers are startlingly revealed in the aisles. The ceiling and dome are decorated with delightful frescoes by Walter Starmer which are continued in the Lady Chapel, where they celebrate as a war memorial a wild collection of ladies, including Harriet Beecher Stowe, Christina Rossetti, Joan of Arc and a Girl Guide.

The Free Church to the north of the square is, rightly, much plainer than St Jude's, with a central dome instead of a spire. The sides are good, but the front is unattractive, and its manse is starkly unadorned.

Free Church

Houses c1910 **R23**
6–10 Meadway, 22 Hampstead Way NW11
Baillie Scott
 Golders Green
Baillie Scott's only group of street houses in Hampstead Garden Suburb (but see **Waterlow Court** R20). After seventy years it is possible to imagine these tiny pebble-dashed cottages with shallow-arched windows and steeply pitched roofs as remnants of an Arcadian village.

Arnos Grove

Piccadilly Line Underground Stations **R24**
1932–3
Arnos Grove and Southgate, Charles Holden; Oakwood, Charles Holden with C H James
Arnos Grove Station has its place in the histories of modern architecture: it was used at the time as proof of the moral fitness of the style for a modern transport system, and, by extension, for modern life. It is now clear that Holden's concerns were always with abstract geometrical combinations, produced by the elemental forms which he gave to the various functions of an Underground station: the canopy, booking hall and covered platforms. At Southgate (picture page 388), these are extended to include two parades of shops and a bus stand. See also the stations at the western end of the line (T24).

Cholmeley Lodge 1934 **R25**
Cholmeley Lane, Highgate Hill
N6
Guy Morgan
⊖ Archway

These well-maintained flats present a non-revolutionary alternative to the modern style of **Highpoint 1** R27. They have an artistic front and a utilitarian back. The front is scalloped to face the view, with red-brick bands alternating with the window strips and continuous balconies; the back is of stock brick with the plumbing exposed.

Hornsey Town Hall 1934–5 **R26**
The Broadway, Crouch End N8
R H Uren
⇌ Hornsey

The Town Hall's tall brick tower and two wings form an asymmetrical composition set back from the busy Broadway behind a 'planned' town square, with further 'municipal' buildings (formerly the Gas and Electricity Boards' offices) on either side and in the same style. The buildings pay homage to Dudok's Hilversum Town Hall of 1928, but also hint at neo-Georgian in the disposition of their windows. The public interiors were lavishly detailed in marble and bronze; their subsequent neglect may be remedied by plans of 2007 to convert the building for varied cultural uses.

Highpoint 1

Highpoint 1 and **2** 1936 and 1938 **R27**
North Hill N7
Lubetkin and Tecton
⊖ Highgate

These two apartment buildings are the nearest realization we have of Le Corbusier's ideas. As the name implies they are positioned on the top of Highgate ridge, commanding magnificent views

Highpoint 2

Highpoint 2, detail of Caryatid porch

of the City to the south-east and of the extensive suburbs of Hendon to the west. During a rare visit to London Le Corbusier congratulated Lubetkin on producing 'a vertical garden city'. Highpoint 1 is the more didactic of the two, representing fully Le Corbusier's *Five Points of Modern Architecture* – *pilotis*, roof garden, liberated plan and long windows. The building is intentionally detached from its immediate surroundings, anticipating the new millennium of *La Ville Radieuse*. The plan is double cruciform with eight flats on each floor. The white-rendered façades are well maintained and, like Nash's Regent's Park terraces, look new.

Highpoint 2, on the other hand, attempts to fit in with its surroundings in both general form and facing materials. The building runs parallel to the street, and its façade is composed of a mixture of tiles, bricks and glazed bricks, a change of style caused by public reaction to Highpoint 1. However, in section the building exhibits further debts to Le Corbusier in its use of double-height 'studio' apartments, and externally it is reminiscent of Le Corbusier's own apartments at Porte Molitor in Paris. In the *porte cochère* Lubetkin incorporated reproductions of two of the Erechtheum caryatids as a humorous rebuke to his stylistic critics, who complained of the absence of historical references in Highpoint 1.

The buildings share a garden, with swimming pool, tennis courts and tea room. They confirm the idea that this particular model of living could be successful when inhabited by the middle-class intelligentsia, but that it could be a wholesale prescription neither for the Welfare State nor for the renewal of the traditional city, as the twentieth century disastrously demonstrated.

Jack Straw's Castle 1964 **R28**
North End Way NW3
Raymond Erith and Quinlan Terry
⊖ Hampstead

The brick south wall is all that remains of this famous eighteenth-century pub with its romantic associations with highwaymen. Its replacement by Erith and Terry had nothing to do with its previous style, but was one of the few large timber-frame structures to have been built in London since the Great Fire. The cream-painted timber sidings, projecting windows and castellated cornice give the building a festive quality.

The upper floors were converted into flats but in 2008 the ground floor, formerly the bars, lay empty.

Houses 1966–8 **R29**
24–32 Winscombe Street N19
Neave Brown
⊖ Archway

Neave Brown went on to design the huge Alexandra Road scheme (E8) for the London Borough of Camden, and this little row of houses shows some of the concerns which there acquired monumental significance. Their chief interest lies in the manipulation and insistent zoning of the section: the top floor contains a main bedroom on the street side and a living room with a view of the garden; the middle and main entrance floor a dining-kitchen and a large terrace; and the ground floor, sunk slightly below the street, a divisible children's bedroom. Externally, they are less successful: the individual houses are at odds with the terrace, and the top and bottom of each house conflict with each other.

Houses 91–103 Swains Lane 1970–2

House 1969 **R30**
81 Swains Lane N6
John Winter
⊖ Archway

Overlooking Highgate Cemetery like a lodge, this three-storey Cor-Ten steel-framed house was designed by John Winter for himself. The frame is extended on either side of large sheets of fixed glass in order to accommodate vertical steel louvres for ventilation. Cor-Ten steel was an American invention of the early 1960s to allow exposed structural steelwork simply to rust in a controlled manner as a permanent finish, thereby avoiding costly maintenance and giving the building the patina of age. This is one of the few examples in London of the domestic use of the material. The absence of opening windows gives the building a very abstract image, recalling the hermetic and 'cool' buildings in Chicago by Skidmore, Owings and Merrill, in whose offices Winter worked as an assistant in the 1950s.

Note Eldridge Smerin's addition of 2008 to the growing collection of modern houses on Swains Lane, a new glass pavilion overlooking the Cemetery to the south-west. Further up still is a row of seven generously wide-fronted houses (1970–72) by Haxworth and Kasabov.

Flats 1980 **R31**
119 Hornsey Lane N6
Colquhoun and Miller
⊖ Archway

Sited on a narrow plot between two existing blocks, these flats for single people were commissioned by the London Borough of Haringey. The planning is straightforwardly modern, with a carefully proportioned façade which demonstrates the form of construction: a frame of load-bearing brick walls and concrete floors. The apertures in the frame are filled with spandrels of glass blocks and simple timber-framed windows.

Section S: Outer London, north-east

At present, there is little significant architecture in this section. It is dominated by the valleys of two rivers running north–south. To the west the River Lea, now mostly tamed by reservoirs, runs towards the Thames; its undeveloped marshes and abandoned watercress farms are slowly being turned into a regional park for recreation on the drained land. To the east lies the Roding Valley, reaching the Thames just to the east of the Beckton sewage works. On a ridge between the two valleys is Woodford, the most prosperous of the suburbs which now cover the land on which building is possible. Its development was prompted by the extension in the 1940s of the underground Central Line running along the west side of the Roding Valley to Epping and Ongar. The motorway to Cambridge and East Anglia (the M11, opened in the 1970s) runs down the middle of the valley to connect with the North Circular Road.

To the north is Epping Forest: originally royal hunting grounds (see Queen Elizabeth's Hunting Lodge just north of Chingford Green), it was made available to the public with the building of the railway from Liverpool Street to Chingford. Bought by the City of London in 1878, it became east London's equivalent of Hampstead Heath: a resort for the crowded poor of Whitechapel and Bethnal Green. It is wilder than the Heath, and has cattle grids on its approach roads.

William Morris Gallery 1762 **S1**
Lloyd Park, Forest Road, Walthamstow E17
⊖ Walthamstow Central

Morris was born in Walthamstow in 1834 and between 1847 and 1856 his family lived in this large, three-storeyed and double-fronted Georgian house which was built in 1762. Now used as a gallery but with very little disturbance to its original domesticity, it contains a marvellous collection of many of the fabrics, carpets, wallpapers, fittings, furniture, stained glass and books produced by his firm Morris and Company, together with drawings and sketches of the designs for them. Furniture and designs by A H Mackmurdo and all the important members of the Century Guild, and books designed by Frank Brangwyn, form related displays.

All these may be difficult to visit because of uncertain and limited visiting hours.

Walthamstow Civic Centre 1937–42 **S2**
Forest Road, Walthamstow E17
P D Hepworth
⊖ Walthamstow Central

The importance of London's local government has declined over the twentieth century, but the town halls which the various boroughs built usually attempted architectural significance and were built in the progressive style of the day. Walthamstow's is a very late example, and its date suggests that it might have been built in the neo-Georgian or even modern style. But although the layout is classical, the first two buildings of the intended group of three were carried out in a rare and late version of a style derived from the comfortable official architecture of Scandinavia.

Newbury Park bus station 1949 **S3**
Newbury Park IG2
Oliver Hill
⊖ Newbury Park
When the railway line serving Newbury Park station was incorporated into the Central Line, as an economy a new station was not built. This splendid new bus station, however, was. It has heroic concrete parabolic arches supporting an asymmetrical concrete vault (compare the inside of Howard Robertson's **Royal Horticultural Society Hall** 09), and very elegantly detailed copper roof covering.

Housing 1990 **S4**
20b Bisterne Avenue E17
Wickham and Associates
⇄ Wood Street Walthamstow
This modest housing development for the London Borough of Waltham Forest caused much commotion when built on account of the strong colour scheme for its exterior rendered walls – a vibrant blue and burnt sienna. The arrangement of six flats planned on three floors either side of a glass-canopied external stair is eminently sane, and no doubt the colours will eventually be accepted.

South West Essex Reform Synagogue **S5**
1990–1
Oakes Lane, Newbury Park, Ilford IG2
Michael Gold Architects
⊖ Newbury Park
The winning entry in an RIBA competition in 1988, this synagogue is impressive for its cool and spartan interior. The circular prayer hall is effectively lit by a series of small windows set in deep conical reveals at high level in the external wall. The play of light emphasizing the building's pure geometry as a setting for the liturgical ritual is free of sentimentality and recalls Gold's theoretical preoccupation with 'people' in architecture from the early 1980s.

Section T: Outer London, west

Enlarged arterial roads going west to Heathrow Airport and beyond overshadow this part of London: the tail of Westway connecting to Western Avenue, and Chiswick Flyover to the Great West Road and the M4 motorway. From sections of elevated carriageway the motorist can see the dormitory suburbs of Ealing, Acton and Uxbridge stretching loosely to the horizon in either direction, unceremoniously absorbing the historic houses and parks of **Syon** T9, **Osterley** T10, **Chiswick** T6 and **Kew** T4. Until the mid-nineteenth century the area was predominantly rural, sprinkled with country houses and their attendant villages close to the Thames, and with the Grand Union Canal passing through open fields on its way to Paddington.

The most significant remains of this more privileged past are to be found in two large houses: Syon and Osterley. They mark the step from early to late Tudor, and both were later successfully converted by Robert Adam. While Syon and Osterley are now embedded in between-the-wars suburbia, Chiswick retains much of its eighteenth-century character, with a large house (Lord Burlington's Chiswick House) supported by a village (the relatively intact Chiswick Mall and Lower Mall).

To the south, held in the bend of the Thames, are the Royal Botanic Gardens at Kew, laid out by William Chambers in 1758–63. Chambers's ten-tiered Pagoda, his variety of small temples, and Decimus Burton and Turner's later Palm House, all set in beautiful gardens, are together one of London's main architectural treasures.

Notable late Georgian architecture includes Uxbridge Town Hall (1789) and a small number of private houses, particularly John Soane's own house at Pitshanger (T11), now a public library, built in 1801–3 overlooking Walpole Park in Ealing, and Berrymead Priory in Acton.

Hammersmith has some good early-nineteenth-century streets and squares (for example **St Peter's Square** T12) but the most important development was in the mid-nineteenth century when the Victorian suburb was given one of its chief models in the curved and tree-lined streets of Norman Shaw's Bedford Park, Acton (T17), the earliest garden suburb in London. As with north and south London, the initiative for twentieth-century suburban expansion came from the London Underground (here the Piccadilly and District Lines). Charles Holden's many stations built in the 1930s (T24) are consistently excellent, unlike later stations on the lines at Hatton Cross and Heathrow.

The 1930s produced the architecture of transport, recreation and workplaces, and its white factories were truly remarkable. Regrettably, with the exception of Banister Fletcher's 1936 **Gillette Building** T27 and the **Hoover factory** T25 by Wallis Gilbert and Partners, only the cherry trees and the directional thrust of the Great West Road remain of this once fine approach to Central London from the west. (Gilbert Scott's monumental Guinness Brewery of 1933 was also senselessly demolished in 2006.)

Further to the north, the new **Wembley Stadium** T42 replaced the original of 1924 and only Owen Williams's structurally expressive **Wembley Arena** T26 of 1934 remains as a testament to the era's optimism with mass society and its institutions. Heathrow Airport was in 2008 the world's largest, busiest and one of the least liked airports. Despite negative press following its opening in 2008, **Terminal 5** T41 went some way to redressing the impression that had previously characterized Heathrow. As the London Docks had given impetus to the expansion of London's East End in the nineteenth century, so at the beginning of the twenty-first century Heathrow extended the westerly limits of London from its centre to the M25.

Perivale Underground Station

Wembley Stadium T42, detail of arch support

St Nicholas started 15th century T1
Church Street W4
nave rebuilt by Pearson, 1882
⊖ Turnham Green

The church forms the charming nucleus of Chiswick village, now passed by, sandwiched between the Thames and the torrential traffic of the Great West Road. The tower is of the fifteenth century, but the body of the church was rebuilt by Pearson in 1882. There is a monument to William Hogarth in the churchyard, and Lord Burlington and his protégé William Kent are buried here. See also **Chiswick Mall** T7, **Chiswick Square** T3 and **Strand on the Green** T5.

Boston Manor 1622 T2
Boston Manor Park, Brentford
⊖ Boston Manor

Originally the property of the wife of William Reade, this large and simple three-storey manor house stands in its own grounds behind a high boundary wall. The Jacobean exterior is brick, with three plain gables on the front and two on the sides, and a surprising mixture of Italian motifs which may have been added later – segmental pediments, niches in the gables, and a modillion cornice above the second storey. Pevsner notes that only Inigo Jones would have used such devices so early in England.

The view from the south-west shows the intrusion of the outside world: the M4 motorway bisects the grounds, and the industrial strip of the Great West Road forms the skyline. Nevertheless, with its attractive small lake full of geese and wild fowl, the park is good for Sunday walks.

Chiswick Square 1680 and T3
forecourt to **Boston House**
1740
Burlington Lane W4
⊖ Stamford Brook

Two- and three-storey cottages flank Boston House, forming a picturesque forecourt. The tranquillity of this once-secluded enclave off the Great West Road is now shattered by the flyover opposite.

Temperate House

Royal Botanic Gardens, Kew 1696 **T4**

⊖ Kew Gardens

Kew Gardens now cover 121 hectares (300 acres), forming an extensive park held by the bends of the river Thames. The river also gives views to **Syon Park** T9 in the west. As a museum of landscape and botanical specimens Kew is unsurpassed, containing specimens collected over two centuries. An excellent map and guidebook are available at the entrance.

The Royal Botanic Gardens have three principal origins: Kew Palace, its gardens planted in 1696 by Henry and Lady Capel, and the park of Richmond Palace to the north. George II lived at Richmond Lodge, with his son Frederick and daughter-in-law Princess Augusta nearby at Kew House. All that now remains of this Hanoverian retreat is Kew House, restored in 2006 and renamed Kew Palace. It was here that the Capel family planted the first specimen trees in the late seventeenth century.

In the mid-nineteenth century Princess Augusta's eighteenth-century gardens at Kew (derived from the work of William Chambers) and Queen Charlotte's gardens at Richmond Lodge (by Capability Brown) passed to the state, under the charge of the great botanist William Hooker (1841–65) and his son Joseph (1865–85). In the first five years of Hooker's directorship the gardens expanded from 4.5 to 31 hectares (11 to 76 acres), and W A Nesfield (father of W E Nesfield) later laid out the four major vistas (Pagoda Vista, Broad Walk. Holly Walk and Cedar Vista) and designed the picturesque lake (1845) and the pond in front of the **Palm House** T15 (1847). The gardens now became a repository of the world's botanical species, with a research laboratory and separate houses for orchids, alpine plants, ferns, cacti and so on. The

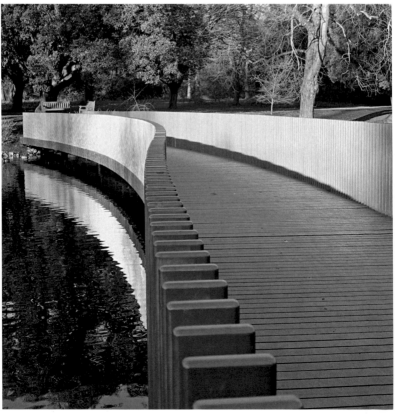

Sackler Bridge

cataloguing spirit of the Victorian age is exemplified by the Palm House, containing every known variety of palm.

The architecture of Kew Gardens is the subject of separate entries: Chambers's **Pagoda** and **Orangery** T8; Nash's **Aroid House** T14; Nesfield's **Temperate House Lodge** T16 and Turner and Decimus Burton's **Palm House** T15. Note also Turner and Decimus Burton's magnificent Temperate House (1862–98), restored in 1982.

At the beginning of the twenty-first century, a masterplan prepared by Wilkinson Eyre prompted a flurry of new architectural commissions: the exquisitely detailed **Sackler Bridge** by John Pawson of 2006 is to be noted, as is the **Alpine House** of the same date by Wilkinson Eyre. In a patch of woodland north-west of the Temperate House, the elaborately structured **Tree Walk** by Marks Barfield and Jane Wernick Associates was opened in 2008.

Strand on the Green 18th century **T5**
W4
⊖ Gunnersbury
A companion to **Chiswick Mall** T7, but even less urban – only a footpath here separates the modest eighteenth-century houses from the river.

Entrance side

Chiswick House 1725–9 **T6**
Hogarth Lane and Burlington Lane W4
Lord Burlington
⊖ Turnham Green

Erect new wonders and the old repair;
Jones and Palladio to themselves restore
And be whate'er Vitruvius was before.
Alexander Pope

Burlington's public career as an architect started with **Westminster School** K41 and continued with the building of this, his country villa, to be used for entertaining, and as a library and art gallery. He had already designed and built the Summer Parlour building (next to the villa) as an extension to the old Jacobean family house (largely demolished in 1788). Work on the new house started in 1725, when Burlington was

Garden side

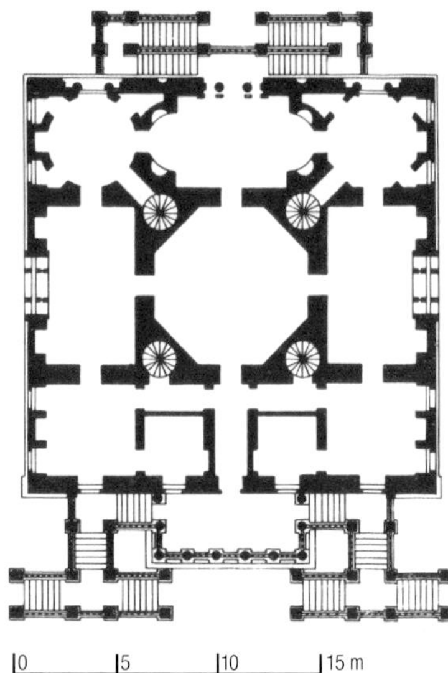

twenty-nine. The design is based on Palladio's Villa Capra ('Rotonda') at Vicenza (its 21m/68ft square plan is the same dimension as that published for Capra) but it also borrows from Scamozzi (Rocca Pisana) and, in the details of the interior, from Inigo Jones. The vermiculated Portland stone ground floor originally housed Burlington's library in the long room facing the garden. The stuccoed first floor has a suite of state rooms arranged round a central domed saloon, reached from a hall via the portico. The character of the outside rests in the way the octagonal drum of the dome pushes through the pyramidal roof, improving on Scamozzi by replacing the oculus with 'thermal' windows more appropriate to the English climate, and in the quirky chimneys housed in obelisks at the perimeter. The fussy arrangement of steps up to the portico, with statues by Rysbrack of Palladio (left) and Jones (right), derives from Palladio's drawings.

The *en suite* arrangement of the first-floor rooms was later fully developed by Adam and is now a cliché, but was then new to England. The design of the interior was under the general direction of Burlington, but his protégé William Kent did much of the detailed design of ceilings and chimney-pieces, borrowing many of them directly from Jones. In the 1950s the rooms were restored and furnished where possible with original items. They have not been lived in since this restoration, and have a curiously cold quality which, however, is probably appropriate to the designers' didactic intentions. The gallery, facing the gardens, is a suite of circular, apsed double-square and octagonal rooms, each lit with a Venetian window. On a summer afternoon it seems a wonderfully evocative and idealized synthesis of English and Italian country living.

Burlington remodelled the grounds, using as landscape architect William Kent, who here developed the 'natural' style to complement the architecture. They are now a public park, with restoration proceeding piecemeal, and Kent's intentions are therefore hard to read. The Obelisk to the west, the Doric column and Deer House to the east, and the Temple, belong to his original decorative scheme. The Inigo Jones gateway, north-west of the house, was brought from Beaufort House, Chelsea, in 1736; and the classic bridge over the canal was built by Wyatt in 1788.

Just to the east of the house, the new café set in its restored landscape was completed in 2009 to the designs of Caruso St John.

Houses c1730 **T7**
Chiswick Mall W4
⊖ Stamford Brook

A short walk from **Chiswick House** T6, the Mall, despite much development, preserves the waterfront of a Georgian village, the street separating the houses from their front gardens on the unembanked river. The best eighteenth-century buildings are Walpole House, Strawberry House and Morton House.

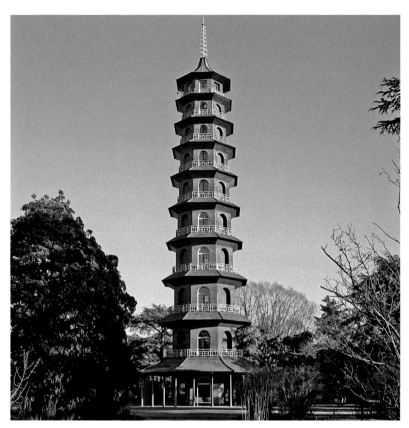

Pagoda and **Orangery** 1761 **T8**
Royal Botanical Gardens, Kew TW9
William Chambers
⊖ Kew Gardens

One of London's great eccentric and eclectic structures, the Pagoda is a vivid reminder that there were other influences at work in the period besides Palladianism. Standing in the south-west corner of **Kew Gardens** T4, at the end of Pagoda Vista, the ten-storey structure of stock brick rises to a height of 50m (163ft). Unfortunately, the eighty enamelled dragons which were originally positioned at the corners of its Chippendale balustrades have been removed. Although Chambers is remembered principally as a classical architect, he travelled extensively in China, and as a result of this interest in the exotic he also built a Chinese Temple (1760), a Turkish mosque (1761), and a Moorish Alhambra at Kew. None of these structures remain today.

The Orangery was for a long time England's largest hothouse. It has seven bays, rusticated walls and arched openings.

Syon House 1761–8 **T9**
London Road, Brentford TW8
Robert Adam
⇌ Brentford Central

The house, built in the fifteenth century as a convent, was altered to its present form – 30m (100ft) square with corner towers – in the mid-sixteenth century. In 1761, at the same time as he started work at Osterley, Adam was commissioned by Hugh Smithson, first Duke of Northumberland, to remodel the state rooms of Syon 'entirely in the Antique style'. Adam proposed a huge dome filling the central courtyard of the existing house. The rotunda was not built, but the perimeter rooms are his grandest in London: the ceilings are higher than those of Osterley, and the sequence more extensive than at Kenwood. Adam here combines classical plan forms with a range of very different decorative schemes. The white entrance hall, apsed at the north end, screened at the south, has the authentic chilly grandeur of English neoclassicism at its best. Nevertheless it is quite small: 11×9×6m (36×30×21ft). The steps behind the screen lead to the anteroom, green and gold, with projecting green marble columns. Some of these are recycled from Rome, and all carry a piece of projecting entablature and a gilded statue, a motif used here for the first time in England. The well-preserved scagliola-work floor is part of the original decoration. The decoration of the dining room is less integrated – only the ceiling unites the two apsed and

screened ends. The drawing room separates the dining room (for men) from the gallery (for women). Its walls are covered in red Spitalfields silk, and the ceiling and fine Adam-designed carpet compensate for their sparseness. The door-cases exhibit another of Adam's decorative sources: Italy. Adam inherited the long, thin shape of the gallery from the Jacobean house. The bays are divided and subdivided with low-relief pilasters, and the intervening spaces are covered with arabesque plasterwork of extreme delicacy.

The screen and lodges to London Road, by which the grounds are entered, were built in 1773. The screen is of insubstantial delicacy and transparency, the heaviest element being the Northumberland lion over the gate. The grounds were laid out by Capability Brown, who gave the house its present view down the Thames. See also **Osterley** T10 and **Kenwood** R7.

Osterley Park 1763–7 **T10**
Isleworth TW7
Robert Adam
⊖ Osterley

Adam's three greatest works extant in London – Osterley, **Syon** T9 and **Kenwood** R7 – are remodellings of existing houses; all belong to the early years of his practice and were started in the 1760s. Of the original house built at Osterley by Thomas Gresham, a successful Elizabethan businessman, only the corner towers remain. In 1711 it was bought by Francis Child, goldsmith and banker, whose grandson commissioned Adam to restyle it.

Adam's first work was the grand Ionic double portico across one face of the original courtyard, raising its level to that of the main rooms on the first floor. Then, in the 1770s, he began to decorate and furnish seven of the nine rooms on the ground floor. The entrance hall is double-apsed, white and boldly decorated. The segmental arches show Adam's use of archaeologically correct Roman motifs and his departure from Palladianism. The library ceiling is flat, not coffered, and decorated in Roman low relief. The bookcases are exquisite. The drawing room completes the rooms finished in 1773; the walls are plain, but the ceiling, the design derived from Palmyra, is one of Adam's most successful experiments with colour – gold, pink and green. The decoration here is thinner, but the furniture is still sumptuous and elegant. The Etruscan room is the only one remaining of the four Adam designed in London; the painted decoration and matching furniture are freely derived from Greek pottery, which was wrongly thought by both Adam and his contemporary Wedgwood to be Etruscan. The remaining rooms are not by Adam: the breakfast room was completed before Adam started, the gallery may have been restyled by Chambers, and in the attractive grounds, the lakes and stables (now tea-rooms) belong to the original house. The conservatory and the derelict Roman bridge (stranded on the north side of the M4) are by Adam. The house is owned by the National Trust.

Detail of the portico ceiling

Pitshanger Manor 1801–3 **T11**
Ealing Green W5
John Soane: restoration by
John Wibberly and Ian Bristow 1986
⊖ Ealing Broadway

Soane rebuilt this house for himself, leaving only the south wing of the earlier house by his teacher George Dance the Younger. Although it is small, the front is particularly grand. Soane used the triumphal arch motif of Ionic columns, set forward from the façade and surmounted by statues. Robert Adam had reintroduced this usage at Kedleston Hall in Derbyshire, and in the south-east anteroom at **Syon** T9. The back of the house is quite different. Horizontal bands of alternate brick and stucco and vertical ashlar strips divide the façade into nine parts, each containing a window.

Soane sold the house in 1811 when he moved to Lincoln's Inn Fields. Following a succession of owners the house was bought by the council in 1900 and used as a public library. In 1980 the library moved out and some of the building's long-neglected interiors were restored. These include Soane's magnificent library and breakfast room. The dark-red porphyry and grey marbling in the breakfast room are particularly dramatic.

St Peter's Church

St Peter's Square

St Peter's Square and **Black Lion Lane** 1825–30 **T12**
W6
⊖ Stamford Brook

St Peter's Square is the very successful result of a uniform plan by an anonymous designer. Although not formally complete and dilapidated in places, it is particularly fine. The three-storey houses on the east and west sides give the impression of large semi-detached villas, while actually forming unusual groupings of three houses. The villas are connected by single-storey walls, giving access to garages or garden studios behind, which have large scrolls at the centre; eagles and sleeping lions adorn the doors, and the gateposts are topped by pineapples. The houses, which are faced with sandy stucco and have white-painted doors, window frames and central balconies, act as a background to this exuberant decoration. On the north side of the square are two-storey variations on the same theme. The result is pleasant and relaxed, conveying, as Pevsner observed, 'the flavour of a suburban Belgravia'. Hammersmith's oldest and most elegant church, the church of **St Peter** (1827–9), by Edward Lapidge, closes the view to the east. Its attached Ionic portico and the octagonal west tower are reminiscent of Soane, and can be seen in deep perspective from the square. The interior is very simple, with the gallery on three sides carried by Tuscan columns, and columns and pews painted in Pompeian red.

The Anglican Chapel

Kensal Green Cemetery opened 1833 **T13**
Harrow Road W10
⊖ Kensal Green

This hygienic, out-of-town cemetery is, like the museum, the railway station and the zoo, among the building types invented in Europe in the early nineteenth century and built for the first time in London in the 1830s and '40s. Kensal Green was the largest of the new suburban cemeteries, laid out by private companies to provide better conditions than those available in central London's scandalously crowded graveyards.

Unlike its contemporaries, Kensal Green has been continuously and well maintained. Its architectural fittings are in the correct taste of the time, although (unlike **Highgate** R9) not particularly funereal; the entrance screen to the road is in Doric, the Anglican chapel is in Greek Doric and the Nonconformist in Ionic. There are fine tombs of the 1830s in classical and Egyptian styles. Architectural burials include Robert Smirke and the Brunels, father and son. See also **Nunhead** X7 and **Brompton** M1 cemeteries.

Aroid House 1836 **T14**
Royal Botanic Gardens, Kew TW9
John Nash
⊖ Kew Gardens
Originally designed as one of the two garden pavilions for Buckingham Palace, the Aroid House was moved to **Kew Gardens** T4 in 1836, its twin remaining at the Palace. The building has six Ionic columns *in antis* and pediments, and was subsequently glazed in order to house plants from the tropical rainforests.

Palm House 1844–8 **T15**
Royal Botanic Gardens, Kew TW9
Decimus Burton, Richard Turner
⊖ Kew Gardens
The finest existing glass and iron structure in England, Burton and Turner's sensuously curved giant conservatory predated Paxton's Crystal Palace by three years. The fine, slender cast-iron work, the complex intersecting geometries, and the sheer size of the glass envelope establish the Palm House as a truly innovative building. All the known species of palm can be viewed from delicate cast-iron galleries, which in turn are decorated with cast-iron insignia of palm leaves, painted white. The combination of delicate structures, both living and man-made, their white and green tracery filling the warm damp spaces, is magical.

Although the building was restored in the 1950s, by the late 1970s it was apparent that despite regular maintenance the high temperatures and humidity had severely degraded the original cast-iron structure. In 1985 the entire building was dismantled down to the main frames, and stainless steel components substituted for those beyond repair. The 5500 components and 16,000 panes of glass were reassembled in 1988.

The Irish engineer Richard Turner was also responsible for the particularly fine botanical glasshouses in both Dublin and Belfast. See also Burton and Turner's **Temperate House** T4 (1862–98).

Temperate House Lodge 1866–7 **T16**
Royal Botanic Gardens, Kew TW9
William Eden Nesfield
⊖ Kew Gardens

This sophisticated small building was as influential in its way as Burton's more famous Palm House. Designed by R Norman Shaw's partner, it is said to be one of the first buildings in the Queen Anne style. The central chimney, coved cornice and roof are exaggerated in their proportions, suggesting a top to a much larger building. The detailing of the windows is particularly fine. Nesfield was in partnership with Shaw from 1866–9 only, and there are no buildings in their joint names. Unfortunately the talented Nesfield died prematurely.

Houses 24–34 Woodstock Road

St Michael & All Angels

Bedford Park started 1875 **T17**
W4
R Norman Shaw, Maurice B Adams,
E W Godwin, E J May and others
⊖ Turnham Green

Only five years after it was started, Bedford Park, the suburb which set the pattern for English low-density development for the following century, had gained a reputation as a colony of the artistic, bohemian and progressive middle classes. The free Queen Anne style of the earliest houses, built from prototypes by Godwin, became identified with bohemianism. This does not seem to have been the intention of Jonathan T Carr, the young developer of the 46 hectare (113 acre) estate, who merely undertook a routine speculation.

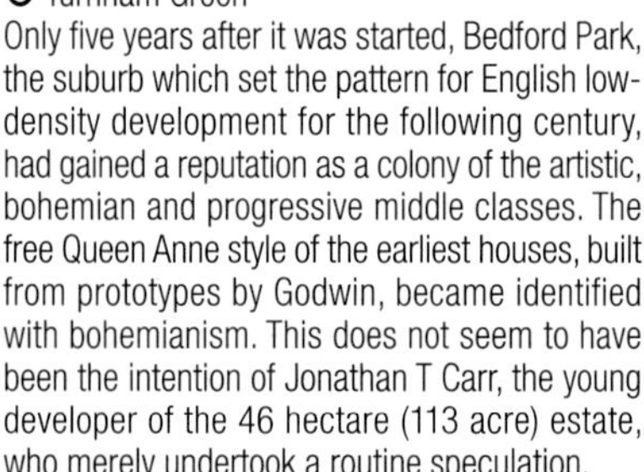

The layout is pleasant if unremarkable, consisting of curved streets with T-junctions, aligned to preserve the existing trees. It is this very vagueness, like that of the earlier and equally influential **Ladbroke Estate** I7, which made it so easy to copy. While Godwin provided the first models, however, it was Shaw's work which set the style in the houses listed below. His group of non-domestic buildings from 1880 (St Michael and All Angels, Tabard Inn and Bank) shows him at his most picturesque, the church exhibiting an extraordinary mixture of late English Gothic, Dutch and Georgian features. Houses by Shaw are: 24–34 Woodstock Road; 5–7 Blenheim Road; 6 Bedford Road; 19–22 The Avenue; 3–5 Queen Anne's Gardens. See also Voysey's **houses** T19, T20.

St Michael,the nave

Rupert Road

Hammersmith Bridge 1884–7 **T18**

W6 and SW13

Joseph Bazalgette

⊖ Hammersmith

A suspension toll bridge built at this crossing in 1825 was replaced by the current one designed by Joseph Bazalgette and opened in 1887. Its piers use the earlier foundations but the original masonry chain supports were replaced by a clumsy, bifurcated design in iron. The bridge proved unable to sustain the loads of modern traffic and attack by bombs and frequently had to be closed for repairs and for restoration, most recently in 2000, after which it was repainted in its original green and gold colours.

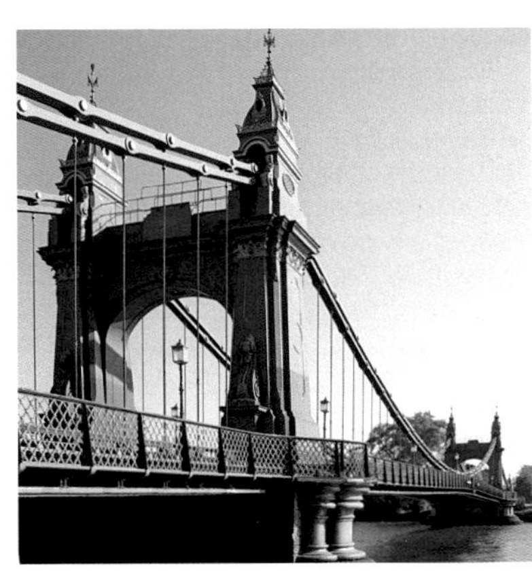

Studio house 1889–94 **T19**

14 South Parade W4

C F A Voysey

⊖ Turnham Green

One of London's outstanding Arts and Crafts houses, Studio House is an early work and, unusually for Voysey, a tall one. Set in Shaw's suburban cosiness, its style – white roughcast and stone trim with banded windows – looks chaste and brittle.

Studio house 1891 **T20**
17 St Dunstan's Road W6
C F A Voysey
⊖ Barons Court

Set back from the corner of St Dunstan's Road behind its Arts and Crafts iron railings, this house is deceptively small. The low, horizontal forms of the projecting eaves and the asymmetrically composed chimney, doors and windows are unmistakable signs of its architect.

See also 14 South Parade, **Bedford Park** T17 and **Annesley Lodge** A13.

Voysey House **T21**
ex **Sandersons wallpaper factory**
1902–3
Barley Mow Passage W4
C F A Voysey
⊖ Chiswick Park

One of Voysey's few non-domestic buildings, this was originally built for Sandersons, for whom he had designed wallpapers. The unashamed 'factory' language of the outside – big bays, large windows, white and blue glazed brick – is moderated delightfully by the soft but assured curves of the segmental arches over the windows, and the irregularly drooping high parapet.

Factory 1929–32 T22
Carillion ex **Pyrene** 1930
Wallis Gilbert and Partners
Great West Road between
Syon Lane and Boston Manor Road W6
⊖ Osterley

This section of the Great West Road, with its dual carriageways lined with buildings, is a fragment of a triumphal entrance to London which was superseded by the M4 motorway. Taken as a whole, the factories are a unique aspect of twentieth-century industrial archaeology: a series of buildings dedicated to the new industries, eclipsed by subsequent economic events.

Following the criminal destruction in 1980 of Wallis Gilbert's listed and magnificent Firestone building, the future of the other factories was uneasy. (Ironically Wallis is recorded as saying that when his factories had outlived their usefulness they should indeed be demolished!) The **Pyrene** building opposite has a fine moated entrance and characteristic rounded corner windows, and the **Curry factory** T28 next door has a sensuously streamlined entrance.

Royal Masonic Hospital 1930–4 T23
Ravenscourt Park W6
John Burnet, Tait and Lorne
⊖ Stamford Brook

The Royal Masonic Hospital marks the retirement both of John Burnet and of his variety of scraped classicism from this famous London practice. The large hospital is laid out symmetrically, and pays homage to the brick style of the Dutch architect Dudok, in the handling of large masses and the raked-out brick detailing, and also to Eric Mendelsohn in the adoption of large curved corner balconies. The firm's extensive and consistent output during the 1930s, of which the hospital at Ravenscourt Park is the best and most ambitious example, was to derive much inspiration from these two continental influences.

Northfields

Osterley

Piccadilly Line Underground Stations T24
1930–3
Acton Town, Ealing Common, Park Royal, Alperton, Sudbury Town and Sudbury Hill
Charles Holden; Northfields and Osterley, Charles Holden with S A Heaps

During the expansion of London's suburbs in the 1930s, encouraged by the extension of the Underground, the station was often the first building of the new suburb's nucleus, standing apart from the existing village (if there was one) and incorporating its own small parade of shops. It was the symbol of the suburb dweller's connection with the metropolis, and the architects used elemental modern and classical languages. The booking hall was usually identified by the single large volume, and sometimes there was a vertical marker as well, like the very tall decorated towers at Osterley and Park Royal (Day, Welch and Lander, 1935–6). The stripped classicism of the style, though sometimes brutal, has worn well and subsequent work for London Transport has not bettered it. See also Arnos Grove and **Southgate** R24.

Hoover Building 1932–5 **T25**
Western Avenue W5
Wallis Gilbert and Partners
⊖ Perivale
The Hoover Factory is a *tour de force* expressing the 1930s preoccupation with representing the factory as a palace. Unlike many of the other *moderne* factories of the period, the Hoover building is not just a façade but a serious attempt to dignify the workplace. The canteen block to the west, with its high, well-lit rooms and richly designed entrance, was exceptional for England at the time – reminiscent of Brinkman and van der Vlugt's Van Nelle Factory in Rotterdam (1927). The principal elevation to Western Avenue absorbs and digests a mixture of modernist influences – the corner windows to the towers at either end call to mind Eric Mendelsohn's famous Einstein Tower in Potsdam (1921), the decorative bands of red and blue tiles set into the white stuccoed surfaces are memories of Josef Hoffmann's Palais Stoclet in Brussels (1905), and the beautifully crafted iron gates compare with those of Mackintosh's Glasgow School of Art. Pevsner described the Hoover building as 'perhaps the most offensive of the modernistic atrocities along this road of typical bypass factories' – this is also a comment on the shift of taste over the years. In 1992 the building was converted into a supermarket and its façade restored.

Wembley Arena **T26**
ex **Empire Swimming Pool** 1934
Empire Way, Wembley HA9
Owen Williams
⊖ Wembley Park ⇌ Wembley Stadium
Despite Owen Williams's claims to pure objectivity, this building has a romantic and expressive view of structure. At the time of its completion it was the largest covered pool in the world. The daring cantilevered concrete roof spans 72m (236ft), and is counterweighted by monolithic concrete seating and massive external piers. The external appearance of these piers, seen in perspective, is truly monumental, and further evidence that Williams was not just solving problems.

Factory ex Gillette 1936 **T27**
Syon Lane W5
Banister Fletcher
⊖ Osterley
Designed by the author of *A History of Architecture on the Comparative Method* (mandatory reading for students of architecture fifty years ago), the green copper dome to the clock tower of the Gillette Factory acts as a landmark on the Great West Road. The three-storey red-brick façade (141m/562ft long) is less memorable: the fine detailing of the central clock tower, the expressive masonry and the entrance steps are not enough to hold the overall composition of Fletcher's principal London work together. See also **St Anne's Vestry Hall** L100.

Factory now **J C Decaux** c1936 **T28**
Great West Road between
Syon Lane and Boston Manor Road W6
⊖ Osterley
The palatial offices of the former Curry building act as a representational front of the business. The warehouse behind (Foster and Partners 2000) is an extremely elegant replacement of the original factory and provided a glazed 'street' to display the advertising company's products, separating it from the 1930s building facing the Great West Road. See also nearby to the west the former **Pyrene factory** T22.

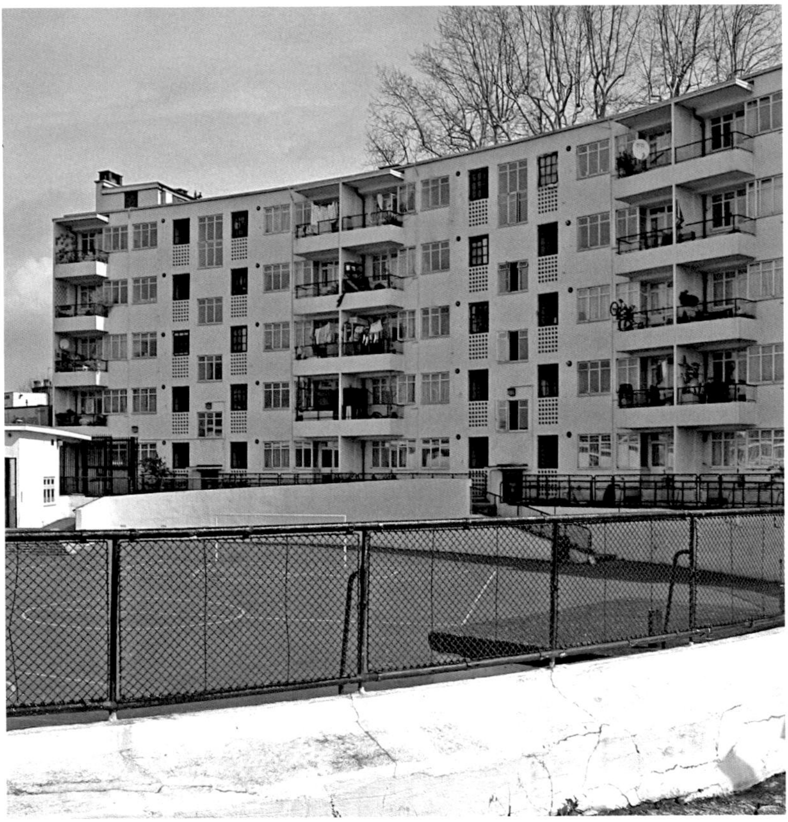

Kensal House 1936 **T29**
Ladbroke Grove W10
Robert Atkinson, Maxwell Fry,
C H James, Grey Wornum;
housing consultant Elizabeth Derby
⊖ Kensal Green
The best example of pre-war workers' housing in London, Kensal House was sponsored by the Gas, Light and Coke Company, owner of this unpromising site next to the railway with its derelict gasholder. It closely followed continental examples (such as May's Frankfurt and the Siemensstadt at Berlin) in both method and form. The method involved research into the ergonomic requirements of the minimum and efficient 'work unit' – the kitchen and bathroom – and the integration of gas-fired hot water and heating. The form is that of parallel blocks: there are two of six storeys running north–south to allow sunlight to reach both sides of the flats, one straight and the other curved with a returned north end. The curve of the western block derives from the circle of the gasholder on whose site stands the nursery school, much photographed for modern architectural histories. With its well-maintained concrete and its assured, repetitive and un-fussy elevations, the scheme still looks good.

Dollis Hill Synagogue 1937 **T30**
Parkside and Clifford Way NW2
Owen Williams
⊖ Neasden
Owen Williams, the architect of twentieth-century building types like newspaper offices (L118), health centres (X10) and covered stadia (T26), had here to reconcile his 'new objectivity' with the archaic programme of the Jewish faith. The hexagonal windows of Dollis Hill recall the apertures in castellated beams (in particular the Findhorn Bridge in Perth, 1926), while the roof was an early example of the use of pre-stressed concrete.

Heinz Research and **Administration Centre** 1965 **T31**
Hayes End Road, Hayes Park, Middlesex UB4
Skidmore, Owings and Merrill with Matthew Ryan and Partners
⊖ Uxbridge and bus or ⇌ Hayes and Harlington
The industrial headquarters building formed in the image of a contemporary palace in its own park was, by 1965, a tradition of the famous American practice of Skidmore, Owings and Merrill – see the Connecticut General Life Insurance Company, Hartford, Connecticut (1954–7) and Reynolds Metal Company, Richmond, Virginia (1955–8). The Heinz building at Hayes was England's first taste of this 'well-made' American tradition but when built, the three buildings, with their slightly tapering white concrete frames, were a slight disappointment. However, the extreme professionalism of their construction was undeniable, and they have worn well.

Highgrove Housing 1972–7 **T32**
Eastcote Road, Ruislip HA4
Edward Cullinan
⊖ Ruislip Manor
The 113 houses built for the London Borough of Hillingdon, set in a sloping meadow in the suburb of Ruislip, were in the line of development which began with the architect's own house in **Camden Mews** C11 in the early 1960s, and continued with research at Cambridge in suburban forms and models in the mid-1960s. The back-to-back semi-detached houses at Highgrove have 9m (30ft) frontages to allow kitchen, dining and living rooms to be side by side, divided or open-plan, but all opening – suburban-style – onto their own gardens.

The houses are in groups of four (not unlike Frank Lloyd Wright's Broadacre City proposals) and the site is organized particularly around a network of paths at right angles to each other. The resulting 'molecular' structure of the site planning was reminiscent of work in Holland by Herman Hertzberger – characterized by planning ideas that were relatively exclusive to the project, making physical external connections (to ordinary city streets, avenues and so on) more or less difficult. The original bright-blue plastic-coated corrugated-steel roofs, which with the regular timber windows gave the buildings their distinctive appearance, were later unsympathetically replaced.

Houses and **flats** T33
for Kensington Housing Trust 1975–80
103–23 St Mark's Road W10
Jeremy Dixon
⊖ Ladbroke Grove

This terrace of forty-four flats and houses set out with the intention of fundamentally reinterpreting the tradition of the London house – the principal relationship to the street, arrangement of front façades and back gardens, and so on. The scheme resembles a terrace of large houses, each subdivided into a pair of narrow-fronted houses above a ground-floor flat. The gabled façades absorb a number of influences: Queen Anne eclecticism, the English Free Style of Norman Shaw, and the ubiquitous speculative builders' architecture of the turn of the century. In opposition to the object fixation of much new housing, this project was admired for its near invisibility.

Civic Offices for London Borough of Hillingdon 1977 T34
High Street, Uxbridge UB8
Robert Matthew, Johnson Marshall and Partners
⊖ Uxbridge

That the imagery of a Scandinavian hospital should be applied to a large bureaucratic institution (with its open-plan offices) is a sad comment on the times and evidence of an architectural loss of nerve. The adoption of 'friendly' forms was intended to make unwieldy local government less inaccessible.

Architecturally the opposite proves to be the case, for in a secular age civic centres are among the last institutions that can legitimately be distinguished from housing or commercial building. But the building was a relief from the banal office blocks normally associated with local authorities and which surround this one.

Offices, **flats** and **restaurant** T35
1984–7 Thames Wharf, Rainville Road W6
Richard Rogers Partnership
⊖ Hammersmith

A utopian development next to the river (see Foster Associates' Hester Road offices N36) provides offices for the architects to the south of the site in a converted factory with a new barrel-vaulted steel roof, and the fine River Café, both overlooking a courtyard open to the Thames. At 1–25 Thames Reach are three new blocks of flats, their planning a textbook example of the compositional methods of the 1960s, in which the individual elements are identified and then arranged to make a picturesque assemblage. Only the elaborately wrought steel balconies between the blocks provide a clue to their authorship.

Offices by Ian Ritchie

6 Furzeground Way

Stockley Park started 1985 **T36**
Stockley Road, Hillingdon UB11
Master planners Arup Associates; Architects Arup Associates, Foster Associates, Ian Ritchie Architects, Troughton McAslan, Richard Rogers Partnership, Peter Foggo Architects, Eric Parry Associates, Lifzchutz Davidson and others
⊖ Uxbridge ⇌ West Drayton

It was only a matter of time before the North American business park made a significant appearance in London's outer boroughs. Stockley Park was the most ambitious of its type. Built on former gravel pits and rubbish tips, it has highly convenient transport connections. Of its 150 hectares (350 acres), 100 are dedicated to parkland, lakes, playing fields and a golf course, part of a joint venture for the reclamation of land for a major public park, between the developer and the local authority. The remaining 36 hectares (90 acres) are planned for a commercial development devoted to the high technology business community. The Park provided seven building zones for new office and workshop buildings, with an eighth for the central amenities building. The new buildings were restricted to three storeys and provided 140,000 square metres (1,500 million square feet) gross floor area.

Arup Associates, Troughton McAslan and Foster Associates designed the first office buildings. Arup were also responsible for the central amenities building. Two other buildings are memorable, the first being 8400 square metres (90,000 square feet) of offices by Ian Ritchie. The double-glazed external wall advances the Pilkington 'planar glazing' system, with its use of clear, toughened, and in some cases low-energy-coated glass. The result is a building form of remarkable abstract purity. In contrast to the rather timid use of solar shades elsewhere at Stockley Park, here the building is animated by a monumental three-storey steel frame supporting large curved and perforated stainless-steel shades on the south-east and west façades. The second building of note is by Eric Parry Associates at 6 Furzeground Way. While earlier buildings were conceived in the spirit of abstract installations, Parry's building was the first to engage the possibilities of the site and to acknowledge the reciprocal relationship between architecture and landscape, and, while the earlier buildings eschewed hierarchy and representation, his was deliberately figurative. The exterior *piano nobile* wall is formed of panels of glass block and clear glass placed in a standard 'stick' system. These two buildings demonstrated clear alternative architectural directions for Stockley Park, which nevertheless did not compromise its overall unity.

Over the twenty years since its beginnings, Stockley Park's landscape has matured, the buildings are now hardly visible behind dense hedgerows and groves of trees, and there is much evidence of wildlife. The most recent addition of note into this arcadia is by Arup Associates of a four-storey triple-glazed circular pavilion that breaks with the two-storey convention of earlier buildings.

Offices 'The Ark' 1988–91 **T37**
Ralph Erskine,
Rock Townsend, executive architects
Talgarth Road W6
⊖ Hammersmith

Erskine's first building in London recalls the sheltering of his Byker Wall housing in Newcastle (1969–80) and, more distantly, that of his 'Arctic City' project of the 1950s. It stands as one of the series of monuments on the road between London and Heathrow, on a site lassooed by railway lines and the elevated road. The idiosyncratic design of the building attempts to provide a form appropriate to the scale of the super-highway. Eight floors of offices, their shape reminiscent of a helmet or shield, are set against the road to defend the atrium to the south.

Hindu Temple and **Meeting Hall** T38
(BAPS Shri Swaminarayan Mandir and Haveli)
1990–5
Brentfield Road, Neasden NW10
C B Sompura
⊖ Neasden, ⇌ Stonebridge Park

In London, Christian Europe's chief denominations were traditionally represented in Westminster; other religions are elsewhere – the Buddhists in Bethnal Green and Islam in Regent's Park (F56), for example. The unlikely location of Neasden for a Hindu temple is explained by its being one of the sub-centres of immigration from the Indian sub-continent. The complex has two parts: the 'haveli' or assembly hall, and offices, and the 'mandir', the temple. The latter, made of Carrara marble and Bulgarian limestone, was prefabricated and carved in India and then constructed on site by volunteers. Neasden's gain of this exotic translation is Westminster's loss.

Chiswick Business Park 2003– T39
566 Chiswick Park Road W4
Richard Rogers Partnership
⊖ Gunnersbury

Stuart Lipton was the *éminence grise* behind **Stockley Park** T36; this is the next chapter in his story of the business park. At Chiswick it is denser, less dependent on the motor car, and a single practice, the Rogers Partnership, was commissioned with a single building idea: elegant rectangular four- and five-storey pavilions. They have emphasized porticos (reminiscent of that by Ian Ritchie at Stockley Park) which also provide solar protection to the offices behind. The plan with its central core and generous floor-to-floor heights provide an idealized working environment. What could have been a 44-storey tower (possibly the genesis of the plan) has been distributed in eleven pavilions around an artificial lake at the centre of the site, an access road and car-parking confined to the perimeter.

Housing 2007 **T40**
Westway Beacons, Banstead Court
Acton W3
Gardner Stewart
⊖ East Acton

The transformation of lightly trafficked arterial roads into six-lane semi-urban motorways represented a gradual increase in the use of the motor car over the last half of the twentieth century. This is nowhere more explicit than where the original semi-detached houses of the 1930s, that once overlooked these roads, should still retain independent access to them. The result is verging on the surreal. A proposed solution was found on the south side of the A40 where Westway turns into Western Avenue. Here, a series of five large semi-detached apartment buildings in series are joined together by generous three-storey translucent glazed entrance halls or winter-gardens, either side of which are mostly blank brick walls; the habitable rooms look south and away from the road. An overall impression is that here is an appropriate scale to be seen from cars travelling at 50mph. One would not be surprised if the provenance of these heroic 'motorway' buildings was the Stirling office of the early 1970s, just following Leon Krier's arrival in London.

Departures

Arrivals

Heathrow Terminal 5 2008 **T41**
Heathrow Airport
Rogers Stirk Harbour and Partners
Paddington Express
⊖ Heathrow

Despite the continued discussion about it being in the wrong place, Heathrow continues to expand. When seen in plan it appears to be thoroughly medieval and representing something of the British character – that is, not entirely logical and making a virtue of necessity. With each successive development and with an increasing scarcity of land, the buildings get larger and taller, culminating in the competition-winning Terminal 5 design of 1989. In plan it is 177×420m (580×1380ft) and seven storeys high. The 45m (147ft) high section is therefore the key to an understanding of the building. Departure is on the top, with arrival at the bottom, the space between devoted to baggage handling, security and shopping. On arrival, bridges from the terminus connect passengers to a five-storey perimeter void in which escalators give direction to the double-height baggage reclaim areas above. This sequence is beautifully and skilfully detailed, reminding one that this practice has been in the business of the well-made for over 40 years. The use of white lacquered backed glass for most of the internal wall surfaces helpfully frustrates the ad hoc application of signs typical of old Heathrow, giving a sense of calm to arriving passengers. The use of circular lighting plates, leaving the ceiling void just visible behind, gives an unpretentiousness to the whole. Terminal 5 goes some way to redress the impression of arrival in a Third World country that had previously characterized Heathrow.

Note the **Stirling Hilton Hotel** by Manser Associates of 1990, by far the best hotel at Heathrow. The built diagram of bedrooms forming a wall on both sides of a large five-storey atrium, glazed at either end, remains impressive. Comparisons have been made with Norman Foster's Sainsbury Centre at the University of East Anglia.

Wembley Stadium 2008 T42
Stadium Way, Wembley HA9
HOK Sport Architecture and Foster and Partners
⊖ Wembley Park ⇌ Wembley Stadium

The momentum of modern times seems to mean that things get inevitably bigger and stadia are no exception. Gone are the Lutyens-esque twin domes of Simpson's original stadium of 1924, replaced after a protracted genesis by the new Wembley. If the stadium is undeniably a dramatic feat of engineering, firstly for its 90,000 capacity in a great three-tiered bowl under a retractable roof, and secondly for its 133m (436ft) high arch as a new landmark visible to incoming flights into Heathrow, it is less convincing as a piece of urban architecture. As with other major sporting venues at Twickenham and Wimbledon, there is an inevitable discontinuity between the idea of a 'coliseum' and the indifferent sea of semi-detached houses in which it finds itself. This is not helped by an absence of foreground and an equally absent-minded perimeter enclosure to the stadium itself. The masterplan proposes a denser urban setting, which it is hoped will go some way to offset these shortcomings.

Northala Fields 2008 T43
Western Avenue between
Kensington Road and Church Road
Northolt UB5
FoRM Associates
⊖ Northolt

As Western Avenue (the A40) makes its way out to the M40, with the arch of the new Wembley Stadium just visible on the northern horizon, to the south four unexpectedly large mounds or tumuli come into view. These suggest the presence of an ancient burial ground that had somehow been overlooked. The mounds are in fact part of Ealing Council's Northolt and Greenford countryside park of 18.5 hectares (45 acres), and protect the rest of the park from traffic noise. The spiral path ascending the tallest is lined by low retaining walls made of gabions (wire baskets) filled with pieces of concrete, providing a robust and characterful detail in contrast to the smooth grass slopes. The gabion theme is extended to all the park's equipment: bollards, benches and even the litter bins. On the flat area to the south, new lakes provide habitats for wildlife and London's first purpose-designed fishing ponds.

From the summits of the mounds, over the uniform sea of two-storey houses set in surprisingly dense trees, greater London can be viewed for the first time from this otherwise flat terrain. Planes can be seen repetitively landing at and taking off from Heathrow; the towers of the City of London are clearly visible against the backdrop of the Surrey hills, as is the arch of the new **Wembley Stadium** T42 to the north. It is from the demolition of the old Wembley that the concrete came to fill the gabions, making Northala Fields a commemorative place after all, and a splendid new London park.

Outer London, east

The historical significance of this part of London is military and industrial: it forms a time corridor which has expanded from west to east along the Thames over 2000 years. The Roman city of London is the western end of this axis, which continues through William the Conqueror's Tower (protecting the city from invasion by sea) to Henry VIII's naval yard at Deptford and the **Royal Naval College and Hospital** U3 at Greenwich, and finishes in the east with the eighteenth-century dockyards and military establishments at Woolwich (U16, U17).

Industrial complexes are often concentrated to the east of cities, and London is no exception: in the nineteenth century the East End became the city's principal dockland and manufacturing area, ('East End' and 'West End' derive from the eighteenth century when the areas actually marked the eastern and western limits of London). A boat trip from Westminster Pier to Greenwich shows the Thames as a former 'working' river, with the magnificent exception of Wren's set-piece design for the Greenwich Hospital.

The docks were planned on the north banks of the Thames (with the exception of the Surrey Docks at Rotherhithe), taking advantage of the marshy ground, the River Lea and the serpentine curves of the Thames. The first were built by the West India Company in 1789–1802, to be followed in 1805 by the East India Docks at the mouth of the River Lea. The East India Dock Road and Commercial Road were built, making connections with the City, and this basic infrastructure was then expanded over the following century. Impressive for their sheer size and the zeal of their Victorian engineers, the docks are best appreciated from the air (see Cameron and Cooke's *Above London*). During the 1960s the docks moved to Tilbury, continuing London's easterly expansion.

The vast area of land vacated by the docks was put under the control of a public Development Corporation which proved incapable of planning much beyond a rudimentary new infrastructure: the Light Railway, the new City Airport and some very expensive stretches of road. **Canary Wharf** U48, the largest single development, was built in two phases, beginning in 1990, with North American investment and mostly North American architects. Buildings across the river on the Greenwich peninsula included the **O2** (the former Millennium Dome) U50 by Richard Rogers and Partners and the Millennium Village to a masterplan by Ralph Erskine. Both projects experienced early setbacks but became working additions to the life of the city.

The medieval fishing villages of Rotherhithe, Deptford, Woolwich and Greenwich, to the south of the river, were relatively unchanged until they became caught up in nineteenth-century London's industrial sprawl. Further to the south and east the land rises in hills and bluffs to the plateau of Blackheath, where **Morden College** X2 and the elegant **Paragon** X5 testify to more gracious standards of living.

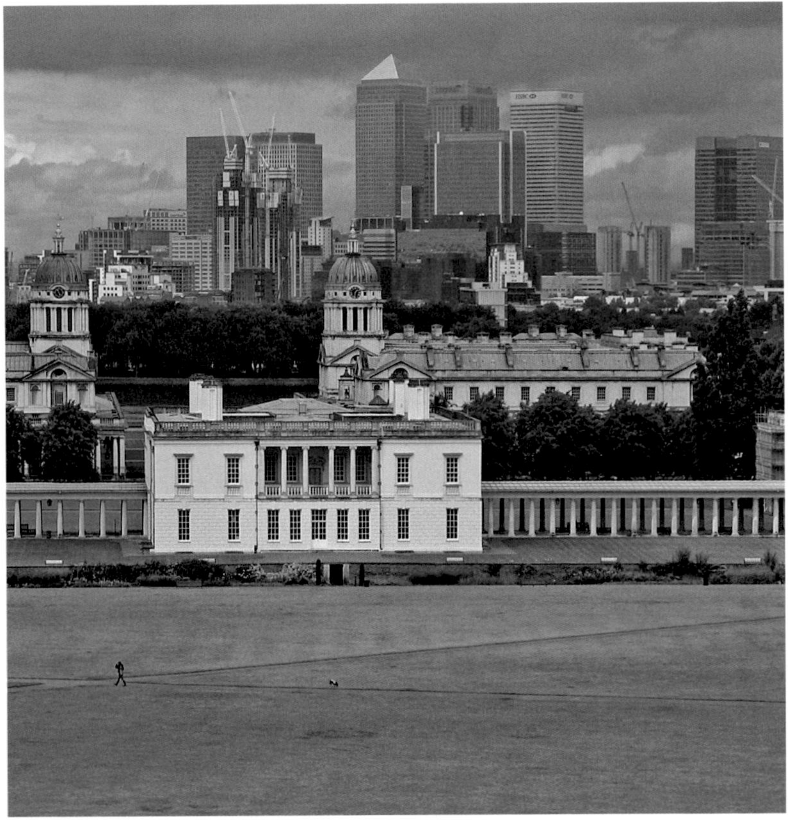

View north from Greenwich Hill; Queen's House U2 in foreground

Canary Wharf U48

North of the river

Hackney, Bethnal Green, Stepney and Poplar, to the north of the river, were villages in the Middle Ages, and the Isle of Dogs (the name deriving from the royal dogs, kennelled here out of the hearing of the royal palace at Greenwich) was pasture and marshland. Hackney has the most distinguished past, which today is hardly discernible. In 1750 the parish had twelve villages or hamlets, including Kingsland, Dalston, Hacklewell, Clapton and Homerton. By the mid-nineteenth century, these areas had lost their identity and were absorbed into the expanding East End of London. Bethnal Green, Stepney and Poplar went the same way, and by the end of the nineteenth century their names were associated with some of the worst slums and overcrowded conditions in the country. Their combined population in 1880 (working mostly in and around the docks) was over half a million – Stepney alone had a larger population than Bristol. The area's chief architectural interest now lies in its philanthropically endowed workers' housing. In 1842, in the reformist climate which brought amenities to the working population of the East End, Pennethorne laid out Victoria Park (87.8 hectares/217 acres). This was London's first Victorian park, and became the largest under the control of the GLC.

Further to the north, the coincidence of the open spaces of the Lea Valley, the high-speed rail connection and the extension to the Jubilee Line established the principal venue for the 2012 Olympic Games at Stratford East. Here, construction was under way in 2008 for an Olympic Village housing 3000 athletes, a new commercial centre and an Olympic Park providing sites for stadia by Hadid (aquatics), Hopkins (cycling), HOK Sport (athletics) among others.

Charlton House 1607–12 **U1**
The Village, Charlton SE7
⇄ Charlton
Following the destruction of **Holland House** I1 by bombing, Charlton remains the only complete Jacobean house in Greater London, and is a perfect example of the E-plan of the period. The hall is in the middle of the plan and is entered through the large-windowed porch on its long axis. To either side, in the wings, are the chapel and parlour, the kitchen and the pantry, with bay windows on the legs of the E.

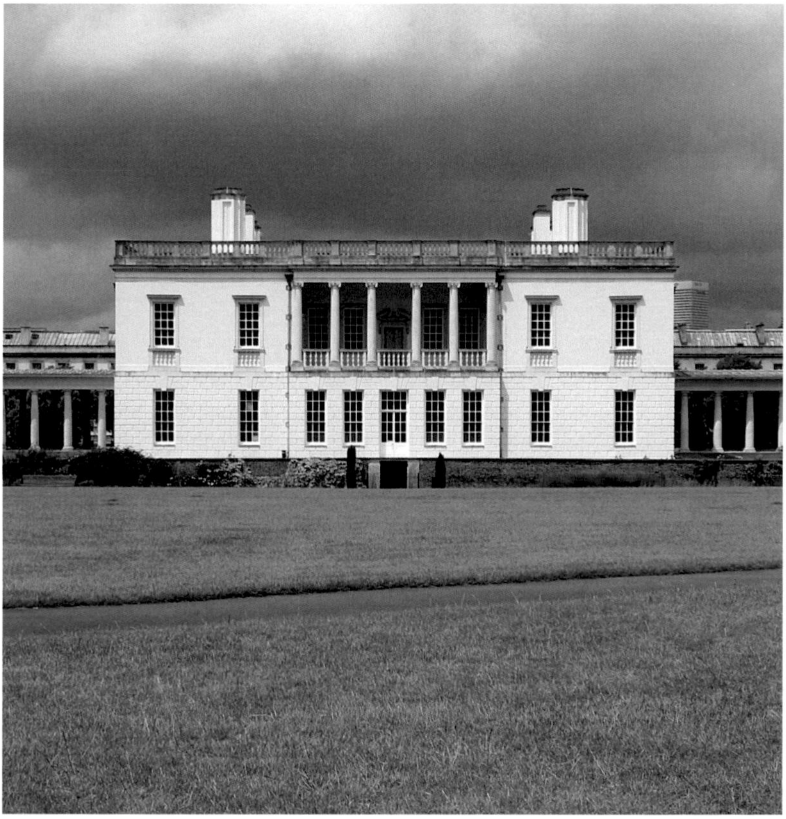

Queen's House 1616–35 **U2**
Greenwich Park SE10
Inigo Jones
⊖ ⇄ Greenwich, or boat from Westminster or Tower Bridge
England's first Palladian villa and Inigo Jones's earliest surviving work, the Queen's House has a long and complicated history. With its proximity to the naval dockyards, Greenwich was always favoured by royalty. In 1613, James I donated Greenwich Palace to his Queen, Anne of Denmark, who was dissatisfied with the large, rambling building. Accordingly Inigo Jones, the King's Surveyor, was instructed to build a more modern house on the site of the palace's southern gatehouse.

Jones's original plan consisted of two parallel ranges, either side of the Dover Road, connected by a bridge at first floor. As well as allowing access on the north side to Greenwich Palace, this would also give the queen unimpeded and dry-shod access to the park on the south. Anne of Denmark died in 1619, and the villa was left unfinished until Charles I decided to complete it for Henrietta Maria's occupation in 1637. Inigo Jones's son-in-law, John Webb, enlarged the house by adding further bridges along the east and west fronts, giving it the apparently square appearance we know today – actually it is 33×36m (110×120ft). Four years later Wren was instructed to prepare plans for a Naval Hospital on the site of Greenwich Palace. The Queen's House was eventually to form the rather modest focus of Wren's truly baroque and palatial design, the finest of its kind in England, best appreciated from the Isle of Dogs on the north of the river. The Queen's House remained the residence of the Governor of the Naval Hospital until in 1806 it was turned into a school for seamen's children. At the same time the Dover Road was moved to the north, where Romney Road now runs, and open colonnades were added in 1807–16 by David

Alexander. These connect the house on both sides to the much larger composition of the Hospital. In 1933 the school moved out of the building and four years later the Queen's House was opened to the public as the National Maritime Museum.

The architecture is remarkable for its restraint and for the absence of contemporary Elizabethan elements (bay windows, turrets and gables). Among its innovations are the strict Vitruvian proportions, rusticated base, south-facing loggia with unfluted Palladian Ionic columns, and the double open staircase with symmetrical curves leading up to the terrace on the north side. The sills to the ground-floor windows were lowered in 1770, destroying the primacy of the *piano nobile*.

The interior is as consistently Palladian as the exterior. The hall, 12m (40ft) square, unlike the traditional hall of the Elizabethan manor, is a grand vestibule with a fine marble floor. However, the gallery supported by brackets is a remnant of the Elizabethan minstrels' gallery, and Lord Burlington, despite his admiration for the house, observed that any room of this size required columns. The most impressive feature is the Tulip Staircase.

Royal Naval Hospital U3
1664, 1696–1702
Romney Road SE10
Christopher Wren, Nicholas Hawksmoor, John Vanbrugh, John Webb and others
⊖ ⇌ Greenwich

The country south-east of London was a favourite retreat for medieval royalty (see **Eltham Palace** X1), and in 1423 the Duke of Gloucester took over a Carthusian establishment at Greenwich. Later, Henry VII and Elizabeth I were born there, and Henry made the original manor into a palace. Inigo Jones built the **Queen's House** U2 for James I's queen, Anne of Denmark, and it was completed after her death by Jones's son-in-law, John Webb. No more building was done at Greenwich until after the Civil War, when Charles II determined to replace the old Tudor palace, using Webb as architect. Webb planned three buildings arranged to form an open courtyard facing the river. This was started in 1664, but only the building nearest the river on the west was completed. The river façade consisted of three bays with a central pediment – the extension eastward is a later addition. When William and Mary came to the throne in 1688 they decided to live at **Hampton Court** V1, where Wren's state rooms in the east wing were just being finished. Greenwich was to be turned into a hospital for sailors, on the pattern of the earlier one for soldiers at Chelsea (N2) but more magnificent; in 1695 Wren was appointed Surveyor-General for the Commission to build it.

His first plan was for a series of buildings on either side of Webb's axis. These would have formed progressively narrowing courtyards, with a large domed building on the axis between the river and Queen's House (a scheme not adopted at Greenwich but useful for Vanbrugh at Castle Howard and Blenheim). Wren's second plan was

The Painted Hall

the one we now see, continued for many years after his death: the completion of the first court by mirroring Webb's first building, and behind this, up a broad flight of steps, two U-shaped buildings facing each other across the axis. The northern legs of the Us contain on the east the chapel and on the west the hall, each marked with a dome at the corner. The spaces between the legs of the Us are closed with colonnades of paired columns (probably influenced by Perrault's Louvre); these form courtyards overlooked by the wards.

The hall is the grandest secular interior of the period in England – a baroque synthesis of Wren's spaces, Hawksmoor's architectural decoration, and the painting of Thornhill (who painted the interior of the dome of **St Paul's Cathedral** L28). The ceiling (1707–26) shows William and Mary surrounded by the four cardinal virtues, while, under Apollo, Architecture makes a rare painted appearance carrying a drawing of the hospital. The hall is connected by flights of stairs to two more painted spaces: the entrance vestibule under the dome and the tall room at the other end, which provides a ceremonial dais for the high table.

Wren's plan continued to be executed by his pupils – see Hawksmoor's extraordinary closing block to the westward courtyard behind the hall. Vanbrugh made plans reviving the idea of a central domed closure to the axis, but nothing came of them. In 1755 the hospital had over 1500 pensioners, and in 1769 Webb's original building was extended on the south side. In the 1780s the interior of the **chapel** U15 in the Queen Mary building was magnificently refitted by Stuart and Newton.

The hospital closed in 1998, and its buildings were partly converted for various educational purposes. Also to be noted is the **National Maritime Museum** (the former Royal Hospital School of 1780), transformed, and its open courtyard glazed, in 1999 by Rick Mather Architects and BDP.

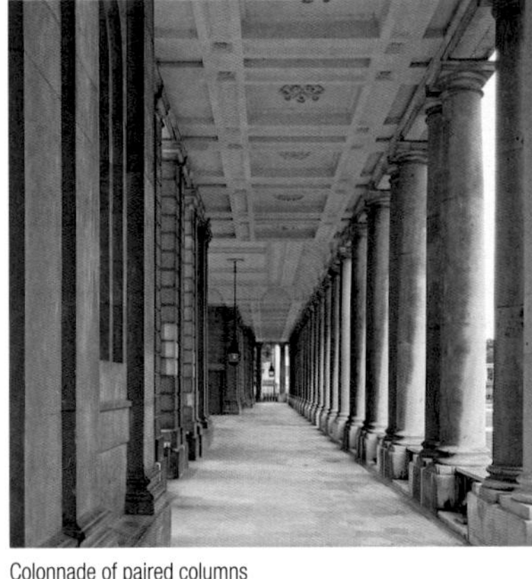

Colonnade of paired columns

Flamsteed House U4

Old Royal Observatory 1675–6

Greenwich Park SE10

Christopher Wren (?), Allies and Morrison

⊖ ⇌ Greenwich

The history of the Royal Observatory buildings is quite separate from that of the Naval Hospital U3, but both have their origins in royal patronage. The attribution of the modest observatory to Wren is speculative. It was built for use by the first Astronomer Royal, John Flamsteed (1646–1719), appointed in 1675, and housed in its square plan a tall, octagonal first-floor room with large windows for observations. Over the following two centuries the site was augmented with further utilitarian buildings which were used for astronomy until the Observatory moved to Herstmonceux Castle in Sussex in 1948. Since then the buildings have housed a museum on astronomy and time, most recently rearranged and augmented with a planetarium (Allies and Morrison 2007). The path of Meridian 0°, a visitor attraction, passes through the museum and is prominently marked in the pavement outside.

Almshouses Trinity Hospital U5

1695

Mile End Road E1

William Ogbourne (master builder), Christopher Wren, John Evelyn (?)

⊖ Whitechapel

Built by Trinity House for retired seamen or their widows, here is a fine example of seventeenth-century planning. Two rows of houses face each other across an avenue of trees, at the end of which is the chapel.

St Alfege 1712–18 **U6**
Greenwich High Road SE10
Nicholas Hawksmoor and John James
⊖ ⇌ Greenwich, or boat from Westminster Pier
Of the intended fifty new churches commissioned in 1711, this was both the Commissioners' and Hawksmoor's first. Developed from his earlier theoretical studies, it set the pattern for the later ones. To the biaxially central space are added auxiliary spaces: the richly decorated, segmentally arched chancel, small transepts, and the two large staircases. The identity of the nave is emphasized by an oval moulding occupying most of the flat ceiling. The interior was gutted in the Second World War, rebuilt and restored by Albert Richardson.

Outside, the portico is at the east end, facing the main road. Its Roman arch rises into the pediment and its Doric order continues all round the church. Set between the pilasters, smooth, unmoulded, round-headed windows contrast with the heavily keystoned square ones. The nearly free-standing tower at the west end was finished by John James in 1730. See also **St George-in-the-East** U9, **St Anne, Limehouse** U10, and **Christ Church, Spitalfields** H6.

St Paul 1712–30 **U7**
Deptford High Street SE8
Thomas Archer
⊖ New Cross ⇌ Deptford
Archer's churches for the Commissioners of 1711, St Paul and the more ebullient **St John, Smith Square** K35, are among the best examples of the importation of Roman baroque to early-eighteenth-century London. St Paul's plan is fluid and derived from Rome's Sant' Agnese, the flat-ceilinged space defined by a Corinthian order. The exterior is more stiff, but the arrangement of tower and steeple (an amalgam of Borromini and Wren) is a relatively early and successful experiment in relating tower to nave (compare with the later **St Martin-in-the-Fields** K40). The drum of the tower continues down to the ground as a vestibule, and is wrapped in a semicircular Doric colonnade. Just to the north is **St Nicholas**, Deptford Green, in the style of Wren and worth a short detour.

The Free School, detail

St Mary Rotherhithe 1714 **U8**
St Marychurch Street SE16
⊖ Rotherhithe
A reminder of a once-active shipbuilding village, St Mary Rotherhithe stands among trees in its own railed and gated yard. Across the street is the **Free School**, founded in 1613, a simple three-storey house with two charming painted sculptures of a boy and girl pupil on its first floor.

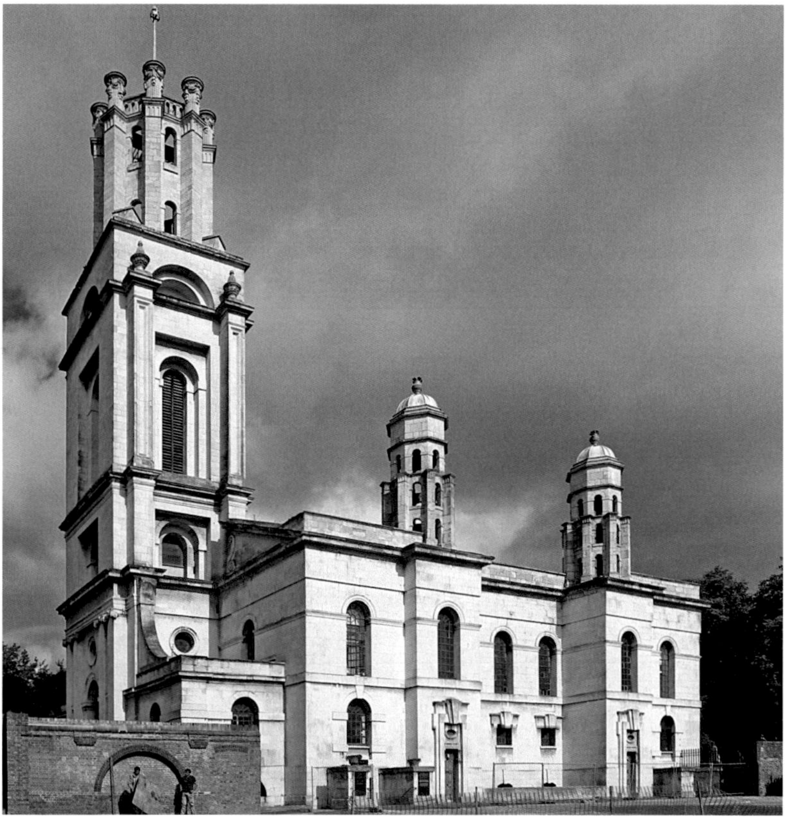

St George-in-the-East 1714–29 **U9**
Cannon Street Road E1
Nicholas Hawksmoor
⊖ Shadwell
Started in the same year as **St Anne** U10 and **Christ Church, Spitalfields** H6, St George's was bombed in 1941 and now houses a small new church designed by Arthur Bailey (1964). The plan has the two right-angled axes of the other churches. The cross-axis is marked with stair towers set towards the corners, not with projecting transepts as at **St Alfege** U6. These towers, together with the horizontal box of the nave and the wide main tower (now lacking its finial pepper pot), make one of the noblest compositions of English baroque. Decoration is restricted to the Corinthian order at the base of the tower, the open octagon with Roman altar finials at its top, and the famous keystoned doorways to the stair towers. The typical chalk-white and soot-black weathering of Portland stone is here shown particularly well. See also U6, U10 and H6.

St Anne 1714–30 **U10**
Commercial Road E14
Nicholas Hawksmoor
⊖ Westferry

The dominant feature of the interior is the ceiling's great flat circle, edged by a Corinthian entablature moulding, whose centre marks the junction of the two cross-axes. This and the Corinthian columns set in from the corners allow the plan to be read as a Greek cross. The interior was gutted by fire in about 1850, but was restored by Philip Hardwick and John Morris (1851–4).

The external composition is not as 'elemental' as that of **St George** U9. The tower is more Gothic in spirit, and is joined to the body of the church with a wide blank stage against which rests the semicircular porch; the stage is echoed by the small attics at the east end.

At the time of writing a phased programme of restoration of the interior was under way.

The Model Room

Royal Arsenal 1717–20 **U11**
Beresford Square SE18
John Vanbrugh (?)
⊖ ⇄ Woolwich Arsenal

The extensive site of the former Royal Arsenal between the Thames and the town of Woolwich is being developed at the time of writing. Three of its best buildings have been restored: the Brass Gun Foundry (1717), the original Royal Military Academy, or Model Room (1715–22), and the Gun Bore Factory (c1720). The Model Room is the most distinguished and the most characteristic of Vanbrugh. Its projecting stock-brick entrance is magnificently robust. On either side are rusticated piers, above which are cylindrical pedestals supporting lions. The high central semicircular arch is concluded by a broken pediment.

Vanbrugh Castle 1717–26 **U12**
Westcombe Park Road SE3
John Vanbrugh
⇄ Maze Hill

Vanbrugh was appointed Surveyor to Greenwich Hospital as successor to Wren in 1716. Overlooking the Royal Hospital he built England's first sham castle, a building of seminal importance in the development of the Picturesque style. Vanbrugh Castle was the first private house to be designed with conscious associations with the Middle Ages, a medieval fantasy rather than the scholarly reconstruction of the nineteenth century. Summerson observed, 'the house is without a scrap of Gothic detail about it', but its steep proportions, narrow, heavy windows and round towers are Gothic in spirit. Vanbrugh's later additions gave the house its symmetrical shape and plan.

Nelson Wharf c1770 **U13**
265 Rotherhithe Street SE16
⊖ Rotherhithe
This fine five-bay house is London's only surviving example of the eighteenth-century merchant ship-owners' style. The separation of living and working accommodation, characteristic of the nineteenth-century city, was yet to take place. See also **Shad Thames** L67.

Tide Mill and **Distillery** 1776, 1813 **U14**
Three Mill Lane E3
⊖ Bromley-by-Bow
These two handsome buildings are stranded in a post-industrial wasteland. The earlier, dating from the beginnings of the Industrial Revolution, spans Bow Creek, whose tide drove its machinery. The later, with its cupola and hoist, was a distillery and is still used by vintners for storage.

Chapel 1789 **U15**
Greenwich Hospital SE10
James 'Athenian' Stuart and William Newton
⊖ ⇌ Greenwich
A fire in 1779 gutted the chapel, designed by Wren and finished after his death by Ripley. It was rebuilt by Stuart, Surveyor to the **Hospital** U3, and it remains his finest London work. With Nicholas Revett, Stuart had visited Greece, and on return had published *The Antiquities of Athens* (Vol 1, 1762). The chapel presents the fruits of their journey: exquisite, archaeologically correct neo-classical decoration laid over a broadly seventeenth-century scheme. The 3.6m (12ft) high doorway between the chapel and the octagonal vestibule is the finest marble carving in the Greek style produced in eighteenth-century England. The organ gallery, carried on marble Ionic columns, has workmanship which is almost equally refined.

Woolwich Garrison **U16**
ex **Royal Military Academy** 1800–6
Academy Road, Woolwich Common SE18
James Wyatt
⊖ ⇌ Woolwich Arsenal
Built to replace the original school within the Arsenal, this design presents a silly contrast to the classicism of the **Royal Artillery Barracks** U17. Wyatt's plan for the parade ground façade is the same, but carried out in brown and yellow brick in thin Gothic style. The centrepiece is a parody of the Tower of London's **White Tower** L4, complete with corner turrets. The bright red-brick end pavilions are later.

In 2007 the building and its site were offered for sale for housing development.

Royal Artillery Barracks 1802–8 **U17**
Grand Depot Road SE18
James Wyatt
⊖ ⇌ Woolwich Arsenal
The magnificent south elevation to the parade ground is among the longer (323m/11,060ft) continuous architectural compositions in London. From a white triumphal arch in the centre spread ranges of two- and three-storey plain stock-brick barracks, connected by lower white colonnades. Behind this façade the barracks were set out as a small town on a grid-iron plan, but few of the original buildings now remain.

Albert Gardens c1810 **U18**
Commercial Road E1
⊖ Limehouse
Albert Gardens is a regular and completely preserved small-scale square, open to the north. Laid out following the building of Commercial Road (1803–10) to link the docks to the City of London, it was rehabilitated in the late 1970s by Anthony Richardson and Partners.

St John 1825–8 **U19**
Cambridge Heath Road E1
John Soane
⊖ Bethnal Green
The conjunction of west front and tower is here resolved with great sophistication. There is no pediment and the square piers either side of the central bay continue past the cornice line so that the square stage of the tower is engaged. The piers continue to form the short tower, and in a manner typical of Soane are detached from it, revealing a tense slice of space between. The tower was apparently intended to be higher, with the result that the circular cupola looks rather squat. The interior was burnt out in 1870 and insensitively remodelled. The window tracery is also an uncharacteristic later addition. See also **St Peter Walworth** P1 and **Holy Trinity** F22.

Licensed Victuallers' Benevolent Institution 1827–8 **U20**
Asylum Road SE15
Henry Rose
⇌ Queen's Road Peckham

Had they been built ten years later these almshouses would have been done in ingratiating Tudor; instead, the two extremely plain yellow-brick L-shaped domestic wings enclose an undecorated court. Architectural richness is reserved for the chapel in the centre, which has a handsome Doric portico and an elaborate sarcophagus on the roof, and the very fine iron railings and gates. It is now being surrounded with Southwark's Pixie-style housing, which has replaced the towers of the previous decade.

St Peter 1843 **U21**
Woolwich New Road SE18
Augustus Welby Pugin
⊖ ⇌ Woolwich Arsenal

It has been said that Pugin's zeal to provide places for Catholic worship often overcame his artistic judgement: St Peter's is a clear example. The exterior, with no tower and a chancel added later by another architect, is most uninteresting. The interior is decidedly mean with cheap cruciform columns and no clerestory.

Museum of Childhood **U22**
ex **Bethnal Green Museum**
1855–6 ,1875, 2000–6
Cambridge Heath Road E1
J W Wild, C D Young and Company, William Cubitt, Caruso St John
⊖ Bethnal Green

A philanthropic social experiment in its day, the Bethnal Green Museum was intended to bring Art to the East End, thereby civilizing the working population. Ironically, the three-bay red-brick façade seemed more appropriate to factory or railway station than to museum. Nevertheless, when seen across Bethnal Green the regular bays of the flank, with a frieze of terracotta inlaid panels below the eaves, have a quiet dignity. Wild's exterior conceals the cast-iron galleries of the original iron museum from South Kensington, designed and built by C D Young & Company. Having proved unpopular as the South Kensington Museum, the building was dismantled and moved to Bethnal Green under the supervision of William Cubitt, in an early example of the economy and flexibility of prefabricated building.

In 2000 the first phase of a programme of work (architects Caruso St John) was completed that included the total rearrangement and redecoration of the interior, and the use of parts of the previous basement. A new single-storey entrance pavilion spanned the full width of the façade decorated with a stone frame enclosing panels of marble 'marquetry'.

Garrison Church of St George **U23**
1863
Grand Depot Road SE18
T H Wyatt
⊖ ⇌ Woolwich Arsenal
The church was badly damaged in the Second World War, and with the removal of the roof it has been interestingly transformed into a commemorative garden. The Villa Giulia in Rome is evoked by the combination of the 'external rooms' of the garden, the Lombard porch and the 'early Romanesque' basilica. This seems an excellent use for obsolete church buildings.

Abbey Mills Pumping Station **U24**
1865–8
Abbey Lane E15
J Bazalgette and E Cooper
⊖ West Ham
Bazalgette and Cooper were engineer and architect to the Metropolitan Board of Works, established in 1855 to deal with London's sewage (see the **Victoria Embankment** K104). Designed to raise the level of the northern outfall sewer, this eccentric building is a good example of their collaboration, and of the split between Victorian engineering and architecture. The exterior is a well-mannered mixture of Byzantine and Gothic, complete with a mansard roof. The large, galleried machine hall – all in cast iron – originally accommodated the massive beam engines, replaced by electric motors in 1933. The building is best seen from the footpath on the former railway viaduct to its north.

To the south is the modern replacement of 1997, Pumping Station F, its decorated gables identifying it as a design of Allies and Morrison: compare the extension to the **Horniman Museum** X9.

Deptford Town Hall 1900–3 **U25**
New Cross Road SE14
Lanchester, Stewart and Rickards
⊖ New Cross, New Cross Gate
Lanchester (brother of the car designer) and Rickards, who won the competition for the design of Cardiff City Hall and Law Courts in 1897, were an influential force both in the classical revival around 1900, and in the establishment of the Edwardian baroque style. Deptford Town Hall was the subject of a competition organized by the newly formed Borough of Deptford, and remains one of the most enjoyable Edwardian public buildings. The seven-bay front elevation has been variously described as playful, nautical, florid and fanciful. It has a central oriel window with statues in niches on either side, and a set-back pediment capped by a clock tower, in the style of Hawksmoor's churches. It is now used by Goldsmiths College.

Hackney Empire **U26**
1901, renovated 2001–4
Frank Matcham; Tim Ronalds Architects
Mare Street E8
⇌ Hackney Central
One of the prolific Matcham's many music halls, used as a theatre more or less continuously, but also as a bingo hall and TV studio in the 1960s. Restoration and extension completed in 2004 enabled its use for musical and theatrical events, touring companies and the traditional Christmas pantomime. The ebullient auditorium was tactfully restored, the foyer and back-of-house upgraded. The Mare Street elevation was extended and returned, providing a façade to the Town Hall square with a bar at the corner, and the theatre's name announced with terracotta super-graphics.

Houses 1935 **U27**
85–91 Genesta Road SE18
B Lubetkin and A V Pilichowski
⊖ ⇌ Woolwich Arsenal
Because they wished to transform the city by the invention and superimposition of new housing types, many modern architects overlooked the traditional terraced house. These four houses are an exception. The rendered fronts and curved second-floor balconies show that the language of **Highpoint 1** R27 is not exclusive to the block of flats.

ex **Greenwich Town Hall** 1939 **U28**
Greenwich High Road and
Royal Hill SE10
E C Culpin and Bowers
⊖ ⇌ Greenwich
A rare example of successfully imported and digested continental modern: the style is from Dudok, but in yellow stock brick. For once, the modern style and programme – a public building to represent a socialist administration – come together in a knowing composition of carefully balanced verticals and horizontals. The tower is as stylish as that of an eighteenth-century church, and serves the same symbolic purpose. See also **Hornsey Town Hall** R26.

Housing 1952 **U29**
Usk Street E2
Denys Lasdun
⊖ Bethnal Green
To many people the cluster block represented just another version of the local authority tower block with the lifts and staircases exposed, but Lasdun's cluster blocks in Bethnal Green were a very early realization of a number of contemporary urban theories.

Lasdun's previous housing, with Tecton, had involved arbitrary pattern-making in the façades (see **Priory Green Estate** G68 and the **Hallfield Estate** I27); the form of the cluster block, on the other hand, derives from attempts to identify each dwelling, connecting these by 'vertical streets'. But its eight-storey tower, a composite of four smaller towers set at different angles to each other, is not a street. Architecture is a precise art and such imprecise images cannot be used as its justification. See also **Claredale Street** U30.

Housing, Keeling House 1960 **U30**
Claredale Street E2
Denys Lasdun and Partners
⊖ Bethnal Green

This area, bounded by Hackney Road to the north, Cambridge Heath Road to the east, Bethnal Green Road to the south, and Shoreditch High Street to the west, contains an example of virtually every English experiment in public housing. Lasdun's second attempt at the articulated tower (the first was at Usk Street U29), Keeling House can be regarded either as an eccentric tower block or as a determined attempt to invent architectural alternatives both to the street, and to the conventional mixed development of the previous decade. Lasdun hoped that the stacked maisonettes, separated by wide bands of concrete, might remind tenants of the two-storey houses in the district, and that the shared landings would foster sociability. Two six-storey blocks of maisonettes in dark brick were part of the same scheme. Keeling House was converted into flats for sale, with a new entrance hall added in 2000 (architects Munkenbeck and Marshall), and the surrounding maisonettes demolished.

Old People's Home 1960 **U31**
Rectory Field Crescent,
off Marlborough Lane SE7
Stirling and Gowan
⇌ Charlton

The least well-known building of this famous partnership. Accommodation for sixty-two people is planned around an internal courtyard, with the height of the building varying from one to three storeys to allow the maximum sunlight into the courtyard. The castellated, stepped engineering brickwork, the forty-five-degree and ninety-degree planning geometries and expressive boiler flue are unmistakable signs of its authorship.

Forest Gate School 1963 **U32**
Forest Street E7
Colquhoun and Miller
⇌ Forest Gate, Wanstead Park

The school marks this firm's departure from the rugged English Brutalism of Lyons Israel and Ellis, for whom the architects had worked, towards their later, cooler, more rational method. Influenced by the teaching of Colin Rowe, by Dutch examples, and by the many brick schemes originating in Cambridge about this time, the plan extends two wings of classrooms from a square, double-height assembly hall. Although poorly maintained and extended, it looks as if it had been carved from shiny red brick.

Housing 1965–8 **U33**
Trafalgar Road SE10
James Gowan
⇌ Maze Hill

Designed by Gowan in the last years of his partnership with James Stirling this formerly handsome courtyard of four-storey maisonettes enclosed an internal court. Their red-brick façades and industrial metal windows are inspired by the 1930s; on the other hand the second-floor access gallery cut into the surface of the block, with its corner bridges, refers back to the Preston housing of the original partnership and recalls the Spangen flats in Rotterdam (1921) by Brinkman. All this was reduced to irrelevance by the later reroofing.

Housing 1968–72 **U34**
Robin Hood Gardens, Cotton Street
and Robin Hood Lane E1
Alison and Peter Smithson
⊖ Blackwall

At first sight just another large and dreary GLC estate: two long cranked slab buildings of drab precast concrete address each other across a no-man's-land of common gardens, distinguished by a large artificial mound. However, this was the Smithsons' final built reality of nearly twenty years of urban theory, beginning with their competition entry for Golden Lane (1953) which projected a network of 'streets in the air'. It was not a new idea, but the reappraisal of the street and its function characterized their frequent writing and contributions to Team X (the successor to CIAM) over the years. Even if it can be justified as a fragment of a larger piece or a city within the city, Robin Hood Gardens must nevertheless be a particularly depressing place to live in, severed as it is from any connections with the existing city by its almost manic defence system of walls and moats. This scheme was an example of the late modernist avant-garde determination to realize a theoretical position at all costs. In this the Smithsons were not alone.

Hostel Thames Polytechnic 1971 **U35**
Thames Street SE18
Frederick Macmanus and Partners;
design by Edward Jones
⊖ ⇌ Woolwich Arsenal

These 250 south-facing study-bedrooms positioned above a communal ground floor took their inspiration in part from Le Corbusier's Pavillon Suisse in Paris of 1927 and the 'social condenser' of Russian constructivist architecture of the 1920s. With other contemporary schemes such as Michael Gold's Clipstone Street **housing** G72, also for Frederick Macmanus, the project represented a search for a lost objectivity.

Thamesmead started 1972 **U36**
Abbey Wood SE2
GLC Architects Department
⊖ Abbey Wood

Until 1985 the GLC was the world's largest landlord and had a huge programme of house building both in London and in the 'expanded towns' outside. By the middle of the 1960s the supply of large sites was exhausted, and the Erith marshes, with their sewage works and disused ordnance range, were identified as a possible site for the new town that the GLC had long wanted to build. The plans followed up-to-date models: two- and three-storey buildings which defined cranking routes or which could be laid out in rows, tower blocks for the childless, and big roads, including a crossing of the Thames to Barking. Artists' impressions showed canals weaving through all this. A factory was set up on site to produce heavy precast concrete units, from which the earlier linear housing and towers were built. The method of building was not robust and its tawdry results have had to be re-faced and re-windowed. After forty years, the best feature of Thamesmead is its mature landscaping.

The **Bexley Business Academy**, Yarnton Way, was one of the first privately sponsored secondary schools promoted by the Thatcher government for deprived urban areas. Completed in 2003, it was among ten such schools in the UK designed by Foster and Partners, better known for their commercial and business work. The three-storey building is axially planned and compact, generous in section and beautifully detailed. Externally, the glazed elevations are protected by a *brise soleil* of vertical louvres which close to double as a security system when the school is unoccupied to give the building a curiously blind, enigmatic character. Internally, the reverse applies: an open-plan, triple-height atrium, bridges, and much transparency allow for optimum control of the 1350 students. There is nowhere here to hide.

Ickburgh School special care unit **U37**
1972–3
Ickburgh Road E5
Foster Associates for the Spastics Society
⇌ Clapton

Re-windowed and with only the corrugated siding remaining of the original cladding, this little school building is now only of interest to Foster completists. The firm's first non-commercial non-industrial building, this small single-storey shed adapted the steel-framed structure of their building for IBM Cosham, Hants, to the particular requirements of severely handicapped children. The plan had fully demountable partitions, WCs in the centre, a ring of circulation round them, and two activity areas facing a small play court. The non-glazed parts of the exterior were faced with enamelled aluminium siding.

Warehouse and **showroom** 1973 **U38**
70–2 Hailey Road, Thamesmead
Foster Associates
⇌ Belvedere

This warehouse, originally designed for a glazier's, is set in the wastes of an industrial estate in Thamesmead, and was a prototype for Foster's later and better known Sainsbury Centre at the University of East Anglia (1975–8). The skin to the building was originally a blue stove-enamelled corrugated-steel sheet wrapped over a system of steel portal frames: by breaking with the traditional relationships of wall, eaves and roof the building managed to resemble an extremely large industrial product.

Unlike most contemporary buildings in England it was meticulously detailed, emphasizing its industrial design lineage. Nevertheless, as with the Sainsbury Centre, it is still possible to appraise the architecture.

The end bay of an industrial hangar is functional, and that of a Greek temple is rhetorical or symbolic: by contrast, the gable ends here and in the Sainsbury Centre do not play a part in an industrial process, nor do they mark a formal entry. The lines of the building could be endlessly extruded; its length is determined only by practical considerations, and the end walls simply mark off a length of an ideally limitless form.

Housing 1982–4 **U39**
60-62 Albion Drive
34–36 and 25–37 Shrubland Road
37–43 Brownlow Road E8
22–5 Church Crescent E9
Colquhoun and Miller
⇌ London Fields

Albion Drive

Taking its cue from the neighbouring mid-nineteenth-century semi-detached villas, this 'infill housing' goes some way to correcting the mistakes of earlier public housing. Instead of distinguishing between people with and without children or between houses and flats, the project proposes a more generous semi-detached villa. This can then be used either to infill small gaps without disruption to neighbouring houses, or to make terraces for the larger sites. The street is thus reconfirmed as an important space. The buildings have a desirably loose fit between plan and elevation, though the central column has always appeared too spindly.

A little to the east the contemporary housing at Church Crescent is further evidence of the intelligent reworking of London's house types. As at **Caversham Road** C15, the overhanging hipped roof, the second-floor loggia and the extensive white-rendered blank panel to the first floor give the buildings a generosity not normally associated with public housing. The brief called only for four large houses, but it is possible to imagine this type forming the basis of a street or local district.

Docklands Light Railway stations **U40**
1987–84
Poplar to Beckton
Ahrends Burton and Koralek
Although much of the new railway ran on existing track, all the stations were new: such a complete architectural programme had not been attempted since the southern extension of the Northern Line in the 1920s (W11). The 'kit-of-parts' used for these eleven stations distinguished them from some others on the DLR lines which combine unsophisticated engineering with shopfitting. Their colours have dulled with age, but the 'cheerful' red, white and blue colours of the railway's livery, relentlessly applied to the architecture, became an irritating cliché (Holden's work on the Northern Line by contrast looks more mature: generally neutral backgrounds were enlivened with brightly enamelled signs.)

The original modest plans for the railway were overtaken by the colossal scale of some of the later developments in Docklands such as **Canary Wharf** U48, and the platforms had to be lengthened to take new, longer trains.

Royal Albert Station

Pumping station 1985–8 **U41**
Stewart Street E14
John Outram Associates
⊖ Blackwall
A shed for automatic pumping machinery decorated in Outram's cheerful, eclectic and thoughtfully detailed architecture, to an allegorical programme which must remain obscure to the uninitiated observer.

China Wharf 1986–8 **U42**
29 Mill Street SE1
CZWG Architects (Campbell, Zogolovich, Wilkinson and Gough)
⊖ Bermondsey
China Wharf is not a Chinese dragon but a housing building of seventeen flats with offices on the ground and first floors. It has three distinct and separate elevations. The façade to Mill Street is clad in London stock bricks with gault-brick and blue-engineering-brick details to match the neighbouring warehouses. The courtyard façade is stuccoed and painted white to reflect light into the area. The river façade is more fully glazed and its concrete frame is painted red.

Housing, Compass Point 1987 **U43**
Manchester Road E14
Jeremy Dixon BDP
⊖ Island Gardens
A further episode in Dixon's reworking of existing housing types and forms, the buildings are arranged on either side of an axis running at right angles to the Thames. The noticeably low floor heights and the absence of chimneys are difficult to reconcile with 'traditional' or historical forms, and the houses' modest styling was only too vulnerable to the exigencies of the 'design-and-build' contract.

Cascades 1987–8 **U44**
2–4 Westferry Road E14
CZWG Architects (Campbell, Zogolovich, Wilkinson and Gough)
⊖ Heron Quays

This heroic housing project interrupted a period in which there was a virtual moratorium on 'high-rise' housing. Cascades recalls ideas in student housing projects from the late 1950s and early 1960s in which the inclined section is almost obligatory. In this respect it is a nostalgic building incorporating various influences – the spirit of Le Corbusier's *Unité d'Habitation* in Marseille, the iconography of warehouses and ships, and a character that is in a way curiously Swedish. If only the inclined shape had been generated by a funicular lift and not a stair.

Reuters 1987–8 **U45**
Aspen Way E14
Richard Rogers Partnership
⊖ Brunswick

Built quickly for a company which deals in information, and intentionally provisional in appearance, this very large building is sited over a dock at a bend in the River Thames. Plant, services and computers are at the lower levels, and above these are offices faced with a changeable system of either glass or opaque panels. The escape stairs are placed outside the main envelope. At roof level, an exposed steel structure cages a variable arrangement of plant and communication aerials.

Like many of Docklands' buildings, Reuters originally suffered from the almost complete lack of a rational, normal context and the site is entered past a bus stop through a small gate set in a substantial steel fence. It has since been joined, inconsequentially, on the west by the overdeveloped block of flats and hotel.

Housing 1987–9 **U46**
Roy Square, Narrow Street E14
Ian Ritchie Architects
⊖ Limehouse

Much of the new housing in Docklands is silly in both arrangement and style, and the sizes of its dwellings tiny. This scheme is one of the better exceptions. Modelled on the generalized 'block', the 77 flats are arranged round and reached from a common landscaped courtyard which is raised above a garage. The style is assured, calm and timeless. The introspection of the scheme can be explained by its hostile and uncertain surroundings.

Finland Quay West 1989 **U47**
Onega Gate, Redriff Road SE16
Richard Reid Architects
⊖ Surrey Quays
This is one of the better housing developments in Docklands. The seven linked pavilions form an emphatic front to Greenland Dock, and unlike most recent housing in Docklands they address the large expanse of water with a robust and appropriate scale. The **Paragon** X5 in Blackheath is a reference acknowledged by the architect. The buildings give the impression externally of large urban villas in multiple occupancy. For the resident the interior gives a desirable variety of living conditions.

Canary Wharf 1990– **U48**
E14
Cesar Pelli and Associates with Adamson Associates (Toronto), Frederick Gibberd, Coombes and Partners, and others
⊖ Canary Wharf, Heron Quays
Canary Wharf's tallest building is clearly visible from the hop fields in Kent and from the M11 approaching London from the north. From the hump of the Blackwall Tunnel approach to the south, it comes suddenly and dramatically into view. This is particularly memorable at night, with the translucent **Millennium Dome** U50 establishing a foreground to the glittering concentration of towers behind. For a moment you might be approaching downtown Houston, Toronto or any other North American city. However, unlike the unfortunate *La Défense* in Paris, Canary Wharf does not directly interfere with any of London's more sensitive historic view corridors. It presents a piece of corporate America in England, and unsurprisingly, the project was initiated by Canadian developers Olympia and York with American architects in attendance –

Cesar Pelli, SOM, KPF, etc. The project was initiated in the Thatcher era when the rest of London's Docklands were being shamefully redeveloped without any credible masterplan.

Built in two phases, Canary Wharf recovered from the recession of the early 1990s and by the end of the decade had become a successful annexe to and rival of the City of London. The accessibility provided by extensions to the Docklands Light Railway (and later to the Jubilee Line) assisted this revival. The first phase was built to an admirable masterplan: a single axis extends east–west on the quays between two docks; a new upper level provided a grid of conventional roads (on which buses and taxis run), 'front doors' to the office buildings, and several excellently furnished outdoor spaces. Below this and level with the quays are extensive and entirely enclosed areas of shopping, modelled perhaps on those of Montreal and Toronto, and a service road.

1 Canada Square by Cesar Pelli and Associates of 1991 remains the best building. It has a straightforward and abstract repetitiveness appropriate to tall buildings – although, from a strictly proportional point of view, it would have been enhanced by an additional twenty floors, and the crowning pyramid might have been more enjoyable as a public place. Foster and Partners' Citigroup to the south was, however, a demonstration that the well-made high-rise building was no longer exclusive to North America. Whereas the City of London with its medieval street pattern has not been ideal for absorbing large high-rise buildings, at Canary Wharf the tabula rasa of the vacated docks and restriction provided by the river gives a more appropriate setting.

The office slabs that filled out the grid in the second phase and which line the dock to the south lack the originals' multi-level circulation and compared with that of the first phase their architecture is unambitious and boring.

Canary Wharf Underground Station

Of the dozen built for the eastward extension of the Jubilee Line, **Canary Wharf Underground Station** (Foster and Partners, 1999) was by far the largest and grandest. By 2008 it had become the Underground's second busiest station. It linked the Underground to the massive development at Canary Wharf previously served only by the Docklands Light Railway. Excavated and built in the former dock, it houses all the functions in a single linear structure: an external retaining wall and a 'gull-wing' roof supported on a central line of massive three-storey-high columns. The three entrances are marked by glazed hemi-domes which allow daylight to penetrate to the lowest, platform, level, and incorporate ventilation extractors. Externally, the roof was landscaped as a small evergreen-strewn park.

Thames Barrier Park 1995–2000 **U49**
North Woolwich Road E16
Patel Taylor Architects and Groupe Signes
⊖ Pontoon Dock

The best modern park in London, appropriately transforming a square of derelict industrial land into a series of distinct and architecturally inventive 'settings'. These consist of a riverside promenade, a raised ground with views of the drama of the Thames Barrier, a sunken green 'dock' of an area densely planted in rows and crossed by bridges, play areas, bicycle routes, ramps, a café pavilion, and so on. Visitors arriving from the north are greeted by a pavement water feature. The whole is treated in a direct and robust manner.

Forming the west boundary to the park, the excellent housing by Barratt Homes, also to a masterplan by Patel Taylor (2001), appropriately introduced stepped terraces which contribute a generosity rare in contemporary housing and regrettably otherwise absent in Docklands. The design recalls student housing projects of the early 1960s.

02 ex **Millennium Dome** **U50**
1997–2000
Greenwich Peninsula SE10
Richard Rogers Partnership
⊖ North Greenwich
Lying across the Greenwich meridian on land poisoned by former industrial activity, this very large tent of twelve 90m (295ft) tall steel masts supporting 100,000 square metres (1,089,000 square feet) of fabric roof was the centrepiece of the government-sponsored celebrations of the year 2000. Closed for six years, it was reopened in 2007 as a 'venue': a successful 20,000 seat performance arena surrounded by a seedy mall of shops and restaurants.

Plans for parts of the peninsula to the south included the Millennium Village, a utopian area of 'sustainable' housing, to a masterplan by Ralph Erskine.

London Regatta Centre 1999 **U51**
Dockside Road, Royal Albert Dock E16
Ian Ritchie Architects
⊖ Royal Albert
On a very particular site characterized by large widely spaced objects and looking south over the expanse of the former Royal Dock, this centre houses accommodation for local, national and international rowing activities in two buildings. To the west, two storeys house the clubhouse, organized around a concrete spine wall and with a first-floor terrace from which to view rowing races and the planes arriving at and taking off from London City Airport. Extending to the east is a long, single-storey boat shed, its walls constructed of sturdy load-bearing 'gabions' (stones held without mortar in wire cages): perhaps a fragment of a landscape as much as a building.

Peckham Library 2001 **U52**
Peckham Hill Street SE15
Alsop and Stormer
⇄ Peckham Rye
This small building is part of an ambitious project of urban renewal and carries a large reputation. It is extremely popular socially; this might be attributed to its would-be populist character and the creation of a generous public loggia providing a place to congregate and to hang out. The library is then raised above on tall spindly *pilotis*. This idea of the levitating rectangle is a Corbusian reference, as is Alsop's preoccupation with brightly coloured 'pods', which occupy the interior. The building was awarded the Stirling Prize in 2001.

Idea Store 2001–5 **U53**
Whitechapel Road E1
Adjaye Associates
⊖ Whitechapel

This is one of a pair of buildings commissioned from Adjaye in an attempt by the Borough of Tower Hamlets to improve the image and use of what were formerly called public libraries. The earlier, at Chrisp Street, Limehouse, opened in 2004. (Although it might be thought that those who have a problem with 'library' might equally be worried by 'idea'.)

Its prominent position, the appearance of a small department store complete with escalator rising directly from the street market and its cheerfully coloured, extensively glazed façades, are intended to propose an 'openness' that earlier libraries were supposed to lack. As well as conventional bookstacks, its five floors contain 'after-school study zones', space for shops or a café, and at the rear a performance studio.

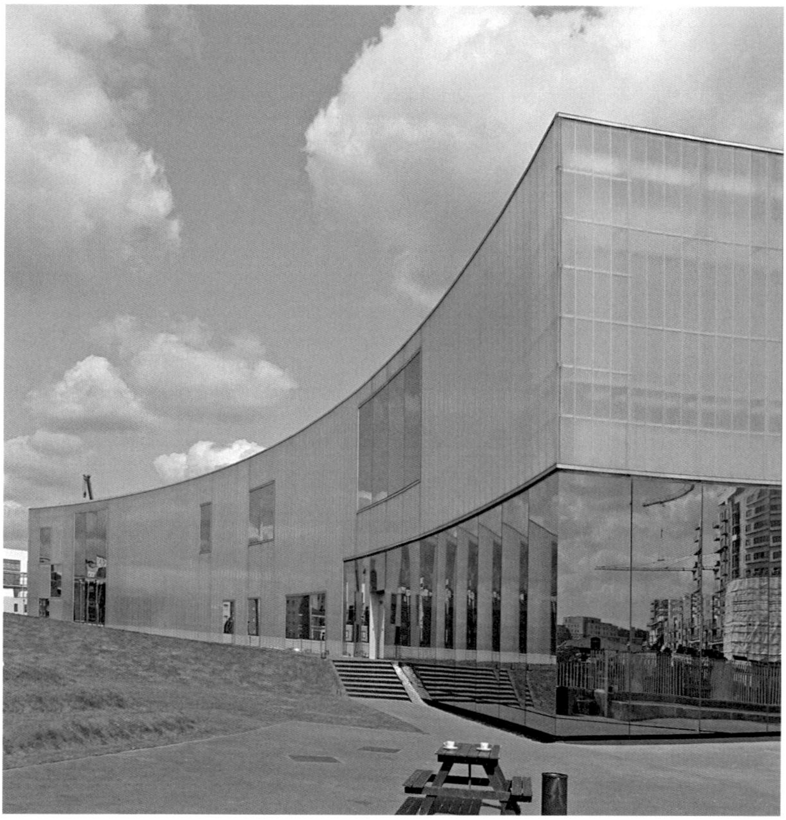

Laban 2003 **U54**
Creekside SE8
Herzog & de Meuron
⊖ Greenwich, New Cross ⇌ Deptford

Rudolph Laban was the father of modern dance in Britain: he arrived as a refugee from Nazi Germany in 1938 and established his school first in Manchester before moving to New Cross in 1976. The centre is now the largest school of dance in Europe. Following an international competition Laban moved from its ad hoc premises in a converted church behind Lewisham Way to this large shed sitting alongside Deptford Creek and confronted by Archer's magnificent **St Paul's Church** U7.

Its concave entrance façade of a combination of transparent and translucent polycarbonate and glass panels, with blushes of colour from the interior, whilst acting as a protective shield against the sun, understates the entrance. The interior, by contrast, is not the expected open plan but a dense arrangement of rooms and corridors partly reminiscent of the labyrinth of the previous home. The detailing is idiosyncratic: a large black matt-vinyl spiral staircase, an electric yellow, jumpy, bendy horizontal handrail for spontaneous practice, and a strong colour coding of the interior circulation – pink, lime and magenta – in collaboration with the artist Michael Craig Martin. The building received the Stirling prize in 2003.

Housing, Donnybrook Quarter **U55**
2003–6
Old Ford Road, Parnell Road E3
Peter Barber Architects
⇌ Bow Road

Those who see Donnybrook as a 'Mediterranean village' might be reminded that white stucco has been a common London material from the eighteenth century onwards and that terraces of houses making streets are equally typical of this city. The project is a sane and welcome rebuke to the arbitrary form-making that characterizes most contemporary housing. However, unlike, for example, the villas of Belsize Park Gardens, the composition of windows appears to be random and the buildings have the impression of having been totally immersed in white stucco, removing the normal front/back hierarchy and contrast of materials.

See also Peter Barber's housing at **Tanner Street Gateway** in Barking, where the same concerns for the street and direct access from it to the houses are demonstrated.

93–115 Evelyn Road

Boxley Street

Housing for Peabody Trust 2004 **U56**
93–115 Evelyn Road E16
Niall McLaughlin Associates
Boxley Street E16
Ash Sakula Architects
⊖ West Silvertown

These two highly contrasting schemes were the winners of a competition run by the Peabody Trust to patronize new young architectural talent and promote fresh thinking about low-cost housing. 'Cool' is an unlikely adjective for the Trust's housing, but McLaughlin's elegantly restrained elevations and generous apartments would be more at home on the borders of a Swiss lake than here in this remote part of Silvertown. The fully glazed façade, (its three horizontal divisions spanning the blocks' upper two storeys) is mostly opaque and the use of dichroic film in its panels, a collaboration with Martin Richman, results in constantly changing colours. Clear windows positioned on the corners give views in deep perspective along the face of the street.

On the corner of Boxley Street to the south, four flats arranged in a pair of two-storey blocks provide a refreshing contrast with their gold anodized window frames and rough-and-ready cladding of gold and silver foil covered in transparent corrugated plastic, designed in conjunction with artist Vineta Hassard.

Ben Pimlott building **U57**
Goldsmiths College 2004
New Cross SE14
Alsop Architects
⊖ New Cross Gate

Goldsmiths is one of London's respected art schools, but its campus is far from consolidated. Its late head, Ben Pimlott, commissioned Alsop to produce a master plan for a new entrance at the college's frontage to New Cross Road. The proposed entrance building was not constructed, but the eponymous seven-storey building behind was, and accommodates mainly studios for students. Its design is abrupt: the north-facing studios are fully glazed while the southern façade is sheathed in industrial siding and decorated with artistic gestures. Another of these adorns the terrace formed by the cut-back of the upper storeys, and effectively prevents its use as a terrace or look-out.

Note to the east, on Lewisham Way, Allies and Morrison's more sober Goldsmiths College **Library** of 1997. The building is a linear glazed box with a continuous brise soleil of tall fins giving a strong character to the street façade.

Blizard Building 2005 **U58**
Institute of Cell and Molecular Science
Queen Mary College, University of London
Turner Street E1
SMC Alsop
⊖ Shadwell

The research building provides laboratories, offices, lecture theatres, etc, for four hundred students, accommodation that would normally be housed in a bland but secure place, but not here. A simple linear public plaza defined by two parallel no-nonsense blocks connected at first floor by a glazed bridge is an introduction to the bright and colourful world of Will Alsop and painter Bruce McLean. Here under the banner of demystification, the building, with strong graphic exhibits and oblique views into research laboratories, hoped to engage the public in aspects of medical education. This contemporary imperative to demonstrate the literalness of what is going on inside tends to reduce the building to a large but inaccessible display case.

Stadium under construction March 2009

Olympics 2012 site **U59**
Lea Valley
Various architects
⊖ Stratford

At the time of writing, plans for the clearance of a large area of land formerly used for industry had been carried out to make way for the construction of a stadium and various other buildings to house many of the sporting activities of the Olympic Games to be held in 2012. While the earlier designs for these were of some interest, constant exercises in 'value engineering' (i.e. reducing budgets) threatens the little they had.

Outer London, south-west

This section contains much good architecture, and is dominated by its huge open spaces: the royal parks of Bushy, Hampton Court and Richmond, and the common lands of Wimbledon and Putney. The last three are on high ground to the east of the Thames, which here is narrow and flows south to north. The tidal river meets its first weir at Teddington (illustrated page 457), near Richmond, which with Kingston is one of the two market towns on the Thames. Both have now been engulfed by twentieth-century London, but have their own histories outside the scope of this book.

Up to the eighteenth century the area consisted of open land: the royal palace at **Hampton Court** V1, manors, and court officials' houses were scattered between the Thames-side villages and market towns. Alexander Pope, Burlington's house-poet, set up house in Twickenham in 1719, quickly establishing it as the Hampstead of its day, and Walpole's **Strawberry Hill** V7, opposite Ham, continued the fashion. During the course of the eighteenth century, the towns and villages were peppered with middle-class and aristocratic houses (for example **Montpelier Row** V5 and **Manresa House** V8).

The nineteenth century brought the London and South Western Railway, running south of Kingston, and making the area suitable for city commuters' suburban houses. Twentieth-century development then joined the towns and villages together, closing round the open spaces. The heroic exceptions to the standard suburban pattern were the two LCC **Alton housing estates** V10 and V12, on high ground overlooking Putney Heath and Richmond Park. The latter is the most successful realization of Le Corbusier's theories in England: the view of the point blocks from Richmond Park remains a powerful reminder of a possible alternative to the existing city.

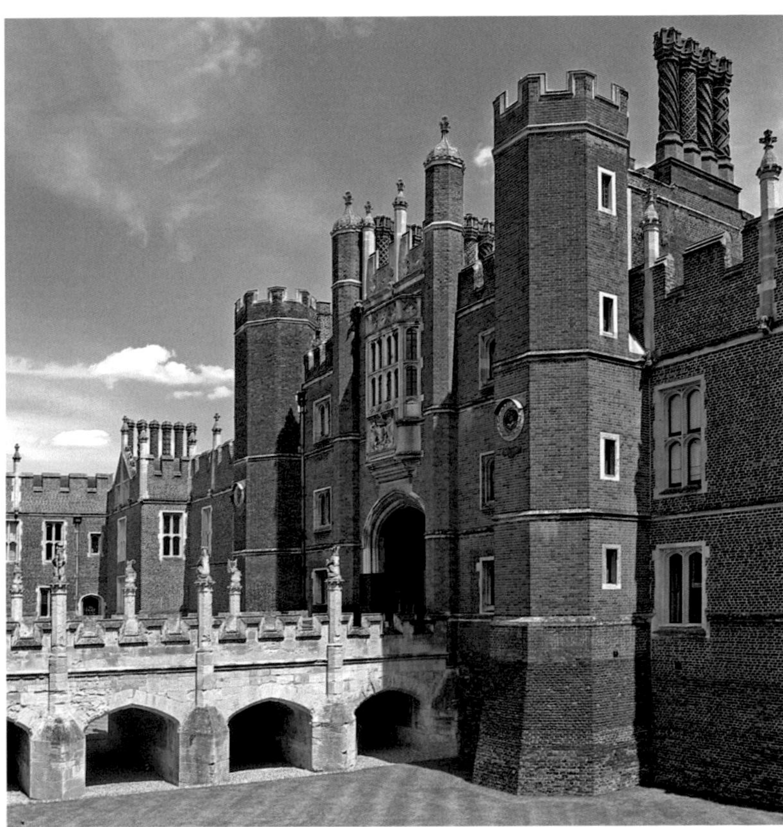

The Great Gatehouse, Hampton Court V1

The King's Apartments

The Queen's Apartments

Hampton Court Palace 1514–1882 **V1**
Christopher Wren 1689–94;
William Kent 1732 and others
⇌ Hampton Court

Hampton Court is England's Tudor masterpiece, and although planned on a regal scale it was not originally a royal palace. The historical and physical development can be briefly summarized: In 1514 Cardinal Wolsey bought a medieval manor from the Order of St John of Jerusalem; in the years that followed he was to make it the grandest house in England, and in 1529 he presented it to Henry VIII in an effort to retain royal favour. Wolsey's palace then consisted of the west front (without wings), the Base Court, the Clock Court (with different buildings on the north and south sides), buildings round the master carpenter's court, the Chapel and the cloisters to the west of it. Henry embarked on further building: the Great Hall is attributed to him, and he added a courtyard on the side of the present Fountain Court, and another north-east of the Chapel. He also remodelled Wolsey's structures around Clock Court and added wings to the west façade. Henry's successors used the palace as a royal retreat, and no further significant changes were made until Charles II ordered the construction of the long axial canal and the radiating avenues through Home Park from the 'French' formal gardens in front of the east block. These were the first moves in transforming Hampton Court from a very large medieval manor into a 'European' royal palace. William and Mary accomplished the final transformation when William decided to make Hampton Court his Versailles. In 1689 Wren started work with plans for the wholesale reconstruction of Wolsey's Tudor palace, and by William's death the structural work was complete on the new Fountain Court, the south range of Clock Court and the new Orangery. Luckily, Wren's comprehensive plans were not to be realized. Minor works continued for the next two centuries and the result is an extraordinary catalogue of English architecture.

The main approach to Hampton Court is from the south-west, crossing the Thames over **Hampton Court Bridge** V9. The immediate view is of the magnificent west façade's many twisted chimneys, turrets and castellations, all in red brick. The perpendicular Gothic façade is the grandest of its date in England. The **Great Gatehouse** leads into Wolsey's relatively modest **Base Court**, whose profile is broken by the west front of the Great Hall, in **Clock Court** beyond. The Base Court's brickwork is decorated with terracotta medallions by Giovanni da Majano, the earliest example of Italian Renaissance craftsmanship in England. Anne Boleyn's Gateway leads in to Clock Court, which has the finest architecture in the Palace, To the north is Henry VIII's **Great Hall**, built over Wolsey's cellars and completed in 1536. To the south, Wolsey's range is unexpectedly concealed by Wren's grand Portland stone colonnade, which forms an entrance to the King's apartments. The new, white, classical architecture of this lofty arcade was as revolutionary in its time as the architecture of modernism was to the Edwardians at the beginning of the twentieth century. Between the colonnade and the Hall to the east are a range and doorway by William Kent, built in 1732, and one of the earliest examples of the Gothic Revival.

With Wren's 31×36m (101×117ft) **Fountain Court** the classical transformation is complete. When it is compared with the court of the Louvre, 91m (300ft) square, which was Wren's model, it becomes clear that the standard bay of Fountain Court is a device for a much bigger idea. As Summerson said, 'the Fountain Court is a rather apologetic substitute for the Privy Court originally proposed, and the crowded fenestration gives an uncomfortably restricted sensation.' To the south are the King's apartments, to the north and east the Queen's, connected by the two-storey communication gallery and overlooking the Privy Garden (restored in 1995 to its state in 1702). Fountain Court leads to the east front of William and Mary's 'Versailles'. Wren was not to build his original designs at Hampton Court, with the grand central dome, end pavilions, and expressive detail, and as a result 'the mobile silhouette and the decorative intricacies have all disappeared ... the skyline is dead level and from an excess of variation Wren has passed over to something bordering on monotony' (Summerson). Despite Wren's lapses, however, Hampton Court shows marvellously the development from a Tudor manor house, built with defence in mind, to a geometrically based, open and confident classical palace.

Ham House 1610 **V2**
Off Petersham Road, Twickenham TW10
⊖ Richmond, then bus
The house was originally built in 1610 for Thomas Vavasour to an early-seventeenth-century H-plan, and approached from the south. The Great Hall is from that date. The house was subsequently altered and expanded and its entrance moved to its present position on the north face. It is now owned by the National Trust, which has put its characteristic enthusiasm and expertise into restoring and maintaining the fine gardens.

From the bank of the Thames north-east of Ham House, an occasional ferry provides access to the opposite bank and Twickenham and **Marble Hill** V6.

Roehampton House 1710–12 **V3**
Roehampton Lane SW15
Thomas Archer, enlarged by Edwin Lutyens
⇌ Barnes
Archer's first London work, built originally as a country house for Thomas Cary, had a dignified brick façade, crowned originally by a 'gargantuan broken pediment' (Pevsner). It was later extended by Lutyens and converted into a hospital, since rebuilt and making the site available for housing development.

St Mary 1714–15 **V4**
Church Street, Twickenham TW1
remodelled by John James
⇌ Twickenham
James was the architect of **St George, Hanover Square** J6, and his work in the small riverside village of Twickenham was clearly of metropolitan character. The vigorous pedimented Tuscan decoration to the sides is quite different from the refinement of St George's, and more like the work of James's contemporary, Hawksmoor.

Montpelier Row 1722 **V5**
Twickenham TW1
⇌ St Margarets
Those visiting Twickenham's parish church (V4) or **Marble Hill** V6 should take in this exquisite early Georgian terrace, the best of the district's many surviving houses of the period.

Marble Hill 1723–8 **V6**
Richmond Road, Twickenham TW1
Henry Herbert, Roger Morris
⇄ St Margarets
The house was one of several built along the shores of the Thames, which it commands across a wide, deep lawn. Herbert was a contemporary of Burlington, an amateur architect, and heir to Inigo Jones's Wilton House, Salisbury. After the publication of Campbell's *Vitruvius Britannicus* in 1715 the house became one of several models for the eighteenth-century villa. Painstakingly restored by the GLC, the interiors are gradually being furnished. The exterior lacks edge and Palladio's exquisite sense of proportion: the outer windows are placed firmly in the centres of their bays, and the ground floor is clumsy. The partnership of Herbert and Morris, Master Carpenter to the Office of Ordnance, went on to design the Palladian bridge at Wilton.

Strawberry Hill 1749–76 **V7**
Waldegrave Road, Twickenham TW1
Horace Walpole and his 'Committee of Taste', including John Chute, Thomas Gray, Richard Bentley, Thomas Pitt and Robert Adam
⇄ Strawberry Hill
As Lord Burlington is associated with the birth of English Palladianism, so Horace Walpole (the younger son of Prime Minister Robert Walpole) is synonymous with the advent of the 'Picturesque'. As an antidote to the prevailing Palladian taste, Strawberry Hill was the most influential Gothic Revival building in England. But like **Vanbrugh's Castle** U12 in Greenwich, it did not use Gothic in the scholarly and medieval fashion of Pugin or Ruskin in the following century. This was a period of pluralism in architecture (see Chambers's **Pagoda** T8 at Kew), and the forms of Strawberry Hill have as much to do with Chinese fretwork as with Gothic tracery. In 1747 Walpole bought a small riverside property, and over the next thirty years made a series of additions, each supervised by his 'Committee of Taste'. Meanwhile members of the committee scoured the churches and abbeys of northern Europe for inspiration – the tombs in Westminster Abbey were to reappear in Strawberry Hill as mantelpieces.

The informal and asymmetrical disposition of the house is Walpole's principal contribution. The entrance, reached from the north past the little cloister, leads into Bentley's Staircase Hall (1753), which rises to an armoury. Beyond is the famous Library (1754) by Chute (Bentley's design was rejected by the committee). This is a remarkable room: the fireplace is borrowed from the tomb of John of Eltham in Westminster Abbey, and the gilded bookcases derive from the screen in old St Paul's Cathedral. The next room is the Holbein Chamber (1759), also by Bentley, with an imitation of the tripartite ogival screen from Rouen Cathedral.

The Gallery, designed by Thomas Pitt, is the most dramatic space of all. The vaulting is borrowed from the aisles of **Henry VII's Chapel** K8 at Westminster Abbey, but the bays, recesses and mirrors refer to the sensuous interiors of Robert Adam. Walpole instructed Adam himself (despite a declared antipathy to Adam's 'gingerbread and snippets of embroidery') to design the Beauclerk Room (1766), where the fireplace is borrowed from the tomb of Edward the Confessor at Westminster. The Chapel (1763) and the Great Bed Chamber (1772) should also be noted. From 1925 the house was occupied (and excellently maintained) by St Mary's University College. In 2002 a trust was formed to restore and care for it and its gardens, and to make it publicly accessible.

Manresa House **V8**
ex **Bessborough House** 1750–68
Roehampton Lane SW15
William Chambers
⇌ Barnes

Notwithstanding Burlington's work at **Chiswick House** T6, this is probably the most authentically Palladian house in London: the proportions of the Ionic portico are copied faithfully from Palladio's work in Vicenza. It is now part of Roehampton University.

Hampton Court Bridge 1930–3 **V9**
W P Robinson, engineer;
Edwin Lutyens, architect
⇌ Hampton Wick

The bridge, the fourth on the site, is a curiously bland design of three broad, very shallow reinforced concrete arches faced with red brick, with decorated stone panels at the piers above the cutwaters. The Lutyens of New Delhi here displayed very little of his characteristic mannered inventiveness (almost as if not wishing to upstage the Palace?).

Housing, Alton East Estate **V10**
1952-5
Portsmouth Road SW15
LCC Architects Department
⇌ Barnes

Neutral and democratic Sweden was the only European country with a significant state housing achievement during the Second World War. It is no coincidence therefore that 'Swedish modern' should be the style adopted by most architects who worked for the Welfare State in the immediate post-war era; apart from the new towns (Harlow and Crawley, for example) the Alton East Estate on the edge of Richmond Park is the definitive version of it. For its residents, the mixed development of towers and terraced houses, set among the mature trees of its semi-rural 11 hectare (28 acre) site (housing 2800 people), must have seemed a long way from the memory of the war-time city. For its socialist designers Alton East's forms embodied the triumph of 'people's detailing'. See also **Alton West Estate** V12.

Parkleys Estate 1954–6 **V11**
Parkleys, off Upper Ham Road KT2
Eric Lyons
⊖ Richmond, then bus south
This estate of 168 dwellings is one of several built by the Span development company, of which Lyons was a director (see also those at Blackheath, X11). The houses are in modest two-storey terraces, the flats in three-storey blocks with H-shaped plans. The row of shops on Upper Ham Road marks the entrance to the site which is laid out picturesquely and after fifty years is now remarkable for its lush and well-maintained landscaping. The whole scheme is an intriguing complement to the nearby almost contemporary, smaller but altogether tougher, **housing** V13 by Stirling and Gowan.

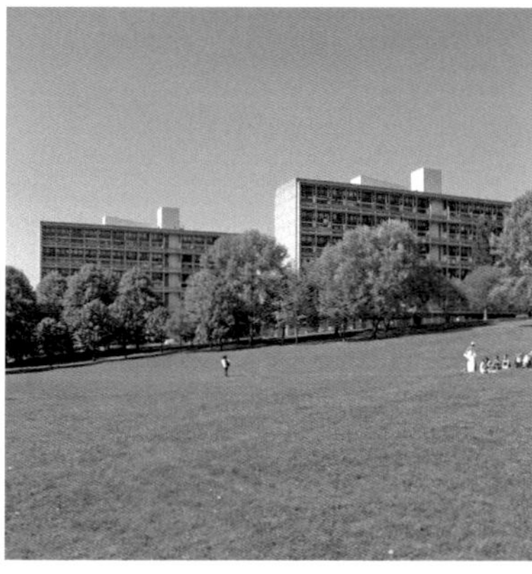

Housing, Alton West Estate **V12**
1955–9
Roehampton Lane SW15
LCC Architects Department
⇌ Barnes
On one of the few sites appropriate to it, Le Corbusier's *Ville Radieuse* nearly found its London embodiment on 40 hectares (100 acres) of rolling land overlooking Richmond Park. About 1850 dwellings are arranged in three building types: the eleven-storey slabs of maisonettes to the north, two clusters of twelve-storey point blocks, and rows of three- and four-storey maisonettes. Schools, shops, a library and old people's dwellings are scattered among these. All the buildings except the maisonettes are made of and clad in concrete, in a style as close to Le Corbusier's own as precise English workmanship would allow. Viewed from Richmond Park, the ensemble does look very like a city of separate big buildings set in parkland.

While the designs were the work of enthusiastic young architects (including Bill Howell, Sam Stevens and Alan Colquhoun among others) anxious that the repetition of the Swedish-style mixed development of **Alton East** V10 should not occur, the layout lacks both a Corbusian geometrical order and a sensible circulation system. The copies of the Unité are nothing like social entities lifted off the ground: too small and without the new social order which the model required, they obstinately remain just blocks of flats – 'workers' housing'. The square point blocks derived from Swedish models are much more successful, and the group set among mature cedars suggests high-style high-rise. The appalling rows of maisonettes, which have weathered very badly and been much altered by their owners, are best ignored.

Flats, Langham House 1958 **V13**
Langham House Gardens,
Ham Street, Richmond TW10
James Stirling and James Gowan
⊖ Richmond

Built in the long, narrow back garden of Langham House (a Georgian mansion overlooking the common) these thirty flats are important in the development of post-war English domestic architecture. In opposition to the limp 'Swedish modern' of the Festival of Britain years, they show allegiance to the Dutch de Stijl movement of the 1920s and to Le Corbusier's Maisons Jaoul in Paris (1956). The careful, mannered, concrete and brick detailing (Jaoul is intentionally far less precise), both inside and out, was later seen as evidence of the emerging 'Brutalist' sensibility. The term 'Brutalism' has generally and inaccurately been applied just to buildings of exposed concrete. For the avant-garde generation after the war the term reflected their frustration with the architectural establishment and their wish to get into better company. 'Mies is great but Corb communicates' was a maxim of Peter Smithson, the most vocal of this generation. James Stirling's essay *From Garches to Jaoul* underlined a similar concern.

House and **guest house** 1970 **V14**
22 Parkside SW19
Richard and Su Rogers
⊖ ⇌ Wimbledon

A fine example of suburban domestic architecture, these houses are a successful attempt to free the London house from its traditional masonry straitjacket. The programme was used as a vehicle for an exercise in possible serial production, but this is a one-off realization. It casually uses non-domestic building techniques – single-span steel frame, huge sliding panes of glass, sandwich wall panels – all of which were by then taken for granted in North America. The arrangement of the separate guest house facing the street, the larger house behind, and the delightful forecourt and lush planting, creates a small masterpiece of site planning.

Offices, **shops** and **flats** 1986–8 **V15**
Hill Street, Bridge Street, Richmond TW9
Erith and Terry
⊖ Richmond

Next to the Thames, this redevelopment of existing buildings and two ranges of new ones roughly encloses three new open spaces. The mostly ill-proportioned façades of the new parts are in an assortment of weary classical styles from a variety of periods and places and in several different materials. The resulting picturesque jumble still has the air of a poor film set. The suspended ceiling grids and fluorescent lighting of the interiors are conspicuous in their illumination of the office floor plates behind.

Several of the pitched roofs which were designed to last hundreds of years were severely damaged in a storm in 1989.

Teddington Lock, the weir and barrage

Outer London, south

'South London' is a series of former villages and early-eighteenth-century suburbs engulfed since the mid-nineteenth century by the massive expansion of London. Those who live north of the river tend to see it as an incomprehensible obstacle to be negotiated en route for Gatwick Airport or the south coast; but for south Londoners it has the advantages of being within easy reach of central London and not too far from open countryside.

Clapham was an early and rather grand suburb, with fine eighteenth-century terraces contemporary with **Church Row** A6 in Hampstead. Mansions for wealthy bankers were built overlooking the Common, and from 1825 Thomas Cubitt laid out the elegant streets and imposing residences of Clapham Park; further south, Streatham was another well-endowed early suburb.

In the mid-eighteenth century Camberwell, Peckham and Dulwich to the east were villages, separated from each other by extensive fields, with hamlets such as Peckham Rye in between. These village nuclei are now hardly recognizable, but the commons at Clapham, Wandsworth and Tooting Bec, and the parks of Brockwell and Dulwich, are clues to a more agrarian past. John Soane's Picture Gallery of 1811–14 at Dulwich (W3) is among the few significant buildings.

The development of the railways and arterial roads in the nineteenth century transformed the area. Ribbon development spread along Brixton Hill, Streatham Hill and Streatham High Road, which today have a character rather like the North American 'strip'. Decaying nineteenth-century semi-detached houses alternate with shopping parades, the spaces between and behind being occupied by large and mediocre twentieth-century local authority housing estates.

Between the wars the Northern Line Underground was extended into Surrey: Colliers Wood, South Wimbledon and finally Morden (completed in 1926) were added to London's apparently endless suburbs, and Charles Holden built more excellent stations (W11).

Bishop's Palace **W1**
c1410–20,1510–20,1765,1867
Bishop's Avenue
off Fulham Palace Road SW6
⊖ Putney Bridge

Fulham's principal historic monument is more of a comfortable manor house than a palace. The estate belonged to the Bishops of London from the end of the seventh century until 1868, when it was taken over by the Church Commissioners. The Palace has lost two of its chief external attractions, as Pevsner pointed out: the direct connection with the river was disrupted when the embankment was built (c1775) and in 1921 the famous Danish moat was filled in.

The courtyard (1510–20) is the principal space, gentle and domestic in scale, and built of brick with a black diaper pattern. The bell tower is eighteenth-century, and Butterfield's chapel (1866) is in stark contrast: Gothic, with hard polychrome brickwork.

Dulwich Village 18th century **W2**
SE21
⇌ North Dulwich

A pleasantly leafy outlying village, whose remaining Georgian houses are now surrounded by twentieth-century suburbs.

Walk south down College Road to the mill pond, opposite **Dulwich College** W6, with its minute and charmingly rural Pond Cottages. Further still down this road are the only remaining working toll-gate and road in London.

Dulwich Picture Gallery and **Mausoleum** 1811–14, 2000 W3
College Road and Gallery Road SE21
John Soane, Rick Mather Architects
⇄ West Dulwich

London's earliest nineteenth-century public art gallery, Soane's Picture Gallery was built for **Dulwich College** W6 under the bequest of Francis Bourgeois, and represents the most advanced stage of Soane's personal abstraction of the classical. The gallery contains the collection of paintings brought together by the art dealer Noel Desenfans, intended for the Empress of Russia but left to Bourgeois, who in turn left them to the College. The building also houses a small mausoleum dedicated to both Desenfans and Bourgeois, and included almshouses – a touching commemorative ensemble. Badly bombed in 1944, it had been renovated by 1953, with the almshouses converted to give extra gallery space (which is not top-lit, and is therefore inconsistent with the rest of the gallery).

Much has been written both about this complex building and about Soane's illusionist devices. The detachment of elements, the hovering planes of brickwork to the exterior and resultant slits of space, and the inventive decorative themes give this disarmingly modest building a pedigree well in advance of its time. The earlier forms of J N L Durand come to mind, as do those of Louis Kahn.

In 2000 the galleries were refurbished, and a new wing added, to the designs of Rick Mather, which contained a café, education studios and more exhibition space. This wing created a new cloistered courtyard between the road and Soane's gallery.

Plan as originally built

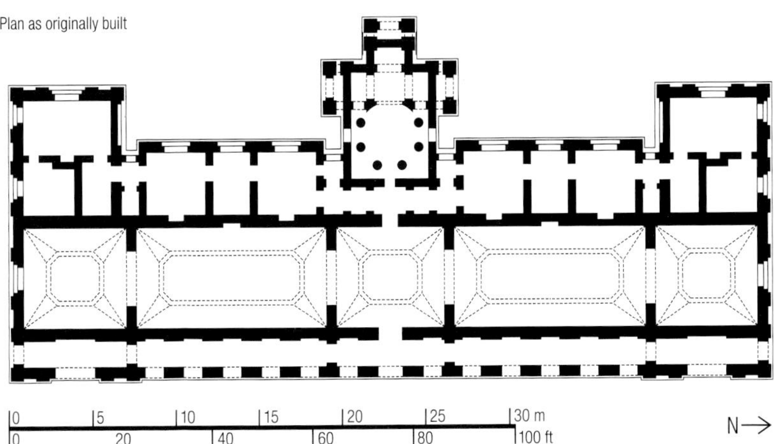

St Luke 1822 W4
Knight's Hill and
Norwood High Street SE27
F O Bedford
⇄ West Norwood

The general feeling of Bedford's many churches is that of correctness: here he manages to make even the usually sumptuous Corinthian look restrained. The order of the portico is an unusual variant of Corinthian, with fewer leaves and square ends to the flutes. The only decorative motif used in the design of the church is the acanthus. The interior was remodelled in 1878.

St Matthew, Brixton 1822 **W5**
Brixton Hill SW2
Charles F Porden
⊖ Brixton

Another 'Waterloo' church, whose grand plain Doric portico is, since the destruction of Hardwick's propylaeum at Euston, perhaps the best in London. A century earlier, Gibbs had shown how to unite tower and portico at **St Martin-in-the-Fields** K40; Porden shows how to disunite them again, by placing his fine three-stage tower at the east end of his temple. Porden did for Doric what the Inwoods so splendidly did for Ionic in their **St Pancras Church** G21 of exactly the same date, the building of which he supervised.

Dulwich College 1866–70 **W6**
College Road SE21
Charles Barry Junior
⇌ West Dulwich

The College was founded in 1619, and the buildings from its foundation to the mid-nineteenth century stand on either side of Gallery Road facing the end of Dulwich Village. The newer buildings, to the south in College Road, conform to the type of the Victorian institution: large, symmetrical and ornate, in Italian Renaissance rather than Gothic style. The central block contains the hall, but the northern block lacks the tower which was intended to make it symmetrical with the southern.

Shaftesbury Park Estate 1872–7 **W7**
Lavender Hill, Eversleigh Road
and Latchmere Road SW11
⇌ Clapham Junction

An estate of 1135 two-storey cottages, thirty shops and a church built by the Artisans, Labourers and General Dwellings Company. Unlike the tenements of similar philanthropic enterprises, this estate of simple terraced houses remains pleasant to live in. The details are Gothic: the street corners have turrets, and the houses have paired entrances under bracketed and steeply pitched porches. The streets are formally planted with plane trees.

Dixcote 1897 **W8**
North Drive SW16
C F A Voysey
⊖ Tooting Bec

All Voysey's familiar usages are evident in this big house overlooking Tooting Bec Common – the white pebbledash, battered chimneys, horizontal windows with stone trim, wide low front door, and heart motifs on the garage doors' strap hinges. But only the design is his; it was built by another architect following Voysey's resignation from the job after a disagreement.

Brixton Town Hall 1908 **W9**
Brixton Hill SW2
Septimus Warwick
⊖ Brixton
A spirited exercise in the Edwardian mixed style. For Warwick's later, calmer architecture see his **Wellcome Building** G64.

Arding and Hobbs Department Store **W10**
1910
Lavender Hill SW11
J Gibson
⇌ Clapham Junction
A fragment of Wigmore Street in Clapham Junction (designed by the architects of the defunct Debenham and Freebody), Arding and Hobbs represents similar Edwardian aspirations towards urbanity. The grand curved corner, topped by a cupola, and the first-floor timber screen have more affinity with Mountford's nearby Battersea Town Hall than with the modest three-storey commercial frontages of nineteenth-century Lavender Hill.

Tooting Bec

Clapham South

Northern Line Underground Stations **W11**
1926
Clapham South, Balham, Tooting Bec, Tooting Broadway, Collier's Wood, South Wimbledon and Morden
Charles Holden
The extension of the London Underground in the 1920s was the initiative of Frank Pick, the Managing Director of the Underground Group of Companies. In 1923 Pick and Holden started a long collaboration. Following his work on the extension of the Northern Line to Edgware in 1925, Holden tackled the southern extension the following year. The stations of Clapham South, Balham, Tooting, Collier's Wood, South Wimbledon and Morden are remarkably consistent in design. The stone frontage, often on a corner site, and the columns supporting a splayed window over the entrance were Holden's above-ground expressions of the invisible but unifying network of Frank Pick's Underground. The columns' capitals are solid versions of the Underground's 'roundel'.

William Booth Memorial Training College 1932 **W12**
Champion Park SE5
Giles Gilbert Scott
⇌ Denmark Hill

Since the destruction of the Guiness Breweries, this group of buildings for the Salvation Army, together with the former **Bankside Power Station** L121, remains one of the largest of Scott's extant London works. Its layout is a distant successor of those of Wren's institutional buildings such as the **Royal Hospital, Chelsea** N2. The college is laid out as a campus arranged around a central entrance building, marked with a square tower, unfortunately close to and cramped by both a main road and a railway line. To the south and to east and west rather severe five-storey dormitory buildings are arranged to form grassed quadrangles, the whole making a 'campus'.

Pullman Court 1935 **W13**
Streatham Hill SW2
Frederick Gibberd
⇌ Streatham Hill

One of the most lively early modern (early for England) designs in London, Pullman Court confidently combines the best of the lightness, picturesqueness and hygiene promised by modern architecture for the progressive middle classes. The three- and seven-storey blocks of flats are arranged with studied asymmetry around a green containing fine mature trees. While the buildings seem rather close together, the ensemble is a successful pioneering design which brings the air of a Mediterranean holiday resort to Streatham.

Six Pillars 1935 **W14**
Crescent Wood Road SE26
Val Harding and Tecton
⇄ Sydenham Hill
The high roof terrace, a wing of eccentric shape (governed by the site), the long horizontal windows and the 'six pillars' at the entrance are the 'modernist' attachments to this otherwise simple three-storey house.

ex **Children's Home** 1960 **W15**
11–12 Frogmore SW18
James Stirling and James Gowan
⊖ East Putney
With the old people's home in Charlton (U31), also 1961, these two houses for abandoned children in Putney were the last buildings of the Stirling and Gowan partnership before it dissolved in 1963. The buildings, since converted into flats and insensitively altered and re-windowed, are in brick and are of a domestic scale, and the outside play areas are partially covered by the bedrooms at the first-floor level. The scheme is modest, but the stepped plan and the development of the corner window anticipate work of both Stirling and Gowan in their later independent practices – Gowan's Trafalgar Road flats U33 in Greenwich, and Stirling's Halls of Residence at St Andrew's University, Scotland (1964).

Pollard's Hill Housing 1971 **W16**
SW16
London Borough of Merton Architects Department; P J Whittle, design by P Bell, D Lea, R MacCormac, N Alexander
⇄ Norbury
During the 1960s Professors Leslie Martin and Lionel March conducted research at the Cambridge School of Architecture into the properties of the Fresnel Square and its applicability to housing layouts. This was a significant contribution to the low-rise high-density housing debate, later published in Lionel March's *Urban Space and Structure*. The resulting perimeter planning technique (essentially a rationalization of the eighteenth-century London square) was first built at Pollard's Hill. The aim was to combine a planning density of 250 people per hectare (100 per acre) in three-storey houses with a significant gain in public open space. Its problems, however, derive from the rigid and indivisible nature of the plan, the 'double-fronted' effect of the Radburn principle and the emptiness of the central space.

Outer London, south-east

Eltham Palace X1 was established on the ridge overlooking the Thames in the fourteenth century, but it was not until the late eighteenth century that this section was developed as a suburb. The village of Blackheath and the heath itself had been the setting for many important events in English history, but by the eighteenth century it was a fashionable suburb of the small town of Greenwich. Architectural respectability of a sort was bestowed by Vanbrugh's building of his own **house** U12, east of Greenwich Park. Sporadic additions were made to the village, but the grandest house and groups are from the end of the Georgian period: the very fine **Paragon** and **Paragon House** X5.

Blackheath was joined by Lewisham as the scene of early Victorian suburban experiments: their leafy, low-density, mildly Italianate housing now provides relief from the carpet of twentieth-century semis of the commuter suburbs, encouraged by the electrification of the Southern Railway, and epitomized by Bromley.

Crystal Palace Park

Crystal Palace Park

Eltham Palace 1479 **X1**
King John's Walk SE9
⇌ Mottingham
High on the ridge which forms the southern edge of the Thames valley, Eltham was a royal palace in the fourteenth century, but the moated palace is of the fifteenth. The Hall is one of the four surviving examples in London – the others are at **Westminster** K5, **Hampton Court** V1 and **Guildhall** L8. It is 30m (100ft) long and 11m (36ft) wide, with a splendid hammerbeam roof. Unlike Westminster it has high windows, except at the dais end where they are much taller. The rest of the Palace has disappeared, except for some fragments, and all the other buildings on the site are later.

In 1933 the palace was leased by Stephen and Virginia Courtauld (Stephen the younger brother of Samuel, of Courtauld Collection fame), and they added two new wings reached by a large, circular and roof-lit entrance hall, its Art Deco finishes restored by English Heritage in 1999.

Morden College 1695 X2
Morden Road SE3
Edward Strong, mason
≈ Blackheath

A very beautiful almshouse group standing in its own extensive grounds, Morden College was founded by John Morden, a Turkey merchant, for less successful retired merchants. He and his wife are commemorated by statues set in a double arch in the pediment above the west door. The buildings have been attributed to Wren, and he was on the Greenwich Hospital Commission with Morden. The central courtyard has low arcades supported by Tuscan columns with small central pediments; opposite the entrance is the Chapel, aligned with a lamp standard in the form of a Roman Doric column in the centre of the quadrangle. Morden College and the **Royal Hospital, Chelsea**, N2 are the best surviving examples of Wren's domestic, as opposed to his monumental, architecture.

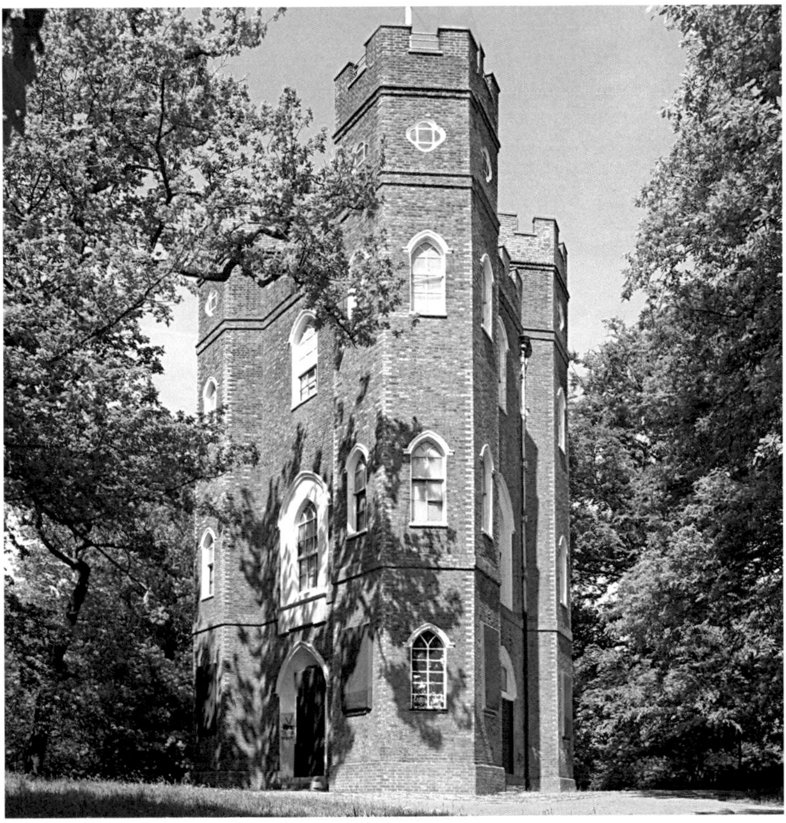

Severndroog Castle 1784 X3
Castlewood, off Shooters Hill Road SE18
Richard Jupp
≈ Eltham

A triangular Gothic tower, secluded in the trees of Castlewood, commands the strategic high ground above Woolwich (Shooters Hill was a sixteenth-century beacon hill). Erected by William James's widow to celebrate the capture of Severndroog Castle, Malabar, in 1755, the tower commands magnificent views over London but unfortunately is closed to the public.

Colonnade House c1790 **X4**
South Row SE3
⇌ Blackheath
A fine detached house facing a small pond on the heath – the triangular composition of one, two and three storeys is held together by the long Tuscan colonnade.

The Paragon c 1790 **X5**
SE3
Michael Searles
⇌ Blackheath
A very grand group: fourteen large semi-detached houses, linked by enclosed single-storey Tuscan colonnades, are set out in a shallow crescent overlooking the heath. The style is the summit of Georgian taste: spare Coade stone string-courses, arched heads to the ground-floor windows and, behind parapets, mansard slate roofs with thermal windows to the attics. Walk round the back, where the houses have pairs of curved bay windows with huge areas of glass. **Paragon House**, in South Row and Pond Road, is a grand, detached version of the Paragon's semis, with the same very large semicircular bay at the back, but with the elegant front door on the side.

Blackheath Park (Cator) Estate c1825 **X6**
SE3
⇌ Blackheath
An early suburb of tree-lined avenues. built on the grounds of Gregory Page's estate following the demolition of the house in 1787. The open pattern of Victorian terraces and villas has now been filled in with more recent suburban housing.

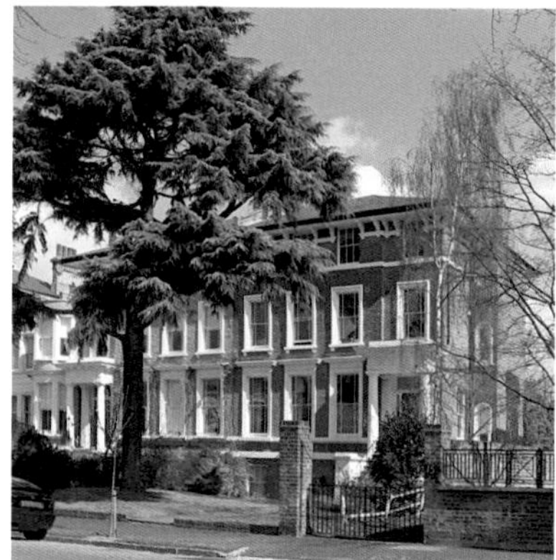

Nunhead Cemetery 1840 **X7**
Linden Grove SE15
J B Bunning
≹ Nunhead

This cemetery, London's second largest, is one of the series laid out in the 1830s and '40s, but unlike **Highgate** R9 or **Kensal Green** T13 it has few good architectural tombs, nor are any famous architects buried there. The entrance has gateposts decorated with inverted torches in cast iron, and with its Soanian lodges is suitably forthright. Abandoned by its owners and unmaintained, the cemetery was rescued and a programme of restoration, including that of the octagonal Gothic chapel, was begun in the 1990s. It was reopened as a public park in 2001.

Red House 1859 **X8**
Red House Lane, Bexleyheath DA6
Philip Webb
≹ Bexleyheath

William Morris and Webb were co-workers for Street, and Morris asked the young Webb, who was then twenty-eight, to design a house in the country for him and his wife; this is the relaxed, comfortable (though large) red-brick result. The style is unsettled, with some medieval and some early-eighteenth-century features, and overhanging barn-like tiled eaves. The interiors are bare, but with occasional crafted flourishes like the brick fireplace. It is an important design: a welcome relief from the contemporary overheated designs of the metropolis, and a reassertion of specifically English domestic values in which some architects today still find inspiration. It is owned by the National Trust and its interior is visitable.

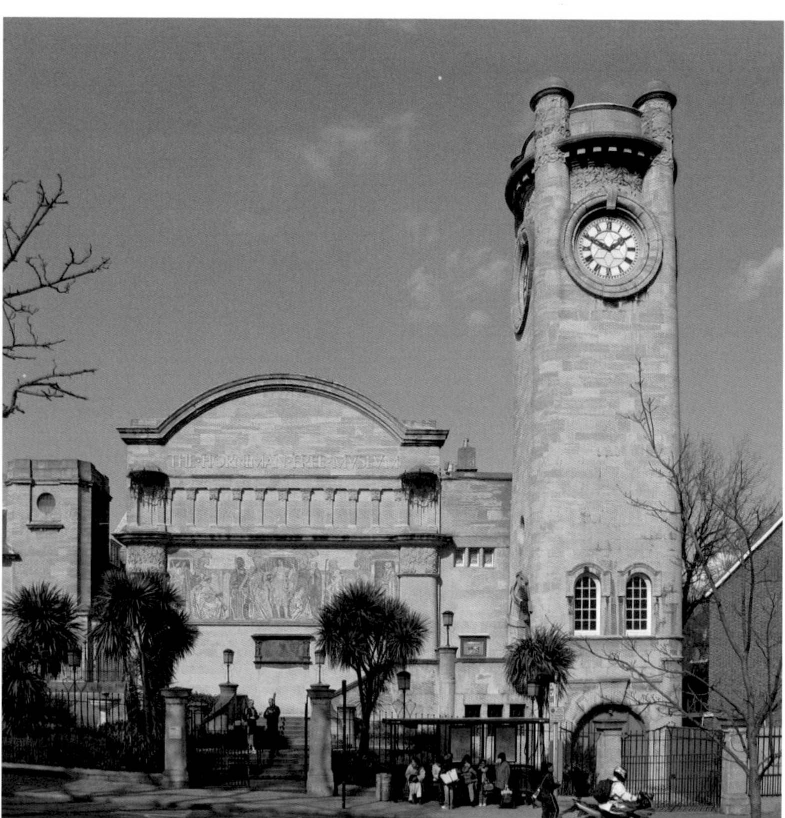

Horniman Museum 1896–1901 **X9**
100 London Road SE23
C H Townsend; Allies and Morrison 2002
⇌ Forest Hill

C H Townsend was one of the most original of the Arts and Crafts architects. The Horniman Museum, contemporary with his design for the **Whitechapel Gallery** L98, is undoubtedly his masterpiece. It has a strong asymmetrical composition when seen from the street; the massive clock tower with its circular cornice is set to one side of the large blank façade. Behind this lie the top-lit galleries, which house the anthropological collection of the client, F J Horniman MP. The exterior shows the influence of the American architect H H Richardson in the almost exclusive use of smooth stone, an abundance of relief ornament, the battered walls and scarcity of openings. The large and central mosaic panel on the outside of the museum was executed by the painter Robert Anning Bell, a member of the Art Workers' Guild. Townsend believed interiors and exteriors could be treated quite separately: the Free Style expression of the exterior contrasts with the interiors, which are simple and functionally planned. Townsend added the lecture hall and library in 1910, using the same materials but a simplified language.

To the west, the addition by Allies and Morrison of 2002 works successfully within the logic of Townsend's original plan and forms a courtyard between old and new. This provides a focus for the enlarged museum, with additional visitor facilities and a new public entrance from the park. The new vaulted gable facing London Road introduces a suitably deferential element into the accretive façade of the expanded museum.

Pioneer Health Centre 1934–6 **X10**
St Mary's Road SE15
Owen Williams
⇌ Queen's Road Peckham

Of all the home-grown contributors to modern architecture in England during the 1930s, Owen Williams is one of the most impressive and enigmatic. His engineer's approach, coupled with a refusal to be part of the architectural coterie, encouraged the Williams enigma. His insistence on invention allowed him to pursue pioneering 'objectivity' without a residue of sentiment for previous styles. The Pioneer Health Centre, known as the Peckham experiment, remains as an example of Williams's inspiration to the new architecture. Doctors I H Pearse and G S Williamson, the Centre's founders, believed that preventive action was the solution to society's ills: the Centre was to provide a place where families could meet to discuss their problems and trained staff could advise on treatment. The extensive sporting and recreational facilities could serve 2000 families at a time, in a catchment area of 5–6000 families. Peckham has parallels with the city clubs of Russian constructivist utopias of the 1920s, but Williams was detached from such theory. His design follows the warehouse or industrial type of his other works, the central space being filled by the grand swimming pool and separated from the other ancillary activities. The exterior, with six gently curved bay windows, has always seemed rather a weak afterthought, and not typical of Williams's logic. The unsympathetic conversion by the LCC architects (c1954) detracted from the structural clarity of the original design.

Housing 1957–9 **X11**
The Hall, The Keep and Corner Green:
South Row, Blackheath SE3
Eric Lyons for Span
⇌ Blackheath

These three middle-class housing schemes were widely copied in form and style. Span was a development company which attempted to modify the standard housebuilder's pattern – separate or semi-detached houses set well back from engineer-designed estate roads with over-generous sight lines and turning circles. Lyons's designs provide two- and three-storey rows of houses or flats loosely arranged among densely planted common gardens, with car movement and parking firmly relegated to the edge of the site. While the layouts have been widely and successfully copied, Lyons's architectural style, with its attempt to extend the range of materials usable for houses (by such means as tile hanging and weatherboarding), subsequently and in other hands degenerated into sentimentality. See also the Span development at **Ham** V11.

Housing 1974–8 **X12**
107 Westmoreland Road, Bromley BR2
Edward Cullinan and Brendan Woods
⇌ Bromley South

This six-storey building of thirty-six flats for a South London housing association has two façades. The front to the quiet suburban street attempts to evoke the classical villa, having a plinth, a principal floor and an attic storey. The composition is symmetrical, with a large double-height central entrance. The back, facing the common garden, is 'democratic', and the individual units are clearly expressed. The front, a rendered wall with openings, has two access galleries connected by stairs, with ramps to the street either side of the entrance forecourt.

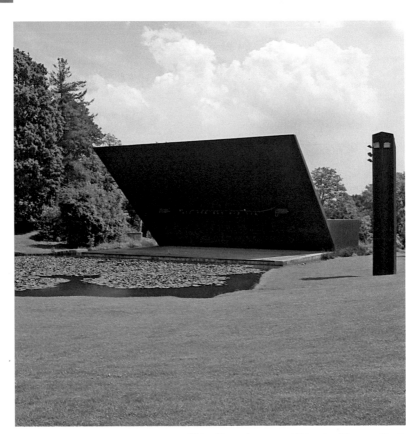

Bandstand 1997 **X13**
Crystal Palace Park SE26
Ian Ritchie Architects
⇌ Crystal Palace

This is not an unknown Cor-Ten (controlled rusting steel) installation by Richard Serra languishing in a remote south London park, but on a summer afternoon it reveals its true purpose as a very successful bandstand, abstract, beautiful and highly practical.

It has a commanding presence addressing a natural amphitheatre and separated from it by a lily pond-cum-moat. This splendid composition is completed by two monumental Cor-Ten obelisks housing the loudspeakers. But then this is not just any south London park: the Crystal Palace was relocated here from its site in **Hyde Park** J2 in 1851 and was used as a performance space and museum before it was destroyed by fire in 1936. Vestiges of its monumental terraces remain, which provide an unlikely setting for the more familiar television transmitter whilst recalling Albert Speer's Zeppelinfeld at Nuremburg of 1935–8.

Appendices

The Great Estates

The boundaries of the Great Estates, often with squares at their centres, gave central London its essential structure and character. Apart from the large, open Royal Parks, the estates contributed the fractured and democratic pattern, unlike the autocratic arrangements of many European cities.

1 Audley
2 Battlebridge
3 Bedford
4 Berkeley
5 Berners
6 Brett
7 Brompton Hospital
8 Burlington
9 Cadogan
10 Campbell Cole
11 Campden Charities
12 Chelsea Hospital
13 Church Commissioners
14 City
15 Crooke
16 Crown
17 Clothworkers' Company
18 Conduit-Mead
19 Cubitt
20 Curzon
21 Day
22 De Beauvoir
23 Duchy of Cornwall
24 Earl of Camden
25 Earl of Listowell
26 Edwards
27 Eton College
28 Eyre
29 Foundling Hospital
30 Gascoigne
31 Gibson
32 Grand Junction Canal Company
33 Gray's Inn
34 Grosvenor
35 Haberdashers' Company

36 Hall
37 Harlar
38 Harrison
39 Holland
40 Hope
41 Hutchins
42 Jesus College
43 Ladbroke
44 Leicester
45 Lincoln's Inn
46 Lloyd Baker
47 Lloyd-Lisson
48 Maddox-Pollen
49 Maitland Park
50 Minet
51 New River
52 Norlond
53 Northampton
54 Phillimore
55 Pickering
56 Portland-Soho
57 Portman
58 Rugby School
59 St John's College
60 Sloane-Stanley
61 Smith's Charity
62 Southampton
63 Spurston's Charity
64 Talbot
65 Temple
66 Thornhill
67 Thurloe
68 Torriano
69 Trinity House
70 Vaughan

The London square: a chronology

From its origins in the Inns of Court and Inigo Jones's Covent Garden **Piazza** K14, and following the destruction of the medieval, timber-built City in the fire of 1666, over the next 250 years the characteristic classical London square often provided the nucleus for the spacious developments of the brick houses of the estates.

- 1600–1700
- 1700–1750
- 1750–1800
- 1800–1850
- 1850–1900

Camden
Barnsbury
Canonbury
Milner
De Beauvoir
Thornhill
Lonsdale
Gibson
Cloudesley
Albion
Union
Wilton
Arlington
Oakley
Harrington
Claremont
Turner
Argyle
Vernon
Myddleton
Lloyd
Euston
Regent
Northampton
Granville
Tolmers
Tavistock
Wilmington
Hoxton
Arnold Circus
ton
Mecklenburgh
Brunswick
St John's
Rosebery
Gordon
Woburn
Queen
Fitzroy
Russell
Red Lion
Gray's Inn
South
Finsbury
Spital
Charterhouse
Bedford
Bloomsbury
New Street
Aldermanbury
Finsbury Circus
Devonshire
Lincoln's Inn Fields
New
Paternoster
Soho
Ludgate Circus
nover
Salisbury
America
Golden
Temple
Covent Garden
Leicester
Trinity
Trafalgar
St James's
Nelson
Parliament
Trinity Church
Merrick
Dickens
Smith
West
Vincent
Cleaver
Avondale
St George's
Dolphin
Lorrimore
Sutherland
Oval
Albert

Four model squares

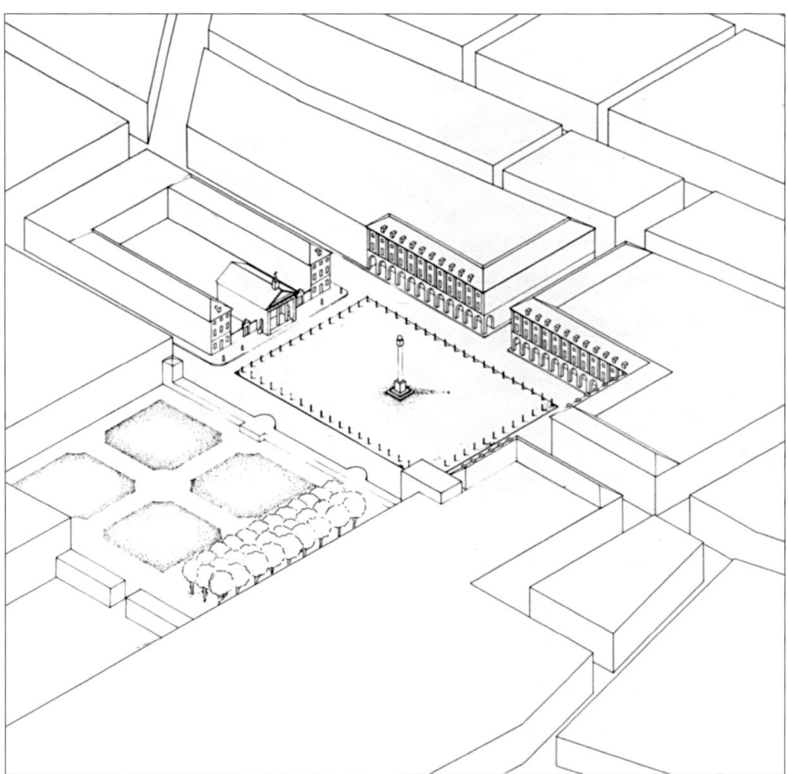

1631 Covent Garden Piazza K14
London's first real square, its arcades and name imported from Italy, was built by Inigo Jones under the patronage of the fourth Earl of Bedford. Jones's **Etruscan temple** K15, of 1631–8, forms the centrepiece on the west side.

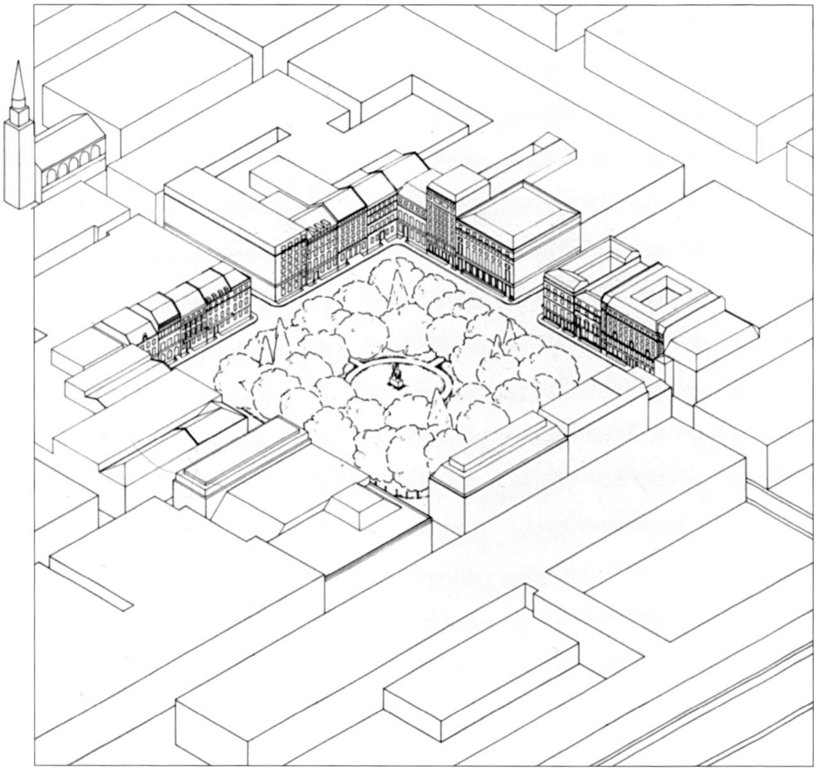

1665 St James's Square K18
The most regularly planned seventeenth-century square in London was developed with individual houses of different designs. It was entered through centrally placed gated streets, their vistas later closed by important buildings.

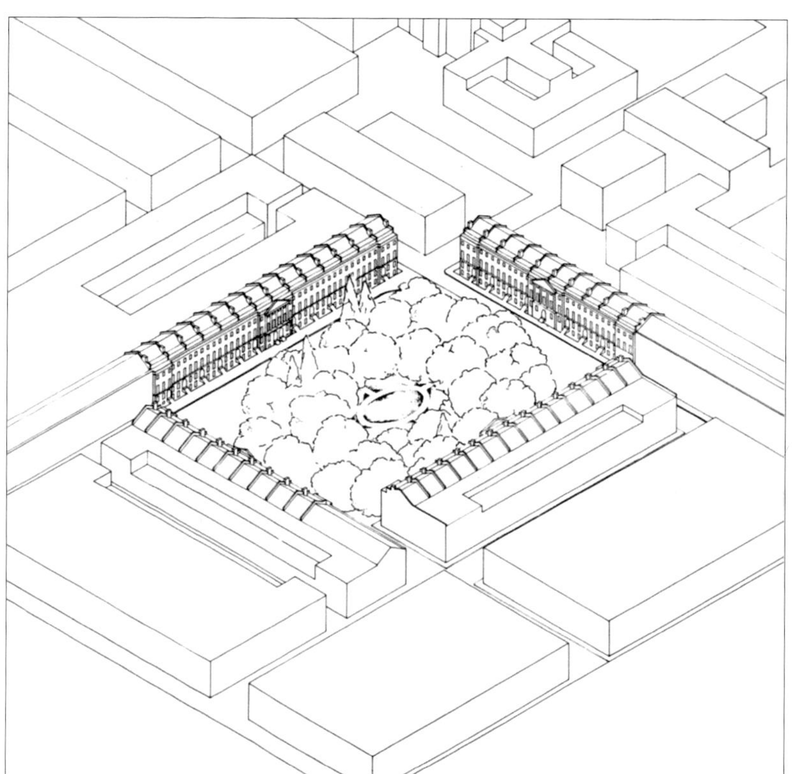

c1775 Bedford Square G12
The façades of the regular four-storey houses make a composition of four palaces facing each other across an oval garden, and the square is connected with the rest of Bloomsbury with streets at its corners rather than its sides.

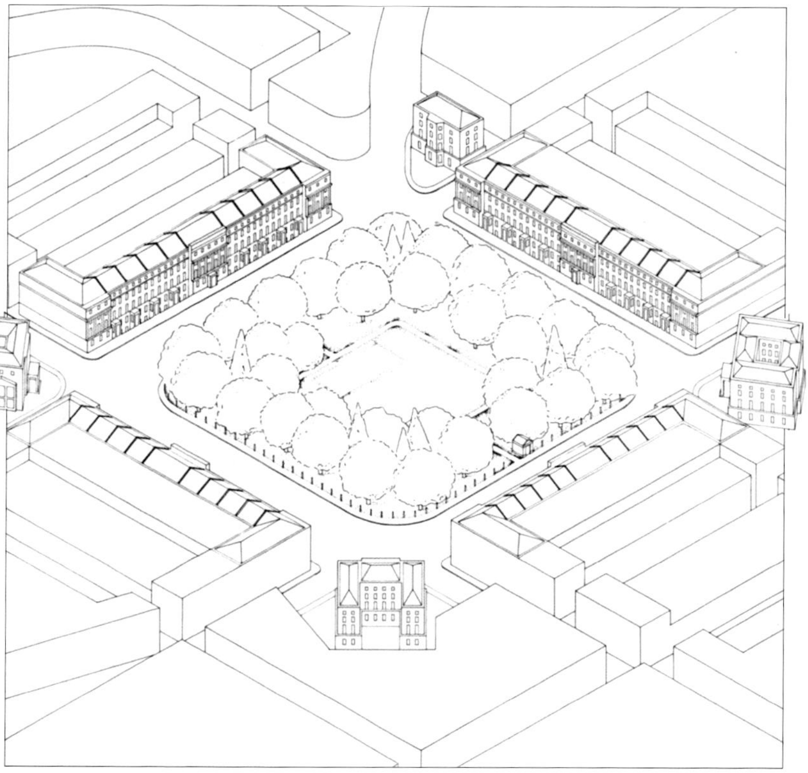

1825 Belgrave Square J24
Breaking the mould of the Georgian square, Cubitt and Basevi introduced diagonally placed, individually designed, mansions at the corners, and projecting porches to the elevations. The square was never gated.

Legal London

The Inns of Court: a continuous promenade between Theobalds Road and the Embankment

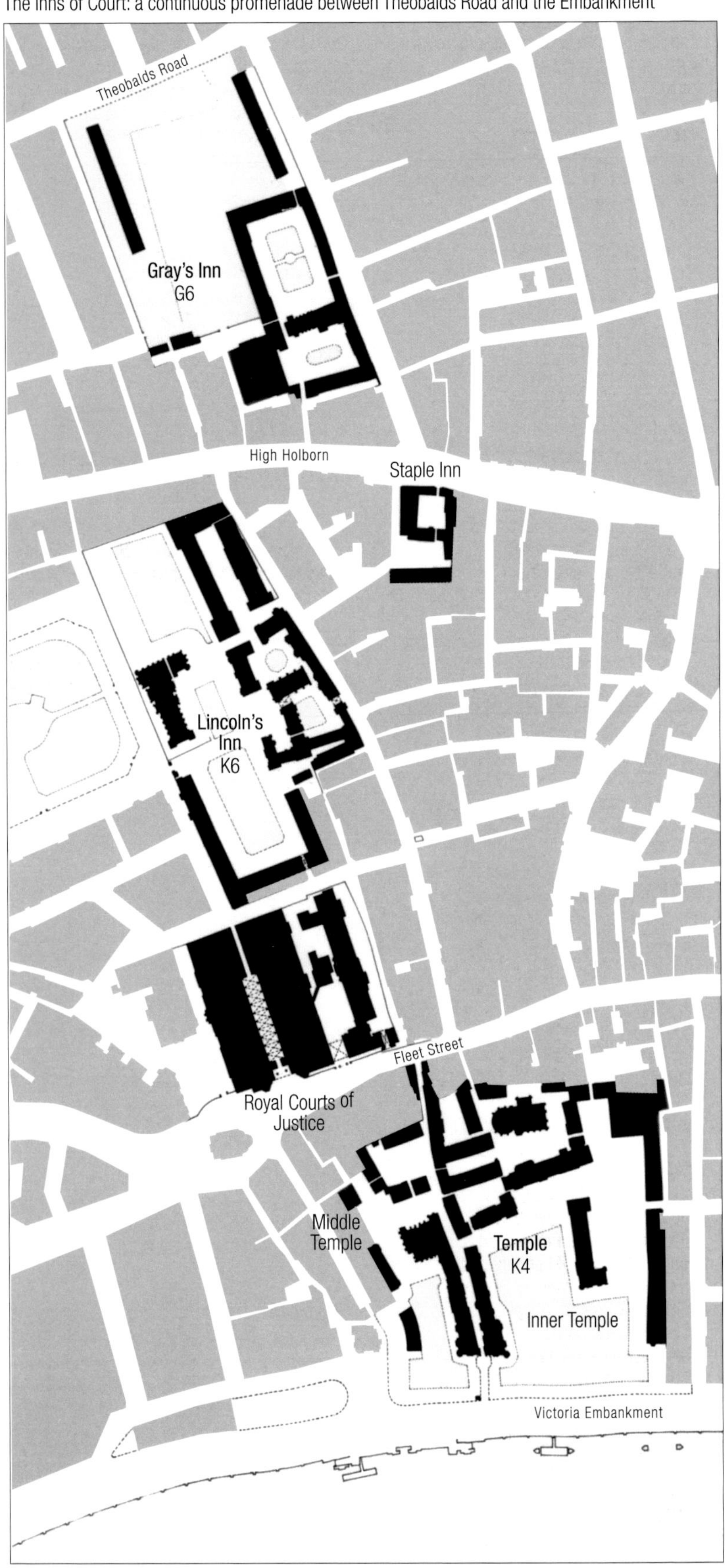

Further reading

The following books have been used as sources. Most of those in the first group are available in paperback, those in the second can be consulted in libraries.

Allinson, Ken
London's Contemporary Architecture
Architectural Press, 1994, 4th ed. 2006

Cooke, Alistair and Robert Cameron
Above London The Bodley Head, 1980

Cruickshank, Dan and Wyld, P
London: Art of Georgian Building
The Architectural Press, 1975

Downes, Kerry *Hawksmoor*
Thames and Hudson, 1969

Fleming ed, *Penguin Dictionary of Architecture*
new impression 1970

Frampton, Kenneth
Modern Architecture, A Critical History
Thames and Hudson, 1980

Hobhouse, Hermione *The History of Regent Street* McDonald & Janes, 1975

Olsen, Donald J *The Growth of Victorian London*
Peregrine/Penguin, 1976

Pevsner, Nikolaus, and others
The Buildings of England: London (6 vols)
Yale/Penguin, 1983–2005

Rasmussen, Steen Eiler *London, the Unique City* MIT Press, 1974

Reattie, Susan *A Revolution in London Housing, LCC Architects and their Work 1893–1914*
The Architectural Press, 1980

Service, Alastair *The Architects of London*
The Architectural Press, 1979

Service, Alastair *Edwardian Architecture*
Thames and Hudson, 1977

Stamp, Gavin and Colin Amery
Victorian Buildings of London 1837–1887
The Architectural Press, 1980

Stamp, Gavin ed. *Britain in the Thirties*
Architectural Design Vol 149 no 10–11, 1979

Stamp, Gavin ed. *London: 1900*
Architectural Design Vol 48 no 5–6, 1978

Summerson, John *Georgian London*
Pelican, revised 1962

Summerson, John *The Life and Work of John Nash: Architect* Allen & Unwin, 1980

Colvin, Howard *A Bibliographical Dictionary of British Architects 1600–1840*
Yale University Press, 1995

Hitchcock, Henry-Russell *Early Victorian Architecture in Britain* (2 vols)
The Architectural Press, 1954

LCC and the Survey of London Committee
The Survey of London (47 vols)
GLC ed Sir Francis Shepherd
Also available online:
www.english-heritage.org.uk/surveyoflondon

Maxwell, Robert *New British Architecture*
Thames & Hudson, 1952

Summerson, John *Sir John Soane*
Art and Technics, 1952

Summerson, John *Architecture in Britain 1530 to 1830* Penguin, 1953

Acknowledgements

A special thanks to Alexandra Boyle and Barbara Mellor for their prompting and managing the first edition; Margot Griffin for the drawings of London by century, Legal London and various plans of buildings; our students at the Royal College of Art of 1980–81 for the comparative city plans, page 6, the Great Estates page 472 and the London squares pages 474–7; and to Celina Ribeiro and Emily MacDonald who patiently and cheerfully typed additions to the text.

The authors would like to thank the following who have kindly supplied photographs (all other photographs © Christopher Woodward):
François Gijzels K5, R9
Christoph Grafe page 12, K90, K163 (lower), K181, T8, T15 (lower)
Jacob Nitsch U3 (Painted Hall)

Tamasin Cole would like to thank Bob Evans for making her life much easier.

The plan drawing of K67 is reproduced by permission of the Trustees of Sir John Soane's Museum, and of W3 by permission of the Royal Academy of Arts.

The maps on pages 11, 13, 17, 21, 25 and 29 are based upon the Ordnance Survey maps, and the maps to sections A–P are enlarged from the Ordnance Survey's 1:10 560 series of 1970.

General index

Numbers alone refer to page numbers. References to entries consist of a letter and a number. Primary references are in **bold**.

A

B

D

E

F

S

Index of building types